Gower
Handbook
of
Customer Service

GOWER HANDBOOK OF CUSTOMER SERVICE

edited by Peter Murley

Gower

Published by
Gower Publishing Limited
Gower House
Croft Road
Aldershot
Hampshire GU11 3HR
England

Gower
Old Post Road
Brookfield
Vermont 05036
USA

British Library Cataloguing in Publication Data
Gower handbook of customer service
 1. Customer services 2. Customer relations
 I. Murley, Peter   II. Handbook of customer service
 658.8'12

ISBN 0 566 07688 8

Library of Congress Cataloging-in-Publication Data
Gower handbook of customer service/edited by Peter Murley.
      p.   cm.
   Includes index.
   ISBN 0-566-07688-8
   1. Customer services–Management.   I. Murley, Peter.
HF5415.5.G69   1996
658.8'12–dc20   96-3978
                                                 CIP

Typeset in Cheltenham by Raven Typesetters, Chester and printed in Great Britain by Hartnolls Limited, Bodmin.

Contents

PART I   CUSTOMER SERVICE IN CONTEXT

1   Evaluating the profitability of customer service   3

Professor Merlin Stone
The worth of a properly serviced customer — How much
difference does good customer service make — Tactical
versus strategic application of customer service — Quantifying
the impact of customer service — How much should you spend
on customer service? — Feasibility analysis — Further reading

2   The role of benchmarking   17

Allan Trayes
Benchmarking in business — Benchmarking versus competitive
analysis — Types of benchmarking — Benefits of benchmarking
— A methodology for benchmarking — Critical points for success
in the process of benchmarking customer service — Gaining
maximum impact on customer service — Classic service
benchmarks — An ultimate measure of customer service
competence — When *not* to use benchmarking — The
benchmarker's code – being ethical — Further reading

v

PART II MEASURING, MODELLING, PLANNING

14 Delivering customer service through projects 174

David Honey
Programme management versus project management — What is
a project? — The principles of planning — Work breakdown
structures (WBS) — An introduction to estimating —
Gantt charts and networks — Quality management within
projects — Summary — Further reading

PART III MARKETING CUSTOMER SERVICE

15 Customer service as a product 197

Jan E. Smith
Branding customer service — Delivering customer
service — Informing the customer — Maintaining the
advantage — Summary

16 Lifetime values and database marketing 205

Kevin Gavaghan
A brief history of profitable marketing — Lifetime
customers are more profitable — Listening, seeing and
learning organizations — The building blocks of lifetime
value — The customer database

17 Using the customer database 221

Professor Merlin Stone
Customer management and marketing system requirements —
The changing analytical requirement — The customer-optimizer
— The systems and management interface — Conclusion —
Further reading

18 Direct marketing 233

Tony Williams
The theory –'the customer service continuum' — The
practice — The challenge – how every company can put the
theory into practice — Further reading

19 Telemarketing 246

Peter Murley
The telemarketing image — The advance of telemarketing
— Defining telemarketing — The way forward

PART V   THE HUMAN INGREDIENT

34 Empowerment

Colin Apthorp
What is empowerment? — Empowerment and culture —
Customer expectations — How to recognize disempowerment
— Countering opposition to change — Empowering
suppliers — Giving managers the skills to empower others
— Resistence to empowerment — The customer's perception
— Putting empowerment into the service environment —
Further reading

35 Teamwork - the FedEx experience

Thomas O'Hearn
Corporate philosophy – people first — Recruitment
and promotion — Leadership and management —
Customer satisfaction — Owning service quality —
ISO 9001 accreditation — Concept of internal customers
— Conclusion – people first

PART VI   MAKING THE MOST OF TECHNOLOGY

36 The call-centre concept

Dr Eve Carwardine
 The evolution of the call-centre concept — Best
examples of US and UK call centres — Customer service
by telephone — The additional benefits of a call centre
— Delivering service via the telephone — Summary

37 Harnessing new technology

Martin Meikle-Small
Automation — The potential interfaces to a customer
— The technology project – how to do it — Summary

38 Toll-free and local charge rate services

Jamie Clyde
The services available — What number should you give
to your customers? — The operational benefit of one
nationwide number — Toll-free outside the United
Kingdom

39 Meeting the fulfilment challenge 561

Peter Hardingham
Planning fulfilment (it begins in the home . . .) — Integrated
communications — A typical 'integrated' fulfilment programme —
What your customers think — Hints for the future – the Internet
bell tolls! — Further reading

40 Forecasting volume in a call centre 572

Peter Murley
The need for forecasting: a cautionary tale — Definition
and development of a forecasting model — Analysis of a
forecasting model — Conclusion — Appendix: Call/activity
types

List of figures

Notes on contributors

Colin Apthorp (*Empowerment*) has his own consultancy business and specializes in organization change, culture change, management development, and teamwork. He works extensively throughout Europe and the United States. Following twenty years' experience in retail banking, he worked for seven years in management training, both as training manager and designer, before establishing his agency in 1990. He has had several articles published, and is currently researching the impact of empowerment upon teamwork in the service and manufacturing sectors for a book that he is writing on this subject.

Christine Barclay (*Culture: the prime differentiator*) is an independent consultant in human resources strategy, organization development and change. She has an MA from the University of Glasgow and an MBA from Cranfield School of Management. Following several years' experience in information services management, both in the United Kingdom and abroad, she subsequently worked as a senior human resources executive across a wide range of industries, including information technology, consultancy, financial services and media. A Fellow of the Institute of Personnel and Development, and a qualified counsellor and psychometric assessor, she has conducted research into the psychometric profile of outplaced executives, and, jointly with Professor Shaun Tyson, published in 1986 *The 'N' factor in executive survival* (Monograph No. 1, Human Resources Research Centre, Cranfield).

Professor Tony Bendell (*Quality as a mind-set*) is East Midlands Professor of Quality Management, and Director of the Quality Unit, at Nottingham Trent University. He is also Chief Associate Consultant at Services Ltd. Active for more than twenty years in implementing total quality management in both private and public sectors, he is a prolific author on a wide range of subjects, including quality management and monitoring, benchmarking, and quality in the public sector. *xxi*

Alison Bond (*Delivering service internationally*) is a partner in Research and Data, specialists in customer service. She was previously Market Information Manager at UK Air, where she developed their customer service databases and customer questionnaires, systems for feedback to staff, and associated motivation programmes, before joining Consumerdata to manage customer service databases and carry out consultancy projects for a variety of clients, including leading travel and leisure companies, retailers and utilities. She is also co-author of *Direct Hit* (Bond, A, Davies, D and Stone, M, published by FT – Pitman, 1995), a study of Direct Marketing.

Jane Carroll (*Learning from successful companies*) was formerly Chief Executive of Forum Europe Limited and Forum Asia Limited, divisions of the Forum Corporation, an international training and consultancy firm that is helping organizations worldwide to become customer driven. She has broad experience in the planning and implementation of organizational change initiatives and in the design and deployment of customized learning systems to improve customer excellence, leadership, management effectiveness and sales productivity. For some twenty years she has helped leading companies to achieve their strategic goals and improve both organizational and individual performance, and her clients have included Standard Life Insurance, Standard Chartered Bank, AMP, E.I. du Pont de Nemours, the Export Development Corporation of Canada, United Technologies and American Express. Holding an MBA in organizational behaviour and marketing from the Boston School of Management, she is a graduate of the Stanford University Business School Executives Program.

Dr Eve Carwardine (*The call-centre concept*) leads the Call Centre division as principal consultant with Opta Consulting, specializing in business planning and the specification and implementation of operational infrastructures. After training originally as a doctor, she worked for Imago Consultants (specialists in workflow and document management), Syntegra (the systems integration business of BT), ICL (a prototype software development house), and IBM, before joining Opta. She has extensive experience of diagnosing business problems in the financial services, utilities and telecommunications industries, providing beneficial IT solutions in support of office automation, document management, productivity and efficiency gains, customer service improvements, and the establishment of new teleservicing and direct sales channels, and she has originated and managed major programmes covering all aspects of business planning, people, processes, and the operational implementation of technology. Her clients, both in the United Kingdom and abroad, have included building societies, retail banks, international wholesale banks, insurance companies, major utility and telecommunications companies as well as law firms.

Paul Chapman (*Roles, not jobs*) left his position as Director of Organization Design and Development at the National and Provincial Building Society in

1996 to pursue a career as a self-employed consultant specializing in organization design and development. He started his business career with Burroughs Machines Ltd (now part of Unisys UK), his last position being that of Financial Controller, before joining Rank Xerox (UK) Ltd as Director in charge of management systems and quality, and latterly, customer support services. During 1989–1990 he led a team at the organization's headquarters in Stamford, Connecticut, which redesigned the business architecture of the Xerox Corporation. He has a BA Hons. from the University of York and an MBA with distinction from the International Business Centre at Buckingham.

Jamie Clyde (*Toll-free and local charge rate services*) is principal consultant with Aspen Consultancy, the independent call-centre technology consultancy. He has considerable experience in the delivery and technical operation of call centres in various industries, including telecommunications, computer and IT manufacturing, and retail finance, and his specialist areas are business justification of technical call-centre investment, the technical design and integration of the component technologies of the call centre, and the implementation of IVR. He has recently given several workshops on IVR and CTI, and has also spoken at a number of call-centre conferences.

Stephanie Craig (*Selection,* not *recruitment*) is a Director of Craig, Gregg & Russell Ltd, a professional consultancy that specializes in applying psychology at work. Previously she worked with the States Services Commission in New Zealand as an occupational psychologist, and then with PA Consulting Services where she was responsible for the development of their Psychometrics Unit. A chartered occupational psychologist by profession, she has many years of experience in the design and implementation of selection and development methods across a wide range of job types and industry sectors. Most recently, she has been deeply involved in helping companies to set up and review their procedures for spotting and developing people with high potential through the application of job analysis techniques and output, which has in turn led to the design or redesign of appraisal schemes, personal development programmes and development workshops.

James Ensor (*The role of logistics*) is the Managing Director of Strategic Vision, a management consultancy specializing in customer service, logistics and marketing, primarily for the food, automotive and IT industries. Possessing particular expertise in pan-European work and in assisting companies to cater for the different standards in customer service expected across Europe, he believes that bridging the gulf between, on the one hand, logistics professionals who work with models, and on the other, sales and marketing people who understand customers, is the key to success in providing customer service.

Ros Gardner (*Public sector service standards*) has worked for Marks & Spencer for over twenty years, latterly as Manager of the Customer Services Department, and before that as Divisional Personnel Manager. In addition to *xxiii* her experience in dealing with all aspects of customer service, she has managed a group of stores and warehouses, and has had particular responsibility for staffing and training. At present, she is on secondment as Director of Field Services for the National Association of Citizens Advice Bureaux, responsible for all operations of CABs throughout England, Wales and Northern Ireland. She is also Vice-Chairman of the Society of Consumer Affairs Professionals and a member of the Citizens' Charter Complaints Task Force.

Kevin Gavaghan (*Lifetime values and database marketing*) is Managing Director of Knowledge = Power, a publisher of business management education on CD-ROM and a consultancy specializing in the use of new techniques for customer and staff communications. Experienced in retailing both goods and services with Marks & Spencer, the Burton Group and Thomas Cook, he was appointed Marketing Director for the Midland Bank, where he was responsible for the development of innovative products, new customer database systems, and award-winning advertising campaigns. He was also part of the concept team that created First Direct, the world's foremost 24-hour bank by telephone, and is strongly committed to the use of technology to raise customer service standards, improve sales and increase productivity. He has a BA Hons. in Modern History from Oxford University and is a Blue in the modern pentathlon.

Nick Gazzard (*Activity-based costing*) is a Partner in the Profit Ability Partnership, the largest specialist ECR/DPP consultancy in the UK. He was formerly an Associate Director with Davies and Robson and Sales Planning Manager with Scott Paper Company where he set up the Space Management Department. Nick has been involved in a range of studies and projects over the past 10 years which included a seat on the UK Institute of Grocery Distribution DPP Steering Group. He is now involved in development work at the leading edge of ECR, Category and Space Management, Activity-Based Costing and DPP with many major blue-chip clients. These include Anchor Foods Ltd, Birds Eye Wall's Ltd, Britvic Soft Drinks Ltd, Crookes Healthcare Ltd, EMI Music, Gallaher Ltd, Nestlé UK Ltd and Safeway Stores plc.

Allison Grant (*Standards, measures and performance indicators*) is currently working in telecommunications, primarily on initiatives to improve customer satisfaction and retention. She was originally in management consultancy, and also with American Express throughout Europe, where she gained substantial experience working on performance improvement in all areas of customer service. She has a European MBA from Strathclyde Graduate Business School.

Julia Hall (*Focus groups*) is a Director of IFF Research Ltd, the specialist business-to-business agency. She has been in market research since graduating in 1985, and now designs and manages a wide range of projects in many different consumer and non-consumer markets. She tackles both quantitative and qualitative work with equal aplomb, but has a particular penchant for the latter type. Currently studying counselling and psychotherapy, she is also an active member of the Institute of Directors and an associate member of the Market Research Society.

Peter Hardingham (*Meeting the fulfilment challenge*) currently a member of one of the UK's first 'virtual agencies' – The Drayton Bird Partnership – Peter works primarily on marketing and communications strategy; and also on direct marketing campaigns and database marketing for clients such as Mercedes-Benz UK. He works with a wide variety of projects and specializes in how customer relationships impact an organization's bottom-line. Peter graduated from the London School of Economics in 1980 with a law degree, and has operated in general marketing, advertising and direct marketing ('through the line'), for some 15 years, working for some of the biggest names in consumer and business-to-business industries, both as a client and in direct marketing agencies. Peter introduced computer software mail order into the high street in Dixons in the early '80s, setting up retail and publishing software thereafter. He worked as Account Director with Ogilvy & Mather and again with Judith Donovan Associates, launching Cellnet Call Connections direct marketing campaigns selling mobile 'phones and introducing direct marketing into Nescafe. His business-to-business experience includes FT Information, Kodak, Inmac mail order (Pan-European) and Trade Indemnity Credit Insurance. Before joining Drayton Bird, Peter was Joint Managing Director of Citigate Direct and during this time he lectured on Pan-European marketing and acted as a judge for the 1995 Echo awards.

David Harris (*The training journey*) was a founder member of Groom House, now a leading organization in the training field, which provides customer service training primarily in the communications and financial services industries. However, he initially spent some twenty years with Rank Xerox, rising to board status first as Director of Operations and latterly as Head of Marketing. During his years with the company, Rank Xerox invested heavily in quality management, customer service, and innovative training, in all of which he was significantly involved, and it was this invaluable expertise that he took to Groom House with outstanding results. After running the Groom House organization for some years, he now spends much of his time on marketing projects and in developing new training strategies for customer service.

Elizabeth Harris (*Accreditation*) is Managing Director of Groom House Holdings, the very well-established training organization that she helped to found in 1987 and which now offers a wide range of training – especially innovative training in the customer service field, and mainly to the financial services and communications industries. Her earlier background included a very successful career as a mathematics teacher, and some eight years as a county and district councillor in local government. Now she is well known in the customer service arena, with emphasis on the development of human performance and, in particular, on the targeting and measurement of that development, using assessment and *xxv* accreditation as the chief vehicles. The expansion of these options owes much to her work in meeting legislative requirements for financial services.

David Honey (*Delivering customer service through projects*) is a Director of Opta Consulting, which specializes in the business planning, specification and implementation of operational infrastructures. He gained supplier experience when working for companies such as Mitel Telecom, Phillips Industries and GEC Marconi, and was a Consultancy Manager with Deloitte Haskin and Sells before joining Opta in 1988. With over twenty-five years' experience of working for both suppliers and end users of business solutions in the areas of computing and telecommunications, he has been personally involved to date on more than twenty major change projects for large customers, covering all aspects of business planning, people, processes and technology. He has an honours degree in electrical engineering from the University of Essex.

Howard Kendall (*Internal service for internal customers*) is the founding director of the Helpdesk user Group (HUG), that has 1 000 member organizations in the UK and Europe. Howard is one of the world's top advocates of the Help Desk as a vital management tool, and is recognized as Europe's leading Help-Desk authority. He lectures extensively at public and in-house events, and is quoted frequently in the trade press, in addition to writing regular articles and manuals on Service Management and Customer Service issues. Howard works with leading organizations and industry bodies to raise the awareness of, and standards in, all service disciplines. He is a service 'fanatic' and keenly supports worldwide initiatives to promote service people to the forefront of business thinking. Managing Consultant with HUG (Europe) Ltd, the leading UK-based help-desk consultancy, he specializes in the practical application of service management strategies, together with the supporting procedures of problem and change management, and help processing in its many forms. With over twenty years of detailed IT experience, he is probably the foremost UK authority on help desks and was the driving force behind the founding and development of the Help Desk User Group (HUG), in which he still plays an active management role. His consultancy work is directed mainly towards the provision, organization and support of customer help services and to the definition and implementation of service level agreements (SLAs), and he is totally committed to the effective business use of computing. He is a very authoritative and entertaining speaker.

David Limbrick (*Mystery shopping*) is currently Client Services Director for the specialist Mystery Customer company BDI Research Limited. Previously he worked in consultancy for the Strategy Services Division of PA Consulting and, more recently, in various marketing and service positions within Barclays Bank where, amongst various responsibilities, he implemented an important mystery customer programme. He has an MBA from Warwick Business School.'

Bill Martin (*Business process engineering*) is currently Director, European

Business Operations, for Dell Computer Corporation, having worked for some fifteen years in the computer industry, previously for industry leaders Digital and Bull before joining Dell, and covering a wide variety of manufacturing, marketing, customer service and operations management roles in that time. As a line manager three years ago he saw the need for new and more effective ways of running parts of Dell's UK business, and from that point he moved into business process engineering, in which field he is now leading a major change programme across Dell's European subsidiaries.

Martin Meikle-Small (*Harnessing new technology*) is a Director of Aspen Consultancy, an independent call-centre technology consultancy. His experience in call centres includes: developing the strategy to introduce a direct telephony channel; cost-benefit analysis to improve existing direct channel operations with technology; voice and host data integration projects to deliver efficiency gains; process-based risk assessment and disaster recovery planning for multisite call centres; and implementation of the technology elements within a coordinated call-centre build project. A combination of in-depth technical knowledge and business acumen enables him to provide a very balanced approach to clients' problems, and his enthusiasm and commitment to act either as a catalyst or project leader ensure that his clients gain maximum benefit from the introduction of technology. He is well recognized and respected as an author on all aspects of communications technology.

Mary Ann Moran (*Using telephone techniques*) runs her own successful consultancy company, based at Henley-on-Thames, which she established in 1993 after a period with Rank Xerox. The company provides training in most business and management areas, and, in particular, in three main fields: all aspects of communication skills; customer care and customer service; and career management. At present the company is employed on a range of contracts in the United Kingdom and across Europe for customers who include blue-chip multinationals, large manufacturers, large retail organizations, and small businesses. She personally is also qualified in personality and ability testing, which supports all her training and especially the career management division of her company's work.

Peter Murley (*Framework for delivering service*; *'Due diligence'*; *Using customer surveys*; *Telemarketing*; *Using control groups*; *Incentivizing success*; and *Forecasting volumes in a call centre*) is currently Vice-President Customer Services for Telewest Communications Group, which is the largest provider of cable television and telephony in the UK marketplace at the present time. Previously, he has worked in the human resources field at senior and board level for a number of international organizations, including Unisys, BIS Software and PA Consultants, and also for a seven-year period as a self-employed consultant, during which time his clients included high-profile market leaders such as Mercury Communications, Mercury Enterprises, Cellnet (TSCR), Energis Communications, North West Water, Videotron, RAC, *xxvii* and First Direct. He was also one of the founder members of the First Direct team, initially as Personnel and Training Director, and then as Customer Services Manager, in which position, amongst various special projects, he was responsible for the company's first customer survey process and the implementation of a continuous improvement programme. Following the success of First Direct, he has gained a reputation for a range of business activities, including: design, development and implementation of customer service strategies; evaluations and audits; development of competitive capabilities and resources; training programme design; volumetrics models; telemarketing; customer system requirement specifications; culture-driven change management programmes; and activation of greenfield sites. As a player in the exciting entertainment and telecommunications sectors, he firmly sees the delivery of service excellence as both a core competence and a crucial competition advantage.

Thomas O'Hearn (*Teamwork – the FedEx experience*) is Vice-President Operations, Europe, for FedEx, based in the United Kingdom. He joined FedEx in 1976 and was appointed to his present position in 1991. In the intervening years he controlled various stations and then districts throughout the United States, and became Managing Director in 1989. Throughout his very successful career with the company, he has been responsible for implementing many of its team management policies, and has considerable first-hand experience of the direct results and benefits of FedEx's 'People–Service–Profit' corporate philosophy to which he is totally committed. He holds a BSc. degree from Suffolk University, Massachusetts.

Roger Penson (*Quality as a mind-set*) is Senior Consultant at Services Ltd, and his background is in the services industry. He has carried out extensive implementation work on ISO 9000 for Lincolnshire and Leicestershire TECs, various Business Links, and for many business clients in the electronics, engineering, pharmaceutical, building, computer and service industries, both in the United Kingdom and abroad, and he has led the successful development of a nationwide quality system involving over 7 000 staff.

Jan E. Smith (*Customer service as a product*) is currently Group Strategic Director for the RAC. Her career has been spent mainly in financial services, and she has held senior appointments with Midland Bank, Lloyds Bank, and the TSB Group, for whom she restructured the marketing department and developed a five-year marketing strategy. When she rejoined the Midland in 1989 her appointment was as Marketing Director for a 'business product to establish the first 24-hour direct telephone banking service'. From this remit was developed one of the foremost brand launches of the decade, First Direct, which won the 1990 Marketing Award for Product Excellence. Following her considerable success on this project, she moved to Mazda Cars (UK) as Marketing Director, and thence to the RAC, where, with her extensive knowledge of financial services and the car industry, her objective is to plan and implement a strategy that will take that organization into the twenty-first century at the leading edge. She is a member of the Institute of Directors, the Marketing Society, Women's Advertising Club of London and the Jaguar Drivers Club.

Professor Merlin Stone (*Evaluating the profitability of customer service; Developing service internationally; Using the customer database;* and *Public sector service standards*) is an internationally renowned specialist and consultant in customer care, customer loyalty and customer information systems, whose clients include BP Oil Europe, BT, Equifax Europe, Hitachi Data Systems, Jaeger, Kodak Office Imaging, Lathams Accountants, Ladbroke Racing, Motorola Cellular Systems, Peabody Housing Trust, Sainsbury's Homebase, VW-Audi, Wiggins Teape and Xyratex. Until 1993 he was Dean of the Faculty of Human Sciences at Kingston University, where he still teaches on a postgraduate management course for public and voluntary sector managers. He is also a leading reseacher on the use of information systems at the point of contact with customers. He is the author of ten books on marketing and customer service, including the best sellers *Database Marketing* (1988, Aldershot: Gower and 1990 London: John Wiley) co-authored by R. Shaw and *Competitive Customer Care* (1992, London: Croner) with L. Young.

Allan Trayes (*The role of benchmarking*) is with United Utilities and prior to this worked for Mercury where he set up a front-office call-centre operation providing customer assistance to the company's residential customers. The operation now has 600 work stations, employs around 1 000 staff, and handles on average 16 000 customer calls each day. He was previously with Hutchinson (Microtel) Telecommunications in the very competitive digital mobile communications market, and Hewlett Packard, for whom he helped to found their Response Centre network and established many of the principles that took HP to the top of the Datapro surveys for customer satisfaction. His work has included: extensive experience as an IT manager and engineer, which has helped him to appreciate the crucial role of technology in the development of call-centre management and customer service; broad use of management techniques such as activity-based costing, 'pull' manufacturing, TQM-based continuous improvement, and intensive training, in a manufacturing environment; implementation of more sophisticated and cost-reducing recruitment procedures such as assessment centres based on core competencies; and the development and understanding of several new concepts of customer administration and management for competitive advantage, including network-based, value-added customer services. His qualifications include MBA, BSc., and CEng. and he is a member of both the Institution of Electrical Engineers and the Institute of Management.

Charles R. Weiser (*Encouraging customer feedback*) was formerly Head of Customer Relations at British Airways, Vice-President of Sales and Marketing for BA's partner, Carib Express and is currently responsible for Consumer Financial Services. He specializes in change management and has been deeply *xxix* involved in change around the world while at BA, including: setting up the Executive Club frequent flyer programme; a strategic review of the airline's European business; the development of the company's Air Miles subsidiary; and the research and development of new product lines in the Leisure Division. During his tenure, BA's Customer Relations Division – which he transformed from a back-office, loss-making operation into a global profit centre worth £460m in revenue – won numerous international awards, including the United Kingdom's 'First Direct Quality Award', the United States' IBM 'Crystal Award' for IT innovation and Harvard Business School's 'Best Practice Selection'. Most recently, he has been closely involved in BA's corporate change programme, Leadership 2000, covering most aspects of the airline's operation. He has an MBA from Lancaster University, and is a fellow of the Royal Society of Arts, a member of the Institute of Marketing, and was recently an adviser to the Federation of Small Business Awards. In addition, he has published widely on customer loyalty and change management.

Tony Williams (*Direct marketing*) is Marketing Director of the RAC. Previously, his career was in financial services, first with TSB where he was involved in the marketing operation which transformed the regionally based mutual savings bank into a fully-fledged quoted bank with a product range to match that positioning. He then moved to the Midland Bank where, as Communications Director, he was closely involved in the launch of First Direct, the first 24-hour, 365-day telephone bank in the United Kingdom, being responsible for all aspects of building the brand and marketing the new service. He is an associate member of the Institute of Banking.

Laurie Young (*Delivering competitive advantage* and *New strategies for customer service*) is a marketeer, specializing in the marketing of services, business-to-business products and customer care strategy. He has nearly two decades of marketing experience. Much of his early career was with BT, rising to the position of UK Service Marketing Manager, and in the process gaining expertise in large service engineering, IT, logistics functions, customer care and quality management programmes as well as all aspects of marketing. He was closely involved in the process leading up to privatization and in the acquisition of Mitel. His final important responsibility was working on the creation of BT's new quality of service strategy based on marketing techniques. Moving on to Unisys UK as Service Marketing Director, he developed a market-led approach to service offering and customer care that contributed very significantly – primarily through a complete corporate brand positioning project – to the Unisys turnround, creating a whole new direction and impetus for the company's UK and European service business. He has an MBA in strategic marketing from Hull University, and is a member of the Institute of Marketing. His first book, titled *Competitive Customer Care* (1992, London: Croner), co-authored with M. Stone, has been very well received.

Foreword

by Kevin Newman, Chief Executive First Direct

Imagine there was a formula that turned lead into gold and that the formula could be purchased as readily as this publication – contained in this publication even. Such a book would surely be the biggest seller of all time. Well, no, actually. If such a situation did exist then the world would suddenly become full of gold and it would lose its value and some other mineral would become precious.

So, let's start in the way we mean to go on. First, there is no magic formula for providing outstanding customer service. Second, even if there were, the search would continue for the 'next level'. Third, reading this book is going to be frustrating in that it will leave the reader asking more questions than he or she started with.

On the positive side, this book has a number of welcome characteristics. In the first place, it is above all honest, particularly in its central premise that delivering outstanding customer service every time – thousands, often tens of thousands of times a day – is exceptionally challenging, and this is why such a service is so financially rewarding. Secondly, it is pragmatic, directed for the most part towards 'real life' rather than academic navel gazing. Most importantly, it recognizes that the key to the objective of providing outstanding customer service lies with the business leader.

As a leader and with responsibility for a business which has set new standards in the provision of personal banking, why do I regard customer service as so important and the role of people as so central to its provision?

The answer to the first question is engagingly simple: it is one of the few enduring elements of competitive advantage. While any business may enjoy a short-term advantage through the development and launch of a new product, inevitably if it is successful it is replicated by competitors. To be successful in the long term the new product must be better than the competition. This is definitely the case in service industries but also the case with manufacturing. *xxxi*

The original Golf GTI is rightly regarded as a classic, mould-breaking car, combining performance with conventional car versatility, a brilliant concept and a concept widely copied by nearly every manufacturer, most obviously in the Ford Escort XR3. It was not that the GTI was first that made it successful over a ten-year period or longer, but that it was better designed and better built than the competition.

Next, people are central to the provision of service – and by people I mean predominately staff, though I also include customers, suppliers and shareholders.

Essentially service has two components: hygiene and motivation. Hygiene is the process of getting something right and is predominately improved through procedures, computer systems, indeed removing the opportunity for human error. The motivational component is how the service is delivered and is usually, perhaps inevitably, delivered by people. Thus the computer system tells the airline how many vegetarian meals to deliver to a flight, the quality of which is a key component to the customers' perception of the airline. Equally important is the role of the stewardess in its delivery – not just whether the meal is hot enough but the quality of her smile. As each passenger is an individual, each will put a different emphasis on the importance of these components, but few people will exclusively rate one and not the other.

Why, therefore, are staff so important? Simply that it is easier to manufacture 1 000 perfect meals than it is 1 000 perfect smiles and the smile thus becomes the key point of differentiation. This book seeks to help us along the road towards achieving this Holy Grail, the perfect genuine smile.

Readers may find some topics in the book familiar, but some of what it says will be new and much will be stimulating. None of the content can, however, be a substitute for an individual's belief in, indeed passion for, providing outstanding customer service.

Preface

The *Handbook of Customer Service* has been created for people at all levels – people who care about the delivery of service to their customers, which in a perfect world should be everybody. Our intention is to provide a source of reference, ideas, best practice and example. The chapters in this book, presenting quite different views and perspectives, illustrate that service excellence is achieved in varying ways. The common thread, however, is the part that people play in its design, planning, delivery and implementation.

The book is arranged around several themes and each chapter has been written primarily with the intention of bringing to its readers practical examples as opposed to just theory or rhetoric. We look at some of the key issues of service: the role of service in contributing to an organization's profitability; the outsourcing of service to third parties for delivery; the international dimension; competitive advantage; business processing engineering; and benchmarking. There are sections on measurement and planning; on active customer service; on cultural and organizational environment; on selecting, developing and keeping staff; and on the faceless service revolution (the use of telephone-based customer service/call centres). Some of the subject matter might be considered as belonging to the marketing or human resource domains, and for this I make no apology. For the topic of customer service is wide and varied, and excellent service delivery relies on strategies and action plans which cross all organizational boundaries.

This *Handbook* contains contributions from a large number of individuals and organizations. All of them were chosen because of their special experience and skills in relation to each topic and the way in which they view customer service relative to their subject matter. I acknowledge my gratitude to all those contributors and to the individuals and organizations who have provided information for inclusion in the appropriate chapters.

This preface provides me with a brief opportunity to comment on the *xxxiii* general status of customer service in the United Kingdom at the present time. Unfortunately, customer service, whilst now firmly on the agenda of many large organizations, is not yet recognized at a professional level. There are a growing number of NVQs covering the subject matter, but beyond that there is very little as yet. Assuming that we really are serious about the delivery of service excellence – and we must surely be – then this must change, and change quickly. If this book helps the process of learning and understanding in some small way, that will be a step forward. To me, customer service is one of the most important facets of commercial success, but in the United Kingdom and Europe its delivery is, on the whole, still well behind our American cousins.

Service is an integral part of branding, image and reputation – all of which have to be developed carefully and cherished forever. Customer service is like a successful West End musical. It depends on a cast with its members working together as one team; and on being led, directed and produced by people with a vision and a flair for what the public want. Success depends on critical acclaim and whether the seats sell out, and is driven by the product, the way in which it is marketed and the quality of its people. Continued success comes from consistently meeting the demands of its patrons, changing accordingly, and recognizing that replacing cast members needs to be done without compromising the mission or values of the whole and without the audience falling away.

Success will have been achieved when we no longer have to ask and define what customer service is – it will be blindingly obvious to all. As Louis Armstrong said, 'If you have to ask what jazz is, you'll never know'.

Finally, I must thank my wife, not only for all her help in reviewing the material for inclusion and in collating the chapters in a consistent fashion, but most of all for her patience and forbearance with me in trying to make this *Handbook* happen.

Peter Murley

Part I
CUSTOMER SERVICE IN CONTEXT

1 Evaluating the profitability of customer service*

Professor Merlin Stone

The adoption of a proper approach to customer service – the management of all customer contacts to mutual benefit – has many long-term effects on your business. For example, measurability of the results of customer service should make your marketing and service functions fully accountable for their expenditure. Understanding what creates customer loyalty, and how that loyalty translates into increased revenue and profits, means that business results can be traced back to activities and its benefits set against costs. Measurability also makes it easier to test the effectiveness of different approaches to customer service, giving you the tools to improve results.

The question of how much customer service is worth, therefore, poses three further questions:

1   How much is a properly serviced customer worth?
2   How much difference does good customer service make?
3   What is the strategic versus tactical application of customer service techniques?

THE WORTH OF A PROPERLY SERVICED CUSTOMER

'Lifetime value of the customer' is not a new concept. Its pedigree comes from direct marketing (especially mail order), where long-term customer behaviour is the key to success, and calculating the difference between costs of acquiring customers and the benefits and costs of retention is the norm. The concept is also widely used in consumer goods brand management, where the key calculation is how much to spend to prevent consumers from brand switching.

* The material in this chapter is based on research sponsored by IBM (UK) Ltd.

Calculating the value of a customer is logically simple: the key is data. The required process is as follows:

- Determine who are your target customers.
- Identify the costs of gaining and maintaining customers, and of selling additional products and services to them.
- Identify the profit contribution arising from the sales made.
- Identify the contribution of customer service to customer loyalty and how that loyalty supports or even creates increased sales.
- Calculate a stream of net contribution over the years.
- Use discounted cash-flow techniques to find customers' net present value.

Using historical data of customers you already have, lifetime value can be calculated and then extrapolated, making adjustments where necessary. Some companies are very uncomfortable about using past data as a predictor of future purchase behaviour. However, in many markets it has proved the most reliable method of forecasting.

Defining 'properly serviced'

'Properly serviced' means that you have:

- Identified the customer's needs.
- Developed appropriate products and services to meet those needs ('appropriate' in the sense of consistent with your business strategy and profit objectives).
- Matched the product to the needs, with appropriate prices, channels of distribution, presentation and marketing communications.
- Understood the customer's need for service.
- Developed a service process which meets the customer's needs.

Good marketing and customer service are not the same thing. For example, if you sell the wrong type of product to customers, or if you try to manage them through the wrong distribution channel, you'll be less likely to satisfy those customers, however much you invest in customer service. If they have a choice, they are unlikely to come back to you.

Your marketing plan, phrased in terms of its impact upon your customers, should tell you the minimum customer lifetime values (LTV) you are trying to create. However, if your marketing has not been properly focused on customers, or if your customer service is weak, your marketing plan will only represent a minimum LTV. In this case, your marketing plan should be revised when you have been through the entire customer service calculation.

HOW MUCH DIFFERENCE DOES GOOD CUSTOMER SERVICE MAKE?

The answer to this question depends on precisely how you do your customer service and how your customers react to your customer service initiatives. There are no absolutes here – every company is different, and so is every group of customers. The effect of good customer service can only be identified through research. This research will typically identify the following factors.

The kinds of contact customers perceive *they have with your company*

This is called the contact audit. Its results often surprise managers because they discover that their customers are in contact or attempted contact with their company far more often and in a greater variety of ways than they believed possible. Further, their customers may often think about contact but be dissuaded by the difficulty of achieving it!

The outcome of these contacts in terms of the relationship

Research is likely to produce a complex picture here. In simple terms, a positive outcome leads to improved customer service, but 'positive outcome' can relate to many policy areas: use of the right contact media; the right frequency and quality of contact; use of customer information to provide the right solution; 'right first time' solutions to problems; and complaints well handled, that is, a negative outcome followed by a positive outcome.

How customers react to these outcomes

Once again, the picture is likely to be complex. For example, well-handled complaints, or time taken to adjust a product to a customer's needs, may do more to reinforce purchasing behaviour than no-problem contacts or products which are from the beginning absolutely right for the customer. Usually, this is because when your customers complain, they receive higher quality attention than is normal. Worse, it may be because the only time they do receive your attention is when they complain!

Moreover you should be interested not only in customers who are directly affected, but also in those who are told by your existing customers how well you handle them. Customer satisfaction leads to recommendation certainly, but satisfaction after good problem-resolution may lead to stronger recommendation than just routinely good service! The key here is to estimate changes in lifetime buying behaviour, both of the customers affected and of those they tell about it. Naturally, the longer your company has been measuring the connection between, on the one hand, good customer service and, on the other, buying and recommending behaviour, the more accurate your estimates will be. However, the key need here is not for 100 per cent accuracy but *5* for a broad understanding of the longer-term profit implications of successful relationships.

The financial consequences

This is the translation of customers' relationship-affected buying behaviour into profit, in accordance with the methodology described above.

TACTICAL VERSUS STRATEGIC APPLICATION OF CUSTOMER SERVICE

Some of the techniques of customer service may be used simply as tactical weapons. However, you can use customer service more effectively by taking a strategic approach and transforming how you do business. The two key strategic factors that must be considered in payback calculations are: competitive superiority; and setting up barriers to competitive market entry.

Competitive superiority

You can establish competitive superiority by building and exploiting a database with comprehensive coverage of your existing and potential customers for your current and future products and services. You might use this capability aggressively, for example to win customers from your competitors (conquest sales) by regular mailings to their customers. Such mailings can ask for information about customer needs, and this information can then be used to design products and marketing programmes.

Competitive superiority can also be achieved through lower costs. In many industries, the field salesperson can only make between two and five calls per day (although in some industries the norm may be ten). A telemarketer can make between twenty and fifty decision-maker contacts per day. The optimum competitive policy is to employ field sales and telemarketing according to their relative strengths, using a customer database to coordinate the two.

Thus the sales force can be used where the face-to-face call is needed. This is likely to be in the following circumstances:

- Where personal service is considered essential.
- An important new contact is being made.
- A difficult and sensitive problem has to be solved.
- A complex presentation has to be made.
- In-depth diagnostic work has to be carried out.
- The customer asks for a sales visit.
- On-site research is required.

A telemarketing team, working off the customer database, can be used for all other calls. Eventually, with appropriate teamwork between the field sales force, the telemarketing team *and the customer* (whose time is also valuable and who therefore wants to be contacted by the most effective means for each call), more complex objectives can be handled by the telemarketing team. The telemarketer may become a full account manager. This approach increases the quantity and quality of contact between the sales force and customers, without increasing the cost. It also provides greater flexibility, enabling sales effort to be redeployed more quickly to meet competitive challenges. The discipline with which sales effort is managed can be increased: for example it can be organized to mount competitive attacks on specific customers known to be dissatisfied with a competitive product.

Neglected customers are a problem for most businesses. In many industrial product or service markets, it is the small business customers who may be neglected. In consumer markets, neglected customers may be isolated households or households with low purchasing frequencies. For both groups, the costs of traditional sales channels may preclude contact that is frequent enough to reinforce buying behaviour, and the customer may eventually switch to competitive products – assuming that your competitors have not fallen into the same trap!

Customer service provides an ideal way of building loyalty and maximizing revenue. For instance, the quality of customer service may be checked by a questionnaire to all customers, which could monitor customer satisfaction and intention to purchase next time. The results of the questionnaire could be used to identify problems and to ensure that dissatisfied customers do not become ex-customers. Such a questionnaire could also be used to structure campaigns aimed at managing the replacement cycle. Mailings could be sent just after purchase, halfway through the expected life of the product, and again close to replacement decision time.

Barriers to market entry

Businesses may find themselves unable to enter a market when faced with competitors who hold a high-quality customer database and use it effectively. In some cases, this database can be a unique asset. The cost of setting up such a database may make entry difficult or prohibitive for other contenders. Conversely, possession of a customer service capability may be the key to entering new markets.

QUANTIFYING THE IMPACT OF CUSTOMER SERVICE

The opportunities opened up by customer service are likely to affect both costs and revenue. Some lead to increased revenue while costs stay static or rise more slowly than revenue. Others lead to falling costs while revenue stays static or falls more slowly than costs. These effects will be achieved by the 7 development and implementation of particular *applications* of customer service, such as telephone-based customer management or telemanagement.

Many of the changes produced have both short- and long-term dimensions. For example, telemanagement may produce cost savings and revenue increases that arise relatively quickly through reducing the cost of contacting and selling to customers and by increasing market coverage. These shorter-term effects are not once and for all, but extend for as long as you continue to use the application. However, greater market coverage and the reduced cost of that coverage may allow you, in the longer term, to enter different product markets. You may be able to sell a wider product range to existing customers. It may also be possible to sell database information resulting from the application.

The revenue and cost changes that might result from different aspects of customer service must therefore be identified and quantified. This can be done, for example, in the following ways:

- by category of customer;
- by category of product;
- by application introduced (for example sales force support, inbound or outbound telemarketing, direct mail);
- by category of change (that is whether it is cost saving, revenue defence, or growth);
- by time period (short, medium or long term); or
- by category of staff, function or marketing channel (for example impact on field sales force, sales offices, retail outlets, physical distribution, marketing communication, market research, technical service).

The cost-reducing and revenue-increasing effects of some changes are inseparable. If more revenue comes from a fixed-cost base, costs fall as a proportion of sales.

The quantification process can be carried out by the following means.

Target opportunities

You must first generate a shortlist of target opportunities for managing customers better. This objective is usually best achieved in management workshops, supplemented where necessary by a series of management interviews and discussions. You may find that many of the best ideas are already present in your company, but have not previously been allowed to emerge because of the way in which your policies are planned and implemented. After all, many customer service applications are the implementation of common-sense ideas through the use of modern information technology. They may involve, for example:

- Reorganizing workflows or changing organizational structure and reporting lines;

- Re-engineering processes;
- Policy development within existing functions, departments, product groups and so on;
- Opening up of internal communication channels;
- Revenue development opportunities;
- Revenue protection ideas; or
- Quality control measures.

The outcome of this step is a statement of your target opportunities, which provides the focus for the rest of the analysis.

Incremental revenue

Existing marketing plans should be reviewed to identify long-term revenue growth objectives and to clarify the basis for revenue growth plans. Revenue growth plans may be based on factors such as overall market growth, specific marketing strategies (product range, price, distribution, advertising and so on), and anticipated competitive changes. Areas to be considered where an improved relationship will make a difference are:

- Improving retention rates by x per cent (even small percentages may have a very large impact on the bottom line).
- Cross-selling (how many of your customers buy both product A and product B. If this percentage is increased, you can usually make substantial additional profits, if only by spreading marketing and administrative costs over larger revenues).
- Up-selling.
- Improving renewal rates.
- Becoming better at reactivating lapsed customers.

This analysis will indicate the areas where customer service may generate revenue growth through improving the effectiveness of policies that are already planned. Figure 1.1 is a checklist containing some examples of other revenue generation or protection areas.

Cost changes

Quantifying the cost savings from implementing an improved approach to customer service prior to implementation is not easy. It is even more difficult if your existing marketing information is not well organized. If you have only recently adhered to the marketing creed, the information required to quantify cost effects may have to be estimated. This may require not only 'reconstruction of figures', based on estimates of staff but also the use of pilot studies, where particular applications are implemented.

Field sales force and sales office

Higher revenue due to ability of sales staff to concentrate calling on higher
revenue prospects
Less lost business and fewer lost customers due to improved customer care,
as a focus on customer service often leads to improved channels for customers
to signal needs
Enhanced new product revenues due to improved ability to target customers for
new products and eventually consequent greater ease of launching new products . . .
Greater ability of sales force to handle broader product portfolio, due to
deployment of response-handling system to inform relevant customers prior
to the sales call. . . .

Market research

Greater ability to identify potential for increased revenue among existing
customers. . . .

Business and marketing planning

More coherent plans to address new revenue opportunities, due to higher quality
and relevance of information, leading to higher success rate with launch of new
products, greater matching of distribution channels to customer needs and so on . . .

Retail

Ability to market additional products to existing retail customers, whether at retail
or through mail order, due to quality of customer information . . .
Higher sales volumes of existing products due to ability to target promotions. . . .

Marketing communications

Greater effectiveness of communicating with customers and prospects,
leading to higher revenue for given cost. . . .

Product marketing

Reduced costs of selling, due to better attunement of channels to customer
needs, leading to ability to capture higher market share through lower prices. . . .

Inventory

Lower stock-outs and therefore quicker inflow of revenue and reduced loss of
sales to competition due to improved sales forecasting. . . .

Figure 1.1   Checklist of revenue defending or increasing opportunities

Typically, a comprehensive exercise to gather and analyse cost information
is required. It will normally cover every channel of communicating with and
distributing products and services to customers, such as sales force, sales
offices operating by telephone and mail, retail outlets, media advertising and

direct mail. The aim is to quantify costs which may be changed by new approaches to customer service. This exercise is based on interviews, questionnaires and analysis of financial and operating information relating to the channels of communication, distribution and service. Such an analysis may have to be carried out by market sector and product line as well as for the whole business, as some of the opportunities may be confined to particular products or sectors.

For example, suppose that you need to estimate the cost-reducing effects of changing the way your sales force services your customers. The data needed include:

- Sales force activity analysis, to find out how your sales staff are spending their time, and in particular, time spent on low productivity activities such as prospecting and converting low-potential customers, compared with time spent on high-productivity activities (time spent converting high-potential customers or preventing their loss).
- Sales revenue productivity statistics, to measure the productivity of the time actually devoted to your customers.
- Data on market size (overall and by product – number of customers and revenue potential), to enable you to estimate the proportion of the market (overall or for given products) left uncovered by your sales force.
- Data on how the activity profile of your sales force changes when you implement customer service and put relevant applications (for example, telemarketing, direct mail) to work.
- Data on the current costs of managing your sales force.
- Information on how the activities which generate these costs affect the productivity of your sales staff.
- Information on how customer service disciplines will lead to a change in the nature and scale of these activities (for example, data provision work by support staff).

Contact strategies

The current method of managing customer contacts should be determined. Future contact strategy options, using customer service, should then be identified, and an assessment made of:

- The capability of existing channels to support revenue growth targets and the cost of resourcing those channels to achieve them.
- The incremental cost of the customer service strategy needed to support the revenue growth target.

With these and other data, cost effects can then be calculated. Consider this business-to-business example (see Figure 1.2). Suppose that a field sales visit costs £250, a highly skilled telephone account management call £8 and a mailing £1 per contact and the spread of contacts throughout the year is as *11*

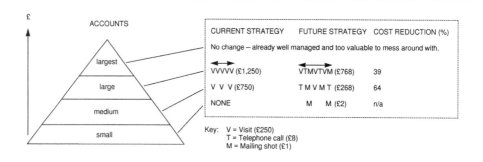

Figure 1.2   Cost effect of contact strategies

indicated. In the future strategy, the large (not largest) and medium-size accounts generate a cost of sales reduction of 39 per cent and 64 per cent respectively. In the low-volume accounts, although the cost of sales (COS) has been increased at least we are talking to them, giving them the opportunity to identify themselves as potential purchasers. Notice that in all cases the number of contacts per year has actually increased. Clearly the measure here will be not just cost of sales but revenue and customer satisfaction. Some customers will wholeheartedly resist being managed by the telephone. Others will actually welcome it! The key is to identify which ones are which.

Other potential cost reduction areas are illustrated in Figure 1.3.

Revenue and cost review

A summary of marketing and customer service activity over the period of the plan should then be prepared, showing the effect on costs and revenues of employing existing methods to achieve targets, and comparing it with the costs and revenues implied by the change in approach to servicing customers. This should indicate the areas where the approach is more effective.

If the analysis indicates the need for distribution channel change, the result might be a wholesale change in the revenue/cost profile. Whole categories of cost may disappear (for example, the abolition of sales branches) and new ones appear (for example, their replacement by a central sales coordination unit). Distribution channel change may create further strategic marketing opportunities, such as the ability to address whole new markets or launch completely different types of product. However, the change may be less revolutionary (for example, retargeting a calling sales force on larger customers, and either supporting or replacing their efforts by a telemarketing operation).

Changing the approach to customer service may reveal many opportunities for increasing revenue and reducing costs but unless these opportunities are firmly built into operating plans as objectives, they are unlikely to be achieved.

Will you achieve any of the following?

Field sales force

- Reduction in number needed for given market coverage. This would be through a more efficient calling pattern and less time spent identifying prospects and obtaining prospect information.
- Reduced staff support required, due to higher-quality information available to sales staff.
- Reduced systems support, due to unification of possible variety of support systems.
- Reduced sales force turnover due to quality of support and consequent higher motivation.
- Possibly broader span of management control and reduced number of reporting levels feasible. This would be due to a better standard of information on activities and effectiveness of field sales staff, leading to lower management costs.

Sales office

- Reduced number of staff required to deal with a given number of customers or support a given number of field sales staff. This would be due to reduction in time spent obtaining and collating information and more efficient prospecting systems.
- Reduced costs of handling customer enquiries due to improved structuring of response handling mechanism, so that customer enquiries go to relevant destination more smoothly without passing through irrelevant hands.
- Lower staff turnover due to higher level of support and consequent improved morale.
- Broader span of control and reduced number of reporting levels feasible, due to better standard of information on activities and effectiveness of office sales staff, leading to lower management costs.
- Reduction in number of branch offices due to ability to cover market better and more 'remotely'.

Market research

- Lower expenditure on external research, due to higher quality and relevance of information available on customers and prospects.

Marketing and business planning

- Reduced costs of information collection and management, due to availability of higher-quality, more relevant and updated information on customers and prospects, leading to possible reduction in numbers of planning staff or in planning component of other jobs.

Retail

- Improved site planning, due to ability to match customer profiles to area profiles more accurately. This might lead to a reduction in the number of outlets to attain given revenue targets.
- Lower surplus inventory, due to ability to target 'sale' merchandise marketing.
- Higher utilization of space, due to ability to market special in-store events to database.

Figure 1.3   Potential cost reduction areas

Product/brand marketing

- Reduced costs of selling, due to better attunement of existing and new channels — some of which are only possible using customer service — to customer needs.

Marketing communications

- Lower costs for achieving any given task, due to greater accountability and to improved ability to identify targets for communication and make communication relevant and therefore more effective.

Inventory

- Reduced write-offs due to reduced frequency of launch of inappropriate products and to earlier termination of dying products.
- General improved forecastability of marketing campaigns, leading to reduced temporary inventory peaks for given products.

Figure 1.3 concluded

There needs to be agreement with the appropriate revenue- or cost-responsible functions concerning how revenue and cost opportunities are to be exploited. It is therefore important for these functions to be involved in the whole strategic appraisal process.

HOW MUCH SHOULD YOU SPEND ON CUSTOMER SERVICE?

Here, the answer is surprisingly simple: **as much as is profitable**. Your research should show you what you risk when customer service fails and what you gain when you get it right. It will also show where problems are greatest and where pay-off is likely to be highest. It will also show what problems are faced by customers and what needs to be done to resolve them. The next step is the financial calculation: How much extra profit you will make? In some cases, the calculation may look one-sided because you may be forced to improve customer service just to meet competitive standards and stay in business. So include revenue protection.

Because of interdependence between different customer service activities and the expectation customers may have for continuous improvement, it may be best to develop a long-term programme of improvement, with recalibration at intervals. This serves to check how customer needs have changed in the interim and to monitor the effectiveness of implementation of your actions.

NEW OPPORTUNITIES FOR IMPROVING CUSTOMER SERVICE

This section should probably be called 'new necessities for improving customer service', at least in competitive markets, since low management awareness of the link between customer service, profit and competitiveness implies a poor outlook for companies whose customer service standards fall behind those of competition.

Management awareness that there is a close connection between customer service and profit, and that the strength of this connection can be quantified – often through the impact on customer loyalty and retention – may lead to new approaches to customer management, starting with the identification of groups of customers who wish to be managed differently and ending with a long-term commitment to achieving differentiated and higher levels of customer service in order to maximize profit. The essence of the new approach is a much stronger customer orientation in business and marketing strategy.

FEASIBILITY ANALYSIS

Two constraints that warrant further research are: technical feasibility; and financial/resource feasibility.

Technical feasibility

Technical feasibility is defined as the levels – frequency, type and quality of contact, planned outcomes – of customer service it is possible to deliver, at different resource levels. Here, levels of customer service should be translated into likely resulting customer behaviour, as your next step is to work out what levels of customer service it is worth providing, measured against the rewards to you in terms of changed customer behaviour.

Financial feasibility

Once the alternatives that are achievable through customer service actions are identified, you are in a position to research financial feasibility.

Customer service requires investment decisions like any other business action and should therefore be subject to the same financial disciplines. This should ensure the provision of the right level of service. It is possible to over-invest in service, with no real return. Assessing financial feasibility requires quantifying the costs of customer service policies and setting them against the benefits (for example, reduced future costs of query handling, increased profit through increased sales). This is not always a question of simple calculations. You may have to make assumptions about the financial and market factors which will apply in the future.

Customer service orientation sounds fine, but red lights may flash for your financial management when this term is used, for it can be a bottomless pit for hard-earned money. Hence the need to justify all customer service expenditure in terms of your financial objectives. The best justification for you is increased business from existing customers, reduction in customer losses and more new customers.

Furthermore, advocates of increased investment in customer service should be asked to justify not only the whole package but every individual element of it. This is the only way to stop incurring unnecessary costs. In this respect, the main areas of cost in setting up customer service include the following:

- systems (hardware, software development and/or licenses, telecommunications);
- specific people training;
- culture shift education programmes for the organization;
- process re-engineering;
- policy development (time);
- setting up new units (for example, telemarketing units);
- closure of old units (for example, branches for instance); and
- redundancy payments.

Each area of cost must be set against the marketing benefits that accrue from it, which lie principally within the scope for customer acquisition and retention. Your ability to acquire and retain customers depends critically on how well you satisfy their needs.

FURTHER READING

MacKechnie, D. (1995), 'Customer Profitability', *Customer Service Management*, **7**, June, 40–1.

Stone, M. and Woodcock, N. (1995), 'Customer Service and Relationship Marketing', *Customer Service Management*, **8**, September, 39–42.

Stone, M. and Young, L. (1992), *Competitive Customer Care*, London: Croner.

Stoner, M. (1995), 'Communicating with Customers to Keep Them Loyal', *Business: Growth and Profitability*, **1** (3), September, 233–42.

2 The role of benchmarking

Allan Trayes

The term 'benchmarking' originated in surveying. A benchmark is a physical line drawn on a landmark that is thought to be a permanent feature of the landscape. Surveyors are then able to map an area relative to the benchmark and, more importantly, anyone else can measure their own position relative to that point, within a three-dimensional space.

The term has been taken and used in a number of other professional fields of activity. The computer industry used it throughout the 1980s to produce comparisons of equipment performance. They speak of 'landmark speeds' and manufacturers have standards that communicate the relative power of the machines they produce. PCs were often referred to in the IBM XT series as the baseline for performance.

BENCHMARKING IN BUSINESS

In business the term has been adopted over recent years by organizations that are keen to know how well they are doing relative to competitors and other industries. In the business context, benchmarking is a process of continuous comparison. The goal is usually organizational improvement through examination of products and services – a review of practices and processes that make up the organization's capability, which results in measurable performance improvement.

The spur to benchmarking activity can arise for a variety of reasons. All too often the organizational performance is deteriorating and there is a belated recognition of the need for change in order to survive. This is not usually the best time to start benchmarking activity. More successful prompts are those driven by natural curiosity to know how the organization compares with competitors and other players who offer excellence in the considered activity. Successful benchmarking starts when the organization is ahead and is *17* prepared to build the structured programme necessary and invest the resources required to get a usable result.

Natural curiosity comes in many forms: it can be kindled by changing market conditions; it may be initiated by a business process re-engineering (BPR) exercise that forces the organization to consider its future mode of operation; it may be the result of regulatory activity requiring changed practice and performance. It may even be driven by internal dynamics that force the question: 'How good are we really?' Even when the organization feels comfortable about itself, its profitability and its competitiveness, there is always the nagging doubt about whether it has a sustainable position.

Benchmarking is a way of satisfying the inquisitive mind, for it provides a means of importing learning from other organizations. It can enhance perspective on industry strategic megatrends and inform management of micromovements within functional domains. It can paint a picture of reality, based on data, informed research and logic that often belies perception and received wisdom. The newly acquired understanding of the organizational context is a much better framework for strategic and tactical decision making that can add greater certainty to desired outcomes. It can transform the way a business is conducted and lead to radical performance improvements on the bottom line.

The positive perspectives and application of benchmarking must, however, be taken in a balanced way. The activity has to be carefully positioned in the successful organization. It is not a panacea. Benchmarking must only be used to inform other activities that are part of the process for change. For it to be successful it must be conducted as a continuous process, and supported by the right investment of both time and money in order to make it a success. Most certainly it is not a one-off activity that is initiated in a time of crisis, for it is a dangerous tool if used improperly, and, employed out of context, it can generate misleading cues and indicate inappropriate change. The activity reveals parts of a puzzle that represents a 'whole market view'. To see only small parts of the puzzle and to make decisions on such data will lead to poor direction and focus. The methodology that follows should avoid such pitfalls.

BENCHMARKING VERSUS COMPETITIVE ANALYSIS

Benchmarking is by nature a cooperative activity, which relies on organizations sharing non-threatening information and data for its success. Competitive analysis has a different aim. It is targeted at discovering what direct competitors are actually doing on a day-by-day basis in your markets. By nature it is more aggressive in the data-gathering phase, and by definition it targets understanding that competitors would rather you did not have. It relies for its success on analysis of public data, interview material, and detailed analysis of data leading to conclusions about the direction or actions of a competitor.

Competitive analysis springs from a militaristic view of competition – to gain advantage, know the enemy better than they know you. Benchmarking, on the other hand, is a partnership exercise aimed at mutual advantage and success.

Often, competitors are natural allies in the benchmarking game. Mature organizations do not see this as a threat, realizing that even though a competitor may understand what they are doing, the competitor still has to make use of that data, which will entail significant organizational restructuring and investment of time and money to achieve. The advantage is not lost. Many markets share data and learning and enable third parties to act as repositories for their own data. An example is the work performed by the Department of Trade and Industry. This has 30 benchmarking initiatives in specific markets in the United Kingdom and the data is readily available. They have identified around 80 independent markets in all, and have taken a leadership role through a desire to see UK players outperform overseas competition.

TYPES OF BENCHMARKING

Benchmarking can operate at a *strategic* level, where the goal is to relate the work to strategic development, organizational redesign or perhaps a substantial process re-engineering exercise. The data will be used in the decision-making processes.

Practical benchmarking can be *external* – often the chief perspective for most organizations – and focus into one of five domains (see figure 2.1 page 21) explained in the methodology below. It may also be *internal,* where comparison is made of functional performance across the organization with the goal of optimizing that performance.

BENEFITS OF BENCHMARKING

A properly conducted benchmarking exercise yields significant insights into any organization's relative performance. The benefits are often gained through shared experiences and are sometimes as simple as not repeating others' mistakes. More often, new ideas are generated by seeing how others have tackled similar problems. There are obvious benefits in discovering how performance rates relative to other similar companies within and outside the specific industry sector, but in addition there are a number of other benefits that accrue:

1 Rapid development for professionals and those working on the benchmarking team. The effect is to import knowledge often only gained by recruiting staff from other organizations.
2 Provision of an excellent database for supporting capital investment decisions. Examples of results of the application of new methods can be used to illustrate the effects of an investment on company performance.
3 Early warning of the onset of a non-competitive position. Understanding industry trends and methods provides a clear indicator of changed conditions. This enables an early response before crisis sets in.
4 A network of contacts is established that facilitates acquisition of data and information when required and that keeps other organizations aware of your own capabilities and skills.

Moreover, starting a benchmarking exercise makes the organization as a whole aware of possibilities outside the normal way of working. This changed perspective is the so-called Paradigm Shift of current management thinking. The cumulative corporate intelligence increases and the organization starts to move into a constant learning mode. This is an excellent basis for building the so-called knowledge-based organization that is the foundation for competition in many modern markets.

A METHODOLOGY FOR BENCHMARKING

Any benchmarking activity, by definition, requires a reference point to be successful, otherwise nothing may be referred back to a common point of understanding so that changes and innovation can be planned and communicated successfully.

An organization intent on starting a benchmarking programme should use itself as the first reference point. This may seem strange, but until the organization understands itself fully it will be unable to make any external or internal comparisons that enable the identification of improvements. Once the initial internal analysis has been completed, there is a basis for comparison and the process of gathering comparative data may begin. The data and knowledge that has then been gained will illustrate accepted best practices and performance in the fields of interest and will indicate significant areas for self-improvement.

It is usually at this stage, that the programme will start to design a model that defines the sum of all the best practices and performance observed during data gathering. This model may then be adopted as the aspirational goal inside the organization and may become the 'benchmark target'. Of course, such a model does not exist in reality but it serves the purpose of producing a focus for improvement. It will inform the organization on how to compete and win and will indicate changes within the organisation necessary to achieve that goal.

'World class' or 'best of breed' as the target?

It is common to talk of becoming world class, and benchmarking is often targeted at producing information which will support that goal. It must be realized that attainment of such a goal is very difficult. By definition you will be attempting to do everything as well as, if not better than, the best you see. This is expensive and usually unnecessary. If you can define what success looks like for your organization, then pursuit of excellence in those elements that deliver success is all that is required. Competitively, it is sufficient to lead your own market in areas of management that produce competitive advantage. You will become 'best of breed' rather than setting the pace worldwide. Adopting such an objective simplifies the benchmark process and enables manageable change.

To become truly world class requires an organizational and cultural transformation that can take many years and cause considerable pain. The root is a passion for excellence that is endemic in the whole organization. It is pointless, however, to set benchmark targets that are unobtainable. Targets that are reasonable and attainable produce more measurable change.

Knowing yourself

There is an increasing amount of work being performed on the subject of organizational competence and capability. Strategic thinkers have suggested in the early 1990s that the organization competes on its competencies (Prahalad and Hamel, 1990), and that a clear view of the 'strategic intent' of the organization is critical (Hamel and Prahalad, 1989) and must be communicated clearly. More recently, Vollman (1993) has linked benchmarking into business transformation at the strategic level. For current purposes, the attention is more practical and the *competence–capability* construct is used to look in more depth at customer service benchmarking, the primary assumption being that customer service is a *competence*.

As indicated already, self-understanding is critical to any benchmarking exercise. In the benchmarking context, the structure of most organizations may be considered using the model shown in Figure 2.1.

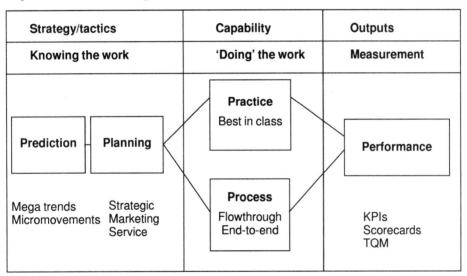

Figure 2.1   The five Ps of benchmarking customer service

The organization operates in a market context and applies a set of capabilities to that context to produce results. This view of the organization considers market movements and changes as external forces that need to be tracked and Predicted. The results are fed into Planning cycles that are used to inform the deployment of operational capability (Process and Practice) and outcomes (Performance).

For most circumstances, organizations manage the Prediction element intuitively. Planning is already quite structured, and concerns centre on whether the right competence is deployed or not. Prediction and Planning form the strategic element of self-awareness and strategic benchmarking is aimed at improving that self-knowledge. Top-level customer service considerations will be included in any strategic benchmarking exercise; the questions asked are usually as follows:

1   Is it good value for money?
2   Is it a competitive variable that can be levered?
3   Is our competence par or better than the market average?

Detailed customer service benchmarking work usually has to answer these questions by providing comparatives of unit costs and a relative quality assessment. In an overall benchmark programme, customer service is usually only one element and the activity should therefore dovetail into the data collection methods of the whole programme.

Breaking customer service down to manageable structure

There is a critical distinction between competence and capability. The organization may often be highly competent in an activity but it may not actually own or be expert in the capabilities that deliver that competence. For example, an organization may be highly competent at delivering customer service but in the extreme case may have outsourced the capabilities for many elements to third parties. Customer service as a whole may be considered a core competence for any organization and a competence that may be successfully compared with others operating in the same market by comparing capabilities.

Figure 2.2 illustrates how the competence of customer service may be viewed as a set of capabilities used to deliver the service to the customer. In answering the question, 'How good are we at customer service?', it is often easier to answer by asking, 'How good are we at capability X, Y or Z?'

Breaking down the customer service competence into its capability set makes it much easier to benchmark the activity, since identical capabilities may usually be identified in organizations with very different service goals and requirements and operating in different markets. A common language can be developed with other organizations since the work is often understood and common at the micro level.

Capabilities can be further classified into a mix of *process* and *practice* as illustrated in Figure 2.2. Processes are the critical backbone of any service operation. How they are delivered to the customer fundamentally affects the customer experience and this is a matter of applied practice, or the way in which apparently identical processes can be operated with differing results.

Processes consist of many different activities performed in sequence. In benchmarking organizations it is often valid to compare process steps or activities directly. Practices are often the result of applied skills and knowledge.

Primary capability	Capability breakdown (Practices/skills)	Breakdown into:	
		Processes/activity	Practice
Call centres	● Telephone call management *Inbound* and *outbound*	Call routing Call completion Wrap-up Fulfilment List building	Salutation Training Calling frequency (*Outbound*)
	● Workforce scheduling	Shift planning Holiday rotas	Employee base Recruitment
	● Demand forecasting	Campaign Management	
Field management	● Engineering	Field repair Installations Maintenance	Problem resolution Escalation
	● Workforce scheduling ● Customer management	Job planning	Documentation Version-control
Parts management and inventory control	● Inventory management	Supplier ordering Invoice payment	Just-in-time Cross-docking
	● Hot-line parts management ● Logistics	'Red routes' Distribution	
Third-party management	● Tender preparation ● Supplier scheduling	Quality control Financial checks	Audits Supplier Evaluate
Complaint handling	● Recovery	Complaint log Compensation Closing	Resolution Escalation Empowerment
	● Data management ● Escalation	Data verification Hand over to executive	
PR and advertising	● Brand positioning ● Campaign advertising ● Media management	No process Media buying Outsourced to HQ	Creative
Campaign fulfilment	● Outsourced to agency	None	Supplier Management
Facility management	● Outsourced to internal group	None	Supplier Management
Information technology (IT)	● Outsourced to internal groups	None	Supplier Management

Figure 2.2   Example capability set for 'customer service competence'

Once again, in benchmarking it is often valid to compare skills directly, even though they may only be one element in an overall practice.

The next step in the methodology is to consider each of the capabilities and start breaking each one down into the processes/activities and practices/skills that make up capability, using the shape of Figure 2.2. Then define the critical success factors (CSFs) for each capability. CSFs may be the result of an exercise to discover what actually is critical to the organization. Sometimes the organization works only with perceived goals or objectives for the processes/ activities and practices/skills. Against this breakdown into CSFs/goals/objectives, a set of quantitative and qualitative measures or comparatives may be described. These will then be the source of the benchmarks used to compare against other organizations. Figure 2.3 provides an example of the layout required.

Competence: Customer service
Capability: Call centres

Activity/process or practice/skill	CSF/goal	Quantitative/qualitative measure
Call routing	All calls to be handled quickly and by the correct agent	Average wait time Number of hand-offs On-call time Abandoned call rate
Call completion	Customers problems to be solved immediately and handled efficiently	Points of failure Call duration Hand offs to support Wrap up time
Employee base	To recruit and retain the right people, doing the right job	Attrition rate Training days Absence rate Management layers Span of control Team sizes

Figure 2.3   Analysis of quantitative and qualitative measures

The benchmarking organization can review the measures set out in Figure 2.3 and develop or discover by research and analysis the common measures used to assess each of these processes and practices in other companies. This analysis will then form the basis of the benchmark data to be collected. The organization collects data on its own performance and tabulates it against the model in Figure 2.3. The data would be laid out as illustrated in Figure 2.4. This analysis may then be used in this form to compare organizations and draw conclusions on relative performance.

Activity/process or practice/skill measure	Company					Own performance	Benchmark target
	1	2	3	4	5		
Average answer (seconds)	10	13	15	16	12	23	14
Number of hand-offs (Average per call)	3	2	3	4	2	7	3
Call duration (Total seconds)	260	380	280	650	420	720	400
Support hand-offs (Average per call)	1	0	2	2	1	3	1
Wrap up time for a call (seconds)	100	130	25	234	123	345	150
Attrition rate (%/year)	11	22	12	8	10	32	15
Training days/year	10	7	12	15	15	3	10
Absence rate (% lost days/month)	3.5	4.2	2.2	3.2	4.2	5.6	3.2
Management layers	5	4	4	6	5	9	5
Span of control	4	5	6	4	5	3	5
Team sizes	8	10	13	14	10	5	10

Figure 2.4 Plotting the results of the comparative analysis measures

The conclusions from Figure 2.4 might be that the company performing the benchmarking has a number of process problems with call centre capability and that the human resources are not managed as effectively as they might be. The benchmark targets now become the goals that this organization will aspire to in future. Programmes of activity may be designed to improve operations to match the benchmark targets based on the conclusion drawn from the comparative data in Figure 2.4.

The way in which the company is improved will be driven by the observations of practice and methods observed when the companies in the programme are studied. Methods will have been documented as a result of observation on visits. Improvement and change programmes will need to be designed to facilitate the adoption of the new methods inside the company.

Internal and external

The method outlined above is equally applicable internally as well as externally, although internally will be used to compare activities and functions. The purpose is usually to transfer knowledge and ability from high-performing units to those that may benefit from the experience of others. Such transfer of learning can be achieved by the transfer of personnel internally to take best practice into the learning unit.

The practical aspects – actually doing it, how, with what and with whom

Once the methodology is understood, the benchmarking endeavour has to be undertaken. There is a simple, defined, benchmarking process that needs to be followed. Spendolini (1992) describes a five-stage model that needs to be frequently repeated for benchmarking to be of value. Other literature describes the process differently, but all indicate the same basic approach. Simply plan what you are going to do; do it; analyse results; and then act. Watson (1993) articulates this very clearly, relating the process to the Deming cycle. If the basic methodology described earlier is adopted to provide the self-awareness and structure to the data required in the benchmarking programme, then the organization is in a good state to enter the process. It will have the necessary approach to make the activity a success, and it will be able to choose the primary areas of comparative data to collect.

The basic steps, therefore, in any benchmarking process are as follows:

1 Know yourself. Use the competence/capability analysis to decide on the data that you need to collect and build the structure of the knowledge base. Develop focus.
2 Win the resources to collect the data. People, time and money are required. Completing step 1 will allow the quantification of need to progress this stage of the process.
3 Identify target organizations to compare against. Plan visits to observe practices and collect process measures.
4 Complete the desk-bound research, perform the visits and write the report.
5 Translate the results into change programmes and action.
6 Start again when you have finished – things have already changed.

These process steps have been extensively described in other literature and the reader is referred to that literature for a more comprehensive understanding and account (Spendolini, 1992; Watson, 1993).

CRITICAL POINTS FOR SUCCESS IN THE PROCESS OF BENCHMARKING CUSTOMER SERVICE

In this context, customer service is treated as one competence in the company set. As such, it should be placed within the framework of an overall benchmarking programme so that appropriate conclusions about performance may be reached. It is not unusual to form a separate team as a subset to the main exercise, specifically to gather the customer service data. If that approach is followed, then the following points need to be considered.

Team selection is critical – there are many models for building teams and they all have something to offer here. The benchmarking task involves collating much detail, and therefore it is essential to engage people who are happy in performing that role and in formatting data in order to share results in a meaningful way with others. One commonly used model of team structuring was proposed by Belbin; Handy (1976) gives a good description of this model and other aspects of team working. In the benchmarking context, 'finisher' and 'resource investigator' are essential types, teams often suffer from too many 'shapers' and detailed work can be missed or not recorded adequately. Direct knowledge and experience of the activity being reviewed is also an essential contribution to the team dynamic. It is usual to include operational management in the team, especially during the visit stage.

The team must consider the whole exercise as a project and set milestones, building project charts and plans, and communicating them. They must also track threats and issues, recognizing that as with all projects, unforeseen circumstances can halt the project and compromise the value of the delivery. It is essential to have a clear purpose to the exercise and sponsors at the correct (i.e. boardroom) level. All visits in particular must be planned well in advance.

Perform the detailed deskbound research first. Much data can be gathered in the business library, while relationships with local universities often yield access to high quality material. Identify appropriate alternative sources of information. Common channels used include: consultancy houses, who often run databases of selected benchmark data built from various assignments; trade associations; common interest groups such as professional institutes; government agencies (the DTI in particular). There are also groups such as the International Benchmark Committee and the San Francisco Consulting Group who specialize in building benchmark reports.

At the stage of actually visiting selected companies, first build a criteria set for selecting the companies to compare against. This criteria set will usually include: similarity of processes (for example – high volume, low complexity); similar market positions; related culture; and same relative state (that is – growth, stable or decline). Be aware that when brainstorming the list, it is common for people's prejudices to be exerted, often unwittingly: people will favour or exclude on the basis of limited information and personal subjective experience. It is important, however, to target organizations that have expertise in your areas of focus. Avoid working with too many companies to start with; six is about right.

When selecting companies, recognize that there are distinct cultural differences that influence behaviours, practices and processes. Customer service is particularly subject to cultural differences. It is conducted by people, for people, and is therefore shaped by the social standards prevalent in the predominant culture. Do not assume that a practice which works well in one culture will be successful in another.

Finally, when producing the report, remember that it has a critical audience, and however fascinating the experience, that audience just wants the facts. The product of a successful benchmark activity is often only a few pages of comparative tables, with opportunities highlighted and explained. Make sure that the backup data is logged and archived effectively. Publishing separate 'best practice' discussion documents often produces significantly more impact on the organization.

GAINING MAXIMUM IMPACT ON CUSTOMER SERVICE

Benchmarking customer service has most impact when it indicates new ways for service competence to support the delivery of the organization's strategic intent. This implies that the benchmark team has fully to understand and subscribe to the definition of that intent and have a clear idea of how the organization views the future position of the customer service. This will indicate expected performance and behaviour and, more importantly, timescales over which transformation and change is required. For benchmarking to make sense, operational management must understand the position and role customer service plays in delivering the strategic intent.

Impact can come from disclosing the opportunity to improve in the organization by demonstrating examples of smoother process flow and significantly better performance measures. Impact can also illustrate discontinuities, ways that other organizations achieve the same results with significantly less resources or with drastically imploded processes. Both of these new views can point to a common organizational problem, pathology, the denial of redundancy and obsolescence in a process. This is often the most dangerous element inherent in organizational resistance, particularly in customer service, since it so adversely affects the customer experience. Benchmarking can be used to indicate important breakthroughs to overcome such creeping torpor.

Typically, radical transformations are found in the application of technology, the management of parts and materials, servicing techniques, and handling the classic processes of customer acquisition and retention. Examples are scheduling and automating field repair management, using 'just in time' parts delivery for field repair and placing responsibility for parts holding with the supplier.

The value of the benchmark practices must be seen throughout the organization for meaningful change to happen. Awareness must therefore start at board level and the board must act as evangelists for the new methods. By implication, this places the board as the earliest audience.

CLASSIC SERVICE BENCHMARKS

As described, customer service as a competence may be broken down into a number of capabilities, each consisting of a mix of process and practice, activities and skills. Service benchmarking that has this defined structure recognises process elements and practice elements within each capability area. Figure 2.5 shows examples of classic service benchmarks used in benchmark projects. These benchmarks are usually well known to most organizations and will often appear on balanced scorecards used in operational areas.

Many 'best practice' benchmarks are difficult to define numerically – organizations will often refer to company X or Y as being best at a particular

Capability	Process/ practice	Classic measure	Expressed as:	Typical value
Telephone call Management	Call pick-up	Grade of service	% of calls answered in x seconds	90% in 20 second
	Lost-call rate	% abandoned calls	% inbound calls lost	<2%
Complaints handling	Customer recovery	Turn around time	% of complaints answered in x days	90% in 10 days
Engineering	Field repair	Mean time to repair	Hours	Depends on products
Inventory management	Parts holding	Days of supply	Days	As low as possible
Employee management	Employee welfare	% absence	% days lost due to absence	3%
Employee management	Employee retention	% attrition	% of workforce leaving per annum	Around 10%
Employee management	Training	Number of training days	Days/employee per annum	10 days
Information technology	Systems availability	% system up-time	Ratio of hours available in service time	99%
Facility management	Environment	Occupancy	Sq ft/person	70 sq ft/person

Figure 2.5   Examples of classic service benchmarks

capability. For example, First Direct, from the banking world, has been used by many as the benchmark in call-centre practice in the United Kingdom for several years. Hewlett Packard is seen as an example of effective field repair management and Dell are often quoted as examples of direct service and supply in personal computers.

Care should be exercised when selecting 'best practice' companies. Best practice has a limited lifespan and good practices can quickly die out. Make sure that information on the company is current.

AN ULTIMATE MEASURE OF CUSTOMER SERVICE COMPETENCE

There is a great desire to seek the ultimate measure of customer service competence. Such a measure would be very useful to the media for league table purposes, and it would be useful to potential investors and customers considering potential new services. It would be useful to organizations themselves to shortcut much hard work in research and relationship management.

Any such measure would probably operate on a comparative basis within a market where activities are sufficiently similar to merit comparison, especially since they will be serving broadly the same customer base. There are already a number of organisations that publish league tables of service standards, including industry regulators and independent bodies in the media who have established themselves as informal arbiters on standards (for example – the DATAPRO survey on computer manufacturers).

There are two questions to be answered. First, is such a measure a desirable thing, and second, if it is desirable, can it be meaningfully constructed, (that is, is it doable)?

Is it desirable?

There is no doubt that people and organizations will concentrate on the data analysis in the measure, to attempt to achieve a high benchmark rate. This is a very useful purpose of the measure. It should be an excellent incentive to improve the standard of service in general. In addition, organizations that are performing poorly will be given an external impetus to improve, while the best will be given a marketing advantage to trade on.

However, the positive aspects have to be balanced by the fact that data can be manipulated by the unscrupulous to tell a much better story than exists in reality. Commercial pressures may well dictate that every loophole in the construction of such a measure will be exploited, which will entail the expenditure of significant resources on auditing and monitoring the measure in order to ensure its lasting integrity.

Any such measure also relies on all organizations openly sharing their data and performance so that the measure may be computed. This is not guaranteed and relies on the goodwill of all those concerned.

Thus desirability is, as always, perceived differently, depending on circumstance. On balance, one standard measure for customer service should provide benefits, but only if its integrity is carefully managed by a respected third party.

Is it doable?

Any 'universal' market service measure should indicate whether customer expectation is being met and indicate satisfaction levels. The nature of customer service is such that assessment is a mixture of subjective review of practices and hard measurement of process performance. Given that practice is a result of management approach and human application, can it be definitively tied down on a comparative basis? The normal approach is the use of survey material and polled opinion, on a sample basis, in the whole market. Statistical methods are used to increase confidence levels in the comparatives produced.

On the hard side, service processes vary across organizations and the points of measure need to be defined very tightly, otherwise there is no like-for-like comparison. An example is the current OFTEL measurement set for telecommunications. These measures attempt to track the length of time taken to provide a new service to customers. The question is, 'When is service provided?' – at the time the customer perceives it or at the time the telecommunications company has finished the mechanics of providing it? And how measurable is either factor? Significant differences exist within companies in the point at which measurement is taken and hence true comparison is difficult.

The conclusion, therefore, is that it is not possible to produce one all-encompassing measure of the competence of customer service. However, individual markets may find a basis for comparison, and league table activity and comparisons will work beneficially in such situations.

WHEN *NOT* TO USE BENCHMARKING

Strategic considerations

Benchmarking is a context-critical activity. The way that it is approached is determined by the drivers of change and the context of the organization. If the organization is highly regulated, such as in the utility sector, the capability focus will be high on process comparison and performance data. This is often because the regulators themselves are interested in league tables of comparative performance. The will to change is therefore driven by the need to impress an external audience rather than to beat competition. Internal benchmark activity, on the other hand, is usually functionally driven and the interest very narrowly concentrated on the practice side.

Figure 2.6 shows how the benchmarking of capability is slanted depending on context.

In a competitive situation, the organization will need a balanced focus on all *31*

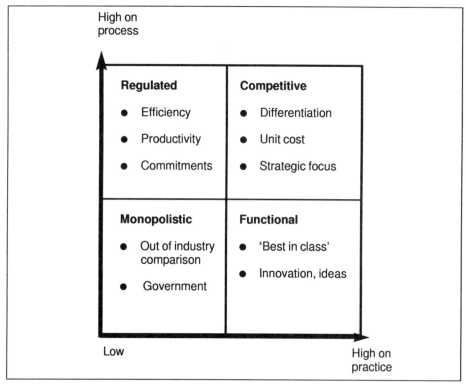

Figure 2.6 Benchmarking of capability in context

aspects of benchmarking. When allied to competitive analysis it forms an important strategic tool that enables the operation to be successful.

By comparison, the monopolistic organization, typically holding more than 80 per cent market share, has little need to benchmark aggressively. It is often the organization that sets the standard of behaviour in the market and it requires simply to be aware of the existence of alternative practices and methods. Benchmarking here is a low-key activity that does not consume many resources.

Practical considerations

It is too late to initiate a programme when the organization is already losing money, people and market share. Crisis management will yield more results and benchmarking can then be used as the organization recovers its position.

THE BENCHMARKER'S CODE – BEING ETHICAL

Engaging in benchmarking involves a significant amount of contact and work with external organizations. Some of these will have a relationship based on commercial terms, such as consultancies and contractors. By far the majority of contacts will, however, be informal and based on reciprocal agreements. Any abuse of such agreements or failure to honour commitments made will prejudice future relationships and bring benchmarking progressively into disrepute.

I suggest that the code detailed in Figure 2.7 should always be honoured. It is based on first-hand experience of what works, and it should lead to pain-free visits for both parties and a useful, non-compromising exchange of information.

Benchmarker accountable

1 Always send a written request and clear statement of requirements to your host.
2 Forward a copy of your questionnaire before the visit at least two weeks before the event.
3 Send a detailed list of visit participants, with job function and area of specific interest.
4 If not requested to do so, offer a confidentiality agreement to ensure that conversations are open.
5 Follow up with a 'thank you' letter and describe the value that you have gained from the visit.
6 Honour your commitments. Forward a copy of the completed report if you agreed to do so and send your own data if requested.
7 Remove any third party's name from shared copies of the final report (for example, use *organization* A, B, C).
8 Do not overplay your welcome by multiple repeat visits. Organizations are not public attractions; they are in business and visits consume resources.
9 Observe the Data Protection Act and reject information that you suspect does not comply.
10 Do not copy any data or information without written permission. *Always* observe copyrights.

Host Organization accountable

11 Respond with written acceptance of the requirements before the visits.
12 Ensure all the people required honour the commitment to speak and present to the hosted organization.
13 Have the guests' written material prepared and ready before the guests arrive.
14 Have your own requests prepared and forwarded before the visit.
15 Be clear, at the start, what you are prepared to share, show and tell and what you are not.
16 If confidentiality agreements have been exchanged, trust the visitor and do not hide information.
17 Do not stage-manage tours so as only to present the good side.
18 Share the learning, the things that went wrong. This is often as useful as the good things.
19 Remember the guests are only human too and do not overload them with information.
20 Stick to the schedule.

Figure 2.7   Benchmarking code of practice   *33*

The essence of benchmarking activity is preparation, honesty and integrity. Competitive analysis is a different activity and should be divorced from successful benchmarking. The objective of a benchmarking visit is not to gain competitive intelligence.

There are some very specific practices that must be avoided, as follows:

1   Do not go 'just to look around'. This wastes the time of both organizations and will provide little insight to a true benchmarking programme.
2   Never take undeclared people on a site visit. This compromises the relationship and is guaranteed to devalue the results through less openness. This is critical if you are invited to any organization that is competitive.
3   Never use a third party such as a consultancy to gather data anonymously on your behalf – such practices compromise all parties concerned.
4   Under no circumstances pass on an organization's data to a third party without first obtaining their specific, written authorization. Any such further sharing should be made anonymous by removing names throughout.
5   Never use devious practice to gain information. Do not ask new recruits to share confidential information. Do not deliberately misrepresent yourself to any organization.

Above all, be sensitive to any perceived intellectual property rights that the organization feels it has and owns. Whilst legislation is still very slack in this area, there is a duty implicit for any organization involved in benchmarking to honour such rights. Apply the rule of reciprocity – if you would not be prepared to share the information you are requesting, don't ask for it.

Further reading

Camp, R. C. (1989), *Benchmarking, the Search for Industry Best Practices that Lead to Superior Performance*, Milwaukee: ASQC Quality Press.

Hamel, G. and Prahalad, C. K. (1989), 'Strategic Intent', *Harvard Business Review*, **3**, May–June, 63–76, Reprint number 90311.

Handy, C. (1976), *Understanding Organizations*, London: Penguin.

Prahalad, C. K. and Hamel, G. (1990), 'The Core Competencies of the Organization', *Harvard Business Review*, **3**, May–June, 79–91, Reprint number 89308.

Spendolini, M. J. (1992), *The Benchmarking Book*, New York: AMACOM.

Vollman, T. E. (1993), 'Benchmarking Core Competency', Manufacturing 2000, executive report series, no. 10.

Watson, G. H. (1993), *Strategic Benchmarking*, New York: John Wiley and Sons.

3 Delivering competitive advantage

Laurie Young

In much of the debate about service quality, there is an implicit assumption that companies should try to provide the 'best' service for customers. Some even talk about exceeding customer expectation, using examples of companies that have transformed their performance by dramatic customer care programmes. The theme of many conferences and much service work is to continually improve service but excellent service is not an end in its own right. Nor is customer satisfaction. It is a means to an end. The aim of commercial enterprises is to make profit and the aim of public organizations is to provide an efficient service within a budget. Service excellence is only required insofar as it achieves these objectives. One of the most important aspects of service strategy and planning is, then, to ensure that the service is always of sufficient quality to encourage customers to prefer it to the competition.

There is undoubted evidence that service excellence will encourage customers to choose one organization over another. For instance, the 'PIMS' database (a rare, long-term study of the relationship between top-level strategy and market performance, established by Harvard University in the early 1970s) showed that product and service excellence increases market share. In other words, if customers perceive the offer they receive to be better than others, they will switch to that supplier and rebuy. There is also evidence that satisfied customers will encourage others to switch to good suppliers. However, it is possible to have very satisfied customers who are not profitable and to invest in high-quality service which does not affect the customers' buying behaviour. It is even possible to overinvest in quality to such an extent that customers find the service unattractive. For example, one company invested so heavily in call distribution systems and staff that there was no delay in answering telephone calls from customers. However, it was found that customers were uncomfortable with the lack of a ringing tone because they had no time to collect their thoughts. Further studies showed that they had only *35* needed sufficient investment to achieve a reply within three ringing tones. This would have been the optimum service because it would have set the necessary standard at the most reasonable cost.

It is therefore important to find out which factors of service influence the customer's propensity to buy and to be ahead of nearest rivals in those factors. It is equally important to stay ahead of perception, as customer needs and competitive response change, by investing in the right improvements. This chapter concentrates upon the techniques to determine competitive service features and how to construct a competitive service programme without over-investing. There are several dimensions to this which start with the development of a clear, competitive strategy.

COMPETITIVE STRATEGY

It is surprising how few companies who consider their service to be an important part of their offer do not think through the place of service in their competitive strategy. Whether it is a manufacturing company trying to use service to 'differentiate' their product, or a service company trying to gain a price premium, their service programmes are often imprecise and vague, rarely giving real competitive advantage. It is essential to develop a clear, competitive strategy for the service of the company which matches the general business strategy.

Each market is a dynamic and interactive system which can be influenced by the players involved. To succeed in generating valuable funds from service, it is important to have a clear idea of where the management team intends the business to go. This involves several elements.

Positioning

Each company involved in a market takes its own position. This can be by design or default. For instance, a company may be the 'market leader', with dominant share and the ability to influence the rules of engagement within that marketplace. Often such leaders set price expectations and service standards. Alternatively, the company may be a 'follower' which is smaller than the market leader and able to earn a profitable existence by providing a healthy alternative either in terms of price or in the features of the service involved. Other competitive positionings include 'least cost' provider and 'niche' provider. It is not always sensible to aim to be the 'best' or leading supplier in the field. It can be more profitable to remain a 'follower' or 'niche' supplier than to challenge for leadership.

However, a company's service strategy rarely reflects its competitive position. Often the service arm of a business aims for the 'best quality' or the 'highest performance' whatever the market position. It is not uncommon for a profitable niche supplier to have a service plan aimed at promoting the best service in the industry or 'delighting' all customers – a position which is likely to be as damaging as it is inappropriate.

The service strategy must match the competitive position or strategy of the company. If a company is market leader it might have to provide the 'best' quality service and behave in the 'best' way because it sets the standard. However, a 'follower' might choose to offer a lesser quality service at a cheaper price. Or a 'niche' provider might choose to provide a quite different service at a higher price. The service mix and direction should be adjusted to match the corporate intent. Figure 3.1 shows criteria that can be used to map a supplier's positioning of its service against competitors.

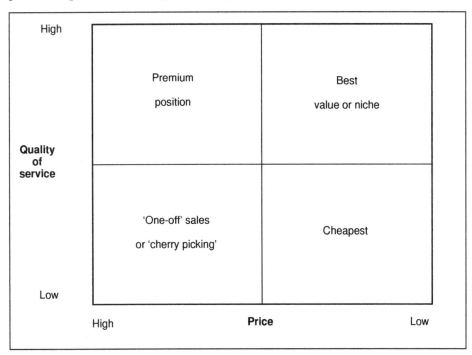

Figure 3.1   Competitive positioning of service

Critical success factors

Any market has rules of engagement by which the participants in the market survive or prosper. For instance, in a professional services industry (such as law or architecture) all participants must meet the necessary legal, or industry, standards in order to be able to participate. Meeting these professional criteria is a critical success factor and it is not possible to trade without them. However, critical success factors are generally less clear, commercial imperatives which are the result of the evolution of forces within the market. For instance it may be a critical success factor that a company should have twenty-four-hour telephone answering or it may need the ability to bring new services to market quickly. In order to use service to gain competitive *37* advantage, a supplier must first decide what are the critical success factors in the market and which relate to service standards.

Differentiation

Differentiation means exactly what it implies: the service must be different from the competition. To take a product example: it would be absurd for the various car manufacturers to sell just one product, say, the Ford Model T. If they were all manufacturing and supplying exactly the same product the customer would only ever be able to choose on price. By offering a multiplicity of products, suppliers are able to earn profit by providing choice to different customer segments.

This, however, is often not the case with service. In the computer industry, at the time of writing, there is very little to choose between the maintenance service of many of the big computer manufacturers. Their services (in fact, the appearance of much of their marketing literature) looks almost exactly the same. Similarly, the telephone service provided by the various network operators and the financial products of many financial services companies suffer from the same commoditization. Through lack of creative design, these companies are failing to provide a unique service and thus allowing their offer to become a commodity. The customer therefore starts to choose on the basis of price and the market becomes generally price sensitive. Whether the service involved is simple maintenance support, or a complex added-value service, it should be unique.

It is possible to make each service unique because each company is unique. Each company has its own core competence and its own culture, which can be expressed in ways that are relevant to customers, thus creating a unique service proposition and a unique brand position. This situation occurs in the more mature industries such as the hospitality industry, where there are offerings as diverse as the Ritz restaurant and McDonalds. Both are excellent service experiences with a particular style and brand positioning. The customer can choose the style of eating experience they prefer, and, in some cases, might go to both (a customer might have a special evening at the Ritz and the next lunchtime take their children to McDonalds). Suppliers should use the unique characteristics of their company to design a unique service offering, at a unique price, for a specific group of customers. The creative skill of good marketing people must be applied to service. If this is not done, the industry is on a path to poor margins, poor profit performance and bankruptcies.

A clear-headed view of herd mentality

It is fascinating how often changes within markets and actions within companies happen because other competitors are making those changes. For instance, at the end of the 1980s many of the British building societies started to buy estate agents. This might have seemed a strategically important and sensible move for the first society which initiated it, but there followed a spate of acquisitions which affected the shape of the whole industry. The property market then moved into recession, and after some years, many of the building societies sold their acquisitions back to estate agents at a breathtaking loss. It was clear that many societies felt driven to make this move because of the changing nature of their marketplace and the speed at which competitors were taking action. They sought to supplement their core service with a risky diversification. The performance of some societies, over the medium term, would have been better if they had taken a different approach.

A supplier may have to move with the market to keep up, but it may also be the case that competitive advantage lies in taking a deliberately different approach from the herd.

Segmentation

Choice of the customers the company wishes to serve is absolutely crucial. Customers have different tastes and appetites. They also have preferences for different service styles and it is therefore not possible to provide a universal service which satisfies all customers. Suppliers should choose a segmentation based on service preference. They should then design the service around the tastes of those customer groups.

Real knowledge of the competition

Surprisingly few companies set up mechanisms to experience the service of their competitors and subsequently adjust their own service in the light of that experience. For example, research by the direct marketing agency Smith Bundy in 1991 showed that only 14 per cent of respondents regularly measured the success of their competitors in customer care (see Figure 3.2). The rest

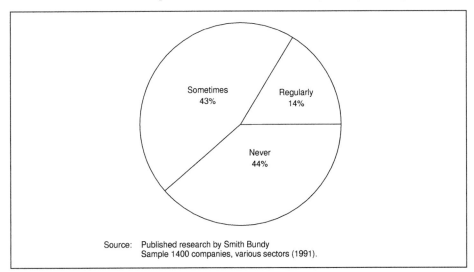

Source: Published research by Smith Bundy
Sample 1400 companies, various sectors (1991).

Figure 3.2   Incidence of measuring competitors' customer care programmes *39*

were divided between never measuring what their competitors are doing and doing so sometimes.

Even fewer attempt to forecast the actions of their competitors realistically. Forecasts must be based on realistic assumptions about the forces which determine competitor action, not theoretical models. For instance, the track record and political power of the members of a competitor's board are a sure indication of their likely actions, whatever their public statements.

SOURCES OF COMPETITIVE ADVANTAGE

One of the most important aspects of competitive strategy is to find sources of competitive advantage which can be applied to the service offer. There are several areas of opportunity open to service providers, including the following.

The core competence of the organization

Each company has a skill or function in which it invests over time because it is seen as the most important task of the organization. Often this priority is made unconsciously because it is so obviously the most important task. It is the area of responsibility which always receives time, attention and investment, almost without question, in comparison with other functions. Because of investment of people and resources, this area will improve in both performance and cost. This progression is represented as an 'experience curve', as shown in Figure 3.3, first highlighted by Bruce Henderson as a foundation for the 'Boston matrix' in the early 1970s.

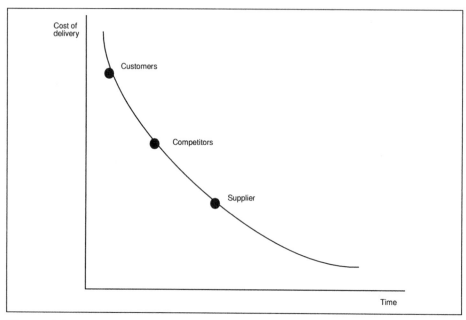

Figure 3.3   A representation of an experience curve

It is around this core competence that the service offer should be built because it will then be the highest-quality offer at the least price. Even if the position on the curve is similar to competitors, it is still possible to use the core competence as a competitive platform because, in conjunction with the corporate identity, it can be built into a unique branded offer that reflects the reality of the customers experience.

Unfortunately, despite the fact that almost all strategy writers emphasize the importance of the core competence, there are few recognized techniques for defining it. Ultimately it can only be determined in discussion, or brainstorming, with senior management. Such discussions can seem vague and difficult but once the 'blinding flash of the obvious' occurs, the simple heart of the company's performance can be exploited as a competitive expression of skill.

The corporate brand

Each company has a corporate identity consisting of its name and any graphical representation of that identity. However, if the core competence of the organization is translated, through that identity, into a number of 'brand values', it is possible to create a corporate brand which will appeal to the target market. This brand has a unique appeal to customers, causing them to relate to it in such a way as to purchase it over time. Loyalty comes from this corporate brand because it gives reassurance in the intensely emotional experience of buying or using service. It is a source of real competitive advantage.

Customer relationships

The relationships a company has with its customers are also a source of competitive advantage. The heritage of contact between the people, processes and systems of two organizations cannot be duplicated. Within those relationships will be some customers who are very loyal and others who could be made more loyal. These customers are a source of competitive advantage because they are more inclined to purchase and repurchase. They are also likely to be advocates of the supplier's service which might be turned into highly profitable growth through a structured relationship programme.

ANALYSIS TO PRODUCE COMPETITIVE ADVANTAGE

Having determined the competitive positioning of the service and decided the sources of competitive advantage, the first step to constructing real competitive advantage out of service is to undertake detailed analysis.

Analysis of competitive service features

Service planning need not be vague or imprecise. Whilst customers often do not have a clear idea of the dimensions of the service they require, or the criteria upon which they buy, it is quite possible to stimulate them to think *41* about the detail of the different dimensions of service. But this must be led by management within the company. They must create a proposition to which the customers can respond.

The first step towards achieving this is to determine the 'features' of the service provided. Each service is made up of features which customers value differently. For instance, a maintenance service might comprise the following features:

- fault reception;
- fault diagnosis;
- telephone manner of receptionist;
- method of diagnosis;
- speed of attendance; and
- speed of repair.

It is not possible to determine these components through research because customers will not be able to envisage them. They must first be identified by specialists in the field: that is, the company's staff. Company representatives should meet to brainstorm all the aspects of the services that the company provides to each customer group, and then create a list of features. Once identified, the features can be confirmed in focus groups with representative customers. They should be asked to rank the value of each service feature and to identify those that are irrelevant or missing.

For example, the most important features of a maintenance service might start with those listed in Figure 3.4. Once these features have been ranked, it is then possible to postulate the value of each feature. For instance, it may be that the service feature 'speed of response' could be provided in two hours, eight hours or twenty-four hours. Having given the features a value, further in-depth research, can be conducted. Customers can be asked three questions:

1 What is the ideal standard for this feature?
2 What is the standard that our company currently delivers?
3 What standard do our nearest competitors provide?

Hierarchy of service features	Priority
Speed of response	1
Speed of diagnosis	2
Time to clear problem	3

Figure 3.4   The three most important features of a maintenance service

It is also possible to stimulate customers to consider the value of service improvements, the equivalent of price decisions. They might say that they require radical improvements in different service features but are unable to make the trade-offs against the cost of improving these features which the company itself will have to make in order to plan investment. The research process can indicate this by imitating the trade-offs that customers must make when paying for the service. This can be achieved by giving them points to spend on different quality improvements. It can give a clear indication of the value of the service in the customers' minds.

The specialist research techniques most likely to yield the type of detailed comparative evaluation that these studies require is 'conjoint analysis' or 'Simalto' research. These techniques force customers to make choices between different aspects of an offering. To continue the example of a maintenance service, the result of this research might yield the data contained in Figure 3.5.

Hierarchy of features	Priority	Ideal requirement (hours)			Our delivery (hours)			Competitor's delivery (hours)		
Speed of response	1	(4)	8	24	4	(8)	24	4	8	(24)
Speed of diagnosis	2	(0.5)	1	2	0.5	1	(2)	0.5	(1)	2
Time to clear problem	3	(2)	4	6	2	4	(6)	2	(4)	6

Figure 3.5   Comparative evaluation of service features

Thus the most important service features have been discovered and prioritized. Each feature has been given a set of values, which have also been subjected to research. The customers have been asked to indicate: their requirement for each feature in an ideal world; their perception of what the supplier is delivering; and their perception of what the competitors are delivering.

Such research needs careful interpretation because, in its raw format, it can give misleading signals. For instance, customers will often have a different view in the rational environment of a focus group to the harsh trade-offs that they will have to make in the real world, where issues such as internal politics affect buying decisions. Also their views of the current delivery will only be perceptions and may not reflect the actual experience of the company they represent. However, the data, interpreted correctly, can give some very useful indications as to the way in which the supplier can plan competitive service. For instance, the 'Ideal requirement' column gives an indication of the customers' needs relative to their price perceptions because they have been forced to show the most important features.

In this example, the supplier is ahead of the competition on the most important service feature (speed of response) but not up to the ideal. Some service gurus would encourage this company to reach the customer's ideal standard, but this takes no account of the level of the investment required or whether *43* such investment might pay back in terms of customers' propensity to buy. Furthermore, this supplier is behind the competition in the second and third service features. It may be that in order to gain competitive advantage they must concentrate on these features and move nearer to the competitive standards in those areas.

The actual investment strategy will depend upon the business strategy, the management priorities, and the culture and politics of the firm. It is, however, essential to have a thorough method of understanding the customers' views of the competitive service standards before constructing a competitive service strategy.

The final possibility of features analysis and design is to work out the emotional requirements of customers and how the values of the corporate brand might meet those requirements. The corporate brand will give customers reassurance and promises of quality. It will also set expectations which can be built into both the performance of people and the design of the service itself. This will ensure that there is a unique offer to the market.

Determining competitive influences – who are the competitors?

Several academic studies into customer attitudes to service have shown that one of the prime influences on satisfaction is the extent to which the experience of the service matches the customers' expectations. It is therefore important to understand in detail the different forces which influence the customers' attitudes to service standards. They include the following:

- *National standards* These are the expectations of performance set by the country in which the service provider operates. They are determined by a myriad of influences that make up the society, including media, family, friends and work.
- *Culture* The expectations of service set by the values of the day-to-day culture in which the customer participates. These values can be different from national standards and can be a subculture within the nationality. For example, there can be a youth culture which creates expectations different from the national standard or there might be a particular organizational style within an industrial sector.
- *Direct competition* The performance and behaviour of the competition creates expectations in the customers' minds. These can create standards which are unique to the industry in which a supplier operates.
- *'Parallel industry'* Customers' attitudes to service can be influenced by companies operating in other industries. 'If the gas board can do it, why can't the water board?' In particular, a monopoly or a public service, which has no direct competition, might be compared to a parallel industry. Customers will make comparisons with similar companies and will be dissatisfied if the supplier does not perform comparably well.
- *Internationalization* The increase in movements of populations creates

in them a changed expectation of service standards. If a consumer in one country moves to another and experiences radically different service performance, they will make comparisons with the service they experience in their home country. They will expect standards in their own country to improve and express dissatisfaction if it does not. Whilst there has always been a minority who move in international circles, increasing international travel amongst a population will have a profound influence on expected service standards.

- *Sector specific needs* The business sector in which customers operate creates unique expectations of service. They might need variation in service features, style or delivery. For example, the service values of a government department are likely to be very different from a city broker. If the supplier does not meet those expectations they will not be thought to be seriously interested in participating in this business sector.

- *Brand* The corporate brand of the company creates expectations. If these are expectations of good service then the customers' experience must match these expectations.

- *Word-of-mouth endorsement* One of the truisms of service is that customers tell many other people of a bad experience but tell fewer people about a good one. This means that, for every experience of the company, there is a potential addition to the word-of-mouth reputation. This is a very powerful and neglected aspect to developing a business. If a potential customer hears a recommendation to use a supplier from someone they respect, they are likely to try the supplier when they have a relevant need. If their experience matches the recommendation they will rebuy and the supplier will gain a loyal customer. Conversely, negative word-of-mouth stories act as a powerful deterrence. Few companies have a strategy to estimate or manage their word-of-mouth reputation, but it can be as strong as media advertising in influencing the purchase decision.

All of these factors will influence the customers' view of service and ultimately affect the competitive position of the firm. It is therefore essential to understand the competitive influences upon each customer group and to work out the relevant investment strategy. The best method of doing this is to build a model of the influences acting upon each customer group.

The model should identify the different customer segments and their expectation of delivery against different service features. The example in Figure 3.6 was the result of the analytical work for the service strategy of a large organization. It identified not only the relative features of service required by each segment but also the influences upon those attitudes. In this example these were primarily: competition, parallel industry and national tastes in consumer segments, whilst sector-specific interests dominated the more business-oriented segments. Once this model was constructed from initial research, it could be used to track the changing attitudes to service in the light of the changing influences upon it.

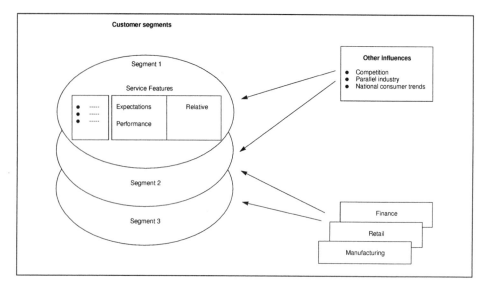

Figure 3.6   Model of influences on customer service standard

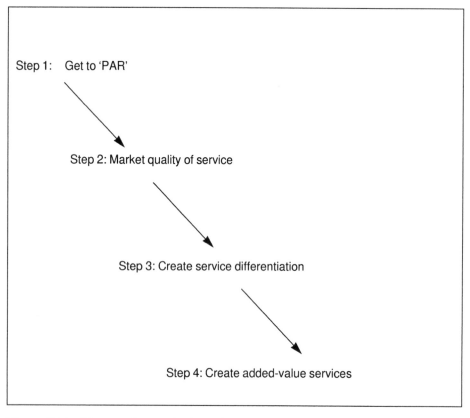

Figure 3.7   The service evolution of an industry

The service evolution of the industry

Industries develop through an evolution of thought and strategy with regard to service standards, which is represented in Figure 3.7.

The first task of a service strategy is to get to 'national par'. National par is a common expectation of service quality that is shared by the population as a whole. It is assumed, ill-defined and emotionally based, but it is none the less a common value. A service which is far below par will become the target of comedians and journalists because they recognize that there is a common experience which can be exploited.

Par is defined as: 'the nationally expected standard of service from a particular industry set by the experience of that population'. Par for the industry can be determined using the features research outlined above. If the industry in general is below par, then the first supplier to move to par will gain market share. This has happened in numerous industries in both national and international contexts. For instance, by redefining its business as a transportation service and setting new standards of care, British Airways gained market share and grew, whilst other international carriers, particularly in the United States, went out of business. The supplier is simply moving to meet the service expectations of customers when others in the industry do not. As a result it attracts new customers, gaining competitive advantage.

Unfortunately the context in which a business operates does not remain static. Once competitors notice that a company is taking a lead through quality or service strategies, they begin to develop programmes of their own. As a result, the service of competitors begins to catch up. They then look for ways to communicate to customers the efforts that they have made in order to attract them back. The industry goes through a phase where it 'markets' the quality of service that it provides. For instance, British Airways advertised the character and responsiveness of its cabin staff, supermarkets advertised their efforts to keep checkout queues low, and the British banks are, at the time of writing, advertising specific aspects of service, such as answering the telephone in four rings.

The problem with this phase of development is that customers will compare the communication claim with their actual experience of the service. If it does not match, the credibility of the whole claim will be undermined. This happened in the 1980s when British Rail launched its ill-fated 'We're getting there' campaign. The campaign claimed that the railway system was progressively improving. However, there was not sufficient improvement in the experience of the UK population to make the claim believable. The campaign became the subject of national ridicule and hostility as a result. Actual experience of the service (particularly if it is a high-volume, mass-market service) must match the communication claim. If not, the 'word-of-mouth' reputation will undermine the service programme.

Once the industry is filled with suppliers communicating common quality of service propositions, it must evolve further. It therefore moves towards service differentiation, which is a process that results from changes in attitude *47* amongst *both* customers and suppliers. If all suppliers are making similar quality claims, then customers choose on the basis of service style and price. They are attracted to an ambience, design or behaviour which suits their taste. Suppliers therefore respond by developing different service offerings for different customer groups. Clearly, if the industry is not yet at this stage, a supplier can gain competitive advantage by anticipating this development, choosing the most attractive segments and designing a service that appeals primarily to them.

The final stage of service evolution is when 'added-value' services are offered to the market. Customers are able to recognize the content and value of the base service and are thus willing to pay extra for added-value service features. This situation is current in the telecommunications industry. Suppliers have taken great pains to define the content and value of the core communications offer as a result of the forces of competition and regulation. They are now designing complex 'intelligent network services' which earn incremental revenue by offering distinct extra features from new technology in the network.

Competitive advantage can be achieved by launching packages of added-value services for the segment that the supplier is targeting. The difficulty is that the incremental value of the added-value features is eroded over time as customers' standards improve. Customers then expect them to fall into the base service. This process is represented in Figure 3.8.

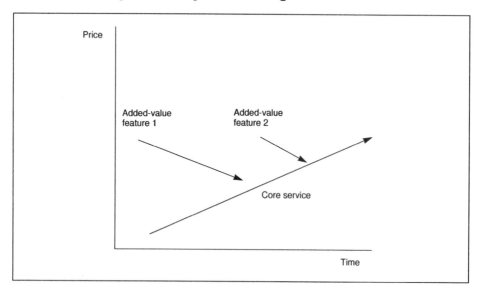

Figure 3.8   The relationship of customer care to added-value services

In order to maintain their competitive lead in their chosen customer segments, suppliers must continue to create new added-value features to distinguish them from the core service. This implies that the ability to design competitive services is a critical success factor of the future service industries.

Companies will have to resource the development processes of their services as seriously as manufacturing companies have resourced product development.

Operational analysis

Clearly the efficiency and cost of all the operations of a service organization can be a source of competitive advantage. They can influence the attitude of customers by the way they operate, stimulating customers to rebuy if they perceive them to be of good quality. They can also add unnecessarily to the cost base and undermine competitive advantage if they are too expensive. It is therefore essential to compare the detailed operational tasks of providing the service to the performance of competitors. The best way to do this is through 'benchmarking'.

Benchmarking is not just visiting organizations in other industries for discussions to share ideas, nor is it research into customer views of competitor service standards. It is a systematic process whereby the performance of one company is compared with its nearest competitors. It is best undertaken by loading anonymous data into a comparative database. This is well developed in mature industries because suppliers have learnt the value of such cooperation. However, the way to progress in an immature service industry is as follows:

1   Write a brief for an agency which describes the service organization involved and its need to benchmark.
2   Gain information on benchmarking organizations around the world and enquire about their skills, resources and experience.
3   Shortlist agencies and send them the brief.
4   Invite agencies to 'pitch'.

The best agencies will have a database comprising data from service companies or the service divisions of relevant manufacturing organizations. There must be a substantial number within the business sector in which the organization to be benchmarked operates for the database to be of value. However, it is also important that it contains data from service companies in a cross-section of sectors around the world. The agency will audit the service organization, and then compile a detailed analysis based on a comparison of the answers with the data in their database. They should be able to compare the client against the best, the average and the worst in its own sector, and also show how the client's operations compare against world standards.

Results of the studies can generate improvements in very specific areas as an integral step of normal business management. It also establishes an intelligence base which, over time, will enable the service provider to develop a methodology by which to evaluate performance measures in a clearly structured way.

The output of the benchmarking study should include a detailed *49* comparative report and interpretation of results. Figure 3.9 shows some hypothetical answers to specific questions asked within a benchmarking study. It can be seen that the performance of the service company involved varied by function. For instance, the company is behind both the sector and world standards in the deployment of technology in the maintenance process. It is therefore behind its sector in the clearance of faults without an expensive field visit. Such detailed results, across a wide variety of functions, enables the management team to take competitive action in the core of its operations.

A PLANNING PROCESS

It is surprising how many companies who are excellent at planning complex, technical products and services are poor at planning their business. However, in order to establish and maintain a competitive service it is essential that a planning process is put in place that allows organizations progressively to select the level of investment in service against competitive offerings. This does not have to be too theoretical or complex. Nor does it have to produce a document which is only used for internal presentations. It does have to be a recognized, practical mechanism to harness the realities of the organization, including politics, into an agreed deployment of resources. Most companies who have made substantial improvements in service over the long term have a cyclical planning mechanism which contains several important steps. Figure 3.10 represents such a process.

The process assumes that there is a strategic review which determines the corporate objectives, the competitive position, the customer segments to be targeted and the sources of competitive advantage. The first step in the planning process is to conduct detailed research into the customers' views of the value of service features. This should also involve the operational analysis necessary to determine the current performance and research into employees' attitudes toward the various aspects of service. Competitor research should also be used to determine competitive standards. It is then important to analyse what to do and to design the appropriate service before implementing and measuring it. This planning process can be repeated cyclically in order to keep the quality of service moving forward in line with changing customer requirements.

SUMMARY

Companies are increasingly trying to use service quality as a means of gaining competitive advantage. Thus they must balance the investment carefully so that it causes customers to choose their offer rather than that of the competition, and in doing so they must take as professional and hard-headed a view of this area of business as any other. This balance is best achieved by conducting research and analysis to determine sources of competitive advantage and competitive strategy. Having carried out this research, a pragmatic planning
process must be adopted that fashions the resulting analysis into a set of

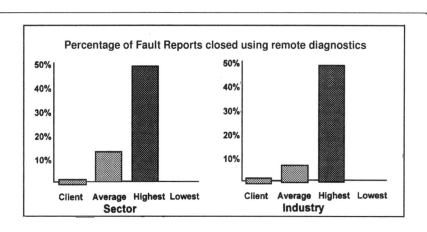

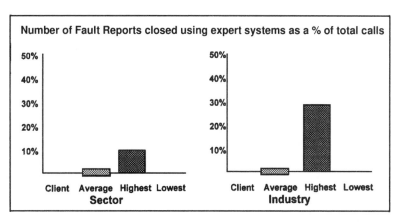

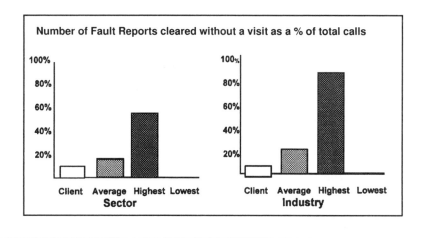

Figure 3.9   Sample results from the benchmarking of the field operations of a service company

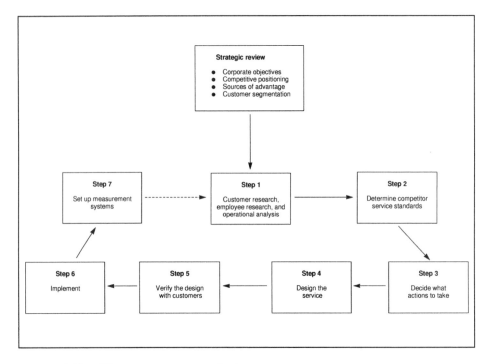

Figure 3.10   The customer care design process

actions capable of producing a unique offer to a chosen set of customers. The customers will then have choice and the suppliers will produce profit. The aim of service strategies is to increase shareholder value, not just to satisfy, or 'delight' customers.

FURTHER READING

Blumberg, H. (1991), *Managing Service as a Strategic Profit Centre*, New York: McGraw-Hill.

Davidson, A. (1987), *Offensive Marketing*, Harmondsworth: Penguin.

Stone, M. and Young, L. D. (1992), *Competitive Customer Care*, London: Croner.

4 Business process engineering
Bill Martin

Much has been said about the importance of customer service over the last decade. Media attention would have us believe that it is one of the highest priorities in boardrooms across industry. Unfortunately, for most of us the reality – scant evidence of significant improvements in the quality of customer service in the United Kingdom – is somewhat different.

Why then, the apparent disparity? Is it a lack of real strategic intent and commitment, or is it more of an execution issue? Clearly there are some companies with a strong desire to be perceived as customer oriented and committed to the highest levels of service. However, the investment and management attention do not measure up to the marketing messages. More common is the actuality of genuine intent, commitment and investment limited by poor execution, resulting in much the same outcome, whatever the intention.

THE PURSUIT OF EXCELLENCE

Being a service leader and continually engaged in the pursuit of service excellence is not easy. Delivering consistently high levels of customer service requires well-designed, cross-functional processes, executed by well-trained and motivated people.

It is often possible to achieve high levels of customer service in smaller organizations, where employee interactions, *ad hoc* communication and customer intimacy substitute for well-structured processes. This informal approach will typically start to develop cracks as organizations reach approximately two hundred people and will positively break down at the three to four hundred people level.

The role of the customer

This operational deterioration may not be at all obvious, rather a gradual decline over a period of time. Typically customer complaints, formal or informal, will start to increase and some form of internal frustration may be evident. However, when immersed in an organization it is often difficult to take an objective view of the impact of internal processes breaking down. One simple piece of advice here – ask the customer. Whether this be through formal surveys or data collection by more *ad hoc* means, it is the single most valuable and objective way of assessing your operational performance as a business.

Allocating responsibility

In one organization a Customer Services Manager has a long-serving and knowledgeable employee who reviews and tracks every customer complaint. The procedure used is very simple:

1 Read the complaint and log it into a customer complaints database.
2 Allocate the complaint to the department responsible for the error or the query.
3 Communicate details of the complaint to the department concerned.
4 Monitor the resolution of the complaint by that department.

Although this employee knows the internal workings of the company well, the difficulty usually starts at step 2: which department is responsible? Not surprisingly, most problems occur where work crosses departmental boundaries. These boundaries are often vague and ill-defined. In most cases there will be a reasonable level of clarity in terms of how work gets done within departments. Little effort, however, goes into clearly defining the boundaries, the interfaces and the issue resolution procedures. The employee is frequently frustrated in trying to ascertain the responsible department and make them accept total ownership of the incident and its customer resolution. If is difficult for an experienced employee to determine how a company works, imagine what it feels like for the customer! This is a manifestation of a larger organization not organized around the customer or the work but around internally convenient departmental structures.

Even today many organizations are structured in functional 'silos', with no emphasis on cross-functional processes nor appreciation for the flow of work through the organization. Unfortunately, the cost of this approach, in terms of rework, productivity and, most importantly, customer satisfaction, is usually masked and not always immediately obvious to managers. If only the real financial impact on the bottom line could be tangibly demonstrated, we would see some considerable motivation to effect change.

INCEPTION OF BUSINESS PROCESS ENGINEERING

So what tools and techniques are available to companies looking to make a step function change in the way they view their business and interact with their customers? The most prominent and talked-about technique over the last several years has been business process engineering. Many companies have invested heavily in business process engineering projects with varying degrees of success. Whilst by no means all projects have been targeted at improving customer service levels, a great many have carried that specific objective.

The 'wake-up call'

Unfortunately many initiatives have been in response to 'wake-up calls' in the face of declining market share, revenues, and profits, or possibly increasing competitor activity. In some cases entire industries have been shaken into action. An example in the United Kingdom is the financial services industry, specifically the banking and insurance sectors. New entrants such as First Direct and Directline challenged both the business models and standards of customer service in their respective market sectors. Both companies, their core strategies revolving around customer service and being easy to do business with, enjoyed outstanding success from launch. They caused alarm bells to ring in boardrooms all round the country, with many organizations forced into reactive and expensive defence strategies, and the words 'business process engineering' tripping off tongues across these organizations.

But deploying business process engineering on a reactive, defensive basis can be fraught with difficulty, with many of the key elements (as discussed later in this chapter) being overlooked in the urgency and desperation for a hasty solution.

DEFINITION OF BUSINESS PROCESS ENGINEERING

What, then, is business process engineering and why isn't it easy? In their book, *Reengineering the Corporation*, Michael Hammer and James Champy define it as: 'the fundamental rethinking and radical re-design of business processes to achieve dramatic improvements in critical, contemporary measures of performance, such as cost, quality, service and speed'. They also suggest another and much simpler definition: 'starting over'. The words in these definitions give many clues as to why this is not an easy process.

Limitations of business thinking

Most managers, particularly in mature and established companies, think in a structured and limiting way, in terms of organization and people, rather than process and work. Few managers think about business and work independently of people and organization structures. Discussions on business *55* processes are invariably translated immediately into the language of organizational structures and 'what's in it for me', whether explicit or otherwise. Business process engineering necessitates a paradigm shift in this kind of thinking.

How many sales presentations consist of the company presenting its product offer, and then going on to describe the internal organization structure, bombarding delegates with names and business cards and achieving nothing? If that isn't enough they then proceed to go through escalation procedures to be used when problems arise and the delegates are dissatisfied customers!

Changing business approach

Progressive organizations have 're-engineered' this sort of presentation into a view of the organization from the customers' perspective: that is, how their particular needs and requirements will be met. For example, one of the core elements of presentations in a company might be how to fulfil the customer's orders, namely, how the process is engaged and how it works start to finish. Without an organisation chart in sight, you should be able clearly to articulate the process, end to end, and precisely meeting the customer's requirements. In many cases it may be of considerable benefit to have the customer walk the process with you. By the end of that exercise, it should be clear that there is no magic or good fortune involved, just a straightforward and well-defined cross-functional process. The customer will then have a much better insight into the business and will leave with a higher regard for the company.

To many, this may appear to be only a subtly different perspective, but that is not the case. Viewing the entire business as a collection of inputs, each with desired, customer-valued outputs, is a considerable shift in thinking for most people. In process terms, this translates into end-to-end, cross-functional processes.

THE SCOPE OF BUSINESS PROCESS ENGINEERING

Business process engineering is sometimes viewed as repackaged organization and methods (O&M), a process improvement technique commonly used in the 1960s and 1970s. Whilst in some respects they may share similar goals (for example, improved productivity, lower cost, or reduced cycle time), that is where the similarity ends. Real business process engineering is much more radical, and has a foundation of innovation and invention rather than simply improvement of what currently exists.

Some business process engineering projects span all large processes, across all parts of the business and in every country in which the company operates. Clearly not all business process engineering projects have such a far-reaching scope, but it exemplifies just how broad and challenging some initiatives can be. The following overview is an example of the re-engineering of a single but core business process.

I recently participated in the redesign of the order fulfilment process in a capital goods supplier. The company had enjoyed good success and considerable growth for two or three years, more than doubling in size in terms of revenues and employees. Its internal operations, however, had not materially changed over this period. The internal structure was aligned along traditional departmental formats: marketing, sales, finance, administration, manufacturing, distribution and post-sales support. Cross-functional processes were not on anyone's agenda. Everything had worked quite well in the past: orders would come in from customers, products were built to order, goods were shipped to fulfil orders, customers were invoiced and cash collected.

Over the previous twelve months, however, not everything had gone so smoothly and growth appeared to be taking its toll. Generally the problem was perceived to be an internal communication problem – departments were not talking to each other. After very limited analysis, the problem was seen to be clearly much more fundamental than the original diagnosis. Within the organization, the employee frustration referred to earlier was apparent, mostly in longer-serving employees: 'Things used to work better than they do today', 'We used to please all of our customers all of the time', and 'I don't know how everything works any longer', were some comments gleaned from the initial research.

The analysis of the current process was an eye-opener for all who participated in it and was equally alarming for those who managed the process. The truth was that there was no process, but rather a collection of variable-quality departmental procedures with no linkages between them. In the past, teamwork, informal communications and solid customer relations had compensated for any shortcomings. Does all that sound familiar?

Some of the key findings, wholly consistent with many other process analyses seen over the years, were as follows:

- Customer needs and requirements not adequately captured and communicated at the start of the process, resulting in ambiguity and pre- and post-delivery issues.
- No individual understood the entire process-order receipt through fulfilment to cash collection.
- A minimum of six different departments were involved.
- Departmental boundaries were conveniently unclear.
- Numerous non-value-added activities, due to not getting it right first time.
- No real customer accountability and poor customer communication.
- No internal ownership of the process.

Room for improvement indeed. The redesign resulted in a process quite radically different:

- Process designed from customer requirement input.
- Single end-to-end process.
- Entire process understood by all who were deployed within it.
- Process had one owner.

- One department was responsible and wholly accountable for every customer order, from receipt all the way through the fulfilment chain.
- Many non-value-added activities eliminated.
- Well-defined feedback loops throughout the process to drive continuous improvement.
- Customer satisfaction levels dramatically improved.

This transition no doubt appears obvious and simple. However, such change is rarely easy to effect in organizations that have operated in functional silos for long periods of time. There are many different aspects to consider, the first being the absolute recognition at the top of the company of the need for change.

RECOGNIZING THE NEED FOR CHANGE

Selecting the right individuals

Business process engineering requires a different kind of thinking, one that does not come easily to many people. Selecting the right individuals for the right project, external or internal, is obviously a critical success factor. Having individuals with an ability to distil an apparently complex business into a logical grouping of major cross-functional, end-to-end processes is a much sought after asset. This is one of the chief elements of any project that spans the breadth of the company. Correct selection of staff for a business process exercise is often the key to the success or failure of large projects.

Simplifying the business process

Most companies manage to convince themselves and their employees that their business is more complex than it really is. Personally I make a point of challenging every claim of how complex our own business is becoming. Individuals involved in process engineering are typically striving to greatly simplify all aspects of a business, placing emphasis on value-added activities and doing everything humanly possible to completely eliminate non-value-added activities.

By definition, business process activities will almost inevitably drive extensive change through an organization. There are therefore many other aspects to be examined. Whilst the 'technical' process engineering work is the backbone of all projects, many other factors can completely derail an otherwise well-executed project. Before discussing some of these factors and how to overcome them, consider this simple example from my domestic life – yes, this sort of work and thinking is not easy to switch off when you close the office door.

My wife has a tray at home which she uses for all incoming mail. Her own administrative system works for her, and she rarely loses or fails to action any
of the correspondence. Without realizing what I was doing, I analysed how

many times each document was touched, reviewed and actioned, and over a week or so, I mentally re-engineered the entire process from receipt to output. I then failed miserably to convince my wife to make my suggested changes. The tray operates today just as it did before my 'value-added' intervention.

Why were my efforts in vain? The changes could have dramatically improved the functioning of the tray, but they were not implemented. Here are the key reasons for that non-implementation, every one of which I have explicitly observed at other times in real business projects:

- No recognition or acceptance of the problem by my wife.
- No involvement for my wife in the definition of the problem or the solution design.
- Poor communication between my wife and me on the subject.
- Significant resistance to change by my wife as a result of being presented with a solution.

Unfortunately there are many parallels that could be drawn between real-life business projects and this simple domestic story.

THE PROCESS OF TRANSITION

In its simplest form, business process engineering has three basic stages:

Step 1

Step 1 is to analyse and document the *current* state; processes, procedures, structures, customer interactions. Typically, data will be gathered from current documentation and extensive interviews with the people carrying out the work.

Step 2

Step 2 is to identify and define the *desired* state. This will often take the form of a vision of where the company would like to be, and in most cases will be radically different from what exists today. Some of the key considerations in doing this intellectually challenging activity must be customer requirements, market characteristics and cross-functional, end-to-end and self-learning processes. The main issue should revolve around what the customer requires and how it can most effectively and efficiently be delivered. Organization structures and jobs should not be a consideration, and hence a constraint, in this vital part of the project.

Step 3

Step 3 is to move from the *current* to the *desired* state. That sounds simple enough, but if the desired state is truly a significant departure from the current one, it is no easy task. There will be a multitude of considerations and factors *59* which will make or break the project. All aspects of the transition must be evaluated and factored into an integrated plan.

I have seen some projects adopt only the last two steps in an attempt to reduce the overall time to completion. This approach can be successful but carries a high degree of risk. Many assumptions will have to be made about the current environment. Thus building the transition plan becomes extremely difficult, will usually take longer, and may result in reworking as a result of elements being overlooked.

THE COMPONENTS OF BUSINESS PROCESS ENGINEERING

The three stages described above indeed represent an oversimplification of a complex task. However, fundamentally, business process engineering has three essential components; *process, people* and *technology*. The weighting of each component varies widely between projects, but all projects must address all three in some way. The simplified three-step outline above relates primarily to the process dimension.

Process

Ideally you should be able to describe your entire business in terms of key processes. Processes should relate to customers in terms of their require- ments and adding value in their eyes. Employees within the organization should think in terms of process and work flowing through the system. They may not be involved in the entire process, but to produce the best results and get the most out of their role, they should possess an intimate knowledge of the process from end to end: what triggers the process – usually a customer – what happens within the process, and what the output is. In conducting interviews to build current state pictures it is usually highly alarming to appreciate how little people within a process comprehend about what goes before and what comes after their intervention.

Here are some of the common pitfalls related to process that I have ex- perienced:

- *The number of business processes* There is no right answer here, but I have seen everything from two to hundreds. I like to see companies try to depict their business through between eight to fifteen principal business processes. This range is manageable and yet not too small where the process is the company.
- *No defined start and end points* Inputs and outputs must be clear through- out.
- *Poor process integration* Processes do not exist in isolation. They touch each other and have dependencies on each other. These integration points must be understood and well defined.
- *Feedback loops* Without measurement and monitoring it is not possible systematically to drive continuous improvement.

People

The most underestimated and troublesome of all three aspects of business process engineering projects tends to be that which relates to changing the behaviour of human beings. Organizational change management – or whatever alternative term you are comfortable with – must not be an afterthought that is integrated into the project close to implementation, as is so often the case. Without the basic foundation of solid communications, involvement, buy-in and ownership by the organization, projects will be considerably more difficult to implement and sustain. In addition to the basics of effective change management above, I would advocate incorporating two vital activities, both of which should start at the earliest possible opportunity in a project.

The first I call *impact analysis*. What are all of the changes coming out of the re-engineering and how might they impact on people, both internally or externally to the business? This is a highly iterative process as new information comes to light and existing information is clarified. Whilst much of the effect will be internally directed, consider carefully the impact on customers and business partners. If the change necessitates some differences in the way you do business with these companies, be sure to involve them appropriately during the planning or implementation phases. The impact analysis should not be conducted in isolation by the project team. Key individuals from the organization and, if required, external partners should be heavily engaged in helping to work through the analysis, clearly articulating the respective effects of various changes. The earlier an impact is identified, the more time there is to determine the most appropriate plan to manage it.

The second activity, derived from the impact analysis, is the *transition plan*. This is people and organization specific and should outline a plan of action for each defined impact. In many cases plans will have a short- and a longer-term component. For example, a project may render a particular job function redundant – let's say that of an expediter. The short-term action may be to stop any future hiring of expediters, with the longer-term plan being constructed around retraining and redeployment of existing employees. You should strive to have the transition plan wholly owned and largely executed outside the project, ideally by the impacted organization.

Research into large projects that do not achieve stated objectives most often cites change management factors as the most prevalent reason for failure. Below are some of the more significant issues I have experienced and some of the ways to stop them being a barrier to success.

Senior management sponsorship

If the project is an important initiative and the company is trying to make a paradigm shift in customer service, it simply must have highly visible support and backing from the top. In some companies it may even be necessary for senior management to have some considerable hands-on involvement in order *61* to convince the organization that it means business. Many companies have some record of initial enthusiasm for projects that never come to fruition, resulting in high levels of employee cynicism. Often, support and commitment will be visible at the start of a project and start to wane shortly thereafter. This situation must be immediately recognized and addressed by the project manager. You will be surprised how quickly the rest of the organization recognizes a drop in commitment or leadership from the top, and how others' interest and attention will begin to drop away as a consequence. Senior management needs to be engaged from the start and remain engaged.

Team selection

As with any team, complementary skills are an important factor. Large projects will often involve external resources as well as internal. Selection criteria should be no different. In selecting external consultants assess the individual more than the reputation of the firm. Also, consultants should be wholly integrated into project teams, not isolated in any way.

Many projects run into difficulty because either the required skills are not present in the project team, or the personalities within that team suboptimize the results. Be sure to have someone on the team who has a track record of leading successful process engineering projects. It would be highly unlikely that an important re-engineering effort would be successful without experienced leadership.

These projects require different sets of skills for different phases and activities within each project. Documenting current processes requires highly articulate individuals with good attention to detail. Developing a vision of a desire demands people with an ability to think outside current paradigms and who can manipulate concepts and evaluate ideas on a constant basis. Customer service-oriented projects require individuals with intimate knowledge of customers and their needs. You may even consider using real customers on the team, probably on a part-time and advisory basis.

Concentrate on getting the right balance of skills and personalities. Personality testing at the selection phase of projects helps in making the right recruitment decisions and also helps the team to get to know each other from the start.

Integration with the organization

Ivory-tower business process engineering does not work. Involving the whole organization at every stage, and continually communicating status and planned activity, is critical.

This is hard work and the need for it will often be questioned. Arguably, it will in fact slow the team down in the research and design phases, but if the job is done well, the benefits will be clear in the transition phase and implementation of the change.

Technology

The third and last factor is *technology*. In many cases this will be information systems-oriented. However, there may be many other aspects of technology which will be critical success factors in projects. Given that this aspect is absolutely project specific, I will make only two general points on potential pitfalls and other points to look out for.

First, be careful to evaluate the people impact, often underestimated, of technology change. It may be wise to integrate many aspects of the technology plan closely with the people plan. As a minimum, pose and analyse the following question for every technological aspect of the project: What is the impact of this technology change on our employees? The response should then be factored into the above-mentioned impact analysis and, consequently, the transition plan.

The second point is on technology test plans and their execution. Faced with tight deadlines and even late delivery, the temptation for all project managers is to compress testing and contingency planning. Do so at your peril! The cost of rectifying a missed problem will magnify every step of the way and could end up being catastrophic at, or beyond, project implementation.

Information systems

Over the last five years we have seen business process engineering play an ever increasing role in the development of information systems. Many factors are influencing this change. For example:

- Information systems are becoming a key competitive advantage.
- The need for information systems to be integrated across the business and to be an enabler rather than an inhibitor to change.
- The need for real-time, enterprise-wide information in global organizations.
- More powerful and more user-friendly client-server software applications are replacing traditional mainframe applications.

Information systems are unquestionably a contributing factor to organizations operating in functional silos. Different functions within a company may operate on different, and often poorly integrated, information systems. This sort of infrastructure can be a serious inhibitor to cross-functional business processes. Many companies today disregard their entire suite of legacy systems in favour of applications that will truly support the running of the business in a way that meets the external and internal demands placed upon it.

It is usually not difficult for a customer to ascertain the level of adequacy of the information systems in a company. The most obvious manifestations are in the provision of information and the number of contact points. Companies with effective business processes, supporting information systems and well-trained employees, will have the information requested immediately available 63 and usually transacted through a single point of contact. This is the most efficient mode of operation, yielding the highest level of customer satisfaction. Unfortunately, we find ourselves encountering the converse situation all too often: being transferred multiple times to unannounced individuals, information not available in real time, having to state details and the subject matter many times, and so on. This is the typical service delivered by companies organized around internal functions and with information systems which do not adequately support their business.

The leading-edge business applications of today require a full and detailed definition of business processes to be completed prior to starting to design or configure the application. This is a significant exercise for most companies as this work typically will not have been done to a consistently high level of quality across the business. Having defined how the company should operate in terms of end-to-end business processes, the application is then configured to support precisely that *modus operandi*. Applications deployed in this manner and well executed can be a tremendous foundation for competitive advantage.

CONCLUSION

With some notable exceptions, the development of customer service in the United Kingdom is still in its infancy. Business process engineering is today the most comprehensive and radical approach to making step function changes in this critical area. The name, like all vogue terms in business, is heavily overused and misapplied. This is not about a minor tweak here and there, or new organization structure – it is a paradigm shift in thinking and operational execution. It necessitates total concentration on the customer and the creation of value – more value than that of competitors. It requires individuals who are visionary and bold enough to challenge and, in many cases, completely disregard what has gone before. It requires skilful and passionate leadership to manage through all the diverse issues that will inevitably be encountered along the way.

The stakes are high. Successful efforts can transform a company. Unsuccessful efforts usually lead to internal cynicism and continued degradation of operational execution.

Senior managers, you own this concept! It has to be led from the top. There is no middle ground – you are either committed to it or you dismiss it.

5 Delivering service internationally*

Professor Merlin Stone and Alison Bond

One of the problems of management literature is that much of it is written by 'Anglo-Saxons' – a convenient shorthand for authors from North America and the 'Old Commonwealth'. Being brutally honest, Anglo-Saxon should be translated as 'white, English mother tongue, from developed economy'. The best-selling American (and sometimes English) marketing textbooks have been translated into many languages and are the staple food of the young marketing student and managers throughout the world. In these books, the service context described is usually (though not always) the privileged service context of the Western consumer, often in an Anglo-Saxon culture. A cultural caveat is usually attached, though, and many readers are left (abandoned) to translate recommended service practices into their own cultures. Alternatively, general market segmentation methodologies are recommended as a way of analysing the needs of different groups of customers – wherever they may live. However, this approach is no longer enough.

THE NEED FOR AN INTERNATIONAL PERSPECTIVE

For a growing number of companies, service planning has a strong international dimension, for a number of reasons:

1   There is a growing awareness of the big differences that exist on both sides of the market – customers' behaviour and expectations, and suppliers' performance. Even within countries, customers are very different – just ask a frequent business traveller about the difference in the behaviour of service staff between London and Manchester, Milan and Naples, Berlin and Munich, Paris and Marseilles! Add the intercountry

---

* The material in this chapter is based on research sponsored by IBM (UK) Ltd.

differences and you really do have a potpourri of behaviour. Here are some examples:

(a) In one country (UK?), looking people in the eye is encouraged, in another (Italy?) it may be considered rude.

(b) In one country, people use very roundabout language (France?), in another they are direct to the point of abruptness (Germany, Israel?).

(c) In one country, people prefer to use first names (USA?), in another not (France?).

(d) In one country, the time taken to deliver a service may be regarded as significant, while in another, it is how the customer is cared for during waiting that is more important.

(e) In one country (UK?), airline passengers trust their luggage to the baggage handling system, while in another (Italy?) passengers try to maximize the amount taken on board, relying on a shouting match with airline staff to achieve their goal.

(f) In one country, customers don't mind standing in the rain and cold waiting for service (UK?), in another they do (France – even Disneyland?).

(g) Most importantly, in some countries, the idea that a customer has rights is much more firmly established than in others – in the minds of both customers and suppliers! The very idea of filling in a customer questionnaire may be seen as fulfilment of a hidden agenda.

2 International trade continues to grow as a proportion of total economic activity. This means that for any product or service, the probability that it has been specified and/or produced (wholly or in part) in another country is increasing. In business-to-business markets, this means that many more customers have direct contacts with suppliers in other countries.

3 International business and leisure travel continues to grow. Customers resident in one country will bring their service expectations to other countries. If they buy or use a particular product or service in several countries, they may expect some consistency of standards.

4 Developments in telecommunications and delivery services have made it easier for service to be provided from one location to many countries. For example, some companies now use a European call centre to deal with service queries, with native speakers of different languages operating from one location. In the computer industry, very high-value spare parts may be kept at a single European location ('end of runway'), to be shipped on demand to customers anywhere in Europe.

5 Developments in broadcast media – particularly cable and satellite services – means that many consumers can be reached with international service messages (branding, service access). But these media also generate international service expectations. For example, service promises for courier companies establish a benchmark by which local offices are

judged. This applies not just to time guarantees but also to image and customer care issues.

Note that these developments affect relations with internal and trade customers as much as with final customers. In many cases, the boundary between these categories of customers is blurred, and particularly in international trade, where the use of third-party distributors and service providers is the normal route to market.

WHAT IS INTERNATIONAL SERVICE?

International service is just one step in the evolution of service. Figure 5.1 gives a comprehensive description of types of service.

INTERNATIONAL SERVICE SUPPLIERS

Let us examine some of the main industries where international service supply is taking place and who is doing well. Our judgement on the latter is based upon our contacts with some of these companies and their research agencies, but is also no doubt coloured by our personal experiences as international customers!

Airlines

For the international traveller – particularly for the most frequent traveller, who may fly around two hundred times a year – there is no doubt that service differentiation has been the key issue in the battle for custom. There is also no doubt that the honours for international service success have gone to those airlines which have decided *which* customers they want to deliver top-class international service to. While British Airways (BA) has done well by concentrating on the needs of the frequent business traveller (for example, the arrival lounge), Virgin has also succeeded by paying special attention to the in-flight requirements of the new generation of travellers (dare we call them the 'West End brigade'?).

This success demonstrates a more general point: that success tends to go to companies which decide who their best customers are and then concentrate on recruiting them, retaining them and giving them the best service. But this is often more difficult to do in an international service environment. Customer databases and other relevant information systems, and the associated relationship management policies, are often organized nationally, making it hard to identify best customers, let alone manage them. However, in the airline industry – international by nature – systems and policies have been designed to cope with the international user. The frequent flyer/loyalty scheme is of course the key. Here, it is interesting to note that the US approach, based mainly on reward, has not been imitated by the leading European contender, BA, which has placed greater emphasis on service differentiation. However, because facilities-based differentiation (for example lounges, privileged *67*

	SERVICE TYPE		
	National	**Multinational**	**International**
To whom?	Customers who experience service in one country only, from company supplying only in that country	Customers who experience service in one country only, from company supplying in several countries	Customers who experience service in more than one country
Examples	Many customers of small firms Many consumer services (for example, retail, financial services, utilities), though this is changing	Customers of multinational consumer goods companies	Users of international travel and communications – telecommunications, air travel, hotels, car hire, courier, freight Users of services of several different national subsidiaries Customers which are multinational businesses and buy from their suppliers' local subsidiary
Main competitive issues	Identify service needs of local customers Monitor competitors' service standards Deliver better service than local competitors Monitor risk of entry from new companies and other industries and countries, and likely changes to service standards	As for national, plus: Develop competitive advantage by transferring (where appropriate) best practice from other countries and (where possible) by exploiting economies of large scale provision (for example, purchasing, inventory management) Overcome inertia often imposed by local employment laws and practices	As for multinational, plus: Identify international service needs of customers Monitor international competitors' service standards Deliver better service than international competitors
Focus of service delivery	Full range of techniques – systems, standards, recruitment and training etc. – used to attune delivery to customer needs	As for national, plus: Head office may focus more on whether methodology being followed and whether right infrastructure exists	Very strong focus on how people from different cultures handle people from other cultures Measurement focuses on customers' perceptions of differences in delivery between countries

Figure 5.1 Definitions of different types of service

check-in) can be constrained by airport provision, there is still a strong reliance on in-flight service provision (for example staff behaviour, use of customer information).

International hotel chains

These companies have been working hard to provide excellent standards to their best customers. The best chains, such as Marriott, have achieved high standards by sticking to what they know best and looking after the needs of the international market. This market consists of not only the individual international traveller, but also multinational businesses which require guaranteed standards (availability, quality and so on) at negotiated rates. Marriott's links with airlines and car-hire companies have helped them in the area of frequent users, via cross-referencing of customer databases.

Car hire

Car hire represents one of the great successes of international service systems. Operating through a variety of ownership structures, the big US-based car-hire providers such as Hertz have used systems, procedures, staff recruitment and training to define standards that international travellers can rely on wherever they hire a car. Of course this service has a cost, reflected in the premium paid for the top international brands. Once again, however, the frequent user (personal or corporate) is concerned to obtain good service and value for money, not the lowest price. It is no surprise that these US providers have invested heavily in branding to ensure that potential customers feel certain they will get the promised level of service.

Interestingly, the principle of focus on best customers has been used by companies like Eurodollar – which specializes in the fleet hire market – to carve their way into a market formerly dominated by Hertz and Avis. The service package provided by Eurodollar is strong on value for money and information systems, providing customers with the benefit of improved management of hire costs.

Consumer credit and charge cards

The international service provided by credit and charge card suppliers has long been centred on the international business traveller, but their attention is now moving to the leisure traveller – the true mass market. For although consumers travel abroad much less frequently than their business counterparts (typically once or twice a year in Northern European states, rather than between ten and a hundred times a year for the business traveller), the numbers are much larger. (Note that in the United States the sheer size of the domestic leisure market makes international travel a relative rarity.)

The most basic international service proposition in this field is that large numbers of outlets should accept the card and that it should be usable in *69* enough cash machines. For a new credit card, such as Japan's JCB, delivery of this service is largely dependent upon partnerships with existing merchant services providers (for example Barclays Merchant Services in the United Kingdom). Beyond this, the service provided is primarily an emergency one, sometimes associated with the insurance provided with the card. In some cases, this is best delivered by a local representative, who may be a national of the tourist's country, or at least someone speaking the language fluently and thoroughly versed in the issuing country's culture. Here, the companies whose main activity was initially in corporate charge cards (for example American Express) may have a competitive advantage. Until recently, this was out-weighed by issues such as value for money when the card is used domestically, but the adoption by American Express of a very attractive loyalty scheme may tilt the balance in favour of such a card for the more frequent leisure traveller.

Business equipment, including information technology (IT) - hardware and software.

Rapidly moving technology has been both the strength and weakness of this sector. Computerized (for example on-line) service systems have been used extensively by suppliers such as IBM to help users get to grips with ever more complex technology, to make equipment more serviceable and software more amenable to remote diagnosis and patching. There are two main reasons for standardisation of international service levels in this industry:

1 There are many international customers (for example airlines, banks) who require the same level of service in every country.
2 The high cost of support resources have led suppliers to search for economies of scale in service provision (for example by concentrating spare parts inventories or technical experts in very few locations (Stone and Wild, 1993)). Such concentrated resources are normally easier to man-age if standard procedures are followed irrespective of the country that the customer is in. This means that on the whole the supplier has to set standards according to the needs of the most demanding markets. While this is very good for the customer and can pose problems for competitors from countries with low service standards, it can be very expensive for the supplier, particularly if service contract prices do not reflect the higher costs of better service. This pressure leads suppliers to seek ways of automating service as far as possible by using expert systems, remote diagnosis and other approaches to minimizing human intervention. The problem is that this approach is not always culturally acceptable.

ARE THE SAME STANDARDS REQUIRED EVERYWHERE?

Notwithstanding the above example of suppliers seeking ways of automating services, the answer to this question is clearly no. Each country and customer type should be treated like a different market segment, as far as is possible.

Thus international customers in the IT industry are provided with customized service contracts, with the service level delivered in each country agreed irrespective of the 'normal' service level. The only problem here is how to ensure that the local service operation can deliver the required service standard. This is usually achieved through standard international systems, recruitment and training.

On the other hand, international travellers expect the same standards of treatment in the air, at the hotel or at the car hire branch, so for these services, achievement of standard levels is important. However, travellers are not completely unaware of cultural differences. International travellers are on the whole a fairly sophisticated breed. They are aware that service depends upon people. They probably do not expect a company to deliver the same standard of service in Moscow and London.

Most service market research shows that on the main dimensions of service (time, quality and so on) customers can distinguish between the different levels of service:

- *Desired level of service* What customers would really like to experience. This is often determined by the best level of relevant experience that the customer has received. 'Relevant' is used because it may not be the same type of service that the customer takes the benchmark from. The benchmark may be taken from a company which the customer uses frequently. For example, desired level of service from a utility may be determined by the level of service received from a retailer (the parallel industry phenomenon).
- *Expected level of service* What customers expect, given their knowledge of local conditions and their experience of service in local and other conditions. Here, the expectation may be based upon experience with a local company from a parallel industry, or even in a 'parallel country' – a country perceived by the customer to be at a similar level of development (for example economic, competition, service practice).
- *Minimum acceptable level of service* What customers expect from the company, given the local constraints (for example staffing, laws) they think it operates under. This is, if you like, the realist's view. Service below this level may lead to loss of business – if the customer has a choice!

Remember, it is your *target* customers' views that are paramount; you are not trying to meet the desired levels of service of all customers. Research is an absolutely vital input to setting service standards (Stone and Bond, 1994). In setting these standards, you may find it useful to complete the matrix in Figure 5.2.

What you are aiming to achieve is part of your branding and what your branding should be is determined by the needs and expectations of your customers. The ultimate branding choice that you have to make is whether you are offering 'Best of British', American and so on, or 'When at Rome, do as Rome does' (that

Standard relative to best local/parallel country competitor for your target market			
Standard relative to best international competitor			
	Minimum acceptable	Expected	Desired

Figure 5.2   Standards matrix

is, conforming to the standards of each individual market). Our recommendation is that if your research shows that your service standards are generally better than those that prevail in the country concerned, start with the 'Best of' approach, as you will find it easier to get your staff behind the idea. But note that 'Best of' does not necessarily mean 'Copy of'.

MANAGEMENT PROCESSES

So far we have discussed international service standards in general terms, without specifying what we mean by 'standards'. There are several ways of interpreting this term.

Detailed performance standards

These are standards which specify precise performance parameters (for example time to answer the phone, time for an engineer to reach the customer or complete a service, customer satisfaction ratings). These standards are usually required where a high proportion of your target customers are international customers who buy centrally and expect the same service standard anywhere in the world. Such standards may be determined through research and may occasionally be built into customer contracts.

Framework of standards

A framework stipulates that in each country, standards will be set for certain named performance parameters but the standards set will vary according to local conditions. This is appropriate where your service is being delivered under very different conditions and where customers will expect these conditions to lead to variations in service achievement.

General principles

This is the most 'relaxed' approach, where an international headquarters lays
72 down certain principles of service but the performance parameters and target

levels are set locally. This would be appropriate where local conditions vary so much that even identifying service parameters centrally would be inappropriate. In general, as a company moves more towards true international service delivery and as its customers become more internationalized, so it moves from setting general principles to setting detailed operating standards.

THE EVOLUTION TO INTERNATIONAL SERVICE

Many companies start by providing national service. The move to multinational and/or international service is normally evolutionary and determined by the extension of the company's activities into other national markets. But for some companies, the move is necessarily very quick (for example a new international courier company, or a new software supplier needing to make support available internationally). To facilitate this move, international distribution techniques are used. Local agencies (franchised or full third-party distribution), working to internationally set standards but within local cultures and employment laws and practices, often provide the best route to international service provision. This is one of the main reasons for the success of many US-based fast-food chains, such as McDonalds.

Cloning is a new variation on this theme. This technique, where a company in some respects takes on the identity of another, is increasingly used in the airline industry. Here, it may take the form of route code sharing, but also the use of other systems, branding livery and training. British Airways is using this technique to raise the service standards of the various companies tied to it via shareholdings or partnerships. Smaller airlines with larger business partners may also use this technique to absorb some of the risk of taking on staff in other countries (for example Air UK's staff in Italy were employed by their partner KLM).

TRANSFERRING SUCCESS

There is no doubt that successful practices can be transferred – as have McDonald's and BA's service standards. The route to successful transfer is the classical service management route of focusing on standards, procedures, systems and, most importantly, people (recruitment, training and motivation), while making allowance for local cultures, laws and economics.With a few stunning exceptions, the transfer does seem to be relatively one way: from the United States (and increasingly from the United Kingdom) to continental Europe and the developing world. In particular, restrictions in Europe on direct marketing practice inhibit companies from following up service individually by writing to their customers to solicit feedback in order to support re-definition of service requirements.

The stunning exceptions include:

- Two total retail service concepts – IKEA in furniture retailing and Daewoo in integrated car retailing.

- The Japanese photocopier/printer maintenance concept – the customer carries out service by replacing a module, rather than the engineer having to call and the service standard becomes a module availability standard rather than time to fix.

These exceptions, however, are a warning that setting and managing service standards are not enough: the total service concept must be kept under review. They also remind us that the most threatening international service concept is usually part of a total business concept designed to be rolled out across the world.

There is a sense in which those international standards that have been successfully rolled out are determined by the culture of the parent company's country, and of course the specific culture of the parent company itself. This company culture will include:

- attitude to customers;
- procedures and systems for managing customers; and
- attitude to and procedures for motivating staff and measuring success.

Rolling out an international service approach successfully therefore depends upon achieving cultural transfer. This usually requires managers to be trained 'back at base' or 'missionary managers' to be sent out to establish strong service practices in the 'outposts'. The latter approach, though more expensive, is often the only feasible route, particularly if the cultural gap is very wide. Training 'back at base' is all too often forgotten. Worse, it may simply be an attempt to achieve the impossible – a virtual head transplant!

FURTHER READING

Davis, E. and Smales, C. (eds) (1989), *The Integration of European Financial Services in 1992: Myths and Realities*, Centre for Business Strategy.

Skarzynski, M. (1995), 'Service Excellence Through Teamwork', *Customer Service Management*, **6**, March, 8–9.

Stone, M. and Bond, A. (1994), 'But How do you Know if Customers are Satisfied?', *Customer Service Management*, **5**, December, 34–7.

Yorke, D.A 'Interactive Perceptions of Suppliers and Corporate Clients in the Marketing of Professional Services: A Comparison of Accounting and Legal Services in the UK, Canada and Sweden', *Journal of Marketing Management*, **5**, (3), 307–23.

6 A framework for delivering service

Peter Murley

The basic tenets of this chapter are that true customer service is less likely to be delivered by organizations which continue to adhere to functionally based structures; that the only way to progress is to develop a common language to describe relationships – a language which eliminates the mysticism surrounding particular functions within organizations; and that structure and complimentary strategies are the only way to success. This requires going one step – or for many, one quantum leap – beyond dejargonizing (a common error of consultants) and towards understanding that the requirement is to create a framework for service delivery which everyone understands and can relate to, as opposed to only a few, select people who use words in the hope that they won't be understood and who devise strategies in splendid isolation.

TRADITIONAL ORGANIZATIONAL STRUCTURES

Traditional organizational structures are nearly always depicted as hierarchical boxes where attention is often drawn to the size of an individual's empire, as opposed to its relationship with the organization as a whole. Figure 6.1 shows in outline a typical traditional structure. The size of a particular person's function or empire is frequently associated with relative importance, or influence, within the structure and sometimes (not always) can help determine who gets paid what. Some of the traditional charts show people with ostensibly identical nomenclatures (for example, director) but on different lines of the chart so as to display their relative importance, contribution, seniority, and so on. The boxes in the plan of the organizational structure are, therefore, different shapes and different colours, and underscore 'functions' or 'specialisms'.

In many organizations this can lead to several people seemingly having the same responsibility and consequently nobody has actual responsibility at all. In other organizations attempts are made to equalize responsibilities in *75*

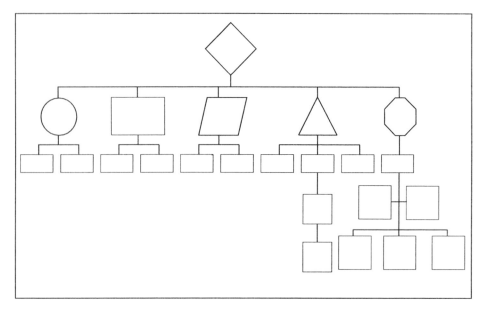

Figure 6.1   A traditional organizational structure in outline

resource terms – such that everyone's box *appears* to be the same size or colour – and this can lead to massive fragmentation and total inconsistency. This is particularly so in the area of customer service, where organizations carve up bits and pieces of direct customer relationship and share out the prime interface roles. As a result they often end up with no customer focus at all, and even worse, a confused set of customers – quite the opposite of what had been hoped for.

Other characteristics of a traditional, functionally based organization are the growth of non-binding and inconsistent cultures, creation of enclaves of independence and existence of ivory towers (that is, remote from the everyday world).

THE 'BRAVE NEW WORLD' – SERVER-BASED ORGANIZATIONS

Organizations for the brave new world must surely recognize that the strength of the organization is greater than the sum of its parts. These 'new world' organizations might best be referred to as server-based – where they exist to serve each other and, particularly, the customer on whose existence we all depend. Good organizations recognize that people are the main centre of activity, that the components of success are inextricably linked with the people partners – customers, prospects, staff, stakeholders, suppliers, the general public 'persona' and, if it is a separate area, the management. In this context, therefore – and starting from the top – a director's prime responsibility is as a team member who is first and foremost a director and secondly a specialist. So, in theory *any* director should be able to do *any* role – it is the skill set as a director which is the important element. Many organizations say this is what they practise, but in reality they don't. Thus many directors have themselves to blame for not being a part of the broader picture, because they always relate everything back to the subject matter which gives them the greatest degree of comfort – their 'specialism' – finance, sales, human resources, marketing, and so on.

The 'wheel' format

The proposition here is that the best organizations must move away from charting to 'wheeling': that is, depicting structures, especially operating structures, as a wheel where each part is critical to the others, and where a missing or faulty spoke will cause the wheel to wobble as it turns. Each part or spoke of the wheel fans outwards and inwards, and in terms of hierarchy the lowest role level in the organization is shown on the rim of the wheel – the part which is most visible or has most external contact. This means, in a customer service environment, that the staff on the telephone or the staff on the retail shop floor are *the* most important links in the service chain as they have the most contact with and the most knowledge of the customer – *not* directors but the front-line staff.

These new, server-based organizations display characteristics of mutuality, enjoy improved communications, create a genuine cultural gel and above all, employ business-oriented directors and staff who share a vision.

People relationships

If, then, the realities and requirements of this brave new world are recognized, is the path to success assured? Well, not quite. The next step is to fashion a structure which recognizes people relationships as opposed to traditional functions, and then to move on to defining a common language that might help each of the components of such a structure understand each other.

The most radical structure is the one that I favour, but I accept that for most organizations an evolutionary approach is likely to be the way forward. The radical approach is one where customer service, finance, sales, marketing, engineering, information technology and so on are no longer named functions at the top of an organization structure. Instead, directors – or whatever the titles or roles are at this level – undertake roles which reflect the company's approach to the people partnership referenced earlier. Thus the key roles may include: director of customers; director of prospects (likely to be teamed with director of customers); director of internal customers (information technology, engineering, purchasing and so on); director of the public persona; director of stakeholders (which would embrace the more traditional finance role); director of suppliers; director of staff. For most organizations a director of strategy is also a plausible role. Figure 6.2 outlines the type of structure I have in mind.

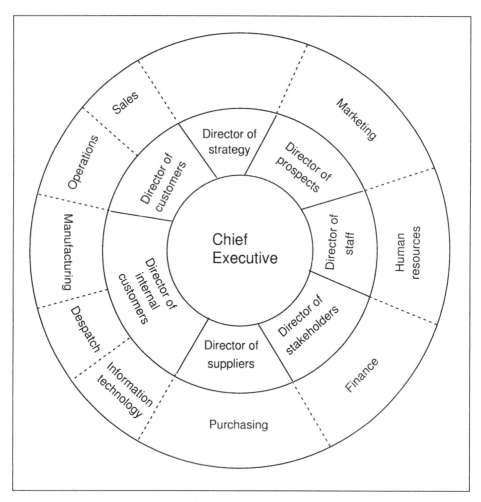

Figure 6.2   Structure for the 'brave new world'

The most likely candidate for the director of customers/prospects is the existing sales and marketing function – although the real task for this function is to understand customer behaviours and how to manage an operational/line unit. The internal customers' role is very important. It is designed to illustrate that such functions are crucial to the delivery of service excellence, but that they are more powerful collectively than they are individually. Internal services as a role area is a start towards ensuring that solutions are delivered which the customers themselves – internal (and ultimately external) in this example – define or contribute to, as opposed to solutions that are delivered to functions without determining their absolute need and the overall strategic intent. In other words this new structural approach may go some way towards reducing the tendency to work on selfish agendas.

A COMMON LANGUAGE

This approach now creates some interesting issues, not least of which is the need to formalize the use of a common language. Even if we could achieve the wheeled structure referred to above, it is highly probable that each member will continue to attempt to protect its so-called expertise by developing its own language, mystical words, acronyms and other myths and fables. In this way outsiders – fellow colleagues from other functions – are held at arms length and can only enter the magic circle if they display an understanding of the language. The development of buzz words and the like is a defensive mechanism and often hides a degree of insecurity, and whilst much of that may be understandable, none of it is of any assistance to the customer. We simply end up with confused messages, outward and inward, and poor communications at all levels, plus an internal infrastructure, one of whose jobs is to try and interpret the different messages into one common language.

At the high level we often have different objectives when we are concerned with functions and this also leads to the use of different words. For example, we often treat suppliers as a necessary evil – they have something we want but we are determined to get it at a price or on a timescale that proves how macho we are as an organization. As a result, we use words in the supplier relationship which do not depict a relationship at all (for example, 'screw them to the ground', 'extract value for money', 'get them to promise or ...', 'deliver', 'get it in writing'). For the staff relationship we use well-worn words such as 'recruit', 'reward', 'promote', 'train', and so forth, and for stakeholders, words like 'nurture relationships, 'make profit', and 're-invest'. The point is that we all use not only specific, highly technical words to create a divide, but also high-level words to describe roles – many of which have various meanings depending on how much we respect the particular part of the relationship chain or on how much we feel it necessary to woo the respondent or flex our muscles.

So what language might be appropriate and how might we then use it in determining the design and development of strategies which work towards one common objective – regardless of the so-called functional contribution. This common language starts with three stages. These stages correlate to language which is very much in use within the marketing arena – for such language best describes the messages which I am trying to relate – and reflect 'lifetime values' or 'lifetime relationships'. Moreover, whilst they are used in marketing (that is, customers and prospects), it strikes me that they are equally, if not more at home, in the other parts of the partnership equation (for example, staff, suppliers, internal customers and so on).

The three stages are as follows:

1 *Tempt-in* Where the objective is to grab attention, gain initial commitment and sell the proposition.
2 *Buy-in* Where the objective is to build the relationship, gain additional revenues or improve the return on investment, and begin to underpin the association.

3 *Lock-in* Where the investment pays off, and where people are wedded to the concepts, the products, the services, the delivery mechanisms, and the methodologies. Where people expect loyalty and give loyalty by buying, committing to or giving more and where they become active advocates of the organization and what it stands for.

THE STRENGTH OF AN ORGANIZATION

The strength of an organization involves many success factors. The four main factors are usually as follows:

1 Technology and its active, beneficial use.
2 Superior knowledge and information such that it beats the competition.
3 Excellence of the product and services portfolio and relevance to the chosen markets.
4 Processes – the detailed understanding of how processes work end to end and in parallel as opposed to function by function and serially.

Overlaying these success factors are what I believe to be four common objectives or goals of all organizations and therefore all functions or directorates within the organization, as follows:

1 Sustainable, profitable growth.
2 Sustainable loyalty, brand values and reputation.
3 Sustainable and controlled cost base.
4 Sustainable competitive advantage.

The most important word in these four common objectives is *sustainable*. Generally speaking, anyone can achieve any or all of these objectives, but the secret lies in *continuing* to achieve objectives, which requires dedication and a willingness to change constantly, day in and day out.

Core actions

The glue which binds the four success factors with the four common objectives or goals is people. People are also the common glue which bonds what are known as *core actions* of organizations. Core actions are those actions which organizations need to take in order to achieve both success and their objectives/goals. These core actions include:

● *Mission* Where the organization is going and by when.
● *Vision* What it will look like when you get there.
● *Strategy* How you will get there.
● *Values* What principles you will adopt and how these will be achieved.

As you can see it follows the well-known principles of how, what, when and where, with the who being the role that everyone plays. People (staff, customers) are the glue, first, because they set the mission, vision, strategy and values (unless of course 'management' are not to be considered as people!). Second, because they determine profit, costs, competitive advantage and loyalty), and third, because they develop and provide the technology, products, services, information, knowledge and processes. All these people elements are integrated back into the server-based structure previously described, in that each of the responsibility groupings – suppliers, internal customers and so on, has at its core, people and people relationships.

With regard to the 'values' of an organization, the best strategies embrace a well-determined approach to how people should be treated, which, within the context of staff, could be said to be the creation of culture. In the context of this chapter these cultural aspects are easily extended into each component of the people partnerships. From experience, the main principles embrace:

- straight talking;
- no reproach;
- constant input sought and feedback given;
- honesty;
- continual development;
- target-oriented, measurement-led and results-motivated;
- investment in people;
- treating people as adults and not idiots;
- 'power to the people' – involvement; and
- constant change.

So the puzzle starts to resolve. We have a new structure, we have determined that people are at the heart of success and we have established a common language.

The result is that by determining core actions, by understanding key success factors, by agreeing common objectives/goals and by defining a common language, we stand a better chance of evolving global policies within a people-focused structure which shares clear, one-purpose objectives (see Figure 6.3).

COMPLEMENTARY STRATEGIES

The last and most challenging part of the puzzle is putting all this together in such a way that each part of the organization can develop its own strategies, policies, processes and procedures so that they are logical, purposeful, and always complement the strategies of the other constituent parts of the structure – in other words, all for one and one for all.

This is a crucial part of the puzzle because all too often strategies are stitched together and form no logical sequence – they jump from one topic or purpose to another. A typical example is the staff policy which develops a selection strategy that offers the 'tempt-in' but forgets the complementary remuneration or development strategy that ensures the 'buy-in'. Strategies *81*

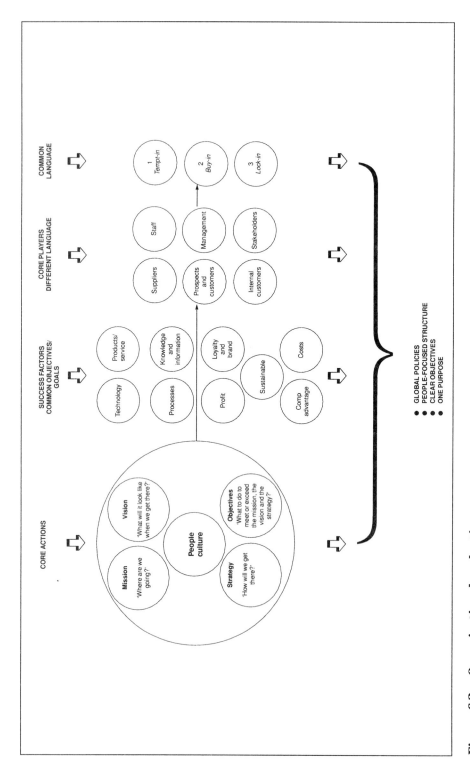

Figure 6.3 Organizational evaluation

which flit from one stage of the relationship to another are not strategies at all but simply actions that address specific moods of the moment or attempt to subdue smouldering fires. Worse still, a staff strategy that takes no account of the future processes of the business, or the researched needs of the customers of the present *and* the future, is not a strategy at all but a miscellany of nonsense. Expand this problem fivefold or sixfold and we then have different directorates going off at various tangents and far from complementing each other. The result is customer resistance, staff demotivation, minimized profits, loss of market share and so on.

So how do you put complementary strategies together? Well, there are certainly several methods one could follow, but taking the principles of this entire structure to its ultimate – and using the two areas of customer and staff as examples (the principles for suppliers, internal customers and so on, are precisely the same) – I would suggest the following procedure.

Let us assume that the staff function have nine strategic roles to play – nine roles as an integrated part of the total organizational strategy – which are :

1 Select staff.
2 Pay staff.
3 Package staff.
4 Incentivize staff.
5 Train/accredit staff.
6 Appraise staff.
7 Develop staff.
8 Involve staff.
9 Measure staff.

These nine roles each require a strategy but the strategy must be developed with the three phases of the lifetime relationship in forward perspective. Thus each strategic area must normally be complete across each of the three stages of the common language. Furthermore, each area of the strategic intent is often linked to another area, or to several others, in such a way that determination of one strategic area must relate to and account for others. It is true to say that tackling the entire strategic framework of nine items across the three stages of the common language – that is, 27 strategic components – is no simple task. With this in mind, development of the matrix approach is possible provided that one tackles each role in a structured fashion, either role by role across each of the three stages or role by role vertically down the matrix (see Figure 6.4).

In either case the inputs and outputs to the strategic process are critical. For example, to determine a broad and then detailed strategy for staff selection, followed by a detailed set of action plans and processes, requires considerable knowledge of the customers, information as to what customers' expectations are and will be for product and service delivery, and so on. Only when this information is known and accounted for can a linked strategy be evolved. By the same token, the elements of the customer strategy will also need inputs *83*

Examples	Staff		
	A	B	C
		Lifetime relationship	
	'Tempt-in'	'Buy-in'	'Lock-in'
1 Select			
2 Pay (£)			
3 Package (benefits)			
4 Incentives			
5 Train/accredit			
6 Appraise			
7 Develop			
8 Involve			
9 Measure			

Figure 6.4   Matrix for strategy development

from the staff area – and, of course, from other areas. Thus, a building block approach is compiled (see Figure 6.5). Each block interlinks with the next one down and the next one across, and also links – in a three-dimensional manner – with others in different topic areas.

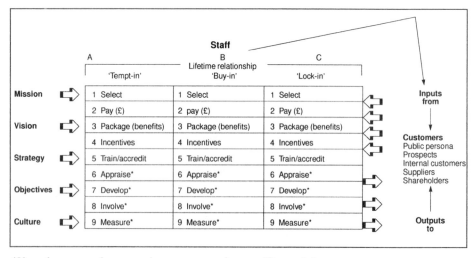

*Use of common language/common words – see Figure 6.4

Figure 6.5   Staff selection matrix

A second example is the area of the customer, the strategic components of which might be as set out in **Figure 6.6** and which would also relate back to other topic areas.

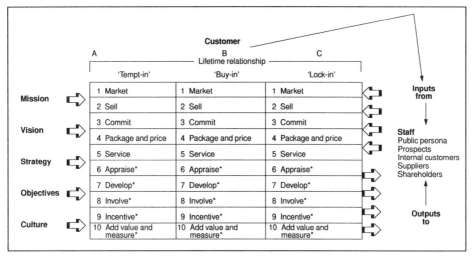

*Use of common language/common words – see Figure 6.5

Figure 6.6   Customer component matrix

Taking the specific example of the selection strategy in the staff area, this strategy needs to embrace a number of stages. For instance, at a broad level these stages might include a plan, an implementation schedule, a benefits, risks and cost schedule, and an input and 'links' reference. Not to embody these elements is to be without a quantifiable strategy, and without a quantifiable strategy the organization will surely flounder. Each strategy must link with the next to be of any real value, hence the reference to 'links'.

A good example of the necessity to create firm links can be gathered from research data. Take a greenfield operation, which is anxious to deliver exactly what the customer wants and in a way that the customer wants it delivered. Traditionally, the marketing area – the customer role in the new structure described above – would gather data concerning customers' priorities relative to the new product(s) and/or service(s) which they are purchasing. This 'priority index' is likely to include such items as quality, price/cost, convenience, consistency, reliability, packaging, design, after sales service and so on. The priority of the indexed items will be determined by a number of factors. The staff role is to ensure that it takes active note of this priority index by building the index requirements into its plans. The staff role should typically enquire for further data – specifically how customers might determine or measure the quality of the service that they expect to be delivered. From this information a service determinants matrix can be drawn up, which may include such items as accessibility, accuracy, consistent communications, competence of staff, courtesy of staff, reliability of the product and the service, consistency and so on.   *85*

We now have a great deal of information about customers' expectations of the service proposition – data which can be built on and honed as the relationship develops, from the 'tempt-in' stage through to 'buy-in' and 'lock-in'. These data, whilst typically considered to be marketing territory, are actually in the domain of every one of the new role areas, as each area depends on the others in order to develop coordinated, structured, consistent and fully complimentary strategies. In the staff area, we would use this knowledge to define the core characteristics or competencies of the staff we need in order to be able to deliver service that meets and exceeds the predetermined expectations of our customers. In this way we have matched people to people and gained core competitive advantage – much more so than on product or price alone. This data exchange is very much a two-way street, in that strategies developed by the staff roles need to be fed back to the other areas who should review their approach accordingly. By these means, the process of continual improvement, change and communication is actively fostered. If, in that process, the traditional functional barriers and ivory towers tumble, then success is assured.

The challenge is to maintain the advantage and develop a constant and sharp edge – and that requires a willingness to be open to change, change and change again, and to accept that learning is a never-ending journey.

7 The role of logistics

James Ensor

Establishing and implementing a first-class customer service strategy is, in many cases, only part of the story. For manufactured goods, it is equally important to ensure that a well-thought-out logistics strategy is in place. Products must be delivered to *where* the customers want to buy them – and in the right size, colour, model or texture – just *when* they want to buy them. For services, it is a question of having the capacity available to meet peak demand. The best customer service strategies will count for nothing if the customer cannot take delivery at the desired time. Given the choice between the 28-day delivery period of traditional mail order and the overnight supply provided by those with advanced customer service logistics, many people will opt for the latter.

THE DEMANDS OF CUSTOMER SERVICE

If the product is a complex piece of mechanical or electronic equipment, such as a car, machine tool or computer, physical delivery of spare parts, rapidly and economically, to where they are needed to repair a failed product, is even more important. This applies also to many services such as airlines, telecommunications or car hire, where the service provider also organizes the maintenance of equipment. Service cannot be provided unless the repair staff, engineer or mechanic is in the right place at the right time with appropriate replacement parts.

Previously, this aspect of customer service was often overlooked. There was the famous story of the Spanish entrepreneur who built a factory to assemble British Minis in Pamplona but neglected to make any arrangements to manufacture or procure spare parts. When challenged, he declared with more bravado than sense that he would build the cars so well that no one would need spares for the first year.

Today, such ignorance has been replaced by a scientific and statistical *87* approach to provision of both original equipment and products and the spares needed to maintain them. With many manufactured products, such as small cars or personal computers – which effectively have become commodities, with little to choose between competing suppliers in design terms or price – competition has shifted to the excellence of the customer service provided and attention has turned to logistics and parts supply.

The same is true of a large number of food products, such as potato crisps, sugar, milk, butter and bread, where consumers differentiate with difficulty between brands and prices are uniform. In this case, the shopkeeper, or the retail chain central buyer, is likely to be more interested in the excellence of the provisioning in terms of reliability of supply. In other words, it is more important always to have some sugar on the shelf, than to have the best-known brand.

The rub is that just as manufacturers have become more sophisticated about the importance of logistics and customer service in maintaining customer loyalty, so have retailers, stockists, garages and other middlemen who deliver the service or the product become more sharp about the costs of actually holding items in stock. Some big British supermarket chains have demanded delivery within four hours of placing an order on suppliers. As the shelves deplete in stores and goods are delivered from the central warehouse to refill them, orders are transmitted in the morning for delivery the same afternoon. Garages and car repair workshops often maintain no stocks at all, but demand a two-hour delivery of all common parts of popular makes of car, which enables a customer taking a car for service in the morning to collect it the same evening.

Pressure is thus placed on the supplier. With most mechanical or electrical components, manufacture can only be organized in relatively long runs. It is very costly to switch over a press-line or a machining cell from making one part or component to another. Equally, delivery in small quantities by emergency motorcycle or van service, whilst feasible, is expensive. Transport operators prefer to wait until there is enough product to fill up a line-haul truck and then despatch it to a single destination.

A LOGISTICS SURVEY

Customer service in logistics is about the scientific method of reconciling these conflicting needs, between the customer's desire for instant supply anywhere, and the manufacturer's need to schedule production and delivery in big lots and to keep the capital and storage costs of stocks under control. Set the customer service targets too low and you will inevitably lose customers; set them too high and costs will rise dramatically, eventually increasing exponentially if you aim for 100 per cent availability.

A customer service study

88 Nowadays the starting point in developing a logistics strategy is usually a

customer service study. Perhaps 200 customers need to be interviewed, some face to face and some by telephone. If it is going to be of any use, this study needs to be done independently; left to the company's own sales force, it will inevitably become biased and distorted. It needs to deal with precise standards, such as percentage levels of order-fill that are desirable, acceptable and unacceptable, rather than broad corporate statements about 'being world-class'. Discovering what standards are actually achieved in practice by competitors is also obviously important, since this will tend to set expectation levels in the market.

Ability to deliver the product or spare part ordered, however, is only one aspect of customer service. As anybody who has taken a day off work to wait for a gas repair knows, it can be equally important that the goods arrive at a precise time and on the right day. The attitude and appearance of the deliverer may also be a factor. Certainly how quickly the supplier responds to the inevitable mistakes when the wrong thing is delivered or the right thing goes to the wrong place can be critical. Generally as suppliers have become more sophisticated about getting the basic delivery of goods and parts sorted out, customers have become more stringent and attention has centred instead on these less obvious details. Without a knowledge of what today's customer expects, it is impossible to set in place the right statistical monitoring mechanisms to check what is achieved.

A survey will inevitably show that different types of customer have widely different expectation levels. This can be due to geographical grounds: customers in remote, rural areas are generally less demanding than those in urban centres. Or it may be due to the type of customer. The managing director's Rolls-Royce will demand and get much more attention from the car fleet manager than the sales rep's Ford.

A Pareto curve

Equally, the loss of some customers will be far more damaging to a business than others. Most food companies' year-end profits would be severely impacted by the loss of one of the top supermarket customers. On the other hand, they can, for a time at least, shrug off the loss of individual corner shops. For this reason, retail customers are classified into A, B and C groups (not, incidentally, to be confused with the socioeconomic groups A, B, C1, C2, D and E): the A group is a small number of important outlets, who provide most of the business; C is a very large number of unimportant ones, each representing only limited business; and B consists of the in-betweens.

In this context, we encounter the nineteenth-century Italian economist Vilfredo Pareto, who developed what is known as the 80:20 rule (20 per cent of customers provide 80 per cent of the business and 80 per cent provide the remaining 20 per cent). Pareto curves are used to divide customers into the three categories. Sometimes, the nature of the market provides the division. A food company, for instance, may supply national supermarket chains, catering groups and corner stores, which could conveniently represent the A, B and C *89* categories. Or a manufacturer may supply domestic, European and rest of the world customers, which again provides possible categories. At this stage, there may be an element of common-sense judgement needed in the otherwise scientific process of categorization.

A Hook diagram

In recent years, a further sophistication has been added to the process of categorizing customers, which is to calculate the total costs of supplying each individual customer and assess what they are each paying. Even supposing that they all take an identical product, some will be far more demanding in their delivery requirements, thus necessitating the holding of larger emergency stocks. Others may require the attention and time of direct salesmen, when the bulk of business is handled through wholesalers. When it comes to logistics, the costs of supplying truck-load quantities into a supermarket depot are far lower than that of van deliveries to corner shops. Most businesses reflect these different costs in the size of the discounts provided to large or straightforward customers. Then again, some large customers are very late payers and this carries a cost, which is reflected in interest forgone.

Thus the Pareto-type display is used to record the gross profit contributed by each individual customer, once variable costs such as delivery have been allocated and the effects of discounts, late payments and non-payment risk calculated. This analysis can radically change the apparent attraction of individual customers: many companies, for example, have only realized when they have studied the costs in detail that the apparently attractive prices often paid by German customers are negated by their preference for having everything delivered in small quantities to each outlet.

The results, known as a Hook diagram, will show that an A group of customers provides the whole net profit of the business, a B group merely contributes to overhead absorption and a C group actually diminishes profit. In this situation, it becomes important to redefine the terms of business of the C customers, either by charging them more or decreasing their service level. Often companies do this by preventing direct sales to customers with less than a specific annual order size and stipulating that they must be supplied through wholesalers.

Profitability v. loyalty

There are certain situations where the propensity of the customer to quit when offered poor service becomes the most critical factor to consider. For instance, British brewers have had three types of customer since the Government `Beer Orders' were introduced. They have their own tied-pub estate, where the tenants may become very unhappy or go bankrupt but cannot easily quit. They have a second group of pubs, where they provide a guest beer or are supplying a free-trade outlet, which buys from several brewers. And many of them have an increasingly important group of customers within the off-licence shops and the supermarkets. In this case, calculation of profitability, which may well be highest in their own pubs, has to be tempered by the degree of loyalty of the customer whose beer runs out during a heat wave.

It is obviously impossible or at least wasteful for a business with hundreds of thousands of customers to assess the profitability of all of them. So it is necessary to construct a good sample, based on statistical probability. For example, with 100 000 customers, a random sample of 200 will be accurate to within 2 per cent above or below the true value 99 per cent of the time. If this is not good enough, a 1 200 sample will be accurate to within 1 per cent on 99.7 per cent of occasions. Just as it is uneconomic to provide 100 per cent service levels, the same laws of probability make it uneconomic to analyse data to 100 per cent accuracy.

So far, we have been considering a company supplying just one type of product, let's say potato crisps, which may need to be sold and delivered to supermarket chains, to pubs and clubs, to off-licence chains and to corner stores. Since crisps sell for low prices and are very bulky, transport costs play a very predominant role in the profitability of customer service. There is no way that a supplier could contemplate dispatching an emergency van with a couple of boxes, just because there has been a run on crisps in Wembley due to a cup final.

However, most customers do not buy just one product. The crisp supplier certainly supplies several types of crisp but may also sell nuts, cheese biscuits and soft drinks to the same customers. In this case, failure to keep the store stocked with low- margin plain crisps could lead to a loss of significantly more valuable soft drinks trade as well.

An extreme case of this occurred some years ago, when the customer was the actor Paul Newman, whose weekend hobby is motor racing. An aficionado of Triumphs, he raced TR6s at club meetings all across the United States and provided the British sports car with millions of dollars in publicity value. Unfortunately, under the stress of racing in a heat, he destroyed a gearbox, and to compete in the final was ready to dispatch his personal Lear Jet to Coventry to collect a replacement. Shamefully, though, the company mechanic simply declared 'we no longer make them'. Newman switched to Datsuns. Today, Triumph no longer sells sports cars.

Providing parts for old or obsolescent machinery can be a big problem from a logistics viewpoint in customer service. Rolls-Royce does set out to provide replacement parts for every car that it has ever made, but this is quite exceptional and can only really be justified for such an expensive car. At the other extreme, the Welsh car company, Morgan, when asked by a German owner to supply a part for a discontinued model, sent a blueprint and machining instructions.

In order to reduce the costs of providing parts for its older designs of watch Seiko, the Japanese watchmaker, supplies a new watch at a handsome discount to customers returning an obsolete model for repair. This has become normal practice in the consumer electronics industry, where the cost of fixing even a minor failure on, say, a computer keyboard may exceed the cost of supplying a *91*

new one. So costs of stocking thousands of obsolescent parts are simply eliminated, although this often gives the uninformed customer a negative impression, unless accompanied by a discount on the replacement.

A SERVICE MATRIX

Most businesses aim somewhere between these extremes, with a stock policy
that differentiates products into A, B, and C categories, in exactly the same way
that customers are divided up. Exactly the same Pareto rules come into play
and it is usually found that 20 per cent of the products provide 80 per cent of
the business and so on. This is true both for supplies of new products and for
replacement and maintenance parts. In both cases, it makes sense to provide a
better level of customer service on A lines than on B or C. Taking these product
categories together with the customer categories produces a matrix of service
levels (Figure 7.1).

Sales volume				
		A	B	C	Service
Customers	A	100.00	98.00	95.00	99.50
	B	90.00	75.00	70.00	86.80
	C	80.00	60.00	50.00	75.60
	Overall	86.40	71.20	63.80	83.10

Note: By dividing customers into three classes by importance and products into three categories
according to sales volume, it is possible to adjust service levels on each to reduce logistics costs
without surrendering competitive advantage. This is usually shown in a matrix.

Figure 7.1   Matrix of customer and product service labels

The C lines are the ones that provide the most problem, since over time they
build up to an enormous number of items, which are sold less and less frequently. Attempts to hold these in a national depot network to meet the occasional requirement rapidly, becomes expensive. A common solution is to
concentrate stocks of these less popular items centrally. Sales rates must be
monitored carefully and lost sales recorded, otherwise the claim will be made,
'We no longer need these – we didn't sell any'. Every six months, depot stock
needs to be checked against demand (including lost sales) and, where necessary, items culled.

Recording the sales rate of slow-moving items may have more impact on profit than watching the fastest movers, which are easy to spot because they rapidly lead to empty shelves. The logistics director of one supermarket chain proudly explained to his managing director that a new computer system would report the ten most popular items right across the retail network. When questioned on the ten least-selling items, he confessed that the system was incapable of this and was fired on the spot.

Properly handled, C line items can be a great source of profit. Well after the transistor revolution, the US military continued to use valve (tube) based communications sets in the field. Those manufacturers who continued to make these obsolete products and ensured that large inventories were maintained in the right places, earned a bonanza.

It is the A lines, however, that are given the most attention. These are the day-to-day fast movers which earn the bulk of the profits for a business and on which its fortune is based. If we are considering spare parts, they are the lines which most often lead to a vehicle being off the road, a machine tool stopped or some electronic equipment dead. These items do not all behave in the same way and may display erratic sales due to a number of factors.

FORECASTING

Occasional large orders from particular customers can distort the normal pattern of supply and lead to undercapacity. One such situation which is particularly irritating, and which can destroy an otherwise good reputation for customer service, is in the supply of airline seats. All airlines sell more seats on early morning flights than they provide, since they have learned that a considerable proportion of their customers fail to make the flight. Forecasting algorithms are built in, which tell them how many extra seats they can 'safely' sell on each flight. American airlines have developed a business policy of paying cash sums to booked passengers to miss a flight when too many people turn up.

But in Europe, latecomers are unceremoniously left behind even if they have arrived in time and have a confirmed booking. The airlines failed to build a Japanese factor into their forecasting algorithms, which was needed on two grounds: Japanese are far more punctual than other nationalities, and also tend to travel in huge parties. On routes such as London–Paris, which have a high Japanese passenger load, this created havoc with the regulars, which no amount of VIP lounge treatment could mollify. These problems could have been solved if an extra or even a larger plane could have been rolled out onto the tarmac in time to cope with the extra passengers.

Just the same thing happens in the supply of goods, where the level of stocks that need to be held in warehouses or rear stockrooms of a shop, depend on the length of the order cycle. With the introduction of 'just-in-time' manufacturing techniques and electronic order processing, these levels have been steadily reduced. Order times demanded by supermarkets and car manufacturers from their suppliers are frequently less than the manufacturing time. Consequently, it is no longer possible to build to order, and demand must be anticipated.

A new premium has therefore been placed on more accurate forecasting in achieving customer service standards. It must be sensibly adapted to take account of known factors that may produce blips in the system. It is known, for instance, that sales of beer and ice-cream are increased by prolonged warm weather but less obvious that sales of chocolate and meat are reduced. Often the increase or decrease in demand can be accurately plotted against a degree rise or fall in temperature and, as weather forecasting becomes more accurate, it is becoming worthwhile to build some of these predictions into supply calculations.

SAFETY MARGINS

Starting with historical records of sales of a product, or demand for a spare part, one can analyse these for various factors. Demand, for instance, may be increasing but it may seem to do this erratically, actually declining in some months or weeks, whilst spurting ahead in others. Multiple regression analysis can separate these apparent meanderings into a regular growth trend, a seasonal factor, influences due to weather, advertising, and sundry other factors. One will still be left with some inexplicable random variations, but they will be much less after these factors have been eliminated than with the original data. Obviously good forecasting is vital for the overall business strategy and for establishing production targets, but it is also an essential input for customer service. To cover these random fluctuations, suppliers must set a level of safety stock above the normal stock-holding.

Seasonal factors are the most obvious element which can vary demand in a regular way. They are important for food, clothing, car sales and vehicle parts subject to accidental damage, but also, though less obviously, for airlines and hotel operators. Stock levels need to be adjusted to account for seasonality. This is done by building in a safety stock level – to be held at or near the point of sale or available for immediate delivery to it – which varies by time of year. Safety stocks, by definition, must relate to the variability of demand, which can be measured statistically. The measure is known as the standard deviation and for sales orders it most often relates to a bell-shaped curve known as a 'normal distribution'. Rarer events may exhibit a 'Poisson distribution', which was first developed through studying deaths by horse-kick in the Prussian army. Once the appropriate statistical function is chosen, one can set a safety stock level at three standard deviations and expect to fall short only once in a thousand times. Safety stock levels can be varied by season, or, as in the case of fashion goods, set for the expected peak and allowed to run down later.

Levels of safety stock should be adjusted with reference to a customer service survey. This should show the penalty of failure to meet demand, which obviously varies by sector. In monopoly supply markets, such as utilities in Europe, regularity of supply was governed by production convenience rather than customer needs. The British Post Office barely attempted to meet demand for its black telephone handsets, since the engineers complained that this would upset their fixed programme of line installation. With deregulation, privatization, and the arrival of competitors offering cheaper phones in many colours and designs over the shop counter, the new British Telecom had to change its customer service mentality in a hurry.

In the food industry, promotional offers often produce a sevenfold and sometimes as much as a fiftyfold increase in sales over short periods. Unless this has been taken adequately into account and stocks provisioned appropriately, the impact of the promotion is lost. Research has been done to show how likely customers are to buy another product or another brand if a food item is out of stock. In Britain, instant coffee and bottled water are the most protected products on both counts, whilst wine drinkers tend to switch brands readily and beer drinkers change to another product. For sugar, stock-outs are most serious of all since there is neither brand nor product strength (Figure 7.2). These factors need to be assessed in considering the level of safety stocks provided.

The situation on safety stock, or safe margin of capacity for a service busi-

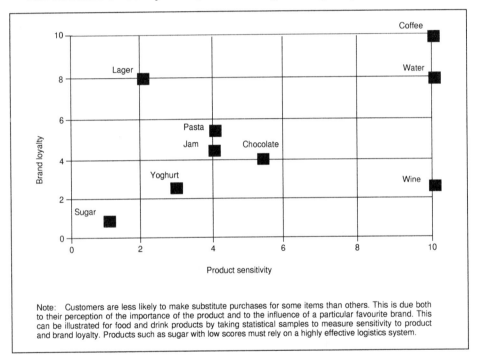

Note: Customers are less likely to make substitute purchases for some items than others. This is due both to their perception of the importance of the product and to the influence of a particular favourite brand. This can be illustrated for food and drink products by taking statistical samples to measure sensitivity to product and brand loyalty. Products such as sugar with low scores must rely on a highly effective logistics system.

Figure 7.2   Customer's perception of product

ness, is complicated where purchases are interrelated. British Telecom was divided into separate businesses once it was privatized. Its new international division commissioned a customer survey using conjoint analysis to try to discover whether its business customers would choose to use the rival Mercury service on calls between London and Paris. Telecom hoped that this survey could be used to set service standards and prices, and determine how much extra capacity had to be laid on. But business customers do not buy telephone *95* service in this way; if they change to a rival supplier they are likely either to switch all calls or to buy call-routing software which will automatically select the cheapest way for each call. Thus a lowering of standards on international lines, leading to more frequent engaged tones, would impact the domestic business too.

THE IMPACT OF LOST SALES

Little research has been done on how much poor service is needed to drive a customer away for good. Partly, this is because most research projects only question existing customers. Lost customers are hard to trace and sometimes so annoyed that they do not want to be interviewed. Yet this is probably the most expensive cost to the business, given how much advertising, sales effort or inducements it takes to gain a new customer. What is known is that customer tolerance acts like a piece of chewing gum. It can be stretched and will gradually recoil part of the way towards its initial position. But successive stretching will eventually break it and at that point it never recovers.

It is recognized that each angry customer dissuades others from trying the service or product – the actual number varying by country and by product. If the customer's views happen to be publicized in the press, or television, the results can be magnified many times. This factor should also come into the cost calculation for lost sales. So the deceptively simple chart, setting off the rising costs of lost customer sales and the declining costs of holding stock as service levels diminish (Figure 7.3), actually disguises some complex and detailed research.

This problem occurs in the supply of car parts, which contrary to popular belief are no longer mainly supplied by car manufacturers, but by factors or wholesalers who deliver to local garages. With 250 000 part numbers for just the more popular makes, it is difficult to keep enough in the right place to give the two-hour delivery which most mechanics want. Local depots can use expensive express services to get it there in time, or sometimes they can buy in from a competitor and sometimes they lose the sale. Car repairs rarely involve one part – a dozen or more could be needed – so one stock-out usually leads to lost sales of many parts. But more ominously, in the fiercely competitive car-parts business, a mechanic who phones a supplier three times and finds that it has not got a popular part will in all probability be permanently lost. Very careful and sophisticated customer service surveys have to be developed to uncover the true costs of logistics failure in these situations.

A more complex question arises in production of aircraft parts, since these are commonly produced on a once-off basis, while the aircraft is being manufactured. Sufficient spares are made during the production run of the aircraft to meet expected spares demand and then all production stops. It is obviously possible to tool up again for a later production run, but this carries a heavy cost burden. Manufacturers use a technique known as maximizing expected monetary value by simulating what would happen when different quantities of spares are needed over a number of years and assigning a forecast probability

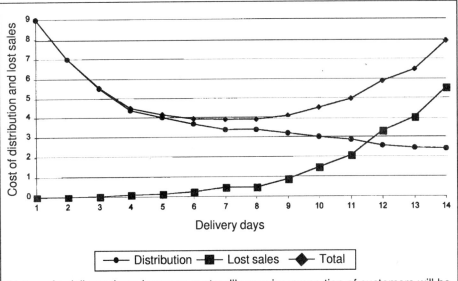

Note: As delivery times increase, a steadily growing proportion of customers will be lost to other suppliers. But, at the same time, the logistics costs, of maintaining stock will reduce. Most businesses aim to have a balance which minimizes the overall cost of both factors.

Figure 7.3   Cost of lost sales and inventory

to each. It is possible then to estimate the costs and sales of alternative strategies to make an informed decision on how many parts should be run off and stockpiled.

Aircraft, which often become unserviceable unexpectedly and in remote places with a large and vociferous passenger-load, present severe problems in customer service. Airlines use logistics techniques to plan spare or relief capacity for emergencies and they also use these techniques to ensure parts and service fitters are available in the right places along their route. Yet unless the customer service strategy is based on a coherent integrated plan, it may reach decidedly non-optimum results. This happened to an American airline whose accountants, tasked with reducing maintenance costs, forbade engineers to fly out to grounded planes if this required an overnight stay. This decision certainly reduced hotel bills – but at a disastrous cost in reputation for customer service with passengers on the abandoned planes.

A consistent failure in retail situations is to adjust the levels of stock to known parameters. It is well known that 80 per cent of clothing sales will be in a narrow range of sizes, but less well understood that perhaps 80 per cent will be in a certain colour. And this size range differs by country (for example, small in Italy, big in Holland). Favourite colours also change by country and sometimes by region within a country. Cars buyers consistently pick a narrow range of colours in each country (for example, silvers and greys in Germany, reds and whites in Britain). Perhaps the most foolish but consistent stocking failure lies in the provision of guidebooks and maps, particularly where the publishers have made things simple by providing a standard rack. Invariably, of course, it is the guide or map to the local area which is out of stock.

STOCK LOCATION AND TRANSPORT

The next question in customer service logistics is where should the stock be held? From the customer viewpoint, it should be located in each shop, each garage, each repair centre, or at least in a convenient depot close by. This has a serious impact on the costs of stockholding since each separate location then has to maintain its own safety stock because demand fluctuates independently at each. Retail space in high-street locations costs far more in rent than warehouses, which are often sited on derelict land that has no other obvious use. The total requirement for safety stock will increase in proportion to the square root of the number of locations. So holding safety stock in 400 retail outlets would need just 20 times as much as locating it all in one central warehouse.

The drawback of the central warehouse is that even with modern electronics it will be the next day before an item can be delivered to remote areas of Britain. In larger countries such as the United States or Australia, it can be much more. This may not be much use to the pub (bar) which has run out of beer, still less to the beer delivery truck, which has stalled because its fuel injector has clogged up. But it may be quite adequate for people ordering stationery or a new item of machinery. Once again the location and number of safety stocks reintroduces the need for customer service analysis. And again, there may be different requirements for the various types of product purchased by any one customer.

Car parts used in accident repair, such as paint, body panels and windscreens, are processed according to the timetable of insurance assessors. Stocks of these can be centralized. Other items such as tyres, exhausts, brake pads and batteries, increasingly bought through quick-fit centres, require local stocks. As these outlets are more highly developed in central conurbations than in remoter parts of a country, it may be economic to vary stocking concentration by region.

Once safety stocks and their locations are planned, it may be necessary to finesse the calculations by thinking about the use of emergency transport or more regular supply to reduce stocks. Twice-daily delivery of components, common in just-in-time supply situations, radically reduces stock levels compared to traditional weekly replenishment.

Reducing safety stock levels to two standard deviations from three will, similarly, increase from one to 25 per thousand the likely failures to meet demand. However, if it is possible to use an emergency form of transport such as a courier service or a parcel carrier, this could be cheaper than maintaining a larger stock. At the British supermarket group Tesco, a world leader in logistics efficiency and customer service, the fall-back arrangement when a small store runs out of bread or milk is for one of the managers to jump into a car and drive to the nearest depot.

Many businesses now use road-map computer programs that can adjust driving speeds for urban, suburban, and trunk roads and motorways, to calculate more accurately the cost and time to deliver goods or parts to specific customers or stocking points. This often leads to a saving in the number of vehicles needed. It can be combined with computer analyses of the number and precise location of depots needed to meet any particular rate of supply response. For Britain, overnight national delivery requires six or seven locations – and one always seems to be sited at Milton Keynes.

Such tools, skilfully used, can greatly reduce the total logistics cost required to achieve any given level of customer service. They can also be deployed creatively to provide different levels of customer service in different regions. In the British Isles it becomes costly to offer customers in Ireland, Wales, Scotland and the West Country a two-hour service response. The same is true of central London and urban areas of the Midlands or Lancashire, where traffic congestion is severe. In France, it is well known that customers in the central Ile de France region are far more demanding than in the provinces. In Germany, the 'Ossies' in the East still expect less than the 'Wessies' in the West. Combining road-traffic computer models with geographically sampled customer service studies, makes it possible to provide customer service where it counts competitively.

CONCLUSION

Logistics strategy is a critically important component in customer service for businesses delivering goods, supplying spare parts, or providing on-site service. But it is just a component and it needs to be integrated into all other aspects of a company's response to its customers. Japanese companies who have led the way in just-in-time logistics in their manufacturing, have also applied these principles in their logistics of supply to customers and to stocking of spare parts. They have discovered that this produces a virtuous circle, where faults in manufacturing are spotted early and corrected before too many defective products are in the hands of customers. With short manufacturing lead times, output can be stepped up or models altered to meet changes in demand. This reduces the number of customer queries or complaints and hence the need to invest in customer response handling. But all elements in the interface with customers need to be carefully analysed and the resources balanced. This requires constant monitoring and regular audits, incorporating a customer-oriented perspective. Above all, internal aspects of logistics planning must be augmented by a detailed understanding of customer behaviour and market dynamics in order to gain the full business benefits.

FURTHER READING

Heizer, J. and Render, B. (1993), *Production and Operations Management* (Boston: Allyn & Bacon).

Hull, J., Mapes, J. and Wheeler, B. (1978), *Model Building Techniques for Management* (Farnborough: Saxon House in association with Cranfield Institute Press).

Sussams, J. E. (1992), *Logistics Modelling* (London: Pitman).

8 'Due diligence'

Peter Murley

Entry into a new market or expansion beyond existing boundaries frequently requires the injection of cash, resources, knowledge, or all three. Often such requirements cannot be met from internal means alone – perhaps one of the primary reasons for taking on a business partner anyway – and even when this is not so, it is often preferable to enter new opportunities with a partner who will share the risk or simply provide the ability to tackle new markets through the power of 'commercial convergence'.

THE EVALUATION PROCESS

Taking on a partner, or indeed a partner being prepared and able to take on you – be it a relationship of absolute equality through to one of absolute inequality – means that one or both sides will need to take honest stock of the other. In other words, the viability of the partnership has to be thoroughly evaluated in a logical and objective fashion. This evaluation often involves seeking and creating synergies.

In creating new businesses, and particularly in takeovers, the fiscal issues are nearly always at the top of the shopping list of at least one of the parties – and correctly so. However, there are other key issues to consider, not least of which are staff, customers and, of course, the service expectations. By considering these issues alongside the financial issues, it should be possible to evaluate a relationship from a much more holistic, 'total fit' perspective: that is, being cognizant of relative strengths, weaknesses, risks and opportunities across a wider range of subjects than just the fiscal considerations.

In whole or in part, the principles of mutual evaluation apply to joint ventures and also to the other key issue – selecting suppliers. This issue is often overlooked or assigned to the bottom of the priority list, yet a bad supplier decision may ruin customer relationships.

EVALUATION CRITERIA

With this in mind (and with apologies to the accountants, whose requirements are only partially catered for in this chapter), the criteria listed below *may* offer you a reasonable basis for evaluation. The headings and examples of questions/areas to cover within each heading, frequently form the framework for what is often referred to as 'due diligence', but could, with adaptation, be applied equally to supplier evaluations. Much of the subject matter of this evaluation process is covered in greater detail in subsequent chapters of this book.

This list of 16 key criteria demonstrates a structured approach to evaluating the suitability of a 'service partner'. Clearly the detail of the evaluation will vary according to the businesses concerned, but as a guideline it may prove useful. The list – which was originally compiled for an assignment that included the need to find a business partner for a minority financial involvement, but one whose skills were vital to the success of the project – is as follows:

1   Client/customer profiling.
2   Revenues and profitability.
3   People and structure.
4   Values, mission and objectives.
5   Performance, indicators and achievements.
6   Growth plans and forward strategy.
7   Planning and project skills.
8   Market and competitive positioning.
9   Value for money (VFM) and understanding of cost components.
10   Skill set transfer and differences.
11   Process engineering.
12   Key differentiators.
13   Quality approach.
14   Technology and systems use and futures.
15   Service investment plans.
16   Character.

1 Client/customer profiling

Here we are trying to establish the other parties involved: that is, the potential 'service partner's' existing base of clients/customers. How solid and loyal they are, and what made them and makes them use this organization. What businesses are this party in and what are the demands of their customers? What products and services are manufactured/sold/marketed? How has this changed over the past 'x' years? What is the penetration of the customer base? How many different products/services does what customer type have/subscribe to?

2 Revenues and profitability

What are the annual revenues by sector, channel, route to market, product, and service? Is it a good and profitable business to be in? How long has it taken to get to this position (for example, profit over past 'x' years by product(s)/service(s))? What proportion of revenue v. profit comes from what product(s) and/or service(s) and customer type? What is the cost to acquire and the cost to service each customer?

3 People and structure

How many people are employed in the organization? What have been the changes in total staff proportionate to revenues/profit over past 'x' years? What are the typical number of customers per staff member (for example, if party A has 10 000 customers, how many staff serve this number)? How are these people treated and rewarded? What is the staff retention rate – current and historical? Is there a flat or tiered hierarchical structure? Are staff customers also? What is the operational experience of their staff? How do people role share and exchange and gain additional skills? Do they reward for extra skills and, if so, how? Is it a meritocracy? How do they share improvements in service delivery? What are staff selection criteria and how are they determined? Are they competency-based? What are the labour costs and on-costs? How is efficiency and productivity recognized, measured and rewarded, and reflected back to customers?

4 Values, mission and objectives

Do they have a mission statement? How robust is it? Why do they have it? How do they use and refer to the statement? Do they have medium- and long-term visions of their future and how are they manifested within the organization? What are the corporate, departmental and functional objectives? How do they overlap and also mutually complement each other? How are they communicated? What is the record of achievement like in the area of communications?

5 Performance, indicators and achievements

What are their performance and work targets and actuals? What do they judge themselves on in terms of key performance indicators (KPIs)? What type and volume of management reporting data do they have/use? How do they target individuals and measure success? How do they measure perceived performance with the customer base? How do they monitor and measure supplier performance?

6 Growth plans and on-strategy

What are their current growth plans and how are these to be funded? Are they *103* evaluating other partnering arrangements? If so, who are they evaluating, and on what terms? Will their growth strategy change as a result of this partnering discussion, and if so, how? Do they currently concentrate and/or intend to continue to concentrate on markets sectors, or does that not matter? How do they go about setting out strategic targets/plans and achieving the objectives set? Are there any staff dedicated to business development, forward strategy, staff involvement and customer knowledge? Do they undertake any competitive benchmarking? If so, how frequently, and who do they compare themselves with, how and why?

7 Planning and project skills

What is their commitment to new customers, products, and services? Do they have new business teams/experts assigned to cover new products/services or changed products /services? How do they make up planning teams and do they have any specific techniques or tools at their disposal? What is their experience at development and *delivery* of fast-track projects? What skills are better/different/worse/ complimentary to ours?

8 Market and competitive positioning

Do they know their market? What research do they do to prove that? Do they survey their customers directly or indirectly? How frequently? What do they do with their results? Who is their biggest competitive threat and how do they intend to (or did they) overcome it? Do they position themselves differently to the others in the market? Why have they been /are they being successful? How do they seek and attract new customers?

9 VFM and understanding of cost components

How do they compare on the costs front? Is the staff structure similar across both organizations? How do they price their products and services? Do they have a full understanding of the costs of acquisition and the costs of service? Do they use or intend to use 'activity-based costing'? How do they reduce costs but still deliver service? Are cost savings shared/used within the business (for example, added profit, reinvestments and so on)?

10 Skill set transfer and differences

How could skill sets be transferred from partner to partner? Where are the key differences and how could we optimize/minimize them? What kind and number of people would each party allocate to the next stage of this evaluation process? What do they do in 'people' terms, that we do/do not and should/would not – and vice versa?

11 Process engineering

Do they use process engineering/re-engineering? Have they got any concrete examples of how this has benefited their business and involved staff, suppliers and customers? Do they use process engineering in the context of systems or the business end to end, or both? How extensively is process engineering being used elsewhere in their particular market and with what impact?

12. Key differentiators

What has to be done to make the other party more competitive in their market sector? How have they achieved that? How do they keep one step ahead of the competition so as to maintain their competitive advantage?

13 Quality approach

Do they employ quality principles? How long have they utilized a formal quality programme? Is this a specific total quality management (TQM) programme or is the general concept of TQM permeating everything in the business? Do they subscribe to quality awards, and, if so, why and how? What advantages have quality programmes delivered? And have they delivered these advantages profitably – in every sense of the word? What issues have quality programmes raised and how have they been dealt with?

14 Technology and systems use and future

What systems do they have – software and hardware? Are they proprietary? How easy will it be to change and update the software? How do they handle change control? How user-determined are the systems now in place? How do they use computer telephony integration (CTI) and calling line indentity (CLI) and power predictive diallers (PPD) and the concept of superoperators (that is, using specifically trained staff with specific skills and attributes, to handle specific calls from specific customers) – call centres? Do they have a specific place for interactive voice response (IVR) – call centres? Where do they see the market going in terms of technology? And their use of available and appropriate technology? Do they have PC-based front-office/customer-facing systems? What is their working environment and do they conform to best practice standards? What are their own system's strengths and weaknesses, particularly with regard to infrastructure and staffing? What are the strengths and weaknesses of their software suppliers (and hardware)? How can their weaknesses be overcome? How do they build futureproof systems (that is, systems which have the potential to adapt to possible future amendments and additions without wholesale change which actively help develop the customer relationship? What are the system integration problems arising from this partnering proposal? How do they integrate management information (MI) outputs from disparate application products?

15 Investment plans

What are their investment plans for the future? What are their expectations for return on capital – amount and timescale? Where do they raise capital? How can they fund multiple and parallel investments, in terms of time, resources and cash? What is their ownership, constitution and so on? Have they made any acquisitions recently, and, if so, how have they integrated from both cultural and customer service perspectives?

16 Character

What is their evaluators' level of comfort with the operation? How do they sit and feel as a whole? Would they make reliable and trustworthy partners? Would they carry their fair burden of responsibilities? Do they really understand *and* listen to their customers? Are their staff happy, professional and dedicated? Is there enough inherent ability/talent within their organization? Are they telling us the truth? Do they care enough about customers and staff?

WEIGHTING OF CRITERIA

It is a good idea to weight each of the 16 key criteria according to its agreed/perceived importance. Figure 8.1 is an example of how these weightings might be agreed.

QUESTION SETS

Question sets are logical groupings of questions leading to an overall evalu-

Criteria		Ranking	Weighting
1	Client profiling	3	0.8
2	Revenues and profitability	3	0.8
3	People and structure	1	1.0
4	Values, mission and objectives	4	0.7
5	Performance indicators and achievements	1	1.0
6	Growth plans and on-strategy	5	0.6
7	Planning and project skills	2	0.9
8	Market and competitive positioning	3	0.8
9	VFM and understanding of cost components	3	0.8
10	Skill set transfer and differences	2	0.9
11	Process engineering	6	0.5
12	Key differentiators	5	0.6
13	Quality approach	2	0.8
14	Technology and systems use and future	1	1.0
15	Investment plans	7	0.4
16	Character	8	0.3

Figure 8.1   Weighting of key criteria

ation of that specific question type. Each set comprises eight questions. These questions can be drawn up from the types of questions listed under each of the criterion headings above. See the end of this chapter for samples of question sets.

One question set is applied to each of the 16 criteria and in the example there are eight questions per criteria. The response to each question is rated on a 1–10 scale. Where 1 is an unacceptable response and, at the other end of the scale, 10 is the best possible response. The maximum score for each criterion is established by multiplying the weighting as a percentage for that criterion by the number of questions in the set. Thus Figure 8.2 shows the maximum scores available for all 16 criteria based on the weightings contained in Figure 8.1.

EVALUATION

The number of evaluators in the due diligence process varies but would ideally be three or five individuals. If the 'due diligence' was, for example, in response to a merger process between two organizations, then this due diligence service and the evaluators would form one part of the entire process. After each criteria evaluation, the evaluators should compare ratings and agree one common assessment, taking into account each other's special knowledge. Thus one total score is derived.

No.	Criteria	Ranking	Weighting	Questions	Maximum score
1	Client profiling	3	0.8	8	64
2	Revenues and profitability	3	0.8	8	64
3	People and structure	1	1.0	8	80
4	Values, mission and objectives	4	0.7	8	56
5	Performance indicators and achievements	1	1.0	8	80
6	Growth plans and on-strategy	5	0.7	8	56
7	Planning and project skills	2	0.9	8	72
8	Market and competitive positioning	3	0.8	8	64
9	VFM and understanding of cost components	3	0.8	8	64
10	Skill set transfer and differences	2	0.9	8	72
11	Process engineering	6	0.6	8	48
12	Key differentiators	5	0.7	8	56
13	Quality approach	2	0.8	8	64
14	Technology and systems use and future	1	1.0	8	80
15	Investment plans	7	0.6	8	48
16	Character	8	0.4	8	32
Total score possible (all criteria)					1 000

Figure 8.2   Maximum scores available from the question sets for all key criteria

The final stage of the evaluation process is to determine the minimum acceptable scoreline, below which a relationship needs to be seriously questioned and possibly avoided. Given that many organizations now conduct regular surveys of customer expectations and satisfaction, together with benchmarking the best service deliverers, an acceptable scoreline may well be one which is linked to the general benchmark rating. In most organizations this is now a rating of between 8 and 8.5 out of 10. In the examples used above this would equate to a minimum scoreline of between 800 and 850.

More structured approaches to the non-fiscal aspects of the so-called due diligence process are long overdue. Apart from forming an important part of any partnering arrangement, this process can set the operational framework and determine action priorities once the partnership is underway. The end result for most organizations is likely to be even greater customer orientation.

There are no hard and fast rules, however, and bearing this in mind you may find that none, or only some, of the criteria or the questions listed are appropriate to your particular circumstances. Whatever your view, everything points to much more structured approaches being taken towards future business partnerships – and quite rightly so. If you have any opportunity to influence the evaluation of another party, are asked to be part of a review body, or if you get involved in any way in creating a 'synergy' of hitherto competing organizations, then remember the importance of customers, staff and suppliers, all of whom are a key part of the service chain.

QUESTION SET 1

Criterion 3   People and structure

Weighting : | 1.0 |

Subject matter :

> **How do they recruit, train, retain, reward and motivate staff? How do they involve staff in the business? What is a typical staff profile – by grade/type?**

Typical questions :   **Rating:**

1	2	3	4	5	6	7	8	9	10

1.

How many staff do you employ (all levels) specifically in the delivery of customer service?

2.

What is the typical number of front-end and support staff per customer(s)?

3.

How are your staff treated and rewarded? What bonus schemes do you have? How do you reward people on a non-tangible level? What is the current staff retention rate overall and at the front-end? How has this changed over the last five years?

4.

What is the organization structure – flat or tiered hierarchy? Are staff the customers also – do you know?

5.

What is the average years of operational experience of management staff and in what industries? What percentage of staff are home grown? How do you train staff and what is the average length of a front-line training course? What are its component parts? How do they receive top-ups and refreshers? What is the ongoing career development plan? Are staff satisfied with development? Do you survey staff and, if so, how regularly?

6. ☐☐☐☐☐☐☐☐☐☐

How do staff role share, and exchange and gain additional skills? How, in turn, are they rewarded for these skills?

7. ☐☐☐☐☐☐☐☐☐☐

What categories and proportions of staff do you employ? Do you subscribe to equal opportunities and agree with returning mothers and ageing groups (including child care/crèche)?

8. ☐☐☐☐☐☐☐☐☐☐

How do you share improvements in service delivery and measure that with the help of staff directly? What are the staff selection criteria – methods/techniques, etc. What are your labour on-costs, and labour costs as a proportion of total operating costs? How is efficiency and productivity recognized, measured and rewarded?

Totals (number of instances at each rating) : ☐☐☐☐☐☐☐☐☐☐

Grand total points :
Weighted at : 0.8   = ☐ **Score   (Maximum: 8 × 0.8 = 64)**

QUESTION SET 2

Criterion 8   Market and competitive positioning

Weighting: | 0.8 |

Subject matter :

> **How do they research and understand their market? What are the threats, opportunities and risks? How will they overcome these?**

Typical questions :   **Rating:**

1	2	3	4	5	6	7	8	9	10

1.

What makes you believe that you know your market? Do you share information with other vendors?

2.

Do you survey customers regularly and what happens to outputs? Can we see some of the data and evaluation criteria?

3.

Who is your greatest competitive threat, why and when (if not yet arrived on the scene)?

4.

What do you intend to do about such a threat - how will you overcome the issues/problems?

5.

How different is your positioning to the market compared to other vendors – unique selling points (USPs) – and why?

6.

What is the secret of your competitors' success/market share? How do you learn any lessons from this and translate it to your business?

7.

What are the market trends relative to your customer types/products/services? How do you see the trends relative to this proposed partnering arrangement?

8.

Do you see any new/ emerging markets for your products/services, and also for those products and services which might make up the new partnering arrangement being discussed?

Totals (number of instances at each rating) :

GRAND TOTAL POINTS :

Weighted at : 0.8   =   **Score   (Maximum: 8 × 0.8 = 64)**

QUESTION SET 3

Criterion 10   Skill set transfer and differences

Weighting: | 0.9 |

Subject matter :

> **How could/would they transfer skill sets across to the business? What are the perceived differences? What is their commitment to the potential partnership?**

Typical questions :

Rating:

1	2	3	4	5	6	7	8	9	10

1.

What do you consider to be the key cultural, social and attitudinal/behavioural differences between our two organizations, based on what you know and what you have heard?

2.

How could we minimize any differences and why should we?

3.

What skills would you allocate to this venture if progressed further?

4.

Why would we find your skills useful versus our own?

5.

How much time and money commitment would you give to the partnership opportunity/venture?

6.

Do you perceive there to be a joint learning experience, or is it all one way and, if so, which way?

7.

What technical skills are transferable and would easily map across the businesses?

8.

What skill sets/approaches are in early development in your sector/your organization that we would be well advised to consider now (for example, to embody in our thinking on this project)?

TOTALS (number of instances at each rating) :

GRAND TOTAL POINTS :

Weighted at :   0.9   =   **Score   (Maximum: 8 × 0.9 = 72)**

Part II
MEASURING, MODELLING, PLANNING

9 Using customer surveys

Peter Murley

Quality is said, by some, to be 'meeting requirements' and several prominent exponents of the mystical art of total quality management (TQM) have defined it similarly. Juran says 'fitness for purpose'. Seven years ago ISO 8402 stated 'the totality of features and characteristics of a product or service that bear on its ability to satisfy stated or implied needs'. What nonsense! Every one of these definitions is inadequate because they are totally impersonal and in no way refer to people indirectly or directly.

Many 'gurus' make a great deal of money from the quality revolution and good luck to them too, but quality is no more a new concept than many of the subjects that we discuss in the 1990s. It just has a different, jazzy and smart name – 'TQM'. A cynical approach, I suppose, but there is in fact little doubt that this is one of the buzzwords of the decade, which of course does *not* lessen its importance. Nevertheless, to jog the memory of those of you who are older than you may be prepared to admit, 1969 was 'Quality and Reliability Year' – so quality is not exactly a fresh idea.

Many of us back the quality theme, however, because we believe we have to follow the trend. Yet quality is far more than just a trend. The reality is that quality is about the whole fabric of the organization and the one positive way forward. Quality is all about a style of management, about effectiveness, and, particularly, about common sense – and lots of it! Unhappily, the quality programme failures are *many* and have been pointed out in recent months by several leading organizations. The quality revolution has not been all it has been made out to be and I believe that this is primarily because it has been implemented by those who have a less than adequate knowledge of the business process in general and of the customer in particular.

A recent survey of 500 of the United Kingdom's largest organizations conducted by Abram Hawkes and Kingston University shows that:

- Only 63 per cent of the organizations have quality performance targets.
- Where targets do exist, only 48 per cent provide any reward for their achievement.
- Quality expectations and satisfaction are not measured universally for staff (69 per cent on expectations, 57 per cent on satisfaction); customers (80 per cent on expectations and 78 per cent on satisfaction); and suppliers (47 per cent on expectations and 37 per cent on satisfaction).
- Only two-thirds of the respondents' TQM programmes had any measurable standards and only one-third applied them across all areas of their business.
- Only 50 per cent felt that TQM had produced tangible results and competitive advantage.

I leave you to draw your own conclusions as to whether these disappointing results are due to overzealous selling on behalf of the TQM consultancy people, or lack of understanding and involvement on the part of the organizations' staff and management, or whether it is a flawed concept where cost exceeds benefit? What drives a business is *people* – staff and customers, in tandem. Programme failures usually occur in organizations which have not concentrated on running their business to provide what the customer actually wants – and the knowledge of what your customer wants always resides with the people who make your business work, namely, your staff. Staff know what customers want because they are in regular contact with them. So my definition of quality is 'consistently exceeding customer expectations'. And the only way that you as managers will achieve this is by constantly staying close to both staff and customers, and involving them in your business.

SURVEYS

People therefore lead you to your profit or success goals, and one method of achieving these goals can be to commit your organization to a survey or questionnaire process. Preferably this process should be ongoing, and should keep you constantly alert by comparing performances from one time period to another, using a core set of consistent, measurable questions and responses and one which involves your staff and customers. A survey process can also help in retaining customers.

Why survey?

A business should ensure that the needs which it is servicing and which it believes are essential, are in fact the same needs that the customer has. The relative importance placed by the customer on each need must be assessed through comparison with customer expectations, and also the company must find ways in which future services, service delivery and products might be differentiated to meet those needs. Less expensive and more efficient ways of providing service have to be researched, and also whether it will cost more to provide service for customers who demand something which they perceive to be different.   However, the list of topics which can be covered in such a survey is considerable. For instance, a good survey can be designed to provide input into mechanisms and measures for rewarding improvement in satisfaction levels: for example, linking results into payment-by-results systems; or rolling into one outputs from the regular survey with reducing cost of service or cost of acquisition (or both) and thus deriving incremental profit. There is quite a lot of competitive advantage in an organization who reward in this way.

There follow two brief examples from First Direct and Cellnet/Call Connections of how involving people in your business through the use of surveys can help.

Involving people through surveys

The bonding of the business, staff and customers at First Direct, began some years ago. First Direct is a service organization first and a banking organization second and is founded on people – staff and customers. It believes that its way forward is to map a business for the future based on the perceptions and the needs of its customers. In June 1990 First Direct decided that a customer questionnaire or survey was a valuable way to cement these foundations.

The process adopted in the initial First Direct survey went some way towards achieving this objective. The survey was defined in such a way as to ascertain attitudes of service quality against a list of what might best be referred to as service criteria or attributes. It gathered data on customers' satisfaction at the time of the survey versus their expectation of service when they first became a customer. These data were assembled on a measurable and quantifiable, as well as qualitative, basis. Other headings covered by the survey included: customer perceptions as to the adequacy of products; future propensity to buy; additional services and products desired; and customers' view of surveys in general.

The second example of a survey is one conducted within Cellnet of the customer base of one of its subsidiary organizations, Call Connections, a cellular service provider. The survey is similar to the survey that First Direct currently conducts, which itself still has some of the elements of the initial First Direct survey but with an increased number of service attribute type questions. The Cellnet survey included a number of open questions where narrative was asked for from the customers. This is meant to encourage customers to express opinions or issues in their own words. As long as these questions are properly interspersed they can provide useful feedback. They also give telephone staff an opportunity to call the customer back personally (where such a survey is returned through the post) and discuss matters on a one-to-one and personal basis. This tactic often gives customers a feeling of warmth and helps cement a relationship.

FIRST DIRECT SURVEY

We will concentrate now on the First Direct survey. From the beginning staff were involved in conducting the surveys, and the company and the staff are involved together in defining what the business would like to know. All good surveys can help an organization establish what it wants to know and what it must know, and indeed in finding out what it doesn't know, but the most important aspect of a good survey and one in which everyone will be prepared to contribute is *feedback*. This involves telling participants what the results are – good and bad. It also requires attention to the development of an action plan to address issues which arise and an ability to avoid complacency about good results. Feedback to customers is not done well in British industry, so surveys – when used properly – are not for the faint hearted! Talking to staff and customers is an important aspect of success. Listening only to yourself, however, and not to others, is a potential route to disaster.

An outline of the stages of the First Direct survey process may help you to plan how you might use surveys in the future.

1 Examination

Any business needs to look carefully at itself and decide where it's going and how it's going to get there. A business has to have a mission in life, which has to be turned into a set of meaningful objectives for the year that can then be progressively shared by both the business and its people.

Everyone must understand the connection between the three components of success: the business, staff and customers. The bottom line of all this for First Direct is that everything that it does is predicated by the customer. And *all* their staff are customers too! It also believes that success is founded on getting the customer relationship right.

So before you start a survey process you should be prepared to examine your current business in detail and come to a conclusion as to whether surveys suit your culture and your objectives.

2 Identification

Given that First Direct believes in the customer as being the reason for and the driving force behind all activities, they had to identify a method of collecting customer views, opinions, attitudes and requirements on a controlled, meaningful and ongoing sample basis. At this stage, you can consider surveying product requirements as well as service-type questions, but there is an argument for doing this separately.

The First Direct philosophy encourages staff involvement and participation and so, in evolving the survey process, they identified the need to include staff in the process at all stages of the survey design, development and implementation.

120   To satisfy these requirements First Direct were looking for a flexible and dynamic tool: one which could be used in a consistent manner for some time to come; which would satisfy and involve both staff and customers; and which would help reward staff for their contribution towards customer satisfaction ratings. They chose a focused survey process in which questions were designed to give good feedback. It's acronym was CFIS – Customer Focused Information Survey.

3 How and what

The how and what included:

- How should the questionnaire be devised – layout, length, structure and so on?
- What kind of questions did they want to ask and why – service, product, 'futures'?
- How should they phrase the questions to avoid ambiguous or biased answers?
- How should they decide the sample – size, criteria?

Four years ago, First Direct did not possess all of the skills and experience necessary to conduct a survey or identify the different stages. They therefore used the services of an expert, who not only helped guide First Direct through, but, most importantly, also ensured that their skills were imparted to the company in such a way that they left First Direct with a high degree of future self-sufficiency.

4 Principles presented

A short presentation was made to the First Direct management group – the small band which runs the day-to-day aspects of the operation – at which the main principles of the survey process were outlined: what the surveys consisted of, how they would work, and the do's and don'ts. The presentation also included proposals on how surveys could be used to good effect within First Direct, and showed examples of outputs. A possible timetable of events was also drawn up: that is, how long it would be likely to take to feed back some tangible results from a representative group of live customers.

5 Task force

A small task force was formed – a group of about six people – which:

- Brainstormed various issues of the business and discussed whether some of these could be addressed within a survey.
- Looked at their own perspective and perceptions of what First Direct provided and how it provided it.
- Considered the broad kind of questions to which they would like to know *121*

the answers – in such a way that the business would be able to move forward and develop around customers.

- Decided to conduct an initial survey of 30 staff so as to gather their views of the levels of service which First Direct and its staff provided and what service quality actually meant to them.

6 Staff survey and analysis

The staff survey was designed and carried out among 30 staff representing all departments within the business. The survey asked a few simple questions:

- How did they rate themselves in terms of service provided to customers? They were asked to remember that rating themselves was the same as rating First Direct.
- What kind of things did they think were important to the customer? What was, in their experience of dealing directly with customers, the customers' expectation level of service? Why had customers joined, why did they stay and what were their priorities?

7 'Protocol' development and testing

Following on from the staff survey, sufficient data was available to enable a 'protocol' or test survey to be developed for customers. This test survey was designed internally, using the expertise purchased externally and was used on 30 customers via a 15-minute telephone call.

8 Protocol analysis and feedback

From this protocol, First Direct then analysed how well customers rated the company's actual service against what they expected when they first joined. The test survey instrument also established if customers had any objections to participating in surveys – either via the post or at the telephone. From this test, a decision was taken to conduct a second test on a further 20 customers in order to gather some additional data and sharpen up some of the questions. Following these customer test surveys, thank-you letters were despatched to participating customers together with a small 'thank you' token.

All the results were then analysed and fed back to staff and the senior management group. In overall terms it was concluded that the survey process added high value and strongly assisted ability to gauge and track customer satisfaction. It also identified the potential for bonding the business with staff and with the customers, and it confirmed results of work already carried out in the marketing focus groups.

9 Evaluation and way forward (1)

The results were evaluated and a forward plan was developed for the future use of surveys.

A discussion was held regarding the relative value of telephone versus mailed surveys. At this stage, therefore, it would be useful just to point out the pros and cons of telephone versus mailed surveys: Telephone surveys provide quicker and better (for example bigger) response and therefore quicker feedback and analysis. Additionally, if you are a telephone-based organization there may be an argument for conducting this kind of business over the telephone. However, it is not necessarily cost effective to conduct phone-based surveys, and there is a chance that – even given a very culture-oriented organization – that the results will be biased: that is, bias either from customers who, if they have a good rapport with staff, do not like to upset them, or from staff who might interpret responses incorrectly and/or complete the form incorrectly on a customer's behalf.

Returning to the development meeting, a sampling was agreed; future frequency of surveys was discussed; decisions were taken regarding who would be responsible for conducting future surveys; how feedback should be handled in the future was determined; and finally an analysis was made of what systems requirements might be in the future.

10 Core survey design

The decision was taken to design a survey and to use it on a widespread basis within the customer base. This survey was to be used to gather attitudes regarding a number of service and product questions to which qualitative and quantitative responses would be used as input to the 1991 strategic business plan. The following steps were taken:

- The final subjects – both product- and service-related – were agreed.
- Thirty questions – mainly multiple choice – were devised. (This is a vital stage, since question phrasing is very important.)
- A decision was made to split the survey into two as 30 questions was considered to be too many.
- A sample was selected.
- It was decided to split the sample into mail and telephone.
- For this first survey it was agreed that all analysis, visualization and feedback to all groups would be done by internal staff.

11 Core survey implementation

- The sample size was 1 500 customers divided into months since first acquired, so as to indicate any degradation in service or differing opinions between different adopters.
- This sample was split equally between survey 1 and survey 2.
- For both surveys, 80 per cent were sent by post and the balance conducted over the telephone.
- Of the 1 200 mailed surveys, 580 were returned within the time.
- Of the mailed returns, 70 per cent were received within seven days of original despatch.

- Of the 300 telephoned surveys, 292 were completed.
- Questions common to both surveys covered service attributes, number of rings to answer, time on hold, length of the survey, and willingness to participate in future surveys.
- Survey 1 also asked questions regarding the ease of the account-opening procedures and the value of the service provided versus other banks.
- Survey 2 asked about new product requirements in the future, use of existing products, and likely date when customers would be ready to buy new services.

Typically, unincentivized surveys result in 15–25 per cent returns in the mail. First Direct response was in excess of 45 per cent and more were returned after the cut-off date. To this day responses are high, due, I suspect, to the way that information is fed back and used to improve the services and products.

12 Core analysis

Since this first survey, a very large proportion of First Direct customers now have their prime banking relationship with First Direct; many have more than one product – that is, two or more accounts; and in addition, over 33 per cent of all customers are recommended by other customers.

Finally, this first survey showed that the length was about right and that 97 per cent would be prepared to participate in future surveys at an average interval of six months.

13 Core feedback

The final survey results were fed back to the following sectors:

- The management group, for feeding into the strategic business plan (for example future product take-up, capacity planning, service levels and so on).
- Managers, to enable them to understand the significance of the results so that they could feed back to staff across the 24-hour shift cycle.
- Staff, who were advised verbally in briefing sessions, and also via a briefing note and a graphical output.
- Customers – 90 000 of them – who received a written statement input giving the good news and the bad news.

14 Way forward (2)

As a part of the survey process – but also because First Direct wanted to formalize its approach to quality – future surveys were embodied within the quality programme, a programme of continuous improvement. A clear decision was taken to use surveys on a regular basis in the future, and over the past few years that has developed to the stage where surveys are a way of life, where the marketing function plays a central role, and where a variety of methods are used.

15 What now?

First Direct have moved on since the first survey, although the principles still hold good. They now conduct four different surveys:

1   Firstimpressions is a census-type survey sent to *all* new customers in the third month of their relationship with First Direct. This survey looks at two aspects:

   (a)   *The account-opening process.* There is a clear perception that it is very difficult to transfer accounts from one bank to another. This survey gathers data on such impressions, which can be used to positive effect in future acquisitions. Among First Direct customers, 80 per cent say that it is a lot easier to transfer than they first thought, which to some degree helps explode the myth that it is almost impossible to do so.
   (b)   *Views of customer service.* The second aspect of the First-impressions survey is to gather input on views of the customer service being provided versus expectations and the propensity of new customers to recommend others to join.

2   Firstresponse, the second survey, is sent quarterly to 1 000 customers who have been with First Direct for longer than 12 months; 75 per cent is via the mail. All analysis work is done by an external organization.
3   The third survey takes place every two months to a small sample size and is conducted by MORI. It is a market evaluation and First Direct partici-pates as opposed to sponsors.
4   The fourth survey takes place annually and is a satisfaction survey that applies the Firstresponse output across the market. It is conducted by NOP and is completed over the telephone.

In addition to these four surveys, First Direct uses focus groups on a continu-ous and rolling basis. This provides them with attitudinal data regarding new products and services. At the current time these groups are helping to build service quality index – some work on which was conducted as part of the pre-launch research. There is no real loop, as yet, to reward staff based on the outputs of these surveys although I believe that the intention to do so still exists.

First Direct do not have customer control groups or 'panels' whereby the same group is asked the same set of questions on an ongoing regular basis. It is thought that this method does not produce spontaneous results and that control groups start to behave in a biased fashion.

SUMMARY

- Ask yourself if you really want to bother to find out what your customers think.
- Ask yourself if you really intend to do anything about the feedback you receive.
- If you answer 'yes' to both questions, then consider the cost of gathering data and the speed at which you wish to gather it.
- If a survey process is what you decide to go for, then give careful thought to the number and type of questions; and when designing the questions, stop and think about bias and what it is you are trying to achieve.
- Try to involve staff within the business in designing the questionnaire and in understanding its value to them and to the business as a whole.
- Design the form, select the sample and define the analysis properly.
- Complete the analysis properly and use external sources to assist you if necessary.
- Ensure that you are serious about feeding back the results, otherwise people will not participate in the future. After all, if you are not prepared to tell the outcomes or do anything with these results, then why did you do the survey in the first place?
- Consider how you might use surveys or other processes for the future (for example continuity of questions to enable comparisons, and tracking of improving or decremental performance).
- Try and incorporate the results into your future strategic planning.
- Consider the impact of surveys on your branding and positioning.
- Think about ways in which you could incentivize and reward results.
- Review your methods continually and search for better and cost-effective ways to move closer to your customers.

Surveys are only one component of a whole series of activities that pivot around the creation of a profitable, thriving business in the most cost-effective and productive way. But surveys can be a very key component because they can draw together, or provide the opportunity to draw together, all the parties to business success. If service, quality, profit and retention are on the top of your list, then surveys may help you. But only if you truly believe that the only and ultimate judge of your products and services are your customers.

Whatever 'the management' does means absolutely *nothing* unless it recognizes that customers keep all of us *in business*, and that lack of attention to their needs and to the quality of service will keep us *out of business*. So get to know who pays our salaries and creates our profits.

10 Standards, measures and performance indicators

Allison Grant

The objectives of this chapter are twofold. First, to define and to distinguish between measures, standards and key performance indicators and to demonstrate the role they play in performance evaluation and improvement. Second, to present the reader with some practical ideas which should help in the development of performance indicators. This development process should be applicable to many organizations, irrespective of the industry.

MEASURES, STANDARDS AND KEY PERFORMANCE INDICATORS WITHIN THE CONTEXT OF THE ORGANIZATION

Definitions

Operational measures and key performance indicators (KPIs) are simple tools which enable straightforward and continual evaluation of company performance and company competitiveness. They can be both quantitative and qualitative, and serve to help management focus on key business issues and re-evaluate company strategy as appropriate.

Key performance indicators and operational measures may often be one and the same. Generally, however, key performance indicators are summary level indicators, whereas operational measures may be detailed, more numerous and analyzed at shorter intervals so that any necessary action can be taken quickly, depending on the results.

Standards are indicators of the levels of performance a company wishes to meet or exceed. They are normally set for operational measures, but they could also be used to add value to key performance indicators. To derive best value from the development of measures, standards and key performance indicators, they really need to be linked and to support one another within the *127* organization as a whole. Figure 10.1 demonstrates how measures 'link' together in a typical organization.

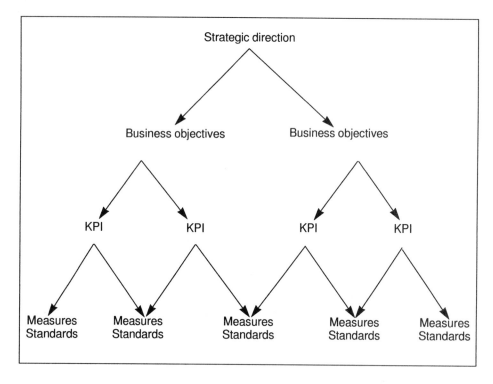

Figure 10.1   Measures, standards and key performance indicators within the context of the organization

Why develop measures, standards and key performance indicators?

Measures, standards and key performance indicators are essential for the enhancement of any organization. Generally, performance indicators help a business to distinguish the factors that create value. They can act as a catalyst for behavioural change and play an essential part in the short- and long-term planning of any operation.

Probably in most organizations, measures, standards and key performance indicators are developed intuitively, without a clear understanding of the links between them. This should never be the case. These measures, standards and indicators should never be developed in isolation. Internally they need to reflect and support both company strategy and the business operation. Externally, performance indicators should be used to take account of customer expectation and competitor performance, external factors that should dictate the standards of performance a company has to achieve.

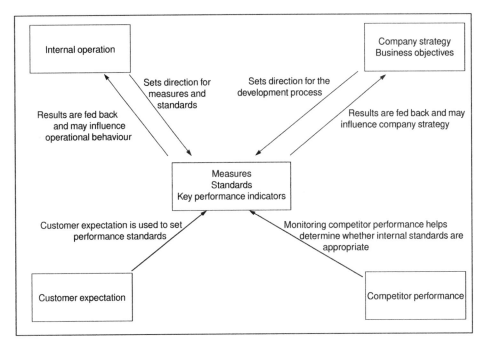

Figure 10.2   The role of measures, standards, and key performance indicators

Figure 10.2 shows how all these factors come into play, and how they can be used not only to support, but also to influence both the operation and the business strategy.

Responsibilities in the development process

It is important to clarify responsibilities in the process of developing measures, standards, and key performance indicators. Figure 10.3 suggests that setting the company direction and business objectives should take place first and is the responsibility of the executive board, which is the group with the strategic insight into the business. Once the executive board has communicated the strategy and the company objectives to the rest of the organization, senior managers and operational managers can set about the task of identifying the appropriate measures, standards and indicators. Operational measures and key performance indicators are not necessarily different; it is simply that key performance indicators are those few manageable measures which senior management and the executive board will wish to see on a regular basis. Operational measures are usually more numerous and are used to manage and react to the operation on a day-to-day basis.

Phase	Tasks	Responsibilities
Phase 1	Setting strategic direction	Executive board
Phase 2	Develop critical success factors	Executive board
Phase 3	Identify and develop key performance indicators	Senior management/ executive board
Phase 4	Develop standards and measures	Senior management/ operational management

Figure 10.3   Responsibility for developing measures, standards and key performance indicators

THE DEVELOPMENT PROCESS IN PRACTICE

Before you attempt to identify the appropriate performance measures for your company, consider the company strategy and the company objectives necessary for successful realization of the strategy. You have to ensure that you understand the company objectives if you are to develop standards, measures and key performance indicators that really support the operation and direction of the business. Very often, understanding the company objectives is not as straightforward as it appears. To illustrate this point, let us take the example of American Express. This company is in the business of offering charge cards, credit cards and travellers cheques, but what are its business objectives? Are they to offer innovative services to support the business traveller, through activities such as partnership arrangements with hotels and airline companies? Or are there objectives to offer financial services to any individual who has the means to pay? If the former is the case, then it would be logical for American Express to concentrate on the creation of measures which evaluate the quality and quantity of its activities supporting the business traveller, rather than indicators which only serve to assess penetration and the competitive positioning of the American Express card.

The assumptions made here about American Express may or may not be true, but they serve to illustrate why you need to understand your company objectives. These objectives set the direction for the development of key performance indicators. If your key performance indicators do not support your company objectives, then there is a chance you are focusing on the wrong measures.

It is also useful to apply the same rule when you develop operational measures. In most organizations it is very easy to develop too many operational measures – too many to be useful. In trying to establish how operational measures support business objectives, you can simplify the task and significantly reduce the number of measures identified. Moreover, by ranking your business objectives in order of importance, you can better prioritize the development of key performance indicators and measures.

Rules for key performance indicators

There are ten rules to follow when developing key performance indicators:

1 Concentrate on developing one key performance indicator at a time.
2 Develop an unambiguous definition for each key performance indicator.
3 Concentrate on developing one key performance indicator at a time to establish owners and accountabilities.
4 Make sure the source of the information is easily accessible.
5 Consider the format of the reporting and ensure the results can be easily interpreted.
6 Create a balance between financial and non-financial performance measures.
7 Develop both quantitative and qualitative measures.
8 Build key performance indicators into personal objectives.
9 Continually evaluate for appropriateness.
10 Create a written and visible record of why and how each key performance indicator was developed.

Concentrate on developing one key performance indicator at a time

Identifying and developing key performance indicators takes time and it is all too easy to further complicate the task by trying to measure everything. To make the task more manageable, identify a few simple key performance indicators that are linked to your business objectives, then try to rank them in order of importance to the organization. Once you have your list, concentrate on one or two at a time and start reporting on them before you move on to develop the others.

Develop an unambiguous definition for each key performance indicator

For each key performance indicator, develop a clear definition and make sure it is communicated and agreed. Without this you may find ambiguity surrounding the results. For instance, if there is no clear definition for a key performance indicator such as 'number of sales within a given period', the organization could be given two different answers depending on the interpretation of the indicator. A finance manager might give you an answer which equates to the number of contracts signed by customers, whereas a sales manager might give you a figure which equates to the number of customers who have promised to sign a contract. Unless the key performance indicator definition is clear and agreed, you could be in danger of receiving two different sets of results!

Establish owners and accountabilities

Each key performance indicator must have an owner who will take responsibility for ensuring that the information is collected on a regular basis. The owner has also to be accountable for the results and for any subsequent action that requires to be taken to improve the results. Single ownership of a key performance indicator also ensures, once again, that two managers do not come up with different results for the same indicator.

Make sure the source of the information is easily accessible

In larger organizations the base information that makes up each key performance indicator could be generated automatically, even though it may not currently be available in the format you require. In this case, work closely with your information systems experts (or with the department who will take responsibility for producing the information) to ensure that reports can be generated automatically using the chosen unit of measure. For those companies not large enough or lucky enough to warrant the expertise of information systems specialists, consider how you will collect the base information. Often the information is there; it is just a question of finding out how to get at it. Managing the maze of information is often one of the biggest problems organizations have!

If the base information just isn't available, consider how the information will be collected. If it has to be gathered manually the exercise is likely to be resource intensive and to produce inaccurate results. In this case, you may wish to postpone the production of the indicator until you can generate the information automatically.

Whenever possible, communicate and agree the source of the information. Once again, this avoids any ambiguity.

Consider the reporting format and ensure the results are easily interpreted

Careful consideration needs to be given to the presentation of your key performance indicators to ensure that the results are easily interpreted and not misleading. For example look at Figure 10.4, which is a graph showing the number of complaints over a period of six-months. Although it appears that the number of complaints has increased over the period analysed, the information is in fact meaningless.

This graph would have been a much more useful performance indicator if the number of complaints had been presented in relation to the number of customers taken on over the six-month period. Without an understanding of the customers numbers, we are not in a position to determine whether the rise in customer complaints, as represented in this graph, is a worrying trend or not.

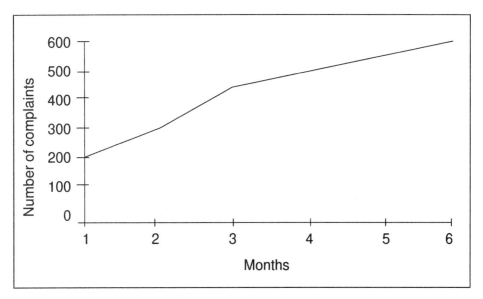

Figure 10.4   Number of complaints arising over a six-month period

Create a balance between financial and non-financial key performance indicators

You should distinguish between financial and non-financial indicators and have a balance of both in your set of key performance indicators. Increasingly, financial indicators are seen as 'lagging' indicators, and usually by the time you see the results it is too late to act. Non-financial indicators on the other hand, can be used to effect change. As an example, the 'number of customer complaints received in a given period' is a good example of a non-financial performance indicator. If the trend in complaints is rising out of proportion with the number of customers, action can be taken to try to rectify the problem. If the company does not monitor complaints and simply waits to see the financial results, the outcome may mean reduced revenues as a result of customer cancellations.

Develop both qualitative and quantitative measures

In your set of key performance indicators you might well consider whether you have a good balance between qualitative and quantitative measures. For example, in addition to identifying 'number of sales' you may wish to analyse 'how well the company is forecasting sales' as an indication of your company's ability to accurately predict future sales. In addition to looking at 'how much revenue', you could also look at 'how well are customers being satisfied' as a qualitative measure which will indicate future revenue.

Build key performance indicators into personal objectives

If your key performance indicators are clearly linked to your business objectives, there is no reason not to include some of them in the personal objective-setting process. For instance, if you have a key performance indicator that deals with customer satisfaction (determined through satisfaction surveys), then you may wish to build a related-performance objective into the personal goals of individuals working the customer service area. This way you will reinforce the importance of key performance indicators in the organization by ensuring that employees have a personal investment in achieving the company strategy.

Continually evaluate key performance indicators for appropriateness

An organization never stands still and therefore you need regularly to check that your key performance indicators continue to reflect your business objectives. When you launch a new product, understand the impact on key performance indicators. If you radically change processes, does this mean a change to the unit of measure for one or more of the indicators? In order for performance indicators to be meaningful they need to reflect your business activity accurately.

Create a written and visible record of why and how the key performance indicator was developed

The development of each key performance indicator is made easier if you can prepare a one-page document defining the indicator, how it is produced, who is responsible and how it will be reported on. The definition document needs to be approved, communicated and reviewed as appropriate. Typically it should answer the following questions:

- What is the definition of the key performance indicator?
- What is the unit of measure?
- Which business objective(s) does this indicator relate to and how?
- Who is the owner of the indicator?
- What is the source of the information?
- At what frequency will the results be produced?
- What will be the format of the reporting?
- Will the information be trended?

Understanding the links between key performance indicators and operational measures

We have already established that key performance indicators and operational measures may often be one and the same, but generally key performance indicators are 'summary' level indicators whereas operational measures may be detailed, more numerous and analysed at shorter intervals. This said, the same rules should apply for the development of operational measures as for key performance indicators: they need to be in line with business strategy and business objectives; and they should be clearly defined and easy to interpret. In addition, operational measures need to be centred on the customer and to take account of aspects of service delivery that are important to customers, such as timelines, courtesy and so on. In this respect, operational measures can act as the bridge between the customer and the business strategy.

Figure 10.5 shows an example of some key performance indicators and operational measures and how they support the business direction. For the purpose of this exercise we have taken the example of an organization in the financial services sector.

Strategy	Company objectives	Key performance Indicators	Measures
To satisfy the UK business traveller by continually searching for new ways to add value and to offer new services.	Offer services to the business traveller which are perceived as offering the most value.	Overall level of customer satisfaction.

Relative positioning of company in the business marketplace (perceived by customers and market). | Levels of customer satisfaction by service offered.

Customer ranking of services compared to competition.

Market share in percentage. |
| | Encourage increased card spend. | Average card spend per annum.

Average frequency of use. | |

Figure 10.5   Examples of links between company direction and performance indicators

Developing performance standards

Standards are indicators of the levels of operational performance a company wishes to meet or exceed. Standards add meaning to operational measures and are useful motivators. They also enable an organization to benchmark its performance against its competitors, as well as better understand whether it is meeting the requirements of the customer.

There are a number of simple rules to follow when developing performance standards. These are as follows:

● Make sure that your standards are in line with customer expectation.
● Make sure your standards are clearly defined.
● Make sure your standards are realistic.
● Try to compare achievements in meeting performance standards with your competitors.

- Make sure your standards are continually evaluated and amended as appropriate.
- Act upon the results when you consistently fail to meet the standard.

Make sure your standards are in line with customer expectation

Standards should never be set without understanding your customers. Ideally standards should be set as a result of detailed research on customer satisfaction and expectation within your industry. In most organizations this understanding will be gained as a result of carrying out customer satisfaction surveys, independent customer research or focus group activity. If in a call centre environment, customer surveys indicate that customers like to have their telephone calls answered within ten seconds, then the call centre standard could be, '98 per cent of calls answered within ten seconds'. Similarly, if customers determine that they prefer to receive goods ordered within five days, then the standard for this measure could be, '100 per cent of goods delivered within five days' or something similar.

Make sure your standards are clearly defined

Definitions are as important in the development of standards as they are in the development of key performance indicators. Carefully defining your standards and communicating this definition is crucial if you want to avoid any ambiguity in the results.

Make sure performance standards are realistic

Do not set performance standards that are either too easy or too difficult. Performance standards that are unrealistic can be very demotivating to employees in an organization, especially when they are so difficult to achieve that the standard is missed time and time again. Standards need to be strict but attainable in order to keep teams or individuals focused on achieving business objectives.

Consider your performance in relation to your competitors

We have already stated that performance standards should be set to reflect customer expectation. It is also worth taking into consideration the performance standards achieved by competitors and by other companies who may be measuring the same activities within a different industry. If other companies are achieving higher performance standards compared with your own and their achievements are in line with customer requirements, it may be that you want to research the reasons why.

Make sure your standards are continually evaluated and amended as appropriate

136 Performance standards should not remain static. They need to be continually

evaluated for appropriateness and may be moved upwards or downwards depending, for instance, on changes to process, improvements in productivity, or an increase or decrease in resources.

Act on the results when you consistently fail to meet the standard

For performance standards to be really useful, they need to be acted upon, particularly when they are not being achieved on a regular basis. Consistent failure to meet realistic standards is the signal that you need to re-evaluate your business processes.

THE REVIEW PROCESS

Measures, standards and key performance indicators need to be reviewed on a continual basis if they are to maintain their usefulness in evaluating whether the organization is achieving its objectives. The review process should take place at senior levels in the organization as well as at the operational level.

It is particularly advantageous to have a reviewer who does not 'own' any of the measures or who works in the organization in a consultative capacity. This way offers a greater opportunity for an objective review of performance indicators.

CONCLUSION

In this chapter we have demonstrated how measures, standards and key performance indicators are a set of simple tools which can be used to evaluate company performance, both in terms of the business direction and the operation.

Operational measures and key performance indicators need to support one another and should be developed in line with business objectives. Standards, on the other hand, need to be developed as a result of clearly understanding customer expectation. Once developed, both measures and standards work together to influence and change behaviour within an organization and to help in the planning process.

Key performance indicators, measures and standards must be developed in sequential order, they should be well defined and communicated throughout the organization, and they have to be evaluated for appropriateness on a continual basis. In addition, the results produced through the development of performance indicators need to be acted upon. Used correctly, key performance indicators, measures and standards can serve as the catalysts for continuous improvement within your organization.

11 Focus groups
Julia Hall

The focus group – or group discussion as it is also called – is a key market research tool. A focus group is a small group of respondents, who, guided by a leader or moderator, discuss a subject in some depth. Originally developed by social scientists, focus groups were adopted by market researchers who have refined the technique over many years. Such groups are a valuable means of gaining feedback about all aspects of suppliers and the markets they serve. Initially the use of focus groups was confined to consumer research, though in more recent years business-to-business researchers have also recognized their benefits.

THE ROLE OF FOCUS GROUPS

Focus groups and customer service

Focus groups are commonly used by marketers to develop advertising and marketing campaigns and to support new product development. However, they also have an extremely valuable role to play in the customer service arena, since they can help suppliers to understand the following factors:

- What customers expect from organizations and what they require in terms of customer service.
- How customers feel about the organization and the service it delivers.
- How new customer service initiatives can be developed in a way which concentrates on customers' needs and opinions rather than on the pre-occupations of suppliers and their internal systems.

Qualitative and quantitative information

Focus groups provide qualitative information. They are used to help build a picture of the whole range of views and opinions about a particular issue and rely on obtaining considered and thoughtful responses from a small number of respondents. These groups will not yield quantitative information and should not be relied upon to show patterns of opinion, the salience of particular views, or the relative importance of specific customer requirements.

The role of researchers

Focus groups are generally arranged through market researchers who, on the basis of the client's objectives:

- design the focus group programme;
- recruit respondents for groups;
- lead or moderate the groups;
- analyse the responses;
- present their interpretation of the findings and the conclusions they base upon them to the client.

FORMING FOCUS GROUPS

Selection of respondents

The individuals who attend focus groups, who are known as respondents, are specially selected and are generally required to fulfil certain key criteria. These criteria are fixed by client and researcher and are designed to ensure that:

- only relevant individuals attend the focus group; and
- individual focus groups are composed of people who are likely to feel comfortable working together.

The relevance of the individual depends on the subject under investigation. In its simplest form this might involve confining investigations to users of a particular product or service. In other cases, the work might need to concentrate on individuals who demonstrate particular lifestyle characteristics (for example, people who take foreign holidays). Another requirement might be to convene groups of individuals who behave in a particular way (for example, those who actively participate in petrol promotions).

The requirement to compose groups of individuals who feel comfortable together is generally met by confining individual groups to people who meet certain demographic criteria such as age, gender, ethnic group, social grade and so on. Since most projects will require information to be gathered from individuals who straddle a range of these variables, it is normal practice to convene a series of groups with each group containing individuals of a similar *139* type. In some cases clients and researchers may feel a need to impose additional restrictions on recruitment. For example, it may be felt necessary to ensure that respondents:

- have not attended a focus group within the last six months;
- have not taken part in research on that subject within the last twelve months;
- are not known to the recruiter; and
- are not known to each other.

No research industry standards currently exist which impose any of these restrictions on recruiters, though many clients and moderators believe they do. There is a widely held belief that the need for these additional restrictions should be carefully considered and should only be imposed if it is felt that they will make a significant difference to the group's value to the research, since they increase the time and cost of recruitment, especially when the individuals whose views are to be researched are hard to find in the first place.

Recruiting groups

Once the criteria for group composition have been agreed with the client, respondents are recruited by the research agency. The individuals who do this work are known as recruiters.

The amount of time needed for recruitment depends very much on the criteria set for respondents. For example:

- An exercise requiring four mixed gender groups of domestic gas users, two made up of ABC1 respondents and two made up of C2DE respondents, will take no more than a week.
- A project which involves recruiting four mixed groups of ABC1 consumers who spend £75 per month on their telephone bill and make a significant proportion of their calls to overseas destinations would take probably two or three weeks to recruit.

The number of groups

Any number of focus groups can be conducted to meet a particular research objective. In extremely rare cases (and if resources either in terms of time or budget are very limited), one group may be sufficient to reveal a range of views and opinions. A single group (perhaps used in conjunction with some one-to-one interviews) might suffice if the work is designed as an exploratory phase of research, which will ultimately lead to a quantified and structured market measurement exercise. However, in most cases two groups is the preferred minimum. This gives broader coverage of respondents and puts the researcher in a better position to identify freak responses. On the other hand, in some cases, two groups can give rise to such a disparate range of views that in analysing the information it is hard to decide where the balance lies. Ultimately, around four groups will probably meet most research objectives, but the number of groups needed will grow if it is important to hold groups with many different types of respondent (for example, customers and non-customers, individuals from the north and from the south, high spenders and low spenders, males and females, teenagers and pensioners and so on).

Geographical spread

The need to spread groups geographically will differ from project to project. In many cases it is advisable to divide groups between different areas of the country, particularly if there is a suspicion that geography may have an impact on opinions. This might well be the case if competitor activity varies according to area or if the client organization has a stronger presence in one region than in another. In addition, there may be a feeling that people living in the north will have different opinions from southern dwellers. (This has certainly been our experience when researching financial products and services.) Another consideration to bear in mind is whether respondents who live in rural locations are likely to behave or feel differently from those who live in a more urban setting.

The number of respondents

There is no hard and fast rule about how many respondents should make up a focus group. The ideal number depends on the type of individuals in the group. Eight to ten is probably the ideal size for a consumer focus group, though if the respondents whose views are required are likely to find it hard to express themselves, it may be necessary to hold a larger group. Twelve should probably be considered as the maximum number of respondents. In a group of more than twelve, some respondents may not get the opportunity to express their opinions adequately. In addition, with a large group there is more of a danger that one or more particularly vocal individuals will take over, while more reticent respondents will retreat. In focus groups made up of business people the ideal number is six or seven. This is because business people are accustomed to working together in meetings and sharing ideas, and are generally much more forthcoming from the outset of the group about their own views and opinions. Thus the smaller business group gives everyone the opportunity to have their say.

Group format

Focus groups are generally conducted face to face. However, it is now perfectly possible to conduct focus groups over the telephone using audio-conferencing technology. This certainly opens up the possibilities for the use of focus groups in business-to-business research when respondents are notoriously difficult to pin down (though the protocols involved in audio conferencing mean *141* that the moderator and respondents would have to be experienced audio conferencers in order to get the best out of this medium). In the future the growth of video-conferencing technology may mean that focus groups can be conducted using this medium, though current availability and cost of this equipment will probably rule this out for the immediate future.

Whether held face to face or over the telephone, the format is the same. A group of respondents discusses the subject in question under the guidance of a group leader or moderator. The moderator is most usually an agency researcher or freelance qualitative researcher with special training and considerable experience in conducting research through focus groups. In some cases, where the client is an experienced researcher, there may be a case for sharing the moderating between independent researcher and client. However, if this is done the client needs to be very clear that the point of the exercise is to listen to respondents and draw out their opinions in a neutral way. Any temptation to be defensive or reply to respondent criticism or dissatisfaction must be firmly resisted.

THE OPERATION OF FOCUS GROUPS

Group venues

There are three options for focus group venues. They can be held:

1 in recruiters' homes;
2 in a viewing facility; or
3 in a private room in a hotel, business centre or other conferencing facility.

While groups with consumers can be held in any of these venues, business groups are more often held in viewing facilities or private rooms in hotels or other conferencing facilities.

Client viewing

When groups are held in homes, it is usual for the moderator to attend alone. However, in some cases it may be acceptable for one representative of the client organization to be present, though, as with client moderating, it is vital that the client agrees to maintain a watching brief, to remain silent and only to respond to or raise questions if the moderator gives specific permission. (This would generally happen at the end of a group when the client is given the opportunity to answer any questions which may have arisen during the course of the discussion). The market researcher's professional body (the Market Research Society) requires that respondents are made aware of the fact that a client is in attendance. In practice, however, a market researcher moderator will generally introduce the client as a colleague.

Groups in viewing facilities offer a much better opportunity for client representatives to view focus groups. Depending on the venue, this involves clients sitting in a separate room and watching the proceedings either by means of a one-way mirror, or through a video link-up. Again researchers are required to state that observers are in attendance.

Groups held in hotels or other facilities also provide clients with the opportunity to view. This can either be done by allowing one member of the client team to sit in on the group or by organizing a video link-up to another room where clients can watch unobserved.

Recording response

Whatever the venue, group discussions are always tape-recorded and transcriptions are often produced. In viewing facilities it is customary also to make a video tape of the discussion.

Group length and timing

Focus groups generally last for one and a half to two hours, though it is also possible to run extended groups which last between three to four hours.

Group discussions are most usually held in the evening and, in general, two groups are held back to back. Groups can of course be held at other times during the day depending on the respondents attending. For example:

- Breakfast groups can work well with respondents who would be unable because of work commitments to attend at other times (for example, we conducted a series of breakfast groups with publicans).
- Afternoon or lunchtime groups may work well with pensioners who prefer not to go out after dark.

Rewarding respondents

When conducting focus groups among consumer or business respondents, it is customary to provide an incentive. Incentives are generally paid in cash for consumers and for some business people (for the latter group the incentive may be positioned as a contribution towards travel costs). However, some organizations, notably in the public sector, have strict rules about accepting incentives and may prefer a donation to be made to a charity on their behalf. The amount paid depends on the following factors:

- The amount of time the respondent is required to spare.
- The venue for the groups (a higher incentive is usually paid for viewing facilities or hotels than for groups in recruiters' homes).
- The type of respondent (business respondents expect to be paid more than consumers and the more senior or hard-to-find business respondents usually command higher incentives).

In some cases additional incentives may be required to persuade individuals to attend the group discussion. This may include the provision of transport to and from the venue or, for consumer groups, money towards baby-sitting expenses.

WHEN AND HOW TO USE FOCUS GROUPS

Focus groups are only one way of gathering qualitative information. The other alternative is the face-to-face discussion or interview when respondents express their opinions and feelings one to one. Researchers both in the agency and on the client side should bear in mind that focus groups may not always be the best option.

In deciding whether the face-to-face or the group option is best the following points are worth bearing in mind.

The pros

- Focus groups provide interaction between people within the group and encourage creative thinking. The group working together can spark ideas which the individuals, if approached in one-to-one interviews, would probably never generate. This makes them an ideal forum for developing ideas for new services or products.
- The group provides a setting in which respondents can listen to the attitudes of others about a particular company and the products or services it provides. This may encourage them to reassess their own position on a particular topic and, ultimately, to come to a more considered view.
- Groups provide the opportunity to demonstrate new ideas for product or service development using facilities that might not be available during a one-to-one interview. This may involve video presentations, presentation and trials of product prototypes, the opportunity to phone into and experience a telephone helpline and so on.
- Groups provide the opportunity for clients to hear, first hand, what customers and potential customers have to say about their company and its products and services.

The cons

- There is always a danger that individuals within the group will take over while others will withdraw, with the result that either extremely negative or extremely positive opinions will obscure the actual range of opinions which is, ultimately, much broader.
- The group forum makes it difficult to assess individual awareness or knowledge of particular products and services on an unprompted basis.
- The group discussion is not a good way to obtain factual information on individual behaviour.

In addition, since a project which involves group discussions, like a project which involves a series of face-to-face interviews, covers only a small proportion of the population, neither technique should be used as a means of gaining a representative picture of how the market behaves or feels. If the requirement is for data which can be used to measure opinion or to assess what real potential a new customer service development has to alter customer behaviour, quantitative research will be required that covers a much larger sample of individuals in a much more structured way.

Constructing focus groups

In constructing a focus group or a series of focus groups to meet a particular research or need, the factors outlined above require careful consideration. On the basis of these, the following questions could be used as a checklist:

- What are my objectives, and are focus groups the best approach?
- How many groups do I need, or can I conduct, within the budget/timescale?
- What are the key criteria for attendance?
- What are the best common denominators for each group?
- Do I need to place other specific restrictions on recruitment?
- Do I need a geographical spread?
- Do representatives from the client organization wish to view the groups?
- Do I need to hold groups in a viewing facility or is a recruiter's home more suitable?
- How easy will respondents be to find, and how much time do I need to allow for recruitment?
- What should I allow in terms of incentives?
- When should the groups be held?
- How long do I need with each group?

What to ask and how to ask it

When running the focus group, the moderator generally uses a topic list of key points to guide respondents through the session. This topic guide should not be confused with a questionnaire; it does not pose specific questions to individuals but is more of a checklist of subjects which can be discussed by the group as a whole.

The areas covered in any set of focus groups will, of course, be dictated by the specific objectives of the research. However, in putting together the topic list it is worth bearing in mind that focus groups generally follow a set process and a well-structured topic guide will take advantage of this.

Forming

Respondents may well be anxious at this first stage and need to be made to feel comfortable. The first thing the moderator must do is explain the format of the *145* group and the rules of engagement! Then everyone needs to be given a chance to speak. A good approach is to get everyone to introduce themselves to the group or, an even better ice-breaker is to ask respondents to talk together in pairs or threes and then to introduce each other.

Storming

During the next phase of the group there is likely to be some tension; respondents will be working out where the power and control lies and establishing boundaries. At this stage it will be important for the moderator to ensure that individuals likely to dominate are reigned in and quieter individuals are given permission and encouraged to speak.

Norming

During this stage respondents and moderator will reach a point where differences are accepted; this is where the group starts to feel more comfy. At this stage the moderator needs to beware of the temptation to trade pleasantries and push the discussion on to the next phase.

Performing

This is the point where respondents can be asked to work through tasks together, though some element of storming may return here. This is the time during which most constructive and creative work will be done.

Mourning

Towards the end of the group – say, with ten minutes to go – the moderator must give notice that the group is coming to an end. Respondents are given the opportunity to adjust views they expressed initially, or say anything that as yet has been left unsaid, or make final comments. Finally, the moderator must close the group and thank respondents for their time and comments.

In putting issues to the group the moderator needs to beware of conducting a group depth interview. The best focus groups require the group to structure a response to feed back to the moderator through discussion. The kinds of questions which should be avoided are ones which start 'I'd like each of you to tell me . . .'. A much more appropriate approach in a focus group situation is 'What do people think about . . .'.

Besides posing questions to the group as a whole, moderators can use a wide range of projective or enabling techniques to stimulate conversation and help respondents to explore their reactions to specific issues. These are often used by researchers who need to get beyond the rational off-the-cuff response to particular issues or who want to understand how customers really view an organization. Examples of these techniques include:

- *Sentence completion*. The moderator asks respondents to complete a phrase such as, 'I never bother to phone the helpline when I've got a problem because . . .'.
- *Word association*. Respondents are asked to shout out words they think of when a particular company is named.
- *Guided dreams*. Respondents are asked to imagine themselves in particular situations and describe how they would react.
- *Magazine tearing*. Respondents are given a pile of magazines and asked to tear out pictures which help describe how they feel when they visit a particular company.
- *Speech bubbles*. Respondents are presented with an illustration of a situation with empty speech bubbles and asked to fill in the words.
- *Personification*. Respondents are asked to describe a particular organization as if it were a person. Would it be male or female, how old would they be, what would they wear, what car would they drive, where would they go on holiday, what sort of house would they live in and so on.

As we have already stressed, because of the extent to which individuals can influence opinions within the group, focus groups are not a good means of assessing the impact of particular activities on individual behaviour. Nevertheless, if it is important to gain a steer on this kind of information, this problem can be overcome by giving each respondent a simple tick box questionnaire to use during the course of the group. This might be particularly useful if part of the objective of the research was to determine which of a series of possible customer service options was most attractive to customers. In this case, each option would be discussed in detail, then each respondent would be asked (individually) to number rank the options according to how attractive each was to them personally. Having completed this task independently, and handed their questionnaires to the moderator, the group then discusses their choices and the reasons behind them.

ANALYSIS AND INTERPRETATION

Conducting focus groups and gathering information from them is a subjective process. The task of analysing the mass of information which results from a programme of groups is an equally subjective task. One key point to bear in mind is that the analysis process begins with the first moments of the first group and is not a discrete exercise that is conducted once groups have been completed and all scripts have been transcribed. During the course of a project, researchers will take notes during or immediately after focus groups on key points which may well form the basis for additional questions to be posed in subsequent groups. These may also start to form the basis of central hypotheses which the researcher will test out during subsequent group discussions and during the analysis process.

If groups are tape-recorded it is usual practice to have these recordings transcribed and to work from the transcriptions in pulling the findings together. *147*

Individual researchers have personal preferences about the best way to condense and analyse the information. Whichever method is employed, the main tasks are the same. They involve:

- Pulling together all comments made on a specific topic.
- Identifying those comments in terms of respondent types or other key variables (such as, customers/non-customers, high spenders/low spenders and so on).

While doing this, certain basic principles apply to the approach adopted, which require that the researcher:

- becomes fully immersed in the detail;
- constantly questions the data; and
- is prepared to reassess hypotheses part-way through the process and, if necessary, rethink the analysis approach, or compare and contrast the responses of different key groups.

Once all the information is collected, the researcher will be in a position to determine the meaning behind it. This is the stage of interpretation. Of course, during the analysis process itself, the researcher will have insights and thoughts about what the data means or why things appear to be the way they are, and these will be noted down as part of the process.

Interpretation is an iterative process. The first part involves the researcher taking the evidence which has been analysed and making subjective judgements about it. The second iteration involves feeding that information and interpretation back to the client. The client and researcher will no doubt go through a further iteration at the debriefing session where ideas are discussed about what the findings mean for the organization and what the best next steps are likely to be.

FEEDING BACK THE DATA

When feeding back data from focus group research, as with any form of qualitative research, researchers must make clear that what is being presented is a range of views and feelings, and, because of the sample from which responses are drawn, is not intended to be fully representative of the views of the marketplace as a whole.

Since focus group research very often forms the first part of a larger research exercise, the best way to feed back the data is probably during a working session where researchers and clients can get together to talk through the findings and discuss their implications for the client's next steps, whether that be implementation of a new approach or the identification of a need to quantify the data.

Since focus groups designed to help clients develop customer service generally have a bearing on customer service staff, following this initial working presentation, the client company should seriously consider communicating the results to those directly responsible for customer service – their customer-facing staff. In our experience this feedback, though it may sometimes need careful positioning, often has a wonderfully motivating effect on customer-facing staff. However, it is only worth providing feedback to staff if management are prepared to act on the recommendations which flow out of the research.

CUSTOMER SERVICE STAFF AND FOCUS GROUPS

Up to this point we have dealt with focus groups which involve customers, non-customers, or potential customers of the organization. At the same time, in developing the research approach, considerable benefits can be gained by convening groups with customer service staff to discuss the following:

- Their role in servicing customers' needs.
- Typical customer service situations in which they find themselves.
- The challenges they most often face in servicing customers' needs.
- The support they feel they need from the organization in order to help them to do their jobs as successfully as possible.
- Their impressions of the views and opinions of the customers they deal with.

It is generally true to say that customer-facing staff have considerable insights concerning, for example, what motivates customers, and what customers like and dislike about dealing with their organization. Yet all too often, company structures are such that this information does not permeate through the organization to those who set policy regarding customer service. By involving customer service staff in the process, this channel can be opened – with valuable results.

Convening groups with customer service staff is just one way to include them in the process. Organizations gain much by involving customer service staff behind the scenes in focus groups and giving them the opportunity at first hand to hear what customers have to say. For example, several companies include videos of focus groups in quality reviews and training sessions with customer service staff, because they are such a powerful way of helping staff to understand the following points:

- What customers expect.
- How they want to be treated.
- How they feel about the way the customer service staff within the organization currently perform.
- Why they are required to follow certain procedures.

FOCUS GROUPS AND STRATEGY

The scope for breakthroughs that create new markets or give significant *149* advantage to an organization has steadily reduced through the twentieth century. This means that strategy development tends now to be a continuum, with radical changes of direction becoming less frequent.

The chief inputs to corporate strategy will always be macro issues such as economic prospects, global trading trends, demographics, technological and financial forecasts, and quantified assessments of customer behaviour and cultural trends. Since market research is a means of gathering information on these issues it can be a contributor to the process of strategic change – albeit usually quite a minor one. Where market research does play a greater part is in supporting product, brand and promotional strategies. Research can also provide important inputs in the critical area of customer service, which in many markets is as important a differentiator as the characteristics of the product or service being sold.

The value of qualitative information gathered through focus groups is essentially in fine-tuning strategy or in helping tactical issues such as positioning or promotion. This is because, as has already been suggested, focus groups are essentially anecdotal and illustrative rather than direction setting. However, as the most 'immediate' form of qualitative research they are invaluable in helping to bridge the gap between the marketplace and decision makers in many companies, and can be particularly valuable in the case of companies where decision making is dominated by engineering, technical or finance people who tend not to have people-oriented instincts.

The customer agenda is more likely to become part of management's vision if they experience this at first hand, rather than if it was reported to them second-hand through researcher's charts or figures or the expert arguments of marketeers. This is why focus groups can be pivotal in helping the development and maintenance of marketing orientation within a company.

FURTHER READING

Gordon, W. and Langmaid, R. (1988), *Qualitative Market Research*, Aldershot: Gower.

Kreuger, R. A. (1989), *Focus Groups: A Practical Guide for Small Businesses*, London: Sage.

Murstein, B. (1965), *Handbook of Projective Techniques*, New York: Basic Books.

Worcester, R. M. and Downam, J. (1986), *Consumer Market Research Handbook*, Maidenhead: McGraw Hill.

12 Mystery shopping
David Limbrick

Five years ago, I was fortunate enough to be involved in the process of designing and implementing a service quality programme for a large high street bank. At the time, the 'what gets measured gets managed' school of thought was gaining in popularity and therefore, as was the case with many similar programmes, a programme of 'external' service measurement was deemed necessary.

In the planning stage, it was taken for granted that we would require regular customer feedback. We were also keen to learn more about 'mystery shopping' (something that was popular in the United States) and how it might help us to provide specific 'service' related information to individual managers. After a number of fruitless calls to the Market Research Society (MRS) and much time spent in searching the business directories, I managed to find a couple of companies, one of whom I currently work for, who claimed to specialize in providing such services. Today, had I been faced with the same challenge, things would be very different. Indeed, at the last count, no fewer than 120 organizations registered with the MRS claim to provide mystery shopping services, of which approximately 40 say that mystery shopping represents a significant proportion of their annual turnover. As in many industries, however, the Pareto principle applies, with only a handful of companies accounting for the vast majority of the estimated £20 million or so spent annually in the United Kingdom on mystery shopping.

This growth represents a considerable success story, for not only has mystery shopping firmly established itself during what was a recessionary period, it has also done so in the face of quiet – and sometimes loud – disapproval from the traditionalists in the UK research industry. Having had a difficult childhood, mystery shopping has come of age! Once the poor relation of the research world, it is now one of possibly the fastest growing sectors of UK research. Partly on the basis of 'if you can't beat them, join them', and partly because of its real market attractiveness, most research agencies are changing their attitudes and extolling the virtues of mystery shopping.

WHAT IS MYSTERY SHOPPING?

The demand for mystery shopping, or mystery customer research (MCR) as we prefer to call it, comes from a wide variety of industries and embraces a very wide range of potential 'customer' strategies. Its scope is such that the term 'shopping', which somehow suggests a predominantly 'high street' or 'retail' focus, is much too narrow. Indeed, in the last year alone, BDI Research, a specialist division of BEM has used the technique to assess a variety of processes, including rail travel, hospital services, new product launch, medical advice, and financial advice, to name but a few.

Mystery customer research is a form of *observational* research. It provides a 'snapshot' of the performance of an individual, an outlet or a process, at a particular moment in time. Mystery customers seek to provide an impartial 'customer's eye view' of a particular business process. Quite simply, MCR is based upon the most basic of ideas, namely, that there is no better way of measuring something than 'going and having a look *or a listen.*' A working definition might be summarized as the 'objective evaluation, by a trained evaluator, of a particular service or service process against a number of predetermined customer-driven criteria'.

MCR must not be confused, first, with the approach taken by some organizations who choose to utilize head office staff in order to provide 'sneak reports' on particular customer-facing processes or members of staff, and secondly, with those approaches which use untrained, poorly briefed, recently recruited 'real' customers to undertake an apparently 'objective' evaluation. Whilst this second type of approach may provide value in some areas, it has a number of weaknesses, not least the reliability and integrity of the data capture. Finally, having recently undertaken a review of MCR in the United States, it would seem that a principal objective of MCR there is not to enhance service nor to provide information on training needs, but to minimize cashier theft and dishonesty – an important task, no doubt, but strictly not one which forms part of MCR in the United Kingdom. The definition of MCR therefore does not embrace 'security checking'.

Unlike customer satisfaction research which concentrates on *subjective* customer attitudes and their 'stated satisfaction', MCR concentrates upon the actual behaviour of organizations and their staff, *objectively* reporting upon the service delivered. Whilst the criteria used in MCR schemes are normally derived from or related to 'satisfaction' criteria, MCR as a form of research is not and cannot be used, contrary to popular belief, for measuring customer satisfaction. Indeed, a serious problem associated with MCR surveys is when one attempts to obtain both objective service and subjective satisfaction feedback at the same time. The latter does not always correlate with the former, and this does little to aid interpretation by staff.

THE GROWTH IN MYSTERY CUSTOMER RESEARCH (MCR)

The reasons for the growth in popularity of MCR are often overlooked, and sadly, this does little for its pedigree or standing in the research community. Clearly the popularity is due, in some part, to the marketing efforts of supplier organizations like my own. However, at the risk of oversimplification, the main catalyst has been from the client side. Faced with the challenge to measure, monitor and improve service, client organizations looked to the research world for help. Whilst customer satisfaction research has a great deal to offer, there has been some debate over its usefulness. Mountains of data and unchanging mean scores often makes such information difficult to use, not to mention almost impossible to action. Increasingly faced with such problems and frustrated with 'mean score hover' – a term used to describe the levelling off of measurement results – client organizations, in an attempt to obtain less ambiguous, more meaningful and actionable information, began to look towards MCR.

Satisfaction tracking suffered from a number of other problems and this provided additional fuel to the demand for MCR. A leading issue for instance, centres around customer response and the fact that response rates, through questionnaire fatigue and a number of other factors, make it difficult to sustain a robust programme. Feedback, and, in particular, the 'loop time' from evaluation to report, is a primary consideration. Even when sufficient responses are obtained, communicating information which is 'old' before it is received is often perceived by those staff who should use it, as a waste. Additionally, interpreting and acting upon information which indicates that '70 per cent of customers are fairly satisfied' can be very difficult. On the other hand, MCR information which identifies that '12 per cent of staff mentioned features 1, 2 and 3' and '5 per cent of staff attempted to close the sale' is somewhat more meaningful and specific. The power of such action-oriented information became the dominant catalyst for the growth in the use of MCR and has arguably been an important factor behind its continued popularity.

Perhaps faced with a limited budget or perhaps due to disappointment with previous measurement efforts, organizations understandably began to consider replacing traditional research programmes with MCR programmes. Big mistake! – Perceptions are a vital ingredient to any customer service programme. Lose perceptions and you risk losing the customer focus. As with MCR, traditional research, when undertaken *correctly*, will also provide clear guidance. MCR and traditional research should *not* replace one another – they do different things.

Integrating MCR and traditional measurement

It is important to remember that no one form of measurement will provide all of the answers. Traditional research seeks to provide feedback on the *subjective* views of customers ('How do you feel about?' and so on), whilst MCR concentrates on providing *objective* feedback on a particular event or experience ('Did 'x' happen?').

Clearly the two approaches measure different factors and should complement rather than compete with one another. Likewise, MCR should not be used to replace internal measures. Rather it should be used to provide information which is either unobtainable from internal measures or which augments the meaning of internal information. Happily, many organizations now take an integrated approach to measurement, balancing MCR with more traditional measurement techniques (see Figure 12.1).

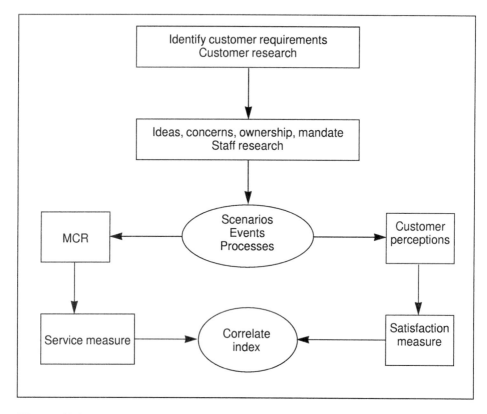

Figure 12.1   An integrated approach to measurement

In many ways the scenarios or events act as a 'common denominator' for MCR and 'event-based' customer measurement. This in turn facilitates the correlation of MCR results with customer perceptions. For example, customers might perceive staff to be 'unfriendly' and rate such criteria as 'unsatisfactory', whilst MCR information might indicate that staff failed to give a greeting or offer a farewell (the latter being identified through customer research as being important determinants of 'friendliness').

Other than investing time in identifying, through customer and staff research, those criteria which determine the nature of effective customer re-
154 lationships, consideration should be given to identifying the most appropriate

measurement approach. Sometimes this may require MCR. At other times it may require a different approach: for instance, post-transaction or event-based research, a powerful customer service research technique, and one which, because of its timeliness and tight 'closed loop', is itself customer focused. At all times, however, the focus of measurement should be on 'action and improvement' and not 'measurement for measurement' sake.

INTRODUCING AN MCR PROGRAMME

When introducing an MCR programme, there are a number of significant areas to examine.

Current state review - building upon existing learning

Invariably organizations have undertaken some form of measurement from which successes have been made. Apart from the real risk of 'reinventing the wheel', failing to recognize and build upon existing learning will impact adversely upon the overall success of the programme. MCR programmes do have a tendency to 'just emerge'. Linking MCR programmes with existing initiatives often helps to position MCR as a genuine development rather than 'something dreamt up by executives'.

Functional workshops - service is about the whole organization!

At the risk of oversimplifying matters, most traditional research projects are handled on an agency market research department basis, with the market research department representing the particular research needs of the client. With customer service, and, in particular, with MCR, this tends not to be the case. MCR, typically, has a much broader audience with many functions (for example marketing, training, operations, and even regional management expressing an interest in mystery customer information). Marketing, for instance, may want to know how well a new product is being promoted in retail outlets. Training may want to know whether staff have remembered what they learnt in training sessions. Sales may want to know whether products are being sold effectively (for example are features and benefits being communicated effectively?) and whether they are complying with industry standards and guidelines. Operations may want to know whether particular operational standards are being met. Customer service may want to identify whether staff are behaving according to customer service policy, whether they are polite and so on. Involving *all* important parties from the outset is critical. Such involvement will help to ensure that maximum support is gained and that return on the investment is optimized.

Much careful diplomacy and pragmatism is required in the early stages, however. Each 'stakeholder' will have individual requirements and priorities. This, together with the 'enthusiasm' that MCR seems to generate, often manifests itself in an initial request to measure 'everything'. Sadly, too many MCR initiatives suffer from trying to measure too many things. Whilst MCR can evaluate many criteria, trying to cast the net too wide will result in poor quality evaluations and unreliable information. The initial task, therefore, is to set clear objectives, identifying the measurement priorities.

At the same time, there is a tendency to add more and more questions as the programme becomes established, without giving any consideration to those questions which need to be removed because they are not working or because they are no longer important. Care needs to be taken to avoid scope creep. Questions should be regularly reviewed in order to identify whether the information they generate continues to be used and indeed whether this information is acted upon. Additionally, it is important to identify whether specific information has actually generated any improvements. Creating a notional 'return on questions asked' ensures that a sensible approach to questionnaire design, is achieved and maintained.

Organizations often wish to concentrate upon the particular service interaction (people skills and so on), but, at the same time, others are also keen for the MCR programme to consider tangibles' (for example evidence of posters, tidiness, amount of coffee stains on the carpet and so on). Clearly such factors are important, but MCR offers greatest value when it focuses upon the customer–supplier interaction. A clipboard or less 'covert' measurement approach may be more appropriate for evaluating 'tangibles'. That said, some organizations still cannot think of any better way to identify how many tables exist in their outlets, or whether light bulbs are broken, than to use MCR.

Staff research - ownership through involvement!

Too often the contribution of staff is underestimated. There are a number of reasons why staff involvement is critical for MCR, not least the real contribution which staff have to offer. Staff involvement is particularly important in helping to:

- identify barriers/obstacles to providing good service;
- design an effective feedback process;
- design surveys and scenarios;
- set effective and realistic standards;
- identify customer typologies; and
- understand visiting/shopping profiles.

In many instances, staff will not have any real knowledge of MCR and the thought of being on the receiving end of a 'mystery customer' can be quite frightening. It is important, therefore, to understand the fears which might exist so that these can be considered during communication and introduction. Without staff involvement, it will be difficult to obtain 'ownership' and support for the programme. Without ownership and support, it is difficult to secure a mandate for MCR, and, as a consequence, action and improvements are not

likely to take place.

Other issues

In many ways what we have discussed so far represents good practice – the foundation stones of any service measurement programme. However, when introducing an MCR programme, there are other issues which also have to be considered.

Scenario design

Unlike most traditional research approaches, MCR tends not to be based on a 'generic' questionnaire but rather on a 'specific' scenario or customer experience. The evaluator uses this scenario as the 'theme' for the evaluation. Each theme has a number of criteria which form the basis of the evaluation. Scenarios might range from the opening of a bank account to the request for a service engineer to come and service the tv in the customer's own premises.

Whilst some organizations are keen to assess their performance against somewhat obscure or atypical scenarios, the starting point for most organizations is to choose those events which are representative of normal business or which form the Pareto proportion of customer experiences. Improvements in this area are more likely to lead to early gains in overall performance.

Each scenario will include a number of measurement criteria. Such criteria will normally have been identified through customer and staff research. In the early days of MCR, such criteria tended to be measured subjectively against rating scales. These days the criteria are much more specific and measurement tends to be based on the objective 'yes' or 'no', with supporting verbatim comments providing additional context and 'flavour'. This objective focus helps to ensure consistency between individual evaluations, and, importantly, begins to generate actionable feedback.

Evaluator selection

Whilst evaluator profiles (for example age, gender and so on) will obviously differ in each programme, one should not underestimate the effect different profiles may have on the nature of the interaction. Selecting appropriate evaluators therefore becomes important.

In many instances, different profiles are used to mirror different customer types. For example, if most of the customers for a restaurant are business people at lunchtime, then the profiles of mystery customers would attempt to mirror this. Likewise, if typical customers are couples, then scenarios would utilize couples.

Geographical considerations whilst perhaps seemingly trivial, are often necessary for ensuring that the scenario will work (for example where the process includes a telephone or postal follow-up). Selecting an evaluator with a 'local accent' or local mailing address can make all the difference in terms of ensuring realism. Most MCR providers conduct telephone evaluations from a central point. The same considerations apply for telephone-based MCR.   *157*

Self-selection is an issue which also needs consideration. In essence, if evaluators are not comfortable with a particular scenario they should not be involved. Among other aspects, a person who feels out of place is much more likely to be noticed.

In all instances, it is essential to ensure that the scenarios and mystery customer evaluations are realistic and that they mirror typical activities. Again, such information can be gained from staff and customer research.

Evaluator training

Before undertaking MCR, all evaluators should be fully briefed and trained regarding the scenario and particular measurement criteria. Training sessions provide an opportunity for client objectives to be communicated and for handling any queries evaluators might have. Training helps to promote a fuller understanding of client objectives amongst evaluators and, at the same time, to secure a greater commitment to the task. Evaluators have to understand the definitions of particular criteria so that ambiguities and inconsistencies are minimized. At the end of each phase of MCR, all those involved must take part in a debriefing session. At this stage, valuable subjective information may emerge as well as particular evaluator training needs. The main objective, however, is for continuous improvement.

Pilot exercise

Sometimes overlooked with traditional research but critical for MCR is the need for a pilot exercise. As with all pilot exercises, it seeks to 'test the system' and, in the case of MCR, to help in refining the scenarios, identifying what does and doesn't work.

Feedback

Most organizations fail to pay sufficient attention to the feedback process. For instance, how the information obtained is to be communicated and, most importantly, acted upon. Even at a time when return on investment is a priority, much information seems to end up on the shelf rather than as raw material for improvement activities.

Research amongst staff will often begin to inform the feedback process. Feedback should be timely – information more than two weeks old tends to have less impact than feedback which is a few days old. It should also be regular. Unless the action-planning process is well established, feedback which is too frequent will cause bottlenecks in this process and staff will soon become frustrated with information overload.

In order to maximize the impact of MCR, the feedback loop (that is, from evaluation to provision of report) should be no more than five days and ideally around 48 hours. Feedback which is this timely is much more likely to be considered than something which occurred weeks ago. Where an element of competition or comparison is required (for example, part of an incentive and motivation programme), league tables of performance are provided, often on a quarterly or monthly basis, depending upon the frequency of MCR evaluations.

In all instances, 'management' and supervisory staff must know how to communicate MCR feedback. What is a very constructive tool can rapidly become destructive if used incorrectly, especially when individual members of staff are identified. Verbatim comments are very important for adding 'colour' to what might be considered a 'black and white', 'yes' and 'no' report. In many instances, these comments act as catalysts for change. Reporting that there was a long queue at the internal cash dispenser of a bank is more meaningful when it is supported with a relevant statement (for example, 'it was raining very heavily outside').

As outlined above, unlike most traditional research, where the client is largely represented by the market research department, customer service research – and, in particular, MCR – has a wider audience. Feedback therefore needs to take into account the research literacy and particular needs of this wider audience.

Contact reporting

To some, a bureaucratic feature of most MCR programmes is the amount of written communication between client and agency. As a discipline, however, this is critical for avoiding ambiguities. There is a need for much more client–agency dialogue than in most research projects, and this in turn requires great commitment from both sides.

Quality control

Often the results of MCR are used to influence monetary bonuses and reward – another reason behind its high profile. MCR is therefore characterized by the emphasis placed upon quality control, and, in particular, on the fieldwork. Minor mistakes, the odd incorrect entry, tend to go unnoticed in traditional research. With MCR, information is scrutinized by every manager individually and any process error will be magnified across the programme. Quality control is therefore critical for ensuring both smooth running and continuous acceptance of the programme.

DEVELOPMENTS IN MCR

MCR, having been around for less than a decade, is still in its infancy. That said, the research world, the incentives industry and business in general, already have a great deal to thank it for. In looking back over the last few years, it is possible to identify a number of contributions made by MCR.

From the client perspective, MCR has begun to provide a rich and valuable source of objective information upon which service management depends. With its unconventional roots, its broad applicability and its often fascinating *159* insight into the service experience, MCR, much more than traditional research, has attracted the attention of staff from a wide variety of functions, which in turn has acted as a catalyst for involving a greater number and mix of executives in the management of service. In bringing functions together, MCR has helped to raise the profile of customer service within organizations, which, amongst other things, has added fuel to the internal customer concept.

From the industry perspective, MCR (and to a lesser extent, customer satisfaction research) in its fight to gain credibility and its attempt to demonstrate high ethical and methodological standards, has introduced a new set of disciplines, many of which are relevant to traditional research. Additionally, and perhaps more importantly, MCR has exposed a greater number of client staff to the benefits of research, thereby broadening the potential marketplace for research in general. Whilst the demand for service measurement acted as a catalyst for MCR, one might argue that much of the continued enthusiasm for service measurement is due to the effectiveness and broad applicability of MRC. Examples of recent trends in MCR include:

- *Training*. Evaluating staff training needs.
- *Marketing*. Assessing how comfortable staff are with selling certain products.
- *Operations*. Incident reporting (for example, do staff report all incidents, both complaints and suggestions), queue handling and so on.
- *Customer relations*. Handling objections and complaints.
- *Telephone delivery*. Overall performance in terms of service.
- *Consumer associations*. Assess compliance and advice given by staff.

The implications of the above on agency staff is that a wider, more business perspective is now required.

CONCLUSIONS

One needs to maintain a perspective! As a research technique, MCR is merely one from a repertoire of techniques that organizations can use. It represents a valuable tool for service management – valuable because when conducted properly it provides objective and usable information. However, if the popularity of MCR and customer service measurement in general is to continue, then research companies, in conjunction with their clients, must work harder to ensure that the information generated is used to influence change, rather than merely to act as a bookend on some dusty shelf. For too many organizations, the philosophy of 'what gets measured gets done' has been replaced by something more akin to 'what gets measured gets measured'. In such circumstances, service measurement programmes represent little more than a 'going through the motions'. Sadly, going through the motions alone won't get you anywhere!

CASE STUDIES

A small number of case studies have been outlined below in order to give an example of the breadth of MCR. Specific criteria have been omitted for reasons of confidentiality.

- *Healthcare provider.* Assessing the service provided by hospitals to pregnant mothers, MCR results identified a number of serious weaknesses in essential 'maternity' processes. Improvements have since been made.
- *Manufacturer of fine furniture.* Products were sold by a number of independent retailers who also sold competitive brands. MCR identified the extent to which sales staff recommended certain products for certain scenarios. Product knowledge on key brands was evaluated together with the approach to discounting.
- *Travel industry.* The whole customer experience from car park to travel was evaluated. The main emphasis was on the levels of service and 'food delivery'.
- *Pharmaceutical industry.* Evaluators enquired about medication for a minor ailment. Compliance to certain standards was identified.
- *Leisure industry.* A weekend break at a holiday park formed the scenario. All customer-facing processes were evaluated against specifically defined service and operational criteria.

13 Activity-based costing

Nick Gazzard

Before launching into an analysis of the potential for activity-based costing (ABC) to add value to the complex decision-making process surrounding customer service, it seems right to first explain briefly what ABC is. I would define it as: 'The computation and allocation of costs to products or services, on the basis of their direct links to activities and resource, by the manner and quantity of their use of the resources.' Couched more accessibly, it is simply costing a product or service on the basis of the amount of resource it uses and the way in which it uses the resource – rather than by some arbitrary convention – with the objective of enabling change.

ABC is capable of working wonders in illuminating the true value – or the lack of it – in the activities of companies in the marketing of their products and services. Having worked with it for over ten years, I have delighted in its ability to redefine corporate perceptions and improve the bottom line. However, it is an area which has much agreement on its principles and little on its detail. For a technique which develops a great deal of detail, this is a significant drawback.

Thus in this chapter I want to help steer you round the typical opportunities and problems in the application of ABC relating to customer service. They are in the main conceptual and perceptual, rather than matters of great complexity in themselves, so this is not a technically demanding treatment.

BACKGROUND TO ACTIVITY-BASED COSTING (ABC)

In general the development of service costing currently lags significantly behind that of product costing. This is mainly driven by the perception that the products in a company are the engines of profit, and that customer services are traditionally considered as *costs*, not necessarily as a value-adding process in their own right, and thus to be minimized and not worthy of detailed analysis.

If we look at both the specific and the related *value* of the activity, as well as its *cost*, there is a significant shift in the paradigm of our perception. For example, Birds Eye Walls, a Unilever company, allowed its customer service level on deliveries to the Tesco retail chain to fall to a level unacceptable to Tesco. The repeated failure to improve, or properly address the issue eventually caused a main board director of Tesco to visit them and leave them in no doubt as to what would happen if this did not improve. The value of customer service went from a proportion of the department budget, to the turnover of a big customer.

This in turn led to a review of the company's processes, a substantial and continuing increase in service, a reduction in stocks of several weeks, and corporate happiness all round. The *value* of these service activities could be measured both in reduced stock levels, lost sales and, of course, keeping the customer from beating the door down! So conceptually, it is crucial to consider the network of activities and functions which interlink to the human resource, not just the cost of the people and facilities, and also to be inventive in looking at interdependencies of service to value generation.

Another aspect of the folly of not measuring the activity value of service costs has shown itself clearly in the last recession. The traditional, apparently cost-effective, or frankly 'easy' option – for specific customer service functions to remain all but unmeasurable other than as say a percentage cost of sales or simply a budgeted cost – led to the inability when needed, for the customer service function to prove its worth in detail to many businesses. This resulted in heavy cutting of staff and services, as the 'hard' benefits of 'soft' departments were not quantified. The true costs of team breakdown and loss of skills and knowledge sets and their eventual replacement, are only now being fully realized and, I suspect, will force a reappraisal of the 'cost' of redundancy.

There is a conceptual challenge, in that 'true' ABC methods cannot easily match existing systems of cost measurement and control, as they do not in general fully absorb costs, and the costs they indicate vary by activity and use of resource, rather than as a proportion of sales. This means they can appear erratic, even where the methodology is simple and justifiable.

Moreover, implementation of ABC projects is often the preserve of finance, who want the safety and comfort of a more traditional framework and will tend to redirect and reapportion their existing cost capture and measurement techniques to report against activities (that is, the cost of sales in total, apportioned to a customer by volume or value share purporting to show the sales resource or activity used by a customer). In fact, the demands made on sales people, the nature of person deployed, and the quantity and nature of their contact, often varies by customer and thus generally has no *causal linkage* to a customer by volume or value *but by type and level of service*. One client of ours discovered to their horror, that the costs of service to one trade sector were often over £4 per case on a product making under £3. The reported average cost was about £0.22, due to various factors!

COST OF CUSTOMER ACQUISITION AND SERVICING - HOW TO ESTABLISH AND MAINTAIN

The most fundamental problem with the costing of customer acquisition and maintenance is that most companies are not structured to enable the collection of sufficient, accurate data. The process of customer acquisition is a complex one, particularly for purely service industries such as advertising or insurance, with the selling process or pitches routinely costing prodigious amounts to develop and execute, and involving diverse people in many areas of the business in highly variable ways, depending on the nature of the approach required, product mix and how exacting the potential customer is. Often there is little hard data to base assessments on and yet tough policy decisions will be made in terms of limiting the number of sales calls, the complexity of presentations, preparatory work and cooperation. For example, 'we must call no more than three times on leads', or 'no software trial goes beyond one month', amongst many more.

These methods are in essence often crude, typically solely experience-based control mechanisms, based on an assessment of costs related to the number of attempts to woo custom. There is a trade-off in terms of the value of the customer and the cost of acquisition, both of which are hard to evaluate. The fundamental issue to be addressed is the relationship of input to output over time and risk. Obviously experience is a critical factor in both cost-benefit and risk analysis but relies too heavily on personal motivation and predilection to be the dominant method for decision making.

Time recording for activity-based costing/management is seen as being too demanding to be cost-effective, or, in diametric opposition to this view, that the potential value of the customer can justify almost any depth of investment in their acquisition – neither view is, of course, correct. There is a balance, but all too frequently this is a judgement made with insufficient or worse, *no* supporting data.

Compounding this common lack of costing knowledge is a proclivity to regard the costing of the business as fundamentally a finance (divisional) function and to see the relationship between the analysis of risk versus the value of the potential business and the investment in its acquisition is rarely, if ever, an integrated one, and is an evolving process between the activators, that is – sales and marketing and the measurers, that is – finance.

The point is that the relationship between cost and benefit in customer acquisition is fluid, constantly in flux as the relationship develops, and may only actually be predicted prior to the selling attempt if the likely level of ensuing demand is known. Anyone selling any sort of service product knows that the proportion of customer sell-ins which conform to this model of predictability are very few.

It thus seems logical to have a system of costing in which the elements of customer acquisition and the associated costs that can be estimated in relation to a 'pitch' are considered as a discrete cost and then, as a subsequent but linked process, computed for the delivery of the service, both as the initial extra effort of establishing good contact and as the ongoing maintenance or 'sustaining' services are evolved. With the inclination in most companies being toward detailed analysis of total expenditure, accompanied by significant wrangling and heartbreak over annual budgets that are never again repeated once the agreed format is approved, the approach of interactive cost management is rarely undertaken but can reap long-term rewards.

For all the advances in modern management techniques, the lack of depth in many core processes is amazing. For example, in a recent CBI survey, over 15 per cent of companies did not know what their costing accuracy was, yet identified overheads varied from under 5 per cent to over 30 per cent of turnover. Surprisingly, most respondents used the same, very general costing methods. Approximately 60 per cent of respondents admitted a varying degree of concern over their costing accuracy, yet a proper debate on methods, accuracy and related issues has still to break through the straitjacket of convention, inertia and paranoia.

This situation is worrying enough at a general level, but it makes the chances of great costing accuracy in relation to a service activity such as customer acquisition virtually nil. With some 80 per cent of companies using either straight budgets or departmental cost centres as their core control mechanism, the mentality of totality – the 'all or nothing' approach – is understandable, for the culture of activity-based costing and management does not exist in a broad, developed, industrywide sense.

THE VALUE OF ABC IN DEVELOPING FUTURE RELATIONSHIPS

Whilst addressed in more detail later in the chapter, it is worthwhile at this stage considering the type of approach which can be made to costing the acquisition of customers, as the yield from any commercial relationship is dictated by the amount of resource required by it.

First, you may consider the costs of the various people involved. How much time each puts in and how much they cost the business, including taxes, perks and so on, and the costs of their line and personnel management. The addition of the latter costs is often a revelation. A bill of materials and external charges, such as presentation materials, promotional materials, research, travel, liaison can also be assembled. Then look at the networking of interrelated people and departments, to fix a quantity of time expended against each pitch.

As previously argued, the time expenditure of people in service is an important element, but one which is rarely measured, ironically because very few people find the time to measure it. Often it seems that time management is more the management of priorities than of time as a resource. Certainly lack of time is one of the highest reported reasons for non-implementation of activity-based cost programmes – the inability to manage time, due to the lack of it!

The adage about how you measure the business is how you run the business, is also true for time, yet except within production and warehousing 'time and *165* motion' is hardly measured at all. Bringing these elements (people, charges and so on) together can provide an assessment of the total 'costs' of the acquisition of a customer, be it a multinational or an individual. This in itself is not difficult to imagine, but how can it be used?

Measurement revolves initially around history and often leads to simple control (that is, these products/customers/pitches cost too much, therefore reduce their quality, or time consumption, or withdraw from the service completely. This approach rarely considers the possibility of re-engineering the approach in detail, service component by component, in order to better utilize resource, cut down wasted time, detail, materials, research. Often a more focused approach, with less material can be more effective.

The usefulness of ABC is enhanced immeasurably by its predictive ability. One of the most important applications of activity-based costing and management is initially to forecast the likely costs based not on history but on a *build-up of predicted use of resources*. Then, during delivery of the service – be it acquisitive, development, or sustaining – as frequently as the *costs or risks* reasonably dictate, first, to use the model to assess the *current* level of costs, and compare these to the costs and returns originally predicted, and secondly, by doing this, to understand the causes of the variances in costs and by this understanding reduce the variance to target and eventually the absolute level of costs.

Ultimately, the objective is to modify service delivery to what the customer most needs, at lowest cost. This exercise needs continuously to be undertaken and reviewed in relation to another key exercise, *that of finding out what the customer most wants and needs.*

When left to hunch, the variance of one customer to another is measured in every shade of emotion from love to hate, but is not readily, accurately or predictively quantifiable as an amount of money. Using ABC techniques, one can quantify the true input of resources, and by comparing input to output, one can identify the worst yield relationships.

THE INPUTS FOR ABC TO WORK

Primarily the inputs to any ABC model must first pass a selection test based on significance and variability. This requires the business concerned to understand what it considers to be significant.

I rarely find clients who have developed a specific, micro understanding of what level of cost, within the complex detail of their business process, they would consider significant enough to measure and act on. By this, I mean that projects aimed at understanding cost are begun with a core understanding of neither the level of detail required, nor the criteria by which the costs become significant to the business.

This is a crucial part of the design process, affecting the fundamental structural approach to the architecture of the system and its inputs. It can make the difference between, on the one hand, a top-down (that is, departmental) or

budget cost centre costing, broken down to products, services and customers, or, on the other hand, build-up costing, where activities, processes and resources are dynamically combined with each other to synthesize costs – in more traditional terms, a cost apportionment model, or a synthetic model, most similar to a form of variable standard costing.

This is a very important design-consideration and output-shaping factor, as the top-down approach will preclude an enormous range of accuracy in many possible detailed analytical techniques because the base costing data will not exist at the lowest level of activity. However, the top-down approach can be perfectly adequate where the collection of detailed data might cost more than the costs the data will eventually measure, or where the control of activity is set by company policy and is highly consistent in the amount of time consumed.

With the level of cost likely to be output from any ABC model being such an important factor in the design of the system, it would be prudent to test assumptions about activity, use of resource and the resulting costs in a spreadsheet or other similar, low data volume, low development cost environment. This 'templating' technique allows for the possible inputs, together with their relationships to activity and the consequent costs, to be easily and rapidly represented to the business.

In addition, as the methodology becomes more developed and the debate about the mathematics, output and application becomes more intense, the ability radically to alter, or indeed dispose of, various possible solutions is useful in delivering speedy low-cost alteration to best meet, define and fully develop the users and technical requirements of the system.

Thus, our recommendation for the first part of the process is one of building a template model based around business processes. For example, the creation of a product such as an insurance policy, would involve the definition of the product development process along the following lines:

- Market analysis.
- Opportunity assessment.
- Risk analysis.
- Hurdle rate setting.
- Product definition.
- Product development.
- Legal consideration.
- Market testing.
- Launch – promotion.
- Ongoing marketing.

Each element of the process can then be broken into its constituent parts: people, equipment, systems, materials and so on. The interactive relationship between *cost elements* (for example *salaries, system costs, software development*) and the mathematical relationship of these defined, interactive components with the *drivers* of cost (for example as *time spent, quantity done, total used*) must then be developed.

As a simple example of an activity-based costing exercise, let's simulate the launch promotion of an insurance product. You have a *direct mail* promotion to plan and execute for selling a new hotline information service. We need to examine what components exist in this exercise, which include:

- Promotion planning.
- Internal research and evaluation.
- Creating the brief.
- Briefing the agency.
- Selecting the agency/mechanic.
- Developing the promotion.
- Selecting delivery method for mechanic.
- Delivering the offer and follow up.
- Evaluating response post-promotion.

If we are to undertake a model of these components, we need to establish what we are going to attach the costs to: that is, what the 'product' is and at what level we want to cost it. In this example, the cost-carrying object must be the *product* (the hotline information service) since this is the purpose and lowest level of the activity you are measuring, as part of the value-adding (or subtracting) process.

As the cost 'vehicle' will be the product, the next thing we need to define is the grouping of the activities into cost groups. How best to organize this is impacted on heavily by the means through which you will manage the costs and activities that you are going to measure. If management is strictly departmental and thus hierarchical and divisionalized, then it makes sense to cluster and group costs within these structural lines. Costs lying outside these groups would theoretically be unmanageable by people within the group and would thus be less likely, or entirely unlikely, to be acted on.

There is also, of course, within any such divisional structure, enormous scope for internal warfare over whose costs were highest, who should manage what, who was causing the most cost, and how departments interact to cause costs for each other. In the early and enthusiastic days of an ABC project, such bickering is not the prime consideration, but as the system grows more powerful teeth, as more measurement becomes based on the increased scope for cost identification and *ownership*, this element can become the largest barrier to the successful implementation of the project.

If the business or function is organized as a unit, then costs can be organized by a process-based grouping, allowing the analysis of the sequence of activities and the management of cost within discrete or overall activity. This situation is obviously preferable, owing to the fact that so many costs do interact with one another and that a cost-reducing action in one process or area of the business may increase costs in another. There may be an overall saving, but this will not cheer the head of a department or division if it impacts negatively on their budget/performance indicators.

168   Divisional organization is fairly simple to illustrate and arrange, as all that is required is to identify the functional 'owner' of the resource being applied – that is, line manager, facility manager and so on – and then evaluate and quantify the resource used and the manner of its use, and allocate costs by a suitably interactive method. The business unit approach is the reverse, where the business process becomes in effect the cost group and 'owner' and all resource time is simply grouped by cost area and subactivity, or some variation on this theme.

For a departmental or divisional example, let us suppose that the promotion planner is based within the marketing function, but that the research and post-promotion tracking is done by someone in the market research department and the selection of the mechanic involves someone from sales. So a potential model structure would resemble Figure 13.1.

Activity	Hours	Resource cost (£)
Marketing		
● Planning time	15	34.30 per hour[1]
● Creating the brief	55	
● Briefing and selection of agency	8	
● Developing the promotion	150	
Total marketing input costs	228	7,820.40
Sales		
● Input to planning	4	40.36 per hour[1]
● Input to mechanic	2	
● Follow-up delivery	180	
● Post-analysis	2	
Total sales input costs	188	7,587.68
Market research		
● Planning time	10	20.47 per hour[1]
● Research and evaluation	15	
● Mechanic selection and development	10	
● Post-analysis	24	
Total market research input costs	59	1,207.73
Total overall costs		**16,615.81**

Note:[1] The costs per hour include NI, cars, overhead for personnel management.

Figure 13.1 Model cost structure for a promotion project involving the marketing, sales and market research departments

This is interesting already insofar as the impression may have been gained that sales input to this promotion is limited by the number of functions within it, yet sales actually incurs 46 per cent of the overall costs due to the relatively high expense of the personnel involved. This immediately indicates that a great deal more time and energy could be spent on research, with little impact on overall costs, in view of the relatively low cost of its personnel.

Placed in a template, these costs can be divided by the volume of product predicted to be sold, and maximum criteria could be set for time worked, covering the promotion overall, to achieve adequate return on capital for the activity depending on anticipated sales volumes.

If this methodology eventually proves satisfactory, then it can be translated into database technology which will allow costs to be developed and shown not only in a hierarchical manner such as above, but also, providing costs are constructed by *process*-based grouping, costed against a product. These costs can then be cross-tabulated and represented both by product and by any grouping of product (that is, region, time period and so on), and by division, function and so on.

If a multidimensional database is used, then any combination of time, structure or reporting is possible. Consideration of the possible combinations required for reporting is *very important*, so that such combinations can be built onto the cost vehicle (that is, at the design stage), since adding extra fields to some database files, particularly mainframes, can be a long and expensive process.

Thus the power of ABC is fundamentally linked to the modelling of the interdependency of one element with another and how they interact. The fact that there are no exact standards for how this will work, or what costs to expect, can make it a demanding process to manage. At this point, therefore, the relevance of such a work-intensive effort to define the costs of the business in such a complex manner may seem questionable, but the potential value is not difficult to imagine. Here are some further ideas to illustrate this point. Activity could of course be broken down in more detail than is illustrated here, and interaction may be considered (for example, the impact of missed deadlines by the various departments on one another, and what costs were caused at what level of failure).

A typical example of such inputs would be the failure of a promotion agency to deliver finished promotion materials, or a delay in direct mail delivery missing the booked advertising slot. This causes delay and increased media costs, with consequent time spent by sales in informing and pacifying field sales staff who have arranged meetings and are waiting to implement follow up calls and delivery of promised materials. The potential impact and increase in costs caused by this chain of interlinked events is not hard to envisage, and this is only one instance of the possible causal relationships that may be considered.

Justification for work in activity-based costing is a precarious occupation. However, there are a large number of published articles available, primarily from examples of projects in the financial services sector and in fast-moving

consumer goods, particularly the grocery sector, where cost is one of the chief issues. Articles may be found through CIMA, the Institute of Grocery Distribution (from suppliers' customer profitability publications.)

Building up these costs in a template, typically a spreadsheet, will enable the build-up of all the applicable processes, components and relationships. In turn, this process will create the inputs to the model, its maths and, most importantly, its output or costings. It will also allow the business to consider the significance and variability of likely costs from the model to the business and thus better justify the development of the model in the first instance.

So, at this point, the sensitivity of the model to changes in inputs should be tested by inputting values at the low and high extremes of the range of values likely or possible in real-world situations. The variability of costs under these circumstances can often be a shocking revelation. Also, at the time the sensitivity of the model inputs is tested, the significance of its output needs to be considered in relation to turnover and profits to be gained from the customer, product or service. The issue of significance is best addressed at this stage, as you will now be in full possession of the components and level of costs and can compare them with other normal criteria for significance.

This raises another critical part of the process, one of *accuracy*. About this time in the project, there will probably be a rift between the camps of the 'control tool' costing and the 'decision support' costing groups. Disagreement may have rumbled on from the start of the project. The 'control-ites' will be suspicious of the lack of systematic precedence for costing methodology and, above all, of the inability of such methods to match to the existing total budgets for the business. The second group will be supportive of the relevance and accuracy in relation to their day-to-day work.

The 'control-ites' may also be concerned at the apparent challenge to the existing systems, often ignoring the potential synergies of comparing the input, or budgeted cost base, to the output, or activity level, measured by the actual value added, or cost added output of the business in products or services. This is due to the fact that fixed overheads and non-product or service-related costs/overheads are either not recovered, or are recovered only in part by such methods. For recovery of costs through this approach is limited to those costs that can be directly or 'causally' linked to activities, products or services and the level to which they are used. For example, a computer for direct marketing may only be used for one hour a week for its purpose, although the overhead cost in the business would cover the whole computer, related software, installation, maintenance and insurance. The output measured in an ABC model would be the one hour of use, costed against the products or services for which it is being used.

In this example, one school of thought would see a radical understatement or recovery of the cost, another an accurate 'billing' of their service or product with its actual use of resource. Both views are correct and complementary. If the two are put together, we get a view which says the cost per item is low but the overhead (that is, the computer) is poorly utilized versus its overall cost.

The model can be made to operate in one of two ways. First, to fully absorb costs, by taking the total costs of a resource (the computer) and dividing it by *171* the total activity (quantity of work related to services/products), as well as looking at the time to achieve one activity (that is, a mailing run), or con-sumer/customer search per service item or product (that is, hours per product or service). Or secondly, to deliberately compare one set of data on overall budgets with summations of activity costs, subgrouped to be within the cost heads of the budget. These two methods can be compared with each other in an exercise similar to constraint theory, trying to best compare input to out-put. In this example, the comparison is between the total cost of the machine and its output of value.

Equally importantly, the 'decision support' group will be unhappy with any model which they feel does not truly represent the specific effort input to a product or service, on the basis that it may over- or underrepresent their input or usage of resource, thus over- or underabsorbing costs against them.

This exercise of grouping and analysing costs (for example labour, equip-ment and so on) from the detail of activities relating to processes, so as to then flow or group into cost heads, is a good indication of how far accounting cost practice has drifted from the actual management of the business, as the two are generally poles apart and profoundly difficult to relate to one another. The exercise of comparison, in any particular detail, is one to do last, as it can be problematic and controversial on a truly grand scale, and needs all the depth of understanding and credibility of an established and proven business tool before exposure to such high-risk use.

HOW TO RELATE ABC TO STAFF REWARD

Most staff reward schemes are based on success. This is of course logical and demonstrably sensible. Sadly, many of the costs in a business, and, in particu-lar, additional, avoidable expense, is tied up in *error, mistake* or *breakdown* in practice. The use of success criteria in staff reward schemes is a well-known and rehearsed subject, so how can ABC add to the incentive vocabulary?

As error is not readily or generally acknowledged, planned for, analysed and the response to it consequently well executed, when it occurs, people are often badly trained in coping with it, and as customers, be they external or internal to the business, are often not at their most reasonable. The stakes for error correction are sky high, both in absolute cost terms for the resource spent in correcting the mistake and in the potential cost of losing an external customer in part or altogether, or ruining a relationship with an internal 'customer'.

The reward for error is of course punishment, or at least chastisement. Thus the 'incentive' for getting things right is actually a negative one, namely, the avoidance of some sort of penalty. ABC, particularly when the interrelation-ship of costs caused by internal or external error is considered, is a powerful means of identifying the cost of error, both direct and indirect, and can be used in two decisive ways:

1   *The justification of a reward/incentive against the ABC quantifiable costs of error*, thus providing a positive and therefore attractive reason for

actively avoiding error and for facilitating the best quality of interaction between customers, staff and resources. This will minimize additional costs to the business, prove a valuable means of removing excess cost, or, better still, will maximize the positive output of goods and services, rather than involve the negative use of time in error correction.

2   *Recognition of previously unidentified areas of cost*, allowing for incentive-based reduction schemes not possible before, directed specifically at the then current areas of highest cost. This will enable a quality circle of highest cost identification, targeting for reduction by incentive, actual reduction, identification of next highest cost, and repetition of the process until costs become impossible to reduce or are below significant thresholds.

With its ability to pinpoint and quantify cost interaction, use of ABC opens up a whole new range of management possibilities, Nevertheless, the whole issue and execution of activity-based cost management must be approached from the perspective of a management tool, whose use will be limited severely if its structure is not in line with the business's actual management and working practice, or where data collection detail is above the level at which the costs are being caused or influenced.

The ultimate incentive is the stability and profitability of the company, the provider of the big reward in commerce – a salary. In addition to specific incentive schemes, therefore, it may be that an increasing proportion of increments such as pay rises, or profit shares are tied into the quantifiable cost and profit benefits measured by ABC.

FURTHER READING

Innes, J. and Mitchell, F. (1991), *Activity Based Costing – A review with Case Studies*, Edinburgh: University of Edinburgh (CIMA).
Institute of Grocery Distribution, *Best Practice In Customer Account Profitability*.

14 Delivering customer service through projects

David Honey

What has project management to do with customer service? Customer service is perceived in terms of having satisfied customers, delighting them and nurturing them – if only life were so simple. If we had a bottomless pot of money we could give it away, which should delight our customers and produce fantastic customer loyalty. Clearly, therefore, cost must come into the customer service equation. Then I would introduce innovation as another important factor. Hence the business requirement becomes cost-effective and innovative customer service. This is where project management comes in, since it gives us the methods and tools required to create the operational infrastructure that will deliver cost-effective and innovative customer service. Project management concerns managing activities to achieve desired objectives within defined constraints such as time, cost and quality.

In the 'good old days' it was possible to deliver high-quality customer service and achieve customer loyalty through personal contact and one-to-one business relationships, relationships that had, in some cases, developed over generations. This is no longer possible in the mass consumer markets of today, although it is still desirable. Consequently, we must turn to other means to deliver cost-effective and innovative customer service and these means involve: people, processes and technology. Note that I have deliberately put people first, since it is people who present the greatest opportunities and the greatest risks in the area of customer service.

Just how people, processes and technology can be applied to deliver cost-effective and innovative customer service is covered in other chapters of this book. Here I will examine the use of project management as a tool to ensure that initiatives in these areas are successful.

Many people would argue that project management is more of an art than a science. Certainly it is not an exact science, since the people and political aspects introduce far too many uncertainties. However, there is no doubt that the application of formal project management methods do improve the success rate of projects. The British Army has a saying which they call the '7Ps': 'Proper Planning & Preparation Prevents Piss Poor Performance'. In the business world we would do well to remember this, since our customers, quite rightly, are very unforgiving of poor performance.

PROGRAMME MANAGEMENT VERSUS PROJECT MANAGEMENT

A great many projects fail for no fault of their own: they become victims of 'circumstances outside of their control' such as other projects, politics and a changing world. The message here is that projects cannot be managed in isolation to each other. A project is part of 'a big picture' and that picture is the programme of projects and initiatives that are delivering the overall business strategy. Figure 14.1 shows some project areas that need to be considered as part of the customer service big picture. These areas are only intended as examples, however. Any significant project, such as the creation of a call centre, will need to cover these areas. These must be managed as an overall programme or else there are great risks that the individual projects will succeed individually but fail collectively – that is, strategically!

There will be interdependencies between the different project areas, which will require particular attention to avoid project deliverables falling between the cracks, or contentious issues being disowned. Figure 14.2 illustrates how the

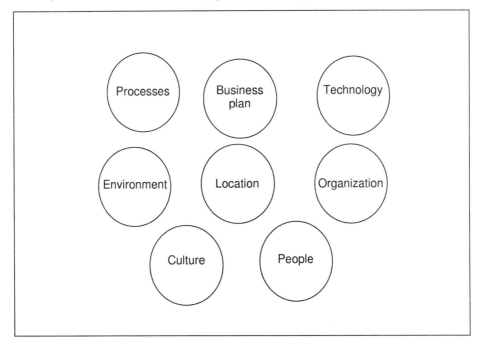

Figure 14.1   Project areas within customer services

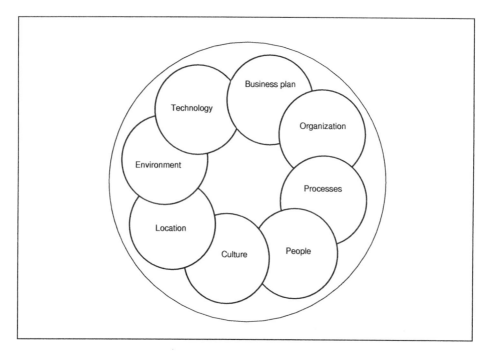

Figure 14.2   Programme Managing 'the big picture'

individual projects could be programme managed as part of the big picture. The sequence of these project areas is not in any particular order and has no significance in the diagram. The message is that the individual project areas must be brought together under a formal programme management framework.

We must never forget that a project is simply a means to an end, not an end in its own right. It must achieve its objectives on time, within budget and to the required quality levels, and those objectives must form part of the big picture, the programme. In any organization it is essential that the management board has good visibility and understanding of the big picture, and the best way of achieving this is through programme management. With programme management it is possible to achieve economies of scale and a sharing of knowledge that is virtually impossible to achieve at an individual project level. If further information is required on the subject of programme management then I refer you to *A Guide to Programme Management* published by the CCTA in London.

WHAT IS A PROJECT?

To place ourselves in context, let us first examine just what we mean when we say a 'project'. A project will have several attributes:

- It will have a set of objectives: for example, 'to provide office accommodation for 450 people' or 'to reduce the number of customer complaints by 50 per cent'.

- It is finite: that is, it will have a start date and an end date.
- It will deliver a set of pre-defined deliverables: for example, a building ready for occupation or a computer system ready for use.
- It will have constraints: for example, the normal ones of time, cost and quality.
- It will be divided into manageable chunks or stages.

Hence, unlike traditional line management, project management can be an excellent discipline for forcing us to be clear about what it is we are actually trying to achieve and what the constraints are for its achievement.

People deliver projects

Projects are no different than any other field of human endeavour; it is the people involved who will ultimately determine whether the projects are successful or not. The use of appropriate methods and tools can bring many benefits, but these pale into insignificance compared with benefits that can be achieved from establishing and managing a successful team.

Given the importance of people to the success of projects, time and effort must be invested in team building and ensuring that the team members have the necessary skills and commitment required to make the project a success. Ideally, a project manager should be able to build a team from scratch, having the freedom to decide from a given pool of resources, both internal and external, who should be on the team and what training is required. Unfortunately, project managers seldom have such freedom and they are typically constrained by the need to make use of resources whose main qualification for a team role is that they are available and there is no budget available for training!

A fact of life in project management is that human resources are a constraint in the same way as time and cost, but more in terms of quality rather than quantity. A common failing in project management is to throw resources at problems without due regard to the quality of the resources and how they are being applied.

When establishing a project it is essential that the people issues and opportunities are treated as a priority. Remember, the crux of the matter is having the right people, doing the right job, right.

Benefits/costs/risks (BCR) analysis

A project is simply a means to an end rather than an end in its own right. It must be justified and the most common approach for justifying a project is so-called cost-benefit analysis. This approach has many limitations: principally, it concentrates on costs rather than benefits and completely ignores risks. A project is undertaken because it is deemed to be beneficial, not because it has costs; hence, benefits must come first. If there are no benefits, then there is no point in undertaking the project. Similarly, there are risks associated with all *177* projects and typically these risks are increasing as the pace of business change accelerates.

Risk assessment and management is a large subject area in its own right; many methods and tools already exist in this area and there is generally no need to invent new ones. However, it is important to realize that risk must be addressed as an integral part of the analysis of benefits and costs and that these three parameters can be traded off against each other: for example, lower risk for higher cost, more benefits for higher risk, lower cost for fewer benefits and so on.

At all stages of a project's life cycle – its conception, during its birth and during its development – benefits/costs/risks (BCR) analysis should be performed. At any stage a decision can be made to cancel a project or radically change its direction based on rigorous and timely BCR analysis. This approach may be unpalatable to many people, but given the accelerating pace of change and the need for flexibility, it is the only way to ensure that sound management decisions are being made and projects can proceed with confidence.

THE PRINCIPLES OF PLANNING

Plans are management documents forming the backbone of the management information system required by any project. The principal objectives of planning are as follows:

- To identify and define the deliverables required to achieve the project objectives.
- To quantify the activities required to achieve these deliverables.
- To provide an estimate of the resources, time and costs required to perform the activities.
- To provide a means for monitoring and controlling the project.

These objectives are achieved by:

- Determining and documenting the scope of the project.
- Defining and documenting the deliverables the project is required to deliver.
- Structuring these deliverables in the form of a work breakdown structure (WBS).
- Identifying the activities/work packages required to supply these deliverables.
- Defining the quality policy to be adopted, since this will have an impact upon activity duration and resource requirements.
- Determining dependencies between the project activities and external activities.
- Identifying required resource skills and estimating required effort for each activity.
- Identifying durations for activities then assigning start and finish dates.

- Identifying management control points.
- Assigning resources and responsibilities to activities.
- Producing cost estimates and a budget.

Without all of these elements the manager is unable to gain an informed approval to proceed and would have no yardstick to measure progress and detect when the project is at risk.

In order to plan a task properly time must be allowed for the planning activity. Therefore every project should start with an initiation stage (stage 0) when time should be allocated to identify the task, to obtain agreement on the identity of the task and to plan it in terms of management, resourcing, activities, deliverables, quality and control. The project may be such that the initiation stage is immediately followed by a feasibility stage to raise confidence in its viability.

Types of plan

Plans are always constrained in one way or another and the common constraints are time, cost, resources and performance or quality. Project plans primarily focus on the time, resource and cost constraints, giving rise to two distinct types of plan:

1 *The activity plan.* This type of plan shows the relationship between activities and time. Usually expressed as a bar or Gantt chart, it is frequently preceded by the use of network analysis techniques in order to identify the dependencies that exist between deliverables/activities, and also to give some indication of the degree of risk (as indicated by the number of critical paths through the network).

2 *The resource plan.* This type shows the resources required to complete the activities in the time identified on the activity plan. This is a tabular summary recording, on the same timescale as the activity plan. The resources covered can be in a wide range, including: human resources identifying both type and quantity; equipment and services; and financial resources for example costs.

It is necessary from the outset to address quality issues in order to ensure that deliverables are of the required quality. To this end it is necessary to consider quality policy and planning, which is covered later in this chapter.

Levels of plan

As previously mentioned, plans are a tool for creating estimates and managing projects in order to ensure that they achieve their objectives within the agreed time, cost and quality constraints. It is important to recognize that the further the plan extends into the future the greater the uncertainties and the more difficult it becomes to estimate accurately. Consequently, it is beneficial to identify various levels of planning and appreciate that these levels *179* reflect the differing needs of the various levels of management involved in the project.

Where a project is of a significant size and duration, it is helpful to break it down into stages and assign stage managers or team leaders to each stage. Taking the project and stage levels as an example, the project manager and senior management involved with the project (commonly a project board or steering committee) need to be able to see the continuing viability of the project and therefore require an overview of the total project, the main deliverables, the activities required to produce them with related timescales, and the total costs. The stage manager, on the other hand, needs to be in control of the activity on a day-by-day basis and therefore requires plans in much more detail.

Planning techniques

Many techniques exist for displaying the different aspects of the plan, including network analysis (or critical path analysis), bar charting (or Gantt charting), resource smoothing (or resource levelling), tabular summaries and graphs. However, there are certain principles associated with the fundamentals of effective planning, as follows:

- *Keep plans simple.* It is a good discipline to keep all graphical plans to a single A4 planning sheet. In this way the plan should be more easily prepared, easily read and therefore more likely to be understood. Anything which cannot be displayed in this way should be summarized and the detail included in a lower level of plan. Similarly, do not use complex symbols or present plans which require considerable education or explanation for them to be understood.
- *Keep plans relevant.* Be aware of the audience for the prepared set of plans and aim to provide an appropriate level of detail. For example, a senior manager will not need to have a detailed plan to make decisions about the ongoing viability of the project or to allocate resources, but a team leader will require far more detail in order to allocate tasks to individuals and monitor their progress. Resist the temptation to just circulate the detailed plans because it is less work. This can result in having to spend a lot of unnecessary time in having to explain to senior management on an individual basis.
- *Do not rely upon pictures alone.* As far as planning is concerned it is not necessarily true that 'a picture paints a thousand words'. Although a bar chart can show what you wanted to happen and then what actually happened, it does not show why you wanted it to happen or why something happened that is different to the plan. Graphical plans should be supported by a short narrative describing the thought that went into the plan, the assumptions that were made and the risks inherent in the plan.
- *Do not plan the unquantifiable.* Perhaps the most obvious and yet most ignored rule in planning is only to plan what it is possible to plan. All too often attempts are made to plan projects which either:

a) extend too far into the future where levels and types of available resources cannot be accurately predicted; or

b) extend beyond key decision points which affect the way forward from then onwards.

For example, plans are frequently constructed which treat the feasibility study as an integral part of the same project and yet the outcome of the study will determine the way the project will develop.

- *Do not plan strategies as projects.* Projects and strategies have different characteristics and requirements, and consequently, strategies should not be planned as projects. As previously mentioned, programmes form a framework for achieving and measuring the success of strategies, and programme management techniques should be used at the strategic level.

With extremely large tasks comprising many but only loosely connected activities, the temptation to treat them as one project should be resisted. An example of such a task would be the development of a new system requiring the procurement of a central computer configuration, the installation of a telecommunications network, the procurement and installation of terminals, and the development of software to run in this environment. These collectively constitute a system comprising a number of projects. A system level plan may then sit above a number of project plans. The basic message here is to divide work up into sensible and manageable chunks.

WORK BREAKDOWN STRUCTURES (WBS)

Purpose

The work breakdown structure (WBS) is a convenient method for dividing a project into its components in terms of work packages, tasks or activities. A WBS reduces the likelihood of something being dropped through the cracks. To put it another way, a WBS is intended to ensure that all the project activities and deliverables are logically identified and related.

Format

The format of a WBS is that of a hierarchically structured diagram (it looks very similar to an organization chart), a box at one level being connected by lines to a number of boxes at a lower level, which themselves represent all of the components of the higher level. As a minimum the box should contain a title and number, the number indicating its position within the hierarchy. To distinguish between internal and external deliverables, different shape boxes are normally used (for example, square and rounded corners).

In general, when constructing the WBS it is useful to think about the main deliverables required from the project and the tasks required to produce them. *181*

Traditional WBSs are structured around tasks, but more modern project management methods, such as PRINCE, structure it around deliverables, which PRINCE terms 'products' and renames the WBS as a 'product breakdown structure (PBS)'.

When the WBS is first drawn there will inevitably be some overlap between areas and it will be necessary to redraw the WBS to reduce the areas of overlap and make it more definitive. In practice it may be necessary to redraw the WBS many times before you are happy with its content and structure. There is no right or wrong answer in this respect; it is simply a matter of creating a WBS that is most appropriate and useful.

Work packages

The more work packages you have in your project, the smaller and cheaper each work package becomes. However, the more work packages you have, the more money and time is spent arranging for these to be properly interfaced with each other and managed. Conversely, if you have only one work package, there is no interfacing overhead but the task itself is large and expensive. Therefore, there is a happy midpoint to be found. The smallest work package is typically an activity that can be performed by one person within one reporting period (for example, one week).

After work packages have been identified it is necessary to estimate how much time and resources are required to complete the specified package of work and produce the required deliverables.

AN INTRODUCTION TO ESTIMATING

A definition and objective of an estimate

An estimate is an assessment of the time and resources required for the successful delivery of a specified deliverable.

The purpose of producing an estimate is to provide information to be incorporated in project plans. This information will include:

- deliverables to be produced;
- tasks to be carried out;
- manpower required;
- cash and other resources required;
- project duration; and
- project timetable (proposed).

The project plans will in turn present the information in a clearly structured form to allow management to take decisions. This will include key decisions on:

- project justification;
- project objectives;

- organization structure;
- resource allocation;
- staff allocation and training;
- project control procedures;
- monitoring and reviews; and
- revision of plans.

Probabilities

An estimate is not an absolute forecast, it is a 'best guess', whose reliability depends on the quality of information available to the estimator and on the estimator's professional skill and experience.

When presenting an estimate, the estimator must establish the quality of the information available and the assumptions which have been made. These will be analysed and presented in terms of the probability that the estimate will eventually prove to have been correct. The usual method is to present the estimate with a plus and minus margin, at a level at which it is, for example, 95 per cent certain that actual events will fall within the margins provided.

Typically the margins might be plus/minus 50 per cent when estimates are presented at the feasibility study stage before a project is approved to proceed, and plus/minus 20 per cent when more detailed estimates are carried out stage by stage through the project.

The estimator's needs

In order to produce a good estimate the estimator needs information and personal attributes. These may be summarized as follows:

- Knowledge of the proposed system.
- Knowledge of the project environment.
- Information about similar projects undertaken in the past.
- Estimating skill and experience.
- Objectivity.

Skill and experience can only be gained by actually doing the job, but all the other items estimators can set out to acquire for themselves. Look for advice and information from all possible sources, both within the organization and elsewhere. Estimators must remember that their job is not to produce an answer that is pleasing or acceptable to management but to produce an answer that proves to be right.

In producing any estimate, the estimator will identify aspects of the project or stage which present particular difficulties because they are subject to large elements of uncertainty, possible changes, or high risk. Examples are requirements which are still under consideration, areas where policy or legislation are volatile, or technical procedures which are unfamiliar, or where staff are subject to rapid turnover.

These areas should be clearly identified when presenting an estimate, and appropriate additions should be made to those areas to allow for the probability that changes will occur and that problems will arise. All standard estimating models list the types of modifiers which may be needed but always remember to look out for ones unique to the project as they will typically represent the highest risk.

Particular problem areas

There are a number of areas which have regularly given rise to problems in estimating for projects and which are worth highlighting, as follows:

- *Inadequate project definition.* In many cases estimators are asked to provide estimates based upon an initial bright idea to do something. It is necessary to identify the lack of definition and qualify the estimate accordingly, in order to show that a clearer definition is required before a decent estimate can be made.
- *Forgetting user aspects.* It is all too common to provide estimates for building operational infrastructure (people, processes and technology) and to forget to allow for the effort required to explain its purpose to users and to prepare and train them to use its facilities and the information that it provides. Make sure that checklists include developing manual procedures, organization changes, preparing and delivering training material, and so on.
- *Data capture and cleaning.* A significant number of information technology (IT) projects have run into problems caused by the difficulty of loading the basic information into the computer system, especially where some or all of that information is currently held manually. Remember that while experienced clerical staff will probably recognize a nonsense figure on a client's file card, a data entry person keying it in among scores of others will not and the system will accept it as fact.
- *Over optimistic estimating.* There is a well-proven tendency for staff estimating a project which they are to manage, to underestimate the required time and resources. This may often be by a factor of as much as 100 per cent. It is caused by enthusiasm for the project and a desire to see it approved, undermining the objectivity which has been noted as a vital necessity for good estimating. When there is a tendency towards palatable figures (rather than realistic ones) it is easy to see that personal and organizational influences may combine to produce substantial errors in the estimating process.
- *Political pressures.* With the accelerating pace of change comes a desire to set a date for a project's completion and then to work backwards to determine what must be done by when. This approach can and has worked on many projects, both large and small. However, clearly there are great risks. If the estimator has the freedom to trade off an imposed time constraint against variable cost and quality constraints, then the

situation is reasonable. On the other hand, if more than one of these constraints are imposed then the situation is likely to be unreasonable. Typically, under such conditions it is quality that is sacrificed, resulting in project deliverables that are 'unfit for purpose' and quite possibly useless!

Remember that by resisting pressure to produce palatable estimates, by identifying areas of uncertainty, and providing management with the means to resolve them by early and clear decisions, the estimator will be doing the whole organization a great service.

GANTT CHARTS AND NETWORKS

The Gantt Chart

The most widely used management tool for project scheduling and control is the bar chart, often called Gantt chart after Henry L Gantt, an industrial engineer who popularized them during World War I.

The principle of the Gantt chart is that vertical lines, forming columns, provide divisions of time and the amount of work to be done in that time. Horizontal lines drawn through the columns indicate the relationship of the amount of work actually done compared with the planned amount. The columns are headed with dates, typically months for project level plans and weeks for stage level plans. A description of the activities is entered into the left-hand column and the date on which an activity is due to start is indicated by a right angle opening to the right. The planned completion date is denoted by a right angle opening to the left. A line joins the right angles to form a rectangle.

As work on an activity progresses a heavy line is drawn to identify progress against the plan. An example of a basic Gantt chart is shown in Figure 14.3.

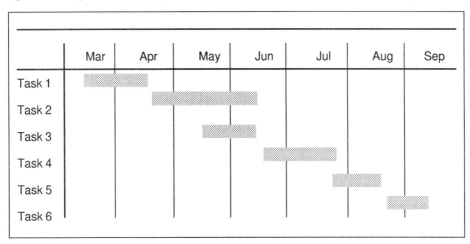

Figure 14.3 Example of a Gantt chart

The majority of PC tools available today use different conventions to those identified above and some even let you define your own convention, but the principles are still the same.

Networks

There are many forms of network techniques but the program evaluation and review technique (PERT) and the critical path method (CPM) are the most common. Network diagram is a generic term for PERT and CPM diagrams, arrow diagrams, bubble diagrams, precedence networks and many others.

The technique employs the use of a diagram constructed to illustrate the dependencies of tasks within a project, as shown in Figure 14.4. The diagram can be used at all levels to show an overall view of the whole project and then to provide a detailed view of tasks at the working level. The diagram, once constructed with times added, can be used to predict the total project duration and finish date. Also, the earliest start, earliest finish, latest start and latest finish times for each task can be determined and illustrated.

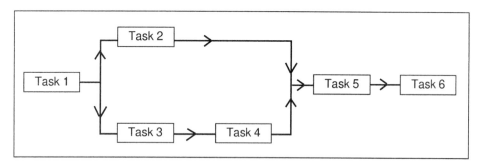

Figure 14.4   Example of a network diagram

Identifying and quantifying the critical path

As a tool the biggest attraction of the network technique is its ability to identify the critical path. The critical path is the path of activities which has no spare time available and late delivery of any one of the critical path activities will result in slippage of the end date of the project. The logic of the above network shown in Figure 14.4 is that tasks 2 and 3 may start as soon as task 1 has been completed. Neither of them can start until then. Task 5 cannot start until task 2, and tasks 3 and 4 have been completed, and task 6 will follow on from the completion of task 5. What we cannot see from Figure 14.4 is whether the critical path is via task 2 or via tasks 3 and 4; this can only be determined by adding the dependency details in terms of dates and task durations. Identifying the critical path enables management to manage by exception and concentrate management resources on the critical tasks.

186   The spare time available on the non-critical tasks is known as 'float'.

Resources on non-critical tasks can be switched to critical tasks at the project manager's discretion, thus keeping the project on target.

The project network is constructed by linking symbols together to form a logical picture of tasks, dependencies and timings. A dependency within a project is denoted by an arrow emerging from one box and entering another box. There are a number of different conventions for linking the boxes together to form a network and for the contents of the boxes.

Figure 14.5 shows a common convention for the details contained within the box. After the project network has been logically constructed the timings for each task can be added. The description of the task (or activity) is written in the centre of the box and the duration of the task in the centre portion above the description. When a project is in progress, a delay of a critical path activity extends the project duration. However, delay of a non-critical task within the limits of available float may be acceptable.

Fortunately, PC-based computerized planning tools take much of the hard work out of calculating the critical path through networks, reporting progress, performing 'what-if?' analysis and replanning. However, in order to use these tools effectively and with confidence a good basic understanding of planning techniques is essential.

QUALITY MANAGEMENT WITHIN PROJECTS

I mentioned earlier that the three normal constraints on a project are time, cost and quality. The consumption of the first two, time and cost, is fairly visible and easy to measure. The last, quality, is the least visible and the most difficult to measure. Consequently, it is the easiest and most likely to be sacrificed to the demands of time and cost.

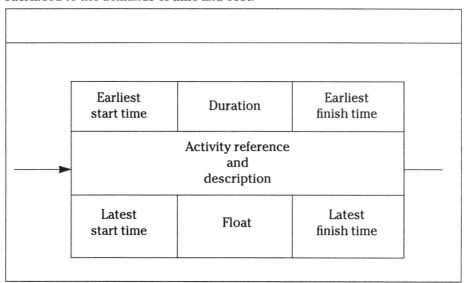

Figure 14.5   Example of a network convention

Time and time again, projects – particularly ones dependent on new technology – have been brought in on time and within budget, only to be scrapped because they failed to achieve the required quality levels. Typically, when the projects came under time and/or cost pressures, areas in the project plan, such as requirements analysis, prototyping, quality reviews and testing, in all its guises, were cut back, which had a direct impact on the quality of the project deliverables.

Given the dangers and risks in the area of quality, it is essential that it is properly prioritized and managed within a project.

Quality concepts

In order to understand the principles of quality management within projects it is first necessary to understand some of the basic terminology.

Definition of quality

There are many definitions of quality, but all of these definitions reach a similar conclusion: that quality is about meeting customer or client expectations of service.

Joseph Juran defines quality in his book, *The Quality Control Handbook*, as being 'fitness for purpose or use'. BSO and ISO take this definition further, 'the totality of the features and characteristics of a deliverable or service that bear on its ability to satisfy stated or implied needs'. BS 4778 and ISO 8402. This generic approach needs refining for every organization, in order to meet the 'stated or implied needs' of that organization and of each project within that organization.

Definition of quality control

Quality control (QC) is the activities and techniques employed to achieve and maintain the quality of a deliverable, whether process or service. It involves monitoring quality and finding and eliminating the causes of quality problems in order that the requirements of a customer are continually met.

Definition of quality assurance

Quality assurance is the process of establishing and maintaining a quality management system (QMS), the assessment of its effectiveness, the audit of the operation of the system, and the continual redefinition of its components to ensure that the QMS supports the organization's quality goals.

Quality control mechanisms

- *Inspection.* A scrutiny of a deliverable, post-production, usually with minimum or no preparation. Identifies errors.

- *Walkthroughs*. A scrutiny of a deliverable, post-production, usually driven by producers to identify errors.
- *Quality reviews*. A scrutiny of a deliverable during production against defined quality criteria. Usually driven independently of producers. Has a very formal structure involving deliverable definition, review preparation, review, and follow-up.
- *Testing*. The measurement of a project deliverable against expected function, data and performance criteria. There are many forms of testing and various techniques and tools. Although this is the strongest quality control technique, as it is the most practised over time, there are still weaknesses in approach.
- *Acceptance criteria*. These are the criteria set up at project initiation and refined during development or procurement. They are targeted by various 'users' of the system, such as end users at operational level and the business at a strategic level. Other users who should develop acceptance criteria for the deliverables are the maintenance area responsible for maintenance post live date and operations, who will be responsible for the day-to-day running of the deliverables. These functions may be run by a large unit or by one person responsible for these functions.
- *Staff development*. Although this may seem out of place as a quality control mechanism, the quality of staff performance is critical to the success of any project. Therefore development plans for the training and experience enhancement of staff should be developed and implemented. Subsequently, this should be tracked to ensure that the expected outcome is being delivered and the staff quality criteria met.
- *Plan monitoring*. Monitoring actual against plan in time, cost and resources is another important quality element, which should be set by the project steering committee or project board.

Involvement of representatives – business/user/technical

At all times the involvement and participation of the three elements – business, user and technical (BUT) – should be considered for the deliverables and services being delivered. This is an essential element of quality planning.

Levels of quality planning

This chapter is concerned only with the quality planning associated with a given project. However, it is worth noting that company/departmental standards should be a strong influence on project standards; the project should adopt a subset of the higher level company/departmental standards, with perhaps supplements specific to the project needs. Obviously, company/organization certification against quality standards such as BS 5750/ISO 9000, and DTI TickIT (this is a Department of Trade and Industry quality assurance checking Methodology), will play an important part in defining and implementing project quality standards.

The quality plan for a big project such as a large call centre is a significant management document required at the initiation of the project. It will identify in detail:

1 *What* the project/deliverable quality criteria are: for example, cost, time, reliability, functionality, and maintainability.
2 *How* these quality criteria are to be developed, controlled, and assured.

Project management and systems development methodologies such as PRINCE and SSADM, together with associated tools, have inherent development and control features which, if assured, will cover many features of *how*. If it is necessary to tailor or supplement these methods and tools, it must be stated in the quality plan and agreed by project management. Establishing *what* the quality criteria are, is project specific, and each of the above aspects will need explicit reference.

The project management impact of quality control

The degree of quality required by the commissioners of the work will influence the planning and management of the project. The higher the quality required, the more effort needs to be invested in planning and control of the development processes and people. It must be borne in mind that this investment in quality should be an investment in effectiveness and efficiency.

Techniques of QC have already been identified above. All these techniques should be considered at the project initiation stage and in all the stage planning activities, and their impact on the process and quality of the development process assessed. The investment in QC should be commensurate with the expected return on that investment.

Decisions on quality controls are made by the project board which consists of representatives from the business, user and technical (BUT) areas. They agree on the rigour of the controls required to deliver a system. The degree of quality control mechanisms must be commensurate with risk, investment and return. The tripartite view of the project board assists in ensuring a balanced view for the degree of control.

The detailed implementation of the quality control mechanisms is the responsibility of the project manager with the assistance of the quality assurance staff from the BUT areas.

Practical quality review

What is quality review?

Quality review is a technique for controlling the quality of deliverables via reviews of documents, for example specifications, standards, test results, and so on. The review process has a defined framework which clearly identifies the roles and responsibilities involved and defines the steps necessary to produce a quality deliverable.

The need for quality review

The fact that people make mistakes in their work should be enough to persuade any organization to operate quality review, particularly as the costs of problem solving and error resolution in operational business systems can be as high as 40 per cent of total operational costs.

Typical problems in customer service systems development environments

- *Incomplete documentation.* This can arise during development or in operation. Many customer service systems have inadequate user and/or maintenance documentation, increasing the risk of misoperation of the system and extending maintenance tasks. This results in a poorer service provider reputation and in increased costs of operating the system. During development, incomplete documentation can cause an extension of development and/or lead to wrong assumptions being made by developers. This can lead to systems being delivered that do not meet requirements, at best, or have significant deficiencies built in.
- *Non-compliance with standards.* Standards are in place to assist development and operation of customer service systems. Breaches of these standards affect the ability of staff to maintain and operate the system.
- *Failure to update standards.* Standards should be practical. If they are ignored because they are impractical and/or out of date they will become unusable and the benefits of having standards will be lost. Quality reviews help identify where these events are occurring and provide a platform for standards maintenance and improvement.
- *Errors detected late in development.* An error detected late in the development life cycle which could have been detected at an early stage in the life cycle, can cost between 100 and 1 000 times more to resolve.
- *Short cuts in documentation.* This is usually caused by time pressure and is not typically controlled. The same problems then occur as identified above.
- *Getting users to sign-off.* This is a problem caused by lack of involvement of user personnel in the development process. The fault here lies with both users and developers. Users don't wish to be involved in 'technical' aspects of the work. Developers will be content only to involve users when it suits the developers. This lack of involvement leads to lack of understanding of what is produced. Users will not commit to something they do not understand or that they cannot be assured is correct.
- *No operative measures of completeness.* Deciding that a piece of work is complete can be a very subjective task. If there is no formal measurement of completeness that has been agreed before the production task, *191*

how does anyone know when the deliverable is complete? If this cannot be measured, then there can be little control over the production tasks. If there is little control, how can the tasks be managed?

- *Circulated documents don't get read.* A common practice is for project documentation to be circulated for approval and/or comment. There is no guarantee that the effort required to review the document will be invested. A cursory approach is usual and in the worst case no effort is made at all. The development then proceeds on probably poor grounds.

- *Excessive requests for change.* Environments which do not have formal change control procedures based on completed deliverables and which promote excessive requests for change are courting disaster during development. The requests for change usually arise as previous work has overlooked requirements or has not efficiently defined requirements.

- *No formal baseline for development and change control.* Should there be no definition of what is considered to be a 'completed' deliverable, then there is no start point for an analysis of the change. The 'baseline' in this context being an accepted complete deliverable.

- *Quality review addresses the problems.* Quality review provides an environment which insists on clear definition of deliverables to be produced. This provides the 'baseline' for control; the assurance that work is complete; that those responsible for deliverable acceptance are active participants in the development; that standards are applied effectively; and that the user and business communities can have confidence that the deliverables are to requirements and can be signed off and accepted. Quality review has been found to be the only structured development technique with constantly high productivity and a low error rate.

SUMMARY

- Customer service: 1st, 2nd and 3rd.

- The only way to deliver cost-effective and innovative customer service is to consider the 'big picture'.

- Set and manage expectations: 'promise low and deliver high', do not overcommit.

- If it doesn't have a beginning and an end, then it's not a project.

- The only thing that is certain about a project is its uncertainty.

- Customer service must be cost-effective to stay alive; to stay ahead it must be innovative.

- Programme management equates to managing the 'big picture' and delivering business benefits.

- People deliver projects; use the right people to do the right job right.

- Benefits, costs and risks go together and can be inter-traded.

- The most useful yet underused word in project management is 'no'.

- The three primary constraints on most projects are time, cost and quality.
- Quality is hard to measure and easy to sacrifice.

- One-page reports are read, two pages are binned.

- No commitment, no project.

- 'Quality' equals 'fit for purpose'.

- Project management is an overhead; the philosophy should be maximum gain for minimum pain.
- Small problems are hard to see but easy to fix. Big problems are easy to see but hard to fix. Fix your small problems before they become unfixable.
- Success = achievement – expectation.

FURTHER READING

British Computer Society (1990), *A Guide to Software Quality Management System Construction and Certification using EN29001*, DTI TickIT, London: British Computer Society.

Central Communications Technology Agency (1990), *A Guide to Programme Management*, London: HMSO.

Central Communications Technology Agency (1994), *PRINCE Overview*, London: HMSO.

Kerzner, H. and Thamhain, H. (1986), *Project Management Operating Guidelines*, New York: Van Nostrand Reinhold.

Rosenau, M. (1984), *Project Management for Engineers*, New York: Van Nostrand Reinhold.

Part III
MARKETING CUSTOMER SERVICE

15 Customer service as a product

Jan E Smith

'Experience is not what happens to you; it is what you make of what happens to you.'
Aldous Huxley

We all know what customer service means to us personally. We know when we receive good customer service, great customer service and dreadful customer service. Every company looking for sales growth and profit recognizes – and usually acknowledges – the immense benefit to be derived from having a reputation for caring about the people who buy or might buy one of its products. Few, though, have really capitalized on this most crucial aspect of business behaviour.

Why is this? Probably because it is exceedingly hard to deliver well at all points of contact with the customer. It requires vision, flair, drive and commitment – real commitment. It is a long-term strategic position to aim for. Quite often, companies are too involved in today's problems to consider tomorrow. Too little thought is given to market positioning and gaining sustainable competitive advantage. The emphasis is on short-term tactical promotions and discounting, or on the latest loyalty programme, without recognizing the greater reward that these strategies would have if they were underpinned by the 'service' ethic.

For those companies that have recognized and acted upon this requirement, such as Virgin and Direct Line, reputation and word of mouth about their service have played a significant part in building their businesses. This perception is critical in establishing a reputation for customer service. Finding out what service people want and delivering that experience is vital. So, too, is recognition of the power of harnessing customer service as part of the company's 'brand' – establishing it as a brand value, driving that value through every part of the business and then promoting it as a product. Your number one product – the product that leads people to you and builds your reputation and customer perception.

BRANDING CUSTOMER SERVICE

Is it possible, therefore, to take the customer service proposition and make it synonymous with your brand – to establish it as part of your product line up. If so, how do you go about it? How do you move from the idea, through words, explanations and promises, to performance?

First and foremost you must believe that service will contribute to the bottom line and that concentrating on customers and their needs will pay dividends for sales now and in the future. A reputation for customer service is your most valuable asset, of greater value than your individual products. Without establishing a service ethic, products will not deliver to their true potential. Once this thinking is accepted by a company, the first step has been taken, but lip service will not do. Total belief is required. To quote Peter Drucker in *Managing for Results*: 'One has to be willing to say – this is the right thing to happen for the future of the business. We will work on making it happen.'

Earlier this year Daewoo, the Korean car company, launched in the United Kingdom. Its *raison d'être is* customer service. Its cars were somewhat dated, based on past Vauxhall design and engines, but it chose to sell its product not through traditional dealership outlets but through its own superstores and, more recently, through Halfords, with whom it has a servicing arrangement. Daewoo's advertising concentrates exclusively on customer service and the myriad of reasons why you should buy from them. Knowing that its product is not as exciting and modern as many on the road today, it has attacked the marketplace on service, and initial indications are that its strategy is highly successful. Market share figures over the first few months of trading are exceptional, showing that people are prepared to buy service first and product second.

DELIVERING CUSTOMER SERVICE

It is obviously easier to achieve customer service in a new company than in one which is long established, as the Daewoo example illustrates. Traditional attitudes – 'this is the way we do things here' – are embedded in company cultures, and people hate change, which makes them uncomfortable. So the first step is: take your people with you. They must understand the necessity for change and be able to relate to it. Your staff are crucial, for you will not be able to deliver service without their energy and belief. The vision in a new company is strong – there is a clear goal and a real desire to succeed, but no room for error and no history to rely on. In this instance, your staff have been recruited to achieve that vision. To enable them to do so, there are a number of areas to be researched and questions asked:

The competition

What marketplace do I compete in? Who are my competitors? How do they operate? What are their strengths and weaknesses?

An intimate knowledge of the market and your competitors is vital. You need to experience at every level their products, how they are delivered and the service they offer. We are all consumers. It is not difficult to judge how you are treated, and how good the service is. Examine that service in detail, step by step along the delivery chain. Remember, it is personal experience that influences buying behaviours.

The customers

Next, who are my customers? Who am I targeting? What sort of people are they? How do they run their lives? What do they really want from me?

Is your product a simple one delivered in a quick and efficient way, or one that is more complex, requiring explanation and care? Whichever it is, you have to establish a real picture of the people you wish to reach, and to know what it is that will make your product the one they will choose. In a mature marketplace it is more difficult to differentiate, but those who put the customer above all will make a strong impression. Tesco has transformed its image and the way it does business over the last decade. There is a genuine feeling now that Tesco cares about its customers and is committed to delivering what they need. Service is as much a part of product line-up as Heinz baked beans or Persil washing powder.

As a new player deciding on your marketplace, establishing a niche and a different way of operating is often easier. Direct Line and First Direct have become brands in the service sector, with customer service as the first product. They were set up in this way with the fundamental belief that to provide a product over the telephone required a high level of service. This was the principal requirement, for poor telephone attitude initially, or subsequent lack of interest and tardiness delivering information, would kill any new venture. Thus delivery to fulfil customers' expectations must be the number one priority. To make an impact, create a new position in the market, attract new customers and retain existing ones, you must follow the words of Pablo Picasso: 'You must do differently from everybody else. You must do everything afresh. You must do it differently and do it better.' So analyse your customers and what they want very closely.

Customer needs

What do your customers want? Find out at all costs – research, test, and research again. It will pay dividends in the long term. It is what people *don't* like about their present service experiences that will give you the best clues. Never ask, 'What do you want?' Most people could not give a complete answer to this question, but they will have very definite views about what they don't like.

In the early stages of research into the telephone banking idea which became First Direct, it was evident that people disliked going into bank branches. They complained about security screens that built a barrier between customer and branch staff, about the lack of tellers in busy times, *199* about queueing, and that banks are closed when 'I' want to do the business. From these and other dislikes, a banking service was designed which eliminated all these complaints and provided personal service from anywhere at any time of day or night, 365 days of the year, and at the end of a telephone. It was a revolutionary breakthrough, and a change to the existing comfortable world of banking which has been copied time and time again in the succeeding years. The simplicity of the service for the customer is a considerable plus. The way of operating which brings customer details onto a computer screen and enables a personal, intimate one-to-one dialogue makes each individual feel special – a person, not an account number. But, at the beginning, it was through combining the list of dislikes about the banking experience of the 1980s that fashioned the new service for the 1990s.

So, don't build complex situations and difficult solutions. *Simplicity* and *care* are two words that can be applied to most great service companies.

Delivering the product

How do I deliver?

First, look at every step. Work though each process and procedure involved in the delivery of your product. You know now what customers don't want, so build on what they would find attractive, and make sure it works. Strip out unnecessary processes and bureaucracy and make life easy. Make it simple to buy because that's the business you're in, selling your product.

Another example from First Direct will illustrate the importance of delivering your product efficiently. In the early weeks after launch, First Direct received thousands of enquiries about its new service. Information packs containing application forms were sent out but many people did not respond – they did not fill in the form immediately and send it back. They were busy people with other priorities. But those who did respond were numbered in thousands: they experienced an account-opening process of up to five weeks – applications to be processed, accounts set up, cheque books sent out, credit cards to be issued. With a new venture like First Direct, you have no way of knowing how robust the procedures you put in will have to be.

If neither of these two examples were they adequate to deal with the reality of the operation and changes had to be made. An outbound telephone marketing team was trained quickly and thoroughly to begin a follow-up operation for those people who had asked for information and not responded, resulting in increased numbers of accounts opened. At the same time the account opening process was examined in detail, bottlenecks in the system were eliminated, and, six months after launch, the service had become much more streamlined and efficient.

So, work out your processes but make sure you monitor them in detail and, if needed, change them quickly! But don't forget one very crucial ingredient.

Who is going to deliver?

Choose your customer-facing staff with care. Just anyone won't do. Staff are your most valuable asset. Recognize the qualities you will need in those who will deliver your product. If unsure, enlist professional help to assist you in profiling the type of people who will add real value to your business. In a new organization it is easier because you can recruit from scratch. In an established company, however, have everyone profiled, and, if necessary, change people's roles. Make sure that the right people are dealing with your customers.

Training

Train them, test them, and then train them again – and if you're not 100 per cent happy, don't use them. Turn the organization on its head. The people who serve the customer are most important. Treat them that way. You won't be managing or directing anything if you don't have customers! So take pride in driving up the standards of service in your sector.

Pride of product

Pride is a great motivator, and a powerful influence in a company. It engenders loyalty to the cause and provides the whole team with deep self-respect. Enter awards for customer service and build quality of approach into everything you do. Quality is not about reading from scripts of the 'Hello, Melanie here. How can I help you?' type. We all hear those words in some shape or form every day now, often uttered in bored, monosyllabic tones. They have become meaningless. You must provide genuine people equipped to deal with customer queries and concerns, people whose product knowledge is without fault. There is nothing more irritating than being asked whether you need help, only to find that you know more about the company, its products and services than the person you are talking to – trained to smile and be polite, yes, but trained in what really matters, no! All-round skills are essential, so don't neglect them. Product knowledge, company knowledge, after-sales service, warranty – staff who deal with customers must be trained in all these areas, and don't forget to constantly measure your staff against your competitors.

How do I compare?

Decide who is an acknowledged industry leader in service, set your sights high and measure your service levels regularly. Is your market share growing? Are people thinking about you? Are they recommending your company? How do you compare against the competition? Measuring success is crucial. Have you failed on any point? Did you miss something in research? If so, take action now. Make changes quickly, whilst you're thinking about it. Your competitor is not standing still and neither are your customers. Make sure you can respond to customer needs. Build a process which allows action at the point of contact, and free your people to take these actions. Reorganize and build a better service environment. Don't create enterprises that are incapable of delivering speed of response. Forget your own ego. You're not as important as the *staff*   *201* who are talking to your customers. Spend money on your staff, invest time and effort in them so that they feel appreciated and understand what you're aiming to achieve. Allow them to contribute and feel proud of their efforts.

INFORMING THE CUSTOMER

How will I tell my customers? How will people know that customer service is my number one product? Well, you can tell them through a range of media: television, press, direct mail. This is basic marketing, but don't forget that you can also take your product to them. It is a two-way dialogue, so don't be simply reactive. Above all, make sure you can deliver to the standards you have set *before* you advertise. Over the years there have been hundreds of thousands of people who have bought products and services from companies whose advertising has promised a listening, caring, special service which they could not deliver. You must live up to your promises, otherwise you are deceiving the customer. Your product might have a guarantee or a warranty, but what about customer service? Make commitments to your customers based on facts and stick to them. Educate your staff in these commitments, train them to deliver the philosophy wherever they are in the world.

Tesco's recent television advertisements cleverly addressed the consumer's potential problems. Two things that worry customers are queueing at a checkout and returning perishable items. In one advertisement Tesco pledged that if more than two customers were in a queue, they would open another checkout. There is obviously a finite extent to this policy but it does make consumers aware that the retailer understands one of their pet hates and is trying to do something about it. The other advertisement showed a woman returning a fresh fish simply because it looked sad! This humorous approach allays the customer's fear of having to justify a returned item in potentially embarrassing circumstances. The whole message from both advertisements is that Tesco, as part of its brand image, is a friendly and trouble-free organization.

Remember, however, that in both these cases, advertising is one thing and delivery is another. For instance, a consumer stuck in a line at a checkout beside a row of unstaffed tills, will experience annoyance and frustration, and probably won't return. Staff must be trained to portray and deliver the company policy. Your company's reputation depends on it.

Word-of-mouth recommendation is imperative. We are all influenced by it and it can prove more valuable than any advertising on television or in the press. Such a reference gives far more information and is based on personal experience – emotional, reactionary. How was I treated? Did I enjoy my experience interacting with that company? Would I want to repeat it? If all or most of the answers are 'yes', then you're doing all right. Customer service is obviously on your agenda as *the* number one product, and it's starting to add to your company's reputation. It is becoming a value of your company 'brand'. If service is the strongest value you have, regardless of what you are selling, you truly have put the customer first. That should be your goal. Don't settle for anything less.

MAINTAINING THE ADVANTAGE

How do I maintain my advantage? Is service an advantage? Never be complacent. Seek new ways to do things. Keep abreast of the changing marketplace. Will my customers change their buying habits? Perhaps they won't shop in my store in future: instead they'll buy over the telephone or from the television screen. How will that affect me? Will I need new people? Do I implement different training methods? How will I cope with different delivery channels? To keep asking questions and adjusting is vital in today's world. Mould the company to accept changing consumer attitudes and needs. Keep abreast of the competition – anticipating their strategies and continuing to deliver service requires constant attention. Remember, you never achieve perfection.

One example of branding customer service (and satisfaction) and keeping ahead was Jaguar in the United States. For years the perception in the United States was that Jaguar was a fine car but unreliable. Hence the joke that if you bought one, it had to be fitted with a Japanese mechanic in the boot. Jaguar took the bold step of guaranteeing that if a purchaser was not satisfied for any reason within a certain time period, they could return the car for a full refund or change it for another. This service strategy was extremely impressive to the consumer as Jaguar sales increased, and only a very small percentage took up the offer. It spoke volumes about the product, and it shifted consumer perceptions about Jaguar's quality standards and Jaguar's concern and care for its customers.

A commitment to service may seem easy – in fact, it's common sense. But how difficult is it to achieve? A recent example of marketing from Hoover may illustrate this point. Hoover agreed to a sales promotion offering two free flights to the United States with the purchase of any appliance over £100. Although there were some caveats to the offer, these were not initially readily apparent to the average consumer. Unsurprisingly, Hoover were deluged with applicants, since it was, on the face of it, obviously well worth paying £100 for a Hoover in exchange for two free flights – even if you throw the appliance in the dustbin. The rest is now history. Huge negative media coverage ensured that, as well as facing enormous financial repercussions, Hoover damaged its brand image in consumers' eyes – and this to a company whose brand name over the decades has become a generic term.

Think carefully about maintaining your advantage. Marketing can destroy as well as build. Always try to deal with your customers honestly. Once they have bought your product, you are at the beginning of a relationship, and your goal should be to make that relationship last a lifetime. Listen carefully to any complaints and deal with them fairly and quickly. The longer people spend complaining, arguing, and documenting faults, the less likely that they will buy again and the more likely they will influence others not to buy. Set out clear policies for your staff and customers about such things as repairs and refunds, yet allow flexibility to deal with individual cases. Statutory law now covers many of these areas but a little extra care and attention is well worthwhile. No matter how small or large the purchase, concern for your customer is evident *203* in how seriously you treat their complaint. Note that Marks & Spencer, acknowledged for its retailing service, encourages its customers to bring back whatever they are not happy with. It puts the customer first.

A lifetime relationship with your customers has its rewards in revenue growth and bottom-line profit as well as pride and satisfaction in delivering services. The longer your customer stays, the more products are purchased, and your initial investment in recruitment is repaid over and over again. Your brand becomes a soulmate, an indispensable part of life, which your customer will not easily give up. There may be better-designed products, there may be cheaper products, but good service is worth paying for, travelling distances for, and simply experiencing. It cannot in itself be bought, but it has a unique value to each individual. It is judged personally. It is of far greater importance than the product it supports, but together the two – product and service – provide a powerful package.

SUMMARY

- *Start with service.* Your belief in its value to your business is vital.
- *Know your marketplace.* How do they think, what do they do, how do they live their lives? And then decide what it is you can offer.
- *Decide how you will deliver it.* Every step of the way.
- *Choose carefully who will deliver for you.* This is at the very heart of your service strategy and will make the difference between your success and failure.
- *Train your staff.* Train them to the highest possible standards and continue to train them.
- *Promote and market only what you can deliver.*
- *Listen to your customers* – especially if they have any complaints or questions. Respond and change if you need to.
- *Allow your staff flexibility.* Flexibility to deal with customers' complaints quickly and efficiently. Encourage them to take decisions which will build your reputation for service.
- *Make lifetime relationships your goal* – founded on service.

These few steps embody a straightforward, common-sense approach – nothing revolutionary. So why do some companies fail to achieve acceptable customer service standards? Mainly because somewhere along the chain something has not been done, or is not happening in a way that best serves the customer. Therefore, be thorough and don't neglect anything. Complacency is an attitude you cannot afford.

Service is your product – service is your *brand*. The future is about service and relationships. These are prerequisites to competitive viability and fundamental to profitable growth in the long term.

16 Lifetime values and database marketing

Kevin Gavaghan

Companies that keep their customers for a lifetime make more profit. They have happier customers and shareholders and more often than not, the best reputation with their staff. In Britain, annual polls by MORI, a market research organization, show that businesses' 'familiarity' and 'favourability' scores correlate closely with their long-term performance, their annual results and the consistency of their share price.

A BRIEF HISTORY OF PROFITABLE MARKETING

In the beginning of marketing, when manufacturers ruled the world, there were mass markets. Later, as retailers moved into dominance, there were 'consumers' and market 'segments'. Now as individual customers exercise their control the focus narrows from niche markets and micromarkets to markets of one. Sophisticated purchasers know that the precise product or service they need is out there somewhere. It is the right colour or size or price and it is available now. The challenge is to locate it, then buy it.

New technologies are now enabling businesses to stop finding customers for their products and instead find products for their customers. The surprising fact is that 'tailor-made' goods and services were always available in the age of handmade service – to those who could afford them; today 'tailor-made' can be achieved by machines which both meet the individuals' needs and still generate economies of scale in production. In the United States, Levi Strauss, the jeans company, is taking measurements and preferences from female customers to produce exact fitting garments. To match the evolving female form of the individual customer is a recipe for a lifelong relationship.

Since 1989, businesses have been preoccupied with recession and competition. Over time, prices and incomes have reduced. Costs have also been decimated as processes are automated and jobs removed. But the angle of income reduction has been steeper than that of cost reduction and margins have narrowed as the lines converge. Worker stress and customer demands for service are now blunting the cost-cutter's blade. To widen margins, companies must now achieve three marketing miracles:

1   Precise identification of their preferred customers.
2   Production of goods and services that add value but not cost.
3   Retention of customers for a lifetime.

All three are now achievable using databases.

LIFETIME CUSTOMERS ARE MORE PROFITABLE

The value of lifetime customers is that they are more profitable. Recruited only once and satisfied at most, but perhaps not all, stages of the relationship, they become frequent purchasers of a company's goods or services and equally regular recommenders of the service to others. On those rare occasions that something does go wrong, the benefit of the doubt is given and the relationship is bonded even more strongly.

Today, most organizations recognize that moving a customer swiftly through from the expensive stage, recruitment, to the welcome, only marginally less expensive second stage, is a complex process with many hidden costs. One global insurance company makes the self-evident point that an 80 per cent customer retention rate means replacing the whole base every five years. Slow that down to 90 per cent and replacement is every ten years. The same company then calculates that with retention improved only 5 per cent, their cost per policy issued drops by 18 per cent.

In a recent issue, *Fortune* magazine set out in graphic form why loyal customers are more profitable. The table shows that while initial sales levels from new customers conformed to a regular and flat pattern over the seven years portrayed, the increasing purchases of those same loyal customers grew from 7 per cent to 23 per cent of total sales by year seven. Costs per customer reduced in almost the same proportions for the reasons just explained, adding to profits. The combined effects of both customer referrals and recommendation to new prospects and the price premiums that may be applied once the relationship is this well founded, added a further 26 per cent to the profit contributions of the loyal customers.

Observation of and by many successful organizations enjoying lifetime relationships with their customers confirms that there are many ways by which they develop those relationships and foster them to ensure long and mutually agreeable times together. Great products, attentive test marketing, regular improvements, excellent service, good stores and merchandizing, interesting assortment, outstanding after sales – all these attributes feature on the list of reasons why customers keep coming back for more. Rarely mentioned but vital to every stage of the relationship – from recruitment through welcome to development and retention – is the customer database. In the relationship between the customer and the organization, the customer database is not only the memory but also the ears, eyes and nose. Imagine any relationship without those tools.

LISTENING, SEEING AND LEARNING ORGANIZATIONS

Loyalty is based on trust, and trust is based on learning. Large or small, organizations are changing so fast that today they rarely have the people, systems and methods which can provide the necessary levels of reliability and responsiveness required to meet the expectations of every customer every time.

As the 'feel-good' factor has ebbed away in most of the developed world and been replaced by the insecurity of threatened jobs, lost homes, reduced income and expectations, and even physical fear, people are turning away from value-added products and brands, and towards value. Peter Wood, CEO of Direct Line, the United Kingdom's fastest growing insurance and financial services group, describes value simply as 'best service, best price – speed to market'. His top 40 executives listen to hour-long, random extracts from 'customer-to-call centre' conversations as they drive to and from work. Like Marks & Spencer's executives' weekly probe into every facet of their customers' satisfaction, the process is one of listening, seeing and learning. Databases, made for the purpose, do all three.

Two marketing managers demonstrate the difference

Two marketing managers who, apart from their names, could almost have been twins, live as neighbours in a leafy suburb in Essex in the United Kingdom. The same age, 41, both are married and have a boy and a girl each. Both are marketing managers on near identical salaries, and have the company BMW, pension and health schemes. Habits, hobbies and holidays are parallel.

There is only one significant difference between them to account for the radically different outlook and aspirations of one from the other. On the customer database of their (mutual) bank, one is shown to have bought the family home in 1984, the other in September, 1989. Negative equity and an overdraft can damage your plans and your purchasing patterns. Recognizing the difference and responding accordingly can also affect a supplier organization's profitable and valued relationship with its customers. But only the learning organization can do this. All need to learn because the pressures on businesses to improve is growing daily.

Six drivers to improve productivity and profitability

1　Owners of businesses are forcing the pace on profitability. Bemused by failures among the business giants and conscious of the accelerating pace of change, shareholders are becoming more expert and more demanding.
2　Competitors, subject to the same pressures, are responding in innovative ways, often forced to by new entrants to the market or global challengers arriving in force accelerate this process.

3   Recession and economic fluctuations (for example, interest rates, exchange rates, house values and so on) cause havoc among predictions, changing the relationship between customer and organization with every rise and fall of markets.

4   Social and legislative change go hand in hand. The social implications of rising and falling markets are codified into legislation to guide or protect consumers – often too little and too late to match the extent of the underlying change. From homes to holidays to PEPS (Personal Equity Plans), boom and bust are matched by the legislation.

5   Information technology (IT) – computing and communications – is changing the rules of the game faster than any other single driver. Accelerating faster than most can accommodate it, ten years from today IT will have caused more dramatic changes in the world we now know than the invention of printing in the fifteenth century. Perfected by Gutenberg in 1487, printing made possible German, French and English versions of the Bible, making the Reformation inevitable within 25 years. The effects have reverberated down the centuries, affecting successive generations of nations in war and peace, in order and in strife, right up to the present day.

6   Service is an integral part of the product, and all organizations are forced to acknowledge this fact. Even food retailers, who have pushed the concept of self-service to an extreme, now recognize this and are restoring customer assistance in all forms so as to keep their customers. Most are using customer and local market databases to learn the precise characteristics of these customers and their shopping patterns. They must do this, not only to keep up with competitor supermarkets but more significantly, to keep up with their customers' changing needs and tastes.

Astute customers, knowing staff

We are overwhelmed with information. New sections in our newspapers, new magazines, surveys, polls and reports, more radio stations and an explosion of TV channels add to the noise and confusion of the modern world. At work the flows of information across our desk are accelerating ever faster. People's capacity to assimilate this information cannot keep up. With a growing sense of unease, people dispose of materials they have not read, conscious that they may be throwing away something of value.

But customers and all other consumers of information are becoming more knowledgeable and more demanding. Our power as consumers is that we each, individually, have a specific agenda. Pursuing that agenda, we read, watch television, talk to friends and colleagues, and develop expert knowledge. We concentrate on learning our special subject – food, wine, travel, insurance, skiing, scuba diving, cars, computers, and so on – better and faster than any generalist member of staff facing us in the store, the bank, the travel agency. The gap between us and them is widening.

But new technologies for both computing and communications now offer methods to ensure systematically that astute customers are met by knowing staff. Imagine the satisfaction one would feel if the next telephone conversation went something like this: 'Right, Mr Smith, I've clearly understood your question and your reason for asking. I don't know the answer but I know a database that does.' The implication is, first, that the customer/product database exists, and secondly, that the service agent knows how to use it.

Customer segmentation and profitable service

Different groups of customers have different needs. Some groups have more to spend and more needs. With them a lifetime relationship can be very profitable for a company. In 1988, for example, Midland Bank in the United Kingdom was able to ascribe a national value to that middle-aged, mid-career group, the 'empty nesters' whose children had left home, of approximately £175 per person per year. This group represented 19 per cent of the bank's customer base, had 30 per cent of the income, but only consumed 20 per cent of the consumer bank's cost allocation, thus yielding 43 per cent of the consumer profit. New products, and in 1989 a new bank, First Direct, were the result.

Other groups of customers offer a very low yield but have lifetime prospects that are disproportionately valuable: for example, students are an expensive but vital investment for banks. In 1988 students accounted for 0.5 per cent of the income, 8 per cent of the costs and 'lost' the bank £135 per customer. But one day, a significant number of them would be valuable 'empty nesters' themselves and would have passed through more or less profitable stages of banking relationship on their way there.

Segmentation is a discipline that has advanced beyond recognition from the early days of definition by home ownership, which included, for example:

- Affluent professional families.
- Less affluent families who own their own homes.
- Poor families who own their own homes.
- Retired homeowners.
- Younger tenants in government housing (ditto, older).
- Young adults in rented accommodation (ditto, older).
- Rural dwellers.
- Police and armed services.

Segmentation by consumption (for example, cars, clothes, electrical goods, leisure) or by lifestyle/lifestage (for example, young, upwardly mobile professionals or double income, no kids and so on) has been layered on top.

So too has been added attitudinal segmentation such as 'traditionalist', 'opportunist' and 'minimalist' in the world of banking and financial services, and other similar terms for parallel worlds of consumption. The important point here is to recognize that all such terms are indications of value grouping, by which businesses can best organize their product and service offers and target their marketing resources.

THE BUILDING BLOCKS OF LIFETIME VALUE

Businesses need to establish three separate but integrated sets of processes before they can fully capitalize on the actual and potential purchase value of their chosen customers. These sets – building blocks of lifetime value – are as follows:

1   The first block consists of the marketing processes – research and analysis to product development and communication.
2   The second block is a complete understanding of the customer's purchasing process from the information gathering stage through comparative evaluation to purchase and after-sales criteria.
3   The third block, essential to ensure that the customer relationship is sustained over time, is the establishment of an integrated marketing, sales and service system that is dynamic and alive to every shift in market conditions and customer mood and behaviour. This model combines elements of the other two blocks, but is both interactive and iterative and uses the learning gained from each experience to refine and improve itself and therefore the customer relationship.

Marketing – an updated classic

The classic marketing model has always recognized that for each market segment – and tomorrow, for each individual – there is a service proposition that blends an ideal mixture, a mixture of products/services; the people with the skills and knowledge to serve them and the processes by which every step of each transaction is carried out to perfection, time after time As customers shop in ways ranging from traditional to innovative (for example, mail order, telephone, store or depot, Internet or virtual shopping mall), the concept of premises expands in extraordinary new directions. Each variant heightens the need for systematic new ways to 'know' and to 'learn' your customer.

In time, the continuous and satisfying performance(s) of an organization in meeting their needs, builds customers' expectations and creates trust. Incremental layers of consistent behaviour are translated into a clear positioning for a company and the development of a brand whose products always match or exceed the promises made in advertising or direct marketing. BMW and Mercedes have spent decades building up six steps in their customers' service proposition and planning ways to prolong the relationship and make a profit. Coca Cola and Kodak, Norstroms, Waltons and Marks & Spencer are equally good, 'old' examples. Direct Line and First Direct, Dell and Microsoft are more recent.

Lifetime relationships are built on the back of products, people, processes, point of sale, performance and positioning that deliver not 'added' value but real value every time. Thus there are six steps in the marketing process:

1   Identify and analyse the customers with whom one will do business.

2   Identify the precise needs and expectations of both current and new customers.
3   Produce products and services that: (a) meet those needs; (b) make profits; and (c) differentiate.
4   Communicate and deliver the products/services to the chosen customers that meet expectations and yield a profit.
5   Commit the sales and the service force to standards of skill, knowledge and performance required to build relationships.
6   Analyse performance in minute and regular detail so as to improve each step at each iteration with each customer.

This last step is increasingly seen as the area in which a company's databases can be used to upgrade performance, productivity and profits in parallel with customer satisfaction. Only by taking advantage of the integrating power of new computing technology will a business realize the full potential of its customers, the productivity potential of its assets, especially people, and the value of all its past investments.

Effective and profitable marketing into the millennium will be a knowledge-based activity. The knowledge lives in the following databases:

- Products and services/sales.
- Service and quality/total quality management (TQM).
- Customer information systems.
- Finance, accounting and operational systems.

Customer purchasing processes

Choose your distribution channel and you choose your customer base. In the development of modern marketing and distribution there was Harrods, 'the top people's store', and there was Woolworths, with Marks & Spencer in between. There was the Queen's bank, Coutts & Co., and Girobank, the post office bank with four or five large clearing banks in between. In the 1980s even these outlets subdivided their distribution networks; within 1 000 variations there were many historic precedents and a few indicators of future success. As a manufacturer, your overriding strategic aim might well be simply 'to get on x's list of suppliers', and not much more.

In 20 years, and noticeably since 1989 when the six drivers described earlier accelerated, most of those easy definitions have been blurred or disappeared. Customers themselves have thrown off the defining characteristics given them by marketers to help identify profit potential. Increased affluence, social mobility and buyer sophistication have been amplified by the fragmentation of the media through which we learn of products and sources.

In all of this, an unseen strand of research and development, concentrated on the customer purchasing process, has changed the rules of the game. The best evidence of this movement has been the proliferation of direct services. Clubs and catalogues are everywhere. In addition to selling financial services *211* direct, the Virgin group in the United Kingdom recently published a 400-page home shopping handbook, listing *over* 1 000 companies in everything from baby products to office equipment, travel, wine and womenswear.

If you were Peter Wood, founder of Direct Line, offering 'best service, best price – and speed to market', where would you start a new business and how would you avoid the capital cost commitment to a bricks and mortar delivery network? One step would be the identification of likely customers and products that met their needs. The other, a detailed analysis of the best methods and costs to match the buyers' needs. Put at its most simple, the purchasing process moves through the following stages:

- Awareness
- Interest
- Offers
- Comparisons
- Decisions
- Purchase
- Delivery
- Service
- (Redress, replacement)
- Repeat.

At a recent conference on call centres in Holland, everybody present noted that the only two stages in this process requiring a physical presence are delivery (and today even that can be achieved by a courier or parcel force service) and redress/replacement. Note that Holland is taking advantage of its location at the centre of Europe, its people's great facility with languages, excellent telecoms and advertising networks, and the proximity of Schipol Airport and courier services, to make itself the European centre of businesses, bypassing the bricks and mortar elements in customer service.

But the more the reliance on traditional methods of sales and distribution is reduced, the greater is the need for integrated customer and product databases to provide service that meets expectations and builds trust in the supplier's brand. Such integration can only be achieved with the third building block of customer lifetime value.

Integrated customer information, sales and service – a live system

By now it should be evident that only by tracking systematically every step of the process, from identification of customer through needs analysis to customer transaction, fulfilment and follow-up, may a lifetime relationship be maintained. At its most comprehensive, the process involves 12 or 13 stages, as follows:

212   1.   *Predictive marketing model.* Banks have for years anticipated customer loan performance by the use of credit scoring tools to assess the likelihood of repayment. As the relationship develops, a second 'score' emerges based on many transactions – the behavioural score which acts like a seeding mechanism in tennis. Analogous to the behavioural score and informed by much cross-referenced information from a number of databases, it is now possible to establish a purchase potential score. This is more than a simple 'profile' score, which only matches a customer against their peer group's propensity to buy a certain product. The purchase potential score assumes that if a control group of customers in a selected decile has purchased 'x' products and represents the high end of the purchase scale, then a similar group of customers at the lower end of actual purchases could be said to have a high purchase potential. In addition, the history of an individual's purchases are traced to ensure that wasteful repeat offers are eliminated. The predictive marketing model recognizes customer groups ranked in order of purchase potential, and refines and updates itself after each iteration with the customer, recording successes and failures and noting specific manual input from service and fulfilment agents.

2. *Business priorities.* Every business seeks to correct anomalies in its performance and status. From balance sheet matching of assets and liabilities, to business mix, margins and brand positioning, there are priorities to guide the strategy and tactics of a business.

3. *Marketing environment.* Shifts in economic conditions such as interest and exchange rates or legislative climate (deregulation, reregulation) are also determinants in the selection of target customer groups.

4. *Customer priority groups.* An analysis, described earlier, of Midland Bank's customer groups led to an intense concentration on higher-value customers disenchanted with traditional banking. The result was First Direct, a 24-hour telephone bank with low distribution costs and high perceived value to its customers. In a market distinguished only by poor service and price wars, the radical proposition offered by First Direct not only retained Midland's total share of market (by switching valuable customers to a new deal), but also created a recruitment vehicle which attracted 75 per cent of its new customers from competitor banks.

5. *Customer scoring.* By adding back the purchase potential scores of individual customers within the customer priority group, First Direct was able to establish specific customer targets and reaggregate them into groups with whom to talk.

6. *Target customer groups.* Back in their new, clearly defined target groups one can begin the next stages of matching products to needs and communications plans to support promotional campaigns.

7. *Products matched to prospects.* Reflecting business priorities, product benefits and features and innovations, each of the target customer groups is matched to products to maximize availability and supply and the capacity of the sales and delivery forces. In the future, this process will be reversed and products will increasingly be matched to customers whose emerging needs have been identified earlier and built into the production process. The winning organizations tomorrow will not be those who are led by their customers but *213* those whose antennae tell them in advance what raw materials to buy and what new products and services to build. (In recent years, car companies have translated 'safety' requirements into ABS and airbags, 'security' into deadlocks on car doors, engine immobilizers and tracker car recovery systems.)

8. *Customer prospects, language and location.* Products matched to customers leads to communications methods and style. Direct responses, tracked by individual respondent and then plotted by like group, now gives a business precise data on the date, day and location of each newspaper or magazine advertisement triggering a call or a coupon. The language and the graphic style can be measured for effectiveness against a 'control' advertisement, quickly promoting successful treatments of a subject over those that waste money and space. Campaigns shorten to bursts of communication, precisely targeted. In terms of 'language' such communications start to become a dialogue where clarity and effectiveness are rewarded with extra sales. Pace of development quickens, boredom is reduced and the whole relationship between customer and supplier is improved qualitatively. The brand's positioning changes to reflect the growing level of trust. Not 'added' value, real value.

9. *Delivery method.* Reflecting the earlier discussion on purchasing processes, delivery methods are evolving to present information and create awareness in new and different ways. Rather than hide competitor information, confident suppliers promote it as an indicator of their candour and their belief in their own product. Decisions are informed by graphic illustration, comparison charts and tables, showing the implication over the long term of actions taken now. All these treatments feed off the product databases which have been equipped to translate text and numbers digitally into new and more friendly forms. Orders are processed via application forms where all the known data on a customer has automatically appeared from their customer file. Transactions are logged by customer membership number and new records created and stored so quickly that the service agent's very next conversation will relay the last exchange in the customer/company dialogue. Choice of order placing medium is at the customer's discretion: telephone only; telephone, telephone, letter; telephone, face-to-face discussion, letter/fax; telephone, computer on-line transaction; on-line transaction only. All are now possible. All ease the friction and reduce the barriers between client and supplier.

10. *Transaction processing/fulfilment.* Previously the largest component, biggest time waster and source of most irritation and least satisfaction, the processing stage is reducing in salience. Confirmatory letters and documents based on single, simple data entry – in the case of direct businesses, an audio log – reduce frustration and improve the value of the relationship. In this instance (and as noted at the beginning of this chapter, in the case of the insurance company), there are double benefits for the supplier. Revenues, short and long term, go up along with increased customer happiness; costs come down, profit and productivity improve. Staff satisfaction should not be ignored. The disciplined, skilled workforce of today take an inordinate pride both in good service and success. This adds more value to the dialogues with customers

whom they 'learn' and 'know' well.

11. *Customer response – immediate after-sales service.* Companies often wait for complaints to indicate problems. Despite every TQM measure, complaints happen and are invaluable sources of knowledge and opinion on one's products. Only now, as responses quicken and analysis tools track developments closer to the point and time of sale, are companies recognizing the power of close-quarter research in improving their prototype products. Engaging customers in research and development has been a recent phenomenon in the computer industry where 'beta-testing' is a norm. The concept of 'proto-cycling' has endless possibilities in every other industry, offering businesses the opportunity to recycle best knowledge and best practice into every stage of the development model. Already a fact in cars, computers and kitchen appliances, the model life cycle is being accelerated to unimaginable speeds. Competitive edge will be measured as much in these terms as ever it has in price or width. The US military describe the difference between the old and the new styles of weaponry in simple terms. With a rifle, the sequence of success is based on 'ready, aim, fire'; with a guided missile it is 'ready, fire, aim' adjusting for enemy countermeasures and barriers in terrain, en route. Thus proto-cycling will increasingly call for companies to fire as soon as they are ready, aiming through the tracking mechanisms of the product and customer systems as they go.

12. *Customer response analysis; long-term service.* In a further extension of the military analogy just described, customer response analysis on a macro level will yield many opportunities to see previously unconnected strands of development, trends that indicate long-term directions and the possibility of different connections. Military intelligence has long relied upon the assiduous collection of data and other inferences to create patterns to guide strategy. New computing powers, especially those harnessed to graphic representations (colours, shapes, movement), yield extraordinary results for military databases. They will do the same for commercial databases.

13. *Update the database.* Repeat the process.

THE CUSTOMER DATABASE

How to build a customer database

In a chapter built on processes, it would be inconsistent not to end with a set of processes by which to build a customer database. The steps are as follows:

1 Recognize the following crucial factors:
   (a) That the lifetime value of the customer is a precious one which can only be extracted with excellent systems, expert analysts and practitioners, and a set of tools that must both grow in capacity and change to reflect new methods and approaches.
   (b) That a full-blown customer database is the foundation stone of every business dealing with customers in groups and customers as individuals. Whether it is British Airways, Tesco or Citicorp, the *215*

British Labour Party, a BMW franchise, the local furnisher and decorator or the radio cab service around the corner, businesses that own and use a good customer database will do better than those who do neither.

(c) That your competitors will not pass up the gold mine that their own customers represent. Having perfected their techniques at home, they will turn their attention to your territory.

(d) That the value of the lifetime relationship is only fully achieved in the development and retention stages, once the more expensive, early stages of recruitment and welcome have been negotiated.

2 Customer-based information is paramount. The relationship is with the customer, a member of the club. The 'member's number', therefore, is the point of reference throughout the life of the relationship. Information is held as follows:

(a) customer details;
(b) product holdings;
(c) product usage;
(d) communication history; and
(e) cross-references to other (customer) databases.

Without the focus on customer membership number, most of the value of a customer information system is dissipated. Even businesses with large stores of historic data have to confront the issue of reorganizing every piece of data that they hold so that it depends on the customer number.

3 Customer database processes fall into three stages, as detailed in Figure 16.1.

Recruitment	Cross-sell	Retention
Via customer offers	Use customer base	Focus on most valuable customers
Via questionnaires	As platform	80 : 20 rule
Via promotions	Segmentation	By segment
Via credit card	Understanding Buying patterns	Learning
Via . . . and so on	Dialogue: ongoing, two-way learning	
Learning		

Figure 16.1   The three stages of customer database processes

4 Data processes to allow detailed analysis in '3D' are assembled and used as shown in Figure 16.2.

This brief outline of data processes clearly underlines the variety of sources that must be systematically combed to ensure that the 'dialogue' between company and customer is based on the latest information.

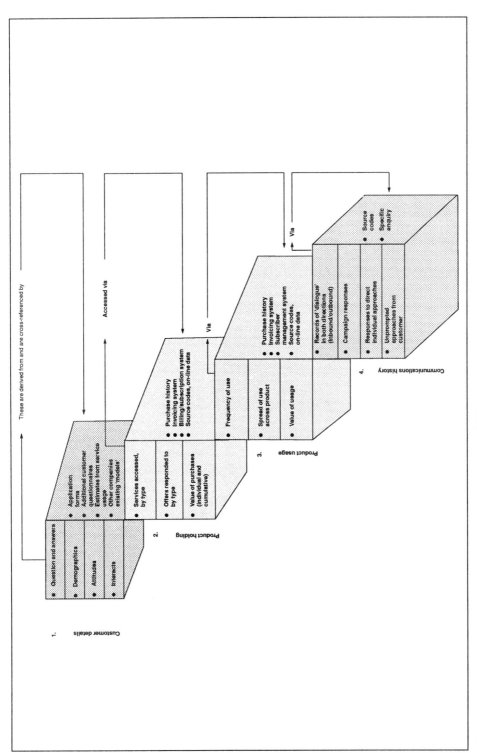

Figure 16.2 Detailed analysis of data processes in '3D'

Interrogation of the customer database

Once the client/company communications channels have been established, usage can be tracked to show which of the various channels is preferred by the individual. Two vital information flows result from assembling and displaying the database in a three-dimensional (3D) model which combines segments, channels and products on each face of the cube.

Customer's product needs and usages are displayed on the faces of the 3D model showing segments and products by:

● frequency;
● individual value;
● cumulative value;
● purchase patterns;
● profitability; and
● source code references.

Customer's communication needs and usages are displayed on the obverse face of the 3D model, combining segments and channels; the information emerging here includes key measures such as:

● cost per response;
● cost per sales;
● customer lifetime value after communications; and
● comparative cost/benefits using different media/communications channels.

Customer database: analysis of deciles

One of the most valuable outputs of the well-formed database is the clear, numerical definition of the relative value and characteristics of the top 10–20 per cent of the customer base versus say the bottom 10 per cent. In the United Kingdom's direct banks and insurance companies, statistical analysis shows that the 80:20 rule applies; in some cases the top 10 per cent of customers are worth up to 50 per cent of the business's potential value.

Knowing who these people are and where they come from is the first step to finding out more about the more valuable customers, and not only cross-selling to all of them, but also recruiting and cross-selling to those who look like them. Equally but oppositely, the bottom 10 per cent once identified may not warrant any expenditure of money, time or resource, because chasing them and cross-selling to them would yield little or no value.

One powerful, recent example of the value of analysis by deciles was demonstrated in the UK business press this year. The general insurance industry has now cross-referenced every insurance customer and prospect by a 6-digit postcode. By matching customers and locations to historic concentrations of risky and risk-free business, companies are now able to identify by individual street the risk and related premium. To see the '10 best streets in the UK' and the '10 worst streets in the UK' identified by name, with levels of risk indicated by more violent shades of red on the A-Z street map, is a reminder of how far and how fast the business of commercially available databases is advancing.

Database tools are available on the open market

Less than 15 years ago the retail director of Thomas Cook's 250-strong branch network in the United Kingdom spent three days with his branch managers on a local catchment area marketing exercise. Each branch manager came equipped with a list of customer names and addresses and their past purchases, an ordnance survey map and a set of coloured pens.

Today, the whole exercise could have been carried out with the help of a CD-ROM from CCN Marketing's MOSAIC service. The CD-ROM cover describes 'Britain's rich and complex social history' and the intense 'variation in local demographics, lifestyles and consumer behaviour'. 'One objective ... to give you the clearest possible picture of each of the 12 MOSAIC groups and the 52 MOSAIC types ... foremost geodemographic classification ... fineness of geographical detail.' The multimedia CD-ROM displays a comprehensive set of statistics, maps and photographs, sound and video 'providing a detailed picture of each of the different target audiences that MOSAIC enables you to identify and target'.

From MOSAIC to MapInfo, the desktop mapping software, new technology that allows you to visualize your data at a stroke. The new 'weaponry' of database technology is already so profuse that a recent trade show was as impressive as the Farnborough Air Show for the awesome display and choice. Like aviation in general and military aviation in particular, the database wars involve an endless process of renewal. Organizations looking to realize the lifetime value of the customer must have a clear strategy based on what Don Peppers and Martha Rogers, authors of a book on marketing technology, called 'The One to One Future: budding relationships one customer at a time'.

Organizing around the customer

In the early 1990s Midland Bank in the United Kingdom debated the virtues and benefits of replacing the marketing director with a customer director, whose responsibilities would have involved a trial reorientation of the bank's information, sales and service systems around the customer. The imminent absorption of Midland into a larger worldwide group precluded this radical development, which would have been based in large measure on the pathfinding work at First Direct, the independent, subsidiary telephone bank.

The technologies to achieve that sort of reorientation are everywhere at the present time. Banks and other distributive businesses will not be competing for very much longer with their peers but with all forms of new entrants and new challengers ranging from AT&T and BT, to Microsoft and Oracle. *219*

Manufacturers will re-enter the fray, throwing off the restraints of their current retail distributors.

All contenders recognize the lifetime value of customers. The tools are now available to realize the extraordinary potential of existing and new customers. Some have brands that may be extended into new fields of commercial customer relationships. First Direct and Direct Line have already shown what can be done from a standing start with current technology. There may be some truth in the observation that 'God created the world in 6 days – but he didn't have an installed base'.

Value

The lifetime value of customers will be realized only by the development of full and open relationships that grow over time. As choice and complexity increase, the answer I want to hear from every sales and service agent in every business I deal with is: 'I understand exactly what you're talking about. No, I don't know the precise answer to your question, but I know a database that does.' As the warm, confident person on the other side skilfully handles my enquiry or request, I will not only enjoy this transaction but look forward to the next.

17 Using the customer database*

Professor Merlin Stone

One of the biggest problems facing companies, particularly the larger ones, is how to make sense of the mass of marketing and service data they now collect. In examining this problem, the first step is to recognize the variety of customer management situations that exist, as shown in Figure 17.1. The figure simplifies the position. So, in mobile customer service, some retailers have home delivery and home service (for example, for domestic appliances). Airline sales forces call on big travel agencies and corporate accounts, and some retail financial services have calling sales forces, but none of these are totally essential requirements. Where addressing customers by name is concerned, retailers are resorting to customer loyalty schemes, while many fast-moving consumer goods (FMCG) suppliers have built or are building databases of customers who are loyal and/or respond to promotions, so as to increase their influence over these customers and support their marketing in the face of pressure from the large retailers.

The situations these companies face lead to a set of general market and customer management system requirements, which we will now examine.

CUSTOMER MANAGEMENT AND MARKETING SYSTEM REQUIREMENTS

From a systems point of view, the situations listed in Figure 17.1 have produced a set of customer management and marketing requirements which systems and software providers (whether external or internal) are being asked to meet. These requirements are as follows:

* The material in this chapter is based on research sponsored by IBM (UK) Ltd.

Key business Requirements	Utilities	Airline	Car makers	Rapid distribution	FMCG suppliers	Large retailers	Regional public sector	Retail finance
Address customers by name, usually at home or business address	Y	Y	Y	Y	P	P	Y	Y
Regular remote debiting of over 1m customers, with need for payment management	Y	N	N	N	N	N	S	Y
Mobile service with customer contact at customer location	Y	N	N	Y	N	N	S	N
Geographical pattern of customer behaviour a critical dimension	Y	Y	Y	Y	Y	Y	Y	Y
Exploding number of product/service categories	Y	N	Y	N	Y	N	S	Y
Thousands of products	N	Y	N	N	N	Y	N	N
Move from monopoly to deregulation, plus large number of major competitors	Y	N	N	N	N	N	S	N
High visibility of customer service, with poor customer care quickly noticed	Y	Y	Y	Y	N	Y	Y	Y
Strong public/government interest	Y	Y	N	N	S	Y	Y	Y
Sector-specific government regulations on handling customers	Y	Y	Y	N	N	N	Y	Y
Large physical network of facilities and/or connections	Y	Y	Y	Y	N	Y	S	Y
Long-term individual customer relationships an essential requirement for performance	Y	N	Y	Y	P	N	S	Y
Individual customers may want to be managed at various points in network	Y	Y	Y	Y	N	Y	S	Y
Need to work with and invoice customers through agents	Y	Y	Y	Y	N	N	S	Y
Need to market to and through large customers and to final consumers	Y	Y	Y	N	Y	N	N	S
Strong risk of commoditization if branding and customer management are weak	Y	N	N	Y	Y	Y	N	Y

Key: Y = yes; N = no; P = possibly; S = some.

Figure 17.1   Customer Management Situations

The database requirement

This category can be split into four very different kinds of requirement:

1 The prospect/customer/agent requirement, relating to information on customers and agents (for example, identification, location, characteristics, needs, attitudes, satisfaction and so on) and their interaction with the supplier (for example, enquiries, purchases, invoices, after-sales service and so on).
2 The product/service/resource requirement, relating to information about the company's products and services (for example, identification, characteristics, production/usage/sales – past, current and forecast – resources required or used, inventories, prices, profit/surplus and so on) and the marketing and service resources used to support them (for example, media spend, overheads).
3 The market requirement (that is, status of the market of which the company's activity forms a part, including both the above kinds of data). This requirement is particularly important for suppliers who are dealing with consumers through agents, such as retailers, as direct customer data may be hard to obtain. Also, the agents' concern for category management and their own competitive position puts a premium on analysis of the relationship between supplier, agent and market data.
4 The management requirement, which relates to data on the company's plans for managing the market and schedules (dates, budgets and so on) relating to those plans.

In nearly all the sectors mentioned in Figure 17.1 (utilities, airlines, carmakers and so on), all these requirements have been the subject of much attention and investment as companies come under pressure to improve customer service, which in turn is often due to competitive pressures. For large companies, the process of matching the customer to the product or service is mirrored by the requirement to match information about the two.

Product/service management requirement

This requirement relates to the process by which the company determines its product or service range and manages it into the market. The best known of these processes is the brand management process, which has recently come under pressure because of customer management requirements, such as category management.

Customer management requirement

The customer management requirement relates to the process of interaction between the company and its customers by which the latter are recruited, managed and kept satisfied. This includes requirements such as order entry, *223* invoicing, sales support, telemarketing, direct mail, loyalty scheme and competitive defence management, promotional management, after-sales service and the like. Here, the main development of the last few years has been the need to integrate what has been called the customer dialogue function, so that customers feel that wherever they are in contact with the company, they are recognized and receive the level of service that is appropriate to them.

For a telephone contact, for a particular customer requirement (for example, bill payment or query, sale, service request, initial call for or response to a marketing or sales initiative), a script is defined for managing the dialogue, supported by interfaces with all appropriate databases and functions above to ensure completion of the dialogue in order to meet customer needs and update the supplier's representation of its relationship with the customer. The environment for call handling usually requires automatic cell distribution (ACD) functionality. The batch part of this function relates to response handling and fulfilment associated with direct mail and may therefore be required to work together with billing functionality.

Agent management requirement

Agents are a special category of customer, whose needs relate mainly to meeting a number of key targets which are precisely defined, rather than final consumers, where needs are often more 'softly' defined. The precise nature of this requirement depends on whether the channel is 'managed'. In managed channels, the supplier's norms, processes and systems for managing final customers are integrated with the agent's (as in the motor industry), and the customer data problem is less severe than in non-managed channels, where data is the subject of competitive secrecy and special negotiation or the intervention of third-party agencies who purchase the data for analysis and provision to suppliers. However, in all cases, the need to analyse the agent dimension exists because of the supplier requirement to be able to determine which agents are successful and how to both exploit and contribute to their success, whether it be directly or through expansion of the category.

Analytical requirement

The customer and agent management requirements are, of course, the two that have led to the explosion in the amount of data available to companies about their interaction with their customers and markets. This in turn leads to the analytical requirement, which exists mainly because of the need for companies to prioritize – strategically and tactically – the various customer management initiatives open to them. For example, for the direct marketing requirement, complex statistical and creative analysis is used to target customers for marketing and sales initiatives (including targeting customers for loyalty and competitive defence initiatives). Lists of customers are then produced for actions in relation to customer dialogue.

THE CHANGING ANALYTICAL REQUIREMENT

So how should companies cope with the very large increase in the volume of data now being recorded in and about their businesses, through research, operations or external data suppliers? Here are two examples of the kinds of data flows that exist:

1 FMCG brand managers can now obtain reports about the performance of their brands (sales, shipments, inventories) within a few hours and sometimes on-line.
2 Many utilities, financial services and industrial marketing companies' managers now have comprehensive databases which record not only purchases but also sales enquiries, responses to promotions, customer service episodes and a mass of detailed data about customers.

These examples illustrate two key dimensions that exist in data analysis – customer and product.

The customer dimension

Companies which have direct contact with final customers (rather than through agents) need to become expert in analysing customer data, in order to answer questions such as:

- Which customers do I want to market to, and which not?
- How do I want to manage my customers?
- Which products and services would I like to sell to particular kinds of customer?
- At what price, through which channels of distribution, and when?

These questions apply whether or not the contact is managed directly or through an agent. The key requirement is that the individual final customer is known to the supplier. The data requiring analysis situation is typically in-depth customer data, combined with sales and service transaction and promo-tional response data. We call these companies the 'customer optimizers'.

The product dimension

Companies which do not know the identity of their final customers, whilst applying customer management disciplines to their immediate direct cus-tomers (for example, retailers), must use product management to get the best results. We call these the 'product optimizers'. Their own and market data on price, promotion, inventory levels and movements and shipments is used to determine the optimum marketing and distribution policy. Their data is organ-ized along the product dimension and the key analysis task is to make sense of *225* the possibly millions (for example, for a grocery brand leader) of transactions each day in which their products are involved.

The hybrid customer and product focus

Some companies are hybrid product and customer optimizers. Many service retailers (for example, retail finance) can identify their final customer individually but must also work hard to optimize product marketing in order to make the best use of their sales capacity. Some retailers focus entirely on product-optimizing merchandising, but others have discovered that individual customer management has become possible through store cards (for example, credit, debit, loyalty). In practice, most companies are hybrids to some degree, requiring both product and customer optimization.

For all groups – both the product optimizers and the customer optimizers, and now the hybrids – the key analytical question is: How can I manage the vast flow of information that I have at my disposal so as to (a) understand what is happening; and (b) take control (as fast as possible) over what is happening and gain advantage over my competition. The answer to this question differs according to whether the company is a product or customer optimizer, or a hybrid (for whom the answer is a combination of the two). It also depends on the situation of the individual company. However, the answers for each type of company have in common the need for a clear *decision analysis framework*.

Decision analysis framework for the product/service optimizer

Here, the volume of data flow is so great that the most urgent need is to distil from the data the scope and scale of any required management action. In many cases, since management does not have a clear idea of the possible full range of required actions because the data indicating the need for action comes from so many sources, required actions are simply not taken, with the result that product/service decisions are not optimized.

In the decision analysis framework for product optimizers, management actions are classed as follows:

- *Nil action.*   No change is required to operating decisions, operating parameters within which operating decisions are taken, marketing and sales policies, or longer-term strategies.
- *Operating action.*   A change is required to adjust one or more variables (for example, inventory levels) within existing operating parameters.
- *Operating parameter change.*   A change is required to the parameters which normally determine operating actions (for example, the lower limit to inventory which triggers replenishment).
- *Policy change.*   A change is required to a marketing or sales policy (for

example, a promotion should be terminated, an advertisement should be rerun).

- *Strategic change.* A more fundamental change is required (for example, a product should be withdrawn or relaunched).

Figure 17.2 gives a simplified example of this analysis framework for a given product of an FMCG supplier.

	Management situation			
	Operating	Operating parameter	Policy	Strategy
Trigger issue	Cash flow slows	Short deliveries to retailers	Promotional coupon return rate too high relative to sales	Continually declining sales relative to category
Data combination which revealed need	Invoice totals Payment totals	Orders Shipments	Sales ex-retail Retail reorders Coupon return rate	Sales trend Category sales trend Usage and attitudes research
Key indicators	Days sales outstanding	Order fulfilment ratio Inventory level	Coupon/sales ratio	Share of category
Diagnosis of cause	Delayed payment by key supplier	Replenishment level set too low	Malredemption ratio abnormally high	Weakening brand values
Action required	Pressure to pay	Increase replenishment level	Kill promotion if possible Do not repeat	Reposition or withdraw brand

Figure 17.2   Decision analysis framework for product optimizers

This classification of management actions can be combined with a categorization of decision areas to produce a clear statement of requirements for the analyses to be undertaken. For example, the decision areas for an FMCG supplier, might be categorized to include:

- packaging;
- manufacturing and inventory volumes;
- distribution strategy and tactics;
- standard costing and pricing;
- promotional pricing;

- promotional offers;
- settlement terms;
- media advertising;
- product range definition;
- individual brand/product definition and positioning, and so on.

Each of these decision areas has its own list of trigger issues and the resulting analysis requirement.

To make the most of the much increased flow of data available to them, product optimizers must:

1 Determine in advance all the possible trigger issues they might be faced with and the possible diagnoses of the reasons for these issues.
2 Use their reporting systems to set up an overall approach for triggering management action, which allows senior marketing management to concentrate on the most serious (not just strategic) issues, and automate as far as possible the process for managing other issues.

Obviously, this procedure represents a big investment, but unless it is done, there will be an increasing tendency for marketing management to revert to the days when they spent too much of their time contemplating screens and reports and too little on making the right policy decisions.

THE CUSTOMER-OPTIMIZER

One of the key requirements for success is the company's ability to classify customers into different groups to be managed differently, either tactically or strategically. Our research suggests that companies which are most successful in this area have developed the following hierarchy of segmentation.

Analytical segmentation

This is the use of customer and market information to identify where there are indeed different groups of customers with different profiles, needs and so on. This approach often starts with very broad questions such as: 'What kinds of customer do we have, what is their behaviour, which products or channels are the most successful?' The segments that are identified in this way may never be subjected to different marketing or customer service policies or strategies. For example, they may be aggregated into a target market for a particular customer service initiative. The main criterion for the successful use of analytical segmentation is that any resulting strategies work overall because they are based on in-depth understanding of customer needs. Analytical segmentation often provides the foundation for the other three types of segmentation.

Promotional segmentation

Promotional segmentation is the identification of different groups of customers for targeting particular initiatives (for example, in marketing this might
be a direct mail promotion, in service it might be providing an enhanced level
of service in an attempt to improve customer retention). A given customer may
belong to a whole series of different segments, according to the objectives of
individual initiatives. The chief criterion for the success of response segmentation is the success of the individual initiative (that is, whether response rates
met expectations, whether customer retention rates rose).

Strategic segmentation

The identification of groups of customers who need in some sense to be handled differently is described as strategic segmentation. For example, in mass-
market financial services, it is particularly important for suppliers to identify
loan customers who are likely to be higher credit risks (in which case they are
usually only accepted as borrowers at an interest rate which covers the risk
premium), or mortgage customers who are likely to be rapid switchers (for
example, of mortgages), in which case they may only be accepted for loans
with higher penalties for earlier cancellation. Conversely, low-risk or in-
frequently switching customers will be targeted and subjected to intensive
marketing, and particular attention might be paid to the quality of customer
care they receive.

The central idea of strategic segmentation is to ensure that each actual or
potential customer is allocated at a minimum to at least one strategic category,
membership of which carries certain implications for the marketing policy
likely to be directed towards them. Also, it is wise to avoid creating too many
categories, with attendant risks of both overlap (a given customer being subjected to too many marketing initiatives or restrictions, which have to be
resolved by prioritization rules) and overcomplexity (because of the number
of segments that need to be addressed with different marketing policies). A
particular issue of importance for both strategic and loyalty segmentation is
the movement of customers between categories.

Delivered loyalty segmentation

Delivered loyalty segmentation is a special case of strategic segmentation
and consists of the identification of particular groups of actual or potential
customers whose loyalty is critical to the supplier. This criticality normally
relates to the volume and profitability of business coming from this group of
customers, but may also be related to other variables (for example, political
sensitivity). Identification of this group is followed by the development *and*
implementation (or 'delivery') of a practical marketing approach, including
branding, relationship management (through whichever channels are *229*

appropriate), promotional management, customer service and systems support, which works to draw that group of customers into a special, long-standing, mutually committed and transcending relationship with the supplier. The components of delivered loyalty segmentation are usually no different from ordinary loyalty programmes. What is different is the *focus of the company* upon the segment and commitment of resources to managing the segment profitably and well. Perhaps the most important feature of such segmentation is the degree of commitment of the company to the segment. This means that the company must have fully bought in to the segmentation approach.

The systems and management characteristics of these four kinds of segmentation are summarized in Figure 17.3.:

	Types of segmentation			
	Analytical	Promotional	Strategic	Loyalty
Technical approach	Can be left to expert systems and data-mining approaches	Expert/data mining approaches may be used, but test results are key	In-depth business understanding required to define issue	In-depth business understanding required to define issue
Senior management involvement	Not required, except to ensure that capability exists	Required if promotions are a large share of marketing budget	Important in defining areas of strategic focus	Absolutely critical because of subsequent commitment to comprehensive loyalty management approach
Customer contact implications	Depends on conclusion	Customers experience correctly defined and targeted promotions	Customers may be required to give more information and should find that they are being offered more appropriate products and services	Customers who are loyal, or who have the propensity to be so, experience more integrated management, whatever the contact point and whatever the product or service

Figure 17.3 Systems and management characteristics of the four types of segmentation

THE SYSTEMS AND MANAGEMENT INTERFACE

So far, we have identified the need for management to anticipate in some detail the kinds of analysis they need to perform on marketing data. But how can management act to achieve improvement in data analysis? Our view is that the answer lies, first, in how the business requirement for data management is specified, and secondly, in the consortium of systems and software suppliers used.

Business requirement

Here, the recommendation is quite simple. It is only too common for large companies, in specifying their requirement for marketing, sales or service systems, to omit the analytical dimension, which leads, as we noted earlier, to this requirement being tagged on at a later stage. In turn, this may mean that some kinds of data are neglected altogether, such that collecting, storing and analysing them is made difficult. The analytical dimension should therefore be included – down to the level of detail suggested in this chapter – for product and customer optimizers.

Systems and software suppliers

Customer and market management systems, most broadly defined, are normally the result of the work of a range of suppliers, typically including:

- *Hardware.* Ranging from mainframes to PCs and including operating system, networking and printing provision.
- *Telecommunications.* To connect sites, customers and suppliers.
- *Database software.*
- *Transaction software.* Defined as anything that handles the flow of product and service to the customer and payments from the customer.
- *Marketing and sales software.* Defined generally as software designed to support the acquisition and retention of customers (in some cases this overlaps with transaction software).
- *Analytical software.* To extract and integrate data held on other software.
- *Data providers.* To provide data about the external world (for example, markets) to match with company data, enhance it and in some cases to help interpret it.
- *Facilities managers (including bureaux).* To carry out work done by some of the above and by the company's managers (marketing and/or systems).
- *Consultancy.* To integrate the whole.

This consortium of suppliers is usually put together very carefully over a period of years, so companies are reluctant to disturb it. Analytical software is often omitted from this carefully constructed consortium, or introduced too late and without the management insight to ensure that analysis provides the required solid foundation for business success.

CONCLUSION

In this chapter, the data analysis problems of large companies have been considered. The conclusions are straightforward, as follows:

1 The analysis required by product optimizers and customer optimizers is different, but many suppliers now realize that they have to do both.
2 Companies should recognize that they will normally need to consolidate and synthesize data from different sources (for example, internal, commissioned market-research, generally available market data and so on) and functions (for example, marketing, sales, finance, customer service, manufacturing and so on).
3 A successful approach to analysis requires the company to define the key analysis dimensions in some detail and then to ensure concentration on a few areas which can be backed by management action.
4 The needs of different users vary and different users will require different tools to support their different management actions. Data, however, must not be dispersed to different users as a result so that the capability for coordinated analysis is lost. Hence there is a need for central consolidation of data to facilitate reporting to all parts of the company.
5 This approach will be much facilitated if the data and analysis requirement is defined as part of the wider business systems requirement, and if the consortium of suppliers is built around this concept.

FURTHER READING

Beane, T.P. and Ennis, D.M. 'Market Segmentation: A Review', *European Journal of Marketing*, **21**, (5), 20–42.

Hopwood, D. and Carter, V. (1988), 'EPOS and its Impact on the Retail Environment', in West, A. (ed.), *Handbook of Retailing*, Aldershot: Gower, 320–33.

Stone, M. (1994), 'Managing Customer Loyalty: Schemes, Themes or Dreams?', *Customer Service Management*, **4**, September, 31–4.

Stone, M., Bond, A., Lockhart, S. and Coombs, J. (1995), 'Retail Customer Loyalty – What Works in Practice', *Customer Service Management*, **7**, June, 22–5.

Stone, M. and Woodcock, N. (1995), *Relationship Marketing*, London: Kogan Page.

18 Direct marketing

Tony Williams

My purpose in this chapter is to show how direct marketing, when fully integrated into a company's business planning and operating philosophy, can have a direct and measurable impact on customer satisfaction and perceived service quality. Through case histories, I will show how direct marketing can narrow the gap between brand image and actual customer experience, thus enhancing the credibility of the brand image while simultaneously maximizing the power of service as a brand differentiator. Lastly, I will offer some practical pointers towards the kind of changes which may be necessary if a company is fully to exploit the potential of direct marketing as a means of creating sustainable competitive advantage in the customer service arena.

THE THEORY - 'THE CUSTOMER SERVICE CONTINUUM'

First, however, we have to place the current and future role of direct marketing in some sort of historical perspective, and to do so, we must take a few steps back.

Divided we were

Once, the marketing mix was an amalgam of disjointed functions. Each function operated within its own narrow remit, making its contribution to the sales effort with little regard for the other functions. This was far from 'total' marketing; the sum of the whole was less than the sum of its parts.

Image advertising, on the one hand, could build a brand identity, while on the other, disciplines like direct marketing and sales promotion could be deployed tactically to boost short-term sales. Meanwhile, the customer service element of the mix – what was occurring at the real-life interface between customer and brand – was for the most part neglected. Treated as a minor auxiliary function, few recognized its key role in the success equation.

The symptoms were plain to see. A lack of emphasis on customer service was creating disharmony. And where there was disharmony, so too was there discord. In many instances, the brand promises being made were not being kept. It was down to poor customer service delivery. An angry letter from a bank manager, a thirty-minute queue at the supermarket checkout, a defective washing machine, or a two-week wait for an automotive spare – any of these failures of customer service delivery were also failures of brand management, but they were not perceived as such. They were seen purely as service level shortfalls. Divisiveness still had its grip.

While advertising agencies carried on producing advertising – commanding the lion's share of the marketing budget – customer service as a vital concept received scant attention. To most marketers pulling the purse strings, it was 'just another department'. Complacency, inertia and a lack of investment fuelled the neglect of the customer/brand interface.

The result? Most organizations were failing spectacularly to invest in managing the real-life relationships with their customers. Relationships to them existed for the most part in the abstract – between the company as an advertiser of brands and the customer as a consumer of advertising. While this partial formula could shift product in the short term, it could not sustain a brand in the long run. This fractured structure was choking the life out of brands.

But that was then.

The customer service continuum

The days of the divided marketing mix have now gone. 'Total' marketing is general practice, and with it, there is a growing realization that quality of customer service delivery is central to the long-term survival and success of any brand. Moreover, first-class customer service is now recognized *as a continuous concept* that must be embraced across all lines of demarcation within the marketing mix. The customer service continuum is with us.

To understand why the perception of customer service has changed, we must understand how the consumer has changed. Five main axioms of behavioural shift point to the emergence of a new, more demanding breed:

1 *Consumers have become more cynical.* Consumers, now well-versed in the tools of the advertisers' trade, are less inclined to believe in a brand promise purely on the basis of traditional advertising.
2 *Consumers are demanding more information.* As consumption patterns move towards service-oriented products, consumers need hard information, not merely persuasive sales patter.
3 *Consumers expect higher standards.* Customer satisfaction, for so long the cornerstone of customer service philosophy, is no longer enough. Anything less than customer delight will prompt defection to other brands. Customer promiscuity is not to be underestimated.

4 *Consumers are more individualistic.* The mass-marketing techniques of yesteryear no longer apply. To build a long-term sales relationship, customer communication must take place on a one-to-one basis.

5 *Consumers need proof above all.* To believe in a brand, consumers must experience the brand promise working in their lives. Without experience, their brand loyalty can't be won.

Recognizing this behavioural shift amongst your customers is the easy part. From now on, the going gets tough.

Like it or not, you can't address this new, more discerning breed of customer with the old tried and tested techniques of customer service delivery. That won't be enough. You must act and you must innovate, drawing on the very last methodology.

It's not just your customer service department at stake, it's your brand's future too, and the quality of your customer service delivery is now an essential attribute upon which that will be judged. Unless your brand meets the delivery challenge, it will wither and die.

Delivering the brand promise through direct marketing

Customer service is no longer the optional extra ingredient in the marketing mix, but a central component of the core brand personality. As such, it must provide the consumer with a real-life manifestation of the brand promise. Direct marketing, by its nature, is a prime way of delivering that promise.

To see why, we will first put the role of pure image advertising into context. Its purpose, as its name suggests, is to create an image of the brand in the consumer's mind. The image thus created forms the basis of the brand's promise to the consumer. Image advertising, because it is an intrinsically passive process, can only present the brand promise. It can't facilitate the consumer's first-hand experience of the brand, so it can't make a direct contribution to the delivery of customer service.

Why, then, can direct marketing succeed where traditional advertising falls short? Let's consider the core characteristics of the medium which make it such an effective vehicle for delivering the brand promise:

- *It engages the customer.* Direct marketing is not a passive medium. It engages the consumer and demands action. Involvement with the brand equals experience of the brand promise.
- *It is a personal medium.* Executed well, direct marketing doesn't just create the impression of a one-to-one medium – it *is* a one-to-one medium. This is central to superior customer service delivery.
- *It is a brand-literate.* High strategic and creative standards in direct marketing ensure that the personality of communications are consistent with the brand identity.
- *It can handle large numbers efficiently.* The increased sophistication of data management techniques has increased the scope for highly tuned targeting, even when handling 'mass' audiences.

235

- *It is measurable.* Direct marketing can be tracked effectively over long periods. In an age where accountability is everything, direct marketing can visibly prove its effectiveness on the balance sheet.

Direct marketing, in short, is an interface medium. It works at the point where customers experience the brand. And, because experience is of the essence, direct marketing delivers real proof that the brand promise can be believed in.

THE PRACTICE

There are six important ways in which direct marketing can facilitate customer service.

1. Listen to your customers, then deliver

There are no exceptions. Listening to your customers is a prerequisite for first-class customer service. Without precise knowledge of what your customer wants, delivering finely tuned customer service is out of the question. Listen well and you receive hard, usable information on your customers. Neglect the listening process and delivering your brand promise is reliant on guesswork.

Direct marketing, with its ability to exploit sophisticated data management techniques, allows you to eliminate the guesswork and apply the 'science' of listening to your customers as true individuals. Then you can deliver what you know your customers want.

One of the most successful cases in point comes from Britain's First Direct bank. As the country's first 24-hour telephone banking service, they eschewed traditional banking values and decided boldly that First Direct would be 'a bank that's built around you'. Implicit in this statement was a pledge to deliver a truly personal banking service. This service would have to be highly responsive. It would have to relate to the customer needs on a one-to-one basis. Above all, it would need to understand and fulfil each customer's individual needs. First Direct were playing a high stakes game. The quality of their service delivery would make or break the brand.

To achieve the required high quality of service delivery First Direct (as the name suggests) made direct marketing the cornerstone of its marketing strategy. They recognized the need for – and so created – a leading-edge customer management database. With this, they would be able to manage information on their customers to such a fine degree – and access it so easily – that they would comfortably achieve the level of personal service implicit in the brand promise. Stripped of the cumbersome baggage of traditional banking and armed with technology and direct marketing know-how, this newcomer would easily outperform other banks in terms of service delivery.

To open an account, all new customers were asked to complete a lengthy questionnaire, or, if they preferred, engage in an informal question and answer session over the telephone. A little arduous on the face of it, but First Direct turned an apparent hurdle into a tangible customer benefit. They made a

236

promise. They promised that never again would they ask customers for this information. It was tantamount to entering into a contract of trust with their customers.

First Direct had a priceless combination: accurate, usable customer data and an implicit degree of trust with their customers. This would provide the launchpad for a finely tuned customer communications programme. They could now execute a highly profitable cross-sell strategy, offering the kind of financial products they knew their customers would be interested in. Having invested in the system infrastructure needed to eliminate the guesswork, they would never have to resort to the indiscriminate selling of financial products that customers loathe so much.

Embracing direct marking in every sense, First Direct turned their brand promise into a readily available reality for thousands of customers. Instead of building a bank according to the bank's needs, they promised and delivered 'a bank that's built around you'.

2. Applying the art (and science) of anticipation

Love, psychologists tell us, is anticipating another person's needs. Any unprompted gestures which demonstrate empathy, generosity or kindness will go a long way in strengthening a relationship.

This may not be a handbook on happy marriages but we can't ignore the parallels. We must be 'relationship marketers' in every sense and, for that reason, we must recognize anticipation as a powerful tool for delivering first-class customer service. Because anticipation is a gesture that goes above and beyond the call of duty, it invariably delights the customer. But it should not have to rely on the quick wits of an individual. Applied as part of a conscious strategy to enhance customer service delivery, it can prove remarkably effective in winning customer loyalty.

Let's turn our attention to the charm of Freeport, Maine, US home to mail-order maestro L. L. Bean. The quaint picture postcard setting is nothing short of idyllic. The locals ooze friendliness. Freeport exudes a truly timeless feeling, as if untouched by progress. Surely not the kind of place you stumble across a thriving mail-order business driven by a relational database? Appearances can be deceptive. Since its birth in 1912, L. L. Bean has used information about its customers to enhance customer service delivery. And in so doing, has achieved spectacular incremental sales. What happens at the company–customer interface lies at the very heart of this success story.

To L. L. Bean, the people they put on the end of their telephone lines are much more than just order takers. Everything about them speaks volumes for the L. L. Bean brand: their charm, their polite telephone manner and, key to it all, their ability to engage in a perfectly natural, no-pressure dialogue with the customer.

Imagine you call them up to place an order. You speak to Ada, a real charmer of a 58-year-old. You want a wool crew-necked sweater. She offers a choice of colours but recommends oatmeal as her own personal favourite. 'Are you buying it for a gift?' she enquires. 'Yes, it's for my nephew's birthday,' you reply. 'Would you care for us to send it to him, giftwrapped?' 'Why certainly.' Ada, still oozing New England charm, proceeds to capture both sets of details (yours and your nephew's) on the L. L. Bean database. Your nephew is subsequently delighted upon receipt of the crew-necked sweater.

Almost a year later, you receive a telephone call – from Ada at L. L. Bean. 'Good morning, it's Ada speaking. Remember me? The oatmeal crew-necked sweater?' The gentle reminder is followed by an offer to send another gift (a pair of cotton drill slacks, suggests Ada) to your nephew for his birthday. How could you turn it down?

It's a remarkably simple success story. By capturing customer data, in this case the nephew's birthday, L. L. Bean can anticipate their customers' needs in a dramatic way. This same attitude of mind, applied to other key items of customer data, would no doubt yield a host of other incremental selling (or rather, service) opportunities.

In terms of delivering the brand promise, the confirmation for me was not the quality of my nephew's sweater, it was the experience of Ada's service, made possible by the relational database that won me over.

3. Make them feel special

The term 'valued customer' is now in all-too-common usage in marketing circles. It is an explicit recognition that customers have a value well beyond that of the first sale. For a growing number of companies, repeat purchasing, cross-selling opportunities, member-get-member schemes and so on, all increase the potential value of one customer. To tap into this potential, most marketers readily accept that a customer must be made to feel special. What is less readily accepted is the means by which you do this.

First, we should be clear about what is entailed in making your customer feel 'special'. It certainly does not mean writing to them 'as a valued customer' and dangling some ill-conceived offer under their noses with no relevance or perceived value. Widespread though it is, this practice is nothing more than tokenism. If you want to capture your customers' hearts and tap into their lifetime values, token gestures are not enough. To make people feel special, you have to do something special. Pamper your customers. Surprise them, delight them, amuse them. Overwhelm them with your generosity (as they perceive it).

Direct marketing, because it lends itself so naturally to a one-to-one dialogue with the customer, can achieve this. A particularly fine example, involving a highly refined application of databased techniques, is American Express's monthly statement mailing. As a vehicle for demonstrating how much you value your customers, a monthly statement mailing has real potential. Too often though, it goes to waste. Companies simply 'piggy-back' a statement mailing with a cheap, non-targeted promotion (one offer for all), creating little interest or response from customers. Enter Amex to buck the trend.

Exploiting direct marketing's ability to deliver customer-specific messages,

Amex now use their statement mailing to communicate offers built around the individual transaction patterns of the cardholder. The data-processing requirement is highly complex, but the idea is beautifully simple. It works like this. Amex track the spending patterns of the cardholder. Then, through their network of third-party partners in the retail section (for example, hoteliers, restauranteurs, car rental agencies) they can create individually tailored offers to match the observed spending patterns. Say, for example, you use your Amex card a few times at one restaurant, your next statement might include an offer of a free bottle of wine when you next dine there. Cheers, Amex!

This is customer service delivery at its finest and direct marketing at its most ingenious. But the essential point is this: Amex customers are more likely to use their Amex card than any other piece of plastic they may carry in their pocket.

4. Match the service delivery to their individual expectations

High-quality service delivery at the customer–company interface is, as we have stated before, the lifeblood of a successful brand. What your brand promises the customer in the advertisements, it must deliver at the interface. If it fails, the customer won't be back for more.

Achieving high-quality delivery at any point of customer contact is not simply a case of applying preset formulas across the customer base. Different customers have different expectations. Some will want the red carpet treatment, others will not. Some will crave extra information, others will shun it. In an age where our customers are as differentiated as our product, delivering service to meet individual expectations is critical to a brand's success.

Direct marketing, because it can reduce a mass audience down to highly defined market segments, can play a pivotal role in achieving differentiated customer service delivery. In practice, differentiated delivery becomes differentiated product.

Again, look how Amex have used direct marketing to reinforce their market presence. While the American Express Card is certainly highly regarded, Amex saw scope for a premium brand to meet the service expectations of their wealthiest customers. Enter the American Express Gold Card, a standard setter for high-end niche positioning. Though the brand promise is announced through glossy awareness advertising, it is *delivered* and *sustained* through the medium of direct mail. Customers signing up for the Gold Card are treated to an exceptionally high-quality customer communications programme. No detail or expense is spared: personalized letters and monthly statements are printed on beautiful embossed paper stock; a suitably intelligent tone of voice is maintained throughout all literature; lavish photography (with lavish budgets) ensures a consistently upmarket look.

The so-called purist direct marketers might balk at the sheer expense involved. How do you justify it when there is no *immediate* payback? Sadly, these folk are the brand-illiterate dinosaurs of the direct marketing world. Direct marketing, because it is an integral part of front-line customer service *239* delivery, must live up to the customer's expectations of the brand. If it falls short, the brand promise falls flat on its face.

Another superb application of direct marketing to deliver appropriate customer service takes us into the fiercely competitive world of first-class air travel. In this niche of the market, a loyal customer is so precious that airlines will spend vast sums on service enhancements, many of them (for example executive lounges, limousine services) highly publicized. But the carte blanche approach – ploughing money into visible service enhancements regardless – ignores the notion of the customer as an individual. It assumes every first-class traveller wants to be treated like an ambassador. The reality is, no two travellers are the same.

British Airways (BA) recognized this and embarked on an ingenious direct-marketing initiative. They asked senior cabin crew to provide detailed input on customer's individual preferences. What was their favourite tipple? Did they usually request a window or aisle seat? Did they like to watch the in-flight movie? Because these people were high flyers in every sense (company directors, government ministers and a surprising number of frequently flying parcel couriers), members of the cabin crew were able to provide detailed answers to such questions.

BA found they had enough useful information to compile a database which was then merged with the BA transactional database. The result? All customer correspondence with this key segment of BA's market could now address passenger preferences in a truly personalized manner. It was a victory in two respects. First, it built loyalty by ensuring truly tailor-made delivery of the BA brand promise. And second, it engaged BA's human software (the cabin staff) in the process.

5. Turn negatives into positives

Even the most visionary organizations can't foresee everything. Accidents will happen. Outside forces may intervene. Unpopular measures are sometimes a necessity. But any problem, however serious, need not become a crisis of the brand – providing it is managed within the framework of customer service delivery.

When a negative threatens to undermine the quality of customer service delivery, the delivery of the brand promise itself is placed under threat. For example, cost-cutting measures may force an organization to withdraw a free customer helpline. A mail order firm might decide it can no longer bear the brunt of a 14-day refund promise and abandon it. In such instances, the company must face reality. The perceived lowering of the level of customer service must be pre-empted with a countermeasure. Attack, using the tools and techniques available to the direct marketer, is often the best form of brand defence.

As a case in point, on its launch in the United States, the Toyota Lexus LS400 executive saloon car was billed as the perfect car. The Japanese, supremely *240* confident of their automotive technology, were challenging Mercedes head on.

Three months later, a minor fault was discovered in a small number of LS400 models. Above a certain speed, the car's aerial was producing a rather distinctive hum caused by vibration. Hardly an earth-shattering discovery, but still one that compromised the Lexus 'perfect brand' status.

To be quite frank, most American or European manufacturers would have let a small issue like this simmer for a while, waiting for customer complaints to dribble in. But not the Japanese. They seized the opportunity to turn a negative into a high-profile brand-reinforcing exercise using direct mail. They wrote to all Lexus owners asking them to leave their cars on their driveways overnight on a certain date, claiming that something remarkable would happen to them. They weren't disappointed. On the appointed evening, Toyota technicians visited the homes of Lexus owners and replaced the old aerials with new aerials (tested in wind tunnels to ensure that all vibration noise had been eliminated). Each car was valeted and a bouquet of flowers was left outside the owner's door. A 'with compliments' note was attached to the windscreen explaining what had been done.

The audacity of the exercise was breathtaking. Yet it was more than just a exercise in public relations. Because it expressed supreme confidence in the Lexus brand, through inspired customer service delivery, it turned a potential brand manager's headache into a highly effective brand-building exercise. And the expense of the exercise – was it really worth it? A quick glance at the increased propensity to repurchase amongst Lexus owners provides a swift answer to that.

Another instance of a negative turned into a positive involves Micrografx, a software supplier specializing in graphics programmes. Like many software suppliers, their free on-line help service was proving uneconomic as it was being abused by unregistered and pirate users. This completely worthless audience was milking the customer service resource to the point where the cost was proving too much to bear.

Knowing that withdrawal would be very unpopular with registered users, Micrografx wrote to them introducing a new concept in user support: a registered user club they named Interface. For a nominal fee, all registered users would be allowed five free calls per year to the helpdesk, while bolt-on benefits such as exclusive product previews, member discounts and invitations to software seminars raised the overall perceived value of membership.

Interface was much more than a token gesture to compensate for the loss of a free on-line help service. It demonstrated quite clearly to the customer that Micrografx were interested in providing a high-quality, value-for-money service for its real (that is, registered) customers. Instead of humble apologies for the loss of one service, Micrografx came up with a superior replacement and emerged from a potential brand crisis in even better shape. That's the added bonus here: when you introduce a perceived improvement in customer service delivery to pre-empt a negative, your customers end up loving you (and your brand) even more.

6. Add service value to differentiate the core product

The proliferation of brands in recent times has left the consumer dazed and confused. Even more disquieting is the proliferation of look-a-likes and me-too brands. The consumer's limited mental shelf space is now overstocked with products that can barely be distinguished from each other. In the age of the discerning, heterogeneous consumer, brands have never appeared so homogenized.

In the quest for real, sustainable brand differentiation, raising the level of service value associated with a product can pay important dividends. Historically, the task of differentiation has been the responsibility of the image advertisers, whose remit has centred on a product's point of difference (and if a product doesn't have one, they'll create one for you). It can still work (sometimes), but it fails to address one issue at the heart of sustaining long-term differentiation: that is the value of service attached to the core product.

We can't fool ourselves. The customer has no way of knowing the level of service value attached to a product without *experiencing* it. A glossy advertisement or TV commercial does not constitute experiencing service, but direct marketing, on the other hand, does facilitate experience. It does provide a tangible, company-to-customer channel through which the customer can get a real taste of service value. That leaves us with only one conclusion: direct marketing, when utilized effectively to add service value to the core product, will contribute to long-term differentiation.

For further enlightenment about differentiation, let us turn finally to the automotive industry – so often accused of churning out amorphous lumps of pressed steel set apart only by their badges.

Recognizing the limits to differentiation achievable through advertising, Vauxhall Motors sought to improve the service value associated with a new car purchase. They opted for a direct-marketing solution. By creating a totally personalized post-purchase communications programme through direct mail, they added real value to the core product. Here's how they did it.

Vauxhall owners are invited to take part in the 'Index' programme when they buy a new car. Owners are provided with a glove box folder for which they can select, every three months, their choice of loose leaf inserts. A range of inserts are made available, covering a wide range of motoring-related subjects: days out in Britain, hotel and restaurant guides, touring in Europe, caravanning – in fact, any subject that might relate to the motorist's lifestyle is on offer.

As a result, the Vauxhall owner is able to build up a totally unique reference guide, mirroring exactly their motoring-related interests.

The single thought underpinning the Index campaign - 'the pleasure of owning a Vauxhall doesn't end when you drive it off the forecourt' – belies its hard-edged commercialism. Here was a channel for ongoing one-to-one dialogue – a channel to deliver a service benefit that could actually be experienced. Through this service, Vauxhall created an enduring point of difference on that crammed mental shelf space. And in case any accountants out there are sucking in their cheeks and whistling, just check Vauxhall's latest customer figures on propensity to repurchase.

THE CHALLENGE – HOW EVERY COMPANY CAN PUT THE THEORY INTO PRACTICE

The following six key reference points will provide an invaluable framework for the brand manager seeking to enhance customer service delivery – and thus the delivery of the brand promise – through direct marketing.

1. Keep the brand at the forefront at all times

Make sure the brand is right at the heart of your thinking. The perceived quality of customer service is seen by the customer as a crucial brand attribute, so service delivery via direct marketing must be consistent with the brand identity, both strategically and creatively.

Define the parameters of your brand identity. What is the brand personality? The required tone of voice? The appropriate look? And what are the customers' expectations of your brand?

Once defined, make every effort to ensure your direct-marketing programme remains within these parameters, while still achieving its delivery objectives. Think back to the Lexus example. The brand parameters demanded that Toyota did not simply send out a letter to customers recalling models for aerial refits. The 'perfect' status of the brand called for something out of the ordinary.

The lessons are simple. Don't be a slave to conventional wisdom by adopting the so-called tried-and-tested solutions. Let your brand guide you to the best route. And let your strategic and creative thinking (again driven by the brand) lead you to the most appropriate solution. Not only will you achieve your customer service delivery objective, but also the brand itself will emerge all the stronger for it.

2. Attention to detail

Be obsessive with the fine detail of service delivery. Remember that every single piece of customer communication will contribute to the customer's perception of your brand, whether positively or negatively.

To ensure that *all* communication is faithful to your brand, start by broadening the definition of your customer interface. Try to list every possible point of contact between your brand and your customer, from the receptionist at your head office right through to the instruction manual or compliment slip included in your product packaging. If anything falls short of the customer's expectations of the brand, find a way to improve it.

If you use agencies, retailers or franchisees at any point of customer contact, make sure they too share your passion for detail. Don't just expect them to act as spokespeople for your brand – provide the right incentives for them to do so. Be rigorous about quality control to protect your brand. Scrutinize all   *243* communication between your company and your customer. Is your level of personalization as finely tuned as it could be? Never settle for the easier but ineffective 'one approach for all will do' route.

This approach may sound like a tall order, but the underlying motivation is sound. Attention to even the tiniest detail will, by enhancing the perception of customer service delivery, work wonders in delivering your brand promise.

3. Initial investment equals long-term payoff

Enhancing service delivery through direct marketing is not a cheap option or quick solution. It is a long-term process aimed at building and sustaining your brand's reputation for first-class custom service delivery. You must therefore be prepared to invest in a first-class delivery infrastructure. This doesn't simply mean investing in the nuts and bolts of database marketing technology, important though that is. More importantly, if you are going to drive your customer service delivery with data, you need the human resource to do it. You will need highly competent data-capture personnel, systems analysts, data analysts and support staff. You will have to invest in training to ensure familiarity not only with the systems, but also with the whole service philosophy underpinning them. This in itself may constitute a challenge to the *status quo*.

Above all, don't be captive to short-term financial targets. You will need budget over and above that required to secure immediate sales targets. Remember Vauxhall's 'Index' campaign. Instant payback never featured among its objectives. The high initial investment needed to achieve the appropriate level of service delivery was justified by higher rates of vehicle repurchase – three, four or even five years further on.

Remind sceptics what you are investing in: the creation of a first-class customer delivery system to sustain the brand. Once achieved, the payback begins. Customer defection rates should drop (and with it the associated cost of retention programmes). Your efforts – and marketing budget – can then focus on new customer acquisition.

Above all, think long term. Enhancing service delivery through direct marketing is not the latest management fad. It should become a way of life for your organization. To command the kind of budget it needs, it must be fully recognized as a valid and valuable long-term business strategy.

4. Agree assessment yardsticks at the start

Always set targets. Senior managers love being able to quantify. They thrive on tangible results-based strategies and see little value in abstract theorizing.

When justifying the investment in a service delivery programme, turn this to your advantage. Show your bosses that direct marketing is, by its nature, a measurable medium. Set out precisely what your success criteria will be: how you will measure the effect on brand loyalty of your initiative; and how you will measure its impact on sales – in the short, medium and long terms. Direct marketing can invariably provide the answers to such questions, so exploit it to the full. And, of course, be certain that your success criteria dovetail with the wider business objectives of your organization.

If securing budget for your initiative proves an uphill struggle, concentrate instead on the merits of a low-cost pilot programme. Present your proposals, along with your assessment yardsticks, and ask for budget to embark on a pilot scheme. If your pilot works, you can go back to senior management with hard evidence of success.

Once your service delivery programme is under way, make assessment yardsticks the objective for everyone involved – project managers, customer service staff, agencies and suppliers. When your human resources are focused on meeting service delivery targets, they are focused on your brand.

5. Educate and motivate internally

Embracing direct marketing to enhance service delivery requires more than a shift in emphasis. For most organizations, it will represent a sea change. For this reason, don't imagine you can execute your service delivery plan single-handedly. You must take people with you, from the boardroom all the way to the front-line salesforce. Educate your senior managers. Use informal tactics and persuasion to make your case. Draw on successful case studies to build up your own argument. Point out how new entrants to your market are embracing the new methodology – and threatening to steal market share. When you frame it in terms of long-term brand survival (and not simply a customer service initiative), the people who matter will sit up and take note.

6. Staff empowerment

Empower your front-line salespeople. They are potentially your most valuable asset in the whole process of enhancing service delivery. Ask them about their gripes. Ask them what they know about your customers (remember how valuable this proved for British Airways). Ask them to tell you how they would perform their roles better – if given the right support. Don't skimp on training or investment in advanced data-capture systems. When you make life easier for them, you also make it easier for them to deliver better service. Widen their scope of responsibility at the interface: the more they can act on behalf of the company, the more they will represent your brand to the customer.

The essence of staff empowerment is this: to your customers, *your staff are the ambassadors of your brand*. When their behaviour, as perceived by the customer, lives up to the expectations of your brand, the brand promise has been fulfilled.

19 Telemarketing

Peter Murley

Telemarketing – a word which, as yet, is still not in the dictionary, and a profession which has a bad and, in some circumstances, well-deserved reputation.

Marketing can be defined as the act of promoting the sales of products through means of market research, advertising, packaging and – inherent in those elements – the whole of the branding issue. Marketing aids both the acquisition and retention of customers.

The telephone is a method of communicating with prospects and customers and educating them regarding certain products and their key benefits, advantages, prices and options. This communication is usually through a call into a service centre of some description – an inbound call – where that awful word the 'punter' is often used to describe a caller, who can be either a prospect *or* a customer. This caller is normally enquiring as a result of some kind of pre-activity from marketing (for example, an advertisement, a piece of direct mail). Or the communication will be via a call from the organization itself – an outbound call – on a cold, warm or hot basis, to try and secure a new purchase, an additional purchase or gain a commitment to buy.

In other words, telemarketing is the art of combining marketing and selling. For this task we entrust, or should entrust, highly skilled, trained and motivated staff to use the telephone and gain business. In the best organizations these people work closely with the sales team; in others, they have taken the place of the sales team; and in a few, the boundaries between sales team and the telephone team are being redefined and working relationships changing. 'The sales person is dead, long live the sales person?'

THE TELEMARKETING IMAGE

However, for the worst organizations – and the worst organizations are those which people remember and on which, therefore, our perceptions are based –

teleselling or telemarketing is unsavoury or tacky and is associated with pressure techniques, appointment setting, down-market products and the visualization of double glazing and shower cubicles sales staff as prime examples of how not to do it.

Teleselling is often viewed as the non-face-to-face version of the idiot sales staff who pressure a sale against a fictitious special offer closing date. For some, teleselling is the art of throwing enough unsolicited rubbish at the wall and seeing how much of it sticks. Unfortunately, in the minds of the public, a lot of it does stick, and this makes the going difficult for those genuinely wanting to do the job professionally. The public often have a hostile view of telemarketing and teleselling – and in many environments the two facets are inseparable – and see the staff involved as a bunch of idiot robots, the equivalent of headless chickens who have no clue as to what it is they are doing, or as smooth-talking trendies who are out to make a few bucks, using their talents to dupe you into buying something you don't want.

However, we must do all we can to dispel such a poor impression. Telemarketing and teleselling has to gain a professional image, and be seen to be practised by professional and adult people talking to other professional and adult people. But *you* are the only people who can change the current image of telemarketing or teleselling – it is in *your* hands and *yours alone*!

Just bear in mind that telemarketing has all the attributes of a real winner – it is highly measurable, monitorable and focused, and it can be an extremely cost-effective way forward, given the right structure and controls and the right mentality.

THE ADVANCE OF TELEMARKETING

Whatever you believe and whatever you may think, telemarketing will shortly burst forth with a vengeance in the United Kingdom. It has arrived and it will not go away. The way people buy and the way they work are both changing. These changes will cause discernible shifts in our attitudes and approaches, and greatly increased expectations of quality and of customer service. With these changes too comes absolutely phenomenal advances in telephony technology, plus the rapid importation into the United Kingdom of proven products and systems from around the world, particularly the United States. And as these new technologies take a fast and firm grip, busy people, working increasingly from home, are finding a greater need to shop conveniently.

Within five years everyone will be involved in some kind of telemarketing, either as the recipient or the provider. In the United Kingdom, those who deliver telemarketing with the most taste and style, who service a true need, will be the winners. Those who use data intelligently and professionally to target their audiences correctly, and persuade them to listen and to buy, will be the survivors and the thrivers. Organizations which have a current customer base now but minimum product penetration will begin to use telemarketing to increase their penetration rates and save money as a result of targeting existing users – a cheaper option than accepting customer defections and then *247* attempting to buy new consumers. So customer satisfaction not only with your products and your services, but also with your professionalism and approach is what will count.

If you want to join in the race, and do it properly, then you have to accept that telemarketing at a professional level will become a core part of your business and one where you will be instantly exposed – exposed because your telemarketeers will be your absolute representatives and can be more powerful than your field sales staff; because it is frequently cheaper but often harder, to close a deal without seeing the customer face to face; because, since there are no second chances in this process, your telemarketeers have to make the first impression count; and because your telemarketeers' knowledge (or lack of it), approach and attitude will act as the brand image of your organization. In other words, telemarketing is a risk as well as a potential match winner.

DEFINING TELEMARKETING

Telemarketing is a thirteen-letter word.

T – telephony, technology and telecommunications

The technology of communication has arrived and the age of the telecommunications monopoly is over once and for all. BT and Mercury have been joined by Energis. The American telecom players are arriving by the boat load – either directly or indirectly – and they have skills, technology and techniques that will set the market alight. Cable companies in the United Kingdom will grow enormously over the next three to five years, for their investment is phenomenal and their potential penetration of the marketplace at all levels is huge. Mobile telecommunications is here to stay and its ramp-up potential is vast. The cost of phone calls is dropping and the attraction of telemarketing is its targeting capability.

E – empathy

The ability to relate to prospects and customers, to make a connection, to understand the requirement – all are paramount in the relationship that telemarketing creates.

L – loyalty

You not only require loyalty from your staff in order to make telemarketing a success, but also from your customers, who in turn will recommend others to your products and services, providing they are happy.

E – energy

248 The amount of effort or energy which people put into telemarketing reflects in its results. Staff involved in telemarketing require masses of energy to deal with a job which, at times, can create negativity and bad feedback. They need both energy and resilience.

M - measurability and monitorability

Telemarketing can be a highly measurable tool, given the right understanding of what it is you are trying to achieve. In many ways, it is far more controllable than many other forms of selling or marketing and its results are relatively *instant*. Telemarketing is *not* an exact science by any means, but is likely to be more exact than some other methods.

A - America

There are so many examples of how good the United States is at service and at telemarketing, yet we still believe that the United Kingdom is not ready for it. Why? What is so different about us? Why is excellent service and telemarketing not for us?

All the good software organizations have helplines and, particularly the American ones, pride themselves on their ability to diagnose and solve problems on-line and in real time. This creates a level of confidence such that the cross-sell is a natural outcome. Some of the largest call centres in the world have a helpline for users on which they will answer literally *any* question, regardless as to whether you have registered your purchase with them or not. How's that for faith in future sales? It is all about perception and what the customer or the prospect remembers as a good experience.

Research in the United States shows that people are more likely to stick with a brand and continue to buy more if they have had a good experience on a telemarketing line with a trained agent. Coors Brewing use interactive voice response (IVR) on an 0800 line to promote beer by running competitions. They can prove its effect on their brand imaging, and the addition of users to their database (for future marketing). Their telephone campaigns sell more beer. The US Stock Exchange can be accessed by IVR or via human intervention in order to gain access to share prices across the world – a telemarketing opportunity.

R - research

Before entering into telemarketing you must research your market and the way in which you intend to deliver your products and services – a golden rule of course in all forms of marketing. Once under way with your campaign, you should continually research your prospect and customer database(s) to provide more and more information, which will in turn help deliver products that customers want. Involving customers in the decision-making process is essential and telemarketing can help you achieve your objectives in this regard.

249

K - knowledge

Knowledge of your prospects and your customers makes the job of selling to them more effective. Moreover, providing your staff with knowledge of your market, products and services, together with your customer and prospect profiles, can only enhance your position and provide greater opportunities to convert opportunities into sales.

E - excellence

The chance to make mistakes in telemarketing or teleselling is enormous – as many organizations continue to prove day after day. Once you have made a mistake it is hard to recover as the message may well have circulated to a wider audience. Getting things right, and right first time, is a rule that applies equally to telemarketing as to any other part of your business.

T - training and tools

Investment in people *must* be backed by investment in training. Results require commitment and commitment needs *attitude*. Attitude, in turn, requires training. The use of tools such as IVR, AVR, ACD, predictive diallers, and software packages will help immensely in telemarketing.

I - in-house

This is probably one of the most controversial subjects in the telemarketing debate. Should outbound and/or inbound telemarketing be entrusted to a third party for anything other than the extremely short term, that is, for the absolute basics or the campaign overflows? If you truly believe that what you are doing or will do in telemarketing terms is at the core of your business, and if it 'adds value', then are you possibly abdicating your responsibility to hand that function over to another party who can make or break you? The people who determine your destiny should be your customers and *not* your suppliers.

There are a number of telemarketing agencies out there who are ready and willing to accept business from you. Some of them are satisfactory, and some are not. Some are better at inbound work and some at outbound – few are best at both. All have particular merit when used for overflow work or for a very specific and limited campaign. Most offer great cost advantages to the small or new organizations in the market, where fulfilment of material – the physical printing and despatch of any correspondence, bills/invoices, letters, order information, rate cards, promotional packs, information packs, etc., – is a requirement and a capability that they do not possess or cannot afford.

Using a third party is of great value in certain circumstances but you *must* choose those circumstances carefully. If you believe in outsourcing, then be selective in what it is that you outsource and tie it into your overall strategy and objectives. Do not outsource just because it is cheaper. The one aspect that an external agency using their own premises may struggle to offer you is representation of your culture and your underpinning beliefs and philosophy – particularly when you are but one client on a long list – *unless* the agency can replicate your culture in some way, perhaps by dedicating a group of staff entirely to your products or services.

However, an important advantage is that agencies do have experience of actually doing telemarketing. They *do* have a reasonable approach to systems and, usually, they *do* have integrated fulfilment and despatch capabilities. My experience in recent years is that new entrants to telemarketing totally underestimate the requirements of systems and of fulfilment, and often struggle to put these requirements together in time. So agencies can help. Those who can replicate your culture and provide true added value to your business are the ones to go for!

N - networking

Networking, not only your system so that data can be shared and used by all staff within the telemarketing/teleselling *and* sales teams, but also networking of information and networking within the industry at large so that you understand trends and developments.

G - gamble

Telemarketing is a gamble and a potentially expensive one. You must therefore plan it properly and think about its use before you jump into it. Like quality, telemarketing is absolutely *not* free, nor is it cheap. By thinking about it, however, you can minimize the gamble.

Finally, for good measure, here are a few examples of how telemarketing is and can be used to good effect:

- People use the telephone to order almost anything and couple it with their credit card. The Government are encouraging catalogue procurement and will use the telephone to place orders. Placing orders gives the opportunity to cross-sell and up-sell more. The possibilities are almost endless.
- Telemarketeers have access to customer data before the call is made, which allows all sorts of opportunities to those who are able to spot those opportunities, use them well. Many organizations rely on the telephone for their complete business and many have grown dramatically in recent years (for example, suppliers of stationery). The best organizations know the users of specific products and target future sales based on that knowledge.
- Financial services are being marketed over the telephone. Collecting debt or overdue accounts can lead to selling opportunities, not least of which is insurance or card protection.
- Even when you can't get through, messages on hold can often tell a tale *251*

of existing offers and products on sale – a continuous marketing message – something the sales person would find hard to do.

- Home shopping is used more and more by people, and telemarketing and teleselling being the reasons for the dramatic expansion in this field. Think of Innovations and other similar organizations, and the way in which they combine a written catalogue with a telephone ordering system. Think of the fact that when you have ordered you are on their database for life!
- Many organizations have systems which spot opportunities for cross-sales at the time of an inbound customer call, based on the profile of the customer and their usage patterns.
- Think of Internet shopping over the worldwide web – the possibilities for telemarketing and telesales are almost endless and growing all the time.

THE WAY FORWARD

One letter that telemarketing does not contain is P. Productivity, profitability and professionalism. The first two can be outcomes but they must be part of whatever your strategy is *before* you decide to proceed. Professionalism is what you must strive for or you will only help to perpetuate the views that others have of telemarketing. Professionalism comes from the level of service which you provide, and that depends on the quality of your staff, the training which you give them, and the investment which you are prepared to make in those resources. That investment is also crucial in systems and many a mistake is made in trying to make telemarketing work properly without adequate systems.

What it all comes down to, however, is people, people and more people. People are your customers, people are your staff. If you recognize their value, then you could well be on the way to success.

Whatever you do and however you decide to proceed – either by yourself or through a third party – don't ever doubt, first, that telemarketing has tremendous potential; secondly, that your product probably can be telemarketed, or marketed in a way that makes use of the power of telecommunications; thirdly, that telemarketing is here to stay in the United Kingdom, and that what you are now seeing is just the beginning of the process; and finally, that if you don't actually enter telemarketing now, then your competitor may beat you to it!

But please think carefully about what it is you will need in order to do the job properly. Think about your market and tailor your activities to meet your requirements and to do what suits your product best. Think about your objectives and rationalize them *before* you go ahead. Consider the options – some may be better, some may be cheaper than telemarketing, so a combination may be your best route forward. Having done all this, decide on the strategy, *plan* your way forward, then review the plans, and continue to plan and review *all* the time – in other words, follow the basic rules of business life.

20 Encouraging customer feedback

Charles R Weiser

Retaining customers over the long term is not simply a matter of measuring the successes and failures of sales and customer service programmes. Listening to customers and building a corporate culture which invites customer feedback, has a fundamental role to play in a company's drive towards both total quality and, ultimately, repeat business from loyal customers. Who wishes to further a relationship in which one partner never hears or takes note of the other?

THE ROLE OF CUSTOMER FEEDBACK IN IMPROVING LIFETIME CUSTOMER VALUES

To understand the role of 'customer listening' in nurturing customer loyalty, it is first necessary to understand a little about the components of a seemingly far removed topic – total quality. There is an irony in the practice of total quality, (that is, the pursuit of getting it right first time) that is not fully evident to many companies which strive for such perfection: total quality demands continual feedback on how a process, product or service has performed, and in particular, its variance in performance against specification. Customer feedback is a vital element of knowing how well a company is meeting its criteria and the promises it is making, and is an indication, first, of how in tune the company is with its customer base, and secondly, of its ability to retain customers who wish to remain loyal.

The man responsible, literally, for the Japanese revolution in quality, W. E. Deming, believed that companies who did not realize that service failures were a natural part of business were doomed to ultimate failure. The Deming cycle, often referred to as the PDCA – plan, do, check, act – cycle, is illustrated in Figure 20.1. It demonstrates that feedback from the market – learning from mistakes – is a key ingredient to achieving total quality. The Deming cycle is not unlike other quality techniques which stress that such 'variances of quality'

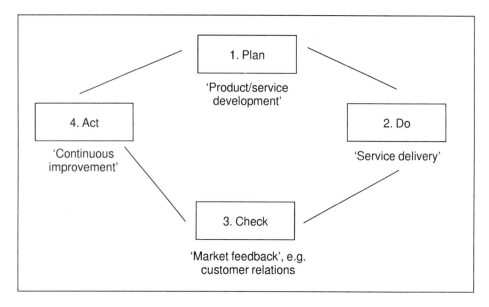

Figure 20.1   The Deming cycle

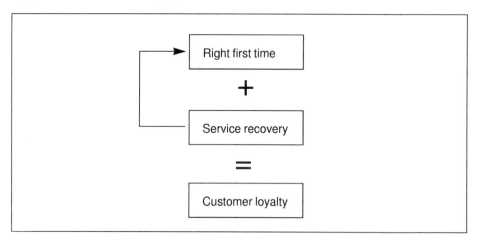

Figure 20.2   The loyalty equation

(whether they be service failures or substandard products) are an inevitable part of business. Hence Japanese industry's long-term obsession with the topic: that is, they believe service failures demand constant attention *because* of their inevitability.

The lesson for business in the United Kingdom is that 'getting it right first time' is a function of learning from service failures. British Airways (BA) employs a similar philosophy in its service quality development. British Airways believes in the loyalty equation as set out in Figure 20.2. This equation illustrates that developing better products and improving service over time is a function of both excellent service delivery and identifying weaknesses in quality.

Figure 20.2 also displays that it is equally important for companies to understand that simply satisfying customers when things have gone right first time is not enough to keep a customer's loyalty. A lesson not lost on Japanese industry from Deming's philosophies was his belief that 'customers that are unhappy and some that are *merely* satisfied switch. Profit comes from repeat customers – those that boast about the product or service' (my emphasis), which helps to amplify Japanese industry's commitment to customer and supplier relationships. Japanese industry's obsession with quality begins with listening to its customers, which, in turn, fosters stronger and longer lasting bonds with those same customers.

CUSTOMER DEFECTION AND ONLY 'GETTING IT RIGHT FIRST TIME'

A company which concentrates primarily upon the first half of the loyalty equation, (that is, 'getting it right first time') can create an unintended side effect – that company can tend to ignore the importance of service failures and the resulting comments from customers. If it only prioritizes the first half of the loyalty equation, the company may not be able to build a long-term, loyal customer base because it is ignoring episodic breakdowns in its relationships with its customers. Like any relationship, denial of the gravity of a situation, or ignoring an issue altogether, can cause strain and angst.

Many companies, in attempting to steer difficult relationships towards harmony, can take the position that the measurement of service quality collated by a customer relations (CR) function, or its equivalent 'service recovery' practitioner, is a necessary evil because a company which is striving towards total quality should not need such a 'CR function' – that is, a company which 'gets it right first time' should not have disgruntled customers. As a result, the function of 'service recovery' and its corresponding information can often be viewed by a company as an admission of failure, and the very existence of such a function might be perceived as the 'wrong' message to send to both customers and those within the company. For after all, the business' priority is 'getting it right first time'. There may thus be a view that emphasis on the 'service recovery' aspect does more harm than good to an already worsening relationship. The second half of the loyalty equation is therefore ignored.

So, if you ask any customer relation-'type' area to list the most significant obstacles hindering the success of their service-recovery function, 'gaining the attention of the business' will usually be near the top of their list. An obstacle of this nature affects the business in two ways:

1 It impinges on the company's level of investment in customer retention techniques, and is therefore important in determining the company's effectiveness in retaining customers who might defect to the competition.
2 It also has a direct impact upon the company's ability to recognize and 255

act upon customer feedback. That is, how likely is the company to 'get it right first time', next time? Does the organization learn?

The general level of neglect of the *function* of service recovery can create a lack of understanding of the principles of total quality and the implication of these principles for the lifetimes values of its customer base are significant.

British Airways (BA) has devoted a great deal of time and thought to the service recovery side of the equation, while others have tended to ignore this quality attribute. Thus BA has developed a revision in the traditional views regarding 'best practice' service recovery and its vital components of measurement and continual improvement. Its research confirms that customer loyalty is not simply a function of excellent customer service.

Figure 20.3 shows that approximately 13 per cent of customers who were completely satisfied ($\sqrt{}$) with BA's service may not repurchase from the airline again – perhaps they changed jobs, found a frequent-flyer programme which better suited their needs, or maybe they just felt it was time for a change of airline. On the other end of the spectrum are customers who have experienced a problem (X). Of those customers who experienced a problem and who chose *not* to tell the airline about their experience, 50 per cent intended not to repurchase from the airline again. However, those customers who experienced a problem and *did* contact the airline with their views tended not to defect from the airline. Only about 13 per cent of these customers intended not to repurchase due to the way their problem was handled, a rate of defection that is identical to the rate of defection of customers who were completely satisfied. *The conclusions are quite compelling: customers who are satisfied rarely write or call to say 'good-bye' when they leave the airline, and more than likely cannot be*

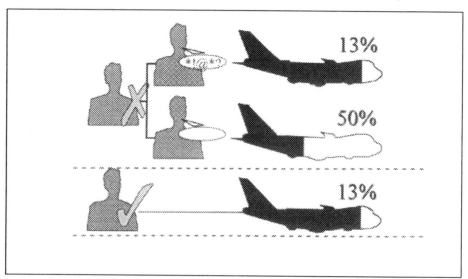

Figure 20.3   Potential defection rates amongst both satisfied and dissatisfied customers

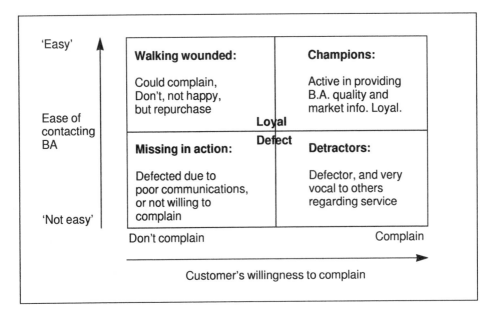

Figure 20.4 How communications channels and willingness to complain affect loyalty

saved anyway, while those who wish to comment due to poor service can be willing communicators and can indeed be turned around.

Given this information, BA has attempted to capture more customer comment through a *listening post* plan, a concerted effort to encourage customer feedback. Through this plan, British Airways has developed a profile of its customer base which can permit it to further refine its products and services (see Figure 20.4).

British Airways wishes to push all its customers into the upper right-hand quadrant in Figure 20.4. Within the champion customer group, they have developed complete profiles of buying behaviours, lifestyle analysis and a host of other demographic and geographic data. In this way, the airline can compare the profiles of the varying quadrants and begin better to understand how best to reach different customer segments and which of these segments are most likely to encounter which service issues (for example, perhaps certain products or services are not meeting a certain customer segment's needs as well as another segment's). This model can compare the profiles of those customer segments and then identify specific characteristics of the segments which may be contributing to service dissatisfaction. The information can then be fed to product development. In this way, British Airways is able to work with its internal customers to devise targeted total quality, rather than a 'blanket approach' which covers *all* processes and customer segments and not simply those that require attention. This approach can be viewed conceptually as shown in Figure 20.5.

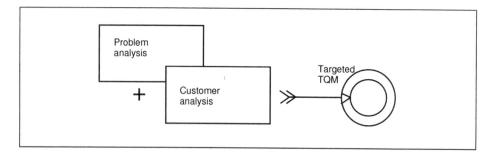

Figure 20.5   Conceptual approach to targeting total quality

COMPLAINTS MANAGEMENT AND LOYALTY: PROTECTING THE CUSTOMER, NOT THE COMPANY

The difficulty that customer relations (CR)-type departments find in 'gaining the attention of the business' hinders their ability to participate in influencing the quality perspective. This hindrance is often the product of company mandates which place the department's terms of reference as protecting the company – not the customer. As a result, customer retention is often nonexistent within CR departments, apart from dispensing cash to keep customers silent. In this instance, customers are not turned around, problems are not fixed and therefore, more customers are at risk of defection. This type of non-customer approach by CR departments can be classified as the 'complaints management approach', which is more concerned with the process than the customer.

In a complaints management environment, the operating procedures of the department are constructed upon a set of success criteria as follows:

- Success: Protecting the company from customer feedback.
  How: Centralization of 'CR' – little analysis and dissemination of customer data.
- Success: Finding culprits for poor service.
  How: Investigation as blame management – who did what and why? No partnership with line areas/product development to fix/prevent problems.
- Success: Providing recompense to ensure customer silence.
  How: Adherence to a strict formula for compensation based upon 'rules'.
- Success: Volume throughput.
  How: Departmental measures concentrate upon 'backlog' and not service levels.

Complaint management departments are not easily accessible to external customers, internal *customers* (for example, line area, product development teams) are not considered as customers, and the department's energy is spent comparing customer activities to the company's 'rules' in order to award recompense. Essentially, such CR departments operate as 'adjudication' or 'investigation' departments, *not* as customer retention units working in unison with the front line or product development to ensure that quality gaps are addressed.

BA's view is that the best way to protect the company is to champion the customer, and they use an alternative set of success criteria for a CR department:

- Success: Championing customer feedback within the company.
  How: Companywide practice of 'CR', extensive publication of service quality.
- Success: Preventing future service problems through teamwork.
  How: Monthly reviews of customer perceptions of service quality with the line.
  Active member of quality improvement and product development teams.
- Success: Recompense to meet customer needs.
  How: No 'CR rule book' – all cases dealt with individually.
  Monthly internal reviews of the most effective means of customer retention.
- Success: Customer retention.
  How: Department measured on customer retention rates and return on investment (that is, how effective the department was in retaining customers with resources available).

BEST PRACTICE IN CUSTOMER RETENTION TODAY: RETAIN, INVEST AND PREVENT

The set of success criteria that characterizes BA's customer retention philosophy – and which the airline believes saves customers from defecting and improves the company's bottom line through improved customer lifetime values – is called: *Retain, Invest, Prevent*.

Retain the customer as job one

First and foremost, retain the customer's business. Do not be distracted by the rule book. BA has invested heavily in technology so that its CR executives can provide the customer with an informed and insightful answer to their service issues and queries without delaying replies. However, the company does not refute the customer's perceptions that expectations were not met.

Human nature plays a large role in service recovery techniques when it comes to replying to customer correspondence or telephone calls. Ask any individual about their skills or competencies, and they will reply, 'Of course I have those', or some such. Anyone who has participated in a performance review will recognize this phenomenon! The same parallel can be drawn regarding customers who are aggrieved over service failures. First, the *259* customer's perspective is that they *know*, unequivocally, what happened. Debating or arguing what the customer perceived to be the facts is a non-starter. Indeed, they were there and it *is* their perception with which we must deal if we are going to save their future business. Secondly, they are upset and a whole host of varying emotions may be affecting their feelings and their demands upon the company. Challenging and/or elaborating upon their views in customer responses draws unintended reactions if communications are not managed properly. For instance, consider the following:

- If the company replies to the customer and claims that the situation was *not* as the customer suggested, then from the customer's perspective, the company is calling that customer a liar.
- If the company relays factual information back to the customer that the latter did not know, this can sometimes be perceived as 'excuses' for poor service (for example, 'The reason why was . . .'). Often, this information can raise a host of other questions that the customer will require to be followed up – questions to which there are often no answers. For example, '*What* type of organization are you running to allow such things to happen for that reason?', '*Why* was this issue allowed to happen?', '*When* did the company know?' '*Why* weren't steps taken beforehand?', and so on.
- If, however, the company simply reports back to the customer that, in fact, events did take place as the customer said they did, the customer can become even more agitated because, well, they knew that!

BA's quality standard is to provide the customer with an open, sincere and non-defensive response to service failures. However, given the infinite variety of customer perceptions and the circumstantial nature of human nature, it continues to be a difficult balancing act to provide 'answers' that do not sound like excuses or draw adverse reactions. To neutralize these factors, BA continually monitors its successes/failures in solving particular service issues – analysing every aspect of the recovery process and researching customer 'dislikes and likes' of the airline's responses and recovery efforts. In a recent survey on complaint handling conducted by BA, its customers were quite clear about what they required from the airline. They demanded that the lengthy and protracted 'adjudication' process was eliminated. In its place, our customers asked that we view their reality as the basis from which we build upon our relationship with them. Thus our customers' requests form the backbone of BA's retention philosophy and contribute to BA's goal of greater customer loyalty.

This research reinforced our belief that, unlike traditional 'best practice' in the service recovery field, our aim should be always to begin from the perspective of championing the customer. The best way we could help our company was to ensure that customers' needs were heard throughout the organization and that we worked with our colleagues to solve problems. If we didn't, overall customer purchases would fall and there would eventually be no customers to champion in future. Customers' needs were quite straightforward:

1 *Apologise and own the problem.*   Customers do not care whose fault it was or who was to blame. They want someone to say they were sorry and to champion their cause. After all, it was the company's product and all aspects of that product should be 'owned' by the company. It is the company's problem that external factors impinged upon the service quality, not the customer's. If the company has suppliers who are letting them down, then sort them out.

2 *Do it quickly.*   Research shows that customer satisfaction with service recovery efforts plummets 30–40 points if a reply is delayed by more than five days. A speedy reply demonstrates a commitment and a sense of urgency to the customer's feelings and to the situation which they encountered.

3 *Assure them it's being fixed.*   The company must know its operations and its services inside out, and must work with front-line areas to permit the company to see the true quality of its service offering. A customer can be brought back to the company if they are confident that a (long-running) problem is in hand, so long as they are convinced by the sincerity of the response and that a timescale for fixing the problem has been indicated.

4 *And do it by telephone*!   Many companies are frightened to talk to their customers because of the emotions service failures create. BA has found that customers are *delighted* to hear from the executives who took time to apologize personally and let them know that we were going to fix the problem they encountered. Telephone satisfaction with BA rates at about 95 per cent today.

In the United States, C. Sewed of Sewed Cedilla (the most profitable US automobile dealership) and P. Brown of the Harvard Business School, reiterate this approach:

1. Apologize when something goes wrong

    - Make it easy for customers to complain
    - Take responsibility (for the problem)

2. Accept that the customer is right

    - Be taken advantage of with a smile
    - Give customers the benefit of the doubt

3. Ask customers what they want

    - Don't guess what customers want
    - Make it easy for them to tell you
    - When the customer asks, the answer is always 'yes.'

Since BA changed its style from a back-office complaints unit to a proactive customer retention unit, customer retention has doubled to approximately 80 per cent. Most of this growth has been achieved through using the outbound telephone to call customers upon receipt of their letter and applying the Sewed and Brown formula. Crucial to measuring the success of the efforts of service recovery within BA has been the retention of future business which would *261* otherwise have been lost. Viewing service failures as opportunities for future business has added another tool in BA's overall kit of influencing customer lifetime values.

Invest in customer retention support

Retaining customer loyalty requires substantial investment not only in marketing programmes, but also in systems and support tools for the other parts of the organization which have roles to play in nurturing these valuable relationships. Thus to ensure that customer retention efforts were not distracted from recovering our customers' business, an enormous amount of time, effort and resources have been spent on information technology (IT) training and work processes. Towards this end:

1 The previous thirteen administrative steps to answering a customer were cut down to three:

   (a) scan-in customer letters or take customer telephone call;
   (b) analyse customer data; and
   (c) respond to the customer

2 A £4.5 million image-based *system*, which eliminates all paper (for example, fax, letters, telexes and so on), called *Caress* (customer analysis and retention system), has been developed and deployed. A customer's entire case history can be logged, held and shared across the organization via one screen displaying all the documents to ensure consistent service recovery.

3 *Training* has turned from writing and punctuation, to interpersonal development, including: allaying customer anger; negotiating a 'win/win' situation for both customer and company; listening and empathy skills; and how to be assertive without defensiveness. Also, guidance is given in how to counsel/support fellow employees stressed by a very difficult and emotionally gruelling job. We cannot take out on our customers the anxieties and emotions caused by our work – we must be able to cope amongst ourselves.

Furthermore, BA research determined that customers were having a difficult time in contacting them. In fact, complaints were actually being received from only 10 per cent of customers. As shown in Figure 20.6, all those below the 'complainant waterline' never truly had their views heard within the organization. Those customers who 'talked to BA' (24 per cent) may have had their problem solved locally, but BA did not record this information corporately and therefore an accurate picture of the true state of service quality was not emerging. The solution was for BA to lower the 'waterline' so that an accurate picture could emerge. Indeed, the 'tip of the iceberg', 8 per cent, represents those 'champions' profiled earlier, and thus, lowering the waterline also created more 'champions' for BA and greater potential future purchases.

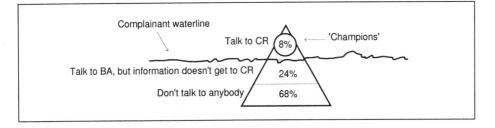

Figure 20.6   The customer contact iceberg

To achieve this goal, two main tactics were employed:

1   Over a dozen *listening posts* have been developed to ensure that we hear from our customers when and how *they* want to speak to us. For example, an *international free-post comment card* was developed to eliminate the trouble of finding stamps in foreign countries, *customer listening forums* take place between BA executives and customers so that grievances are aired in person, and a *'fly with me' programme* was introduced so that executives and customers can fly together and problems can be experienced at first hand.

2   A 'Recovery Point' programme was instituted by the organization to ensure that those customers just below the waterline not only had their problem solved, but also that BA received all the information necessary to gain a clear view of service quality across the network. 'Recovery Point' essentially allowed front-line staff access to similar recovery resources as customer relations.

Prevent problems of a poor relationship, don't cure them

Most companies are not able to see past the present customer problem with which they are dealing. The cornerstone of BA's strategy is to capture 100 per cent of all customer information and ensure that this information is acted upon, in partnership, with front-line areas. A complaint management system – as opposed to a customer retention philosophy – only serves to promote:

- *Blame across departments.* 'Answers' to customer problems are sought, not solutions.
- *Lack of local ownership of problems.* Non-CR areas are encouraged to think: 'CR will deal with our (local area) problems – our job is to get on and serve customers.'
- *Fear.* The CR department wants to know, ultimately, *who* didn't deliver.
- *Myopia.* Front-line departments spend their time on single incidents, rather than viewing the entire picture and current trends in order to conduct problem solving.

Moving from *cure to prevention* and eradicating blame from the customer   *263* retention process are essential first steps. As we witnessed earlier, service failure is inevitable, but it can serve a useful purpose so long as it furthers the continual improvement process and customers are convinced that these processes are taking place. Through demonstrating openness to customers, so trust and loyalty are built. Practising complaint management promotes division within the company and an unwillingness to share data amongst departments, and reinforces the general view that 'getting it right first time' is mutually exclusive from the practice of service recovery and its accompanying information. Customers notice the difference.

However, moving from *cure to prevention* is not an easy task. Openness and an ability to recognize and accept customer data are indispensable for continuous improvement, which, in turn, promises greater repeat business as service problems are eradicated. There is a 'feedback learning curve' (see Figure 20.7) that all organizations must go through when they move from practising the old style of customer relations to the new.

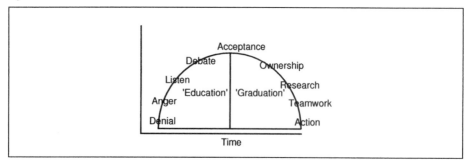

Figure 20.7   The feedback learning curve: coming to terms with customers' views

If service recovery functions are practising blame management it is no wonder they cannot 'gain the attention' of their organization – who would want to listen? It is the job of such functions to champion the customer through the departments that are creating the service or product failures. This partnering cannot be done unless an organization is able to 'educate' itself on how to negotiate the *feedback learning curve*. The management of the company must role model this shift in emphasis to overcome the fear element and to abolish blame management. Once this process has begun, departments will then begin to view the data in an objective, non-threatening light and head towards 'graduation'.

All organizations will find that their varying units will be at different stages of the learning curve. BA has claimed its learning curve through its 'Winning for Customers' programme, which facilitates the education and practice of service recovery and customer loyalty in conjunction with a wide array of internal partners – from human resources to finance, and from information management to service delivery and sales. Some examples are as follows:

● *Service partner agreements.* Internal clients (for example, catering, operations) meet monthly to review the 'state of the nation' from the customers' viewpoint.

- *A customer retention index.* Market research which measures the cost of customer defection both from not 'getting it right first time' and from poor 'service recovery'.
- *100 per cent analysis programme.* All customer comments – however small or large – are placed into the corporate *Caress* database so that internal customers can decide which problems they will wish to tackle, given full information on trends, costs, and so on.
- *Return on investment scenarios.* To report to the company how effective customer retention efforts have been (that is, how much business has been saved given the amount of resources exerted) and which service improvements, based upon recorded service failures, will provide the greatest return for the money invested.
- *Devolve CR 'ownership'.* Through encouraging the entire organization to recognize the lifetime value of its customers (BA knows the approximate lifetime values of the majority of its customers – from gold card holders, to high-street travel agents, to once-per-year holiday travellers), local areas are encouraged to undertake service recovery functions while also reporting service failure statistics so that the company has a clear view of service quality.

TOMORROW'S HISTORY IS TODAY'S ISSUE

Customer loyalty is a holistic, companywide endeavour. Attracting customers is often viewed as *the* challenge for most organizations and, once they are retained, the 'task' is often deemed complete. There is another side to this equation, though, which reads: 'Keep the customers you've got – someone else wants them, too.' It may very well be that this second half of the equation holds the key to prosperity for most companies. It is no secret that the companies with the best customer reputations have progressive 'service recovery' and customer-listening ethics which are themselves market leaders: for instance, Marks & Spencer, Royal Dutch Shell, Rank Xerox, Unilever, Nissan UK – and a host of others (my apologies to those I have excluded). Each of these companies has excellent products and services because of the feedback mechanisms they employ that permit them proximity to the marketplace, which, in turn, permits them to provide the best quality possible. The mission within these companies is the *ideal* that service/product failure should be made extinct – though of course this will never be entirely possible. So, like Japanese industry, they will continue with their mission to eradicate error through customer feedback. As we have seen earlier, the Deming approach applied by Japanese industry has rewritten the rules of the quality revolution – it is a lesson in history that we ignore at our peril. (Indeed, a little known fact is that Deming's approach in statistical process control – the basis from which the PDCA cycle measures success – was actually invented in the United Kingdom in 1934!). *265*

In BA's case, the company has pushed itself towards *its* goal of retaining life-time customers through continual quality improvement by:

- Championing the customer internally after service failures.
- Attacking the 'iceberg waterline' with 'listening posts'.
- Eliminating blame management in service recovery.
- Empowering everyone to own the customer's problem.
- Managing service improvement by fact through 100 per cent analysis.
- Encouraging partnering between operational and product development areas.
- Measuring the success of improvement efforts through the customer retention index.

To retain customer loyalty and to stay in business, companies can no longer afford to 'protect' themselves from customers who have experienced problems. The history of the corporate world is littered with companies who chose to ignore their customers' feedback and relegated the role of 'customer relations' to that of corporate buffer zone. The best way to ensure the longevity of any company is to recognize the contribution of service recovery and accompanying customer feedback. *Never* be satisfied with service failure, but zealously seek it – and encourage your customers to point it out to you. If you don't, your customers *will* tell someone – and that is most likely to be your competitor. The rest, as they say, will then be history.

FURTHER READING

Deming, C. E. (1986), *Out of the Crisis*, Cambridge, MA: MIT Centre for Advanced Engineering Study, 88, 178.

Sewell, C. and Brown, P. (1991), *The Golden Rules of Customer Care*, London: Business Books.

21 Public sector service standard*
Professor Merlin Stone and Ros Gardner

In the last few years, the public sector has attempted to achieve something not far short of a revolution. Until the early 1980s, public and private sectors were seen for government policy purposes as two extremes of a spectrum. The differences are summarized in Figure 21.1.

This is, of course a simplified view. Even then, it was recognized that some public sector bodies, such as nationalized industries, had 'customers'. However, their monopoly positions often allowed them to behave as if customers were supplicants for service rather than customers with rights. Meanwhile, in the private sector, standards of service were often poor, so the public sector was not put under pressure to emulate the private sector.

Today, public sector organizations – from government departments and local authorities, through the many agencies (some new, some venerable) to the few nationalized industries left – are keen to emulate what they see as the private sector's good practice and achievements in customer management. This also applies to the many voluntary sector agencies who are increasingly contractual agents of the public sector, particularly in the 'caring sectors' (for example, health, social services and so on). This chapter examines some key issues relating to this drive.

THE ARRIVAL OF THE CITIZENS' CHARTER

The Citizens' Charter was launched in 1991 by the Prime Minister, John Major. It aimed to establish a ten-year programme of radical reform of service standards, particularly in the public sector. For the public sector, its innovation was to introduce principles of customer service to management. Initially, its focus was on:

* The material in this chapter is based on research sponsored by IBM (UK) Ltd.

Policy attitude	Private sector	Public sector
Customers' status	Customers are won by hard work and may be lost to competition if they are not supplied with the right products and services, under the right conditions.	The sector serves a number of publics. In each, a defined set of individuals have a right to receive the service but on terms and conditions established by law, regulations or historic practice.
Customer feedback	Solicited often as a key indicator of performance.	Solicited exceptionally if service provision under review.
Output measurement	Measured in terms of what customers are prepared to and actually do pay (i.e. revenue).	Measured by inputs (e.g. manpower, equipment, buildings), rather than outputs (e.g. healthy citizens, educated citizens).
Costs and investments	Costs and investments (to secure inputs) are evaluated relative to what customers are prepared to pay for the outputs created by the inputs.	Costs are to be tightly controlled, according to government-agreed budgets. Investment permission is granted, taking into account the overall public sector borrowing requirement. Needs for service are only one factor to be taken into account.
Willingness and ability of individuals to pay for services	A prime criterion for determining which products and services shall be produced, how they will be marketed and serviced.	Normally irrelevant, except in a few cases where means testing is used to measure ability to pay. However, ability of consumers to influence in this way the type and quality of service they receive is deliberately minimized

Figure 21.1   Differences between the private and public sectors

- better services;
- more information;
- better management;
- market testing; and
- rewarding performance.

Changing needs and expectations

One of the main reasons cited for the introduction of the Charter was the heightened awareness of customer service issues and the expectation of consumers that public services should meet some of the service standards being proclaimed (though not necessarily delivered) in the private sector.

Customers' needs and views of the public sector change constantly. They have responded to:

1 Propaganda encouraging them to demand more from the public sector (the Charter itself has added to this and heightened expectations yet further).
2 Consumerist research and pressure groups.
3 Media pressure.
4 Publication of customer charters by a large number of private sector companies (not least the privatized utilities) .

One of the problems that the initiative encountered early on was what we call 'the mirage effect'. As improvements in public service become more common, citizens' expectations increase. Paradoxically, therefore, one of the first effects of customer service initiatives is usually a rise in complaint level as expectations run ahead of performance. So, while public sector managers thought they were arriving at the oasis of satisfied customer expectations, every time they reached the goal set previously, the mirage moved once more to the horizon. This, of course, is why service improvement initiatives must be given time to work and why progress must be through continuous improvement, rather than trying to achieve the impossible perfect in a short time.

In the private sector, companies have learnt to set incremental goals, because so much learning takes place, by both customers and suppliers, on the road to improvement that setting tightly defined long-term goals is inappropriate. As customers and suppliers explore new dimensions of service, different sets of needs and barriers to their satisfaction are revealed, suggesting different routes forward. It is arguable that, at the beginning, the Charter initiative did not recognize this point.

The bad press

The initiative was launched in a particularly hostile media environment. The public sector has always received bad press, for political reasons. When the Left is in power, the Right's media supporters highlight the sectors alleged profligacy and failure to deliver. When the Right is in power, the Left's media supporters emphasize how poor service is an inevitable consequence of tight budgets and new management systems.

Negative media attention is one reason why, as one senior police officer put it to us, the public's perception of management practices in the public sector is at least ten years behind the reality. In fact, from our experience of dealing with both sectors, we would say that the average public sector manager now has to perform a more difficult job than their private sector counterpart. This greater difficulty derives from:

- Constantly changing priorities, mandated not just by governments (the Charter must take some of the responsibility for this), but by the very fast learning curve that all levels of management have had to go through. This means that some changes are driven by learning which approaches do and which don't work.
- Sheer number and complexity of objectives – some managers are given very large numbers of often incompatible objectives, the achievement of some of which they can do little to influence.
- Having to achieve outcomes and levels of performance from staff who have not been recruited or trained to achieve them, without having the powers of redeployment or the training budgets more typical of private sector organizations of similar kinds and sizes.

MANAGING BROADLY BASED CHANGE

Most managers in the private sector would readily acknowledge how long it has taken them on the road to service improvement and how far they feel they have to go. Many, however, have learnt how to manage broadly based change in the interface between their organizations and their customers. There is of course no secret recipe for this. The key is that improving service is not a question of applying a veneer but of building the improvement into overall objectives and all individual functional objectives, plans and implementation, and ensuring that communication, training, staff involvement and measurement are to the fore.

Some public sector service improvement programmes start with the question 'What can we do about complaints?' This has the benefit that it deals with the area of greatest risk and media attention and creates an in-depth dialogue with the public that provides useful information. Nevertheless, concentrating on complaints can lead to a negative tone in discussions of customer service; it may also lead to the fact being overlooked that, for example, those who are complaining are not those for whom the service is most beneficial. So, once complaint management is in place, we advise that the next question that should be asked is: 'What are our overall objectives, what is the role of customer service within these objectives, and how can we change our service so that it meets our target customers' needs better?'

THE ROLE OF THE CHARTER IN STIMULATING CHANGE

As far as the Citizens' Charter is concerned, its main achievements may seem small compared to the kind of change envisaged. However, we would argue that broadly based political initiatives cannot achieve this kind of change by themselves but they can stimulate it in the right environment.

The most noteworthy achievements of the Charter have been as follows:

- The 'Plain English' initiative – we can now understand much more of the documentation that comes from public sector organizations.

- Establishing local standards for a variety of public sector bodies.
- Publishing best practices – a recognition that laying down standards is not much help to managers; they also need to know how to get there.
- The issuing of charters (for example, the Patients Charter, the imminent Job Seekers Charter).
- Improved adjudication procedures (for example, Inland Revenue, Benefits Agency).
- Improvements in processes for handling the public, (for example the police, British Rail, London Underground).

The Charter Mark is one part of the initiative which has been particularly strongly questioned. The criteria by which a Mark is awarded are, we believe, sound. They are:

- Standards.
- Information and openness.
- Consultation and choice.
- Courtesy and helpfulness.
- Putting things right.
- Value for money.
- User satisfaction.
- Improvement in the quality of service in the previous two years.
- Innovative enhancements to service.

The central issue from a customer service perspective is how user satisfaction is measured, whether the standard really is high enough and whether the Mark has sufficient weight in the overall set of measures. However, when we ask managers what it means to them when their organization receives the Mark, there is no doubt that they have had to work hard to improve their approach to managing customers to gain the award. There is also no doubting the damage done by withdrawal of the Mark, although as yet this has only happened to one organization – British Gas.

Changing the complaint culture – for customers

One of the central ideas of the Charter was that customers (particularly in the public sector) needed to express their views more, and often had problems in doing so (for example, didn't know who to complain to, were afraid to do so and so on). This was the idea behind the Charterline, which was a telephone service launched in the spring of 1993. However, this proved not to be a popular service – customers just did not use it. The cost per call was estimated at £70 and it was discontinued after nine months.

Changing the complaints management culture

The Charter's Complaints Task Force was set up in June 1993 and asked to *271* report by June 1995. It targeted the complaints handling system of public and private sector organizations. Its aim was to find out whether the system was accessible, simple, speedy, fair, confidential, effective, and informative.

The Task Force works by informal reviews (it has visited 26 public and private sector organizations) and formal reviews (by questionnaire, visit and full report – covering 60 public sector organizations). In four public services, it has facilitated exchange of best practice and consideration of issues. It will also have produced six discussion papers, including ones on 'Motivation and attitude', and 'Redress and compensation'.

The Charter's failures

Apart from the Charterline, it is probably fair to regard other failures as:

- The wide disparity in service levels achieved. Local authorities have mostly improved by leaps and bounds, while the courts and education are still very slow to improve. This could be due to the strong vested professional interests in the latter two.
- The continuing public cynicism about the charter.
- The resistance by some public sector staff to being identified through name badges.
- The very slow attitude change.

CALLING OR TREATING PEOPLE AS CUSTOMERS

This area is one in which the Charter has had some successes, although there is still some resistance to it. In some public services, staff are prepared to call citizens almost anything but customers. This contrasts with the private sector, where the discipline of regarding staff who are dependent on a department's services as internal customers is also now well established. This latter practice has its origin in manufacturing industry, where staff further down the production or distribution value chain were actually receiving goods or services from those further up it. It has now – particularly under the influence of quality programmes – been extended to many other 'dependency' relationships within organizations, to the extent that in some private sector organizations staff are described, for example, as their line managers' customers for appraisal.

One of the most commonly observed facets of customer service is that 'your customers get treated like your staff'. Many public sector middle managers have complained to us about the authoritarianism and political manoeuvrings of their superiors, with hidden (usually political) agendas rife. While middle managers are struggling to improve services to customers, their superiors are engaged in self-preserving power struggles, in which middle managers (and customers) are casualties. This is an area the Charter will find hard to address.

THE PRIVATE SECTOR MODEL – A CAUSE FOR CONCERN?

One of the problems the Charter faces is that the discipline of treating the public like customers is sometimes rejected by public sector managers because a strange picture of 'model' private sector supplier–customer relationships has been painted for the public sector. This model is a 'capitalism red in tooth and claw' model, where customers aim to beat suppliers down to the lowest price and suppliers aim to get away with murder (including that of their competitors). The blame for this lies partly with politicians whose own experience of industry is limited (yes, there are many on the Right in this position).

This oversimplified model overlooks some key points about private sector markets, such as:

- Customers' relationships with suppliers are just that – a relationship, which may exist for many years or even a lifetime, during which both sides make commitments to each other, exchange information and develop dependence. The key to the relationship is that both sides derive value from it over its duration, even if sometimes the relationship is strained.
- The relationship is often not founded on supply at the lowest cost but on best value over a sustained period – taking into account the customer's costs of dealing with the supplier.
- Supplier and customer usually spend time learning how to deal with each other.
- Suppliers don't necessarily want to keep all their existing customers, and customers may not be satisfied with all their existing suppliers, but the costs of achieving change in the required direction may be too high for either party.
- Most customers recognize that meeting all their needs all the time is not easy and expect a reasonable standard of performance and steady improvement. However, they are very intolerant of poor *relative* performance: that is, when they can see similar organizations doing a much better job with similar resources.

We believe that public sector organizations trying to improve customer service should first consider different customer–supplier models: which, if any, might be helpful to them, and what the benefits of achieving that kind of relationship would be. If this is not done, staff may be put under pressure to achieve an inappropriate relationship. We believe also that the Citizens' Charter should open up this agenda beyond its current rather strong emphasis on individual transactions.

STAFF WHO DEAL WITH CUSTOMERS

In the private sector, customer management is usually such a critical contributor to business success that the role of staff in managing customers cannot be *273* ignored. Most larger organizations in the private sector accept as normal the idea that staff who handle customers must not only be trained to do so, but should also be recruited specifically for the job. Here, personal attributes and skills are more important than knowledge. Putting it simply, some people like dealing with people, others don't. Some people are good at it, others are not. Some who like to do it are actually very bad at some aspects of it because, for them, dealing with people means ordering people around.

In the public sector, there is often no chance of ensuring quickly that all staff who deal with customers have the right characteristics, skills and training. The solution here is prioritization, which means identifying posts where customer-handling is critical, and finding ways of reallocating staff to ensure that those most suited are in 'front office' posts, with the right training, while other staff do the valuable work of processing in the 'back office'. This might involve using assessment centre techniques to identify these staff. Once again, the philosophy of continuous improvement is the key. Mass training programmes aimed at improving general customer-handling skills are very definitely not the answer. Highly focused programmes, customized to the needs of the particular situation and delivered only to priority staff, are.

Empowerment and all that

There is little doubt that giving customer-contact staff as much leeway as possible to improve customer service works, despite its well-known problems (encouraging internal 'them and us' – 'I try hard but the organization makes it hard for me to please you'). The answer here is not to let the information get lost in the problem resolution. At Marks & Spencer, the process is aimed primarily at separating complaint and customer from information, so that the complaint is quickly resolved (ideally at first contact) and the information logged for reporting and analysis. However, in the public sector, the issue is more complicated than in the private sector. Thus, where private sector customer service norms indicate that a concession or change should be made, similar action in the public sector may create a precedent, so that many other citizens claim the same treatment (for example, news travels fast on housing estates), or a perception of inequity, and it may even break a law. This notwithstanding, we believe that it makes sense to work out (with customer-facing staff) what discretion they could be allowed and what they feel they could handle.

The problem of the professional expert

Many public sector staff are highly trained experts (for example, police officers, teachers, social workers, doctors). They have been extensively trained and this usually leads them to have a view about what it is 'right' to provide citizens with. This strong view was best revealed to us when a student from the Health Service, carrying out as part of a university assessment a survey of general practitioners and their procedures for ensuring that their elderly patients received adequate care, established that she could ask what the GPs were doing but not why they were doing it. This was, she said, described as the 'impertinent why' in the Health Service. Doctors were the best judges of why and didn't want any prying into this area!

The problem of the public sector expert was first dragged into the public domain back in the heady days of the 1960s when challenging authority, as embodied in professional staff, became fashionable. For us, the issue is the serious one of encouraging excellent professional staff to see that understanding the customer's point of view, and changing the way staff work to meet customer requirements, is not a challenge to their professional skill but may help them achieve their objectives more successfully. In practice, the changes usually relate not to the 'core service' (for example, the medical diagnosis and treatment) but to the way the service is delivered (for example, how long patients queue, what information they are given about their treatment). It is no surprise to us that the Charter initiative has been most successful in areas not dominated by professional experts!

THE CUSTOMER

Who is the customer?

If staff can be led to see citizens as customers, we are then faced with defining the customer. This requires two steps:

1 *Defining the universe of potential customers.* All those citizens who might be beneficiaries of or affected by the operations of the public service.
2 *Defining the target market.* Those whom the service is primarily intended for.

The police provide a good example of the problem of definition. Their customers include those on remand, convicted offenders and their families, actual and potential victims, and the taxpayer, who is receiving insurance-type protection for a fee. Also among their customers are agencies who depend on the police for maintenance of law and order, or resolution of problems (for example, sports ground owners, social services).

This complex set of customers is characteristic of the public sector. There is no point in trying to simplify what cannot be simplified. The solution is to identify the different sets of customers and to achieve some prioritization. Thus, in cases of serious fraud, the approach may be to concentrate on convicting fraudsters to prevent them offending again. This may be best done by fixing on one offence where a conviction is almost certain and concentrating public resources on obtaining evidence for this case alone. This procedure may mean that one victim gains a better outcome than others (those whose cases aren't chosen), but that future victims are saved. In fact, recovering assets from fraudsters is best left to highly specialized legal practitioners through the civil courts. In cases where it is very hard to prioritize, guidance from government or direct from the electorate may be required.

Are customers of the public sector different?

Although in most respects the customers of the public sector are the same customers of the private sector that have been the subject of so many marketing and customer service initiatives, there are differences in the *average* customers of each sector – or at least in their *target* customers. Whatever the other differences between Left and Right, they do agree that it is the role of the public sector and its agents to support in various ways those citizens whose needs are met less well (as employees, dependants of employees, consumers and so on) by the private sector, although the Left would be more concerned to establish some public services as a right for all rather than as support for the weak.

There are two issues raised by this view of the public sector:

1   Many public sector customers find it hard, for a variety of reasons, to manage their relationship with large organizations of any kind. Examples of these reasons include:

   (a)   language difficulties;
   (b)   cultural antipathy to complaining or dependence;
   (c)   lack of knowledge and skills required to manage the relationship;
   (d)   lack of permanent address;
   (e)   inability to pay transport costs to point of delivery of public service;
   (f)   lack of awareness of the consequences of actions; and
   (g)   lack of will or ability to control actions to within social norms or to terms agreed with a public sector organization (this could even be as simple as failure to get up in time to queue for benefit).

2   Services designed to overcome some of these problems have to be so 'favourable' to the customer that they are also very attractive to citizens who are less in need. At the extreme, this leads to the phenomenon where the socially privileged may be the first to take up a public service and the best at managing their relationship with it, so that they get far more out of it than those for whom the service was designed. Perhaps the best example of this is how the 'middle class' (political correctness now requires us to put this phrase in inverted commas!) manages its relationships with the (broadly middle class) education and medical professions. This class generally demands higher standards of medical and educational practice and is more prepared to intervene if its requirements are not met. The professions themselves are happier dealing with middle-class customers, with whom they feel able to discuss problems more 'intelligently', for example.

There is no easy solution to this problem. We believe the only (and difficult) answer is that of the marketer. If the services are targeted at a particular section of the community, then the *whole* of the marketing mix must be attuned to that community. This provision includes the language (for example, English or not, style and so forth), how customers are persuaded to take up the service, how the relationship is managed with them after the 'sale', and so on. Customers who are not in the target market must be dissuaded from taking up the service. This is not just to conserve resources, but also because we know that if the service system is designed for one kind of customer and in practice most customers turn out to be of a different kind, the system will consume increased resources in trying to adjust itself to do what it was not designed to do. This targeted marketing and 'de-marketing' means being very selective, and of course in the past this has caused trouble for the public sector with those on the Left who believe that certain public services should be available as of right to all, free.

This aspect of public sector service has not been specifically addressed by the Citizens' Charter, which has concentrated largely on service to the 'average citizen'. We recommend that this be taken up by the Charter.

THE CURRENCY OF THE PUBLIC SECTOR

Many public services are in principle free but obtaining them often imposes other costs. These costs are the public sector's currency: that is, what the citizen has to pay to obtain the service. The main costs are *time* and *information*. Both may be used to ration the service.

Time

The commonest time cost is *time spent in a queue*. One recent example we came across was that of a secretary who was temping, had been ill over Christmas and was finding it difficult for a variety of reasons to get started in the New Year, so she had a week of sickness and two weeks without work before resuming. She went to try to establish whether she was entitled to benefit and was so disgusted at the queues that she decided that she would rather not bother. This example illustrates several points:

- Queues are often not for obtaining service but for eliciting information about the service.
- Those who can telephone during working hours (not from a public call box) can avoid this queue (even though this often means waiting in telephone queues when you should be doing something else) – of course, there is a class bias here.
- Queues impose two costs – time and stress, and stress is increased by uncertainty. In other words, if you queue for a long time and are uncertain about what you're going to find at the end of it, its far worse than queueing for a definite benefit.

Of course, had the secretary in question been working and trying to establish her entitlement to benefit for a recent period spent unemployed, the time might also have cost her money.

Information

The more a citizen knows about how to deal with a public sector organization, the more successful that citizen is likely to be in obtaining the service. Information is acquired by spending time learning how the 'service system' of the public sector works. Of course, education and social class both affect how easy it is to obtain information and these are currencies that are much more difficult to acquire.

Therefore, public sector management should consider what currency their service requires and whether it is appropriate, given the nature of the service and its target market. Some customer research is usually essential here. Focus group discussions are usually the best for revealing currency and relationship issues. If the research reveals that the currency is inappropriate, then ways of changing it must be developed. In some cases, these changes can be as simple as improved information dissemination (for example, print, helplines), in other cases improved queue management.

We believe that this area should also be examined by the Charter. It is, in a way, the other side of the coin of service to the underprivileged citizen. The Charter should investigate not only what level of service is given, but also what it costs to obtain it and who has enough of the relevant currency to do so.

STANDARDS

The drive for improved performance has led to many public sector managers believing that the only way to improve performance is as follows:

1 Set standards by which their organizations are to be judged.
2 Measure the performance of the organization as a whole and the individuals within it according to these standards – often in a very public manner.

The Citizens' Charter has contributed to this belief. It leads to a culture in which the generally (there are exceptions) sensible approach of 'if you can't measure it, you can't manage it' is transformed into 'if we're not measuring it, we're not interested in managing it'. The best example of this that we have encountered was an organization where if a citizen wrote in with an enquiry, it would never be answered, because prompt complaints management had been given top priority while the efficiency of handling queries from the public had not been raised as an issue and was therefore not being measured.

There is also a tendency to 'hide behind targets'. So, if a senior manager is asked how well the organization is doing, the answer is a reference to improved target achievement. Target achievement can always be manipulated; just as in the private sector, improved revenues and reduced costs can be achieved by 'milking the market'. In the private sector, qualitative and quantitative market research are key components of measurement. Qualitative research is by its nature more open-ended and reveals customer concerns clearly and in depth. How far these concerns are shared by other customers can then be confirmed by quantitative research.

For this reason, the Citizens' Charter should look at the cultural impact of highlighting certain areas for measurement. This will require commissioning independent research.

CUSTOMER SERVICE MANAGEMENT

Compensating customers

Although a basic lesson from the private sector is that good complaints handling is one of the best ways to secure customer loyalty, this does not mean that compensating customers by small payments is the best approach. In the private sector, the most powerful antidotes to complaint are recognition and remedy: that is, recognizing that the customer is worth listening to and that the grievance is important and remedying the problem. Indeed, one of the reasons why complaining customers are usually more loyal if their complaint is dealt with properly is that the complaint leads to them receiving some attention – an otherwise rare occurrence for some organizations!

Paying small sums in compensation is like giving coupons to gain brand loyalty – it is a sales promotion technique which doesn't change what a customer thinks about the product. Compensation reinforces the customer's feeling that 'they oughtn't to have let it happen' and makes the customer suspect that the reason why 'they' are doing it is to buy people off because they can't get the service right. At worst, giving compensation can create 'compensation addicts', who become expert at obtaining compensation. In marketing, it's always better to give improved value rather than a price reduction. This is a lesson that the public sector should follow.

The Marks & Spencer model of refunding works very well in the retail sector. Refunding for merchandise is not the same as compensating for a service that has not satisfied. Customers of Marks & Spencer stay loyal partly because they know that merchandise can be returned without question (subject to it being in new condition) and that when problems occur, they will be resolved satisfactorily. But when they leave the shop, they also have the merchandise itself as the sign of quality. When a public sector customer experiences poor service, they are led to question the quality of the supplier because they have nothing tangible as evidence of quality 'in their hands'. For them, recognition and redress are very important – particularly since they will often be worried about whether their case will ever be properly dealt with.

Case processing versus transaction processing

In research on the role of information systems in customer service management, we identified many differences between the following processes:

- *Transaction processing*, where large numbers of individuals are being *279* managed through many simple transactions (for example, in the private sector, a supermarket check-out, a paying-in counter at a bank, booking a business flight; in the public sector, refuse collection, paying council tax).

- *Case processing*, involving an in-depth relationship with customers, including the collection of much information about them, evaluation of this information by the organization and often a permanent change in relationship with the organization (for example, in the private sector, taking out a mortgage or a life insurance policy; in the public sector, registering a benefit claim, going into hospital for a major operation, being arrested). Here, customers require much more information before their case can be correctly handled. During handling, more information is exchanged and a relationship develops.

Many private sector models of customer service come from transaction processing rather than case processing (for example, retailing). Most serious public sector customer service problems are in case processing, which puts particular stress on the information processing capacity of the organization. For example, good customer service practice (based on customer requirements) is that customers should be able to obtain information on the current status of their case. For this reason, the Charter initiative needs to analyse the difference between these two environments and encourage the development of standards appropriate to each.

Note that once a customer complains – even in a transaction processing environment – a case has been created. It is not surprising that transaction processing organizations often have the greatest difficulty in dealing with complaints. However, because they are attuned to the need for processes and systems to deal with customers, once they recognize complaints-handling as a processing problem, they can develop very good systems and processes for managing it.

The role of communication

Good customer service depends partly on how information about the situation at the customer interface flows up and down the organization and is acted upon. For the public sector, this is a crucial area for action and has been a primary concern for the Charter. Particular priorities are as follows:

- Information systems should be as far as possible designed to collect, quickly and efficiently, information about the quality, and not just the quantity, of customer interactions. Complaints management systems should enable staff to log all the essential details so that they can be acted upon individually *and* analysed to aid the process of reducing or removing the cause of the complaint.
- Staff should be selected and trained to accept as well as give information in the language and culture of the customer. This may mean selecting from the same ethnic group as customers.

- Internal communication about customer-related issues should receive close attention. In many cases it suits staff who are not at the customer interface to ignore problems at that interface. There should be a clear process for communicating problems and achievements at the customer interface, for resolution of individual cases, and for making policy changes. Staff focus groups reveal very quickly what the current process *actually* is, as opposed to what it is in theory.
- In large organizations, and particularly ones with many geographically dispersed staff (for example, in local branches), communications media will need to be used to ensure a good two-way flow, which may involve much larger budgets than management has been accustomed to.
- In certain parts of the public sector, and particularly those concerned with legal and distress issues (for example, police, social services, health), communication poses special problems. More open communication can backfire because sensitive information becomes too widely available in the organization, with the risk of it reaching the 'wrong' person. However, this does not negate the general principles of this chapter. Here, improving communication requires special care, with more pilot projects and research of customer reactions to change. However, our experience is that customers in these areas do need more information about how their cases are handled (for example, what is agreed so far, next steps, who is responsible, possible delays). Some customers would like choice about how much information they are given (for example, prognosis for their case).

Role of research

Throughout this chapter, the customer's viewpoint is seen as the most important single factor. Yet we can only know the customer's viewpoint by listening to customers *and* to customer-facing staff. As we mentioned above, customer and staff focus groups are an essential starting point for any public sector customer improvement programme. These groups reveal in depth what the real concerns of customers and staff are. Staff are often far more critical of their organization's approaches to handling customers than the customers themselves. As we have suggested above, the Charter initiative must continue to stimulate the use of independent research to provide an accurate picture of customer views.

GETTING THE SIMPLE THINGS RIGHT - THE ROLE OF THE CHARTER

Our experience of the most successful public sector customer service initiatives is that they have deliberately been kept simple, concentrating on top priorities as revealed by customer and staff research. Getting the most important and obvious things right seems to be the best approach. Of course, this does mean that you have to keep going back to customers to see if you are still dealing with their priorities.

How far has the Charter contributed to getting things right?

The Charter has certainly stimulated a 'great debate' on customer service, particularly in the public sector, and generated enthusiasm and motivation. It has triggered specific improvements in some areas (for example, Inland Revenue, Health). However, the failure of Charterline, the continuing poor public perception of many public sector bodies and staff, and customer cynicism, pose a continuing challenge. There is no doubt that the initiative is worth maintaining – provided that it is backed by resources and political commitment. However, it must develop beyond what is perceived to be a strong emphasis on standards and compensation into the area of cultural change. Perhaps this can be achieved by closer working with other government initiatives, such as 'Investors in People' and the professional and managerial associations which help form organizational cultures.

The training, motivation, recruitment and selection implications of the Charter findings are particularly significant. Improving service is concerned with the following imperatives:

1 Making sure that it is worthwhile for an organization to do it – usually true in the private sector, often not so clear in the public sector.
2 Setting up the right systems and processes.
3 Recruiting, motivating and training people and structuring and managing organizations.

These points should all be at the centre of Charter activities, but as a government body, the Charter can make the most progress with the third of these.

We believe that there are two other areas that warrant investigation:

1 The introduction of the quality culture of staff involvement and continuous improvement. Staff who service customers are often best at developing and improving service standards, working with customers to do so.
2 How the Charter model might change with the possible change in the party of government. The Left has always been extremely confused about why the private sector should want to do anything but make short-term profit and have clearly not thought deeply enough about why long-term relationships between customers and suppliers work. They tend to use simple economic models (both sides have invested in the relationship), which though of value, do not explain the psychological side of mutual dependence. Nor does the Left understand that organizations which hold information about customers do not do so just to threaten their civil liberties – they also do it to improve the service they give to customers.

Finally, to achieve maximum impact, the Charter has to:

● Concentrate on a few areas where very significant improvements can be achieved.

- Follow them through to show that the improvements are achieved: that is, that they work for customers.
- Make sure that these achievements are publicly demonstrated and then learnt from.

FURTHER READING

Bendell, T. and Kelly, J. (1994), 'Customer Service in the Public Sector', *Customer Service Management*, **3**, June, 40–3.

Bendell, T. and Penson, R. (1995), 'Customer Charters – A Good Idea or a Waste of Time?', *Customer Service Management*, **8**, September, 43–5.

Bichard, M. (1994), 'Putting the Customer First', *Customer Service Management*, **3**, June, 12–14.

Cooke, M. (1995), 'Customer Service Goes Underground', *Customer Service Management*, **8**, September, 47–50.

Cooper, A. (1994), 'Winning The Charter Mark', *Customer Service Management*, **4**, September, 46–8.

King-Taylor, L. (1994), 'Focus on the Metropolitan Police', *Customer Service Management*, **5**, December, 25–8.

Logan, E. (1995), First-Class Approach at Royal Mail, *Customer Service Management*, **8**, September, 6–8.

Thomson, K. (1993), *Managing Your Internal Customers* (London: Pitman).

Turnbull, D. (1994), 'The Challenge of Improving Customer Service in a Regulated Utility Environment', *Customer Service Management*, **2**, March, 48–50.

Part IV
THE CULTURAL DIMENSION

22 Culture: the prime differentiator
Christine Barclay

Culture is an important determinant of corporate success. In *In Search of Excellence*, Peters and Waterman (1982) identified culture as pivotal to company success:

> Without exception, the dominance and coherence of culture proved to be an essential quality of the excellent companies. Moreover, the stronger the culture and the more it was directed towards the marketplace, the less need there was for policy manuals, organization charts, or detailed procedures and rules. In these companies, people way down the line know what they are supposed to do in most situations because the handful of guiding values is crystal clear.

Culture makes a difference *internally* – to a company's staff – by determining their working environment and influencing their commitment to company goals; it also makes a difference *externally* – to a company's competitors, suppliers and customers – by influencing their perception of the company and determining their expectations of, relations to and interaction with it.

WHAT IS CULTURE?

Theories, definitions and descriptions of culture abound. Due to its acknowledged importance in organizational and management theory, many of the management gurus have sought a definitive definition. Ed Schein (1990) of MIT characterizes culture as:

> A pattern of basic assumptions invented, discovered or developed by a given group as it learns to cope with its problems of external adaptation and internal integration that has worked well enough to be considered valid and to be taught to new members as the correct way to perceive, think, and feel in relation to these problems.

Charles Hampden-Turner (1994) defines culture and the way it functions in this way:

> Culture comes from within people and is put together by them to reward the capacities they have in common. Culture gives continuity and identity to the group. It balances contrasting contributions and operates as a self-steering system which learns from feedback. It works as a pattern of information and can greatly facilitate the exchange of understanding. The values within a culture are more or less harmonious.

Andre Laurent (1990) of INSEAD describes culture thus:

> An organization's culture reflects the assumptions about clients, employees, mission, products, activities and assumptions that have worked well in the past and which get translated into norms of behaviour, expectations about what is legitimate, desirable ways of thinking and acting. [These] are the locus of its capacity for evolution and change.

Charles Handy (1976), eschews a rigorous definition because, according to him, 'A culture. . . is something that is perceived, something felt'.

Given the difficulty in finding a conclusive, all-encompassing definition, culture has come to be shrouded in considerable mystique and complexity, but unnecessarily so. We accept quite readily the sociological concept of culture and subculture when it comes to society in general. All of us intuitively know what culture is through the everyday experience of being part of society. Culture, in all its dimensions, is all around us; we are part of it, we interact with it. It is the way society coheres, the way society functions, the unique way one society presents itself to the rest of the world. It is the embodiment and manifestation of a society's fundamental values and governing norms. It is the way we do things, the way we behave, what we believe, our values, what is acceptable and what is not, our institutions and the principles upon which they are founded, our body of law, our language, politics, power structure, history and heritage. It is the framework and guiding principles of our society. Culture is the unique character of each society manifested through the daily activities and routines of its members.

So too with organizations. Organizations are mini-societies, each with its distinctive cultural pattern. Organizational culture is about the way things are done, the shared values underpinning behaviour, the processes and procedures which are established explicitly and implicitly to encourage, reinforce, regulate and sanction behaviour and action. As well as reflecting current organizational reality, culture also reflects the founding principles upon which a company was built, its shared history and experience.

How to recognize culture

Company values take time to evolve into a shared, unwritten code of behaviour. Although hard to define and 'as different and varied as the nations and societies of the world' (Handy, 1976), culture is recognizable. There is a vast difference between the culture of an advertising agency and that of a local government office, which shows not only in the dress and language but also in the pace at which business is conducted.

Culture is recognizable through:

- management style;
- employment policies and practice;
- attitude to customers;
- corporate style (for example, dress, language, literature, logos, advertising, recruitment brochures, annual reports, telephone answering techniques);
- people and personalities;
- corporate priorities and budgets; and
- pace and energy levels.

However, culture is more than just the sum of these distinct variables. Due to their interaction and interplay and the beliefs and values that underpin them, culture is an altogether more pervasive and intangible phenomenon. In companies with a strong and cohesive culture the immediate, most significant and most forceful indicator of culture is the atmosphere: how the environment of the organization feels to an outsider on first impression.

In one remarkable, value-driven company – the information technology consultancy, The Instruction Set (now part of Hoskyns) – the culture was palpable. Without exception, all visitors to the company – interviewees, head hunters, consultants, suppliers, customers – would comment on the atmosphere of friendly professionalism and youthful energy and excitement. Obviously there was more to the company and its culture than this intangible impression, but no one felt the need to describe the culture more fully. The feeling experienced was so strong that it sufficiently characterized and differentiated the company in the minds of outsiders. It created a unique and lingering impression.

Culture is affected by a variety of factors, all of which to a greater or lesser degree influence it and determine its unique character. For example:

- history and ownership;
- size;
- technology of production, operations, product, communication;
- business goals and objectives;
- environment (for example, economic, market, competitive, geographic, societal);
- people (for example, their personalities, expectations and aspirations); and
- the values, beliefs and cherished philosophies of the founder members and key people in the organization.

Even within the same industry, cultural variations can be found. IBM, for instance, has historically had a paternalist culture: employees are expected to *289* devote themselves totally to the company, and, in return for hard work and loyalty, they are looked after and rewarded well. Apple, by contrast, has grown dramatically over a relatively short period of time to challenge the established giants of the industry by encouraging an entrepreneurial, team-spirited, informal culture.

Different cultures are reflected in diverse structures and systems. There have been several attempts to define and classify different types of culture in terms of organizational structures, and to deduce the relationships, interactions and communication and business processes which derive from them. Roger Harrison (1972) and Charles Handy (1978) have each devised similar four-quadrant models to graphically represent the relationship between the degree of organizational centralization and degree of formalization. Handy categorizes the different cultures as Apollo, Athena, Zeus and Dionysus, corresponding to Harrison's classifications of Role, Task, Power and Atomistic cultures.

Useful as such models are in helping to identify patterns and facilitate comparison, they can detract from the main point, namely, that the essence of culture is intangible. By its very nature, culture defies such neat compartmentalization, generalization and prescription. Structures and processes may reflect culture but they are not synonymous with it. Equally, to categorize culture in terms of organizational structure and infer the cultural patterns likely to be associated with it, can at best only approximate to the reality of any specific organization.

How is culture established?

Culture develops out of the original objectives established by the founders of a business, combined with the shared vision, values and aspirations of its founding members. It is a product of conscious strategy and unconscious motivation and need. As a company grows, its culture adapts to changing circumstances and values under the influence of the most dominant group.

Culture cannot be blueprinted or imposed. It comes from within the organization and its people. Structures, business processes, policies and procedures can be designed and implemented with a particular cultural context in mind, but culture itself develops as an interaction with and in response to the framework they provide. Structures and systems themselves cannot determine or prescribe culture.

In a greenfield site or start-up situation it is possible to articulate a vision of culture, reinforced by supporting structures, systems and policies, that may encourage the evolution of a culture which approximates to that vision. However, culture can only grow out of a vision by its internalization, acceptance and enactment by the people of the organization. For this to happen, the underpinning values of the vision must be shared by and be in accordance with, the aspirations and expectations of those people. The resulting culture, however, will never be absolutely identical with the original ideal, since everyone involved in the process of making the vision come alive will to some extent influence its reality.

How does culture work?

Culture is pervasive and indistinguishable from the reality of the organization. It is manifested in the patterns of interactions between people, their approach and attitude, their priorities and preoccupations, the language they use, the various rituals of their daily routine, their overall style. It provides the frame of reference for the way people work and operate within an organization and the way they interact with the world outside.

With its shared values, culture is what defines and unifies the social dimension of an organization. Formally and informally it regulates behaviour and communication.

How does culture develop?

Culture is organic and dynamic. Just as in society, culture evolves over time in response to environmental factors, within and outside the organization. In the course of their daily routine and practice, its members interact with and influence the culture of the organization and are in turn influenced by it. Culture develops out of and through social interaction, the 'ongoing, proactive process of reality construction' (Morgan, 1986). As an organization grows and employs more people, its culture develops gradually and naturally. Even imperceptibly, it is in a constant process of adaptation.

Not only is this inevitable, it is necessary. The culture suited to a small entrepreneurial company employing few people is unlikely to be appropriate to a larger, more established and complex organization.

Larry E. Greiner (1972) maintains that organizations move through five distinguishable phases of development. Each phase:

- Contains a relative calm period of growth in which different management styles, priorities, organization structures and control mechanisms are required.
- Ends with a crisis of management, the resolution of which brings into being the next phase.
- Is strongly influenced by the preceding one. Therefore, management with a sense of an organization's history can anticipate and prepare for the next development stage.

By acknowledging the inevitability of the evolutionary process, preparing for and managing it, management can mitigate the potential crises inherent in growth and change to ensure a smooth transition to the next stage of organizational development.

Peters and Waterman (1982) share this view of the importance of managing the evolutionary process to ensure that the focus remains clearly on business need and objectives: 'To the extent that culture and shared values are important in unifying the social dimension of an organization, managed evolution is important in keeping a company adaptive.'

Nurturing the values of the organization, and sensitively and subtle 'managing' the internal environment of which culture is part, and which it influences and in turn is influenced by it, is a fundamental responsibility of management.

DIFFERENT CULTURES: CAN THEY COEXIST IN THE SAME ORGANIZATION?

A strong cohesive culture gives an organization the sense of identity, confidence, impetus and strength to compete successfully in the marketplace. However, as an organization grows and matures, it is inevitable that different subcultures develop. Culture is formed by the dominant group to serve a purpose. With growth, comes structural and professional differentiation. As various groups, professions, functions, departments and divisions become established, the purpose of their everyday reality gradually diverges. To suit their needs, they may develop different ways of behaving and working. Their orientation to the market, their priorities, time horizons, degrees of formality, and interpersonal and management styles may differ from those found elsewhere in the organization and from the 'official' or dominant culture. The organization develops into a network of systems and subsystems, each potentially with its own culture.

Some cultural differentiation within the organization is, therefore, inevitable. However, for the wellbeing of the organization, the degree of differentiation is all important; the greater it is, the greater the potential for conflict. As Handy (1976) says: 'Organizations that are differentiated in their cultures and which control that differentiation by integration are likely to be more successful.' Without integration, differentiation will lead to fragmentation, unhealthy internal competition, communication breakdown and potential disintegration.

The key to successful coexistence and organizational cohesion, therefore, is integration of the various subcultures into a strong 'parent' culture. Cultural diversity within subgroups can be tolerated provided their values are fundamentally consistent with the values of the dominant culture and that relations external to the subgroup conform to the overriding cultural norm.

Inevitably this will lead to some tension at times within the organization as internal norms spill over into external relations, but these tensions can be a healthy challenge to some of the basic assumptions inherent in the predominant culture and can encourage appropriate adaptation. According to Peters and Waterman (1982), successful organizations have found ways of breaking down functional divisions so that different professionals can act with reference to a common and integrated set of norms and priorities.

The extent to which diversity weakens or strengthens the organization is dependent on the quality of leadership at the top, the clarity of its vision and the ability of management throughout the organization to coordinate relations within and across functions.

CHANGING CULTURE

Can it be changed?

The essence of an organization is its culture. Therefore, any effective organizational change implies cultural change.

The impetus for organizational change tends to originate from outside the organization, in the form of legislation, competition, consumer demand, and technological developments. To respond to these impulses, new organizational structures, new business processes, and new attitudes may be necessary. Culture is of crucial significance to an organization's ability to adapt, evolve and change, and as such it must be recognized and treated as a powerful business variable, every bit as important as the quantitative variables that management takes for granted as its responsibility to manage. It is the function of management to anticipate change and prepare for it by ensuring a cultural environment flexible enough to respond and adapt in a relatively painless way.

The stronger the culture and the bonds which bind it, the more resistant it is likely to be to influence from outside and the more insular and exclusive it is likely to become. Initially, this has positive implications for the commitment and loyalty that can be generated and harnessed to the objectives of a fledgling business. However, as the business develops and its needs and priorities change in response to the external environment, without management vigilance such cohesion may also hold the seeds of introspection, inflexibility and resistance to change. There is always the danger of a strong culture evolving to suit the agenda and aspirations of the most dominant group, rather than supporting the needs of the business.

Culture is therefore too important to organizational health and development to be left to evolve by chance. Being value-driven, however, culture does have an imperative of its own, so managers can only manage the process of cultural evolution to the extent of controlling some of its behavioural and structural manifestations. They can challenge the underpinnings and suggest alternatives, but, unlike other business variables, culture cannot be controlled, managed or actively changed. 'Managers can influence the evolution of culture by being aware of the symbolic consequences of their actions and by attempting to foster desired values but they can never control culture in the sense that many management writers advocate' (Morgan, 1986).

Culture can and does change: that is, it can be *influenced* to change, but it cannot *be* changed. It does not exist independently of its members; rather it is the manifestation of the values and ideals of the group. Culture will therefore change only where there is a willingness and commitment to change. Full commitment requires more than an attraction to some future reality. Inherent in change, especially change effecting fundamental, ingrained and cherished values, is an element of stress, tension, fear, discomfort, and uncertainty. Thus however attractive the new prospect may be, there also has to be a conscious disengagement from the comfort and reassurance of the traditional and familiar values and ways. Any change programme, if it is to result in lasting change, *293* must take account of this push as well as pull effect. It must articulate a vision of a better future, based on a different set of values, to capture attention and stimulate interest whilst simultaneously generating, by comparison, a degree of dissatisfaction and disillusion with the *status quo*. It must stimulate commitment to new values whilst encouraging disengagement from old ones.

Change will only take place when the opinion formers and culture shapers in an organization can be persuaded and influenced to identify with and enact a more compelling set of values than those which to date have served them well.

Culture change and leadership

Successful change is a function of the quality of leadership not only at the top of an organization, but also throughout it. It depends upon the leaders having the following attributes:

- Appreciation of the power of culture and its importance to the life and wellbeing of the organization.
- Respect for people and their values.
- Willingness to listen.
- Sympathetic understanding of the degree of reassurance, comfort and security which resides in an established culture and the insecurity and inherent fear of change and the unknown.
- Appreciation of the conservative force of well-established vested interests.
- Ability to devise and communicate convincingly an enticing and meaningful vision of the desired future position.
- Ability to persuade and influence the culture makers and opinion formers to champion the cause of change.
- Ability to appeal to the 'hearts and minds' of all employees.
- Total commitment to effective and harmonious change.

How to change culture

Culture involves people – not structures, systems or procedures, but the people who design and operate them. Change is a behavioural phenomenon, not a systems one. Behaviour derives from attitudes, which in turn derive from values and beliefs. Therefore, changing attitudes is a prerequisite of successful cultural and organizational change, not a result or consequence of it. Success or failure depends on people's willingness to change their views and to identify and cooperate with a changed environment.

Any programme for change which targets operational processes and information technology (IT) applications, without taking account of the fundamental fact that all business processes comprise human processes, is doomed to failure. Any strategy which focuses on structures and processes without paying concomitant attention to people and culture, may, indeed, *294* have an impact on the organization, but not the impact intended. It is more likely to provoke cultural entrenchment and resistance than adaptation and change.

Not until a sufficiently high number of individual employees are persuaded to accept a new process, 'internalize it' into their value system, and 'make it their own', does it become part of the 'new culture'. It is the process of accepting and enacting that makes the changed process eventually become part of 'the way things are done'.

There is no magic formula for culture change, no single model that can be prescribed to suit all situations. The solution lies within the problem itself. The answer to what change is needed, how change can be effected, and what techniques and processes should be used, lies within each unique culture. The first step towards effective change, therefore, is to understand in detail the prevailing culture.

All too often, the mistake is made of assuming that official statements or traditional descriptions of the culture of an organization represent the true picture. It is necessary to probe behind these assumptions before planning a change programme. As well as identifying aspects of the culture which may block change, this will also highlight where there are levers for change within the existing culture. Identifying and making use of these methods in the name of change, makes the process easier. It will also provide clues on how to go about it.

The tools and techniques

The tools and techniques used do not have to be complicated. I have used successfully various straightforward means to get beneath the surface of an organizational climate whilst also catalysing the process of change.

Example 1 – consultation and involvement

The IT division of a well-known financial services company, with a reputation for technical innovation, was faced with the prospect of radical change – to its skillbase, manpower profile and strategy, project management practices and procedures, management style, organizational structure, performance assessment, control systems, and to the locus of ownership and power shifting to the end business user – due to the introduction of state-of-the-art technology and its application to business processes.

By means of confidential structured interviews with all middle and senior managers and randomly selected junior managers, and with more in-depth follow-ups with those acknowledged to be opinion formers, role models and resisters to change, I was able to survey the potential for change, identify likely barriers to change and catalyse the process of disengagement through encouraging individuals to question and challenge the *status quo*.

My coordinated findings and impressions were then presented to the same managers in mixed level groups, where discussion was facilitated to open up dialogue on a strategy for change.

Being commercially aware, they could well appreciate the business rationale for change, but were worried on a personal level about the changes to their role and skill profile that were implied in the shift from task to people management and by their lack of confidence in their abilities to make this transition successfully; they were apprehensive about the communication and business skills required at a fairly junior level to support the new customer focus; and they were concerned about the obsolescence of traditional, highly valued, technical skills. This information and their suggestions signposted the next stages of the change strategy, as follows:

- To identify the competencies required to manage in the new environment, through consultation with a cross section of the management team.
- To introduce development centres for all managers across the division, involving and cascading down from director level; to assess management ability against the identified competencies and to design individual development plans. As well as being participants, selected managers from all levels were trained and used as assessors, to reinforce the development of people management skills and promote commitment to the process.
- To design an integrated performance management and career development system which would reinforce the new management style and role and clarify career paths. The new appraisal system, incorporating the principle of self-assessment, was designed with the cooperation of a small, voluntary and interested management task force. It was then piloted in two out of five divisions, using volunteer appraisers. The complete system was implemented among the 600 staff in small work groups, led by trained 'tutors' taken from all levels of management.
- To produce a strategy for technical reskilling and non-management training, through consultation with management across the divisions, incorporating decentralized budgetary accountability to further reinforce ownership.

Managers were encouraged and empowered to champion further change not only by appealing to their 'hearts and minds', but also through recognizing that new skills and reinforcing systems were required to enable them to enact the new attitude change and carry it through into behaviour. Throughout, the key to changing attitudes comprised consultation, involvement and targeting interested parties who had organizational influence to 'champion' the new processes. The time taken was well spent because it demonstrated to the staff that they mattered, and that the company was prepared to invest time and money in their development and would support them through the transition phase.

Example 2 - the value statement

296 Faced with a new senior management team, and the business challenge of

building up a strong roster of successful artists, the chairman of one of the largest media companies in the United Kingdom had a vision to create a company that would be differentiated from its competitors in terms of its commitment to staff and their development. He envisaged a company which attracted talented people to join and stay as long-term players because they felt valued, were developed and enjoyed real job satisfaction, and where the quality of internal relationships between staff would be mirrored in external relationships with artists, customers and suppliers. He wanted the company to become the first employer of choice in the industry.

I drew up a corporate value statement using data generated during a previous director workshop to produce a company mission statement. It encapsulated the values and cultural aspirations for the company of the chairman and senior directors. The principles embodied in the statement were:

- Commitment to customers and artists.
- Commitment to staff; respect for each other.
- Quality.
- Professionalism.
- Teamwork.
- Management through partnership.
- Two-way feedback and communication.
- Decentralized responsibility and accountability .
- Responsibility for self-development.
- Commitment to and participation in company success.

However, it was appreciated that this was more a statement of intent rather than a description of current reality. Like its competitors, this company in the past had experienced and suffered from the culture of the entertainment industry in general: high staff turnover, especially at junior level and in the creative departments where poaching by competitors was the norm, short-term rolling contracts for key staff, which did not promote a sense of security or encourage long-term company loyalty or commitment, little investment in staff development, and high salaries used as bait to lure talent away from the competition and to precariously retain them once enticed to join.

Rolling several steps into one – testing current reality, presenting a vision of an alternative environment and beginning the disengagement process – I used the dissemination throughout the company of the value statement as the catalyst for change. Everyone in the company was invited to attend a three-hour, cross-functional and multilevel discussion group, where the value statement and its rationale were presented. Discussion was facilitated around the following elements:

- Whether the values and the environment that were initially envisaged actually reflected the true situation.
- Those aspects of the current culture likely to block, and forces conducive to, the enactment of the values.

- What each individual and each group as a whole could and would commit to in order to move the current environment closer to the vision.
- Those aspects beyond their control, mostly involving financial investment rather than behaviour change, which senior management would have to influence.

Feedback from the groups was collated – their own commitments to change and their suggestions for management attention – and passed to the board for review and discussion. Issues requiring further investigation into feasibility, cost and strategy were grouped and passed to one of the directors to 'champion' and take forward. To continue the process of involvement and empowerment, an open invitation was extended to staff on all sites to participate in task forces set up and chaired by the respective directors to drive the issues forward.

The process of consultation, involvement and participation generated enormous energy, enthusiasm and commitment, and successfully initiated the process of working together across functional and geographical boundaries to create a working environment which everyone could be proud of. Change was seen in a positive light, with any cynicism and resistance being talked out and worked through in the various groups and task forces. The exercise had impact not only on the way things were done, but also on the perception employees had of their ability and confidence to influence events.

Example 3 – catalyst of change

A young, entrepreneurial IT consultancy had reached that stage in its development where it faced the challenge of sustaining into its next phase of growth the strength of its distinctive character which had differentiated it and fuelled its ambitions and success to date.

The company had a strong culture from the beginning under the charismatic influence of two of its founders. They were visionaries not only about technology, but also about people, organization and business. Their joint vision and reputation was what drove the company forward, attracting talented employees and prestigious clients alike. It was a company suffused with a passionate belief in its pioneering mission at the forefront of technology. The conviction that it was different and better, which its employees lived to the full and demonstrated in everything they did, was what formed the basis of its reputation amongst clients and competitors.

However, as it approached its fifth anniversary, the company had begun to recruit professional managers, to organize functionally, and had been forced by reality and necessity to relax its elitist recruitment policy. Rumblings were beginning to be heard from the 'old timers' about 'the good old days'.

When I had first become involved with the company I had been asked to produce a culture statement, encapsulating the ideals of the founders. All new recruits to the company received a copy. The principles embodied in the culture statement were: customer first; excellence; teamworking; professionalism;

and profitability. It was my belief that, essentially, the culture still reflected these values and that they continued to be enacted in the conduct of business. However, with increased size and more sophisticated structures and management systems, the immediacy of earlier days and some traditional team-reinforcing rituals, customs and practices were less feasible. This was beginning to generate the perception that the company was becoming bureaucratic, less involving and less team-oriented. Time was also playing tricks on recall: memories of 'how it used to be' had become somewhat distorted and rose-tinted over time. Some of the mythology which had helped forge the strong culture was now getting in the way of its natural development.

However unfounded, those perceptions would nonetheless influence behaviour and were potentially potent demotivators. They could not be ignored or dismissed. All the illusions, misperceptions, fears and concerns had to be brought out into the open, worked through and turned into positive energy, constructive suggestions and commitment for the next phase of growth and company success. Life had to be breathed back into the culture statement to make it once more the foundation for all practices in the company.

In mixed-level, cross-functional groups of about fifteen people each, the whole company was taken off-site for two-day team-building workshops. Using a proprietary organizational climate questionnaire (Sashkin) and referring to the culture statement, they were encouraged to compare the founders' vision of the company and its culture with current reality. Working in small groups, they were asked to discuss what needed to change and to come up with constructive suggestions as to how it might be done, with an emphasis on what they could and would commit to do, both individually and as a group. At the end of the intensive workshop each group presented its comments, recommendations and commitments to the managing director and chairman, who in turn briefed the rest of the senior management team.

One of the most significant outcomes was a recommendation to radically change the remunerations strategy and introduce a team-based profit-sharing scheme, rather than a scheme for individuals. Following this, the sales team opted to align its remuneration structure to the general company policy, rather than move to a more conventional, commission-based, sales incentive plan.

Again, the process of consultation in a group setting – however painful and uncomfortable it was to release pent-up frustrations and emotions – was powerfully cathartic and catalytic in generating positive energy for and commitment to the ethos and success of the company.

These are only a few examples of how pragmatic, workable, straightforward change strategies can be devised and implemented successfully by 'listening' to what the existing culture of an organization is 'saying'.

PREREQUISITES FOR CULTURAL CHANGE IN AN ORGANIZATION

Irrespective of company size, industry sector or whether single or multi-sited, *299* the essential elements for successful change are the same. Whilst the logistics of the process may differ, consultation, two-way communication, and employee and management involvement, are still the indispensable conditions for successful change. They underpin and reinforce all other prerequisites.

1 Clear business objectives and vision

Top management must be clear about, and in agreement on, business objectives, and have a vision of the kind of environment necessary to achieve them.

2 Top management agreement and commitment

The top team must be in agreement on the need for change and be committed to changing the culture, the organization and their own behaviour if necessary. They do not have to be the initiators of change. Recognition of the need for change may well come from operating managers who are closer to day-to-day environmental and organizational reality, but senior management must be active champions of change.

3 Definition of the current cultural climate

The emphasis must be as much on where the organization is coming from as on where it is heading. The strategy for change must be based on an analysis of the present state of the organization and its culture and a diagnosis of its strengths and weaknesses.

4 Total management commitment

As first-line contact with the people, managers must champion change through their own behaviour, the promotion of an environment conducive to new behaviours, and through the behaviour they encourage, promote, reward and punish in their staff.

5 Total employee participation

Depending on the size of the organization it may not be feasible, possible or even necessary, to involve everyone directly in the discussion/consultation process. At this stage, staff may be involved indirectly through appropriate representatives (indeed, these companywide surrogates can be invaluable at the implementation stage as informed and committed champions of change). It is essential, however, that everyone participates directly, at the very least, in the training and communication processes. All staff must feel, and actually be, involved at some stage and feel able to make their voice heard at any stage.

6 Cross-functional champions and sponsors

300   No one individual can effect or implement change. Change can only come

about from a team effort where responsibility and ownership are shared. Identifying and empowering champions early in the change process is one way leaders can generate widespread organizational commitment to a new strategy. However, to ensure that the impetus for change and the momentum of the implementation team are sustained, all change needs a strong individual – clear and steadfast in his or her vision, and with organizational power, credibility and clout – to sponsor the cause of change and consistently push it forward.

7 Two-way, open and honest communication

Nothing more quickly destroys credibility and generates cynicism and distrust than management paying lip service to consultation. The parameters of consultation must be communicated upfront and honestly. The boundaries should be set as widely as possible but if any areas are inappropriate or off limits they should be spelled out and the rationale given. Similarly, if suggestions are made which are not to be implemented, reasons must be fed back. Management must be prepared to listen and to act where appropriate; and where action is not appropriate, they must be prepared to explain why. Whilst the formal communication processes used must be structured and co-ordinated, there must always be sufficient flexibility to accommodate informal dialogue also. Finally, as much attention should be given to the process of communication as to the content. Whilst 'the medium is the message', it is also an important part of the change process.

8 Long-range strategy, short-range plans

There must be a long-range flexible strategy, which can change and adapt in response to feedback and suggestions. Short-range plans and benchmarks ensure that the target remains realistic. They provide regular opportunities to communicate achievement, thus sustaining motivation and momentum and generating an ongoing sense of partnership, cooperation, respect and gratitude.

For change to take place, employees must be made receptive to the idea of change, and must understand the benefit to them that change will bring. They also need help and support to implement change into their own work situation.

CUSTOMER SERVICE AS PRIME DIFFERENTIATOR

It is true that a strong, cohesive culture can give an organization a head start in the competition stakes. Unlike product innovations and novel marketing strategies, which give competitor advantage temporarily – until the competition catches up – culture cannot be copied. As Peters and Waterman (1982) state: 'The excellent companies had gotten to be the way they are because of a unique set of cultural attributes that distinguish them from the rest.'

However, uniqueness itself is not the key differentiator. Whether or not competitor advantage can be won and sustained depends on the nature of the culture and its underpinning values. Unless the culture is outward looking and responsive to changing circumstances, its strength will be lost in introspection and entrenchment. The most compelling cultural focus – external, with inherent flexibility and the power to integrate internal diversity around a powerful umbrella ethos – is the customer. Customer service is the value that drives and differentiates excellent companies.

REFERENCES

Graves, D. (1986), *Corporate Culture: Diagrams and Change*, New York: St Martin's Press adapted from R. Harrison (1972), 'Understanding Your Organization's Character', *Harvard Business Review*, May–June, 119–28.

Greiner, L. E. (1972), 'Evolution and Revolution as Organizations Grow', *Harvard Business Review*, July–August, 37–46.

Hampden-Turner, C. (1994), *Corporate Culture: How to Generate Organisational Strength and Lasting Commercial Advantage*, London: Piatkus.

Handy, C. (1976; 3rd edition 1985), *Understanding Organizations*, 3rd edn, Harmondsworth: Penguin.

Handy, C. (1978), *The Gods of Management*, London: Souvenir Press, adapted in D. Graves (1986), *Corporate Culture: Diagrams and Change*, New York: St Martin's Press.

Laurent, A. (1990), adapted by C. Hampden-Turner op. cit. in P. Evans (ed.), *Human Resources Management in International Firms*, London: Macmillan.

Morgan, G. (1986), *Images of Organization*, London: Sage.

Peters, T. J. and Waterman, R. H. (1982), *In Search of Excellence: Lessons from America's Best-run Companies*, New York: Harper & Row.

Sashkin, M., *Pillars of Excellence: Organizational Beliefs Questionnaire*, Bryn Mawr, PA: Organization Design and Development.

Schein, E. (1990), 'Organisational Culture: What Is It and How to Change It', in P. Evans (ed.), *Human Resources Management in International Firms*, London: Macmillan.

FURTHER READING

Hampden-Turner, C. (1994), *Corporate Culture: How to Generate Organisational Strength and Lasting Commercial Advantage*, London: Piatkus.
Handy, C. (1976: repr. 1985), *Understanding Organizations*, 3rd edn, Harmondsworth: Penguin.
Morgan, G. (1986), *Images of Organization*, London: Sage.
Peters, T. J. and Waterman, R. H. (1982), *In Search of Excellence: Lessons from America's Best-run Companies*, New York: Harper & Row.

23 Service as a cross-functional responsibility

Laurie Young

Customer service is different in nature and importance at different phases of a company's development. In its early years, a company is likely to set up a department to provide 'service support'. This is normally to handle technical difficulties with the product but it might also be necessary to manage telephone enquiries from the public and resolve problems with bills. The people in these departments become very effective at handling upset customers and restoring goodwill. However, as the company grows and the industry matures, these methods of service delivery become ineffective, even if the departments involved are highly efficient.

At the time of writing, the mobile service providers in the telecommunications market are blooming. Most of them are young companies with service support functions who provide connections to the network, resolve billing enquiries and handle fault reports. As the market begins to mature, however, they are rethinking their service infrastructure.

The margin on the sale of mobile telephony is falling rapidly and the suppliers are therefore having to think through how they create profit. Answers include 'using service to differentiate' or 'improved customer care'. Some want to design a service environment which appeals to target customers and can be used as an infrastructure through which low margin products can be sold (a warehouse of telephones for example). This latter concept is modelled on the fast-food industry where, for example, McDonalds has created an appealing service infrastructure through which high-volume, lower-margin goods can be sold. The various expressions of new service models have not yet been decided but are beginning to evolve in this young industry.

So, as industries evolve, it becomes increasingly difficult to assign clear responsibility for the new concepts of service in a traditional structure. Suppliers may need to look for new methods of managing service that go far beyond the original, functional roles. The company has to create a vision of *303* new service paradigms, gain acceptance for those concepts and design a new organizational approach. This chapter examines the drawbacks to a functional organization in delivering service; and methods by which cross-functional service strategies can be developed as the nature and significance of service changes.

THE FUNCTIONAL ORGANIZATION

The functional model of the workplace, where people carry out a specific business role in departmental structures, is a feature of a 'bureaucratic' organization. Bureaucracy has been used as a derogatory term in recent times and it has been postulated that newer, 'network' organizations need to evolve in the information age. However, this organizational structure is very common and has been a very effective way of progressing industrial enterprises. At the turn of the twentieth century, one of the early specialists in organizational behaviour, Weber, pointed out that bureaucracy combined with functional hierarchy is a very efficient way to organize. By breaking down tasks into specialist functions, companies have been able to increase their effectiveness and their profitability. It may therefore be the most effective way to organize in certain phases of market and company development.

The people who work within a functional organization are organized into specialist departments, which might include marketing, sales, operations, finance and so on (see Figure 23.1). The benefit of a functional organization is that the people involved have a clear view of the nature and aim of their daily tasks. The mechanisms and approach of, say, a human resources function are similar in different organizations and different business sectors. They have been learnt over years of industrial experience and are now represented in, what is considered to be, a modern, professional approach. A similar evolution of technique has occurred in other functions such as accountancy, marketing and sales. Individuals are able to move into companies from other industries and apply a cross-sector set of skills which are of immediate benefit.

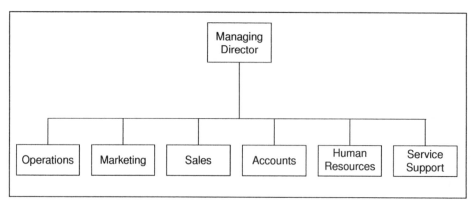

Figure 23.1   Representation of a functional organization

This facility is particularly important in the early growth of a company because it allows the directorate to concentrate on the prime tasks. For example, at the time of writing, cable television in Britain is a young industry. Their immediate task is to use investment to put the infrastructure of a cable network into the streets. By organizing into functional roles they are able to maintain this task as the prime focus of the organization and allow functions like accountancy or human resources to establish recognized procedures or practices with minimal involvement. Specialization therefore becomes the method of progressing the organization.

SPECIFIC SERVICE FUNCTIONS

Although there might be a large department in a functional company called 'service', it may not be responsible for all the service tasks. There are often different aspects of service, in different parts of the organization.

Customer service

This group is specifically responsible for the management of complaints or difficulties from the customer. They are often brought into the process after the normal line operations have failed to handle a customer's difficulty satisfactorily.

Service support

Support service is generally the function dedicated to resolving any technical problems with the product provided. The task is to take reports from customers about difficulties with the performance of the product and to resolve them as efficiently as possible. It might also involve the deployment of resource to prevent difficulties arising in the first place. The function can range from telephone support, with people able to resolve difficulties via remote technology, to a large 'field force' organization equipped with technical people able to visit customers' premises to resolve problems. The principal objective of the role is to get the customers' equipment back into operation as speedily as possible, but because of the technical expertise of this function, it normally has other related responsibilities such as the original installation of equipment or special technical projects.

Arrears

This is a specialist billing function responsible for debt management and the chasing of late payments. Although normally part of the finance function, it is increasingly recognized as an important part of service because it is a non-sales customer contact which can affect propensity to rebuy.

Telephone reception

This function can range from the 'PABX' operators, who receive general telephone calls to the company from the public, to specialist telephone reception teams who receive calls from customers for specific purposes. Although clearly a service role, it is often without a recognized functional home. For instance, PABX answering can be combined with the receptionist's task, or it can be part of 'buildings facilities management' or 'customer service'. Sometimes it is subcontracted or left to unmanaged temporary staff. However, as it is without a clear functional home, it is often neglected. Although an important – sometimes a first – interface with the customer it can be left unaware of organizational roles and staff changes. It often involves minimal training and few clear measures of success. This can lead to lost sales opportunities and lost customers because a poor impression is created in the customer's mind by people who are poorly briefed, managed or trained.

Although the general 'PABX' operators might be neglected, many companies are aware of the need to provide efficient management of specific calls from existing customers for service assistance. They often provide a dedicated telephone number with trained and experienced people who are able competently to handle telephone enquiries. This needs to be backed by good processes such as efficient call management, access to up-to-date customer information and the ability to set back-office procedures in motion. It is increasingly seen as an important specialist component of the service recovery function; some organizations are developing highly sophisticated 'help desks' or dedicated support units for important customers.

WHEN SERVICE IS BIGGER THAN ONE FUNCTION

The difficulty with creating organizations to manage service is that it can be such a broad set of responsibilities. The word 'service' can include any, or all, of the following: pre-sales support; after-sales service; customer service (complaints handling); the service environment; customer care strategies; relationship management; and added-value services.

Service recovery is only one, limited, version of service. A good service director soon begins to realize that service, like the management of a company, is a holistic interdependent system: a change in one part affects others. Uncoordinated tactical changes can have negative effects. For instance, a reduction in inventory to save costs can cause poorer service and thus lose customers. Or poor performance by either the PABX function or the billing department might cause customers to criticize the company's quality of service, even if they are not part of the service director's responsibilities. The director must therefore attempt to define the framework of service for the company at each phase of its development, based upon a knowledge of the strategic significance of service to the market. They must then set overall quality goals for this new service paradigm and all the associated processes to
deliver it.

There have been few models or tools to help make these important decisions. A method of proactively planning different service paradigms is needed. One technique which is effective is the 'feature analysis' model.

The various types of service (from simple maintenance recovery, through to a 'service only' offering) are represented in Figure 23.2. They use 'features analysis' to identify service components and illustrate different manifestations of service. This concept suggests that the 'offer' of a company comprises three sets of features:

1 *Core features.* The hub of the offer.
2 *Augmented features.* The way the offer is presented to the customer.
3 *Emotional features.* The way the offer appeals to the customers' psyche.

These features might be physical or conceptual and the 'offer' will therefore range from a predominantly physical product to one which is predominantly service. In each case, the customer buys the complete set of features and it is the combination of all three levels which set value perceptions.

In diagram 1, Figure 23.2, service is only an emotional reassurance that support will be available if the customer buys the product. However, in diagram 2, service is much more an integral part of the offer: the supplier has used service support features to 'differentiate the product'. Diagram 3 represents a substantially different proposition where an integrated service experience has been designed to appeal to a distinct customer group through which the product is sold. Finally, diagram 4 represents a service-only offer, such as management consultancy.

The way a company organizes responsibilities for each of these expressions of service will be different. In the case of diagram 1, a functional organization is likely, whereas diagram 4 will probably be supported by the sort of matrix structure found in most professional services firms. The difficulty arises in organizing service for diagrams 2 and 3; or if the company has to shift the nature of its offer from one to another.

Service can therefore evolve from the routine and mechanistic acts of a young company (represented in diagram 1) to cover all the attitudes and relationships of a mature company with its customers (diagram 3). Full, profitable service management is thus much broader than mere service recovery. It is different in the following ways:

1 Profitable service is holistic. It encompasses the whole relationship with the customer, whereas service recovery is the restoration of a specific process which is only part of that relationship. The service recovery is finished once the issue is resolved.
2 Profitable service is an offer to the customer which integrates environment, people, location, processes and product into a unique experience that the customer finds attractive. It can be a prime distribution mechanism in its own right. Service recovery is a much more limited aspect of this.

High Product Content

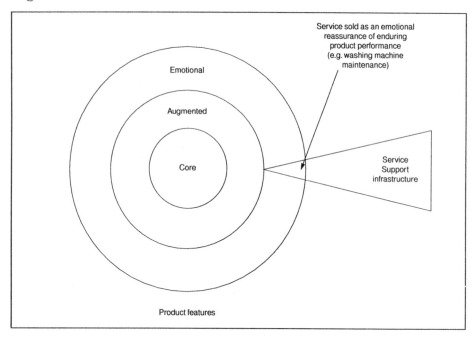

Service used to differentiate a product

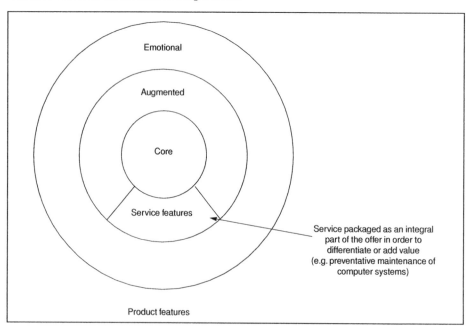

308   **Figure 23.2   Models of different service manifestations**

Low margin product sold through a service environment

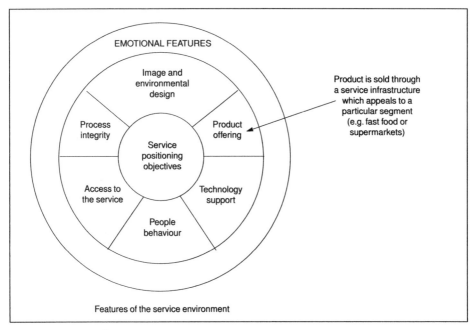

Features of the service environment

Service only or 'added value' offering

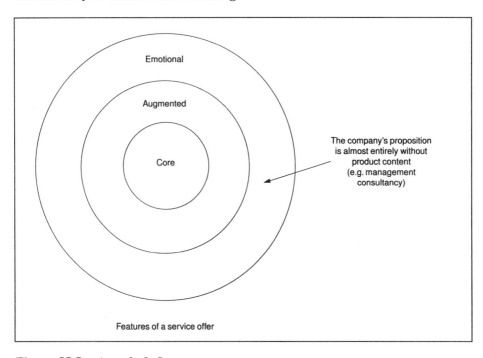

Features of a service offer

Figure 23.2 (concluded)

3   Profitable service is a value proposition which the customer finds attractive and is willing to pay an appropriate price for. Service recovery has a track record of servility, and, as a result, the managers responsible for it tend to undervalue their service, turning it into a commodity.

4   Profitable service is a cross-functional issue because it embodies the entire relationship with the customer. Service recovery is largely limited to the specific service functions listed above.

A broader definition of service is therefore needed. I would define it as: 'A proposition to the customer of features and benefits, beyond the physical product itself, which incur costs and are manageable'.

Service is concerned with the way in which the physical product is treated and delivered. It involves the manner, knowledge and attitude of the people involved in delivering it and the physical environment through which it is delivered. Even more broadly, it can be the nature of the relationship between the company and its customers; and the strategies or programmes which create profit from it. Most importantly, service is a holistic balance of features that meet customer expectation and changes as markets change.

IMPEDIMENTS TO SERVICE CAUSED BY A FUNCTIONAL APPROACH

There are signs that the functional model of organizational design is not always meeting current business requirements. For instance, in recent years many companies have reorganized frequently (some as much as once a year) because organizational structures have had to be adjusted to meet the rapidly changing demands of their business environment and their customers. There is also such a diversity of shape and responsibility in functional organizations that it is clear that no one structure meets all organizational needs. In addition, in almost any functional organization there are jobs that simply do not fit into traditional roles. For example, there are often people who have special project responsibility or new, unassigned functions such as 'total quality'. So functional structures have not always been equal to the general needs of modern business.

In addition, a functional organization can cause difficulties when it comes to providing excellent service. There are several reasons for this:

1. *Limited vision.* People working in a functional department concentrate upon their own tasks and develop a narrow perspective. They don't see the entirety of either the customer's requirements or the offer their company can make to them. Even functions that are charged with service responsibilities only constitute part of the customer relationship. For instance, as the service director is primarily interested in service recovery, they establish skills, processes and resources in order to recover service to the customer. Once service is restored, the service director will move on to the next recovery task. However, there may be other difficulties in the relationship that the customer has with the company or there may be opportunities for revenue to be developed from service initiatives but these are not in the immediate focus of the service director.

2. *Limited responsibility.* Functional departments are responsible for efficiently completing their task and no single person is therefore responsible for the customer's entire experience. People inside functions can damage service by not playing their full part in the customer relationship whilst still fully completing the job they are employed to do. For instance, there are occasions when the service director's tasks might interfere with other relationships with the customer. A sales team might want to sell a piece of replacement equipment to the customer. If the service director provides excellent preventive maintenance it makes their task harder.

3. *Vested interests.* In order to get their own point of view accepted, people develop political power and interests. Self-interest can be put above service to the customer. Even if they advocate the legitimate interests of their functional perspective they can damage the full service to the customer. The interests of the function are progressed rather than those of the customer.

4. *Limited job scope.* A function is designed to undertake a group of tasks that are part of the company's total operations. The jobs and roles inside a functional structure will therefore perform only a small part of the total tasks needed to serve a customer. As procedures evolve, people can take actions which look sensible from a functional perspective but which achieve nothing, and in fact look ridiculous, from the customer's perspective. Employees who are motivated to serve customers will therefore be continually frustrated and looking for ways to manage actions outside their immediate responsibility.

5. *Limited service offer.* As has already been discussed, service changes in significance for a company as market dynamics change. If the company is continuing to offer a form of service which no longer suits market requirements, it has a limited service offer and will fall behind any competitor that is more in tune with customer need. Some employees will be frustrated and look for ways to 'improve' service; others will regard it as the responsibility of a specific department rather than a cross-functional issue.

6. *Limited view of customer needs.* There can be a mismatch between the company's perspective of the service and the customer's perspective. One example is the timing and duration of the service. Customers might have a very different view of the transaction period from that of the supplier. For instance the 'perceived transaction period' of the customers of the cable TV offer clearly begins with the arrival of contractors in their area to dig the streets. Whereas the marketing people in the industry have often assumed that it begins when they send their first mailer, after cable has 'passed the home'. By then, customers may have already decided not to purchase because of the performance of the contractors.

A typical functional structure is likely to be operations driven and with largely financial goals. Top management will tend to have an autocratic and non-participative style. They are also likely to have a low degree of customer contact. This is communicated down the organization so that departments who do not deal *311* directly with customers (or those that perform a specific, limited customer task) see themselves as unable to affect customer satisfaction. In particular, in a functional organization, no one is responsible for the holistic design of service.

An organizational capability must be developed which concentrates on customer satisfaction, with profit resulting from accomplishing these goals. Companies have to develop an all-embracing relationship with customers that is more than just the achievement of individual product sales. Individuals need to be made responsible for the full service offer to one group of customers. Service then embraces the complete relationship of the customer to the company, whatever service paradigm is used to construct the offer.

THE IMPLICATIONS OF A BROADER SERVICE VISION

As an industry evolves, customers become more demanding and margins might come under pressure. There will also be pressure for service standards to increase. In these circumstances the company should consider taking a view of service which is more than just recovery and more than functional tasks. In order to achieve this broader service orientation it must begin to think about service in a new way. For instance, it must consider the following.

Start customer-focused planning

In a functional organization, business planning tends to be a functional responsibility. For instance, there will be a marketing plan, a sales plan and an operations plan, which are integrated into a company plan to meet corporate objectives. The difficulty with this plan is that each function has its own perspective and the perspective of the customer is lost. It is also difficult to realistically integrate the disparate functional plans. (Even if they are integrated, the resultant document does not always make a satisfactory plan. And, once funds are approved, functional heads can go back to their original intentions.) However, the most significant difficulty is that at no point does the planning process take a complete customer perspective.

The plan will contain objectives, product actions, sales targets and marketing programmes but will rarely take an open-minded view of the customers or orientate the business actions around them. This ought to be turned around and companies should consider a customer-focused planning process, in which they would first understand the needs, requirements and opportunities amongst customers and then design functional plans around those.

Customer segmentation

If service is a significant aspect of the offering with cross-functional perspective, then companies must accept that they cannot design a service for everyone. The segmentation of customer groups becomes a crucial strategic issue. The company must decide which customers it intends to serve and how it intends to serve them. It must choose its segments and direct the resources of the whole organization at those chosen segments. It follows that some customers will be attracted to the service and some will not.

The integration of service into the offer

As demonstrated in Figure 23.2, a change in the significance of service will involve a change in how the company creates value. The product managers will need to consider ways in which service can be engineered into the product, or plan a completely new framework of service delivery. They will have to learn the techniques of service development and concept construction, which are different from product management.

The organization structure

As a company matures, the emphasis of its management and organizational priorities have to change. In its early evolution it will tend to be product driven because it exists to bring its new concept to market. If it is successful it will become sales driven during its growth phase. However, as sales slow, and the market reaches maturity, it will have to become more customer orientated and service will become more significant. This is represented in Figure 23.3. The

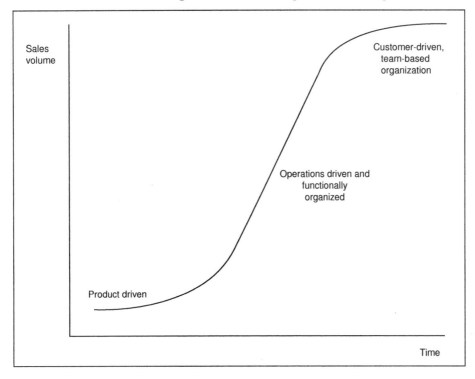

Figure 23.3 Changes in organizational focus in relation to company maturity

company changes from a product-driven environment through an operations emphasis to more of a customer emphasis. The characteristics of each are set out in Figure 23.4.

Product driven	Operations driven	Market driven
1. The customer is the distributor's business	1. Customer is the sales department's business	1. The customer has to be everyone's focus
2. Demand is opportunistic	2. Operations drive customer demand	2. Customer demand drives operations
3. Business is organized around product development	3. Business is organized around functional specialisms, operations around product groups	3. Business is organized around customer groups
4. Operations are orders driven	4. Operations are sales transaction driven	4. Operations are customer relationship driven
5. Business focus is on product development	5. Business focus is on immediate customers	5. Business focus is extended to ultimate end users
6. Marketing is unlikely to exist	6. Marketing consistency is lacking	6. Marketing is consistent and integrated
7. Service is erratic and unskilled	7. Service exists in functional departments	7. Service is part of relationship management

Figure 23.4   Changes in organizational philosophy and emphasis

There seems, then, to be an evolution of organizational focus and culture as companies mature. Survivors become more market-driven organizations with a broad definition of service. They tend to create business teams who are dedicated to serving discrete markets or groups of customers. The organization has to be leaner and responsive due to the need to perform in a lower margin environment. Employees have their attention set on satisfying customer needs. Management is more inclusive and less hierarchical because there is an awareness that the motivation of employees affects service and ultimately profit. Their style is consultative and participative and their diary is as full of customer contacts as internal meetings. Departments who do not deal with external customers understand their role in affecting customer satisfaction: they are involved in internal customer satisfaction.

An organization structure evolves which reflects these requirements. Managers are likely to represent the need to be 'non-hierarchical' by inverting the organizational roles. They will also suggest that boundaries between the company and its environment are more blurred. However, the most significant change is that the organization is likely to be configured around customer groups, with cross-functional teams dedicated to them. These groups might be full business units or small teams. This is represented in Figure 23.5.

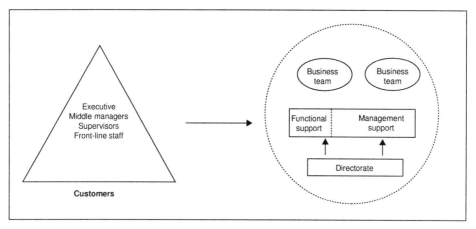

Figure 23.5   Changes in organizational emphasis resulting from a broader definition of service

HOW TO CREATE A BROADER SERVICE EMPHASIS

If the management team begins to realize that service is becoming a much broader issue than mere service recovery, they must begin to develop mechanisms by which it can become a cross-functional responsibility. They must look for cross-functional tools and levers in order to begin the process. These include the following.

Vision

Amongst the leading opinion formers in the organization a new vision must be created of the significance of service. This will involve clearly understanding the evolution of the market and the company's position within it. Colleagues must be educated in the changed requirements of customers through publishing research and through opening the organization up to the debate about the relation of service quality to profit growth. A new service paradigm, which will create competitive advantage and meet changed customer requirements, must then be defined and designed. It must be tested on customers and then sold to colleagues in order to provide a common direction for all employees.

Business planning

By vigorously participating in the corporate planning process, service directors can ensure that service is seen as more critical to the core offer. They *315* should challenge assumptions about target customers or the elements of the company's offer. The planning process should be renewed so that customer segmentation and research into the target customers' service needs occur early in the planning cycle. Planners should be made aware of the ways in which service can be integrated into the company's offer. The process should ensure that the resources of the company are deployed to meet the identified needs of those customers.

Political support

Politics, and political strategies, are a fact of commercial life which are rarely discussed in management texts. Yet they are often the subject of discussion in the workplace. Frequently, the implication of these discussions is that company politics is wrong. However, as all businesses are organizations built upon economic power, the key to achieving success with any initiative is to manage power. This is neither right nor wrong; it is merely a fact of life. As a change in service paradigm will cause changes to functions, job content and processes, the exercise will be intensely political. People will feel that their status and security is threatened. It is necessary, therefore, to plan a clear political strategy and to gain allies for the programme.

There are a number of people in other functions who could be allies to the positioning of service across functional responsibilities. For instance, the marketing director would be a natural ally. The marketing process begins with customer analysis and a vital emphasis in the marketing profession is the 'marketing concept', which seeks to orientate all functional activity around the customer and the market. In addition, there has recently emerged an emphasis inside the marketing community on relationship marketing. This concept suggests that, by concentrating on marketing to existing customers, the company can grow more profitably because it is far more costly to recruit new customers than to manage the relationship with existing ones. Similarly, the quality director should also be a natural ally because of the emphasis of the function.

Manage processes

A business process consists of people, using procedures, materials, information and technology to produce a specified business result. It is a recurring sequence of activities that add value and have measurable inputs and outputs. However, processes are also independent of the functional organization and often cross several functional lines. If they are managed carefully they can be used as a cross-functional lever to improve service.

Many business processes flow horizontally through an organization, resulting in vague ownership. With a vertical management structure, problems occur at the functional interfaces because there are usually very few defect measures at these interfaces. Root causes are therefore hard to identify and quantify. In fact, problems arising from difficulties with process performance at functional interfaces often take a long time to diagnose.

Notwithstanding the current emphasis on process re-engineering, by introducing the concept of 'process management' and by designing processes to serve the customers, it is possible to deliver improved service because the process is independent of functional responsibility. Service directors can get individuals in other functions to see the significance of their own participation in the process chain and the process will then manage the delivery of service to the customer.

The first step in improving business processes is the identification of a 'process owner'. This process owner does not have to have line responsibility for all aspects of the process but is responsible for the overall workings of the process and for its ability to meet customer requirements that have been agreed upon. The owner can be the manager with the most resource invested in the process, or the one feeling the most pain when things go wrong. They should be at a high enough level to see the process as part of the larger business picture and able to influence policy affecting the process, so that resources can be committed for improvement. The owner must be accountable for the process from its beginning to its end.

The objective of process management is to improve the effectiveness, efficiency, control and adaptability of the business processes in the following way:

- Charge line management with the responsibility to continually improve the effectiveness, efficiency and control of their business processes.
- Designate an owner to discharge this responsibility.
- Define and document the interfaces, boundaries and information flow of the process.
- Identify and collect data on defect-oriented measurements of the effectiveness and efficiency of the process.
- Apply quality tools and techniques to remove defects in the process.
- Evaluate future process requirements and devise and put in place means to eliminate constraints and deficiencies.

Each process usually has two sets of customers:

1　The 'company', which has requirements for the orderly functioning of the business. These requirements include policies, practices, laws, ethics, budgets, corporate instructions and so on.
2　The 'user', who is the person or function who actually uses the process output. These requirements relate to the functional aspects of the service.

Having determined the customer requirements, the process owner must decide on the level of service to be provided. For instance, what functions, response times, reliability and availability are needed to meet the requirements of internal or external customers. This design of the service will depend on such things as the resources the business is willing to invest, the expected return on that investment, the users' expectations and the relationship that *317* the service has to the objectives of the enterprise. The level of service should be decided through a negotiation with the customer, resulting in a mutual understanding of the needs and constraints of both the process owner and customer.

Take advantage of fashions in management thought

It seems that there have always been fads in management thought. In recent years these have included total quality, customer care and BSI registration. The latest is 'process re-engineering'. A fad first appears as one item on conference agendas but soon has whole conferences dedicated to it. Articles, 'experts' and books then appear. Finally, it is being offered as a service by all the large consultancies.

It is surprising how easily senior executives will invest resources in these new concepts even if they do not show the benefits that their proponents promised. Like dieters, the companies involved (particularly at middle management level) assume that they are the reason the wonder theory is not quite as good as promised. For instance: 'Our process re-engineering project will not make a radical difference because it is staffed by people who have a vested interest in the functions being re-engineered' or 'The politics here means that our TQM programme isn't as objective or systematic as the Japanese one, so it won't work as well'. As a result the concept soon becomes 'perceived wisdom' – difficult to challenge until it falls out of fashion. Eventually sceptical articles appear (such as 'Does TQM really pay back?') and the fad loses its prominence.

There are also minor fads, which tend to stay within the functional specialism that created them. They are often created by the supply side, who debate them in specialist journals and commission self-fulfilling research on the subject. They then become common currency amongst the functional specialists inside client organizations but do not come to dominate company thinking. For instance, at the time of writing, the latest fads in the information technology world are 'outsourcing' and 'client-server' architectures. In marketing it is clearly 'customer loyalty'.

As fads generally have cross-functional support, they can be used as the basis of gaining cross-functional action to improve service. For example, process re-engineering can gain improvement in process, improving service, because the concept starts with a discussion of customer requirements. Similarly, TQM emphasizes the co-ordination of cross-functional resources to meet customer requirements.

SUMMARY

The word 'service' covers a wide variety of activities from 'after-sales service' to 'added-value services'. Recent management thinking seems to have lost sight of the fact that functional specialism and bureaucracy are very effective ways to organize and achieve business objectives. A specific service department might therefore be appropriate in certain market conditions and at certain stages in a company's development. However, as a company grows and evolves, the service paradigm with which the company operates must also change. It will change in both content and strategic significance. Levers must then be found to ensure that a full perspective of service is understood and managed by the company. These are likely to be cross-functional and have far-reaching implications with regard to the shape and nature of the organization.

FURTHER READING

Armistead, C. (1994), *The Future of Service Management*, London: Kogan Page.
Maister, D. (1993), *Managing the Professional Service Firm*, New York: Free Press.
Rust, R. and Oliver, R. (1994), *Service Quality: New Directions in Theory and Practice*, London: Sage.

24 Roles, not jobs
Paul Chapman

If Frederick W. Taylor, the inventor of 'scientific management' at the beginning of this century and Arthur Sloan, head of General Motors in the 1930s, credited with developing the functional/divisional organization design, were to look down from their celestial resting places (assuming they ever got there) they could pronounce themselves satisfied that their ideas had stood the test of time. Whilst they may rest in peace with a wry smile of contentment, those of us still around and responsible for leading and managing today's organizations and institutions, public and private, might question how it is that, in a world which has changed so dramatically in the last 50 years (and continues to do so at an accelerating pace), we still base the way we organize work on designs and beliefs developed for and from a world so fundamentally different.

WHEN PRODUCTION WAS KING

Taylor and Sloan's designs for organizing work were developed for a world in which production was king. Demand for the goods which could be produced, following the nineteenth-century expansion of the world economy made possible by the Industrial Revolution, was almost infinite, certainly practically insatiable. The virtuous circle (see Figure 24.1) was almost perfect. The rules of the game were set by the suppliers, whose primary aim was to mass produce as many of the same goods as possible at the lowest possible cost, and lack of intense competition meant that prices could be set according to the profit the supplier wanted to make. Henry Ford's statement, 'any colour, so long as it is black', may be apocryphal, but it does nicely sum up the prevailing condition that choice was the supplier's perquisite, not the customer's.

Mass production at low cost – making the same things many thousands of times – meant as far as possible eliminating errors. Calibrating machines to achieve this is a relatively easy proposition; calibrating fallible human beings

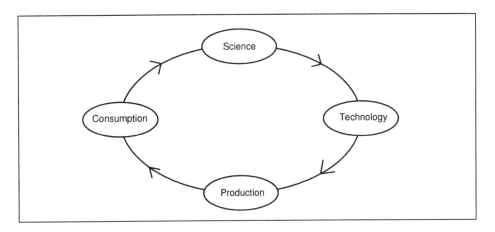

Figure 24.1   The virtuous circle

to the same standard of error-free work is a little trickier. Nevertheless, this is what organizations attempted to do, by breaking down the work to be done by people into easily learned, easily repeated tasks. Thinking, decisions, improving the way work was organized were matters which owners and their salaried managers worried about; the majority of the workforce simply did what they were told to do and were paid for the work produced.

Stark and simplistic as that may sound, if you look carefully at the way work is organized in many of today's organizations, even in the so-called service sectors, you will find that very little has changed. Managers decide how the work will be done and who will do it, and check the outputs before allocating further tasks. Those tasks are organized into a number of specialized 'jobs', but only the managers see the way each job relates to others and that information is jealously guarded in case someone decides that they can do away with the linking middle man.

REFORMING THE SYSTEM

There have of course been attempts to change this approach to work organization, going back as far as the research of the Tavistock Institute in the 1950s, which showed that when groups of workers were given responsibility for a total operation, the quality of their work improved, as did their morale. The total quality movement (TQM), various human resource (HR)-based initiatives, information technology (IT), and, more recently, business process re-engineering (BPR), have all in different ways addressed various aspects of the way work is organized and the work/human interface. Each has its supporters and detractors but it would be fair to say that no single approach has been universally recognized as providing radical, sustained improvement in effectiveness, efficiency or ability to satisfy customer requirements. The reasons for their lack of total success are, I believe, two-fold:

1. All organizations consist of three basic resources: people, processes (that is the way work gets done) and the systems to support the way these two work together. The complexity of modern work means that these resources are integrally related to each other, and changing one without understanding the impact on the others can have disastrous consequences. (One particularly ludicrous example I remember was in an American restaurant, where the old-fashioned waiter's pad and pencil had been replaced by a bar-coded menu and a bar code reader pen. Once the first two customers had asked for a variation to the set menu – not a particularly unusual occurrence in a table service restaurant – pandemonium followed, and order was only restored when the waiter retook all the orders using a good old-fashioned pad and pencil.) Yet each of the approaches I have mentioned above only addresses one of these resources. They do not address the issues in a holistic manner, so the benefits achieved by improving one aspect are dissipated by the lack of integration with the other two.

2. Most organizations tend to apply their chosen approach to improvement in pilot mode, either to a small part of an individual function or to a small subsidiary operation. This is doomed to failure from the start because:

(a) those with a vested interest in preserving the *status quo*, with the emphasis on 'status' as in 'most to lose', will make every effort to ensure that it fails;

(b) the best people will see it as a pilot, not of the mainstream, and will stay closer to the functional homefires to enhance their career prospects; and

(c) a radical reorganization of the way work is done in one small part of the organization cannot possibly interface effectively with the rest of the organization.

Shareholders' memories are short – you are only as good as your last dividend forecast – and their minds are wholly occupied with short-term results. It is a very brave chief executive, therefore, who would be prepared to make wholesale changes in the way the organization works – its people, its processes and its systems. Radical change is thus not likely to come from the core of our large companies owned by shareholders looking for constant incremental improvements in the value of their invested capital and their dividends. We will probably have to look to more unusual sources for new ways of working. For example:

- Greenfield operations, where the expectations are not preset and there are no established work patterns (for example, direct line personal financial services start-ups).
- Operations still owned by their originators with a vision of how things should be and little to lose except their own stake (Virgin and the early Body Shop spring to mind).
- Organizations which can take a longer-term view of their success but which, because of this, are usually seen as old-fashioned and

bureaucratic (for example, government departments) and mutual (that is owned by their members) institutions such as building societies.

Whilst these examples might provide the models for how work should be organized, they are hardly in the corporate mainstream. But if the way work is organized has been successful in the past and if radical change is so difficult and unproven and if the shareholders are probably not going to like it, why change? What imperative should drive the directors of companies comfortably placed in their chosen markets to jeopardize their livelihoods by leading radical transformation of their organization. The answer is two words – customer service. The rules have changed and will continue to change at an accelerating pace. Increasing competition, increasing information available to customers, and the increasing ability of customers to articulate their dissatisfaction through improved education and forums available, mean that customer expectations are radically different now than they were fifty years ago.

THE DEVELOPMENT OF CUSTOMER SERVICE

Increasingly, our public institutions – the courts, the police, local and national government, the banks even – are required to have greater accountability to the public, and because of this they have been shown to be fallible. Whilst the vast majority of people still believe (at least in democratic, non-totalitarian countries) that these institutions provide the most effective means of safeguarding the social infrastructure, as they are increasingly asked to take greater personal responsibility for their own financial, social and physical security, so individuals expect a degree of accountability and improvement in the way these institutions fulfil their responsibilities. The same is true of their expectations of companies supplying goods and services to satisfy their requirements. The difference is that whilst they will complain vociferously at any questionable actions, they will continue to trust in the great public institutions. Conversely, if their expectations of a company are disappointed, they will simply walk away. It is often said that companies should worry less about those people who shout loudly when they are not satisfied with the goods or services and more about those who say nothing but simply take their business elsewhere.

Customers have choices: they feel they have a right to information on the goods and services they have ordered or bought and are no longer frightened of 'the people who know better', 'the men in grey suits'. Recently I read a newspaper report of an incident where a UK clearing bank had used the funds in a child's pocket money account to sort out an irregularity in the parent's account. People were rightly outraged. Then I thought that my father's generation would probably have assumed that 'there is more to this than meets the eye' and 'the bank knew best'. They certainly wouldn't have dared personally to question the bank manager's judgement. As anyone who faces customers on a regular basis will tell you, this is no longer the case. The customers are not always right, but they do have a right to express their views on the quality and value for money of the goods and services they are buying.

THE PROBLEM OF THE OLD HIERARCHICAL APPROACH

In attempting to resolve the issue of the increasing willingness of customers to exercise their right to complain and go elsewhere, some companies have made the assumption that if they train their front-end staff to deal with these situations in a friendly, courteous way, they will be able to satisfy their customers' requirements. Whilst this might (and it is a big might) appease the customers' immediate anger and frustration, it will do nothing to improve the ability of the organization to understand the customers' requirements and satisfy them. These issues lie much deeper inside the organization and need much more radical treatment than teaching sales assistants to smile.

Because our organizations were designed to satisfy the requirements of mass production of the same goods to the same standards, control of costs, quality and resources were the overriding feature. The most effective way of exercising this control was to divide the organization into a number of functions, each charged with unique control of a particular aspect of the business (for example, sales, finance, production, distribution and so on). As these organizations grew and diversified the goods and services they offered to compete with their rivals, so these individual functions developed their own rules to control their individual aspect of the business. Only at the very top of the business, where the heads of these functions came together, did anyone have any idea of how all these rules were supposed to work together to manage the business – hopefully!

Within these individual functions, in order to exercise even greater control, the objectives of the function were broken down into even smaller independent units or departments, so as to ensure that any one person's 'span of control' wasn't too wide and that the job was 'doable' and to prevent fraud or collusion. Thus organizations could be described by the classic 'organigram' shown in Figure 24.2, where each box describes the limits of power and authority of the name or job title in the box. Even the computer technology designed to support the organization worked in the same way, with a mainframe as the centre of all knowledge and power and 'dumb' terminals able to interrogate this central intelligence (see Figure 24.3).

Whilst these so-called command and control structures enable control to be exercised vertically *downwards* through the establishment of individual functional objectives, they do not in any way represent a model of the customer's view of his or her requirements. The customer's process is quite simple:

- Choose the goods or services.
- Order the goods or services.
- Receive the goods or services.
- Pay for the goods or services.

So how do they get a view of that process in the organization described above? The simple answer is that it isn't possible, because that process has been fragmented into a set of rules and procedures, often with a purpose that has

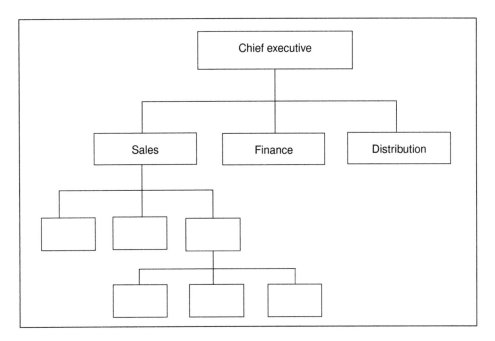

Figure 24.2   The classic 'organigram'

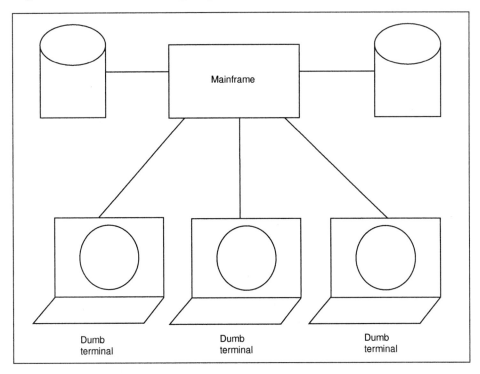

Figure 24.3   The technological 'organigram'

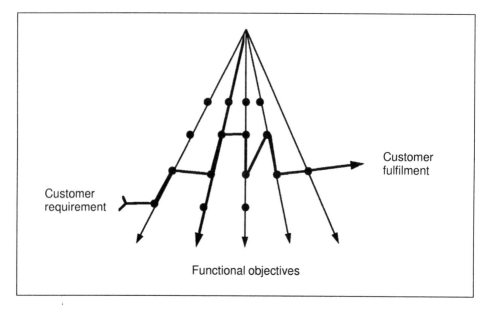

Figure 24.4   The functional process

nothing to do with satisfying the customer's requirements, and defined and managed in a number of different functions by people whose tasks have been vigorously defined and limited in their 'job description' (see Figure 24.4). Here are two examples from my own experience:

1.   In my role as chief accountant for a large computer supplier, I was responsible for the Credit Control Department – six people. Every order, large and small, current or new customer, was rigorously credit checked through Dunn & Bradstreet, bank references, personal guarantors and so on. When I asked the obvious question 'How many orders do we turn away?', I was given the (equally obvious in hindsight) answer that 'Oh, we haven't done anything that radical for years'!

2.   When I worked for a big supplier of reprographics, communications and printing equipment I was involved in redesigning the orders and billing system. The average order to delivery time was 28 days and this held true whether the order was for a simple stand-alone fax or a sophisticated, configured electronic printer. The actual time taken by the warehouse and delivery process, including configuration, was only two to four days, the rest of the time being taken up by sales management, pricing, finance and so on.

Whilst, when things go right, it may not matter to the customer too much that they can't see the process of requirements to satisfaction in this organization design, it matters a lot when things go wrong. Back, then, to the sales assistants who have been taught to smile. Since their tasks, powers and authority

have all been carefully defined by their job description, all they can do is continue to smile and promise to try to find out what went wrong – not usually to put it right, since this is someone else's job. The forlorn cry of the angry customer, heard thousands of times a day in every business is, 'I want to see the manager', forlorn because of the mistaken belief that the manager will have the authority and means to put right the wrong. Not so – they can only take it to the next level of authority. Customer helplines are one response to bridge these internally erected barriers, but usually they also have their powers carefully defined and limited and become just another link in an increasingly long and frustrating chain of inability 'to see the customer's view'.

REORGANIZING THE RESOURCES – PEOPLE, PROCESSES, SYSTEMS

The work I have been involved in at National & Provincial Building Society (N&P) over the last five years has convinced me that there is a better way but that it requires a completely different organization design to the traditional 'pyramid' hierarchical approach and a new way of organizing the key resources of the organization – the people, the processes and the systems. It starts with defining the organization's commitment to – even obsession with – understanding customer requirements and providing goods or services to satisfy them. This is the *direction* the organization is single-mindedly and uncompromisingly to pursue. Clearly the direction will pay due regard to the other significant stakeholders – the members, shareholders and employees – but the pursuit of customer satisfaction has to be the overwhelming and overriding consideration – an end in itself, not a means to an end.

Redefining the organization's objectives – the direction

Equally clearly, the direction must contain more than a wish statement of how the organization would like things to be. It must describe how it will achieve the satisfaction of customer's requirements:

- *The mission.* Describes the purpose of the organization in terms of customer satisfaction.
- *The goals.* The qualitative and quantitative goals which will measure the fulfilment of the mission or purpose.
- *The strategy.* The way the organization will go about implementing its purpose – the key processes and resources used.
- *The values.* The set of beliefs which every employee should subscribe to as the distinctive way in which they will conduct business.
- *The philosophy of management.* The commitment to the way those values will be adopted in the management of the organization's affairs.

It is not sufficient for a small group of directors or a team of management consultants to develop and document this direction simply for publication in the company's annual report. Every employee must understand the direction, not *327* in a 'learned by rote' fashion but fundamentally how it will change the organization's approach to its customers and most important of all, how they will contribute to its fulfilment (that is, what their role will be, how this integrates with all other roles in the organization, and their contribution to the fulfilment of the direction through their individual responsibilities).

The 'understanding process'

At N&P we set about achieving this understanding through what we called the 'understanding process'. This simply consisted of every team in the organization (some 500 teams in all) meeting regularly – fortnightly initially but latterly monthly as part of the Society's management process – to consider three questions, in the context of the direction:

1   What have we done well which we can learn from (as a team)?
2   What have we not done well, which as a team *we* can improve?
3   What other issues, concerns, opportunities and ideas do we have?

The outputs of all of these sessions (supplemented in specific circumstances by extended sessions with mixed teams led by individual directors) were consolidated and regularly reviewed by management teams to measure how well the direction was understood and how effectively it was being implemented.

Different organizations, with different cultures, will go about achieving this understanding in other ways, but the essential elements of the process are that it must be two-way (sometimes called '360-degrees feedback') and it must be used to measure the 'mind-set' of the organization. Had we implemented this process immediately following the agreement of the direction, the feedback on the mind-set of the organization would have been fairly straightforward – instead the reaction we received, after some delay, was, 'very interesting, but we've seen this sort of stuff before and how is it relevant in our case?' In other words, we still had some work to do in order to create a framework that would enable people to understand how they would contribute to the fulfilment of the direction.

THE ROLE OF THE INDIVIDUAL

In common with most large organizations in the United Kingdom, N&P had made its contribution to the job evaluation industry. The Society was divided into a number of separate businesses – Mortgages, Life Insurance, Visa, Savings and Investments – each with its own hierarchy from managing director downwards (and its own customer base!) in a framework of 18 grades or levels, with every job in the Society defined in terms of:

- specific tasks or activities to be achieved by the job holder;
- the qualifications necessary; and
- the level of importance in terms of budgets, number of people managed and strategic significance.

Only accidentally and only for those jobs tasked with direct customer interface, did these job descriptions define what needed to be done in the context of the customer's view of the process. Whilst they described in excruciating details the limits of power and authority, what tasks were to be performed and *how* they were to be performed, they did not define the *role* which the individual needed to play in fulfilling the direction.

The distinction I am making between a *job* and a *role* is not mere semantics. Again, other organizations might use different terms to describe their approach. What is important, however, is the distinction that needs to be drawn between, on the one hand, a specific description of activities to be performed and how they are to be performed, and, on the other, the documentation of a set of responsibilities which need to be fulfilled if the individual is to make the appropriate contribution to the fulfilment of the direction.

The difference between a job and a role

Let's look at the difference between a job and a role in more detail and demonstrate why it is essential to define work in terms of the latter, if the organization is to create the flexibility of mind-set and resource management needed to satisfy ever-changing, increasingly individual customer requirements.

Job descriptions

Job descriptions define work in terms of specific tasks or activities to be performed and *how* they are to be performed. Following the Taylor/Sloan models, they attempt to break the work down into repeatable/learnable components. Although they will often define who the job holder reports to and who reports to the job holder, this is in the context of levels of authority and control, not how the tasks or activities to be performed relate to other tasks and activities in a complete operation or process.

When the nature of the work changes – through a change in markets, a change in organization, or through the automation of the tasks and activities using computer technology – then the tasks and activities are no longer required and the job disappears. It sometimes seems to me that the leaders of our big corporations are obsessed with redundancy. They seem to believe that the only way to improve efficiency and effectiveness is to reduce the workforce. If people are seen as simply cogs in a machine, which is the way many job descriptions are phrased, then if technology changes the number of cogs needed or the way the cogs work together, it is logical that the jobs performing the redundant tasks are no longer needed. If the jobs are no longer needed, nor are the job holders.

Describing people simply in terms of a specific set of tasks or activities they are expected to perform, hugely undervalues the contribution they can make to the success of an enterprise. It also creates barriers to change and the flexibility needed to respond effectively to individual customer requirements. Turkeys are not noted for voting for Christmas, nor will people voluntarily or *329* enthusiastically become involved in change to create greater effectiveness in the organization if the certain outcome is loss of their job and security. Similarly, when the only likely 'reward' for stepping outside the limits of their authority defined in the job description is likely to be disciplinary action, 'jobsworth' becomes the order of the day (that is, nil initiative, nil cooperation), to the detriment of customer service. It is not only unreasonable, but also highly unlikely to be a sustainable *modus operandi*, on the one hand to expect individuals to take responsibility for customer satisfaction with all the flexibility of mind-set and action that requires, whilst on the other demanding that they, on pain of death, operate within strictly predefined rules, procedures and limits of authority.

Role statements

In contrast to very detailed job descriptions defined in terms of specific activities or tasks, roles are described in terms of the responsibilities which need to be fulfilled for the role holder to make the agreed contribution to the fulfilment of the direction. The roles required by the organization are determined by its direction; thus as long as the direction remains the same, those responsibilities will need to be fulfilled. The role statement describes *what* has to be achieved, not *how* it is to be achieved. The 'how' is determined by the team, supported by a common set of tools and methods used by the whole organization to agree team design, design of the process and the systems needed to support these.

In an organization which is role based, the team design becomes as important as the design of the process or the system, because it is the combination of the roles in a team (the people), the process and the systems as an integral whole which will achieve a complete end-to-end process or capability. The combination of all of these processes and capabilities, linked through their agreed inputs and output, fulfils the direction of the organization.

Teams are thus the basic 'unit' of organization design, not only responsible for the achievement of a complete customer-focused process or capability, but also responsible for the improvement of the way that process or capability works. Improvement is an integral part of every team's agreed achievements and responsibilities, and the team is responsible as a whole for the performance of the individual role holders in meeting their agreed contribution to the team achievements. No organization is immune from changes in markets and customer requirements, or the impact of technology on its operations, and so no organization can guarantee to protect all of its employees from the impact of these. However, in an organization where the roles define 'what', not 'how', where the ability of the role holder is defined in terms of a wide set of competencies (see below) rather than a narrow set of skills and qualifications, and where the teams themselves are responsible for improvement, there is a much greater opportunity for all employees to understand the direction and circumstances and to seek opportunities to determine how their competencies might continue to add value to that direction in the changed environment.

Redundancy isn't the only option – it is, sadly, one – but if the organization has a belief that its direction is right and if everyone understands that direction and is a willing participant in the improvement of its fulfilment, then other options become possible

Assessing the role – the competencies

The abilities needed for a particular job tend to be defined in terms of qualifications, specific skills acquired and experience. In a stable market where change and the pace of change are almost imperceptible – I can't actually think of any examples of such markets – then the past might be a good guide to the future. In such a situation, 'graduate with recognized accounting qualification and five years minimum experience of multicurrency operations' might be sufficient guidance as to whether a candidate would fit the requirements of a job.

In markets where the prevailing circumstances are change, competition, uncertainty, rationalization, customer service focus – and I can't think of any markets which *don't* meet these criteria – it becomes more important to understand *how* these skills, qualifications and experience will be applied by the candidate in fulfilling the responsibilities of the role. This is assessed by the *competencies* needed to fulfill the role. Competencies focus on the softer, behavioural aspects of an individual's capabilities (for example, teamwork, coaching, creativity, conceptual thinking) and how skills are applied (for example, planning, project management, measuring). The competencies required by the organization, and how those competencies are required to be used in every role, is determined by the direction of the organization and the nature of the roles required to fulfil that direction (see below). It follows, therefore, that since every organization's direction will be different according to its individual markets, circumstances and 'culture', there can be no one universally accepted set of competencies which can describe 'a good manager' or 'a good customer service adviser'. 'Beware of Greeks bearing gifts', or, more particularly, consultants selling competency systems tried and tested through a number of organizations, which purport to show that certain clusterings of predetermined competencies can be used to assess the capabilities of your workforce. The competencies needed to fulfil every role effectively in your organization can only be determined in the context of your direction, your customers and your culture and history – the 'way we do things around here', as it has been described by Tom Peters.

Nor do I personally believe that it is appropriate to have one set of competencies for managers and another set for the rest of the workforce. This limits flexibility in the organization and perpetuates the belief in a 'them' and 'us' mind-set. In N&P we have defined one set of competencies which is used to describe the requirements of every role, and every individual's competencies are regularly assessed against the competencies required for the particular role they are currently fulfilling. From the comparison of the competency profile of the role and that of the individual, development needs are identified and plans determined for the individual in the context of their aspirations. I would *331* add that this competency assessment is more often than not done in the team, with the team leader as coach/facilitator of the process – as is the assessment of individual contribution to the team's agreed achievements. Not only are teams far more rigorous and objective in assessing competencies and contribution than any individual manager can be – and I have never yet met a manager, including myself, who was comfortable with one-to-one assessments of performance, particularly where this was significantly above or below the norm – but also there is far less likelihood to be bias in the individual team's assessments or across teams, providing everyone uses the same set of tools and methods consistently. The role of the human resources advisers thus becomes that of developing the tools and methods and facilitating consistency of their use across teams, rather than, as in many organizations, being seen as the 'owners' of the assessment process and consequently a convenient escape for team leaders from their responsibilities in assessing and developing their people.

The nature of the role

If the same set of competencies are used to assess every role and every individual, how do you assess the relative worth or value of each role or individual? Job descriptions tend to define:

- the level of budget controlled;
- the number of people supervised;
- the significance of the role to the delivery of the strategy or goals; and
- the powers and limits to authority.

From this description, job evaluation committees can then have endless arguments in laborious detail to determine the grade or level of the job and thus the pay and benefits which go with it. With so much depending on the way the job is described, there is bound to be constant upward pressure on managers to 'talk up' the job (as a one-time member of a number of Job Evaluation committees, mentioning 'strategic' a lot of times, adding capital and revenue budgets together, and counting part-time staff as full time – even going as far as employing two instead of one – are all memorable favourites). The real issue is that the whole process encourages the kinds of behaviour in managers, and in staff waiting to succeed them, which are likely to sabotage the organization's drive for flexibility and efficiency. The need is to achieve more with less by improving the way things are done, not to maintain or increase the numbers of people and the budget because the manager's grade and therefore pay and benefits depends on this.

In contrast, the degree of competency required for a particular role is determined by how that role plays in the organization design – the nature of the role. To understand this, it is necessary to see the whole organization, as well as its constituent elements, as a process. All processes have the same steps, whatever they are trying to achieve, as follows:

1 *What do we want to do.* The purpose of the process.
2 *What do we need to do it.* The requirements and resources needed to fulfil the purpose.
3 *How are we going to do it.* The detailed planning of the implementation of
the activities.
4 *Doing it.* The implementation of the activities.

Generically, each of these steps needs to be constantly measured against the
ever-changing circumstances of the organization and its environment and
improved accordingly (see Figure 24.5).

The way competencies must be applied to fulfil each of the steps listed
above is different, and applied to the whole organization we can see that only
four types of roles are required to achieve its direction:

1 *What* roles, responsible for creating the direction of the organization and
facilitating, measuring and improving its understanding and achievement.
2 *With* roles, designing and developing the tools, methods and capabilities
to fulfil the requirements of the direction and managing its implementation.
3 *How* roles, organizing, planning and leading the implementation of the
capabilities.
4 *Doing* roles, implementing the processes and capabilities.

To fulfil the requirements of each role type, the competencies required by the
organization will have to be applied differently. In N&P, we have taken the concept one step further and designed the whole organization as a process in
which each of the role types participates in the management of the organization according to the nature of their role, and each type of process required
(direction, management of implementation and implementation) contains the

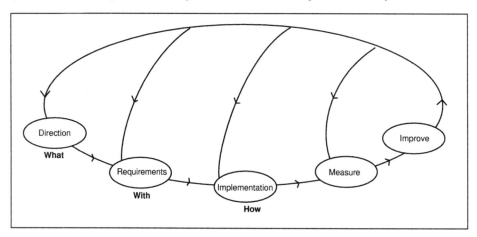

Figure 24.5   The process model

same three steps *what, with* and *how* (see Figure 24.6). This concept then translates into an organization design based on a backbone process (see Figure 24.7) focused on the customer and described in terms of a set of management processes that integrate through the appropriate roles and teams, coming together in a series of events defined and driven by the processes (see Figure 24.8).

The last diagram of the management processes which integrate together to form the N&P organization design (Figure 24.8) is, I know, a long way away from the traditional organigram shown in Figure 24.2, and I should place two health warnings on it.

Adapting the design to the organization

First, the design is unique to N&P and is an integral part of the way we have chosen to address the challenges we face in our market: namely, to create an organization capable of competing in an environment of change where the basis of success is understanding and anticipating customer's requirements and fulfilling them to the customers' satisfaction. Our direction, our organization design, our approach to our people and our approach to understanding customers' requirements have all been developed and implemented against the challenges we see in our own marketplace and they cannot be taken as a blueprint to be applied generically to organizations whose direction, culture and background may be entirely different. The principles behind the organization design should nevertheless be relevant to any enterprise facing a similar challenge: that is, probably *every* institution, public or private.

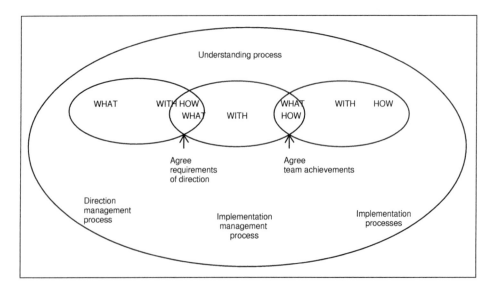

Figure 24.6   The process design

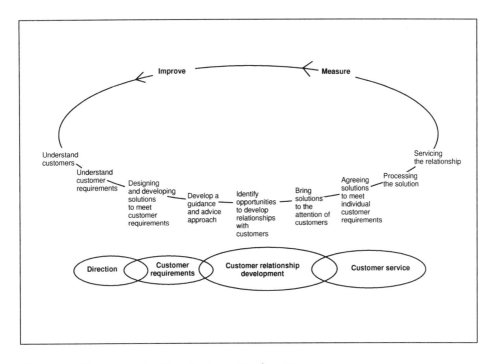

Figure 24.7   Organization design - the 'backbone' process

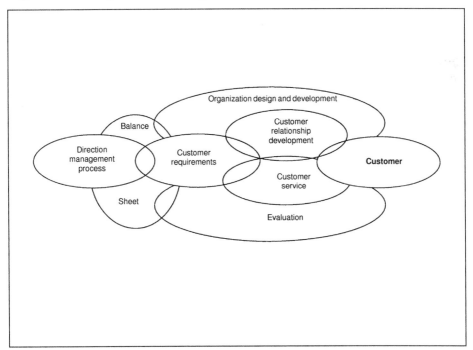

Figure 24.8   Example of an organization design model

Integrated roles

Second, it has taken over four years in N&P to implement this integrated approach to developing and improving people, processes and systems through the process-based organization design we have created. The design has gone through a number of iterations as we have learned how to improve it through the feedback from the understanding process I mentioned earlier in this chapter. Quick wins are continually gained along the way, but the pursuit of improvement is a long and never-ending challenge.

The ability to learn, adapt and improve our organization design – as we developed our understanding and increased our capabilities to respond to ever-changing circumstances and customer requirements – would probably not have been possible had we not taken the crucial initiative, once we had agreed and committed to the direction, of defining the work to be done as a series of integrated roles, detailed in terms of responsibilities and the competencies required to fulfill those responsibilities, rather than as a set of non-integrated job descriptions that simply define in mechanistic terms the tasks and activities to be performed. It is this definition which begins to create the flexibility and adaptability needed to allow every individual to see the value they can add to the organization's achievement of its direction, and it is this approach to defining work, as part of an integrated approach to managing people, that will enable N&P as an organization and each of its employees to adapt successfully to the ever-changing environment in personal financial services.

Integrated roles is an essential first step for any organization facing the challenges of today's environment of change, uncertainty, intense competition and focus on customer service, an environment which demands increasingly from its people flexibility, responsibility and, most important of all, an understanding of their own worth and ability to add value.

Role integration is important but it must be accompanied by equally fundamental changes in all the other human resource policies, procedures and systems which have been developed and implemented over the years to support a now extinct way of working.

Reward

With only four types of role, rather than the traditional multiple grades or levels, increasing reward through promotion through the grade structure is no longer viable. Arguably, it was in any case always an illogical proposition, since as people moved up to the next job level, their immediate contribution was liable to decrease while they negotiated the 'learning curve'. Whilst I would not go as far as to say that people should initially be paid less when they change roles, there is no basis for making such a move a justification for an immediate increase in reward. In a role-based organization, an essential element of reward must be based on development of competencies, to encourage people to move across the organization. Each role has a different competency profile and individuals need access to all those profiles (which they have in N&P) in order to develop their own aspirations in the context of the steps they must take to develop their competencies. Competency against the requirements of the role can be measured regularly and increases in reward made according to development of the individual's competencies.

There must also be a variable element of reward based on the organization's or the team's performance against the agreed plan or team objectives. The size of the variable proportion of total reward can be changed according to the expected contribution of the role to the successful achievement of the direction, but the criteria for variation (up or down) must be the same across the whole organization to avoid an 'us' and 'them' attitude and to ensure that everyone is heading towards the same goals.

Finally, individual contribution to the team's achievements must also be rewarded. Ideally, this should be agreed within the team that has decided what the contribution should be, again within parameters developed for the organization as a whole.

Benefits

If you look at the benefits offered by most organizations as part of the reward package – car, family health cover, mortgage assistance – they are based on a profile of the average worker as a middle-aged, middle-class married man with significant family responsibilities. When they were developed, this may have been true – but not any longer. For example, in N&P we offered a low-interest mortgage to all employees, and discovered that over 60 per cent did not take advantage of this benefit. This shouldn't have surprised us since 80 per cent of our employees were female, many part-time, and many under 30, and since one of the 'rules' of the scheme was that it had to be the first, primary mortgage. Rather than trying to develop a set of benefits to suit everyone's personal requirements – an impossible task with a significant overhead – it is easier and more effective to translate the benefits package into a cash equivalent fund with which each employee can buy the benefits they want from a menu of constantly increasing and improving benefits – just as customers should have the ability to choose to spend their cash on a range of options based on their own personal circumstances and requirements.

There is no reason either why benefits should improve based on grade or time served. As with any other element of reward, individuals should be able to improve their benefits based on their contribution and development of their competency (and therefore potential to contribute). If, as they grow older, they feel the need to secure a higher pension, they simply increase the amount of their cash fund that they wish to spend on their pension rather than on another benefit.

Development

Training and development in job-based organizations tends to be concentrated on the specific tasks and activities defined by the job, and often supplemented, *337* almost as a 'reward', by non-specific, non-focused development such as sponsored MBA courses. Training for a specific task is only of value for that task, and retraining needs to take place for new tasks. In a role-based organization, more emphasis needs to be placed on developing the competencies required by the organization to enable flexibility, and also to give the context for specific skills training. Figure 24.9 shows how we approach the development of people in N&P, as a continuum, starting with understanding the organization, through competencies, specific capabilities required by individual roles, and finally the 'programme' information required for time-based projects or events.

Changes in reward, benefits and development are needed to ensure that the benefits of changing from defining work through activity-focused job descriptions, to responsibility-based role statements are fully realized. Figure 24.10 illustrates the transition which has to take place to create the kind of flexibility needed if the organization is to respond effectively to the challenges

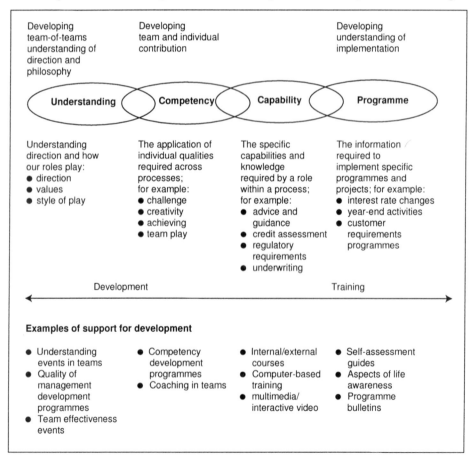

Figure 24.9   The continuum approach to development

Organization element	From job-based organizations	To role-based organizations
Work description	● Tasks or activities ● How	● Responsibilities ● What
Organization design	● Departments or functions of similar skills	● Teams requiring mixed roles based on a complete process or capability
Requirements	● Specific skills acquired ● Qualifications and experience	● Competencies ● Team-based behaviour
Reward base	● Output ● Level of authority ● Time served/promotion	● Contribution to team achievements ● Nature of role ● Competency development
Mind-set	● Limit of authority ● Functional focus ● Compliance ● Individual performance	● Understanding requirements ● Understanding direction ● Improvement ● Team effectiveness
Focus	● Specialization ● Functional objectives	● Integration ● Contribution to organization's goals

Figure 24.10 The transition from the job-based to the role-based organization

of ever-changing customer requirements and market conditions, where customer service is the only viable differentiator.

Creating the kind of organisation and culture shown in Figure 24.10 is no guarantee that the organization will be more responsive to customer requirements. There are many other elements that have to be put in place to improve customer service. For example:

● New customer based processes, adaptive to different customer circumstances.
● New products built on an understanding of customer requirements.
● New technology to help the customer and the organization understand requirements and respond to them.

One thing is certain, however. If the organization does not change the way it sees and manages its only differentiating asset – that is, by allowing people to make the most of their potential to add value – it cannot expect those people to fondly embrace exhortations from their directors and managers to adapt and *339* be more responsive to customers, unless those same directors and managers are prepared to demonstrate the tangible benefits of doing so, and are prepared to remove the barriers – the pointless controls, the internal rules, the 'us and them' culture, the patently unfair reward schemes and rules – which stand in the way of people's inherent desire and competency to create, to add value, to be customer-focused.

CONCLUSION

Frequently, when I have spoken at seminars about the kind of ideas in this chapter, people respond by claiming that they have tried these approaches but their employees are much happier knowing the limits of their authority, being told what to do and how to do it. I don't accept this and believe it is an excuse to avoid the tough decisions that this approach requires.

For example, I live in a small market town in North Yorkshire and every bank holiday weekend I am amazed by the number and variety of events local people have organized – market fayres, gymkhanas, festivals, shows and so on. Many of these events involve thousands of people and their successful implementation requires the same kind of competencies and skills as those needed to manage large organizations – planning, project management, logistics, marketing, finance. Not surprisingly, very few of these events – in fact, none at all to my knowledge – are run by chief executives or finance directors. Instead, they are run by 'ordinary' people, the same people who on returning to work on the Tuesday morning are told to hang up their brains with their coats in the cloakroom and just get on with doing what they are told to do through their job descriptions. What an awful waste of talent and potential competency, which, in the right conditions and with the right motivation and incentives, could transform the way work is done and thus the performance of the organization.

There is an imperative to transform our organizations to enable us to compete effectively in the global marketplace. The final word should be left with someone from outside the Western business community and, although these sentiments were recorded without the speaker's knowledge, they should ring alarm bells in every boardroom in the United Kingdom, Europe and North America:

> We are going to win and the industrial west is going to lose. There is nothing much you can do about it, because the reasons for your failure are within yourselves. Your firms are built on the Taylor model: even worse, so are your heads. With your bosses doing the thinking while the workers wield the screwdrivers, you are convinced this is the right way to run a business. For you the essence of management is getting the ideas out of the heads of the bosses into the hands of labour.

> M. Konosuke Matsushita,
> Matsushita Electric Industrial Corporation
> Japan

I hope we can respond to that challenge. I believe we can, starting with the method of approach to people and organization design described in this chapter.

FURTHER READING

Davis, S. M. (1987), *Future Perfect*, New York: Addison-Wesley.
Drennan, D. (1992), *Transforming Company Culture*, London: McGraw-Hill.
Handy, C. (1976), *Understanding Organizations*, Harmondsworth: Penguin.
Morton, M. S. Scott. (ed.) (1991), *The Corporation of the 1990s: Information Technology and Organization Design*, Oxford: Oxford University Press.
Zuboff, S. (1984), *In the Age of the Smart Machine*, Oxford: Heinemann.

25 Quality as a mind-set

Professor Tony Bendell and Roger Penson

For an organization to survive and prosper, every member must have quality in the forefront of their mind, at all times. Vague, short-term notions of quality, driven by management fad, will not survive. The blunt warning implicit in the previous statement is 'No quality mind-set, no survival!' If you are not prepared to begin changing your organization mind-set, your competitors will move in and whatever grip you believed you had on the marketplace and customer loyalty, will slip away.

So, what do we mean by 'quality' in a customer service environment? How do you achieve the mind-set, and in whom?

DEFINING THE PROBLEM

Establishing the definition of quality in a customer service organization can be a complex and time-consuming affair, not least because it can be difficult to convince the 'back-room' staff that they have the greatest impact on customers' perception of quality whilst not necessarily ever meeting one. In addition, the usual cry of 'How can we measure something as intangible as service?', especially from front-line staff, also confuses the issues, as it tends to imply that the 'intangibles' are immeasurable. For example, 'How big a smile is required to ensure quality?' This is one of the problem areas – establishing what the customer's definition of 'quality' is in comparison with the perception of service staff. Perhaps the smile is not the most important element and there are tangible elements to quality service which need defining.

Whilst customers are not necessarily party to the internal organization which provides them with continuing reassurance, they quickly feel the effects of a lack of commitment to their needs. One thing that the long recession has taught them is to become more specific in their definition of quality and to be much more selective in how they spend their hard-earned money. They have developed a 'nose' for quality – or, more particularly, the lack of it. Many customers will tell you, when they cannot express it any other way: 'I always buy from X, you can smell the quality', or perhaps more often, 'I never use Y, their quality stinks!'

THE MEANING OF QUALITY

What do we mean by 'quality' – a much abused word? First, any attempt at altering the mind-set of any level of staff must begin with establishing what marketplace the organization believes it operates in. This is an important consideration whatever your market, be it 'cheap and cheerful', 'exclusive and expensive', or anywhere in between.

There are as many definitions of quality as there are individuals, so an agreed understanding of the organization's marketplace in the minds of senior management must be made. The definition should relate to the organisation's specific business objectives (which must in some way closely reflect the needs of the marketplace) for it to have any chance of success. Then it must be compared with the actual marketplace view, once established, and be used to drive the concept of quality through middle management and the rest of the staff.

This move to define the marketplace must be led by senior management and is driven by the need to assess what the customer perceives as quality. It is a difficult task, and will require the use of a wide range of tools, such as surveys of existing customers, salespersons' surveys (when did you last consider tapping this reservoir of information?), attempts to question potential customers, even an approach to customers who 'quit'.

How to establish the marketplace view of quality

In this project, the development of research methods to establish the marketplace concept of quality must be a priority. Questioning existing customers can be a dangerous game – many companies, if pressed, would hardly dare! There is, however, a vast range of data already within the organization, from spending patterns in relation to service lines and product types, customer complaint records, even payment histories, which can begin to give you some evidence of what your customers think of you. The ease with which you can access this information will depend on the construction of your database. The more difficult it is to access, the further you have been from a commitment to quality in the past!

These records should be explored first, to ensure that your direct questions to customers are about services/products which still have life left in them. In addition, the size of the customer, the geographic location and the type of complaints, should all be considered, in order to devise a strategy for gaining serious answers.

Obtaining an accurate view demands careful construction of questionnaires, with emphasis on the twin pillars of product quality (for even the world's oldest service industry is assessed by the quality of the product which supports *343* it!) and the standards of service, including the speed at which the service is delivered. Opportunity for 'self-expression' in the reply should not be ignored, since this often defines areas of concern that the organization may never have thought of. Often a specialist is required, to ensure that questions are not 'loaded' to produce the required answer. Specialist companies are also often valuable in retaining the anonymity needed to elicit the truth from important customers who quit. Reasons given face to face are frequently the least unkind that the customer can think of. After all, they had invested some of their pride in buying from you. To find it misplaced can be painful for them as well as you.

Do not disregard the views of the employees – even those who never see the customer – in your investigation. They are also part of the marketplace, even if your final customer never meets them. It is easier to begin a review, directed by the result of the customer surveys, based on product, since this offers a tangible way to involve all staff. The move to 'pure service' elements becomes easier once the products have been assessed, for you have already begun to effect a change in the 'mind-set'.

In the case of a nationally known laundry service, actual photographs of rental textiles were circulated across the country. Each carried a number code. Approximately 500 staff were asked to rate the finished articles according to cleanliness and appearance, on a three-point scale of more than acceptable, acceptable, and unacceptable. The question was asked in terms of, 'If I were staying at this hotel/using these facilities, would I be happy with this product?' When the returns were analysed, there proved to be a broad consensus of what was/was not acceptable. The ratio of returned internal questionnaires was 88 per cent. The previous practice of ignoring staff views had consistently overlooked the potential commitment of staff to quality issues and the desire to accept ownership of these issues *at the point where decisions would be the most cost-effective.*

MAKING USE OF THE INFORMATION

Having established the marketplace perception of product quality and the outline of service quality demanded by the external customer, and having reviewed how far this perception is shared by middle management and operational staff, the next step is to find out how close the organization comes to meeting or exceeding that view, and how much effort is believed to be required in order to close the gap.

The answers will dictate the main areas for review, which should be prioritized as dictated by the effective sequence of events in the business flow. It can be extremely frustrating for staff to find that the action plan has been phased so that 'you can't get there from here'. No area should be excluded, even if there appears to be no criticism of it. The survey will also reveal to staff – and particularly operational staff – how important their activities are in providing quality products, on which the service is based and where the most

cost-effective decision points are to understand (as a result of the survey data) and prevent poor quality. This information must be used to compare the provision, state and operational responsibilities applying to the equipment used to manufacture the product.

The opinion that quality is 'only another fad' can be heavily discredited at this point, when operational staff:

- are seriously involved, at their different levels, in identifying the problems they face daily;
- are asked to contribute to, and participate in, a documented plan to overcome these problems; and
- are shown that their internal suppliers and customers not only are involved in recommending and agreeing what their responsibilities are, but also are identifying the physical and organizational changes required to support the initiative and their fellow staff.

Most staff, in these turbulent times, like to have a clear picture of 'What do I do Monday?' This is especially true of operational staff, whose general expectations are that they be given clear instructions for work, which, once given, never change. The route to successful creation of quality as a mind-set demands that you break that particular mould, steering their thinking away from the narrow and mundane, and encouraging continuous improvement as a way of life. But first you have to give them the confidence to review their working practices and take the first tentative steps to creative responsibility.

Operational staff are usually very pragmatic. They deal in the everyday practicalities and often contribute, and expect to receive, practical answers to their problems. Allowing them to contribute lays the foundation for future developments of quality awareness in all corners of the business. If management support and action is sufficient, it begins to constitute a reskilling of staff whose experience may well have been one of gradual denial of skills and downgrading of respect and responsibility in the minds of middle and upper management.

'Pure service' elements of quality, often so difficult to grasp at operational level, will almost automatically begin to develop. By starting from the physical aspect, the ice is broken. If sufficient trust has been established, then the more 'ephemeral' aspects – such as timeliness, reliance on information provided, levels of support and interest from related departments – begin to come to the fore. These elements naturally lead on to mutual identification of Rudyard Kipling's 'Six Honest Serving Men' – Who?, How?, Why?, What? Where? and When? – as applicable to every aspect of the business and for which a properly controlled and coordinated management plan should be drawn up. When operational staff begin to question the appropriateness of the actions they normally undertake, especially if they begin to suggest taking responsibilities for activities they may have previously refused and suggest how they can be supported and provided, then you will know that fadism is dying gracefully. Fadism will be further weakened if this questioning is done jointly and in the open.

The key to establishing the mind-set on quality as a concept throughout all *345* phases of the organization's existence, therefore, is to underline its relationship to *product* as much as *internal service*, especially since there are very few *services* which do not depend on product for at least a part of its success. *Service* can and should be thought of as the mechanism by which the internal customer passes the product (or service) on to the next member in the chain and, ultimately, to the external customer.

To follow this proposition, concentrate first on product-related procedures and the internal activities which move the product through the chain to the end user. Secondly, consider how much authority should now be given to relevant staff in operating these procedures and whether the identified staff have the interpersonal skills to exercise appropriate decision making within the reformatted work teams. This, in turn, raises the need to delegate responsibility downwards, to the lowest effective point. Revision of the information systems will therefore be necessary to ensure that the required data is available which will enable the correct decisions to be made. This realization marks the watershed in establishing quality as the culture – the transition from lack of trust between owners and staff to a more meaningful relationship capable of withstanding the pressures of continuous improvement.

Once this relationship has been achieved, then the route towards meeting or exceeding the customers' expectations must be mapped. Every aspect of the business flow throughout the organization to the customer should be examined, including whether the organizational structure and the tools, activities and responsibility levels within it remain adequate to meet or exceed customers' expectations.

At this point, you should make sure that you appreciate, first, the enormity of the task on which you are about to embark (everyone must be involved at some stage), and secondly, the fact that this may be a 'one shot' exercise. In other words, you have only one opportunity to get it right. A second time around, and staff commitment is likely to be almost nonexistent, and even possibly negative.

Recognizing these points and their implications in tracking back the application of 'quality' through the organization, from point of sale to concept and provision, will begin to make a difference to the mind-set. There are wide differences in the means to achieve this end, which is quite acceptable providing that the end is achieved, and that your staff recognize your sincerity in the matter and reciprocate your trust.

SYSTEMS FOR CHANGE

What approaches have been used to change the mind-set and what are their strengths and weaknesses? There is no guaranteed way of achieving cultural change and reliance on a particular method can only limit the scope for action and consequent results. Past (and current) methods include:

1 *Customer care programmes,* which tend to concentrate only on the customer/service interface and do not seriously address the underlying issues.

2 *Total quality management*, which, as its name implies, aims at involving every (TQM) member of the organization, but which can suffer from lack of clear direction – both because of its interpretative nature, and from top management, who occasionally get disappointed by the slow progress of results.

3 *Quality management*, which has at least a framework from which to sys-tems-develop approach but which, in interpretation and definition, has a strong tendency to cause rigidity of action and the restricted exercise of responsibility.

Of these three options, TQM is probably the one with the most potential for encouraging the widest adoption of a quality culture that will match the com-petition. It is also, however, the one most prone to failure, partly because of its openness of interpretation, and partly because of the long-term nature of the approach and consequent lack of recognition of immediate, tangible results (which are possible – even if only in apparently limited areas). Senior manage-ment support for TQM frequently fades rapidly, and it is then regarded as just another management fad, in the process spoiling the reception of the next initiative to be tried.

Unless there is a controlled plan, which concentrates on specific issues iden-tified by the research on quality, is based on a thorough understanding of TQM principles, and is committed to both training facilitators and allowing the time to bring groups of staff together to discuss and resolve the issues, then all that will result will be a forum for complaints, with no mechanism to gather ideas for analysis. Dominant individuals will further damage the commitment to change and senior management will not gain the confidence needed in the abil-ity of staff to accept, share and contribute to the changing culture.

Provided that the tools and skills to manage a TQM programme are available and that the groups are allowed to devise appropriate measuring systems, cap-ture objective evidence, discuss and analyse the results and plan an alternative strategy, – with the full support of a senior management player (who is there not only to encourage, but also to ensure the overall objectives continue to be met), then the first steps can be taken. The important issues here are, first, to maintain the attention of the groups on the specific established aims, and sec-ondly, that the results should be published without the groups being damaged by incurring ridicule or by having their efforts otherwise ignored or belittled from any source. Additionally, gaining some early wins and publicity for achievement reinforces the message that senior management are adopting a serious approach to the whole business of cultural change.

Forward progress is eminently desirable. However, TQM programmes can suffer from lack of direction, particularly if there is difficulty in relating a specific activity to the next one in the business flow. This is when a structured system like ISO 9000 can be utilized and its value appreciated.

Quality management systems benefit from clear direction embedded in the published standard and the acceptance of agreed timescales to which every-one is generally committed when seriously pursuing this option. Moreover, the *347* presence of a recognized external body hovering in the background also concentrates the mind. Its greatest strength lies in the definition of areas within the business which must be addressed. However, the very need to document actions and responsibilities can easily smother the process of changing to a 'quality mind-set', a process which demands a lively recognition of the need for (and exercise of) flexibility of action within often quite loosely defined bounds by many different types of staff. The same question must be asked repeatedly: 'Is this action adding value to the service?' If the answer is 'no', then the validity of that activity, indeed of the whole department, must be rethought in terms of meeting the final customers' needs. Without continuous effort to concentrate on the external customer, the attention drifts back to the internal requirements, and the cosy inward-looking needs of the department or the business tend to dominate.

All change costs money. Spending a small amount as a means to gain commitment on the 'shop-floor', and to establish the belief (frequently missing) in management goodwill, is money well spent. It may well surprise you how quickly the shift to 'real' concerns occurs and how the depth of interest and skill in approaching these matters is consequently revealed. Once the genie is out of the bottle, however, it is impossible to put it back! Should the apparent commitment falter, the first result is usually a return to 'work to rule' by disillusioned staff. This will set back the timescale for change by many months. The next event is usually the sight of the more capable and committed staff leaving to work elsewhere. This leaves a pool of workers with less skills in surviving change and an increased resentment to what they begin to see as an imposition if another attempt is made to implement change. Management commitment, interest, support and guidance is essential if the movement towards the change objective is to continue, plus the recognition that a 'quality' wall is built of many small bricks, over a long period of time, and requires a good foundation.

The tendency is for groups to test the strength of management goodwill in the early days of change. Working conditions, not necessarily revolving round pay, are usually frontrunners when the opportunity occurs to raise an issue. The natural argument runs like this: 'If you want us to improve the quality of our work, it helps if we have that broken window repaired/uniforms provided/ canteen painted and so on'. This type of argument can be 'legitimized' by the view that concession on these 'minor' items will be seen as contributing directly to the depth of support operators feel management is giving them.

From the basic issues outlined above, it would seem probable that the flexibility of the TQM process, coupled with the rigour of an ISO approach and a tight hold on the overall strategy of meeting the needs of the marketplace, is potentially the most effective way of establishing the quality culture in all staff. So, what means can we use to establish that (quality) culture? Let's concentrate on success!

BARRIERS TO CHANGE AND STEPS TO SUCCESS

348   In many instances, senior management 'grew up' with the organization. What

was once an easily directed business, however, revolving round a small team of tight-knit staff, has now grown to a three- or four-layer organization, and herein lies the problem. The management skills and outlook, which were once perfectly acceptable for the immediate, hands-on approach, is now stretched to breaking point. Senior management is now torn between maintaining the day-to-day approach and the need to plan for the future. At this point, the recognition of the need to change their management approach should dawn.

How this can be managed is not so easy to conceive, and so the rush to grasp a concept begins. The buzz words of 'quality', TQM and all the fashionable phrases circulating 'out there' are all part of 'management fadism', since they are often adopted with little understanding of how they relate to the needs of the business, or the requirement for senior management to move from 'benevolent dictator' to supporter and guide. Nevertheless, this change must be understood and agreed by all members of senior management – the necessity to speak with one voice is paramount.

One of the principal dangers of a management style change, or a TQM programme, lurks in the handing over of responsibility for identifying problems (and solutions) within the organization, often interdepartmental, to operational staff. This is often the signal for the destructive 'let's find someone to blame' approach, which is hardly likely to underpin the need for cultural change to shared responsibility. It is frequently known as 'hand grenade management,' since there is a definite enemy, a simple way of causing damage and everyone hears the blast. The services of the Red Cross are usually an extensive requirement afterwards!!

Ideally, senior management, believing in the future of their business and recognizing the need to become the supporters of staff rather than dictators, must not allow themselves to feel threatened when seeking the views of middle managers and others. This genuine willingness to ask questions – in the full knowledge that there may be some very awkward questions, and some that they may not have even thought of – listening to the replies without condemnation, and steadily and carefully reviewing the answers, must be clearly observed and recognized by all concerned, so that it favourably influences the views of operational staff and lays the foundations for permanent cultural change at a later stage. Middle management must be taken into the confidence of senior management when the latter begin the process of outlining the change programme. Middle management will have to sell this process to operational staff and gain their cooperation. Benefits must be clearly spelt out, to the individual, the department and the organization. It must be made very clear that there is no hidden agenda behind what will often appear, to the uninitiated, as just another cost-cutting rationalization programme.

In addition, responsibility for the project must be allocated to a respected senior figure, who should have a clear vision of the future and the ability to communicate this vision consistently and well to all levels in the organization. Published guidelines for the project, together with a logical action plan and achievable targets and timescales, are also essential prerequisites.

The logical order for reviewing the need to meet the customers' *349* expectations for quality, and hence to work on the mind-set proposals, evident in the ISO 9000 standards, has to be linked to the TQM approach of training facilitators in order to manage the staff skills required to review every aspect of the business. The cascade approach, convincing middle management of the overall objectives in an unambiguous manner, rather than wall-to-wall banner headlines, is the most effective method since it allows damage limitation during the senior management concept development and middle-management initiation stage, before any resistance is obvious to everyone.

An awareness of the actual business flow within the organization and an identification of the critical success factors within each activity are pivotal to the project. It is often surprising how little senior management actually know about how the business runs. This is often due to the restricted areas of interest each director has, coupled with the impression that, 'When I was running that department we always handled their activities this way'. The failure to recognize that times have changed, and activities along with them, is part of the problem. Activities have often changed to meet some internal need, have taken place step by step over a long period of time, and, in doing so, have often drifted substantially away from serving the customers' needs. Frequently, the chief needs of the internal customer have also been ignored. The surprise which occurs all round following the review is therefore usually substantial. However, provided that there is a clear understanding of the needs of the external customer, underlined by total management support of the project, this surprise can trigger a serious bout of organizationwide soul searching, driven by the goodwill which arises from the healthy concept of self-preservation and survival in all staff.

Once the concept is agreed and an outline action plan defined and published, progress must be made in a way that encourages every view, whilst acknowledging that not every view has the same value and some that sound good will not be commercially viable. A range of skills, many of them new to all levels of staff, will have to be identified, notably based on: the ability to flow-chart the actual needs of the business in direct relationship to the customer's requirements; identification of the critical success factors; and the invention and application of workable performance measurement systems to establish whether performance can be achieved with the current organizational and procedural arrangements. The ability to introduce and manage brainstorming techniques – to resolve performance failures and capture ideas for driving continuous improvement – is critical, requiring formal training of appropriate staff, who themselves should be capable of becoming trainers. There must be no delay between such training and the implementation of these skills – partly to ensure that the fresh ideas do not get stale, but also to demonstrate the serious intent behind the move.

Once this process is in hand, the opportunity to develop, almost subconsciously, the cultural shift towards individual responsibility should be seized. This is most effectively done by supporting the small steps in process or procedural improvement, providing or enabling improved tools and techniques, openly assessing the results of these in brainstorming sessions, sieving the results against staff requirements, customer expectations, organization objectives and objective evidence, and acknowledging that practical benefits take time to show through.

It is a necessary requirement that clearly defined objectives, methods and ways of measuring the results must be agreed and operated within these groups and that group members are allowed to publish results. Open discussion on the perceived benefits, both within the group and wider, to ensure that one man's benefit is not another man's loss, must be encouraged.

It is at this point that senior management will be most effective if their actions are seen both to support the stated objectives and to allow operational staff freedom (within the agreed boundaries) to make decisions regarding the way in which the activities should be done. In other words, provided operational staff suggest workable ideas, which fall within viable cost structures and meet the visionary objectives set by senior management, there should be little or no 'interference' or undue criticism by senior staff on the methods recommended. Laying the foundations of the role reversal from dictators to supporters of staff has begun, and the notion that this is 'another management fad' begins to fade.

One of the problems that is difficult to avoid is how to stop the new order becoming cast in concrete (usually pre-cast!), which in turn is overtaken by the changing market requirements, and indeed by your competitors. This situation is often seen in rigidly documented quality management systems. It merely substitutes one inflexible structure for another and fails to address the need for all staff to be constantly improving their own expectations, performance and methods of work. A lifeless quality management system is usually the first sign that management has succumbed to the short-term 'fadist' method of working – especially among those who should be leading.

The end result of reviewing an organization's structure should, quite naturally, be directed to change. It should be an established result of change that continuing change is inevitable, probably permanent but survivable because all parties trust one another. This change should move the whole staff towards the realization that each individual can and must influence the way things are done to satisfy the customer. This relies on and results in an awareness of the importance of each other, each department and the contribution all make to the objective of quality customer service – in other words, the culture.

HARNESSING OPPOSING FORCES

How can the opposing forces of stability and innovation be harnessed together, to encourage increased expectations and superior performance in a fast-moving environment? It is not easy, particularly where there is a need to demonstrate a documented system to customers and potential customers.

The key issues always are: How can this culture be 'captured', to define it for existing employees and especially new recruits? How much responsibility should each person bear (or even, can they bear)? What reaction should there be from supervisors/managers to whom they report, if the individual has made *351* a decision in good faith which goes beyond the prudent or acceptable? The answers to these questions pose the greatest test of the success of senior management in changing the organization mind-set from management fad to permanency.

The tendency for senior management is to require all changes to be documented and controlled. That way some sense of continuity appears obvious and everyone has a clear understanding of their tasks and responsibilities. The resultant system, however, driven by documented job descriptions and specific procedures, slowly declines into that inflexible state that change was expected to cure.

Striking a balance between bureaucracy and anarchy is obviously essential, probably with a slight tendency towards the latter! Anarchy requires support with a mission statement for the organization, underpinned by published mission statements for each department, which themselves have been agreed by related departments. These statements will ensure a level of interdepartmental understanding of each other's purposes and how they are mutually supportive.

Mission statements, particularly the internal ones, should indicate the existence of published measurable outputs from agreed inputs, support the operation of performance measurement, and, most importantly, provide the opportunity to compare their clear objectives to the current and changing needs arising from within the organization and the marketplace.

In the usual order of things, however, the responsibility structure and job descriptions are reviewed/revised to ensure support for the mission statement(s), training ensures their role is understood and that skills are appropriate – and gridlock commences! Individuals are encouraged to see themselves within a limited sphere, with little opportunity to contribute their ideas for continuous improvement.

The key word here is 'roles', a topic dealt with elsewhere in this book. Traditionally, these have been clearly defined, often in much detail. Usually, the lower down the organizational tree you are, the more your role has been circumscribed. For the culturally inspired organization, the reverse is actually needed, because the freedom to initiate new ideas is most required on the 'shop floor', where the actual work is done and where usually practical inspiration (which separates the companies who can, from those who can't) most often strikes. Unfortunately, the responsibility for vision and strategy, which is owned by the directors, is often confused by the latter with the hands-on dictator style approach. This view, if not curbed, tends to dominate the operational staff and denies them their essential imaginative contribution.

The ability to invent new ways of working is what drives the small steps that make up a valid, fluent quality culture. At the same time, the role restriction required in senior management – to keep them pointed in the direction of strategy and vision and maintain the excitement they must engender in all levels of staff – should discourage them from concentrating on the day-to-day operation and prevent them from mistaking action for progress!

352 Where there is a need to document the management system, this should be

written in a way which identifies the department roles and outcomes – including current performance targets – and should carry the absolute minimum in description of specific activity. This can best be done by identifying the mission statement in the purpose section, followed by the responsibility at the highest level within the department to ensure the relevant operational responsibilities and actions are fulfilled, and the steps by which these are undertaken. Ensure that everyone in the department knows these details and how they can influence their achievement, either by the exercise of personal decision-making skills, and/or through team working or membership of 'quality improvement teams' and so on.

The end result should be documented, and workable guidelines drawn up, based on expected inputs and required outputs, with appropriate performance targets and measures indicated. An overall responsibility defined at department head level, resulting in a clear understanding of how the organization functions in a lively, responsive manner, together with culturally embedded acceptance and ownership of the decision-making requirement at every level within the business, will form a positive basis for educating new employees, as well as an objective basis for reviewing the continual need to meet the changing requirements of the business and the marketplace. In a documented system, 'less is more'. However, the need to provide information on which employees can make appropriate decisions implies that this information should be:

- current and specific to the individual's needs;
- easily obtained and understood;
- in a format which allows decision making at the most effective point within the business flow; and
- obtained from data which enable all relevant aspects to be included in the decision-making activity.

New employees will need to be prescreened for flexibility of mind and interpersonal relationship skills. They will also require to 'shadow' members of their team for a while in order to immerse themselves in the new culture, whilst getting to grips with their role in the department and organization.

Management fadism will have truly died when front-line staff and middle managers alike have access to and cooperate in the sharing and use of management information apt for their purpose. Previously, access to such information will have been largely denied, or produced in an unhelpful format, as a means of enabling senior management to 'control' the business.

SUMMARY

The only route to establishing quality as part of the mind-set is to develop a clear vision, in all staff, of the organizational aims and objectives, recognizing that this must change over time to reflect the developing needs of the marketplace and the activities of the opposition. Ensure that your staff are aware of *353* the continuing vision and strategy and trust them to develop flexibility of mind in exercising their decision making within a mutually supportive team, to whom you have given the authority to act within generally culturally accepted reasonable bounds. This must become as essential and as natural as breathing.

Courage will also be required, to support the long-term effort (an effort that will never actually end, but should require less energy for better results) to share this vision with all staff and to become a supporter of staff whom you must now begin to trust with your vision.

26 Using control groups

Peter Murley

Change is a necessary part of every modern, forward-looking organization and a vital part of change involves revising attitudes towards the business partners (for example, customers, staff, suppliers and so on) and adopting new ways of working. Some of these new working methods will be simple adaptations of a current procedure or process, whereas others will involve dramatic reworking of processes to ensure that the business can continue to meet and exceed its customer requirements, satisfy staff and at the same time continue to be efficient and cost-effective.

The problem with many organization structures is that they are organized around specific functions or skill sets and, whilst change is accepted, the method of implementation is 'all or nothing' as opposed to testing and experimental. This approach has inherent risks, not least of which is wholesale retraining in some instances and potential excess and unknown costs. For most greenfield organizations a part of the project plan involves a 'dress rehearsal', which, as the name implies, is a dummy run of the project at both macro and micro levels before its wholesale launch. This usually involves a group of test customers – often referred to as early adopters – who, amongst other points, are asked to respond to the product(s) and services, the method of delivery and the proposition itself.

For existing organizations, it is often the case that some functions believe they know better than others, and although they test market response to a changed or new product or service prior to full launch, it is usually through methods which rarely involve the staff who are the actual, practical deliverers. As a result, the launch may or may not be costly and/or effective; it may or may not have the support of staff (who may or may not be trained properly to accommodate any new skills and/or knowledge); and it may or may not pick up some of the subtle infrastructure issues which are so frequently missed.

So, how can this difficulty be overcome? Well, one way is to adopt a control group approach. This approach essentially enables tests and experiments to be undertaken within a carefully considered and representative group of prospects and/or customers. Assuming that the tests prove successful, they can be presented to the entire organization in the form of an already established blueprint, complete with known cost impacts, risks and benefits. Furthermore, for organizations who say they believe in empowerment, then the control group approach can bring the practicalities of empowerment into sharp focus – in fact, it takes empowerment to the next step, where staff have a very decisive, practical and influential role in changing the way the organization works and treats its customers. A control group can set the example for the rest of the structure, and can start to quickly change attitudes/methods, approaches and indeed the whole culture of the structure, from the inside by a steady growth, as opposed to attempting to do everything at once and trying to be all things to all people.

This chapter looks at some of the issues and requirements of establishing and operating a control group.

WHAT IS A CONTROL GROUP?

In the context of this chapter, a control group is a group of people within a customer service operation or a call centre, or any other part of a structure, where change management is the order of the day. Control groups are most frequently used in acquisition and/or telemarketing/teleselling environments, or where an organization wants to try out new things but believes them to be potentially costly and where gain/offsets are not clearly understood or believed. Other uses for control groups include testing markets for new product or service introductions or for functionality, special offers or implementation of new technology to the customer base (for example, use of IVR and messaging in a call centre). Additionally, control groups can test: new business processes in a controlled environment; new reward, motivation and compensation plans; different approaches to gathering customer attitudes; training programme effectiveness and so on. They can also be used effectively in the customer servicing arena – that is, in the ongoing relationship with the customer post-initial sale – to test changes to various processes and procedures, including complaint handling. In this way, customers and staff alike can have a genuine input into shaping a truly workable process which satisfies all parties and maintains that essential competitive edge.

A control group affords a professional testing ground for new concepts and ideas or changes to existing practices, but with a significantly minimized risk to the organization and to the customer base. Although a control group can, in some circumstances, be an entirely separate part of the business activity, it is normally composed of people who should, directly or indirectly, remain an integral part of the function(s) from which they are drawn.

Structure

A control group operates best in a flat hierarchy where its members can deliver benefits against the backdrop of a team of equals – a team where all ideas can be discussed openly in the group and where the best ideas emerge naturally and are honed by the group members. If the organization is not truly committed to listening to and empowering its staff, then it may well struggle with this concept and its practical application.

Although generally relatively small to begin with, control groups should nevertheless be of sufficient size to operate within the same working hours framework of their colleagues elsewhere within the organization. The groups *can* operate within a different working hours pattern, but this may create an elitism which is to be avoided where possible. Furthermore, any attempt to operate a controlled environment relies on consistency and where a customer base is passed from one group to another, depending on the hours of work of the control team, such consistency is not possible. For example, if a group of, say, three people are chosen to work in a control group then they would be unable to cope if they had to be available for 24 hours a day, seven days a week – there simply are not enough of them! If the 'business as usual' operates 24 hours a day on a shift pattern process but the control group operates only five days a week for eight hours a day, then not only is the 'control' invalid (customers would experience a control group *and* a non-control group methodology) but those on a shift pattern may begin to resent those who are not.

A leader or a manager should be appointed for the group who is well versed in existing company processes and procedures and who has a good understanding of the company structure and likely problems the group will encounter. This manager will have to be able to resolve problems and persuade others to the course of action which the team and/or its sponsors have agreed on. An important point to bear in mind is that the control group team members and the team manager will be reintegrated back into the main body of the organizational structure at some time in the future (or vice versa) and therefore it is essential for them to work amicably and cooperatively alongside other teams and colleagues within the organization and not to alienate them.

The structure of a group should be made known to the entire business – in more or less detail depending on the audience concerned – and communication regarding progress must be on a regular and formal basis.

Infrastructure

This properly constituted control group will need to maintain ongoing relationships with all parts of the business. Members of the group may well have closer and more frequent contacts with more people, different people and often more senior people than would their colleagues, and they will frequently have more knowledge about the business than more senior people in the organization.

A group will often need to establish within itself a 'master of all trades' capability, while at the same time always seeking to gain help, advice and *357* cooperation from others. An example of this is documentation fulfilment, where maintaining independent stocks of brochures, forms or whatever for group use, or dispatching self-created and signed letters in personally stamped and sealed envelopes, may well be what is required (one of the tests may be the ability to enact faster fulfilment times or to personalize responses and so on).

Normally rather more so than any of their colleagues working elsewhere in the customer services structure, a control group will have very frequent contact with the IT/IS function (for example, for trialing screen changes, for system enhancements, to record customer survey results, for implementing proper measurement systems).

Objectives

The broad role of control groups can be to trial, measure and report against any and every issue, change, new product or service – indeed, on anything which will add value to the company or the customer, increase penetration, gain loyalty and/or improve perception by prospects and customers. 'Anything' is any project, trial, test and so on, which the control group are asked to undertake by their direct or indirect manager or management or any authorized person(s) within the business as is agreed. These trials, projects or tests would have a 'sponsor', or 'client', that is to say someone (or someone representing the business or a part of it) who has a desire to test something prior to general release. Tests, trials and projects undertaken by the control group need to be prioritized, agreed and authorised within a previously agreed budget.

In telemarketing and teleselling environments, control groups will usually test several acquisition/up-selling/cross-selling methods/propositions at one time and maintain extremely detailed statistics to prove, for example, highest percentage penetration, in fastest turnround time, for least cost and maximum benefit. Such data may be profiled against socioeconomic groupings of, for instance, customers. Examples of testing could include: whether conversion from enquiry to take-up of offer is best when the offer to a new customer is made against a cash incentive or a gift; whether such conversion is more likely to be successful via a telephoned enquiry or a mailed enquiry; whether chasing a promise to buy is best via a telephone call from the company or via a letter followed by a telephone call. The variations for tests and trials are considerable.

Administrative structure and discipline

Inherent in the running of the control group is a strict adherence to detail. At least one of the members of the control group should have the desire and the ability to keep and maintain detailed records, including a diary of events and dates such that every action taken has an effective audit trail. It is a *key* responsibility of the entire team to ensure that before implementing any ideas first tried and tested in the control group they should be *proven* to work to the benefit of all parties, and that they add true value to the relationship with the customer and/or the business. Implementing poorly prepared and incorrectly proven theories will be to the distinct disadvantage of everyone concerned and will perpetuate or increase any negative customer perceptions and feedback. In the process, it will underline any negative reactions by the organization itself towards the control group theory. The objectives of the exercise must be constantly reinforced.

Importance of measurement and reporting

Determining measures and reporting on those measures is a crucial part of the entire control group process and requires some detailed attention at the start of a control group concept.

Every time the control group agrees to test a new capability, implement a change or whatever, it is an absolute requirement that alongside the administrative structure is described an appropriate series of measurement devices. Control groups frequently learn more – in the early stages at least – from having to compile manual tally sheets to gather data than from relying on inherent management systems. In fact, in many cases, a sophisticated management information system may not actually exist anyway, and the control group is established to help define the requirements of such a system from a practical perspective. Using manual tally sheets, if done within the culture of the established control group team ethic, enables members to track progress instantly and to share such information with team colleagues.

Whilst the use of manual tally sheets is advisable, the team will need to consolidate reports and data into one format/reporting device. The team usually needs, therefore, a PC with suitable database, word-processing, mail-merge and spreadsheet packages.

For each item taken into the control group, the team (via its manager) must agree on the success criteria: that is, how do we know whether the trial is a success and thus how can we determine its presentation? This requires that the sponsors – those individuals or teams or functions that ask the control group to test out a theory or a principle or set of principles – clearly state their requirements, date deadlines, cost implications and so on. The experience of the control group(s) can help the sponsors in outlining their requirements.

Data gathered in the control group must be compared with that from the operation as a whole (that is, the rest of the function(s) *not* taking part in the controlled experiments). Without such comparative information, success or failure will never be known. This requirement could prove somewhat difficult in an organization that has limited data, poor systems or a lack of measures, but it is an essential challenge. A current position based on as much historically factual data as possible has to be agreed, so that the outputs of the work of the control group can be genuinely compared. Taking decisions based on results of control group outputs which turn out to be worse scenarios than is currently the case would be retrogressive. To avoid this situation, it is often advisable to start by testing the more established procedures/processes – *359* those which are known by fact or by anecdotal evidence. Some of the more difficult aspects can be left until later – although they must absolutely *not* be avoided. An alternative is for the control group to test out internally two or three variations of one principle – that is, a control group within a control group.

Continual change and improvement

Implementation of change and the improvement of existing processes, procedures and methods of working by trial, test and experimentation are the chief functions of control groups. The best groups *know* their customers and use such knowledge intelligently. They are also made up of staff who are close to their customers – they can put themselves in the customer's place, largely because they too are customers.

Members of a control group should be selected for their willingness to test out new ideas and principles and to take risks along the way. They must also be active questioners.

The organization has to be ready for control groups and what they can do. The existence of the control group often challenges the organizational structure which it operates, and in a very real way the control group is also used for testing the culture and devolution of responsibility and authority within the organization.

The best control groups operate with an exclusive customer base allocated to it for the duration of the control exercise – in a call centre this typically might be based on STD codes of customers, so that any calls from the agreed STD set are automatically diverted to the control group at all times. In this way customers need not know that they are part of a control group, and are therefore likely to act quite normally. The chosen grouping of customers/STD code(s) should be as representative as possible of the cross section of customers throughout the entire business. As a second best alternative, a group's customer base could be requested to make contact on a specific/dedicated inbound telephone number, but this is rarely the best way forward.

Control groups should normally cover both calls *and* correspondence. Team members with less experience on calls than correspondence, or vice versa, will need to ensure that they all exit the control group process familiar with and capable of handling all tasks within both areas.

Control group size

The size of a control group depends on many factors but should probably be restricted, at least initially, to between six and twelve operating members. Exact numbers will depend on days and hours of operations, spread of and type of customers, staff skills and so on. In addition to this, the team will need other specialist members, or at least to be able to call upon the services of

others as required. This will include a marketing/sales expert, someone from systems, and one person from human resources/training. The group will also probably need someone specifically to manage the project plan and task inter-relationships.

The control group concept, once established, could develop to take in more than one group. In organizations where customer service extends beyond staff who are working in a customer service/call centre, considerable value is added, if the group includes other staff who have a regular and important customer contact role. An example of this might be an installation and/or main-tenance team in an organization where customers are acquired and serviced through the telephone but where the product requires installation and on-going in-home maintenance. In these circumstances, the control group team may have minute-by-minute contact with their colleagues in the maintenance/installation team – wherever they are – and that the latter only perform work for the exclusive customer base which has already been created within the control group(s). All members of this entire virtual team must know each other and attend a certain number of compulsory face-to-face meetings of all members to establish the team bond. The virtual team must be managed by the same structure as described above, regardless of functional reporting.

RESPONSIBILITY AND AUTHORITY

The manager of the control group should have complete authority to do what-ever is deemed necessary to test any and all activities which have been previ-ously agreed and prioritized, and to measure results. This will be done within the overall framework of any other improvement/change projects.

The general rule is that any responsibilities and authority given to the con-trol group(s) manager are automatically vested in the control group team members. At the very least, the control group manager would be given higher decision-making authority (for example, ex gratia payments, refunds and so on) than other line management counterparts, as this higher authority may well be part of the control group process itself.

We have discussed elsewhere that empowering staff at all levels to make decisions, including those which result in financial awards, results in faster decision making, happier customers and less cost – not more.

THE MEMBERS OF A CONTROL GROUP

A control group(s) should comprise of individuals who are motivated by, thrive on and are excited by change – for there will be a great deal of change in a very short timescale. A control group appointment is not for those who want an easy nine-to-five existence or who prefer regular routine, formal controls, firm guidelines and minimal surprises. Control groups and their staff take risks!

Skill set(s)

Members of a control group should fit the following descriptions:

- Risk takers who can turn risks into opportunities and gains for them-selves, for their team, for the company and for *their customers*.
- People who are flexible in approach – prepared to switch and swap tasks and roles on a regular basis.
- People who are prepared to deal with the unexpected.
- People who can apply innovative solutions to dynamic situations, and articulate them and report back on them to implement for the future and for other team members.
- People who can take on routine tasks one minute and tasks that will extend them the next.
- People who are willing to stand up and be counted.
- People who are prepared to make mistakes once.
- People who are self-motivated, who can constructively criticize self-performance and that of team members.
- People who can demonstrate good administrative skills.
- People who are literate, numerate and articulate.
- People who can create and maintain strong customer rapport.
- People who make clear decisions and stick to them.
- People who are prepared to put themselves out in order to solve *their* customers' problems without trying to shift the responsibility elsewhere (that is, task ownership and follow-through).
- People who are not intimidated by rank and hierarchy and who are pre-pared to tackle and resolve problems within a supportive team culture.
- People who work well in a team – as an active, weight-pulling member, as a coach, as a mentor, as a counsellor, and as an individual with individual style and flair.
- People who are not afraid to speak actively to customers – to make out-bound calls and use 'selling skills' to gain confidence, commitment and so on.
- People who are prepared to take the rough with the smooth, and to take setbacks as part of the journey to success.
- People who are proactive in sharing knowledge, experience and skills, and do not feel in any way compromised or threatened by imparting such understanding to other team members.
- People who believe in customers first, team second, self last.

Training

The first control group established should consist of staff who are experienced individuals, who have undertaken standard training programmes, and who are fully 'accredited'. Subsequent control groups can include less experienced individuals. In both cases the skill sets listed above are prerequisites.

Control group staff should be expected to develop their career and interests whilst within the control group and will be encouraged to do so as normal practice and as part of the control itself. All staff appointed to a control group should undergo a minimum of three full days induction programme whereby the structure and principles of the control group concept are outlined and imparted. This induction should include an introduction to the practical aspects and should include role plays (for example, fictitious or real examples of how to identify and prioritize issues for testing within the control group; how to set measures; how to review progress and report against measures and so on). All induction training should be in formal sessions (but not all talk and demonstration), and should be an ongoing part of the control group process, particularly as more groups are established and/or as team members rotate.

Considerable value is likely to be gained in the early stages of the control group programme from undertaking three further programmes, as follows :

1 *Telephone techniques.* Even though telephone techniques should have been covered in the normal run of customer service training modules, there is much advantage in message reinforcing from a fresh, external perspective, using perhaps slightly different approaches and techniques.

2 *Proactive, outbound calling.* New skills and techniques need to be imparted with specific regard to proactive, outbound calling, to cover, for example, customer surveys and active pre-issue calls (for example, anticipating problems and implementing preventative techniques). These outbound skills are quite different to inbound and demand a new and supplemental approach to telephone techniques training. The skill set is different, and, generally speaking, only between 10 and 20 per cent of customer service staff at the telephone will have the skills to perform such tasks. Moreover, some may not want to acquire them and this must be taken into account when selecting staff for the control groups.

3 *Team building skills.* Decision making, problem-solving exercises and training, using specific case studies and role plays.

Two other areas of training may well be beneficial at this stage:

4 *Representation of data.* At least some members of the control group are likely to benefit from training in the input, analysis and graphical representation of data in meaningful ways.

5 *Presentation skills.* Training in presentation skills will enable members of the control group to represent outcomes to others and gain exposure to some of the senior management within the organization – good for both sides!

Commitment

The best control groups work in an environment where everybody commits to the group's principles completely (although not without question!). In an *363* environment where committing to a working hours schedule which maps that of the larger customer services/call centre operation but without the benefit of a larger team that that implies, staff may have to work abnormal times at short notice and perhaps for minimal – if any – cash recompense.

Team members are likely to have to commit themselves to a certain number of intensive team meetings outside their normal schedules. Whilst these should be kept to a minimum, operating across a wide band of opening hours will inevitably create such demands. These total team meetings are critical to the ongoing success of the control group concept and provide a full opportunity for each team member to make a full contribution by being involved at all levels of the plan. Everybody works together on an equal basis, and all inputs are welcome, good and bad. One of the control group manager's roles is to prioritize ideas and to give reasons for decisions and why some ideas are not workable.

Rotation

Every effort should be made to ensure that as many customer services staff as possible become involved, or have an opportunity to become involved, in the control group(s) at some stage.

Everyone has something to offer – even the cynics. Furthermore, using the same team members each time will result in a potential innovative stagnation, and will also create resentment and a potential elitist view. These factors could contribute to the quick decline of the control group, as could a lack of regular and consistent communications to the wide internal world.

CONCLUSION

There are many areas of detail which must be considered and planned before implementing the control group approach recommended in this chapter. These areas include: deciding upon the degree of formality, nature and regularity of communications regarding the progress, successes *and* failures of the control group; detailing the initial roles and tasks which the group will be undertaking and the prioritization of such roles and tasks; the detail of the success criteria, measurements and comparisons that will be made, together with full details of the reporting procedures and mechanisms to be used; and a full and detailed plan for the gathering of the customer voice, the dissemination of gathered data and the use of such data in progressing further work of the team. In addition to all this, the control group manager and the team must give careful thought to the following items: their physical requirements and environment, equipment required, technical interfaces and so on; agreement on a workable budget that will allow the team to act as a responsible, cost-effective and targeted part of the business; and committing the whole concept, timing and detail to a project plan and using such a plan as the absolute basis for ongoing progress.

In short, the concept requires some careful thought, but the outcome is likely to be positive, refreshing, informative, challenging and dynamically exciting. This kind of approach starts to put some of the responsibility and power back in the hands of the people who have direct and detailed day-to-day understanding of work processes, procedures and customers – the front-line staff!

27 Internal service for internal customers

Howard Kendall

Organizations today are conducting their business in ways that would not have been understood, or indeed accepted, a few years ago. Nowhere has that been more apparent than in the use of technology, or in the ever growing demand for better standards of customer service.

Whilst the demand for better service has now achieved reasonable levels of acceptance in some organizations for the *external* customer, many still do not pay enough attention to the needs of the *internal* customer. An internal customer is essentially any employee of the organization. This person, or group of people, forms part of the delivery cycle to the external customer, whatever their function, and if they do not themselves have the correct level of service to allow them to operate at maximum effectiveness, the external customer is impacted. This obviously can lead to *customer dissatisfaction or loss* – and that is unforgivable when the situation is under our control.

So the need is evident: if we are to give premium service to our external customers, the internal customers must have it as well. But what do we mean by premium service to our internal customer and where does a help desk fit into providing it?

THE NEED FOR AND SCOPE OF THE INTERNAL HELP DESK

Premium service to our internal customers is no more and no less than con-tinually delivering to them the tools, resources and support to allow them to do their job in support of the overall organizational goal – to the highest standard possible. It really does not matter what role the internal customer has, be it accountant, assembly worker, computer engineer or maintenance person, to name but four. Each has a role to play in the organization's success and support for them is crucial.

To ensure that this support is delivered, use of the internal help desk is vital. We will go on to examine the objectives, but the scope of each help desk, whether a single unit exists in the organization or multiple units, depends on the services being delivered to each person. There should be a help desk, or structure of help desks, for *all services* provided to them. So help-desk scope should be defined by the service needs of the internal customer and the objectives developed to fit that scope.

Examples of services that may require internal help desks are computer and telephone technology, building services and equipment, production/assembly lines, payroll and personnel, purchasing/ procurement, sales and marketing. In each organization the requirements will be different but these are a good place to start.

HELP-DESK OBJECTIVES – BASIC SUPPORT AND ADDING VALUE

The help desk, at its best, should achieve the following benefits:

- A superb service to internal customer relationship.
- Best use of business technology and other delivered services.
- Ever-increasing service quality – and less wasted effort.
- Reduced problem impact on service and customers.
- A clear organizational focus for service, internal as well as external.

Whilst senior management teams may have generally been committed to providing the best technology and services for their people, often the support for them is regarded only as 'nice to have' rather than an integral element. Organizations are, however, waking up to the fact that if they spend millions on state-of-the-art technology and services, a little further investment in high-grade support pays enormous dividends. And it is what the internal customer wants that is important, namely, that the flow and quality of the technology and services to their desk should be just as reliable as the pen and paper. If there is a problem with any of them, or they need information on how to do something, then they need help fast! If not, the time lost is often the difference between success and failure in the business. The basic support to be provided at the help desk is:

- A rapid professional reply.
- Comfort and understanding.
- Confidence that if a solution is not instant, it will follow in an acceptable timespan.
- Added value – probably information.

Many help desks passed this somewhat elementary stage of development years ago. Others have still not yet mastered even these simple requirements. However, these basic elements must be achieved, for then it will be possible to *367* develop the added-value elements that will build up the benefits identified at the start of this section.

This will entail adopting a service quality enhancement project role at the help desk, which, in addition to the day-to-day role, will enable development of proactive relationships with internal customers in order to learn how best services to them can be improved. The help desk can then act as the project driver to ensure that enhancements are implemented successfully. These enhancements might range from improving the information to the customers so that they can help themselves to make better use of the services, through to providing or developing better services or discovering new areas of business use alongside existing services.

DEVELOPMENT AND IMPLEMENTATION OF A HELP DESK

Before we start to develop the help desk, it is necessary to look at the issues that will influence the unit in the support it is required to deliver, as follows:

- What is the mix of services provided and how wide geographically are they delivered?
- What is the level of support required for each service in all of the business areas?
- Is this level currently being met anywhere and do customers know where to go for the support?
- Are support skills, tools and so on able to be provided internally through existing resources?
- Are there other support teams in the organization, locally or anywhere else in the world, that might be combined?
- Are there outside support services that are an alternative?

This range of issues provides several important questions to answer and also indicates some of the main topics currently being discussed in the help-desk 'industry'. The variety of support now needed in many organizations is not inconsiderable and the wide range of needs highlights the following pivotal areas that must be addressed.

Structure

Is it possible to deliver support for all these needs from a single help desk? Do solutions need to be delivered at the front-line help desk, or should we concentrate on providing a slick, professional call management and simple advice centre, supplemented by second-level specialist support teams (or indeed external support service providers)? Could support be through a single catch-all help desk constructed on a countrywide or global basis?

The answer, of course, is mostly dependent upon your own company and its business support needs, but many organizations are now reconsidering use of
the 'catch-all, fix-all (or most)' type of help desk because of the high level of

commitment and resources required to perform to an acceptable standard. And the professional 'front-end' help desk, using excellent staff to provide an effective frontline to a highly skilled matrix of specialist support centres – inside or outside the organization – is growing in popularity. This makes sense in many cases, as few organizations have the desire, number of staff and/or correct combination of support skills to dedicate to front-line help alone.

Process

After considering how the structure may be developed, the process requirements should be the next step. Figure 27.1 illustrates the classic elements of the help-desk process that are easily adapted for use in any organization. The issues to consider at each stage are as follows.

Call/problem/issue collection – the primary role

It is important to capture all problems and issues. The help desk should be able to resolve a high percentage of the calls they receive (first-level problem resolution), particularly on simple or regular faults, leaving the support players to concentrate on the more complex, or high-priority issues.

The problem calls received at the help desk, and those problems passed directly to the support layers must all be categorized, logged and prioritized before being passed on to the resolver. Problem category and subsequent prioritization will depend on a number of factors including:

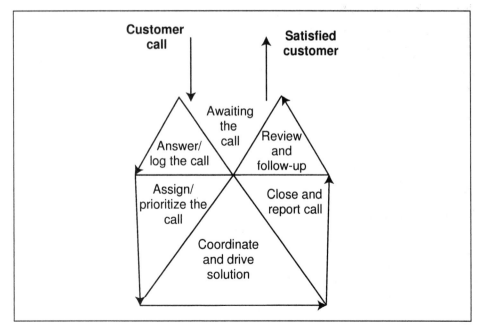

Figure 27.1   The help-desk process

- business area affected;
- impact on that business;
- number of customers affected;
- which support groups are aligned to support these issues; and
- how frequent the problem/incident is.

A sample of priority codes is shown in Figure 27.2. These examples can be adapted depending on specific needs. No more than five or six priority codes should be used – more simply leads to confusion at the lower end, plus lack of use!

Code	Definition
1	Major service loss
2	Service impact or potential total service loss
3	Problem requiring resolution but has bypass
4	Problem with no immediate impact

Figure 27.2   Sample of priority codes

Problem logging

Every problem that is reported must be logged, and the record on the log can then serve as the base document for the tracking and progressing of the problem. This applies even more in today's service culture, in which you cannot afford to lose track of any customer issue.

Logging can be paper-based or automated. By whichever method, however, the logging of the problem is the first checkpoint for the process, and at this stage it is possible to assess the reported problem in order to establish its completeness for processing, and then to assign it to the appropriate support person. That person thus becomes the problem owner, responsible for providing a resolution in the time frame specified by the priority code and liaising with the help desk to keep everyone fully up to date.

Coordination

The motivator behind each step of the process is the help desk, responsible for the maintenance of the log and the recording of all detail for each problem record. This process is crucial if meaningful analysis is to be performed at a later stage.

Resolution

The help desk will necessarily spend a large proportion of its time monitoring and chasing the progress of problems towards resolution, and is responsible
for ensuring that the problem owner acts promptly to resolve the problem.

The problem owner can take the following actions:

- Bypass the problem, updating the problem report with recommended actions to prevent recurrence.
- Provide a solution, detailing the actions on the problem report and making recommendations as appropriate.
- Eliminate the problem by changing something outside the direct problem area, detailing actions taken and making recommendations.
- Reallocate the problems to another person if the original assignment was wrong or they cannot resolve the problem due to more urgent commitments.
- Escalate the problem, even to a 'crisis declaration' if necessary, to ensure that the correct management and specialist resources are made available to resolve the problem.

When the problem is resolved, the problem report must be returned to the help desk for analysis.

Problem escalation

Escalation and priority issues are very emotive, yet critical to the success of the whole problem management process.

Providing the help desk with automatic priority allocation, and with subsequent escalation requirements for specific problem types, is essential. It enables staff to react positively in each problem situation – eliminating the question, 'Who should be told, and at what stage?' – and removes the need for arbitrary decisions. In fact, it becomes a routine operation.

Each organization will have its own priority and escalation settings, but in every case these should be set and agreed by the management team. This will not only ensure that each manager is committed to the process, but also adds authority to the assignment and prioritization of problems to the help desk. The management team must:

- identify problem categories;
- identify/create support groups;
- allocate categories to support groups (establish ownership);
- determine escalation procedures; and
- link escalation process and periods to priority settings.

The benefits achieved by an effective priority and escalation process are:

- reduced management involvement;
- minor problems stay minor;
- consistent priority allocation;
- management reporting is improved; and
- it caters for 'one-off' situations.

Problem reporting

Problem reporting covers all stages of the help process, from the initial report through to the detailed analysis of past problem trends.

Gathering sufficient information is vital at all stages and this process must start with the original problem report. At an absolute minimum it should contain:

- the originator's name and contact information, plus a description of the problem/issue;
- an indication of priority; and either
- note of an unsuccessful resolution action attempt; or
- note of a successful resolution action, and recommendations to prevent recurrence.

When the original problem passes through the help desk the following should be added:

- assigned problem/log number;
- date and time on receipt; and
- initial problem area classification;

and for those problems that were not resolved by the help desk:

- the person to whom the problem was initially assigned;
- priority; and
- date/time of problem allocation.

The problem is then able to be filed in the problem log. As the problem log will act as the base for the control of all problems within the problem management cycle, it must be constructed to allow outstanding problems to be highlighted quickly and then progressed by the help desk.

The initial problem area classifications should be reviewed in the light of the problem resolutions and the time frame in which returned and relevant data then transferred to the problem log. For example:

- resolution action;
- final assigned problem area;
- 'time to fix';
- impact on service level (s);
- recommendations to prevent recurrence.

The completed problem log should be analysed to provide reports of:

- problem incidence;
- classifications;

- impact;
- trends;
- backlog; and
- recommendations (reviewed/actioned/rejected).

This sequence illustrates clearly that the problem log forms the essential basis for all subsequent reporting and analysis requirements.

Problem reporting is an aid to effective decision making for management. So what do management need to have reported from the system – and when? Common reporting includes the following:

1 A daily briefing – to stay abreast of problem situations, both new and ongoing.
2 High-priority notification of crisis situations requiring immediate management involvement.
3 Regular summary reviews of the totality of problems over a period for assessment of priority and impact.
4 Review meeting support for individual or regular meetings with management, customers, or suppliers.
5 Trend analysis by various different criteria to aid forecasting of future workloads, staffing levels and delivery needs.

These are the typical reporting requirements and reasons why from problem management. *Ad hoc* reports will undoubtedly be required for the one-off situations that occur in every installation.

Problem reviews

The basis for all problem review meetings should be the analysis produced from the problem log. Note that three reviews are required in most cases:

1 *Service department problem review.* To cover all problems and recommendations that occurred within the service delivery function.
2 *Customer problem review.* To cover those problems that were caused as a result of customer actions.
3 *Supplier problem review.* To cover all service elements supplied from external sources.

Process changes

The classic help desk process, if run well, works. Does it need to change? Quite clearly, the answer is a resounding 'No!'

What is necessary, however, is for us continually to analyse all areas of the process and determine how we can improve them. Figure 27.3 identifies the potential improvements that we can make, and what the benefits might be.

373

Area	Improvement	Benefit
Priority	Ensure that each help-desk person and all support team leaders really understand and subscribe to the priority system. Also build in regular reviews of perceived priorities with relevant customer groups.	Priority issues are resolved in right time frame. Customer priority is accurately reflected.
Logging	Ensure adequate information is recorded at each stage, particularly on resolution action and improvement possibilities.	Helps resolve future issues. Establishes trend information.
Review and action	Better use of the initial help-desk information to support and influence management action. We are still making uninformed decisions when the evidence is there to use.	Correct actions and decisions. Wider awareness of all service issues.
Customer feedback	Build a regular means of gaining customer feedback on IT and help-desk services. Visits, questionnaires, calls will all play a part.	Customer trust, understanding and commitment. Early warning of problems.
Customer information	Providing the customer with regular and/or standing information on services, news, education and self-help details. Provision of 'one-stop-shop' facility to aid choice.	Better informed customers. Less problems/complaints. Greater customer choice. Better business performance.
Support groups	Keep support groups on the ball by information transfer. Let them know results of their good (and bad) efforts.	Better morale and communication. Problems fixed quicker.

Figure 27.3   Potential improvements to the help-desk process and accruing benefits

HELP-DESK SERVICE QUALITY MEASURES

The measurement and judgement of the success of a help desk has long been a very subjective and sometimes emotive area.

Clearly, to be able to gauge the success of any department is most important, and in this respect the help desk is no exception. Yet how are we to measure the success of an area that does not produce anything that is tangible? Let us consider the activity areas involved, and the possible measures that could be taken in each area.

- calls taken;
- enquiries/problems logged;
- complaints/customer satisfaction;
- problem resolution time;
- problem status;
- service(s) performance levels.

Possible measures in each area are as follows:

Calls taken

The volume of calls is a poor measure. It is dependent on too many variables (for example, customer literacy, help desk scope, type of organization and so on). Better call measures include:

- time to answer call;
- call length;
- calls abandoned; and
- call type.

Enquiries/problems logged, and problem resolution time and status

Again, volume is not a reliable indicator, unless broken down. The likely areas we can concentrate on are as follows:

- problems by support group/customer group;
- problems solved within time bands/priority;
- outstanding/recurring problems;
- enquiries versus problems numbers; and
- problem impact on services.

Service performance levels

Should help desk performance be linked to the service level achievement? The help desk is clearly there to ensure that service is delivered to the correct quality and that problems/enquiries are resolved with minimum impact. This now *375* happens in some organizations – help desk performance success is service success and vice versa. In the new service culture this is a good way of focusing effort on the help desk. What is important, however, if this process is to be developed, is that all staff pull together with the help desk to achieve service goals. Help desk failure/success will then reflect on everyone! It could be the best way of service-oriented, open and honest management.

Customer satisfaction/complaints

Our one time measure of success but the most difficult to assess. The use of a survey questionnaire (see appendix example) is the only real way to do this. This can be done every quarter/half-year, as appropriate.

So, performance measurement is difficult for the help desk, but not impossible. It is, though, still almost impossible (without a vast process study) to place an accurate financial value or payback period on a help desk. The same, however, is true of quality and customer service – would we abandon them?

Other issues

Other issues will include physical location and layout, together with automation requirements and the recruitment and retention of staff. Staff for customer service are addressed elsewhere and the help-desk requirements mirror those closely.

Location and layout

In today's advanced telephony environment, the layout is more critical, with the layout for optimum staff performance being crucial. Specialist help should be sought for the design of your desk layout, particularly for large staff numbers, but main criteria would include excellent interstaff visual contact, ample workspace on desks, and provision of 'head-up display' information about service status.

Automation requirements

Automation requirements are likely to include the provision of sufficient telephone capacity, using some of the sophisticated tools now available (for example, automatic call distribution, computer telephony integration, call queueing, voice processing and others). The provision of a suitable computer system will also be essential, for logging, tracking and analysing the calls and problems that come in. All automation requirements can be evaluated with the help of an expert consultant or a relevant user group, who will help you to avoid the many expensive pitfalls in making the wrong purchase.

LESSONS ARISING FROM HELP DESKS

Being points of communication, help desks have grown a new breed of professional staff. The industry across the world has its own membership forums where members:

- Meet, talk to and visit other help-desk professionals.
- Receive up-to-date information on all help-desk aspects.
- Look at the vendor marketplace for support tools.

This is a clear lesson for us that pooling knowledge in a specialist niche can help all of us to improve performance. In addition, help desks have become quite sophisticated in their management of internal customer relationships, often using service-level agreements (SLAs) to replace contracts for internal use. This gives a clear understanding of what service is expected and can be delivered.

Automation tools, particularly logging and tracking software, have become an industry in their own right. There are numerous options available and there is some sophisticated usage going on, including the use of case-based reasoning and knowledge-tree tools to allow higher diagnostic capability on the front line with lower-skilled staff.

So there are lessons that can be applied to the external customer market as well, but perhaps the primary lesson is the use of a sound structure and process, which ensures that a consistent response is given regardless of the personality involved. As with any service role, the *successful organization* has an effective, dynamic *help desk* with skilled staff, *all* of whom regard *service and the help desk as a profession*.

28 Learning from successful companies

Jane Carroll

In today's very competitive and rapidly changing business environment, developing long-term relationships with customers has become crucial not only to business success but often to survival. Companies that have embraced a strategy for building customer retention and acquisition hold exceptionally strong beliefs about the importance of service excellence, which they view as a fundamental way to differentiate themselves from competitors, accelerate growth and improve profitability. This philosophy underlies the operating principles of such organizations.

A NEW ROLE FOR CUSTOMER SERVICE

Until the 1990s, customer service was traditionally considered as a post-sale capability that dealt primarily with the resolution of problems or provision of ongoing technical assistance. Now, this definition is too limiting. Today, service excellence embraces the entire organization as a delivery system for customer satisfaction. This is a paradigm shift in how companies should think about their business. The ability to provide consistently outstanding service must extend far beyond the front lines to include every employee, every system, every organizational process, main suppliers and, most of all, customers themselves.

Companies in the vanguard are proactively making important changes to facilitate this new role for service. They are developing systems that will continually track and understand what their customers need and value. They are examining how they can do a better job of building customer loyalty. They are improving customer-driven processes and eliminating those which have no value to customers. They are training their people to achieve service excellence. They are exploring how to anticipate and respond successfully to differences in customer requirements on a global scale. They are empowering their technical people and other staff members, and instructing them in the critical role they play in customer retention. And they are teaming sales, service and technology functions much further upstream in ways that are cost-effective and add value to customer relationships.

What lessons can be learned from companies that have been successful in their transformation to customer-driven organizations?

Since 1976, I have been associated with the Forum Corporation, which has done widely acclaimed work in helping organizations achieve superior results by becoming customer driven. We also conduct extensive research on what is happening in the field. Forum invests more than US$1m annually to study the changing expectations of customers, and to identify and understand the behaviour of people in companies that consistently provide outstanding customer service. This chapter is based on what we have learned from our work with clients and on the results of our global best-practice research on how successful companies are managed.

CUSTOMERS, PROCESSES, PEOPLE

Companies known for high levels of customer service do things differently from other organizations. They create predictably positive experiences for customers by concentrating simultaneously on the needs of their customers, on continually improving business processes that help them serve customers well, and on providing everything their employees need to exceed customer expectations.

Concentrating on customers leads to a deeper understanding of customers' businesses, expectations, perceptions and priorities for improvement. To do this well requires building superior relationships with customers and having a reliable system in place to bring both present and future customer expectations into the organization. Success depends on how well an organization listens to its customers. Companies that continually seek customer input, convert what they learn into actions that improve processes, and enhance the abilities of their people to deliver outstanding service, survive even in the toughest times.

Concentrating on processes means understanding which processes deliver outputs that are valued by customers. Successful companies study their critical processes with great care and identify those that cause customers to become dissatisfied and leave. Then they aim at eliminating, re-engineering or continuously improving those processes so that the organization services customers more reliably, quickly and at a lower cost.

Successful companies *concentrate on people* by providing support and encouraging employees to act on behalf of customers. Part of this empowerment involves building effective leadership throughout the organization so that all employees, both as members of their work units and as individuals, thoroughly understand their roles in achieving and sustaining service excellence and are inspired to take part. By tapping the experience and energy of management and employees, both as individuals and as teams, companies more easily find better ways of serving customers. As a result, they achieve *379* lower costs of doing business, higher customer retention, better overall quality, higher employee morale and increased employee loyalty.

Concentrating on customers, processes and people involves a series of five key actions that characterize virtually every company which has successfully achieved a high level of customer service excellence. These actions are:

1 Deploying a clear, compelling customer-keeping strategy to everyone in the organization.
2 Saturating their organization with the voice of the customer.
3 Building strong leadership and employee involvement.
4 Developing a plan and reliable process for continuous improvement.
5 Providing continuous learning at all levels.

DEPLOYING A CUSTOMER-KEEPING STRATEGY

One of the most common reasons companies fail in their efforts to improve customer service, is that the link between the initiative and corporate strategy is weak or misunderstood. A company's strategy has to be clear, relevant, have service improvement at its core and be connected to the central business issues of the corporation. It must also be communicated effectively to everyone in the organization – it cannot be an abstraction understood by only a few people at the top. To be successful, a customer service strategy must be accepted and implemented by everyone.

Creating a vision of better service

A highly effective way of translating a strategy so that everyone understands their responsibilities is through a vision statement. Such a statement must be clear, understandable and aligned with the company's values. It should engage people throughout the organization, be memorable and be linked to customer needs. Moreover, it should set a goal of what the organization wants to be in the future.

Look at a few fine visions and notice how they have both inspired people and helped them understand what they had to do to serve the customer. For instance, the vision of L. L. Bean, a leading US direct mail retailer, is: 'Sell good merchandise at a reasonable profit, treat your customers like human beings and they'll always come back for more.' And the motto that Ford Motor Company adopted in the 1980s is unbelievably powerful: 'Quality is Job 1.'

Demonstrating a commitment to the vision

However, a vision statement ultimately makes little difference if it can only be found on a bronzed plaque bolted onto the wall at corporate headquarters or printed on a laminated card for employees to carry in their wallets. In fact, thinking of 'vision' as a noun is somewhat misleading. Try this redefinition as a verb: vision is the process of involving a company's people in decisions about where the organization is headed and determining how each employee can help achieve strategic objectives.

Johnson & Johnson, a large manufacturer of medical supplies, showed great feeling for and interest in its customers in its statement: 'We believe our first responsibility is to doctors, nurses and patients, to mothers and all others who use our products and services.' A trial by fire for this vision was the 1982 crisis precipitated by an unknown person who put cyanide in some capsules of the company's leading analgesic product, Tylenol. The tainted medicine killed five people.

The entire Johnson & Johnson organization mobilized within hours to withdraw all Tylenol in the distribution chain. The company chairman kept the public updated on all details of the problem with hourly, nationally broadcast news conferences. Within a week, the company had begun redesigning Tylenol packaging to be tamper-resistant. Production resumed within a month.

Throughout the crisis, Johnson & Johnson maintained its vision: 'our first responsibility is to doctors, nurses and patients ...'. Little thought was given to cost. After the crisis was past, financial analysts recognized that the fast, unselfish action had helped Johnson & Johnson retain the loyalty of millions of customers. Soon after consumers heard about the poisonings, a survey found that half of all Tylenol users said they would never use the product again. Three years later, however, the company had recovered almost all of its share of the US analgesic market.

In contrast, consider the West German car maker, Audi, which faced accusations a few years later that 'sudden acceleration' in its cars had caused several deaths and hundreds of injuries. Witnesses reported that while trying to park, their Audi automobiles rocketed forward for no apparent reason. Audi's own studies indicated the problem was driver error, occurring most often when the drivers were people with specific physical characteristics. The car maker believed that drivers simply were stepping on the accelerator when they meant to step on the brake.

But claiming that technically 'it was not at fault' was not enough. Audi sales in the United States dropped from 74 000 automobiles in 1985 to 26 000 in 1987, and even professional parking valets were refusing to touch the cars. In contrast to Johnson & Johnson, Audi showed no vision (see Figure 28.1). It simply issued a news release suggesting that driver error was the reason for the problem. Customers felt insulted and betrayed. Under government pressure, Audi ultimately did modify its foot pedal controls, and the 'sudden acceleration' incidents stopped.

British Airways achieved success by deploying its service strategy through a clear vision and by constantly repeating this vision. Chairman Sir Colin Marshall began the carrier's transformation from inefficient bureaucracy to customer champion with seminars on its vision, 'Putting People First', which 35 000 employees attended. A year later, every employee attended another programme on the same topic. Other versions have followed each year. This constant, consistent communication has had positive results: employees are committed to putting customers first and the airline's customers are exceptionally well served. *381*

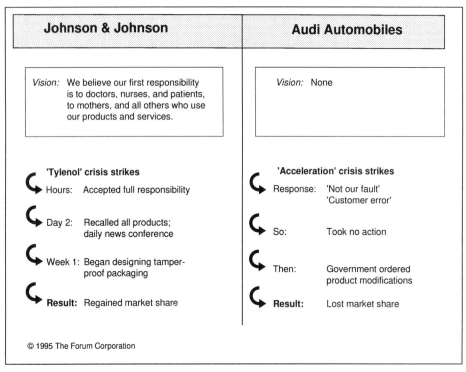

Figure 28.1   The value of living a vision

SATURATING THE ORGANIZATION WITH THE VOICE OF THE CUSTOMER

Ted Levitt, retired professor of marketing at the Harvard University Graduate School of Business, said: 'Industry is a customer satisfying process, not a goods producing process.'

This statement captures the essence of how to achieve customer service excellence. The best companies are managed from the outside in, not from the inside out. They have extraordinarily powerful connections with their customers. They listen carefully to their customers and bring their customers' collective voice into their organization (see Figure 28.2). The goal is for people throughout the organization, across functions and at all levels, to understand and act on what customers need and expect.

Outstanding companies have achieved this kind of customer-driven behaviour by, first, carefully targeting whom they want to be their customers. Second, they have invested in learning what their customers need and expect now and what they will need and expect in the future. Third, these companies have been able to inspire everyone in their organizations to measure every action against customer needs and to strive constantly to exceed customer expectations.

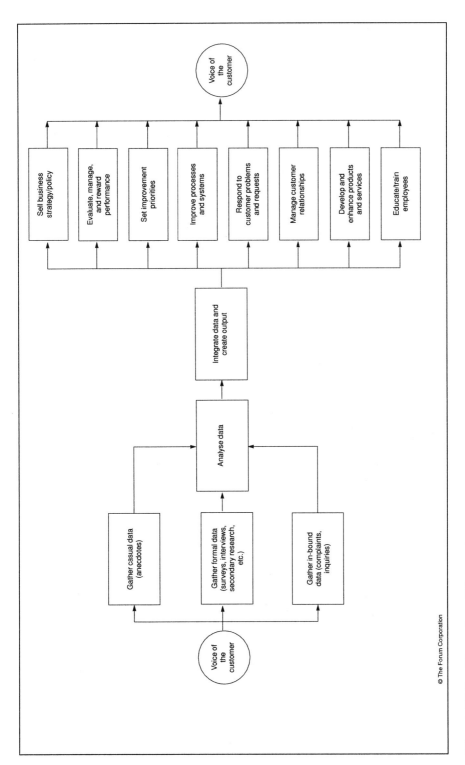

© The Forum Corporation

Figure 28.2 The voice of the customer process

Who are your customers?

There are essentially three categories of customers. *Final customers or end users* are those who ultimately use a company's products and services. *Intermediate customers* are those between the company and final customers (for example, retailers, jobbers, distributors, agents). *Internal customers* are people inside the organization who take work from someone else and carry out the next function on the way toward serving intermediate and final customers.

For organizations as a whole, prioritizing customer groups is generally a top management decision. For corporate leaders, choosing the customers on whom the company will focus is a decisive opportunity, since doing it well can lay the foundation for success. Thus Jan Carlzon revolutionized the money-losing Scandinavian Airlines (SAS) by recognizing that business travellers were the key to its recovery. Amid a steep worldwide recession in the early 1980s, Carlzon saw that business people were the only stable source of revenue on SAS's routes. He declared that the airline's goal was to become 'the best airline in the world for the frequent business traveller'. SAS's EuroClass, the first business class, became an industry leader and helped increase the airline's earnings by $80 million when most competitors were posting huge losses (Carlzon, 1987).

For some companies, intermediate customers are worth every bit as much as final customers. A mortgage banker, for example, may find that the most valued customers are the real estate agents who recommend their services to home buyers; or a packaged food manufacturer such as Birds Eye Wall's must please the decision makers in supermarkets who allocate shelf space among product lines. Finally, based on the company's vision and top management's understanding of who the company's customers are, individual work groups identify their key internal customers.

Understanding customer needs

Service-focused companies require to learn several important aspects concerning their customers. They strive to understand, first, the needs and expectations of their intermediate and final customers and which needs matter most; second, how they are doing in meeting their customers' service expectations, particularly in comparison with their competitors; and third, what they must do, in order to go beyond what the customer needs and expects.

One of the tragic but inevitable events in business is losing a customer. The greater tragedy, however, is losing a customer and not knowing why; or worse, not even knowing they are gone. Much can be learned from lost customers: for example, why did they leave, and why did they choose their current supplier? When thinking about the impact of lost customers, it is helpful to think in terms of lifetime brand loyalty. If a customer organization is retained over its normal lifetime as a buyer of products and services, what is the revenue stream gained from that relationship? Answering this question provides a clear understanding of why customer service is so extraordinarily important.

Gathering data about customers

Customer-driven companies use multiple means for gathering customer data. Generally, these methods fall into three categories: formal, inbound and casual.

Some examples of *formal channels* are convening focus groups, sending out questionnaires and setting up systems to capture direct customer feedback. A sale rung up at a Benetton clothing store anywhere in the world records the type, colour, and size of the item. Regional agents report the computerized data to the home office in Trevino, Italy, so rapidly that factories can make more of a popular item and restock stores thousands of miles away, literally within days.

Inbound channels include reviewing complaints, unsolicited comments and suggestions. As seen in Figure 28.3, depicting results from a National Consumer Survey conducted in the United States by TARP, there is a strong relationship between complaining and customer loyalty. That is why companies providing outstanding customer service invest in complaints. Some companies actually

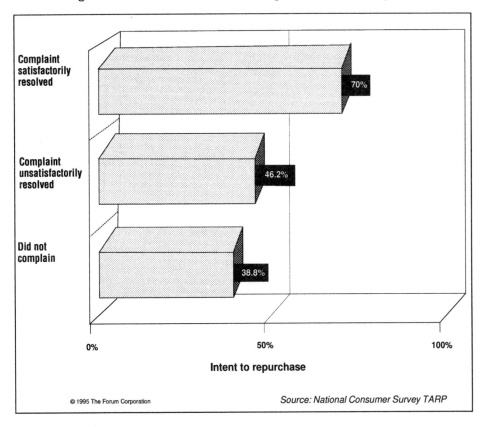

Figure 28.3   Relationship between customer complaints and customer loyalty

telephone customers just to solicit criticism. Nissan phones each person who buys a new Nissan automobile or brings one to a dealer for significant work under warranty. The objective is to resolve all dissatisfaction within 24 hours (TARP, 1995).

An example of a *casual channel* is the data that executives, sales representatives and service providers learn when they meet with customers. It is critical to have a reliable process to capture this information and disseminate it throughout the organization so that it can be acted on as appropriate. Hearing a customer directly affects people much more than a thousand carefully crafted reports and charts. One junior employee for a medium-sized manufacturer of industrial filters launched a revolutionary customer focus movement in her company by dragging the CEO out to see and hear a few real customers.

Capturing the voice of employees

Companies which are successful at delivering outstanding customer service also recognize that employees are valuable sources of data about customers, and that their voice must be heard. They have an intimate knowledge of how work gets done and are more likely to understand what might be getting in the way of consistently meeting or exceeding customer expectations. Employees can provide rich data on a wide range of factors: for example, those aspects of products and services that are most important to customers; perceptions of product and service performance; gaps between the organizational mission and customer satisfaction; ways in which management can help employees improve product and service quality; and ideas about top priorities for improvement. In many cases, employees are aware of opportunities where quick solutions could yield immediate rewards.

After Nissan opened its automobile factory in Smyrna, Tennessee, they inventoried all the different problems within the operation. Next, they did a correlation study to see who was aware of which problems (see Figure 28.4). They discovered that top management was aware of only 4 per cent of the problems; general supervisors, 9 per cent; and first-line supervisors, 34 per cent. The front-line employees, however, were aware of 100 per cent of the problems. Any top management team, through its own means, will never be aware of more than a small fraction of the problems. So it is imperative to listen to people at all levels in the organization and empower them to solve problems they face.

Ongoing measurement

The best companies are skilled at obtaining customer data, but more importantly, they excel at *using* customer information. The purpose of measurement is action and improvement. The best companies realize that the essential goal of a customer-driven measurement system is to collect the right information and use it to drive actions that will improve service to customers.

Measurement is critical to evaluating and demonstrating the need for

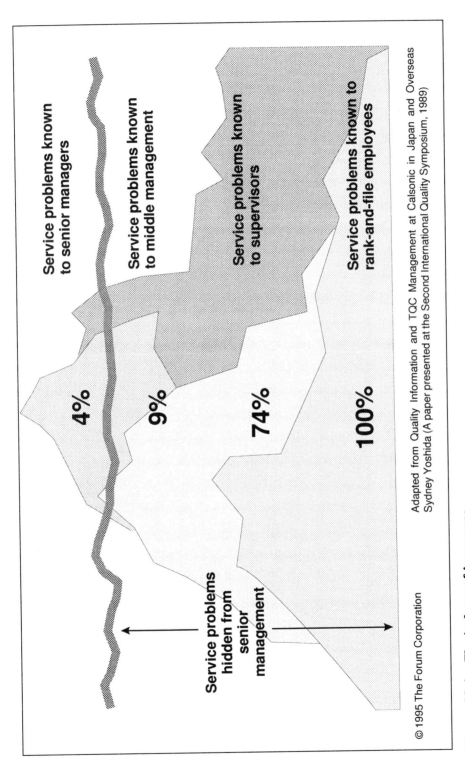

Service problems known to senior managers

Service problems known to middle management

Service problems known to supervisors

Service problems known to rank-and-file employees

4%

9%

74%

100%

Service problems hidden from senior management

Adapted from Quality Information and TQC Management at Calsonic in Japan and Overseas Sydney Yoshida (A paper presented at the Second International Quality Symposium, 1989)

© 1995 The Forum Corporation

Figure 28.4   The Iceberg of ignorance

change, evaluating the impact of change, ensuring that gains made are sustained and establishing priorities for improvement. The implications of not measuring are a poor understanding of customers and processes, less ability to meet and exceed customer expectations, and spending time and effort improving aspects of service that have little or no value to customers.

A balanced business scorecard

The most successful companies understand that financial measures are results that are recorded well in arrears of the organizational actions and customer decisions that lead to them. Thus, financial outcomes are lagging indicators that arrive too late to help prevent problems and assure organizational health.

Top companies balance traditional financial measures with customer, process and people measures. They employ a balanced business scorecard to provide a balanced view of their business. To support the scorecard, they treat measurement as a management system, establish systemwide standards, methods and processes to gather data directly from their customers and eliminate wasteful data gathering and reports.

The impact of listening and responding to the voice of the customer and measuring results on a continual basis, is well summed up in the words of Peter Hughes of Texaco in Swindon: 'Once you listen to the customer, then you can begin to change the culture to one that is geared to giving the customer the best possible service.'

BUILDING STRONG LEADERSHIP AND EMPLOYEE INVOLVEMENT

Companies managed around principles of service excellence describe their organizations as both customer focused and employee focused. They recognize that success requires the creation of an environment in which everyone in the company is willing and able to carry out the vision and strategy. The ability to bring people together to accomplish a common purpose in the midst of conditions of great change is *leadership*.

Leadership in companies which excel at customer service extends well beyond the boardroom. Progress depends on encouraging personal initiative and building leadership skills throughout the organization. Today's business environment is simply too complex for a single, heroic individual to master. And customer service strategies rely on decision making at every level. A few individuals at the top, no matter how talented, cannot implement them successfully.

A pivotal outcome of strong, effective leadership, therefore, should be total employee involvement: a cascading of knowledge, understanding and commitment down through the organization, from level to level, work group to work group, individual to individual. For the corporation, employees who thrive on change provide a competitive advantage that is strong and sustainable.

Although outstanding leadership can effect miraculous change, it is not itself a mysterious, inborn quality. Leadership can be learned, and developing leadership from within is invariably faster and more reliable than selective recruitment. Still, it is not easy. It demands executive persistence, management courage, careful preparation, constant communication and a highly emphasized, contextual leadership development effort.

Through its global research of over one hundred leading companies and relevant consulting experiences, Forum has found broad and deep leadership a chief characteristic of success.

Interpreting conditions affecting the work group

There is strong correlation between leadership performance and a passion for having better information. The goal is not information for its own sake but to make sense of the world and to make good decisions. Specific leadership actions involved include:

- Seeking information from as many sources as possible.
- Knowing how the work group supports the organization's overall strategy.
- Analysing how well the members of the group work together.
- Knowing the capabilities and motivations of individuals in the work group and of oneself.

The ability to win the confidence of the work group correlates highly with the practice of interpreting. To build that confidence, leaders continually reassess information about the external environment, organizational issues, work group activities and themselves. To do this correctly requires careful listening, creative information gathering and a willingness to accept criticism.

Shaping direction for the work group

Leaders in service-focused companies work with others to shape a vision for the future of the work group. To spark commitment, this vision should integrate the work group's short-term and long-term goals, the tasks at hand and the expectations of each group member. Leadership practices that help shape a vision and strategy to give meaning to the group's work include:

- Involving the right people in developing the group strategy.
- Standing up for what is important.
- Adjusting plans and actions as necessary in turbulent situations.
- Communicating the organizational strategy.
- Creating a positive picture of the group's future.

There is a strong correlation between worker involvement in shaping a vision and the group's ability to see it through. Employee involvement is by far the most powerful way to secure the commitment and initiative of every member of the team.

389

Mobilizing individuals around a common mission

To move from vision to working reality, leaders in successful companies are able to rally the work group as a whole, aligning members with the overall direction. This means involving people not just as listeners but as thinkers, doers and leaders themselves. The ultimate goal is to foster a sense of ownership in every worker. Each member of the work group should feel both committed to the vision of service excellence and responsible for its success.

Specific leadership practices used to mobilize individuals with different ideas, skills and values around a common objective include:

- Communicating clearly the results expected from others.
- Appealing to people's hearts and minds to lead them in a new direction.
- Demonstrating caring for the members of the work group.
- Demonstrating confidence in the ability of others.
- Letting people know how they are progressing toward group goals.

Interestingly, Forum's research found that mobilizing people is the most difficult leadership task for managers to master. One reason is that traditional business education concentrates on critical thinking and number crunching, and not on appealing to people's hearts and minds. The danger of non-mobilization is that workers will become frustrated, time will be used inefficiently and service improvement projects will never move beyond the manager's own desk.

Inspiring others to achieve results

Inspiration can move nations, and to achieve customer service excellence, it is a central requirement. Business leaders generate inspiration by:

- Promoting the development of people's talents.
- Recognizing the contributions of others.
- Enabling others to feel and act like leaders.
- Stimulating others' thinking.
- Building enthusiasm about projects and assignments.

The complete leader

In customer-driven organizations, the absence of any one of the four elements described above renders leadership ineffective. For example, the leader who shapes a clear vision, mobilizes the work group, and inspires people, may still face frustration and even failure if he or she does not accurately interpret customers' needs and the marketplace and organizational conditions.

DEVELOPING A PLAN AND PROCESS FOR IMPROVEMENT

Businesses today are in permanent white water, adrift in rapids that seemingly have no end. Customers, especially, are churning the waters: their demands for speed, quality and service are increasing dramatically. Organizations that can adapt to these turbulent conditions will thrive, usually at the expense of those that cannot.

All the successful corporations of our time are characterized by smart, aggressive management of change. If you ask General Electric's Jack Welch what the key competencies are for any business organization, he is going to say the ability to drive change and create speed, simplicity and self-confidence. He has made his formula work and so have quite a few others.

In general, companies successful at achieving service excellence have also been successful at creating and implementing a plan for change. They have avoided failure by paying attention to vital factors that ensure effective trans-formation. As a result, they are prepared to respond effectively to ongoing change in an organized, optimized way. They are managing change instead of letting change manage them. They have proven that organizations which can combine predictive ability, (for example, forecasting shifts in customer needs) with an aligned response to change are likely to come out way ahead.

No one set of steps to effective change will be right for everyone. There are, however, guidelines and lessons learned from successful companies that can be used as building blocks of a change process for almost any organization. Critical to successful change of any kind are alignment, improvement and mea-surement; these three streams of activity are present in every stage of any effective change process (see Figure 28.5).

Stage 1 - Building the foundation

Alignment is the most crucial stream during this stage and it has to happen early on. To achieve it, the leadership of the organization has to make a com-pelling case for change. To build the foundation for intentional transformation, some basic questions must be answered, for example: is there a clear need for change? How can we make everyone see it? Is the senior management team truly committed? Without good answers to those questions, the effort will stall and quickly die.

But early alignment is just part of the challenge. At the same time, some serious *improvement* efforts should be launched. Early success in improving customer-pleasing processes, service excellence and product quality can eliminate the risk of messages about alignment being seen as empty and mean-ingless.

Nor can *measurement* wait. The measurement stream must start right from the beginning, not to immerse the organization in its faults but to establish baselines for future comparison. Any meaningful change is impossible to per-ceive without a context for measuring progress. There should be baseline mea-sures on people, processes and customers. The voice of the customer is *391*

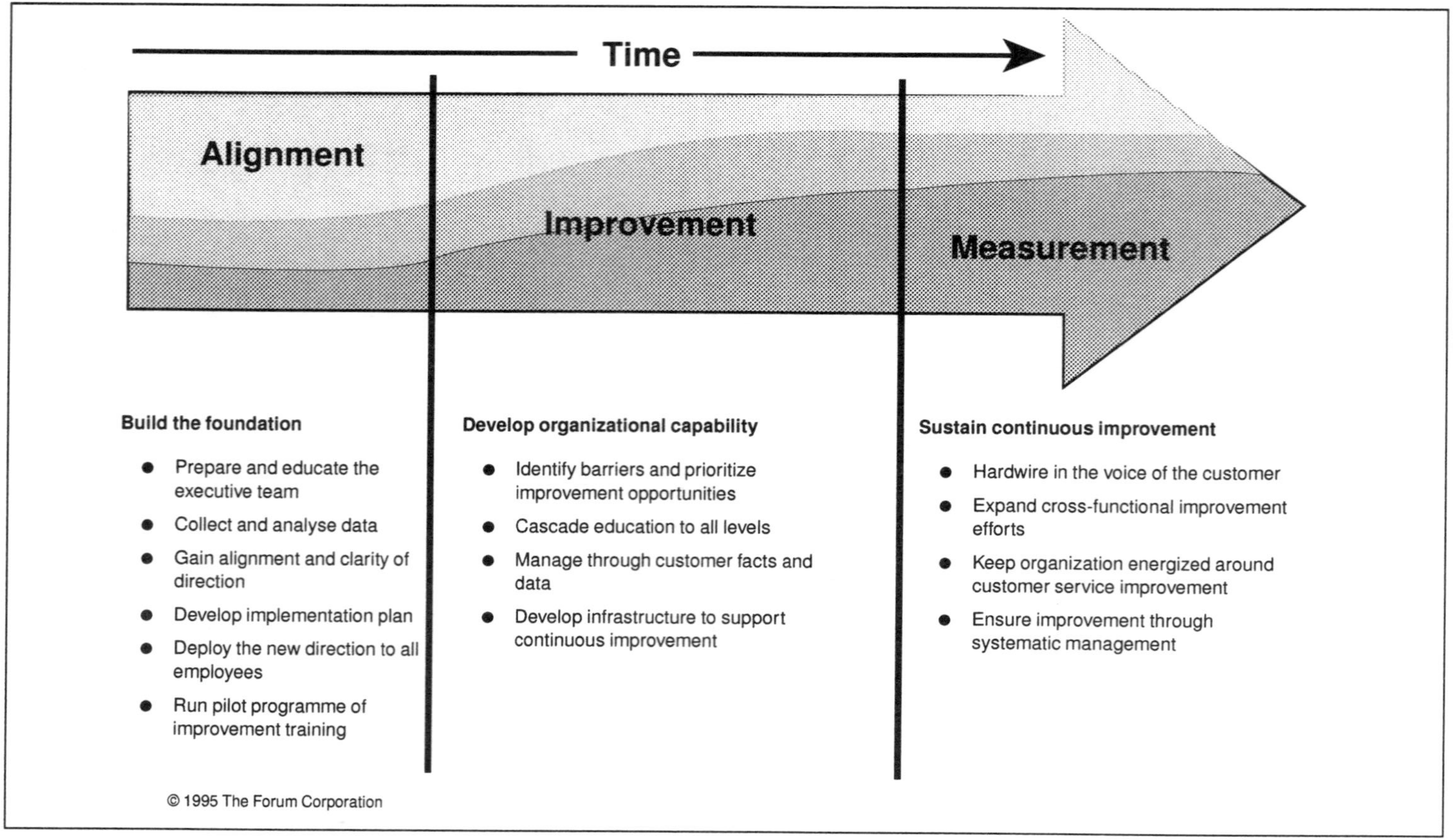

Time →

Alignment

Improvement

Measurement

Build the foundation

- Prepare and educate the executive team
- Collect and analyse data
- Gain alignment and clarity of direction
- Develop implementation plan
- Deploy the new direction to all employees
- Run pilot programme of improvement training

Develop organizational capability

- Identify barriers and prioritize improvement opportunities
- Cascade education to all levels
- Manage through customer facts and data
- Develop infrastructure to support continuous improvement

Sustain continuous improvement

- Hardwire in the voice of the customer
- Expand cross-functional improvement efforts
- Keep organization energized around customer service improvement
- Ensure improvement through systematic management

© 1995 The Forum Corporation

Figure 28.5   Implementing a customer service strategy: key actions

especially critical to access from the start because customer-driven change is the purpose of the entire process.

Stage 2 – Developing organizational capability

Building on a solid foundation, the second stage is a period of tremendous acceleration. Both people and processes come together and propel the organization rapidly toward its objectives. Alignment activities must continue but the main emphasis is on developing the capability of the organization. An important goal is to improve the company's ongoing capacity to manage change by gaining new insights into what customers will want, at the same time developing the required skills and knowledge employees will need to meet those new demands and helping employees apply their new competencies quickly to improve work processes.

All of this takes enormous effort, but there are ways to make the effort pay off and quickly. Increasingly, companies are letting managers train their own people. This builds credibility, and the immediacy of the learning is unmistakable. Done correctly, essential skills training for thousands of people can be under way in a very short time. It is a fast and long-lasting approach that builds the confidence, competence and commitment required to make change happen across the organization.

The measurement component continues to grow because valuable data are being gathered all along the way, and processes are being created to feed those data back into the organization. Measurement is becoming integrated into operations and therefore becoming much more purposeful. People measure what they need in order to pursue changes that, through effective alignment, they believe in wholeheartedly.

Stage 3 – Sustaining customer service improvements

By now, improvement efforts should be sweeping through the organization like waves hitting a beach. People and processes are adapting quickly to the emerging environment. So it is important to put in place the processes necessary to sustain performance at the new level. New reward systems are needed to support new behaviours, and operations systems must support new objectives.

This is the stage at which empowerment – one of the world's most abused concepts – truly becomes possible. Many companies try to achieve empowerment too early. Telling people they are empowered without providing clear alignment, necessary skills and competencies, and meaningful measurement capabilities is a cruel joke perpetrated on the workforce. On a macro level, at least, change management has to follow this rational, carefully sequenced model.

Ultimately, there is a shift from measuring past results to measuring processes that help forecast the future. These are the key processes that will help capture and maintain advantage in the marketplace. I know of a chief executive who reads an incredible number of customer surveys every month to *393* make sure that he is thinking ahead about what will be required in order to stay in front of the competition. Time and time again, his company implements improvements months before competitors have even considered such changes.

A reliable process for improving service

Most companies that have sustained service quality improvement efforts attribute part of their success to the work of teams throughout the organization. In the early phases of the effort, the results of *pioneering* teams can demonstrate the benefits of being service focused and using a common systematic approach to process improvement. Conversely because of this visibility, stumbling in this area can have significant consequences in terms of higher levels of waste, employee turnover and cynicism, and organizational inertia.

Customer service improvement teams in leading companies use concrete skills and tools to do their work effectively. Teamwork, and a common approach to uncovering and resolving customer issues and problems, are paramount. The following eight-step method typifies that used in many companies for improving customer service. It is based on Forum's extensive research on what distinguishes best-in-class customer-driven companies and our own work with large companies that are implementing service improvement strategies:

1   *Pick the issue* Once a high-priority process affecting service excellence has been identified and selected for improvement or elimination, there must be clear definition of the issue and a deep understanding of its impact on customer satisfaction. Then a preliminary project plan for the team's work must be developed.
2   *Research the current situation.* Document the current process, collect comprehensive facts and data on the issue, create an informative display of the findings, and analyse data for insights into possible causes for the service problems.
3   *Obtain root causes.* The key actions in this step are to identify and gain an understanding of all probable causes, choose the most likely causes based on facts and data, and then go beyond symptoms to identify and select root cause(s).
4   *Generate possible improvements.* Produce a list of possible improvements, choose the best improvement and set a clear goal, and design a comprehensive action plan to pilot an improved process.
5   *Run a pilot.* Design a limited test of the planned improvement. Take measurements at specific points and compile a detailed record of activities and results.
6   *Examine results.* Evaluate the results in terms of the goals of the pilot and compare also with pre-pilot data. Communicate the results to all those who provided data on which the pilot was based. Note any positive or negative effects and then make a decision whether to move forward, rerun the pilot, or reassess root causes.

7   *Set up transfer.* Prepare documentation of the new, more reliable process. Communicate details of the new process and obtain approval for widespread implementation. Design a system for continuously tracking the improvements.

8   *Seek further improvements.* Identify and implement ways to improve the team process. Identify important next steps to ensure that the barrier does not reappear. Celebrate the team's work.

Through all phases of change, during alignment, improvement and measurement, top companies do not settle for initiatives propelled by singular events. Change management is not creating a new vision, launching a new training effort or affecting a handful of process improvements: it is crafting a more fluid, focused and adaptive organization so that, no matter what the next big change looks like, an organization's people and processes will continually adjust (see Figure 28.6).

PROVIDING CONTINUOUS ORGANIZATIONWIDE LEARNING

Today's leaner, faster business environment has created a need for continuous learning. Companies that have successfully aligned their organizations to deliver excellent service to customers, support learning and link it directly to relevant business issues. As a result, they realize the rich individual development of their employees and impressive business results because of the skilled, knowledgeable actions of those employees.

Training contributes high tangible value to the service improvement efforts of companies, quickly and often without the need to increase staff. How do top organizations conduct their learning programmes? What do they teach and to whom? Where does training fit into the customer service strategies of world-class companies?

To find some answers, the Forum Corporation has studied corporate training organizations that are well known for making strategically vital contributions to their companies' success. These studies have revealed the best practices evident across some of the world's most respected and valued training organizations, including those at Motorola, American Express, DuPont, Sun Microsystems, US West, PPG Industries and John Hancock Financial Services.

How the best organizations learn

In top companies, the process of learning is continuous and reaches all levels of the organization. In my view – and this is substantially supported by the results of Forum's research – the most successful training systems reflect five core principles of effective adult learning, as follows:

1   *Learning is a transformation that takes place over time.* The most effective customer service training is supported and implemented as a continuous process of deliberate and relevant learning experiences and tailored to individual skill levels.

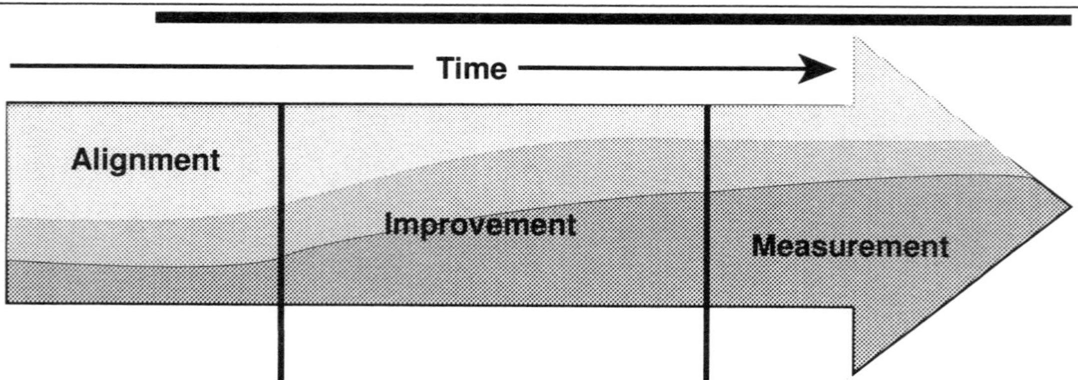

Time

Alignment

Senior team:

- Has knowledge to make informed decision on service strategy
- Has clear vision of the future
- Understands degree of organizational readiness
- Has clear priorities for pilot improvement teams
- Agrees to move plan ahead

Everyone in the organization

- Is aligned around a common vision of the future
- Understands their role in newly focused organization
- Is enthused by early success of pilot improvement teams

Improvement

Senior team:

- Understands what is working and what is blocking improvement
- Is actively engaged in removing obstacles to improvement

Facilitators and team leaders:

- Are able effectively to lead and coach improvement teams

Everyone in the organization:

- Has the skills, knowledge, and capability for total involvement in improvement efforts

Measurement

Everyone in the organization:

- Is energized to continuously improve customer service
- Understands their customers' requirements
- Through teamwork, focuses on solving service problems and improving customer-pleasing processes
- Continuously monitors improvements and levels of customer satisfaction

© 1995 The Forum Corporation

Figure 28.6   Implementing a customer service strategy: outcomes

2   *Learning follows a continuous cycle of knowledge, action and reflection.* People learn to serve customers better by doing just that. Then they can examine and assess their actions, which leads to new understanding, which in turn guides future actions. All elements of this learning cycle should be seamless and totally integrated.

3   *Learning is most effective when it addresses relevant issues.* People learn in order to respond to challenges in their environment (that is, the need to provide better service to customers). Top companies accelerate customer-driven learning by linking all training to individual and organizational objectives.

4   *Learning is most effective when people learn with others.* People who learn together share and build on one another's perceptions. Group training for members of service improvement teams, for example, increases the likelihood of understanding and cooperation back on the job.

5   *Learning must take place in a challenging and supportive environment.* It is easy for people to fall back on old ways of serving customers and not stretch to find new ways of thinking and acting. On an organizational level, support systems and resources for service-oriented training must be in place to facilitate new programmes, encourage high performance, assign relevant projects and reward results.

What people in the best companies learn

Providing a quality learning experience is simply not enough for training to have a meaningful impact on service improvement efforts. The training is only effective when it is linked to the roles individuals being trained must play in helping achieve service improvement objectives. Figure 28.7 shows examples of key areas in which training takes place in companies where service excellence is a strategic objective.

How each employee can achieve service excellence

Everyone in a customer-driven organization must consistently provide a level of service that meets or exceeds customer expectations. This collective responsibility is a logical extension of the principle that anyone who interacts with a customer becomes a service provider and is able to grow the customer relationship. Companies must therefore ensure that all employees understand how their customers define outstanding service, how they can deliver excellent service and, in general, how to recognize and close gaps in service quality.

How to plan and implement a service improvement initiative

Top executive teams must fully understand what it means to be customer driven, why excellence in customer service is important, and all aspects of senior management's role in assuring a service improvement effort is successful. *397*

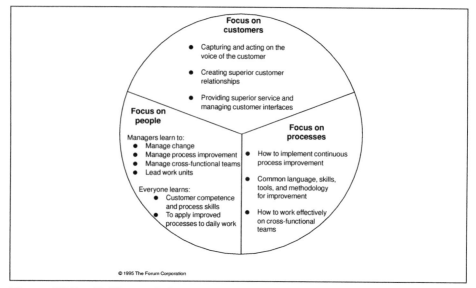

Figure 28.7   Skills needed to achieve and sustain service excellence

Making total customer satisfaction a reality requires extensive knowledge and insightful perspectives of how it will happen. Subjects for this training might include lessons learned from best-in-class companies, how to build and improve reliable processes, and how to involve and train employees to deliver outstanding service.

Leadership capabilities

I have already discussed in some detail the need for companies to create an environment in which all employees are aligned with the company's vision, and empowered to make decisions and implement actions that contribute to customer satisfaction. Training in this regard is concerned primarily with how to involve others in applying the corporate service improvement strategy at the work unit level and how to guide the development of leadership abilities in others.

A reliable method for process improvement

High-performing organizations recognize that improvement from within reduces costs for customers without resorting to unpopular practices such as head-count reduction or spending freezes. Therefore, these companies are providing their employees with the skills, tools, common language and methodologies to reduce the waste and improve the processes most important to customers.

How to capture the voice of the customer

Middle and upper-level management must have skills for gathering customer data, turning the data into action steps that improve service processes, and enhancing service-driven performance within their work units. This is also important for those managers whose units serve large numbers of internal customers.

Customer-retaining sales skills, disciplines and tools

Salespeople are a critical component in the establishment and advancement of long-term customer relationships. They must learn diagnostic tools and key disciplines that help them develop customer-specific selling strategies based on what customers value. They must build trust and commitment with customers, and orchestrate an organization's total resources to ensure outstanding service to customers.

Customer interface skills

Front-line service people must continually develop and refine skills, attitudes and perspectives necessary to create consistently positive interactions with customers. Necessary skills include how to understand the customer's point of view, improve teamwork and relationships with co-workers, handle complaints, assess challenging situations, deal with difficult and angry customers, solve complex problems, and minimize the impact of costly service mistakes.

How to work effectively on teams

In addition to training in many of the competencies already mentioned, members of service improvement teams receive training in skills needed to work collaboratively and cross-functionally. Team leaders must learn skills for moving teams forward, for managing the balance between technical and team issues, and for managing team meetings.

A new learning standard

Customer-focused training is not an abstract concept. It encompasses a set of specific and constructive behaviours consistently exhibited by training organizations in high-performing companies. Significantly, these behaviours can be emulated by virtually all training organizations. By moving closer to the business, segmenting customers to provide custom solutions, and supporting the company's strategic objectives, training organizations direct their efforts toward outcomes that are important to customers and therefore to the company's success.

Move closer to the business

Top companies operate their training organizations much like market-oriented professional services firms with customers, competitors and costs at the hearts of their business model. Typically, corporate training professionals spend much more of their time consulting with internal customers on where value can be added and less time on delivery of training. 'We create a business environment for training,' says Ed Trolley, Human Resources and Development, Dupont/Forum Partnership. 'When your costs are simply allocated, people can get lazy about it. But when your survival depends on customer satisfaction, it forces a whole different behaviour.'

Segment customers to better understand needs

Customer-driven training organizations are markedly more responsive and able to measure the effectiveness of the training they provide. Across the board, their customers have voiced new and heightened expectations for speed, method of delivery, demonstration of results and relationship management. So, the training groups work hard to precisely identify distinct customer sets, understand the specific requirements of each, and determine how well training is meeting those requirements.

Carve out a strategic role

Top training organizations view themselves not solely as implementors of change, but as leaders of their company's customer service strategy. They see their role as supporting current skill and knowledge needs and also identifying and developing the emerging skill sets the company will require to advance their service capabilities faster than competitors. They also share a considerable emphasis on competencies, which they believe are the bridge connecting learning with fulfilment.

At Sun Microsystems, the training group's planning model mirrors that of the company's customers. This model requires training to answer questions like: Who are our customers? Who are our competitors? Why will customers buy from us? What must we do to make this happen? Do we have the necessary skills and abilities to totally satisfy our customers, again and again?

Corporate vision and values

We have already stressed that a vision and set of values lie at the heart of a truly customer-driven company. Training in these organizations not only reflects the vision and values, but also effectively enables the companies to live up to their ideals.

Corporate commitment to training

Training organizations in companies with high levels of customer service spend 3 to 5 per cent of payroll on education and training. Motorola's current policy provides at least 40 hours of training each year per employee, and the company expects to quadruple that commitment by the year 2000. Motorola and other companies with such commitments recognize that their expenditures on learning are an investment. They shape training solutions knowing that, for the companies they serve, learning has become a high-stakes business strategy.

Modelling excellence

The leaders of successful organizations value learning and demonstrate it in their daily behaviours, decisions and actions. At Xerox, the cascading of Leadership Through Quality from top management down through the rest of the organization, has clearly established managers as role models of learning and teaching.

CONCLUSION

Imagine an organization where every individual, every work unit: understands exactly how it contributes to adding value for the customer; knows how to measure its performance daily; knows where to make improvements for the greatest impact on performance; and has extra time every day to engage in new continuous improvement and innovation activity. This is the customer-driven company.

Some years ago, my associate, Richard Whiteley, was taping a television interview on the subject of his best-selling book, *The Customer Driven Company: Moving from Talk to Action*. At the end of the session, the interviewer asked, 'Do you think this is a revolution?' Richard thought for a moment and replied:

> I am not sure of the proper label, but I do know that it is tremendously important. It is significant enough that organisations are going to have to change in momentous ways. They are going to have to change their behaviour, their attitudes, their structures, their compensation systems and their values. They will have to change their very culture to make customer service work.

REFERENCES

Carlzon, J. (1987), *Moments of Truth*, New York: Harper and Row.

FURTHER READING

Donovan, P. and Samler, T. (1994), *Delighting Customers*, London: Chapman & Hall.

Gale, T. B. (1994), *Managing Customer Value*, New York: Free Press.

Hessan, D. and Whiteley, R. C. (1996), *Customer Centred Growth: Five Proven Strategies for Building Competitive Advantage*, New York: Addison-Wesley.

Lele, M. M. and Sheth, J. N. (1987), *The Customer is Key*, New York: Wiley.

Sewell, C. and Brown, P. B. (1990), *Customers for Life*, New York: Doubleday.

Whiteley, R. C. (1992), *The Customer Driven Company: Moving from Talk to Action*, London: Century Business Press.

Part V
THE HUMAN INGREDIENT

29 Selection, *not* recruitment
Stephanie Craig

Selection is about choice. It involves the ability to choose the very best people from a pool of suitably qualified applicants. Within this concept of choosing it is implicit that the selector:

- knows what is needed for success in the job;
- attracts the right candidates;
- has information on the relative merits of each candidate to guide the choice; and
- has a reasonable number of suitable candidates to choose from.

This sounds very straightforward, yet the research, the popular press and our own experiences illustrate clearly how difficult it is consistently to select the best people.

Research describes the predictive power of selection on a scale where plus one is perfect prediction (that is, selection of the successful performer) and minus one is a perfect mismatch. Whilst figures vary, the most frequently reported sets of figures indicate predictive power for various selection techniques as shown in Figure 29.1. The range is from total chance for astrology and graphology up to reasonable confidence in prediction when using structured interviews, work sample tests, ability tests and assessment centres.

MODEL OF THE SELECTION PROCESS

There is a well-established model for the selection process. This model uses all the selection process, which has been shown to work most effectively. Any employer should use this method. In particular, employers of customer service people find the model most useful since frequently the selection is:

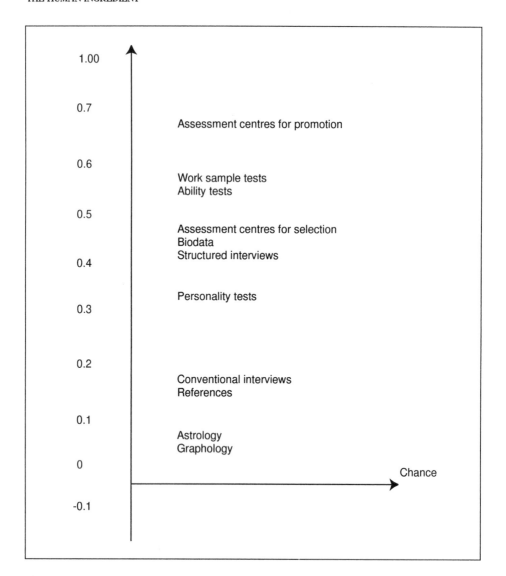

Figure 29.1 Predictive power for various selection techniques

- of large numbers of people;
- into similar posts; and
- of people who are in the front line, either in direct personal or telephone contact.

Having a systematic approach to selection, using the model, ensures greater accuracy and streamlines the administration of the whole selection process.

This model, as it frequently applies to customer service positions, which tend to involve large numbers, is shown in Figure 29.2. It is a series of successive sieves that are used once the candidate population has been attracted.

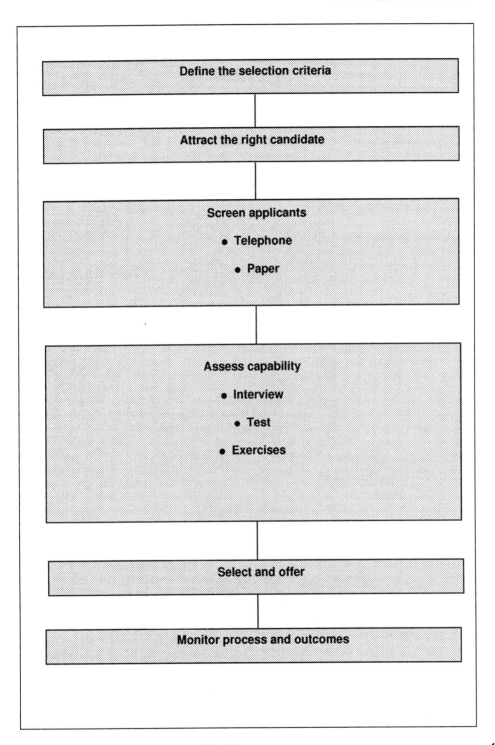

Figure 29.2   A model of the selection process

The numbers filtered out at each stage depend on the volume of candidates and the number of positions on offer. The selection process, as shown, uses objective measurement, and therefore allows cut-off limits to be raised or lowered to suit the volume and calibre of candidates.

During the process, the model moves from determining what kind of recruit will be most successful in the job, through to making an offer to the very best. The effectiveness and the fairness of the process must be monitored throughout the selection activity, with information collected at each stage and analysed once full outcomes are known. Each phase of this selection model is addressed in the following sections of this chapter.

SELECTION CRITERIA

Defining selection criteria?

The selection criteria provide the standards against which candidates are assessed. The term 'criteria' refers to what the recruits will do and how they will have to behave in order to produce successful outcomes. Selection criteria, therefore, include:

1 *Activities* A detailed description of the specific tasks or roles to be undertaken by the job holder in order to meet the strategic objectives as set out for the customer service area.
2 *Competencies* A detailed description of all the knowledge, skills, abilities and personal characteristics which are required by the job holder to enable them to perform the activities successfully.

The principal themes which will ensure that selection criteria are comprehensive and accurate are as follows:

- *The activities must be described in detail.* The definitions should be specific, concise and unambiguous.
- *The activities should be forward looking.* Strategic intent should be translated into specific tasks or else the strategy remains merely as an intention.
- *The competencies are derived from the activities* (that is, they are not merely 'nice things to have'). The competencies are those aspects of a person's knowledge, disposition and skill base which will enable them, perhaps with some training, to perform the tasks well. Without an adequate level of the competencies, a position holder will struggle to succeed.
- *The competencies need specific behavioural definitions.* They should be expressed in terms that will allow their level to be, in some ways, observed and measured.

Using selection criteria

The activities clarify the role requirements, which enables advertising to be specific, job descriptions to be written, promotion requirements to be determined, and the selector to match the relevancy of a candidate's experience against the role requirements.

The competencies provide the more obvious standard for selection: they set the content and tone for the selector. Selection methods are designed to collect information on the level of competence shown by the candidate. In addition, competencies provide information to the job holder on how they might improve their performance. Review of which competencies are associated with which activities sets out for the job holder the 'how' to do the job better, not just 'what' to do better.

Having selection criteria which give clear, concise behavioural descriptions is vital for selection and ongoing people management. We now turn to the processes used to develop selection criteria which meet these requirements.

Developing the criteria

The process used is known generally as job analysis, which is a system of collecting objective information on what people have to do and the competencies they need in order to be successful. Within this process description there are many different methods used, which divide, roughly speaking, into three different types. Some analyses may employ all three types.

The interview

The most frequently used method is the interview. This method tends to produce rich information, but it is sometimes not too amenable to analysis. The interview is typically structured with the job analyst seeking questions of job holder and/or supervisor about the duties and responsibilities, the competencies, and the environment and/or conditions of work. The interview can be individual or group, and may use either job holders or others who know the job requirements and demands very well.

The disadvantages of the interview method are that it is time consuming and, depending on the structure used, can be difficult to analyse. These disadvantages can be solved, however, by applying an exacting structure and reporting schema. With structure, the interview has both predictive power and richness of data.

Ways of structuring the interview vary. The structure may be prepared specially for the job in question, or it may be derived from the recognized methodologies of *critical incident* (Flanagan, 1954) or *repertory grid* (Kelly, 1955), both of which are used very frequently and may be used together in the same interview. These two methods are particularly adept in eliciting the competencies. Another structured interview approach is *functional job analysis* (Fine and Wiley, 1977), which uses a standardized and controlled language for *409* describing and measuring the tasks performed on a job by a worker. In this approach, which is highly structured and task-oriented the interview write-ups can also be scaled to allow for quantification of the data. Activity information is obviously well covered by this method, but the competencies have to be inferred from the activities, which requires considerable skill and introduces subjectivity.

The interview approach has been adapted by a number of researchers and users. For example, Boyatzis (1982) and his associates at McBer & Co. used the critical incident structure supported by a personality measure, the *thematic apperception test* (Murray, 1938). This particular structured interview has later become known as the 'Behavioural Event Interview'. The Management Charter Initiative in the United Kingdom uses functional job analysis in the production of the management standards, and it employs repertory grid, critical incidents, group interviews and workshops in the production of the personal competencies (MCI, 1990a, 1990b, 1991).

The questionnaire

The second most popular method is the questionnaire. This method uses either an existing questionnaire or one designed or tailored to meet a specific need or job. Questionnaires have the advantages of being relatively easy to analyse and of providing quantitative information. The most widely used of the existing questionnaires is the *position analysis questionnaire* (PAQ) developed by McCormick, Jeanneret and Mecham (1972). This is a standardized and structured job analysis questionnaire containing 194 elements, of which 187 concern work activities and situations. The items are organized under six headings: information input, mental processes, work output, relationships with other persons, job context, and other characteristics. Ratings are on extent of use, amount of time, importance to this job, possibility of occurrence (hazards), applicability and special codes. There is a management version of this questionnaire known as the 'Professional and Managerial Position Questionnaire' (Mitchell and McCormick, 1979).

Another existing job analysis questionnaire is the *work profiling system* (Saville & Holdsworth, 1988). This questionnaire has an item bank of 800 tasks that are divided into three groupings: managerial and professional, service and administrative, and manual and technical. Ratings are sought on time spent on and the importance of each task, together with data on job context. This method facilitates objective deduction of the competencies required for successful performance by the use of fixed associations between the task and the competencies.

In contrast to existing job analysis questionnaires, considerable use is made of specially designed or tailored inventories, which are used primarily in respect of a particular job or level. The content of such a questionnaire is thus more specific. For example, one specially designed questionnaire derives its content from previously conducted, structured interviews – especially those using repertory grid – or from in-house desk research. The approach is called *repertory grid job analysis* (Smith, Gregg and Andrews, 1989). Lists of job activities or roles, produced by interviews, are placed along the top of the grid, and the competencies, again elicited by the structured interviews, are placed along the side. Respondents, who are usually supervisors and managers, rate on a seven-point scale the level to which each competency is needed in the performance of each activity or role. The advantage of this latter method is that it combines the production of a large amount of rich qualitative data from the structured interviews and then allows clustering and quantification by the analysis of the grid.

Observation

The third type of method is observation, which is often used in support of an interview or a questionnaire. It is rarely used on its own, however, as it requires spending considerable time in observing different job holders. Nevertheless, it does provide an interesting slant on what people actually do, rather than what they say they do.

There are numerous other, less frequently used methods (for example, diaries). The general consensus from research suggests that flexibility is required as no one technique is likely to be appropriate across all areas of use.

Applicability to customer service

The three main types of method – interview, questionnaire and observation – are used to elicit and to define the activities and competencies in customer service roles.

There is a particular constraint which occurs frequently with customer service roles: that is, that the roles are often not in existence at the time of the study, or a pilot is operating that may not provide the model for future full operations. The job analysis is then necessarily constrained in scope, but it will often play an even more integral role in guiding the selection, remuneration and management of staff. The output of the job analysis, so used, will greatly influence the culture of the centre.

The most frequent approach used for customer service roles is, in my experience, a combination of the interview, structured by repertory grid, followed by a questionnaire. The questionnaire is most usually specially designed and uses the outcomes of the interviews as the content (that is, repertory grid job analysis, as described earlier). The interviews are often conducted with those responsible for planning the customer service centre. As these people only see the expected tasks from their own personal perspectives, all interview data must be combined and the sum represented to each person so as to ensure that all individual concerns are adequately addressed. This requirement is especially relevant in respect of the activity data. The competency data is frequently more easily agreed as the planning team often have a strong sense of the culture and style they want to inject into the customer service centre. *411*

This cultural element will be present in many of the descriptions of how people in the centre should behave if the centre is to gain competitive advantage.

As a general point, those chosen as interviewees and respondents to any questionnaire must be:

- *knowledgeable*, particularly of the position demands and tasks involved;
- *respected*, so that their involvement in the analysis is seen as positive; and
- *influential*, insofar as they can persuade others that systematic job analysis followed by the design of systematic selection processes are worthwhile.

Some customer service outcomes

A review of several job analyses conducted for customer service positions shows the following:

- The activities are very dependent on the nature of the position and the employing company.
- The competencies show some common themes.

Not surprisingly, the activities differ according to the role. The content of the job is of paramount importance. The activity emphasis is not just on 'handling enquiries' but on providing specific information that meets and exceeds a customer's needs. The detail of the customer service role will vary from position to position and from organization to organization.

The competencies, however, exhibit common characteristics. The language in which each are expressed vary according to the role and organization, but there are clusters of similar meaning. Thus the competencies tend to include the following themes under the headings of social, personal and work-specific.

Social competencies

These competencies refer to the different aspects of behaviour required in social interaction in customer service roles. This group is probably the most fundamental of all the competencies in that it is hard to see how a person might perform to even the most basic level without these competencies. The different elements which are common to all customer service positions are as follows:

- *Social confidence.* For example, being outgoing and friendly, able to quickly develop effective relationships with a range of people, able to feel and to show interest and warmth towards others, and able to set people at ease.
- *Listening skills.* They include attending to what people say, reflecting back and asking questions to clarify understanding, and taking in all the information without modifying it according to personal values or views.

- *Empathy and helpfulness*. Namely, being able to see things from the other's point of view, understanding the feelings and frustrations even when those may be felt to be unreasonable, being sympathetic and concerned, putting the customer first, and being driven to help the customer and to resolve any difficulties for the customer.
- *Communication skills*. In both written and oral communication, the required skills cover the ability to communicate clearly and fluently without the use of jargon and to pitch the communication to suit the customer and the media being used.
- *Teamwork*. Basically, an enjoyment in working with others, a willingness to share workload and to help each other, and a sense of belonging to a team and pride in that team's effort.

Personal competencies

Involving the personal skills and abilities needed to achieve outcomes in addition to the social competencies, the different elements of personal competencies are as follows:

- *Self-assurance and resilience*. In other words, being able to take a firm stand when necessary, being assertive, being confident in oneself whilst aware of personal limitations, being able to transmit confidence and certainty, and being able to handle rejection and setbacks.
- *Persistence and control*. Having the energy and stamina to keep going despite setbacks and the monotony of routine, not giving up and having the tenacity to keep trying to find a satisfactory solution, being self-disciplined and in control of feelings and reactions, and staying calm and unflappable despite provocation and pressure.
- *Enthusiasm*. This competence includes the ability to maintain and present a consistently positive attitude, to be enthusiastic and project interest and excitement, to be energetic and to have the stamina that will sustain this energy and enthusiasm over time.
- *Thoroughness*. For example, being able to set priorities, being systematic and methodical, attending to details and facts, being precise and accurate, being able to spot mistakes, being concerned to produce quality work, not bending the rules and procedures, being conscientious.
- *Practical intelligence*. The ability to think quickly, to spot the key points, to use past experience as a guide, to absorb and understand quickly product and technical information, and to handle straightforward numerical calculations.
- *Initiative and decisiveness*. In general terms, these attributes involve taking the responsibility for acting without prompting from others, accepting and adapting quickly to change, being alert to the neccessity for doing things differently with different circumstances and people, making decisions on the basis of the information available at the time and standing by those decisions until further information necessitates amendment. *413*

Work-specific competencies

While this set varies from job to job and organization to organization, all these competencies have to do with the acquisition of the knowledge and necessary specific skills, as follows:

- *Technology skills.* Encompassing a range of skills from being comfortable dealing with technologically sophisticated products through to specific knowledge and experience in the application of the technology used.
- *Product knowledge.* Again this element is highly dependent on the nature of the position, but it will include being up to date with all relevant aspects and being willing to learn in order to add to the knowledge base.
- *Business awareness.* An attribute that will include having a broad understanding of the business and the marketplace and appreciating the many levels of interaction with the customer. It may also include being commercially aware and keen to impact on the bottom line.

These lists of competencies are neither exclusive nor exhaustive. Organizations will have different competencies according to their specific needs and culture, and will also express the competencies differently, both in the content of their definition and in the way they are labelled. However, the competencies not only provide the standard for how people need to behave in order to be successful in the customer service position, but they will also begin the process of developing the culture of the customer service area.

ATTRACTING THE RIGHT CANDIDATES

The larger the number of applicants, the greater is the choice and the probability of selecting the very best people. Increasing choice through numbers has two aspects to consider, namely:

1 how to target the right applicant population; and
2 how to handle the numbers if you are successful in attracting a wide range of people.

Many selection processes have very tight, narrow bands within which applicants are sought. This is the technique most companies use to attract just enough of the obviously right people. Most advertisements are explicit on the experience and qualifications required. Often these minimum requirements are placed at the top of the range to reduce the number of people applying, whether or not the level of qualifications or depth of experience is really necessary.

Customer service roles present a unique recruitment opportunity for many people. Minimum standards, experience and qualifications are often all that is
truly necessary. The real selection decision is on behaviour. Is an individual

predisposed to and motivated by a customer service role? Social skills, interest in people and empathy are likely to be worth more than tertiary education.

Many customer service roles are new, so directly relevant experience is not really possible. In some instances there is a positive desire to recruit people from backgrounds other than those that may appear relevant. The new style or theme of the organization may run in direct contrast to that of a similar, more established organization or even group within the same organization. There may be a strong desire not to recreate the same culture and procedures in the new organization.

Without the hard facts of experience and qualification to guide advertising, there is a tremendous danger of opening the floodgates to large numbers of truly unsuitable people. The need is to combine access to the broader range of people while maintaining the quality of the applicant.

Knowing the applicant population

A job analysis begins to define the applicant population. The activities set out the tasks people may have handled at some stage in their experience of life. This experience is not limited to a conventional job. It may have been gained in the home, through social or charitable activities or suchlike. The competencies define the style of the person sought.

The combination of information on the activities and competencies enables pen pictures to be drawn which can guide the advertising media used and the content of the advertisement. Creative advertising and multimedia can be used to reach the largest audience. This can involve radio and press advertisements, and posters in bus shelters and tube stations, to name the more obvious.

Extending the range for the applicant population offers ultimately greater choice for the selector. It also offers a high degree of fairness and equal opportunity as the population has not been officially stratified by experience and qualification, neither of which may be equally achievable by all sections of society and which in any case may not be needed for these customer service roles.

Interesting the applicant population

Within the wider audience reached with advertising and publicity, the more appropriate people must be persuaded to present themselves as applicants. The competency profile can give an indicator of the prime motivators of those most likely to succeed in the particular customer service role. These prime motivators can, likewise, be built into the advertising and publicity content.

Dealing with the numbers

Broadening the band of potential applicants reached by creative and multimedia advertising, if successful, will bring large numbers of applicants. This *415* can present a huge administrative burden unless systematic screening and assessment processes have been designed and are in place by the time the advertising campaign begins. The next section addresses these processes.

SCREENING APPLICATIONS

When faced with large numbers of applications or the prospect thereof, the recruiter needs to find a screening process which will provide sufficient, relevant information to enable an informed decision to be made and the process needs to be quick and accurate. Ideally, the process should:

1   *Inform the recruiter.* Many screening systems, especially standardized application forms, offer too little information that is immediately usable for a customer service role recruiter. Education, other than having adequately completed secondary level education, may not be important. Equally, an applicant's experience outside conventional employment may be as important as that gained through the paid employment they have had. The screen has to allow the recruiter to learn of the full range of an applicant's experiences as they may be relevant to the role, and also something of the person's interest in and attitude to customer service. Additionally, there may be an opportunity to assess telephone manner and speech.

2   *Be quick and easy to use.* Screens, typically application forms, can take considerable time to read and consider the relative worth of the information offered. Often the process has to be conducted by a senior person as the information can be complex and presented in very different ways by different people. Screening can be conducted in such a way that it enables quick scanning and scoring by a person who is relatively inexperienced in personnel matters.

3   *Be accurate.* The chief source of error in screening is inconsistency in the standards applied. Inconsistency will be introduced when there is more than one screener and it will be introduced when screening takes place over several days, even when it is done by one person. Accuracy can be achieved by setting a standard format or 'scoring system' for all screeners to use. This moderates bias and prevents the 'creeping scale' which occurs when each applicant is compared with and pegged against the previous applicant screened.

Options for screening

These options fall into two broad categories: screening by paper or by telephone. The position may require that both types of screen are used. Broadly speaking, face-to-face customer contact positions tend to use only paper screening processes, but telephone contact positions often use both and usually the telephone screen precedes the paper screen. Three types of screen are described below.

Telephone screen

This type of screen is used most frequently as the first sieve for any telephone-based customer service position. The screen typically addresses three areas, as follows:

1 *Essential minimum criteria.* These may be a willingness to work shifts, to work in a non-smoking area and any other such minimum or essential criteria which have a proven performance, social or legal requirement.
2 *Relevant experience.* Questions may be asked about the range and nature of experience in particular highly relevant areas. The applicant is able to draw on any personal, social and work experiences in order to answer the questions. The types of questions used could include the following:

   (a) 'Have you dealt with customers or the public in a service or retail capacity?'
   (b) 'If yes, is/was it mainly by telephone or mainly face to face?'

   (These questions could be scored separately or together depending on the weighting one might wish to give to them.)

   (c) 'Have you ever worked in *xyz* services sector?'
   (d) 'If yes, is/was that mainly by telephone or face to face?'

   (Again, these questions may be combined or scored separately.)
3 *Telephone manner and voice.* Whilst no questions are asked, an assessment can be made on clarity of expression, use of language, structure of response, tone of voice and projection of friendliness and enthusiasm.

The questions used are crafted to be unambiguous, simple to ask and straightforward for the candidate. The scoring system allows for a reasonably wide range of points to be achieved. The final cut-off uses the total score – no one response can reject an applicant.

Telephone screens need take no more than betweem four and seven minutes, and frequently the whole process is operated through a computer-driven screen where the questions are presented in a set order and the responses scored automatically. This latter approach means that all scoring is applied consistently and turnround can be very quick.

Application form screen

The application form may be the first or the second screen depending on whether a telephone screen has been used. Typically, the application form is redesigned to include not only the conventional education and employment areas but also areas which address the activities and competencies more directly. An application form, so designed, may have a mixture of response formats from the chronological record of education and employment through to *417* multiple choice or tick box. The amount of blank space to be used at the applicant's discretion is limited; blank space often leads to errors in reading and understanding handwriting, together with difficulties in comparing the information given by one applicant with that offered by another. The principles behind these redesigned application forms are as follows:

1   If information is sought in relation to the activities and competencies, direct questions can and should be asked on the subjects. The underlying premise for the question content around the activities and competencies, is that an individual's past and present biographical and experience record will give a strong indication of the type of situation the person is drawn to and/or avoids, and also of the style of behaviour the person is likely to have developed over the years.
2   The format should enable easy comparison between applicants as information is given in the same place and, generally, to the same degree of detail.
3   The format should enable easy use of a numerical scoring system, again using the activities and competencies to suggest weights.

Examples of the questions and scoring using the activities and competencies are as follows:

●   The activities and competencies may suggest specific opportunities/ events/experiences in which a person may have been involved. The nature and degree of involvement may be scored or it may be a simple score as shown in the following example:

'Have you experience of explaining complicated products/procedures to others?'

	None	Some	A lot
	☐	☐	☐

This type of question uses the sum of all the experience shown by assigning weights to none, some and a lot. It is the total score on which decisions are made. No one response can give an adequate measure on its own.

●   The activities and competencies may suggest situations which would have been part of the applicant's experience, and a description of what a person had done may be sought. These type of questions are harder to score but they do provide rich, qualitative information. For example:

'Describe a situation where you have persuaded people from different backgrounds to work together.'

This type of question has instructions which asks the applicant to state clearly the situation, to say what they did and what the outcome was. It is scored by scanning for key phrases and specific points made.

The application form total score is again the one that is used for decision making. No one item is powerful enough to act on its own. The accumulated points total, derived from responses to many questions and the use of variable weights, is the decision indicator.

Telephone interview

The telephone interview may be used after a first screen that uses an application form. It is most frequently used for telephone contact positions where the face-to-face impression made is not a principal determinant of a person's likely performance. Face-to-face impressions will be relevant in telephone-based customer service roles, but only as they affect the relationships with internal customers and colleagues. In many instances, this is not as relevant as the impact made over the telephone.

The telephone interview tends to begin the more thorough investigation of capability. It is used between the initial screen and the more time-consuming final assessment of capability, and it can range from a relatively brief discussion of a person's education, experience, knowledge and skills required, through to a much more detailed examination.

The first format will simply give the opportunity to confirm details given on an application form or curriculum vitae, and will add flavour to the straight facts given on experience and education on the application form. This type of interview need take only about 15 minutes and in some instances it is scripted. The script applies typically when there are education and experience areas that need to be addressed and which may not have been covered adequately in the application form or curriculum vitae.

In contrast, the fuller interview may take up to an hour to conduct and it should follow the same structure and process that apply in the face-to-face interview, which is addressed in the next section of this chapter. The key difference is that assessments of interview style, as opposed to reported behaviour, are based on the impressions made by the voice and on oral mannerisms in the telephone interview, and users of the technique will quickly become aware of how limited is the range of impressions that can be made over the telephone. This factor emphasizes how vital it is for all telephone users to be able to fully exploit that possible range. Conversely, the range of impressions that can be made in a face-to-face interview are far more varied. As a result, these impressions are frequently given more weight in the selection process than might be justified. Interestingly, there is often a tendency for recruiters of telephone-based staff to feel uncomfortable until they have 'seen' the person, despite the relatively low impact that the face-to-face impression has in such roles.

In summary, screening can be conducted relatively quickly and accurately using paper and telephone processes. Paper screening is used by nearly all recruiters as it provides not only the screening information required but it is *419* also the written record of an applicant's background. Telephone screening is often added to the paper sift as a means of gaining more and different information on applicants. The typical patterns for telephone-based positions are as follows:

- Telephone screen
- Application form

or

- Application form
- Telephone interview

Thus the screening phase with its two processes will dramatically reduce the applicant numbers to a manageable number of broadly suitable people. The processes described will have sifted through the richly varied applicants to select out those who do not meet the broad specifications for the positions. It is the next phase of thorough assessment which sets out the full range of applicants' capability to allow the recruiters to make informed choices.

ASSESSING CAPABILITY

The preceding phases will have given adequate opportunity for the collection and confirmation of information on applicants' education, experience and the knowledge components of competencies. This final phase is devoted more to the exploration of applicants' skills, abilities and personal characteristics. These are the more complex competencies and require more sophisticated assessment processes and more time.

The assessment processes used for assessing capability are typically those of the structured interview, tests and assessment centres (which use multiple techniques including exercises that simulate part of the job). Each of these processes offer reasonable evidence of prediction but they can also be time-consuming.

Customer service positions often follow a process which combines the techniques into an assessment day called a selection workshop. In its design a selection workshop is very similar to an assessment centre. It will allow for large numbers of applicants to be assessed thoroughly, but over a short period of time. Equally, the workshop can be used with very small numbers of applicants.

The typical selection workshop includes tests and a structured interview. Some workshops also have an exercise. Each of these are addressed below, along with the process for final decision making.

Tests

Tests should be chosen, administered and interpreted by trained users. There is a professional and ethical obligation to use tests appropriately and within the scope intended by the designer. Their misuse can lead to legal difficulties and abuse of equal opportunities.

There are three categories of tests: ability, aptitude and personality. Most selection workshops have one example of each.

Ability tests

The ability tests used are usually for the assessment of quickness and accuracy in verbal and numerical reasoning. There are numerous examples of excellent short tests from which to choose those suited to particular needs. Whenever possible, the chosen tests should be administered to a large number of people in the same or very similar job type so that job standards and cut-offs can be set. If this is not possible as the positions are new, the publisher reference points (normative data) should be applied with caution. A lower limit cut-off only is recommended until such time as internal norms can be developed.

Aptitude tests

The aptitude tests used are usually related to clerical abilities and keyboard skills. There is often a need in customer service positions for a thoroughness and quickness in clerical activities such as checking and filing. The keyboard also has to be handled with speed, confidence and creativity. Many customer service positions do not expect keyboard experience and they provide a detailed training programme to acquire the specific knowledge. However, some selection workshops do seek information on applicants' relative capability in handling either the mental processes involved in operating a keyboard or the operation of an actual keyboard with a timed example using the kind of information involved. The latter is usually set up as a work sample test. Again, these tests should be given an internal trial to set in-house norms. Without these, reliance on publisher's norms requires caution.

Personality tests

The personality inventories used in these selection workshops could be as varied as the ability tests, but, typically, a narrow band of well-known instruments are used. As the customer service area has expanded, at least one test publisher has produced a personality instrument designed specifically for these positions. Saville and Holdsworth (1988) have produced the customer services questionnaires from the relevant items in their large, omnibus personality questionnaire called the 'Occupational Personality Questionnaire'. The scales in the customer services questionnaire are:

- *Relationships with people*
  Need to control
  Sociability
  Group orientation
  Attitude to authority

421

- *Thinking style*
    Understanding people
    Mental awareness
    Attitude to change
    Approach to organizing
- *Emotions and energy*
    Emotional sensitivity
    Need for results

Other publishers of such tests may make specific references to customer services in their supporting literature if they have not actually produced a subtext for the area. For instance, the 'Hogan Personality Inventory' has extensive data on customer service staff.

Personality tests require high levels of knowledge and interpretative skills. Any prospective user, therefore, must consult a qualified person who can recommend the instrument that is most able to provide information on the competencies, guide the administration of the test, and facilitate the provision of interpretation and feedback to the applicants.

The combined use of ability, aptitude and personality tests will give clear indicators of the relative positioning of applicants on many of the competencies.

Structured interview

This interview draws its description from being structured around the competencies. The interview is tightly managed around the need to collect information of relevance to the competencies using preset questions, or a range of preset questions and preset behavioural indicators or response evaluators. This type of interview is more directed in its focus and less open to spontaneous questioning than is a conventional interview.

A typical structured interview will seek to measure between four and six competencies over a 60–90 minute period, with about 15 minutes spent after the interview on evaluation. Each competency will be explored by using three or four questions with supporting probes. Each question will ask the applicant to illustrate their competency by reference to a specific example which describes:

- What the situation was.
- What the person did.
- What problems were encountered.
- How the person resolved them.
- What the outcome was.
- What was learned from the experience.

Responses to the questions and probes are evaluated by the preset behavioural indicators. These are operational definitions of the competency: they give illustrations of high-performing behaviour and low-performing behaviour. As the process is relatively standardized, the interview can be conducted by a wide range of people, who do not have to be personnel specialists but do need to be trained. As a result, line managers often conduct the interviews, achieving the necessary levels of accuracy and gaining a strong sense of ownership and commitment whilst doing so.

Exercises

The use of exercises is considerably less frequent in customer service positions than the use of the other techniques mentioned. Where exercises are used, it is often to gain more behavioural evidence on how a person actually responds to typical situations in customer service roles. The exercises divide into three sorts: individual analyses, role play and group.

The *individual analyses* are usually used to measure an applicant's ability to assimilate a high quantity and complexity of information and to pull out the main points. This type of exercise is only used in positions which call for this capability and the exercise itself will simulate the nature of information processing involved.

The *role play exercises* are used more frequently in customer service roles. This involves a role play of a typical customer contact situation. The applicant's behaviour is observed and evaluated. Role plays can be very effective as they put the applicant into the same environment and with the same stresses the job holder faces. Behaviour so observed is usually very informative. Role plays are, however, very difficult to handle when large numbers of applicants are involved, and the more role players involved, the less standardized is the experience facing each applicant.

Group exercises are used only when the need for teamwork is a performance imperative. Most customer service positions require people to work as individuals in their contact with customers whilst maintaining good relationships with colleagues. Their performance will not, however, be substantially enhanced if their relationships with colleagues are excellent rather than merely good. Where co-working, sharing workloads, and handling different but interacting aspects of a role are required, then investigation of team working skills through an observed group exercise will add value.

Final evaluation

Once assessment has been completed for one group of applicants, the final evaluation stage occurs. This aims to pull together all the information on each applicant, and to record and offer it for comparative review. The review can be strongly numbers driven as all the assessment results can be presented on a rating scale. Using the same rating scale for all aspects of the assessment means that individuals can be compared directly. Final evaluation may involve the following:

- An assessor synthesizing all the results of two or three of the applicants, determining the degree to which they meet the standard and making a recommendation whether to offer or reject each of the applicants.
- An administrator recording the numbers or ratings achieved by each applicant onto flipchart-sized matrices, together with the recommendation made by the synthesizing assessor.
- An administrator will facilitate a discussion between the assessors on the recommendations and will guide the final decision making on which applicants should be offered positions.

This process enables quiet time for consideration, followed by consensus decision making. The matrix provides a record of the ratings and the packs of detailed applicant data provide the qualitative information. Both can later be used to review the final numbers of applicants offered positions.

MONITORING PROCESS AND OUTCOMES

There is a requirement to monitor all aspects throughout the selection process in order to ensure both *process efficiency* and *equal opportunities*. The numbers collected will serve both purposes. The monitoring system must, however, be set up *before* the selection process begins. Often it is impossible to monitor once the process starts if the data have not been collected fully at each stage.

The monitoring information needed for each applicant is as follows: name; sex; race; age; marital status; and disabilities. Data under these headings have to be collected at the application form or screen stage, otherwise it is not possible to monitor the progress of any one individual or grouping through the selection process. For data-processing purposes, the name is omitted and each person is coded for ease of later analysis.

The figures involved at each stage have also to be recorded. These figures include the following:

- Number of applicants to the telephone screen.
- Scores, by applicant, on the telephone screen.
- Number sent application forms.
- Number returning application forms.
- Scores, by applicant, on the application form.
- Number asked to take the telephone interview.
- Scores, by applicant, on the telephone interview.
- Number invited to the selection workshop.
- Scores, by applicant, on the structured interview.
- Scores, by applicant, on the exercises.
- Final scores, by applicant.
- Recommendations and offers, by applicant.

Obviously, not all of these assessments processes will be used, but considerable quantities of data can and should be collected.

The analyses for process efficiency and for equal opportunities will allow the user to determine which parts of the process have been most and least effective in predicting the final assessment outcome (that is, accept or reject), and which, if any, suggest adverse impact. Immediate review of those parts which appear to produce adverse impact is vital. The system needs to ensure that equal opportunities are provided for all who have the essential competencies needed for successful performance.

The data so collected and subjected to short-term analysis on process efficiency and equal opportunities, have to be kept and reanalysed, using real performance data, in order to determine finally which parts of the selection process are most effective and most efficient. This type of analysis needs figures, and also sufficient time to have elapsed in order to have available established and accurate performance information.

SUMMARY

Informed choice is only available to the selector if the following apply:

- A job analysis has been conducted to determine what people have to do in order to be successful (the activities) and how people have to behave in order to perform the activities well (the competencies).
- The activities and competencies are used to determine the profile of the prospective employee and to design the assessment methods.
- The job analysis has been used to inform the advertising strategy so that the widest range of potentially suitable people are reached.
- The telephone screen or application form is used to reject those whose background and experience does not reach an adequate level of relevance.
- The telephone screen (for telephone-based positions) is also used to reject those who fall below the minimum standard on voice and manner.
- The selection workshop is used to thoroughly assess the applicants on their relative capabilities on the competencies.
- The final evaluation enables comparative judgements to be made and consensus achieved on decision making.
- Each phase and outcome is monitored to ensure equal opportunities and process efficiency.

REFERENCES

Boyatzis, R. (1982), *The Competent Manager: A Model for Effective Performance*, New York: Wiley Interscience.

Craig, Gregg & Russell Ltd (1986, 1992, 1995), 'Hogan Personality Inventory', Tulsa: Hogan Assessment Systems Inc.

Fine S. & Wiley W. (1971), *An Introduction to Functional Job Analysis: A Scaling of Selected Tasks from the Social Welfare Field*, Washington DC: Upjohn Institute for Employment Research.

Flanagan J. C (1954), 'The Critical Incident Technique', *Psychological Bulletin*, **51**, 327–58.

Gael, S. (ed.) (1983), *Job Analysis. A Guide to Assessing Work Activities*, San Francisco: Jossey-Bass.

Kelly, G. A (1955), *The Psychology of Personal Contracts*, New York: Norton.

McCormick, E. J., Jeanneret, R. P. and Mecham R. C. (1972), 'A Study of Characteristics and Job Dimensions as Based on the Position Analysis Questionnaire (PAQ)', *Journal of Applied Psychology*, **56**, pp. 347–68.

MCI (1990a), 'Management Standards: The Standard Project.', final report, October, London: MCI.

MCI (1990b), 'Personal Standards Project', summary report, July, London: MCI.

MCI (1991), 'Management Standards: Implementation Pack', London: MCI.

Mitchell, J. L. and McCormick, E. J. (1979), 'Development of the PMPQ: A Structured Job Analysis Questionnaire for the study of professional and managerial positions (Report No. 1)', Occupational Research Centre, Department of Psychological Studies, Purdue University.

Murray, H. (1938), *Explorations in Personality*, New York: Wiley.

Saville & Holdsworth Ltd (1988), 'WPS Manual' and 'Occupational Personality Questionnaire', Thames Ditton: Saville & Holdsworth.

Smith, J. M., Gregg, M. and Andrews, D. (1989), *Selection and Assessment: A New Appraisal*, London: Pitman.

FURTHER READING

Arnold, J., Robertson, I. and Cooper, C. (1992), *Work Psychology: Understanding Human Behaviour in the Workplace*, London: Pitman.

Boam, R. and Sparrow, P. (1992), *Designing and Achieving Competency: A Competency-Based Approach to Developing People and Organisations*, Maidenhead: McGraw-Hill.

Smith, M, Gregg, M. and Andrews, D. (1989), *Selection and Assessment: A New Appraisal*, London: Pitman.

30 Incentivizing success

Peter Murley

Theory says that money is not the main motivator of the human race, but for many the truth is that the lack of it is a considerable demotivator. For many of us the theory is just that, a theory, the practicality being that money is what drives us forward. It is a necessity. It pays the bills. Having a little extra money enables us to enjoy a few luxuries. Having a reasonable surplus may hasten that early retirement, or may attract the envy of others. Many of us dream of untold wealth as a result of winning the lottery or the football pools so that we can do all the things we ever wanted to do, and more besides. But even after achieving our new riches, most of us would still undertake some form of work. In our new world we might even try to ensure that those with whom we worked also had the right motivation and incentive.

As a 'boss', however (if such new found wealth took us in this direction), you would soon realize that in addition to receiving the regular pay cheque, your staff actually thrive on being involved, asked, consulted, communicated with, empowered, believed, trusted, cared for and recognized. You would quickly find out that what really makes the difference (apart from the regular cash to fulfil the basics) is simple recognition – simple recognition of a job well done, a pat on the back, a thank you or a lasting reminder, and so on. And, as with so many aspects of life, little and often frequently has high impact.

THE VALUE OF RECOGNITION

As a member of staff you hope that practical recognition of your efforts and success (and failures) comes from 'the management'. More meaningful recognition, however, often comes from a colleague or a customer. If it were possible to find ways of motivating and recognizing people so that all parties (peers, customers, management and so on) can contribute, then one might evolve an organization that truly lives, eats and breathes a service culture – but that is 427 surely just a pipe dream! Even those who win the lottery and decide to fulfil their greatest ambition to be, say, a world-class concert pianist without any financial reward, would soon become very depressed unless recognition of their ability was forthcoming in the shape of a genuine round of applause, an ovation, a mention in the press and so forth. Such 'cashless' recognition is nearly always more rewarding to the ego and spurs on an individual to even greater achievements and future triumphs.

The best organizations have developed service cultures to an art form. They understand and can fine tune the 'people motivators' and take a proper balance between cash and non-cash incentives.

This chapter, therefore, provides you with a set of examples, or ideas, for recognizing success, achievement, teamwork, customer service or whatever. Some of these ideas add little money to the wallet, whilst others do, and many simply seek the middle ground. The overwhelming emphasis is on rewarding genuine achievements – and *not* just because another year has passed, another year's experience has been gained and a few grey hairs added. These service-related salary increments should be consigned to the bin of history. Another year's service, pure and simple, does not necessarily equate to greater wisdom – more often than not it relates to complacency and perpetuation of bad habits. Worse still bad habits pass to the next generation and beyond.

None of the examples given are relevant only to specific job roles, grades or degrees of seniority. Whilst clearly these examples could be applied in line with rank, they are equally applicable at all levels. You are left to decide whether different treatment at different levels is fair and equitable!

There is just one caveat, namely, that everything must be delivered within a framework of commercial reality. An organization can provide, or seek to provide, the best customer service in the known universe, but be doing so at a high financial loss. In this instance, rewarding service without allowance for fiscal performance would surely be irresponsible and of itself be a contributor to such failure.

Whether or not they result in cash awards, incentives are not free to the organization, but the non-cash variety can have a disproportionately higher impact motivation than cash in some circumstances. Incentives must fit the organization, its structure and its mission as well as its style, and not vice versa. Moreover, as an organization and its cultures grow, change and develop, so must incentives adapt to suit this evolution. This chapter should be read against such a backcloth.

The following examples constitute my top incentives and are not intended to comprise an all-embracing of current trends. Nor has any account been taken of tax implications and the like, where these may be applicable.

FREE SHARES

This incentive involves the allocation of a number of shares to eligible members of staff. Such shares can be cashed in at an agreed time or can be retained on an ongoing basis.

Often this benefit is awarded according to rank/status and/or length of service and is usually based on an actual number of shares or more likely a percentage of base salary converted to an actual number of shares according to the share value at the time of allocation. An example would be 'free shares to the value of 10 per cent of annual salary as at 31st March 19XX'. With salary at £30 000 and share value as at 31 March standing at £3 per share, this would equate to 1 000 free shares. Often free shares require a minimum length of service before eligibility.

For organizations which operate cash bonus schemes (for example, salary of 'x' plus 20 per cent on-target bonus against pre-agreed criteria), it may be of value to permit a proportion of the bonus to purchase shares (and might, for example, be based on service standards), which would then attract a proportion of free shares. This encourages monies to stay within the organization and also recognizes staff's investment in the business (given the possible risk attached). An example might be 'salary of £30 000 with a 20 per cent on-target bonus provides £6 000 cash, of which 50 per cent (£3 000) can be used to purchase shares for which the company will contribute one free share for every four purchased'. Thus a £3 000 (50 per cent) bonus would, at £3 per share, produce 1 250 shares. In this example it may be that cash-in of the shares (or at least the 250 free shares) would not be permissible for, say, two or three years from the date of award.

Shares are a positive way to feel a part of the wider organization. They provide an opportunity to invest (with the inherent risk), and their value is one good indicator of the perception of the organization within the market at large.

Free shares can be allocated as a benefit regardless of company performance – that is always 'x' per cent of salary every year – or as a variable percentage allocation, within an agreed range, dependent on achievement of specific targets (for example, personal, department, corporate).

SHARE OPTIONS

Share options may, as with the example above, cover specific criteria (for example, length of service, achievement of objectives and so on), but involve the allocation of a number of options on shares which can be exercised within an agreed time frame, which is usually referred to as a 'resting period'. They are usually granted after completion of one year's service or more (that is, to indicate a degree of commitment) and might be for a fixed amount or a percentage of salary or a multiple of salary and so on.

An example might be 'share options to the value of 15 per cent of base salary will be granted and can be exercised 36 months following award'. At month 36, monies can be used to buy shares at the agreed price on month 1 or, as is often the case, shares are purchased in month 36 at month 1 price and sold at the same time with the benefit (if positive) being the difference. With a base salary of £30 000 and options at 15 per cent, the monies available for shares options at month 1 is £4 500, which at £3 per share buy price would buy 1 500 shares. If, at the buy/sell time of month 36, the shares were worth £4, then the gain would be *429*

£1 500. If at month 36 the shares were offered at a sell price of £3 or less (that is, the month 1 price or less), then the options would be unlikely to be exercised.

With annual share option awards, staff may hold several batches of exercisable options – all at different prices depending on the buy price at the time of the award.

Share options are a considerable incentive to those staff who have an opportunity to influence share value, and they have been the cause of some controversy within the 'utilities' sector. One way to reduce any such controversy is to make such a scheme available to all staff proportionate to their salary, contribution or whatever, rather than to a few. That way everybody can feel part of the organization, its success and failures.

SHARE SAVES

A share save is a simple scheme whereby staff are permitted to set aside a fixed monthly sum directly from their monthly or weekly salary for a set period of time, say five years. At the end of the five-year term, the accrued amount is used to purchase shares in the organization at an agreed rate per share, which is usually the buy price at the beginning of the savings period.

An example might be as follows. Maximum 15 per cent of a month's salary (based on £30 000 per annum) is £375 per month. Over five years (assuming base salary constant) this amounts to £22 500. With the buy price at the start of five years at £4 per share, this equals 5 625 shares. If at the end of the five-year save period each share is valued at £5, the 'gain' would be £5 625.

Several organizations offer 'guaranteed share save' schemes whereby should the value of shares at the end of the period be less than would have been the case if the monthly savings had been invested with an agreed percentage interest rate, then the total of the savings will be returned *plus* the agreed interest rate. This is, in effect, a no-lose scheme.

BONUS

Bonus comes in many forms and we cannot hope to list all the variables in this chapter. However, many organizations have yet to realize the value of a bonus and the ways in which it can help to sustain loyalty. The best bonus is one which is related to achievement of previously agreed objectives. A reasonable element of the bonus awarded should therefore be about objectives that the member of staff concerned can directly influence.

Some years ago bonuses were only available to the top echelons of the organization and although the use of bonuses has grown considerably many still view them as a perk of the more senior staff. At the bottom level, awards like attendance bonuses were created in the 1960s and 1970s: that is, effectively paying people an amount of money for turning up to work and doing what they were already contractually paid to do! In manufacturing environments another form of bonus, piecework, has been used for many years and is a way of rewarding increased output against standard production times.

The most common, or popular, bonus payment systems fall into four categories: profit, personal, team and service.

Profit related bonus payments are awarded according to the profit of the organization as a whole or to an agreed business unit. They usually take the form of a percentage of basic salary which is related to the percentage of profit achieved. For example, a net profit target of 10 per cent of revenue might equate to an on-target bonus of 10 per cent of base salary, and achievement of a 15 per cent net profit may equate to a bonus of 15 per cent. The amounts will usually depend on what proportion of the total operating and capital costs are represented by total salary costs.

Personal bonus can be on top of or in place of the profit bonus and is payable on achievement of pre-agreed personal objectives. These personal objectives may or may not be fiscally related and will depend on the role of the job holder. In roles where a budget is part of the responsibility, the personal bonus may well relate, for example, to underachievement of costs budget or overachievement of revenue. In non-budget roles, bonus awards may be based on such items as successful, on-time, implementation of a project plan, improved customer retention rates (where this can be directly attributable to the job holder), and so on.

Team bonus can also be a stand-alone or cumulative part of the total bonus payments available and is related to achievements of a predefined group of staff that make up a team. Items such as number of complaints successfully resolved, retention rates, product penetration rates, team productivity/efficiency, and team utilization rates, all spring to mind as possible examples.

Service bonus is discussed in more detail below under 'Service attributes', but is an important part of the next generation bonus schemes.

Most organizations use bonus payments in fairly standard and predictable ways. The real challenge, therefore, is to come up with diverse schemes which are interesting and which offer staff a genuine opportunity to contribute to the business. An example of this might be as follows:

Example

There are seven role levels in the organization, as follows:

1 Team player
2 Team coach
3 Team coordinator
4 Team manager
5 Team director
6 Team managing director
7 Chief executive.

This example will deal with role level 4.

Stage 1 Base salary/package

Base salary:	£30 000
Benefits:	

Car:	value equivalent £5 000	
Medical cover:	value equivalent £1 000	£11 000
Other benefits:	value equivalent £2 000	
Pension:	value equivalent £3 000	

Package value excluding bonus:	£41 000
Target bonus:	25 per cent
Target value package:	Base × 1.25 + benefits = £48 500

Based on the above, two further options are available to staff who wish to risk more on the bonus element. *Option two* is to value the cash equivalent of the benefits at 85 per cent of the value shown; *option three* leaves the benefits value at 100 per cent but with a proportionately lower bonus. Thus the base package options are as set out in Figure 30.1.

Salary	Option 1	Option 2	Option 3
Base line	30 000	30 000	30 000
Bonusable base	30 000	39 350 (85% of benefits)*	41 000 (100% of benefits)*
Pension	3 000	None	None
Other benefits	8 000	None	None
Bonus target	25% × 30 000	25% × 39 350	20% × 41 000
Bonus	7 500	9 837.50	8 200
On target (Equals approximate equilibrium) . . .	48 500	49 187.50	49 200
Bonus x 2	15 000	19 675	16 200
Excess Achievement (Equals proportionate recognition of 'risk taker')	56 000	59 025	57 400

* Benefits are £11 000 in total plus the base line salary
Note: Converting benefits to cash is often referred to as café/menu style)

432 **Figure 30.1 Base salary bonus options (café/menu style)**

Stage 2 The bonus elements

The bonus target (assuming the highest risk is selected) is 25 per cent, which is divided into the four categories previously described, each attracting a percentage of the total bonus, as follows:

Category	% of bonus allocated
1 Profit (company)	30
2 Personal	15
3 Team	25
4 Service	30

Therefore, as shown in Figure 30.2, if the year-end achievements are as stated, then the resultant bonus would be 26.4813% of £39 350 (the optional bonusable base) = £10 420.39.

	Category	Year-end achievement (%)	Bonus calculation			
			Allocation achieved (%)	Total (%)	% of bonus target	Total (%)
1	Profit (company)	120.000	30 × 1.20	36.000	25 × 0.36000	9.0000
2	Personal	75.000	15 × 0.75	11.250	25 × 0.11250	2.8125
3	Team[1]	100.00	25 × 1.00	25.000	25 × 0.25000	6.2500
4	Service	112.25	30 × 1.11225	33.675	25 × 0.33675	8.4188
Total						26.4813

26.4813% of £39 350 (the optional bonusable base) = £10 420.39

Note: [1] *See under* 'Service attributes' and 'Service attributes and cost-related bonus'.

Figure 30.2   Calculation of bonus percentage

Stage 3 Bonus payable – options

In the example above, the bonus achieved is £10 420.39. This bonus could be paid in any of the following three ways:

1   Half as cash with the balance increased by 'x' per cent (for example, 25 per cent) in value terms and used to purchase shares, with a resting period of, say, three years (see 'Share saves' above). Thus the member of *433*

staff concerned can take £5 210.20 as cash and the balance of £5 210.20 will be increased by 25 per cent to circa £6 512.75, which at £4 per share will purchase some 1628 shares with the option to exercise in three years at the sell rate at the time.

2 Half as cash with the balance consolidated into basic salary (thus attracting increased pension contributions).

3 Half as cash with the balance (plus a contribution of 'x' per cent from the company) to be used to purchase additional pension benefits as, for example, a once-off and charge/commission-free amount.

A tiered approach to bonuses, using the above examples, is demonstrated in Figure 30.3 – assuming that there was an agreed need to differentiate bonus amounts by role level, which for some organizations is a moot point.

Bonus payments are normally made on an annual or six-monthly basis but could also be quarterly. In the above examples the four categories may be payable within different time frames (for example, the 'service' element is particularly appropriate on a six-monthly or quarterly basis). If bonuses are collated and paid on a frequency less than annually, rules must be established regarding, for example, clawback. Thus if category 1 was excellent but categories 2, 3 and 4 show the proportional annual achievement to be below target, then bonus payments might be made in the face of poor or declining performance. Generally speaking, though, clawback is not a recommended course of action except in pure sales roles where unit sales may be key bonus drivers.

SERVICE ATTRIBUTES

More and more organizations are conducting surveys, or questionnaires, to canvass the views and opinions of their actual and prospective customers relative to service standards. The most appropriate data to gather from customers and prospects relates to quantitative and qualitative information regarding product and/or service *and* expectation – not just one, but both.

Role	Role title	BONUS Profit (Company)	BONUS Personal	BONUS Team	BONUS Service	BONUS as a % of Bonusable Base
1	Team player	10%	10%	35%	45%	10%
2	Team Coach	15%	10%	35%	40%	15%
3	Team Coordinator	25%	10%	30%	35%	20%
4	Team Manager	30%	15%	25%	30%	25%
5	Team Director	40%	15%	20%	25%	30%
6	Team MD	50%	15%	15%	20%	40%
7	Chief Executive	70%	10%	5%	15%	50%

434 **Figure 30.3   A tiered approach to bonuses**

These two measures, satisfaction and expectation, can be made in a number of areas referred to here as 'service attributes'. In surveys conducted on a continuous, regular basis – say, quarterly – and against a valid and representative sample size, service attributes would be common to all surveys at all times, thus ensuring that data can be gathered and compared to show, for example, improvements in or degradation of service.

Service attributes will vary widely depending on the market sector, products, type of business and so on, but typically *might* include (for a service delivered over the telephone) the following items (for established customers/users of the service):

1 *Speed* of response (seconds delay before pick-up by a customer services representative).
2 *Knowledge*/understanding (of the member of staff responding to the call).
3 *Problem* resolution (that is, was the reason for the call satisfied?).
4 *Follow-through* of promise (that is, did member of staff do as requested?).
5 *Timeliness* of written correspondence (if correspondence was required as part of follow-up).
6 *Accuracy* of data (that is, was the action taken and correspondence sent an accurate reflection of the request?).

For newly acquired customers one would consider additional attributes covering, for example, speed of fulfilment (that is, time to receive product for use), ease of understanding of bill/invoice and so on. Also, within a retail environment one would expand in/amend the service attributes to suit (for example, time (in bands) before gaining attention of sales person, professional approach and so on). Once established, each, say, quarterly survey could cover a range of different questions, but the core service attributes would always be included for comparative purposes.

Many organizations only gather satisfaction ratings against service attributes, but 'exception' data is also of great importance, serving *inter alia* to establish priorities for service delivery by understanding the relative importance of each issue that is in the customer's mind. Figure 30.4 shows an example of a satisfaction rating. Using an agreed rating scale – in this example, a scale of 1–10 (with 1 being poor/unacceptable and 10 being outstanding) – the six attributes can be rated against satisfaction *and* expectation. This data can be used very effectively – not only for the marketing and sales areas and for direct customer feedback together with corrective action plans, but also most significantly for the meaningful reward of staff involved in the delivery of the service which is being assessed. Thus, in the example shown, the overall satisfaction rating was 109.125 per cent which if the bonus trigger (that is, any lower than the trigger = £0 bonus) was 100 per cent, then achievement of target would equate to a 9.125 per cent annual bonus (of 'x').

However, the payment of bonus based solely on service satisfaction ratings is not necessarily the most effective or cost-effective way forward as no account is taken of the costs of providing such service. It is advisable, *435*

Target overall rating 8 (satisfaction) for the year

Attribute	Quarterly 1	
	Satisfaction	Expectation
1 *Speed* of response	9.4	9.0
2 *Knowledge*/understanding	9.3	8.8
3 *Problem* resolution	8.6	9.7
4 *Follow-through* of promise	8.9	7.8
5 *Timeliness* of written correspondence	6.8	8.6
6 *Accuracy* of action	9.4	9.5
Overall statistical average (against sample sizes)	9.1	8.9

Note: With attributes 3 and 5 requiring priority attention, further analysis, action and so on.

Quarter	Overall rating
1	9.1
2	8.4
3	8.4
4	8.9
Annual statistical average	8.73
Target	8.0

Achievement % (actual/target)	109.125%

Figure 30.4   An example of satisfaction rating of service attributes

therefore, to embrace a further measure so as to provide the commercial equity between service and progressive cost efficiency. An example of this is shown in the next section.

SERVICE ATTRIBUTES AND COST-RELATED BONUS

Whilst clearly organizations can elect to apply bonus against whatever criteria they feel are suitable, it might be foolish to do so without regard for continued attention to costs and profitability. Thus the award of bonus against service attributes could, in this example, be balanced against other elements.

In the example shown below it is assumed that the organization has the ability to establish accurately (through, for example, activity-based costing and the detailed understanding of business processes) the 'cost of acquisition' (that is, the cost of acquiring one new customer) *and* the 'cost of service' (that is, the cost of servicing, on an annualized basis, each customer post-acquisition). For many organizations, a lack of understanding of these two global cost measures, let alone the great detail necessary to establish the final costs, will prevent the use of such a bonus system. However, even if the data is not used for such reward purposes, it is doubtful if organizations can run an effective business without such understanding. An example might be where the launch of a particular sales campaign adds the required gross sales but at such an acquisition and ongoing servicing cost that it would have been more prudent to have not proceeded.

Example

	Target	Achievement
Cost of acquisition	£25	£23
Cost of servicing (annualized)	£40	£41

With servicing cost weighted as twice as important as acquisition cost then bonus attributable would be as follows:

Acquisition = £23/£25 = 8% under budget @ 1 weighting = 8% positive
Servicing = £41/£40 = 2.5% excess (over budget) @ 2 weighting = 5% negative
Overall 3% positive = bonus 103% (with 100% = £0 bonus)

If we now continue the service attributes rating described in Figure 30.4 and apply a weighting factor the following emerges:

Cost of acquisition = £23/£25 = 8% under @ 1 weighting = 8% positive
Cost of servicing = £41/£40 = 2.5% over @ 2 weighting = 5% negative
Service attributes = 8.73/8 = 9.125% over @ 1 weighting = 9.125% positive
Satisfaction:
    = overall achievement 12.125% positive
    = bonus   112.125%   ([1]see Figure 30.3)

As described above under 'Bonus', this rating can now be applied as one part of the service formula, or could be used as a stand-alone bonus against specific guidelines/rules.

The bonus payments described in this and the previous section may appear complex. However, whilst they depend on the existence of regular and accurate data, the availability of spreadsheets and databases makes the analysis task a simple one. The real issue is how to simplify the message so that staff fully understand the principles and workings of the implemented scheme(s) and accept it.

SKILLS ACQUISITION AND ACCREDITATION

For many years, industry has paralleled the military in its use of hierarchy and rank. The army, so it is said, needs 20 ranks in order to maintain respect, *437* discipline and a host of other so-called important standards. For those of you who still work in such hierarchical institutions, it is usually quite interesting to see how presentation of the *status quo* becomes the very powerful motivator, usually at the expense of the customer: for example, note how much energy is wasted in formalizing the criticality of the chair of command or how in many cases the existence of such a long and rigid structure actually exacerbates the issue of communication.

Conversely, on the radical side of the fence, of course, there are those who do not believe in structure or form, but in the survival of the fittest – almost an organization where any order of seniority, however limited, is despised.

Perhaps the truth lies somewhere in between. Yet in service-led organizations, and arguably in others – if indeed there are organizations other than service-led ones – it is vital to be able to encourage the right people to stay in the right roles, as opposed to having to tempt them with additional responsibilities and fancy job titles, which for many is, if anything, demotivating, even though it might be socially acceptable. Moving people up an artificially created ladder with excess rungs (including, for example, taking sales staff out of their roles because they 'earn too much' and moving them to management positions) is simply maintaining ill-conceived structures and taking the easy way out. Despite being ill-equipped for the task, people will often start to climb a ladder against their better judgement frequently with disastrous results.

Some of the more forward-thinking companies have evolved a five- to eight-tier organization structure that enables individuals to grow in terms of their skill base and knowledge whilst still retaining an original level or role. It is a structure which retains people where they are best suited but does not penalize them financially. Such organizations also have a different approach to roles and tasks and how each role is described relative to the next in the structure (see Chapter 24).

Referring back to the seven-tier role structure described above under 'Bonus', one example of a skills acquisition/accreditation-based rewards might be as follows:

Role 1 Team player

Requirement for role is a basic seven-week training programme for new tiers, plus:

- Accreditation 1 – New account enquiry.
- Accreditation 2 – New customer acquisition/sale.
- Accreditation 3 – New customer account query (basic level).

Over the first six months of employment, role 1 holders are *required* to:

- Attend all product updates (minimum four).
- Complete six hours of distance learning.

- Pass accreditation 4 – New customer account query (complex level).
- Pass an applied knowledge accreditation.

After the first six months of employment, role 1 holders can undertake additional accreditations (subject to any rules/guidelines published). The following list of accreditations are available to all role 1 staff and count for 'points' as indicated. A total of 100 points will result in a salary increase of $£x$ or a salary increase of $£x/2$ plus a grant of shares to the value of $£y$.

Points	Accreditation	Includes
26	5 – Credit card payments	20 hours home study
43	6 – Back office account query resolution	15 hours CD-ROM training
47	7 – Team motivator training	40 hours distance learning
55	8 – Coaching course	1 week off-job 'own time'
25	9 – etc	
60	10 – etc	

To a large degree the data above equate well to NVQs (National Vocational Qualifications) and to some excellent work which has been done by the Management Charter Initiative (MCI) in setting standards.

Customer and peer points

For many, this system of reward has considerable attraction, not least because it is, or can be, a direct reflection of the views of those who are the ultimate judges of the service provided.

To a large degree the actual recognition is of more importance than the amount or the value. Much will depend on the culture of the organization and the ease with which 'points' are meted out. If it is considered very easy to gain points, or if it is easy to 'persuade' others to part with points, then their relative worth declines. If the criteria by which points are awarded are clear and fair, and result in the equitable recognition of 'excellence', then there will be an inherent value in each point and a respect for the overall system itself.

Points award schemes are used by several organizations in the United States. A number of (points) vouchers are given to regular customers (for example, regular product purchasers/service users, who themselves may be on a points-based loyalty scheme), who, if or when they receive excellent service, can hand over their numbered voucher to the member(s) of staff concerned. These points can be used in a number of ways, but typically would not be for cash. They could, for example, be used towards gifts from a catalogue (which might also be used to add up points from other bonus/recognition schemes) or purchase of shares. Attachment of points to individuals or teams can also be used to recognize the best or most consistent service deliverers and to reward them specifically.

Points schemes can also involve staff and suppliers whereby either can, *439* individually or as a team, reward the other when excellent 'internal' service is provided.

As with most good schemes, a few rules may be necessary but the fewer the better. A 'no rules' points scheme for staff and suppliers would work well if, for example, each were allowed one voucher per month for them to award at their discretion, as opposed to the provision of too many to sprinkle around like confetti!

OTHER FORMS OF INCENTIVE AND MOTIVATION

Product incentive

Simple and liberal use of branded gifts to recognize good individual or – perhaps more appropriately – team performance.

The impact of small, reasonable quality items is a tangible but cost-effective way of recognizing achievement (as long as everyone has an equal chance of gain). The scheme has minimal cash value; and is brand supportive in that it can usually create an external awareness of the product or the organization, that is to say a wider audience than just recipients.

Sometimes it might be of value if, instead of products, product points were distributed, which can be accrued for larger items. This decision clearly depends on what the incentive is aiming to achieve.

Achievers club

For some unknown reason the 'achievers club' has been the traditional pre-serve of the salesperson. And the achievers clubs are not always the allocation of a few pounds for the best performers but frequently involve the provision of expensive 'business trips' to exotic locations where everyone can get together, exchange important commercial information (!) and if there is time, relax and have a few drinks! A somewhat cynical commentary, perhaps, but a view held by many.

Meanwhile, the people who are talking to customers who use the services or buy the products, or to the prospects who want to do so, are left at the end of a telephone or in the retail unit without recognition of their contribution. So why not extend the achievers club concept to everyone: one per department or function; one per geographic location; one per quarter. Whatever the criteria, *all* those involved in customer service should surely be treated with a degree of equality.

An achievers club can be the exotic business trip; the award of money; the allocation of points for selection from a range of items; some free shares in the company; a long weekend for the family (who often live and breathe the culture more than their partner!); a bunch of flowers; a team day out; a simple plaque and enrolment in the club itself. Some of this has a distinctly American flavour which does not always travel well, but in this instance, the taste is just as sweet on this side of the Atlantic – not in all organizations and countries but in many.

And for those organizations where such an approach doesn't work, then maybe it is time to change the culture and the way people behave?

Dreams

We all have 'dreams', many of which are surprisingly humble and inexpensive, while others seem impossible and grandiose.

If one can establish the dreams of staff, then it might be possible to make them come true, in whole or in part. Relating dreams to specific recognition programmes (for example, employee of the month, or the achievers club) can be a powerful motivational tool. For example: the dream of owning a Porsche might be partly fulfilled by having the use of a chauffeur-driven one for a week; becoming mayor of your town or city may be achieved by shadowing the real mayor for a week; having dinner with the national rugby team; meeting a film star and going to a film première – all these might be dreams which could be brought to life.

Sponsoring a deprived child through a specific education programme is another way of making a dream come true. Such sponsorship is also excellent PR for the organization concerned, as well as helping to underline the company's social commitments to the community as a whole. Staff motivation will also be enhanced, which must at least put this form of recognition on the agenda.

Anniversaries

Remembering personal birthdays, anniversaries or other memorable dates by simply sending a card, a small gift, flowers and so on, is another excellent form of recognition.

Monthly specials

Staff at all levels – or specific staff in specific functions are involved each month in the achievement of some kind of global objective. This global monthly objective might be linked to the overall objective of the department, team, organization or whatever and may well be accompanied by decking out the department, service centre or retail unit with colourful, themed items affirming the monthly target.

An example might be 'Mad March' for new acquisitions. The work units are decked out in green (for example, PCs, ceiling and wall displays and so on) and one simple objective might be to acquire 'x' number of new customers. Every time anyone enters the department there is a live reminder for them of the target/objectives. At the end of the assessment period all those involved (which should also include those who, whilst they may not directly influence the acquisition of new customers, have/had a team role to play – that is, *everyone*) receive a gift, provided that the target was achieved. Gifts are usually small and may include, for example, a specially labelled bottle of wine, a points allocation or whatever.

As with all the awards, one can mix and match ideas and rewards as part of a progressive package or just use awards on a one-off basis when required.

Local money pots

The provision of small sums of money to agreed teams or departments for disposal as seen fit.

The money would usually be allocated according to team size, say, £500 per quarter for a team of ten. The team leader/coach would have full authority to use the money for a number of agreed options or award schemes but could also devise very specific targets provided that they met the previously agreed criteria. For example, they may spend £100 on the purchase of a series of small rewards (for example, sweets), or they may decide to award £200 to the best performer of the quarter, with the balance of the money going to the remainder.

Various methods of collecting information on which to base the awards may be employed by the team leader, including perhaps the use of team games which record successes. For instance, the use of a tennis game (played on a mobile white board located within the team area), in which completion of certain work activities scores a specific number of points and the winners are the first to six games and at least two games ahead.

Other awards could include team t-shirts (named teams or emblems); retail vouchers; travel miles/vouchers; team meals and so on.

Events and milestones

Events

There is a wide range of events in which the organization can take part, such as Children in Need, Remembrance Day, Telethons, Guy Fawkes Night, Easter Sunday (Easter bonnet), American Independence Day, and many others of varying significance.

These events can serve a number of purposes, primarily the following:

- Raising money for charity. For every event in which the staff raise '£x', the company has an opportunity to contribute also (for example, matching the amount raised by the staff).
- Providing an opportunity for staff to enter into the spirit of the celebration, at work. This might involve dressing up for the specific events.
- Enabling the best teams, departments, individuals or whatever, to be recognized in some way for their efforts or contribution – or even, say, for being 'the worst dressed team'!

Milestones

442 The establishment of clear milestones within the annual set of objectives.

These can be fiscal milestones but are often more meaningful to many staff directly involved in customer service if they are related to matters such as: number of new customers acquired; number of products purchased; number of unresolved queries as a percentage of queries; number of work activities/minutes of time per annum; number of customers serviced per member of staff and so on.

CONCLUSION

In this chapter we have touched on some of the ways of motivating staff through recognition of their success and contribution to the delivery of service excellence. The best ideas come from matching the needs and requirements of *your* customers to the objectives of *your* business with the help of *your* staff. What works for one will not work for another, but the best incentives need good communication and good communication is not easy. It requires actually thinking about and planning the best way forward – the way that satisfies, wherever possible, the expectations of all business partners. Therein lies the challenge!

31 The training journey

David Harris

The beginning of the training journey should be viewed as the meeting of two paths: the one trodden by the company and the other by the individual. The paths overlay each other and the journey should be purposeful and productive.

Previously, many companies have viewed training and training investments as a necessary evil, but circumstances have changed and nowhere more so than in customer service. No company now believes it can achieve outstanding customer service without a substantial investment in the training of people. In turn, the shortage of employment opportunities and the need frequently to change career direction has made people much more receptive both to personal development and to better and more frequent training.

Tom Roth suggests that in these circumstances a new style of contract of employment is being forged between company and individuals, with three central clauses:

1 Employability of the individual, replacing security of employment.
2 Commitment to the job, replacing company loyalty.
3 Contribution of real value, replacing efficient job performance.

In his view, development and training are the solution, and nowhere more so than in achieving *quality customer service*.

THE COMPANY AND THE INDIVIDUAL

Thus in a changing business environment:

- Companies are looking for performance through commitment. Investment in training will make a decisive contribution towards achieving this objective.

- People are looking for involvement, if not job security. Certainly commitment to training is a significant step in this direction.

This new consciousness will attract two new disciples: the non-training company, and the non-trained individual.

Companies venturing into customer service training for the first time will have regard for the level of investment and the return on that investment, the implementation and follow-up of the training programmes, and, of course, the content and quality of the training programmes themselves. One unqualified payback for every company is the contribution that quality training will make to the culture and values of the company and the commitment and motivation of the individual. The individual, venturing into customer service training, might have other considerations. This could well be their first exposure to quality, structured training and, when effectively delivered, this training will give new stand-alone life skills that will add to the employability of the individual and, essentially, to their human worth. People returning to employment, changing careers or merely looking for stability will also find real benefits in personal development through quality training programmes.

So, we have the meeting of two paths, where the company and the individual set out on the most effective, productive and enjoyable training journey. The role for the training profession is in ensuring that both the company and individual really appreciate the benefits of treading the same path together.

OPPORTUNITIES FOR TRAINING

Induction training

One might describe the training programme at the beginning of a career in customer service as akin to climbing mountains. It is the induction into a new type of job, perhaps a new style of company and certainly, when done properly, it will be the beginning of a new life experience.

Induction training for customer service occurs in two modes. First is the start-up mode, either with the setting up of a new unit or group to service a new product or strategy, or alternatively, with the determination to fundamentally improve customer service by reorganizing and starting afresh. The second mode for induction training in customer service is what might be described as maintenance: that is, recruiting additional people or replacing people who have moved on or left the group. The same programme in principle would obviously meet the requirements of both modes. In practice, start-up programmes tend to be rushed and incomplete and have usually been modified and upgraded several times before they reach maintenance mode.

The mix

What should an induction programme for customer service look like? It seems it could last from one week to twelve weeks, with a potluck mix of knowledge and skills content.

445

Let us go back to that image of the two paths meeting. What are we trying to achieve? Balanced customer service people with the right mix of attributes – technical knowledge, interpersonal skills, self-management ability and flexibility – so the training programme should acknowledge these requirements and be designed accordingly.

Too many induction programmes are top heavy with technical knowledge and far too short in other areas. Why? Because of general belief that people need all this information. Well, they might, but at the induction stage, training programme planners should be strict in applying a 'need to know, nice to know' filter to the quantity of technical knowledge in the induction training programme.

New or improved interpersonal skills are, for many people, difficult to acquire, so more time than initially seems necessary or feasible should be allocated to this area of training. For the best use of allocated training time, the concept of threading – that is, giving a balanced mix of knowledge and skill through many of the sessions and, in effect, utilizing time more than once – is a way to run productive programmes. Self-management tools are essential for customer service people, although training people to use them frequently usually means overcoming a degree of scepticism. There are, however, many such tools that can be used to develop and maintain confidence and assertiveness, they are a must in induction training for new customer service staff.

Finally in our mix, how do we develop the fourth attribute, flexibility? The answer lies in structured practice sessions with a variety of customer scenarios that require customer service people to mix their knowledge and skill in order to be flexible in resolving customer issues.

Figure 31.1 gives an indication of a possible content mix for an induction training programme.

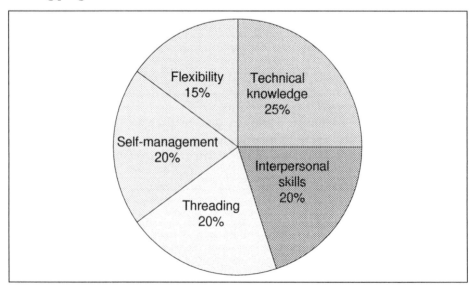

Figure 31.1   Induction training mix

The time

Having looked at the balance of the training mix, the other important design criterion is the amount of time required or the length of the training programme. People new to formal training will take longer to absorb and practise the skills they need, yet at the same time they will quickly become tired and find it difficult to concentrate. The other part of the equation is affordability: how long can you afford for people to be in training and how much can you spend internally or externally on developing and running training programmes? The best solution, certainly for new start-up training, is to select the middle ground and hold back both time and budget in reserve, which will enable you to revisit unsuccessful parts of the training programme or people who need more support. A middle-ground programme might last four weeks and the chart in Figure 31.2 shows how this programme might be organized in terms of content and mix.

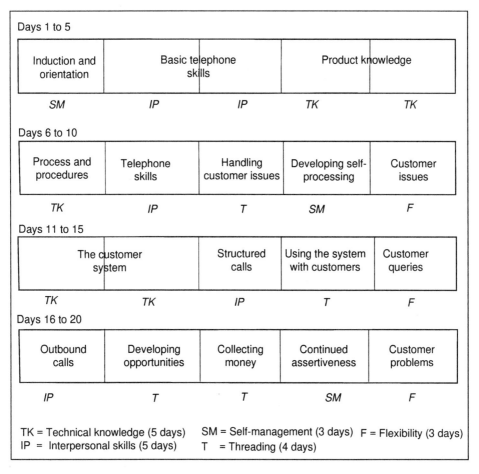

Days 1 to 5				
Induction and orientation	Basic telephone skills		Product knowledge	
SM	*IP*	*IP*	*TK*	*TK*

Days 6 to 10				
Process and procedures	Telephone skills	Handling customer issues	Developing self-processing	Customer issues
TK	*IP*	*T*	*SM*	*F*

Days 11 to 15				
The customer system		Structured calls	Using the system with customers	Customer queries
TK	*TK*	*IP*	*T*	*F*

Days 16 to 20				
Outbound calls	Developing opportunities	Collecting money	Continued assertiveness	Customer problems
IP	*T*	*T*	*SM*	*F*

TK = Technical knowledge (5 days) SM = Self-management (3 days) F = Flexibility (3 days)
IP = Interpersonal skills (5 days) T = Threading (4 days)

Figure 31.2 Induction training programme

Structured training

People already giving customer service will be using a variety of approaches when dealing with customers, with varying degrees of success. Structured training will improve their effectiveness, but here our journey will be through hills and valleys, or perhaps peaks and troughs is a more apt description of this situation. To persuade people of the need to improve their performance, the optimum approach is to use objective performance measurement instruments, sharing results and feedback with customer service people and letting them take ownership of this need for improvement.

Two approaches are equally valid. First, internal orientation assessment: that is, taking a measurement of the view of their customer service staff and examining their views as to the level of customer service performance or their own personal attitude towards customer service. The second approach is to use one of a series of methods for validating customer service performance, from mystery shopping through to a more focused approach, in order to help generate training needs.

With the information we have from whichever feedback method we have used, we can structure an objective case for a new training initiative with customer service people who are performing in a less than adequate manner. Technical knowledge may need augmenting, but people have the ability to acquire and retain knowledge and usually the gaps will be due to lack of understanding caused by poor presentation of data. The two areas that experience suggests will call for most work are interpersonal skills and self-management. However, such has been the improvement in interpersonal skills training in the last few years that finding new ideas and techniques to attract and interest customer service people is not difficult, so long as the skills are valid and relate to the job in hand. Self-management programmes are more difficult. The scepticism mentioned in induction training will probably have transformed into cynicism when dealing with more experienced service staff. In these circumstances, feedback findings really help, particularly if from an orientation assessment. The developer has first to decide on an appropriate technique and use feedback data to validate and justify the training, and secondly, to ensure that the training is of such quality that the self-management techniques are taken on board and then regularly maintained.

Continuous training

The third type of customer service training that the best customer-focused companies undertake is the continuous training of good staff to maintain and improve the service they provide – continuing our journey over the lowlands. At this stage, people are usually very available and receptive to additional training. The developer's role is to find new valid techniques that will be recognized as improving skills in key areas, and assuming of course that there will be continuous quality presentation of new technical knowledge. Developers must identify new approaches to the development of interpersonal skills, new ways that will continually improve the human aspects of the customer service environment.

So, in summary, the three types of customer service training journey are:

- *Climbing mountains.* Inducting new people in customer service skills.
- *Hills and valleys.* Improving inadequate customer service skills through a structured approach.
- *Over the lowlands.* Continuously developing the performance of existing quality people.

THE FOUR DIMENSIONS OF CUSTOMER SERVICE

The ways to establishing outstanding customer service is by developing and balancing the four dimensions of customer service, which are shown in Figure 31.3. Training plays a significant role in three of the four dimensions: systems and organization, environment and human performance in quality service. These dimensions will not be achieved without significant people performance, performance that will necessitate a substantial training input.

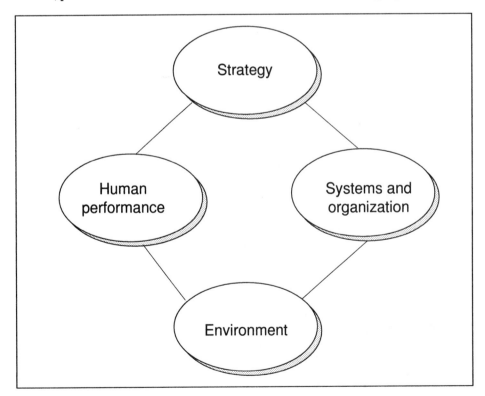

Figure 31.3   Four dimensions of customer service

SYSTEMS AND ORGANIZATION

The elements of this dimension, as shown in Figure 31.4, include customer interface systems, customer management systems, job role management, customer information management and customer process and procedures.

Customer service people will need initial training in customer interface systems and job role management. Customer interface systems require keyboard skills, systems awareness and screen management, all of which can be acquired using self-teach, demonstration and practice sessions. Job role management is a fundamental part of induction training, requiring an understanding of leader and team member relationships and job roles, responsibilities and empowerment. Over a subsequent period, people should be introduced to the customer management systems to the depth required for their job role. Particular attention should be paid to the accessibility of these systems to the customer interface system and any gaps that might exist; these efficiencies should be highlighted and alternative actions to cope with any shortfalls should be initiated to make the training credible.

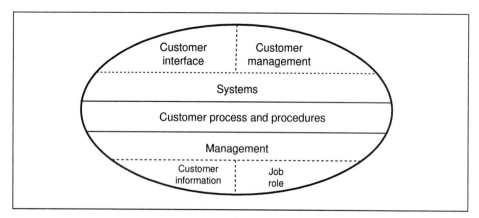

Figure 31.4   The elements of the systems and organization dimension

One of the critical areas of customer service is customer information management, and that is the next step in the training process. If communication channels, such as complaint procedures, query elevation and high-level technical support, have not been proceduralized, the deficiencies are quickly highlighted during training – perhaps better here, however, than later when dealing with customer issues directly. Further downstream, process and procedures for providing customer service start to crystallize. While these processes and procedures are hopefully not too rigid, they should begin to provide the certainty of giving quality customer service, establishing guidelines for empowerment, guaranteeing service levels, and, at the same time, keeping costs under control. As these processes are developed, self-paced learning materials that should be 'trainee friendly' can be produced for use with both new and existing customer service people.

THE ENVIRONMENT

This latest edition to the dimensions of customer service, in many ways carries the critical training load. The previous induction programme outlined, does not include training in any of the elements of customer service people environment, concentrating only on specific human performance. New programmes will require adjustment and probably extension to take in additional training for the people environment dimension.

Let us now consider each of the four elements of this dimension, and as set out in Figure 31.5, their respective training requirements.

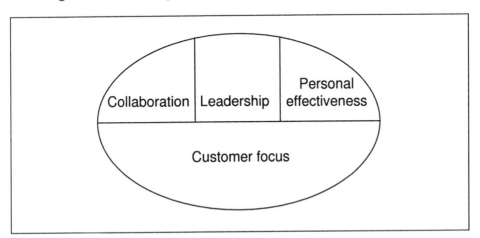

Figure 31.5   The four elements of the environment dimension

Leadership

It is fact that situations which generate outstanding customer service are typified by high-quality working team leaders. Note the two main aspects, 'high quality' and 'working', the latter implying that they have the same, if not better, human performance attributes than members of their team, providing a training lead in itself, however. At this stage we will analyse 'high quality' and the aspects that make a high-quality team leader in customer service.

As shown in Figure 31.6, there are six leadership skills that work especially well in leading customer service teams: working style, motivation, team management, performance goals, coaching, and counselling.

Working style

There are several different systems for determining working style; whichever is chosen it should provide a basic tool for the team leader in understanding the following factors:

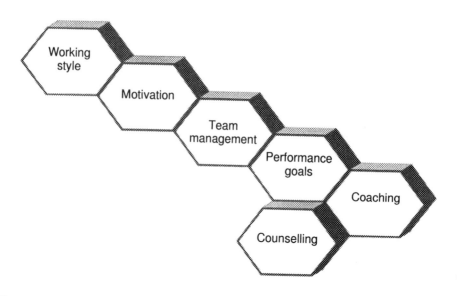

Figure 31.6   The six leadership skills in customer service

- How people are different.
- Why they are different.
- How those differences will be reflected to the customer.
- The best ways of dealing with different people.

The members of the team should themselves be training in working style technology, helping them to deal better with each other and the customer.

Motivation

A great deal has been written and much training has been carried out over the years on the subject of motivating people. While the motivation of customer service teams is critical, simplicity of approach is the best solution. With a working-style methodology in place, the team leader is better equipped to identify the state of individuals and what will work best as motivation.

The next steps for the leader are to identify circumstances and weigh options that will enable team leaders to be trained in a simple, flexible motivation approach on the back of working style.

Team management

Team leaders must be trained in the simple process skills of planning and organizing team activity. These skills, coupled to monitoring skills, enable the team leader to draw out the best in operational terms from the team, other than the use of people management skills. The team leader should be able to set the ground rules for acceptable team behaviour, utilize a process for team decision making, and have an effective method for running team meetings.

Performance goals

Teams are at their most productive when working towards committed, performance goals, both as a team and as individuals. Team leaders are trained in the process of identifying and setting individual performance goals, while at the same time maintaining the momentum towards achieving the goals of the team. The important issue in productive performance goal setting is the alignment of the goals, from company mission right through to the goals of the individual. Team leaders can be trained both to set goals in alignment and to identify and amend the productivity losses that can result from misalignment. Training also covers the communication of goals and the techniques for gaining the commitment of the individual to their achievement. Monitoring progress and giving feedback completes the cycle of managing performance goals.

Coaching

Team leaders and their supporters – the more senior members of the team – have to be able to coach team members to produce continuous performance improvement. To achieve quality coaching three elements are required:

1 An acceptable coaching model.
2 The ability of the coach to identify types of behaviour and if necessary pattern better behaviour.
3 The ability to give non-emotive objective feedback.

The need to achieve elements 2 and 3 means that the training has to be focused and practical in developing and testing the coach's behaviour. The payback to any team leader in developing good coaching skills can be seen in the motivation and performance of team members to achieve behavioural improvements, particularly when used in support of structured training.

Counselling

The final behavioural skill of the customer service team leader is that of counselling, which might be defined as productive communication, for use in a variety of circumstances from performance review through to disciplinary interviewing.

By using a working-style approach, the team leader, through personal versatility should be able to achieve quality communication, which, when linked with pre-planning and objective setting, gives a framework for counselling. Training in the business counselling skills required by a customer service team leader, involves substantial practice and feedback in order to develop those skills.

Collaboration

The second part of the environment dimension is collaboration: that is, working together as a team to produce maximum effectiveness. Collaboration should be seen as the most productive way of working and a better option for the team than cooperation or competition.

Customer service team training through collaboration, centres initially on team members' differences as individuals and the issues that these might cause. However, people soon become aware of the benefits differences can add to a collaborative approach. Thus team members have to learn to appreciate the value that different types of behaviour bring to the group and to develop methods of contributing and innovating which are truly collaborative.

Personal effectiveness

The third aspect of the environment dimension is personal effectiveness, which is a combination of a series of skills, an aspect of self-management and an attitude of mind. To develop effectiveness – that is, the ability to make a quality contribution – people should first be given a set of guidelines that show the way. Their performance then has to be monitored and feedback provided on the level of effectiveness of their activity. Elements of personal effectiveness training concentrate first on interpreting the working style and building the job picture; secondly, on examining process effectiveness in both technology and procedures; and thirdly, on linking this with an attitude of mind for achievement in producing customer service.

Customer focus

The final element of the customer service environment is customer focus itself, and whereas it could be argued that customer focus is an attitude, a well-structured training programme will help to build the concepts of customer focus. The team should formulate its own vision for customer service and identify the critical success factors that will make the vision come true. Identifying customer types and determining segmentation make customers, and their needs and expectations, more of a reality and enable customer service people to put themselves in the customer's shoes, thus enabling them to recognize what it will take to move customers from indifference to satisfaction. Customer service teams that have experienced this type of training are best equipped to deliver the personal levels of customer service which customers are coming to expect.

TRAINING FOR HUMAN PERFORMANCE

The fourth dimension of customer service is human performance, and here good training is most needed. Previously we looked at the four aspects of human performance and examined how they might be allocated in an induction training programme. In this section we will look at the training techniques and opportunities that exist for each of the four aspects of human performance detailed in Figure 31.7.

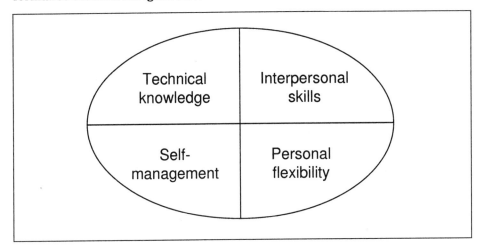

Figure 31.7   The four aspects of the human performance dimension

Technical knowledge

The technical knowledge aspect relates all the information necessary to give customer service, including: products and services; policies and procedures for customer management; product application and usage; an awareness of competition; and knowledge of the company's sales and marketing strategy.

At induction, the amount of knowledge given to new people must be balanced against what they can absorb and time spent on training other aspects of the human performance. People readily pick up knowledge and retain it over time, which in this situation can result in experienced customer service personnel becoming overly reliant on their technical knowledge to the detriment of other aspects of human performance.

The development of training for technical knowledge requires the developer to be both creative and ingenious in order to avoid boring repetitive training interventions. Appealing to a spectrum of learning styles makes the training most effective. Initial knowledge can be learned through a variant of self-teach methods (for example, distance learning, computer-based training (CBT) and, most recently, compact disc, either in the ROM or interactive version). Paper-based distance learning, while less complete than technology-based training methods, has the advantage of simplicity and ownership. It can be utilized at a variety of times and situations and does, in itself, remain intact as a longer-term memory jogger. Computer-based training (CBT) can be developed into a much more complete and reactive way than paper-based training, with the advantage of being able to monitor the progress of participants, both in terms of time committed and results achieved. The drawback with CBT, as with all technology-based training, is the availability of equipment and the restrictions on time when it can be used.

Compact-disc-based products, while relatively new, are beginning to make an impact as exciting and dynamic training vehicles, particularly where the long-term audience is large and the knowledge required is going to remain relatively static. Self-paced training makes the bank of knowledge available to the participant, but technical knowledge training requires additional activities to make it live and to put the knowledge in context when dealing with customers.

It is in the areas of self-paced and technical knowledge training that developers need to be at their most creative in devising a variety of interventions that will encourage learning and maintain interest.

Interpersonal skills

Customer service needs good people skills and these skills can be developed for face-to-face contact, but increasingly, quality customer service is being supplied by telephone.

Looking first at face-to-face skills, the interaction training has to be linked to a proven interaction model in order to give the participants a structure and a set of tools to manage the face-to-face situation. If the structure can be supported by a type of self-profiling, it gives the customer service people better understanding of the effects of their behaviour. Using a proven interaction model (for example, social styles), a training programme can then be tailored to reproduce a variety of circumstances that are likely to confront the customer service person, and can indeed be extended to develop skills in gaining additional business opportunities, should that fall into the job role.

Telephone skills have become recognized as significantly more important in providing customer service, and training to achieve these skills is becoming increasingly more sophisticated and effective. Surprisingly, most customer service staff who work with the telephone benefit from a basic programme that substantially improves voice and telephone management, which are skills that can be checked and refreshed on a regular basis.

The debate as to whether to train people to use a structured approach to calling, or a scripted approach, is well known to customer service people. The human performance dimension comes down heavily on the side of structure rather than script, recognizing the customer service operator's need for flexibility in customer dealings.

Techniques in telephone training, using well-structured material and up-to-date methods, produce substantial improvements in both telephone skills and telephone productivity. The concept of threading enables these programmes to be enhanced with additional technical knowledge of customer circumstances, thus making the learning both productive and realistic.

The use of mechanical monitoring and recording processes enables interpersonal skills training to be conducted in a broader and more intense fashion. However, to ensure the continued success of the training, experienced interpersonal skills trainers must be available to facilitate the programmes and give feedback.

Self-management

The self-management skills of the customer service people, the third aspect of the human performance dimension, are the skills that enable the successful customer service person to continue giving quality service through the working day to the widest variety of customers. A portfolio of self-management skills would include assertiveness, self-talk, job picturing and mind-setting.

The development of this programme needs input from people experienced in these techniques. This help is now available as part of the training in vocational job roles.

Personal flexibility

The final attribute of human performance is personal flexibility. Personal flexibility is derived from strong abilities in the other three aspects of human performance, giving the customer service person the confidence and wherewithall to be continuously flexible in order to meet the requirements of the customer.

Improvements in using and developing flexibility come through acting and reacting to a variety of customer issues set out during the training programme. Performance in handling these customer issues during training can be monitored or assessed during these training sessions.

SUMMARY

The training journey in customer service has taken us in the direction of quality and achievement. New programmes are now required to identify the critical success factors that will enable us to reach these two goals.

The development and implementation of programmes needs to be done against a background or process that ensures a successful outcome. The closed-loop development process shown in Figure 31.8 sets out a mechanism

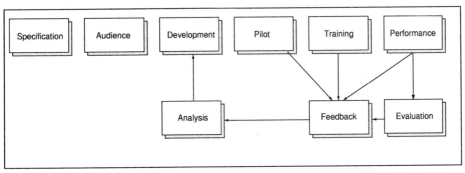

Figure 31.8   The closed-loop development process for a successful training programme

that will facilitate the development and delivery of a successful training pro-gramme. This closed-loop process depends on structured, objective feedback from trainers, participants and line managers to ensure that programmes meet and continue to meet expectations in the training of people and to further the development of an environment through which we can deliver quality cus-tomer service.

32 Using telephone techniques
Mary Ann Moran

In all large companies customers are being lost every day because of the way in which they are dealt with over the telephone. The sad thing is that the companies concerned often don't even recognize the symptoms, let alone the causes.

Most organizations subscribe to the view that customers are key to their future – 'without our customers we wouldn't even be here.' More and more, organizations are 'meeting people' over the telephone. It is therefore crucial for companies to ensure that every time customers call, they are dealt with in a professional and effective way, leaving them enthused with the 'feel good' factor. Thus every company that uses a telephone, and especially those who employ it as their main customer contact point, must regard the telephone as one of the most important tools they have in delivering customer service.

Unfortunately, one area which is frequently overlooked is investment of money and resources into training telephone skills techniques. All too often such investment is overshadowed by heavy marketing expenditure, expenditure which is frequently wasted through the inability to reinforce the brand due to inadequate telephone-based service.

Moreover, many companies invest much time and money in developing customer service charters and producing supporting documentation for this message to their customers. Some train their staff in what marketing messages and mission and vision statements actually mean; others may even train staff in how to deal with customers face to face, but because it is assumed that everybody can 'use' a telephone when they join an organization, then the techniques of delivering service via such a medium are not widely considered as important – not important, at least in terms of the immediate 'induction' training, compared to knowledge on, say, products, systems or other job tools work (for example the PC, the physical telephone system, voice mail and so on).

THE INCREASING IMPORTANCE OF THE TELEPHONE

As customer expectations grow there is, at last, a realization that in every walk of life, the telephone is becoming more important and that all business entities have an increasing dependence on the telephone as a powerful customer communication tool. To ensure that the telephone is treated as a vital element, it is essential that organizations effectively develop the way in which they staff it, so that any and all issues and problems can be more easily resolved.

Why has this change come about? What are the techniques which staff must have in order to ensure that every encounter over the telephone actually builds on and enhances the relationship between customer and supplier?

Dealing first with the 'why', from both the customer's and the supplier's perspective, there has been a demand for improvements in both the speed and efficiency with which information and service is delivered. The world is now firmly dependent on the telephone as a rapid means of doing everyday business. Where customers may have been happy to accept just basic information, they now demand to be treated with respect, to be listened to and for promises to be kept. This, coupled with increased competition and greater variety of product and services, has led customers to realize that they have real choices – choices involving more than just the price.

SKILLS, ATTITUDES AND BELIEFS

Companies and their staff must ensure that they are seen as the organization that treats customers differently, and so become the premier choice in their chosen marketplace. How do they achieve this objective?

Once a company has the infrastructure and the vision of a customer service culture, together with the internal procedures and systems to support it, they must concentrate their efforts on enabling staff to develop skills, attitudes and beliefs to deliver customer service 'messages' in a way which will ensure that the customer feels 'valued' as a result of the call. Traditionally, possessing 'good customer service skills' has meant ensuring that customer needs are met (the reason why the customer called in the first place), either by giving them the appropriate but basic information they require, or by just being 'friendly' over the telephone. The real challenge is to move towards exceeding customer needs – to deliver the unexpected and to satisfy every time.

When we are on the telephone there are a number of specific techniques that are vital in delivering customer service excellence. These techniques cover all areas, all situations which could impact customer satisfaction levels, and include the following:

- The knowledge and ability to recognize customer types.
- The ability to adapt to all situations that may be encountered.
- Developing each individual's own personal approach from their voice (for example, volume, tone, attitude).
- The ability to control both oneself and the way the call conversation

progresses so that the customer is led or guided through a process which ensures that all their needs and expectations are met and, where possible, exceeded.

● The ability to make decisions on behalf of the company within any appropriate guidelines, thus ensuring that the company, as well as the person, satisfies the customer.

We will now examine each of these areas in turn and determine what techniques should be developed, and how this can be done.

DIFFERENT CUSTOMER TYPES

First, let us look at people's ability to recognize the different customer types. Many training organizations have classified the different types of customers that staff are likely to meet. These classifications range from just two or three types to twenty or thirty. The greater the number of classifications, the more difficult it is for individuals to recognize the correct grouping for a customer. Nevertheless, each customer type can be broken down into smaller categories, and this subclassification can sometimes aid the staff member in dealing with the issues and identifying the right action in the right circumstance.

Most types of customer that staff will meet or speak to are normally in a reasonably rational frame of mind when they call in. However, there are occasions when something has occurred which causes the customer to step out of the rational mind-set. When this happens that customer then becomes either very uncertain, hesitant, and perhaps even fearful of using the telephone, or, at the other extreme, aggressive, demanding and irate, frequently attacking the member of staff personally during the course of the call.

For the demanding customer, whatever they are demanding has to be done (as long as it is within certain predefined boundaries) and this requires whoever is dealing with them to focus on doing it in a way that delivers service. The unsure, hesitant or fearful customer needs to speak to someone with a patient and calm approach, someone who can let them know that it is acceptable to be unsure, while the attacking/aggressive customer must be calmed down to a rational frame of mind that will enable them to vent their frustration in a constructive and less personal fashion. One of the classifications that is often forgotten is the rational customer because they can be quite easy to deal with and therefore an assumption is made that everything is satisfactory. However, even these customers still require something 'extra', something special that will move them to become advocates for the company and its service. Finally, there is also, of course, the more positive customer – one who is very satisfied and who may even call to thank us for something that has been done or a promise kept.

STAFF BEHAVIOUR – ADAPTING TO SITUATIONS

Once we have identified the customer types we are dealing with and have *461* recognized their requirements, we then have to adopt the right approach, which may well require us to use types of behaviour that are not our natural choice.

Each of us has a preferred way of operating. For example, some relate closely to people and are very good at building relationships, whereas others are comfortable with a more pragmatic style, staying with the facts and being almost clinical or procedurally oriented in their procedure. Each of these approaches may be acceptable for particular types of customers under particular circumstances. However, it is never possible to guarantee that a specific call answered will provide the right combination of circumstances and customer type.

This brings us to our next criterion of behaviour, adaptability. As we have already mentioned, it is not always possible to meet our ideal combination of circumstances and customer type, which means that telephone staff must be able to adapt their own preferred choice of behaviour in order to deal with all possible combinations.

What we have to consider is the ease with which people will be able to adapt, given that there may well be an initial mismatch between the member of staff's preferred style of communicating and the customer's desire to be dealt with in *their own* preferred style.

The most effective deliverers of customer service excellence are those individuals who can naturally and fluidly adapt their behaviour to deal with the customer in the way that the customer *wants* to be dealt with. For instance, from the customer perspective this may require that their call should be answered in the first place by an individual with a good technical understanding. Thus in order to deal with this situation, the member of staff may well have to adapt their preferred style of operating and talk to the customer in more technical terms – being careful, though, not to use company jargon. However, when the next customer calls in – someone who likes to pass the time of day and wants a more personal touch – the staff member is able to adopt their preferred style of behaviour using their personal approach skills to ensure that the customer is satisfied. But on each occasion, for every call taken, the process must be transparent. Customers must feel that the staff member's approach is genuine every single time.

All members of staff have therefore to be able to work in ways that may not always feel comfortable to them, but at the same time be able to do so in such a manner that the customer is unaware of any concern or anxiety. This adaptability or ability to deal with customers in the way they *want* to be dealt with, is probably one of the most important techniques. Staff do need, however, to be aware of their natural choice of behaviour so that they become aware of what it is that they do to reinforce this preferred choice. They can then start to learn and practice the skills that will enable them to adapt and choose between behavioural styles when dealing with customers. They can acquire this knowledge of their preferred choice through tools such as personality testing and observation of calls, based on certain criteria to identify the different preferred

styles. Lastly, after being trained or coached in the new skills and techniques, staff are then responsible personally for practising those skills, so that they become equally adept in all areas.

One important consideration for organizations is the recruitment of new staff or training/retraining of existing staff. Not all people are willing to try new things and work 'outside their pigeon-hole' (that is, to do things in the way they perceive things 'should' be done.) Some people have very fixed mind-sets and often do not see the need for a change in approach. Staff who are fixed in a box are less likely to be able to deliver customer excellence when they are on the telephone, than those who have a willing and flexible approach, who can see that there are many different ways of dealing with customers, and who appreciate that they can actually develop all the necessary skills. Customers also often have fixed views, of course, but as the customer is always right, we have to adapt to them and not the other way round.

THE NATURAL DEVELOPMENT OF CUSTOMER SERVICE EXCELLENCE

What skills and techniques need to be developed such that delivery of consistent customer service excellence is a natural outcome? Well, there are a number of ways that we can look at this. For example, without learning any new skills, every individual, no matter how long they have been working with the telephone, should analyse each area of their own personal approach to see if they could do it differently, and, more importantly, be consistently better at it.

However, the most important attribute is the way in which we approach and speak to our customers. In this respect, there are many things that can be conveyed by our voice and they all contribute to how our customers feel and whether they will be satisfied at the end of the call. First, do we sound as though we can actually deal with the call? A high squeaky voice might convey immaturity to some listeners and may cause an aggrieved customer to demand to 'speak to a supervisor'. To avoid this problem, practice lowering your vocal tones. In addition to sounding 'mature', individuals must sound as if they want to deal with the call. Disinterest, which can be easily identified in someone's tone of voice, is another critical aspect. Each call should concentrate on achieving customer satisfaction, and staff must therefore ensure from the onset that they sound interested in dealing with the customer and happy to deal with each and every call. One of the simplest techniques in this context is to begin each call with a smile, for it is very difficult to sound uninterested or reluctant to take a call when you are smiling. Just fixing a grin on your face is not enough, however. Staff must not sound insincere, and words must be spoken with sincerity, so that customers really believe the messages they convey.

Another facet that requires some thought is whether the actual sound of the voice is interesting to the customer. For instance, if the voice is on one level all the time, it sounds monotonous and can suggest boredom. To relieve this impression, the tone should be varied so that the operator's voice sounds more melodious, is easier to listen to, and offers a more welcoming approach. If *463* staff feel that they have a 'boring' voice but find it difficult to vary their tone, emphasizing various key words can help as a starting point.

There is another useful tactic similar to that of 'smiling' outlined above. When customers call organizations, they are not normally looking for trouble. They generally have a query that they want dealt with on the spot in a professional manner. Thus to make certain that this happens, staff should try to 'enjoy' the call themselves, right from the point of answering the telephone. If this enjoyment is conveyed to the customer, it also helps the voice sound less monotonous.

How do people manage to convey enjoyment over the telephone for each and every call, especially in difficult circumstances where the mind can subconsciously start to wander, leading people to say things that might express negative attitudes or disinterest to the customer?

In such circumstances, what tends to happen is that in our minds ulterior thoughts start to undermine the way in which we deal with customers. For example, someone may have spent a long time on an earlier call helping a customer decide on the way in which they pay for a product or service, and at the end of that call, as far as they knew, the customer was satisfied. The customer then calls back in an irate frame of mind (having just spoken to a 'friend' who tells them that they have done the wrong thing and may have been misled), complaining about the company and accusing the staff member personally of 'sharp practice', 'incompetence', 'being useless', 'don't know why you were employed' and so on. As a consequence, the telephone-based staff member starts having thoughts like 'What do they think they're saying', 'How dare they talk to me like that', 'I worked so hard to sort this out, how dare they say I'm wrong' and so forth.

When this occurs – and it often does – it is very easy to listen to your own subconscious, rather than listen to the customer, with the result that delivery of service excellence is not the outcome of the call. These subconscious thoughts must therefore not be allowed to impact negatively on the way in which the customer is handled. Here are two ways of ensuring that your inner voice makes only positive statements:

1   Individuals should believe that in some way they will be able to satisfy every customer, and that part of the enjoyment of their job is to meet the challenge of discovering how this can be achieved. Certainly, this process is not easy to start with and it does take some time to perfect, but as with all skills and techniques, it can be developed with practice and patience.

2   Individuals can cultivate a positive frame of mind and concentrate on the customer by constantly listening positively and proactively to what the customer is *actually* saying. By listening to and appreciating the real truth, the real reason why the customer called and not any blustering that might accompany it, the staff member can look for bridge-building opportunities with that customer which will resolve the problem.

The final area associated with the voice concerns the clarity with which words are actually spoken and this aspect is determined by three factors: pace, volume and enunciation.

First, how quickly does the individual actually speak? Most people when they are speaking on the telephone do so at the same pace as they do face to face (that is, their ordinary rate of speech). We should remember, however, that when people are communicating face to face the understanding of the message is largely conveyed by the body language that is being used to support the spoken words. On the telephone the element of body language is missing. Although, therefore, we do not change the rate at which we speak, it can appear to the listener on the telephone that we have accelerated because, due to the missing element, it is more difficult to understand the true meaning of what we are saying. Thus if people just speak at their normal pace it can lead to real confusion from the listener's perspective, and if this confusion continues, it can infuriate customers. This situation may result in an angry person on the telephone as opposed to the pleasant customer who rang initially.

The voice should be slowed down a little over the telephone in order to maximize the opportunity for the customer to understand what is being said to them immediately, and not by having to ask people to repeat what they have just said. This will make the customer feel more comfortable.

Secondly, the volume at which people speak can also lead to a lack of understanding from the customer's point of view. Some people have naturally soft voices, while others have somewhat booming voices. Both extremes on the volume scale can cause people – both staff and customers – to mishear what is actually being said. Staff have to be sure that they project their voice in a balanced fashion so as to be fully understood. Good ways of deciding the correct level are to practise with a friend or colleague, or to tape your voice calling another extension in order to check whether you come across clearly during the conversation.

The difference between projecting and shouting must be clearly understood. Individuals should never feel that they have to shout in order to be heard over the telephone. Shouting can in fact cause their voice to rise in tone, so that, as discussed above, they sound immature. The voice has to be projected from the heart of the body, not shouted from the throat.

Assuming that pace and the volume are correct, the third and final factor that we should look at is the enunciation of words. Again because of the lack of body language over the telephone, staff have to enunciate every word with care – and probably more energetically than they would face to face – to ensure that the correct words are heard. They have almost to imagine that they are sending the word away from their mouth.

THE CALL STRUCTURE

So far we have discussed how to recognize and deal with different types of customers; we have looked at ways of approaching and speaking to customers; and we have considered how we should remain positive and in control of *465* ourselves under difficult circumstances. What else can help to deliver service excellence?

Although we have looked at actual staff approach, we have not yet looked at how staff can guide customers through the call, how they should greet them, and how they should leave the caller with a warm feeling when they terminate the call. For customers to be truly satisfied they must feel that they have been looked after throughout the call and have not had to flounder and think of what to talk about next. With the skills that staff have or can develop, together with a proper call structure, everyone should be able to guide the majority of customers to complete satisfaction. The call structure, in association with various skills, is a significant contributor to that customer satisfaction.

The call structure involves skilful questioning techniques, active listening and building a rapport with the customer. By these means we can ensure that the *real* reason(s) for the customer's call is (are) discussed, and that the conversation is not simply superficial. Effective questioning and listening will provide clues to any additional, sometimes hidden, needs the customer has.

Once the member of staff has fully understood the customer's requirements, the call structure then moves on to ensure that solutions to the questions asked or issues raised are presented in a way that the customer can understand and appreciate. This requires, *inter alia*, that the answers should be presented in plain English, uncluttered by jargon. The customer has to comprehend in detail what it is that is being proposed and why this proposal is the best solution for their situation. Only when a customer truly appreciates that this is the case, will they leave the call satisfied.

EMPOWERMENT OF STAFF

However, in presenting the solution, staff may often have to do or say things that are not within their usual parameters of operation. Companies therefore have to empower their staff and allow them the flexibility necessary to respond completely to customers' needs. This means that in presenting a solution that may have bent normal company rules the staff member must have the confidence that the company will support them in that decision. Moreover, the ability to provide instant solutions will often deflect customer aggravation.

Of course, meeting their needs will not alone ensure a customer's satisfaction; as we discussed earlier, that is only one side of the equation. The way in which the customer has been dealt with has an equal impact. Because perceptions of customer service have changed so dramatically in recent years, customers have a mental checklist of what they expect to happen: that is, a warm, friendly, welcoming greeting from someone who listens and deals with them with empathy; who has a personal approach; and who does something extra or unexpected. When all these criteria are met, a customer is more certain of obtaining satisfaction.

Finally, once the solution has been presented, the customer must be asked whether they are satisfied. If the answer is 'Yes', the call can then be progressed to its natural conclusion and positive links made between the company, the staff member and the customer. If the answer is 'No', more questioning is necessary to try to find a satisfactory solution. If at all possible, no customer should leave a call without having received full satisfaction.

As soon as the customer has expressed their full satisfaction, the call can then be closed as smoothly and as positively as it started. The start and finish of a call are of crucial importance, as these are points at which the customer gains their first and final impressions of the company and its 'brand' image. The call therefore needs to be particularly positive, enthusiastic, and enjoyable at both the start and finish in order to generate in the customer the confidence that will allow them to continue to trade positively.

CONCLUSION

Change does not happen overnight for either the company or its staff. However, as long as there is:

- a commitment of time;
- a willingness to develop and learn new skills and ways of operating; and
- a commitment from everyone within the company to take on responsibility for providing consistent service at *all* levels of the business,

then you should soon be ready to deliver customer service excellence at the telephone.

33 Accreditation
Elizabeth Harris

Once it is established that an organization should concentrate on customer service, then its perpetrators must next consider all the accessories required. We need technology, surveys, mystery shoppers, structure, statements, brochures, customer-focused incentives, and, of course, the inevitable vision and mission statements and so on. Unfortunately, in the pursuit of outstanding customer service, too many good ideas conceived in management think-tanks come to grief through lack of trained and motivated implementors.

FIVE STAGES TO CUSTOMER SERVICE

The five stages on the road to this desired customer service are: vision; selection/recruitment; training; evaluation; and accreditation.

The vision

The result of many hours of management team effort, the vision must be translated into tangible customer experiences. What do you want your customers to perceive? What do you want your customers to receive? How does this outstanding customer service manifest itself?

The selection and recruitment of customer service staff

The answer to the questions above provide the basis for the selection criteria for your staff. They tell us what *competencies* they will need to display; and in turn these will determine the training design. Figure 33.1 illustrates how these competencies are central to customer service focus.

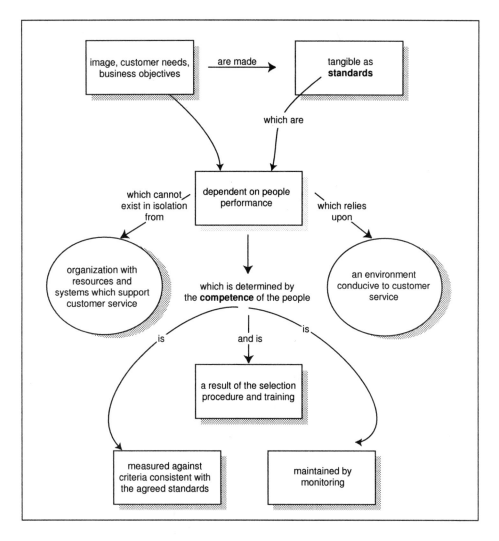

Figure 33.1   The relationship of competencies to customer service focus

The training programme

No matter how sound your selection process, if you mean to be at the leading edge in your field by stamping your customers with your own superior brand of service, you will need to undertake a comprehensive training programme that will equip people with the competencies you have identified.

The concern in this chapter is for the *outcome* of the training. However well developed, tried, tested and previously successful the training has been, the truly focused customer service organization will never rest on its laurels and take training for granted. Built into the training programme must be the facility to measure continually the standard and quality of the output.

Along with developments in computer hardware technology, however, has come the creation of a whole new method of customer communication which, sooner rather than later, will dramatically affect the success of marketing policies. This new arena is commonly known as the Internet, or the World Wide Web. The World Wide Web is the newest information service to arrive on the Internet. The Web is based on a technology called Hypertext and most of the development has taken place at CERN – the European Particle Physics Laboratory. The World Wide Web is basically a universe of information which is accessible through a computer network and works on the principle that information placed on the 'web' is available to any authorized user, in any country, from any computer and via a simple program. As we all know, the creation of a worldwide system of computer communications in the early 1990s was initially driven by the use of military data links by the educational institutions, initially in the United States and then around the world. After that, it was not long before the communications possibilities for the rest of humanity became clear. Now it is possible for any one of us with the correct equipment to send and receive messages and files from anywhere in the world – at local telephone call charge rates!

One of the most common uses for this new technology has been e-mail between company sites and employees. More recently, 'viewer' programmes (known as 'browsers') on the Internet have made it absurdly easy for anyone to exploit the facilities offered on a highly interactive and graphically organized interface. Just as the domination of Microsoft Windows has continued apace, so too will these browsers bring about enormous increases in Internet traffic.

But what will we talk about? At the beginning of this chapter I put forward the idea that in a retrogressive development parallel to the increasing communications possibilities, the substance of what we communicate has suffered rather than benefited. For the future, the area of transactional relationships has to be a clear exception to this decline in standards.

In transactional relationships we already have a great deal of experience of the new electronic world (for example bank transfers, ordering theatre tickets, playing computer games, satellite television and so on). The idea of expanding this range to include most of our everyday transactions (for example shopping, organizing travel, reading books on-line and so much more) will not be difficult for consumers to assimilate in the medium to long term.

Whilst this development may take a number of years to become fully apparent, we must take heed now of what it will mean for customer relationships and fulfilment strategies. These relationships will become 'real time' in their nature. When consumers decide for example, that they would like to apply for investment in a new financial instrument, or for details on the latest fashion craze, they will expect instant satisfaction. Increasingly, they will be offered this satisfaction over a Web site provided by finance companies, retailers, and almost any other company you can imagine. Indeed, already we can order flowers, wines, computer equipment and much more over the combination of telephone line and computer equipment that allows communication on the World wide Web.

PROGRAMME EVALUATION

Name .... Date .... (please tick as appropriate)

What was your overall view of the three days programme?	Very good	Good	Average	Poor

Was the content relevant to your job?	Completely	Mostly	Partly	Not at all

Did the trainer(s) meet your requirements?	Completely	Mostly	Partly	Not at all

Was the time available used?	Very well	Well	OK	Badly

Overall the course material was:	Very good	Good	Average	Poor

Were the three days well structured?	Very well	Well	OK	Badly

Please tick appropriate box

SETTING THE SCENE 6 5 4 3 2 1

Made me appreciate the reasons why I am attending the training; what my objectives are.							Already knew why I was attending the training: aware of my objectives.

THE TRICKY TELEPHONE

Made me aware of the tricks of the telephone and how to overcome them.							Already aware of the tricks of the telephone and can overcome them.

FEEDBACK

Made me aware of the importance of constructive feedback and gave me a structure to follow.							Do not see reason for structured feedback. Irrelevant to the course.

Note the even number of tick boxes to discourage the instinct to sit on the fence.

Figure 33.2 Programme evaluation form

External observation

Bringing in others to observe can be extremely helpful and supportive. The observation can be informal or formal, objective or subjective. Visits to the training sessions, discussion with trainers and participants, using the 'accreditation tool' (see below) at predetermined stages – all can give useful feedback during the training process.

One caveat, however, is not to use observers too frequently, since overuse can create inhibiting factors. One manager decided to attend some training sessions from the beginning in order himself to learn all he could on the subject. He proceeded to take copious notes on the content, purely for self-use. On the third day several participants approached the trainer and said that they could not attend the training any longer. The customer services manager was deemed to be writing reports on what they did or said in order to use the notes as evidence and they felt unable to contribute in such circumstances.

The other risk is observers who arrive mob-handed, practically outnumber the participants, and then disrupt the training by whispering amongst themselves.

Instruments

Use of inventories and surveys are increasingly popular. Carefully constructed questionnaires are issued to participants for self-evaluation or handed out to peers, supervisors or subordinates for a different view. This feedback can measure skills improvement, and, most important, it can give an indication of less tangible outcomes required from the training.

An example of this is an *orientation* assessment via a survey before, immediately after, and sometimes following, the training. This can give information about the participants' approach to customer service and serves as an indication of whether desired changes in attitude have been achieved.

These evaluations are crucial, for while we would expect trainers to continue the selection process, conducting information assessment during training, this alone is no guarantee of the external quality of the service delivery.

Accreditation

Through accreditation we can secure a greater degree of success for the training outcome. It is the basis for the continuing delivery of service excellence. It pushes your customer service providers on to greater heights. Thus the rest of this chapter is dedicated to this vital ingredient.

WHAT IS ACCREDITATION?

Accreditation is the process by which the customer service provider is assessed against the identified competencies.

This assessment is undertaken by a series of simulated customer interactions or calls, each carefully prepared so that the provider has been observed and evaluated in as many customer situations as possible. (For the purposes of this chapter, the example of telephone-based customer service delivery has been used for the accreditation. However, the principles are easily adaptable for roles which involve minimal telephone interaction, such as retail sales). The calls are arranged as a series in increasing order of difficulty, so that the provider progresses through set levels of accreditation. This means that once past a predetermined threshold level, the service provider may be released to receive simple calls if the system can be set to facilitate this.

The idea of progressing or developing through levels of accreditation softens the pass/fail perception. When this process is being used at the end of a training programme, it should be rare for a first-level fail to occur as the trainers should have identified potential failures during the learning.

The following activities are prerequisites for this accreditation process.

Identifying what is to be accredited

The elements that have to be identified for accreditation include:

- The situations which may need to be handled, or sorted into levels of difficulty.
- The competencies essential for handling those situations in the way that the organization wishes.

Figure 33.3 shows an example of a competency list for the purposes of accreditation.

Designing accreditation tools

Accreditation tools, against which the assessment can take place, are required for the following purposes:

- Documenting the competencies and performance criteria.
- Checking for objectivity and consistency.

The detail of the accreditation tool will depend on the requirements of the organization. In some cases, accreditation details will need to be very detailed (that is, for compliance/legal reasons) and in others a simple tick box document will suffice. Figures 33.4–33.7 give four examples of accreditation tools.

Creation of the customer scenarios that form the background to the situation require the following elements:

- Credible customer data (for example names, addresses, contact numbers, history and circumstances).

473

GENERIC COMPETENCIES

Real-time

1   Salutation/greeting
2   Listening skills
3   Caller identification (criteria match/spend profile)
4   Questioning skills
5   Rapport
6   Confirming/summarizing skills
7   Satisfaction (of customer)
8   Anchoring
9   Promise
10 Close/wrap

Reflective

11 Positive statements
12 Data accuracy on screens (spell, field completions, etc.)
13 Flow
14 Objection handling
15 Benefit statements
16 Data captured for closing screen
17 Data asked for — complete against script?
18 Knowledge — products
- Services
- Company
- Market/competition
- Process

Figure 33.3   List of generic competencies for the purpose of accreditation

- Profile for the role play.
- Characteristics, personality, behaviour, opinions, social style, circumstances relating to the call.
- Ensuring the system environment to enable the scenario, including data entry if necessary.

See examples of customer scenarios in Figures 33.8 and 33.9.

Training the accreditors

Accreditors must be trained in the following skills:

- Understanding the accreditation documentation (tool).
- Understanding the skills and training messages.
- Briefing the scenarios.
- Role-playing for consistency and objectivity.
- Identifying the different behaviours required for each accreditation level.

Competence	Performance criteria	Pass/threshold competent		Conditional pass/needs development		Fail		Supporting information
Closes the sale	1. Recognizes and acts on buying signals	Yes, and can give examples of others	☐	Sometimes	☐	Not at all	☐	
	2. Summarizes agreement to buy	Yes, structured with benefit links	☐	Yes, structure and/or benefit needs development	☐	Not done	☐	
	3. Checks understanding with customer/client	Yes, always, and matches	☐	Sometimes	☐	Not done	☐	
	4. Explains next step and timescales	Yes, fully	☐	Sometimes and/or step or timescale missing	☐	Not done	☐	
	5. Thanks and anchors customer/client (name/company/product/help)	Yes, effectively using the key areas	☐	Sometimes and/or could be more effective with key areas	☐	Not done	☐	

Figure 33.4 Accreditation tool – sample 1

Member of staff:	**Accreditor:**				
Date:					
Competence Area:					
Telephone communications	Exceptional	Above average	Average	Below average	Unacceptable
Salutation					
• Follows format • Hello – Company name – How can I help?	**Comments**				
Invitation					
• Questioning/listening skills • Request customer name/ account number • Carries out verification process	**Comments**				
Resolution					
• Information clear/concise • Positive • Power words	**Comments**				
Satisfaction					
• Checks with customer • Questions/listens	**Comments**				

Figure 33.5   Accreditation tool – sample 2

Competence Area: **Telephone communications**	Exceptional	Above average	Average	Below average	Unacceptable
Wrap-up					
● Anchors ● Company name ● Themselves	**Comments**				
Voice					
● Tone/pace/volume ● Sincerity ● Enthusiasm	**Comments**				
Builds rapport					
● Use of customer name ● Introduction of own name ● Empathy: 　■ Emotion 　■ Values 　■ Language	**Comments**				

Figure 33.5   (continued)   *477*

Competence Area: **Product/systems/procedures**	Exceptional	Above average	Average	Below average	Unacceptable
● Knowledge of product(s)					
● Knowledge of system(s)					
● Knowledge of procedures					
	Comments				

Competence Area: **Complaint handling**	Exceptional	Above average	Average	Below average	Unacceptable
Ability to identify and handle complaints using the model (CLEAR)					
● Clarifies ● Listens ● Empathizes ● Acknowledges ● Reacts	**Comments**				

Competence Area: **Difficult situations**	Exceptional	Above average	Average	Below average	Unacceptable
Ability to identify and handle positively					
● Rejections ● Put-downs ● Criticism	**Comments**				

Figure 33.5 (concluded)

ACCREDITORS CHECKLIST

	√/×	
Call structure		
Salutation		
Wrap-up ● close		
● anchoring		
● personal messages		
● customer satisfaction		
Communication cycle ● questioning		
● listening		
● informing		
Customer relationships ● rapport building		
● trust		
Difficult situations ● rejection/put-downs		
● criticism		
● complaints (model CLEAR)		

Figure 33.6   Accreditation tool – sample 3

479

ACCREDITORS CHECKLIST
(Continued)

	√/×	
Handling objections		
● identification		
● model		

Voice		
● tone		
● pace		
● volume		

Data accuracy		
● spelling		
● filed completion		

Company messages		
● personal		
● benefits		
● positive		

Knowledge		
● products		
● services		
● market		
● process		

480   **Figure 33.6   (concluded)**

- Observing, avoiding inferences, documenting evidence.
- Analysing, scoring, prioritizing, weighting.
- Giving feedback.

Depending on where we recruit our accreditors, they should each participate in the soft skills training modules so that an assessment can be made regarding their understanding of the messages. In addition, if necessary, they should demonstrate a full knowledge of product, procedure and policy, and they should of course display full commitment to the desired customer culture.

Planning the accreditation timetable

When any significant numbers of people are to be accredited, this becomes a truly herculean task, which includes:

- Persuading accreditors to block time for the exercise.
- Sorting calls and allocating to accreditors.
- Ensuring a mix of accreditors for each acreditee, so as to obtain a range of feedback and a fairer result.
- Planning the logistics so that calls can be undertaken in a non-threatening environment.
- Allowing time for preparation, reflection, feedback and recuperation.
- Building in time for coaching between calls.
- Allowing time for repeat calls.
- Setting aside slots for counselling.
- Contingency for any possible occurrence.

Organizing resources

Resources to be planned and organized include, for example, the following:

- System time, telephone lines.
- Space.
- Equipment (recording/playback).
- Documentation.
- Copying for feedback.
- Refreshment.

Communication

Tasks to be covered under this heading are as follows:

- Briefing and check understanding of participants.
- Information and schedule of participants with follow-up for confirmation.
- Information and schedule to accreditors with follow-up for confirmation (don't just think they'll turn up because they said they would).

Name of assessee:	Name of assessor:

4 = Really good, gave you a warm feeling and impression
3 = Good – better than we get in most places these days
2 = Not up to the standard we require
1 = Unacceptable

Be sure to expand notes box to give feedback to the Customer Service advisor/representative

Definition of high score	4	3	2	1	Definition of low score	Comment/feedback
Salutation						
Words					Incorrect, inaudible	
Tone/pace/volume — Correct and clear					Unattractive, unsure	
Enthusiasm — Warm, confident, placed well					Too slow/fast	
Overall first impression — Infectious enthusiasm / Wow					Indifferent	
Invitation						
Used open					Question not appropriate	
Question early — Good open early						
Obtained name					Not at all	
Used name — As often as appropriate						
Tone/pace/volume — Maintained good level					Dropped off altogether	
Enthusiasm — Excellent					Indifferent	
Directed questions to issues — Took control					Lost control	
Issue						
Active listening — Ums/ahs support statements					Silence or interrupted	
Showed interest — Questioned and empathized					Unrelated response	
Clarified — Probed issues / Phonetic for facts					Face value, no hearing check	
Resolution (a)						
Information gathering — Questions asked smoothly					No attempt to build rapport	
Address keyed — Explained fully					Just asked for method	
Postcode						
Confirmed back address — Quickly without repetition					Questioned whole address	
Confirmed back telephone number						

Figure 33.7   Accreditation tool – sample 4: qualitative assessment form (telephone response)

Criteria	Positive		Negative
Resolution (b)			
Rapport and trust	Pastimed as appropriate		No attempt to build rapport
Pastimed (kept customer interest)	Matched		
Matched voice (tone/pace/volume)	Adapted to customer		Mismatched
Matched language	Made trust statements		None offered
Resolution (c)			
Use of real terms	Used real terms		Used jargon
Use of power words	Included power words		Name used
Questioned understanding	Restated and questioned		No test of understanding
Gave accurate information	Fully accurate		Gave inaccurate information
Satisfaction			
Ensured total understanding	Explained process		No explanation given
Question for satisfaction	Questioned and repeated		No test of satisfaction
Question for further help	Offered further help		No offer
Anchored	Anchor name/product/company		No anchor
Wrap-up			
Explain next step	Detailed what to expect next		No explanation
Signed off/thanks	Gave name and ended on high		Just said goodbye
Screen check			
Speed of entry	Efficient, no undue delay, filled gaps		Slow, tedious and silent gaps
Completeness	All information completed fully		Too many missing items
Accuracy	Spelling and facts all OK		Types and mistakes

Knowledge gates

○ ○ ○ ○ ○
○ ○ ○ ○ ○

Summary

Knowledge score ☐

Overall score ☐

Overall feeling/area for improvement/area for congratulation

Figure 33.7 (concluded)

483

Account No: 50000000
Company: Bodge & Son

Account status: Active
Product: Widgets

Script: Dolittle & Dally

Mr Robertson, a partner at Dolittle & Dally, Solicitors, is on the telephone. We have only, so far, dealt with Mr Hamish Fletcher, the other partner, who agreed the contract and the terms. Mr Robertson is a somewhat obnoxious character, who wants to complain about almost everything, although he is unable to provide any specific facts regarding the problems. He complains about the cost: 'It has not been as cheap as promised', 'We've used your widgets for nearly a year now and only signed up with you because you had plans to provide better widgets – what's happened to these plans? You conned us.'

He claims that the service is totally unreliable and that business has been lost as a result as customers have taken their custom elsewhere. He demands compensation for loss of business. He claims that when the business extended and had a second 'gold' widget installed, the installation engineers were rude and foul-mouthed in front of the female staff. He insists that when he rang up before, asking about widget extension modules, the member of staff he spoke to 'hadn't got a clue'. He doubts that you are any better. Finally he wants to close the account there and then, with no early termination penalties (he is only three months in to a 12-month contract), claiming his firm signed up on the promise of gold widgets which have not materialized. 'We could take you to court over this for breach of contract.' What does the member of staff do/how do they respond?

Request to system re account/history build:

Ensure name on account is Mr Hamish Fletcher.
Ensure one widget is selected.

Figure 33.8   Customer scenario 1

- General information to the rest of the organization.
- Preparation for feedback channels on successes (and others).

Allocation of a coordinator and administrator

- Accreditation involves reams of paperwork and continuous checking. Make sure there is someone who takes an overall view and a different someone who will churn out the documentation.
- Computer-based documentation is used more frequently now, but printouts are still required for confirmation, signature, and simply for keeping in your pocket!

THE ACCREDITATION PROCESS

First, the accreditors meet their accreditees and discuss the procedure. The accreditor's objective is to allay fears and settle nerves that may have a detrimental and possibly uncharacteristic effect on the call.

Account No: 50000222
Company: Bodge & Son

Account status: Active
Product: Widgets

Script: Scientific Systems

Scientific Systems is a large organization which supplies complete computer systems and software support to other firms, both large and small, throughout the country. There are several regional offices, from which sales staff operate.

The customer, Mr Woods, is ringing up on Friday at 9.00 p.m. as he has been called out to his office. His customers have been trying to contact his technical help desk but have been unable to do so as the widgets have, yet again, failed. It is vital that the widgets are working, as Friday night is one of the busiest nights of the week. The customer will not wait for a call-back and insists on holding on the line as the member of staff concerned progresses the fault diagnosis regarding the failed widget. He then insists on speaking to his Account Manager, as he perceives this to be a major problem. He is also asking why the agreed compensation for widget failures has not been automatically forwarded to him relative to last month's sorry events. He is not a happy man!

Request to system re account/history build:

Build history:

Monthly bill:	£230 570.00	Dated: 01/01/1999
Payment:	£230 570.00	Dated: 24/02/1999
Monthly bill:	£127 863.25	Dated: 02/02/1999
Payment:	£127 863.25	Dated: 28/03/1999

The member of staff concerned will need to access these bills in full detail.

Build current adjustments as follows:

Goodwill credit: £500.00   Dated 30/03/1999

Build account notes as follows:

01/04/1999	20.22 Problem report re gold widget no. S1276777. Engineering advised. Resolution within 8 hours.
30/04/1999	Credit account £4,000 against S1276779 gold widget. Cheque sent in post.

Current balance: £500 credit

Figure 33.9   Customer scenario 2

Ground rules

Next, ground rules are set, the procedure reviewed, and understanding established. For example, in the early calls, if the interaction begins to deteriorate and the accreditee is floundering, it is advisable to stop the call and begin again. This stage would then need to be repeated to convince both parties that a real customer situation could have been handled. Obviously when this *485* occurs it is documented, and if it happens more than once the occurrence must be taken into consideration in determining whether the accreditee is passed for that level of accreditation.

Making the call

The call is now made, and for each call, the accreditor is asked to look for a general core of competencies and, in addition, specific skills for that particular call. The tool is used where performance criteria are defined, behaviours described and the appropriate result recorded. The accreditor is expected to make the best effort in dramatic acting so as to give a credible impression of a customer. No allowances should be made for the fact that this is not a real situation, and the two parties should not step out of role until the call is ended.

Immediate post-call activities

Reflection and preparation

By pre-arrangement the accreditees reflect on the call and prepare to receive feedback, including the identification of their own areas of excellence and improvement and errors in terms of fact and procedure. Meanwhile, the accreditors listen to the recording of the call, score the real-time competencies and reflect upon the overall effect of the interaction.

Feedback

Immediately following this preparation, and while the call is fresh in their minds, the two partners to the call meet for feedback and to agree the next step. This could have a number of options: repeat the call, coaching from the trainer or more of the same, move to next call.

Accreditors debriefing

At the end of each stage of the accreditation process, or at suitable elapse of time, the accreditation coordinator, trainers and accreditors must meet together to review the process and flag up areas of concern and/or preferably share call highlights and successes.

Action

Finally, the whole process comes to an end, actions are agreed/decided and certificates for levels of accreditation awarded. In parallel, an action plan is drawn up for the personal development of each accreditee and dates set for the next round of accreditation.

Ongoing use of accreditation

At this point it is up to the organization on how to proceed. Once the tools are in place, supervisors/team leaders/team coaches can use them for assessment and coaching purposes, bringing in the trainer accreditors, trainers or trained satellite trainers (that is, phone-based staff who have a team-based responsibility for aspects of the training process) for ongoing accreditation either on an individual basis or to undertake a further block accreditation. Elements can be used at recruitment and at the relevant stages during training. The continuing maintenance of the quality of customer service depends on careful planning and monitoring of this activity to ensure that each individual is regularly assessed and that the quality recognized by the accreditation does not deteriorate. Figure 33.10 shows an example of the application of the accreditation process.

1 Recruitment and selection	Assessment with accreditations if appropriate to evaluate existing skills.
2 Pre-programme learning	Knowledge testing with opportunity to accredit further to test existing skills.
3 Training programme	Ongoing informal/formal evaluation. Stage accreditation.
4 Post training	Full accreditation.
5 Continuous development	Formal and informal assessment for coaching accreditation for maintenance, reward and development.

Figure 33.10   When to apply the accreditation process

APPLYING THE ACCREDITATION PROCESS

Recruitment and selection stage

If experienced staff are employed, the accreditation process can be evolved in order to ascertain:

1 whether the experience is valid;
2 what training is needed; and
3 how soon customer calls can be taken.

Once the process is in place and thereafter available for use, it becomes an invaluable tool for the champions of quality to demonstrate the risk of launching people into the customer service area without thorough training.

Too often, in times of stress, the call centre manager is persuaded to put any available bottoms on seats to cope with an excessive call load, regardless of the effect on the customer. Inappropriately experienced staff are thrown in at the deep end merely to address the immediate situation. They can sometimes do more damage to the organization than unanswered calls.

If their lack of skill can be objectively demonstrated, this action can be avoided or at least undertaken from a position of awareness. Accreditation results can give information on which to base decisions about such manning issues. If the risk is then taken to place less than competent staff before the customer, the resulting inadequacies of service will not be entirely unexpected. It is also more likely that necessary training will soon follow.

The preprogramme learning stage

Providing that the desired route is taken and the new recruits undertake the training planned for them, then prior to their joining the course, they can complete various distance-learning assignments. This affords the accreditation process another opportunity to show its worth.

Even very skilled staff can demonstrate poor customer interface because they lack confidence in their knowledge of the product(s), the company or the process(es). In this case, small inputs of distance learning can bring about an improved accreditation result.

Each stage in fact provides opportunities to identify less competent recruits that may be improved via coaching and training.

The training

We have already explored evaluation and indicated that staged accreditations must be built into the comprehensive call centre training programme. As each stage is reached, an appropriate measurement of competence is made. Remedial action can then be taken before undesirable behaviours become habit. The measurement also serves as a method of highlighting inadequacies in the selection or training programme.

Post-training

On completion of the training, before any certificates are awarded and certainly before 'real' customers receive the benefit of our service, the full accreditation process comes into play. Recruits undergo a series of simulated customer interactions in the manner explained earlier. During this process, knowledge, behaviours and attitudes are threaded together and measured.

Continuous development

Once the accreditation process is in place, the simulated calls, the accreditor expertise and the related document will provide support for continuing maintenance of standards and the further development of staff. Alongside the everyday assessment and performance monitoring of the people carried out by their team leaders and coaches, accreditation is applied at intervals either to revisit the existing levels of competence and check that they have not slipped, or to take the customer service provider on to the next stage of development. In, for example, financial institutions where advice is given on investments, this ongoing competence assessment is a legal requirement and the accreditation tool can be used to demonstrate compliance.

In addition to the use of accreditation, other forms of performance monitoring will be in use in the good customer service/call-centre environment. Informal assessment plays a big part, with informal and formal coaching a planned regular activity. Monitoring should be carried out, first, by listening to calls with and without the knowledge of the member of staff concerned, and second, by posing as a customer and giving subjective feedback. The latter method should not be confused with mystery shopping exercises which should give feedback on the organization's overall performance. Individual strengths and weaknesses should be identified informally and addressed, once again by means of a carefully planned and regular monitoring exercise.

The accreditation process alone cannot bring about outstanding customer service. However, with all other elements in place – strategy, systems, organization, environment and training – accreditation is an important ingredient in promoting and maintaining the delivery of service to the standards to which the organization aspires.

34 Empowerment

Colin Apthorp

People cannot be empowered – they empower themselves by choice, providing that:

1　They are given information and training.
2　Responsibility is delegated to them and they are coached sensitively to use delegation as an opportunity for development.
3　They have access to role models through managers providing examples of confidence and maturity.

People have to be challenged to release their full potential, whilst being supported through honest feedback and counselling – but not challenged and then blamed when things go wrong.

As customers we now expect a different form of service from that which we were previously prepared to accept. Yet as suppliers we seem uncertain how to meet our own expectations. Staff, suppliers and customers know that the solution to satisfying this new expectation for smooth (not necessarily faultless) service lies in creating empowered service cultures. The question is: how do we achieve those cultures?

WHAT IS EMPOWERMENT?

The Concise Oxford Dictionary defines 'empower' as 'to authorize, license, give power to, make able'. For the individual, it is about enablement and the freedom to operate within personal boundaries. For the organization, it is culture change and the bravery to create and manage the empowered service environment. In this sense, empowerment is, 'building an organization in which individuals take control over and more responsibility for the results of their work; can use more of their talents and creativity; keep learning'. The key factor is *enablement*.

When power goes to employees, they feel more responsible, show more initiative, do more and enjoy work more. However, true power is only passed on when employees are *enabled* to use it, and that requires their understanding of the business goals, together with ample opportunities to learn and purposeful (confident) managerial support.

There is nothing particularly new about all this. Organizations have been searching for this release of employee creativity ever since people began to work together. The trouble is that managers in these organizations have been afraid to unlock this creativity. For too long creativity has been viewed as a threat to management power, and, sadly, during this time managers have believed that the successful management of staff is dependent upon the ownership of power. The culture of 'command and control' enablement grudgingly given – if given at all – is part of a power struggle and not part of a shared process of business development.

In 1994, the MCB University Press organized a European conference in Nottingham entitled 'Empowerment in Organisations'. The conference delegates and speakers arrived at a simple definition of empowerment as: 'a group phenomenon, creating increasing levels of employee involvement'.

Any customer when in conflict with a service provider is seeking nothing more than true employee involvement. The customer is involved in a service failure with no choice about the level of involvement. In other words, the customer's involvement is absolute. But how absolute is the involvement of the individual providing the service? Is this individual a junior or senior member of staff? What is the response to the customer? Is there resistance to involvement? Is there a desire to put things right or to avoid blame? The answers to these and other similar questions is to give the customer the opportunity to examine the culture of the organization simply by the way the customer is treated.

EMPOWERMENT AND CULTURE

Culture in commercial and industrial organizations can be defined as, 'the way people behave towards each other, or treat each other'. This is the internal culture, and what customers usually experience is the interpretation of this internal culture into the provision of an external service. What most customers do not think about, as they experience poor service, is that they are indirectly measuring the extent to which power is a protected commodity inside the service provider's organization.

How responsive to customer complaints is the organization, both in terms of time allocated and creativity of solution? Hierarchical company structures tend towards hierarchical ownership of power. Executive power resides at the top and is apportioned selectively and traditionally down through the many levels of increasingly junior management. Everyone knows their place and their job description will describe the restricted scope the individual has for decision making and solution implementation. Oh yes, and there will be almost no evidence of informing, training, coaching and so on – or certainly not as a means towards employee involvement.

As companies delayer more and more, as businesses expect their people to demonstrate innovation, creativity and flexibility, the anachronistic relationship between management messages about empowerment and traditional management power-based behaviours causes more and more confusion for staff and customers alike.

CUSTOMER EXPECTATIONS

Just what *do* we expect as customers? Efficiency, responsiveness, satisfaction? Probably most of us would settle for being understood and made to feel of value to the service provider. As human beings, we have a basic psychological requirement for a sense of self-worth, that wonderful feeling of recognizing that being wanted and valued by others really does say something about one's own value to one's self. We leave school being told that we are about to enter the adult world. We arrive in our first job to be treated as an incompetent child; little wonder we have difficulty in adjusting to this new 'offer' of involvement (empowerment)! So what's different about being a customer? Well, as customers, we suddenly have control once again – the customer is always right.

Customers sometimes know and sometimes don't know what they want. True or false? Actually, the whole statement is both true and false. As customers, we may walk into a shop without much notion of the particular product we are looking for. However, we will always have a clear notion of the type of service we expect to receive. We will, if asked, describe this expectation as (variously) courteous, helpful, polite, purposeful and so on.

A disempowered member of staff may still have a sufficiently high sense of self- worth to be polite and courteous, but they will find it difficult if not impossible to be helpful and purposeful. Who owns the decision-making ability to say, 'yes, we can put that right' to the customer?

As customers, our expectation is that any 'reasonable' request can be met by the person we are dealing with. Sadly, the service provider's culture may not understand this, or may understand it but not have the bravery to act upon it!

What, then, is 'reasonable'? There is no real problem in explaining this, since most businesses have their standards of performance quite well defined. Even those without clear definition will have an ability to describe these standards implicitly to staff. After all, without some ability to behave 'reasonably' towards its customers, the service provider will rapidly go out of business! Staff therefore have a sense of what the company accepts as reasonable behaviour from customers. The worst scenario is that in which the staff member has acquired this sense or understanding passively, without the support of a robust communication process. At best, however, the staff member clearly understands the full range and scope of service as it is available to be provided to any expectant customer.

Thus we begin to distinguish between the empowered and the disempowered service culture. The way in which managers treat staff (and each other) will be greatly influenced by the quality (for example, scope, range, frequency, relevance and so on) of the organization's internal communication system; the channel through which all staff receive information and supply feedback. This system is an essential component in the empowered culture and one which every one of us, as customers, expects to exist to the highest standard in an organization. Of course, as customers, we don't always realize this until we fail to get the service response we are looking for. In other words, customers expect perfect communications inside organizations. Conversely, organizations are confused about the true value of perfect communication and generally do not communicate very well.

HOW TO RECOGNIZE DISEMPOWERMENT

We have already seen that protecting a power base is paradoxical to the philosophy of empowerment. It is unfortunate that the word chosen to describe the philosophy and practice of 'employee involvement' has to include any reference to 'power' whatsoever. We know that empowerment describes a group phenomenon and enabling behaviours, both of which contradict the underlying principle of protecting a power base. So, how to recognize disempowerment as a customer?

The overseeing tendency

A large hotel chain carried out a survey of their conference customers. This also made them aware of the critical role of conferences for their profitability. Most problems were found to be related to the fact that hotels are production (for example food and beverage, room occupancy, housekeeping and so on) oriented. Individual guests seemed less dissatisfied by this attention to getting the product right. Conference guests – usually not paying individually but as part of a corporate package – tested the service element more fully. Hotel staff should have been given the responsibility of tackling dissatisfaction and additional demands quickly and politely in order to protect the corporate conference bookings and should have been empowered to make decisions during customer interactions. Instead, the hotel hierarchy placed functional managers as overseers and arbiters of customer complaints.

Lack of involvement

The above example describes how managers traditionally become involved in customer service difficulties: that is, they know their place, which is to oversee and step in when conflict occurs in order to 'pass judgement'. Employee involvement becomes compartmentalized. The staff member hands the problem to management. Management steps in, removing the need for the staff member to form a decision (and thereby the opportunity to learn), and the decision having been made, management then hands the placated situation back to the staff member. Discussion of the situation will, all too often, be dealt with as a blame-oriented reprimand of the staff member some time later.

Confused messages

'I want you to take full responsibility for this,' says your manager. Next day, you are expected to explain every move you made in the last twenty-four hours to the same manager.

This confusion is a particular risk during times of change. Culture change gives managers implied false messages about their loss of power. They become confused and create confusion in others simply by no longer understanding how to apply enabling behaviours without giving constant instructions. This aspect of culture change represents the biggest challenge to most managers.

Managers become pawns in the game of culture change. Their confusion causes them to give conflicting messages to staff:

'Take the initiative'	'Don't break the rules'
'Mistakes help you learn'	'Mistakes are costly'
'Show more flexibility'	'Don't break the mould'
'Think holistically'	'Just get results'

The left-hand list concerns empowerment, whilst the right-hand column describes traditional 'command and control'-based thinking. However, the values in the left-hand column require some management bravery to turn them into practice.

Working in organizations is not easy. Customers want responses from the left-hand side, and staff and managers are unsure how far to go. In this sense, the 'bubble' of empowerment is constantly being inflated and then 'punctured'. Customer expectations are not met because traditional behaviours stifle the expectation. Staff expectations are not met because their actions are restricted at the point of customer interaction. Confusion reigns!

The tendency to hinder

Service is nothing without underlying sales, creating the customer population. Most organizations recognize this philosophically, but do not extend this recognition in order to build a more integrated internal service base. Sales teams 'hand over' the results of their efforts to service providers who are frequently operating in a very different compartment inside the organization. Sales departments are frequently driven by performance measures through numbers, or value, of sales. Service is (or should be) driven by quality of service performance. There are clearly conflicting internal goals of quantity and quality which are kept apart. It is, after all, easier to manage a business in which functions are clearly compartmentalized rather than one in which functional distinctions blur and 'dovetail'.

Placing barriers between functions hinders empowerment. It prevents sales and service people sitting down together to discuss their best combined approach to customer satisfaction. There is a lack of fit between what an intended new orientation of empowerment demands and the existing functional processes of the organization. Thus these aspects of organizational performance hinder employee involvement and the development of flexible responses to customer needs.

Many traditional organizational and employment practices operate as considerable hindrances to true empowerment. Restrictive functional divisions, hierarchical and status-oriented pay and benefit policies, lines of communication heavily dependent upon union representation, are all examples of hindering tendencies. Empowerment programmes should become institutionalized, woven into the practices and values of the organization, a natural part of common work practice, in order to indicate deep culture change.

COUNTERING OPPOSITION TO CHANGE

'It cannot work here.' 'Our industry is too different.' 'We cannot manage quality that way.' Change is likely to be challenged. It should be – an organization with 'yes' people surrounding those in office will sooner or later be in trouble. However, less positively, good ideas and solutions will also be opposed.

Changes in market conditions must be responded to for commercial survival. Companies in a monopolistic situation may find themselves beginning to operate in a more competitive environment. Competition can be unnerved by a flexible, less predictable response, the type of response that often comes from an innovative, creative organization that is also able to deliver its response rapidly to the marketplace. Organizational and cultural practices may oppose employee-formed creativity (at the very least, it will not be rewarded) and the traditional thinker is disadvantaged by more innovative competitors. This form of opposition may be expressed in various ways: unsupportive technology, authoritative legal and administrative practices, adherence to historical beliefs and values. These are rational arguments which are sometimes found to have some real foundation. However, the opposing tendency stops these rational arguments being challenged and the opportunity for positive change is lost. In the service environment, customers frequently do expect to be treated with knowledgeable respect – behaviour which organizations guarantee to deliver through their managers but do not guarantee will come from employees, especially the less experienced. This is a rational argument which totally ignores the ease and worth of empowering all staff from the first moment they arrive in the organization.

Empowerment is liberating: it challenges the structure of power, status and privileges by challenging the organizational hierarchy. The core value of empowerment is that people can make judgement about service, can make decisions, and can control (or manage) themselves. In 'opposing' organizations, all this threatens management, particularly middle and junior management who are not given the education they deserve in order to become guides and coaches rather than commanders and instructors. Thus opposition is most frequently expressed through middle and junior management fear and confusion.

The principles and practices which create empowerment must be fully *495* understood so that disempowerment can be recognized and reversed. New territory must be explored and charted in order to build a visible and tangible process of empowering practices. A strategy for empowerment in the service sector must be based upon staff operating:

1 in a free-moving environment without the hindrance of restrictive practices;
2 amongst situationally supportive leadership behaviours recognized by their flexibility and appropriateness;
3 to the full extent of their individual and collective potential;
4 in the belief that their actions are valued by both the customer and the employer; and
5 in a way which truly reflects their desire to identify with the aims, objectives and values of the company.

EMPOWERING SUPPLIERS

The service chain is not complicated. It may be somewhat complex but this complexity is usually a reflection of the sophistication of the end product, not of the function of delivering service. Suppliers can rapidly become confused as they find themselves dealing with a customer going through culture change. Our current experience of culture change seems to require organizations to spend some time in a state of chaos as they 'defreeze', 'learn', and remobilize. How should the supplier interact with a customer in chaos? Probably the supplier has no mechanism to enable the process of responding to new and apparently irrational customer demands. You may know how halving delivery times will benefit your own customers, but have you explained this to your supplier? Suppliers all too often find themselves to be the losers in the effort by some organizations to gain the competitive edge through internal empowerment. Companies must remember that 'empowerment is a group phenomenon'. It must embrace all contributors to the customer service chain, particularly when the chain is complex. Service organizations which are concerned primarily with their own culture as an influence upon their own customers, build barriers between themselves and their suppliers, thereby making the process of delivering high-quality service stressful, time-consuming and costly.

Suppliers must be integrated with the culture change (empowering) process. They must be communicated with openly, frequently and honestly. They must be a collaborator, not an enemy. Customer service staff, however well intentioned, cannot demonstrate confidence and honest ownership of decisions if they have no faith in the supplier's ability to support them. Suppliers cannot provide the desired level of support if they do not understand the extent to which the customer's staff member is being empowered, and why.

Many large service organizations have been pleasantly surprised by the response they have received from their smaller suppliers when they talk to them about empowerment. When observed from outside, however, this is not particularly surprising. Smaller organizations find empowerment easier to put into practice and small supplier organizations are often further down the road to true empowerment than their larger, corporate customers. The message for large organizations is not to expect lack of understanding or resistance from suppliers – the reality is often just the opposite.

GIVING MANAGERS THE SKILLS TO EMPOWER OTHERS

Managers have to be able to make sense of the future in order to cope with and contribute to culture change. The future must, therefore, be described and 'available' to managers so that they are themselves empowered through the vision of customer service. The traditions of 'command and control' are based partly on the philosophy of 'daily orders': that is, managers being managed hierarchically and therefore managing others hierarchically, and communication being seen almost completely as a cascade of instructions without any invitation or opportunity for feedback. This situation leaves managers unable to release their own true potential and therefore unlikely to look for and release the potential in others.

Empowering managers are identifiable in that they:

- develop people's self-worth and their belief in their value to the organization;
- search for everyone's true potential;
- trust people to make their own decisions;
- talk about mistakes as part of the ongoing development of people; and
- interpret communication primarily as listening.

The danger is, of course, that managers display empowering characteristics only when commercial life is 'easy' and competition is not threatening profits. The challenge is to empower staff to take risks and potentially make mistakes during those times when commercial success is much harder. The paradox is that this is just the time when staff empowerment pays off. Empowered staff 'manage' the customers, while empowered managers 'manage' the business. The roles and responsibilities compliment each other rather than oppose each other.

RESISTANCE TO EMPOWERMENT

But what of those people who do not want empowerment and who are reluctant and even resistant to an empowering culture change?

The easy option here is to return to the opening words of this chapter! There is an underlying message here that managers must make the choice about making self-empowerment available to people. There are no guarantees that all staff will enthusiastically embrace a wide range and scope of new-found responsibility and authority, but is that what true empowerment is really about? No! True empowerment is based upon: *managers creating the empowering environment in which staff will choose to demonstrate their true potential.*

Everyone has their own individual level of true potential. Of course, as we mature, we become more and more conditioned by the environment and role-modelling behaviours around us. If these factors are in opposition to the 'empowering model', then we will resist empowerment when it is offered. If the role modelling is empowering, however, then we will be positively influenced through a demonstration of the value our organization places in the release of our full potential.

The short answer to unblocking resistance is to believe that no one is truly destructive to the requirements of customers and that everyone, therefore, has a contribution to make. Also, it is essential to build 'empowerment behaviours' into the policies and practices of good service business management. For example, does the recruitment and selection of staff include 'empowerment screening' processes, such as questions or exercises, to determine an individual's ability to value themselves?

Here are some questions which managers in the service environment should ask themselves:

- Do I give my staff time to understand customer needs?
- Have we discussed and defined customer service together?
- Have I described my perception of the scope and range of empowerment that is available to them?
- Have I used empowerment as an excuse to stop managing people?
- Do I simply blame people when they make mistakes?
- If I were a customer of my own service, how empowered would I want my staff to be?
- Are there any 'restrictive practices' blocking true empowerment of my staff?
- What can I do to unblock any barriers?

THE CUSTOMER'S PERCEPTION

Why do customers prefer to do business with empowered people? The benefits for customers are dramatic. For example:

- All staff are responsive to customers' needs at the moment of need. Customers do not have to wait for requests and resultant commands to be passed up and down a militaristic chain of command.
- Higher quality levels, all staff being 'share-holders' in the quality of service provided.
- Responsiveness is noticeably improved. Responses become more sensitive (empathetic) and flexible (tailored to the individual customer).
- Listening shifts from an internal focus to an external focus. External customers have more influence over the policies and practices of the business than internal (systems and procedures) factors.

In the context of customer service, customer satisfaction is measured to a great extent by the customer's ability to 'feel' satisfied. 'These are good people to do business with' is a tangible statement of a customer's perception of excellence. (Note 'a customer': that is, this statement is not necessarily an expression of total satisfaction from the entire customer base.) Herein lies the most powerful message of all about empowering staff in the service sector: *'It's not what you do, it's the way that you do it – that's what gets results'*.

Empowered staff should recognize that customers are individuals with individual, subjective needs and expectations. There can be no manual on staff empowerment, only constant role-modelled behaviours which are clearly responsive to customer 'whims'. We are all customers of each other and the best empowerment message we can tell ourselves is that which acknowledges our individuality.

As suppliers we always seem to know what is right for our customers! When we become customers however, our perspective changes, for customers are always very right-brained, irrational, unreasonable and demanding of perfection. There is thus always the potential for a mismatch here unless empowered staff can apply their own creative and flexible responses to customer needs.

PUTTING EMPOWERMENT INTO THE SERVICE ENVIRONMENT

Are there decisive actions service organizations can take in order to place empowerment at the centre of their cultures? Remember that empowerment is a group phenomenon and that staff and managers must therefore be offered empowerment collectively. Most businesses would recognize that this means working with people in teams and giving teams the sense of direction and purpose they require in order to choose to empower themselves.

An example of empowerment for teams would be built around the following steps:

- A clearly stated mission for the company.
- The opportunity for teams to decide what their role and contribution is towards that mission.
- Flowchart the progress of the team outputs.
- Identification of each team's customers and customer chain.
- Measurements of performance.
- Question what each team believes its customers expect of it.
- Teams take ownership of increasingly 'localized' customer surveys.
- Teams are given the authority, responsibility and know-how to be able to respond to survey results.

These steps allow teams to describe the values that they want to bring to their service culture. Because these steps are based upon clarity of company mission and the team's own contribution towards achievement of that mission, both company and team values become aligned. Alignment of values and beliefs is absolutely essential to the success of empowerment in the customer service environment. There will be no demonstrations of truly empowered *499* behaviours from individual staff if those staff are not part of teams which share belief in the values held by the business. Anything else is simply a superficial or cosmetic response to customers.

Superficial or 'thin' responses are vulnerable and become transparent when viewed through the customer's eyes. There are no short cuts to take when building a culture of empowerment in the service sector. This is why it is vital to take progressive steps to build a substantial and well-formed 'model' of empowerment. It is essential also to carry out constant maintenance to this model. Is everyone in the organization given a full sense of their own value to the business? Does substantial communication take place as a three-way flow – up, down and across the service provider's entire organization? Are managers constantly role-modelling empowerment behaviours. Are service teams operating with belief in the value of their actions? *Is empowerment truly your way of life?*

FURTHER READING

Brower, M. J. (1995), 'Empowering Teams: What, Why and How', *Empowerment in Organizations*, **3** (1).

Byham, W. C. with Cox, J. (1992), *ZAPP! The Lightning of Empowerment*, New York: Balantine Books.

Covey, S. R. (1992), *The Seven Habits of Highly Effective People*, London: Simon & Schuster.

Goldzimer, L. S. (1990), *Customer Driven*, London: Hutchinson Business Books.

Ripley, R. E. and Ripley, M. J. (1992), 'Empowerment, the Cornerstone of Quality', *Management Decision*, **30** (4).

35 Teamwork – the FedEx experience

Thomas O'Hearn

There is no secret to whatever success FedEx has enjoyed. What we do is in all the books. Our secret, if we have one, is just doing what they say.

Frederick W. Smith
CEO, FedEx

This quotation is an obvious starting point for what I have to say about the role of teams within FedEx. What my organization does is textbook stuff – you can read about it in any one of a thousand books that have been published on the subject of team work within organizations. All we do is apply it to our day-to-day business.

What is our day-to-day business? Well, if you don't already know, FedEx is the world's largest air express transport company. In fact, some say we invented the industry, but that's another story. At the time of writing we move approximately 600 million packages and 200 million kilos of air freight every year to and from destinations in more than 200 countries. To help us do that, the company has a fleet of nearly 500 aircraft and more than 110 000 employees.

It doesn't matter which way you look at it, with annual revenues of $8.5bn, FedEx, established in 1973, is now a substantial business and is growing all the time. The secret behind the company's rapid growth has been a total commitment to excellence – a satisfied customer after every transaction – and the only way that that can be achieved is, in turn, through total commitment to the people who make service happen day in, day out. To quote CEO Smith again: 'When people are placed first, they will provide the highest possible service and profits will follow.'

CORPORATE PHILOSOPHY – PEOPLE FIRST

FedEx's corporate philosophy, as expressed by its founder, is: people–service–profit. Simply, if you treat people fairly in terms of the way that they are managed and compensated for the job they do, if you communicate with them effectively and treat them with fairness and respect, then they are likely to be committed to the company and to its service excellence objectives, with the consequence that profits will follow. You can have all the technology in the world, but in a service business like FedEx, ultimately, you're only as good as the people who run the business.

Putting people first is hard work. Teamwork, the active and continuing involvement of people from across the business, is one of the intrinsic elements that supports the people–service–profit ethos, turning it into a practical management tool (as opposed to an abstract corporate concept) which directly affects every aspect of the organization.

RECRUITMENT AND PROMOTION

Cultivating a 'people first' environment starts with recruitment. FedEx expects its employees to be team players, which isn't to say that the organization wants to stifle individual creativity. In fact, far from it, but as the whole business is run on the basis of teams working together successfully to fulfil set objectives, identifying and selecting team players is critical. Line managers are ultimately responsible for recruitment decisions, with input from personnel as necessary. However, choice of candidate is based not solely on their skills, but also on their ability to fit into the existing team. As such, it is not unknown for members of a team to sit on the selection panel, with the final choice being a 'team' decision.

Whenever possible, FedEx strives to reaffirm the corporate philosophy, namely, that 'the people who are now working in the company are the future of the company', by encouraging promotion from within. An on-line computer job posting system provides non-management FedEx employees with a clear window on to the current paths of advancement open within the company, and that includes management.

Promoting people with solid day-to-day experience of the sharp end is a valid decision, whatever your business. However, making the transition from a non-managerial to a managerial position can be fraught with difficulties. No matter what the industry, failure rates can be as high as 80 per cent or more. But is it simply a question of not everyone being suited to management roles, or is it a lack of support? I suspect it is a bit of both. To provide support and help successfully evaluate leadership potential, FedEx operates the Leadership Evaluation and Awareness Process (LEAP) for all employees interested in entering first-line management. Team involvement has a distinct role to play in this process.

LEAP candidates attend an introductory 'Is Management For Me?' one-day class that familiarizes them with managerial responsibility. Assuming an individual candidate doesn't drop out at this point, the next stage is to complete leadership awareness activities. This is a three- to six-month period during which the candidate is coached and evaluated in leadership attributes. At the end of the agreed period, the manager makes a written recommendation supporting or opposing the candidate's bid for management.

Equally important is 'peer assessment'. Who better to ask if there are any obvious management strengths or failings in the candidate than those they currently work with? Asking the team's opinion helps maintain their integrity at a time when they may feel threatened by the impending departure of a key member. A minimum of three and generally no more than ten of a candidate's co-workers are selected by their manager to complete confidential assessment forms indicating whether they think the person is or is not a promising prospect for management.

A group of trained managers serve on the LEAP assessment panel to which candidates present written and oral arguments on specific leadership scenarios. They are then interviewed by the panel and a consensus decision on whether the candidate is suitable for managership is reached. Before issuing its opinion, the panel compares its decision with the findings of the peer assessment and manager's focused recommendation. The LEAP assessment panel is also used for external candidates for management positions, although peer assessment is not applicable for these.

So, as can be seen, there is 'team' involvement in both external and internal recruitment.

LEADERSHIP AND MANAGEMENT

Communication

FedEx views managers as leaders, and believes that leadership is not about power and building empires, but rather, that management is the ability to communicate the company's vision of excellence. The managerial role is to communicate that vision of excellence in such a way that others feel motivated to achieve its success.

Good managers are 'coaches and counsellors' rather than 'doers'. The people within a manager's team are the experts at their particular job, while the manager is their support, there to advise and guide the team. How many times have you met managers who are superb administrators, working the system day in, day out, but who are poor managers of people? Throughout industry and commerce around the globe there are companies which perpetually have demoralized staff, the result of managers who have no concept of leadership, communication and delegation skills.

Leadership development

Within FedEx the emphasis is on delegating more responsibility to teams, thus leaving managers free to concentrate on taking a more effective role in the training and personal development of their staff as well as forward and continued business improvement planning. To that end, all managers attend courses at the FedEx Leadership Institute which deals specifically with how to lead people, concentrating on the real meaning and practical application of leadership. The philosophy is a simple one: lead effectively, improve the skills of the team, and you improve the job being done, which takes us right back to *503* the underlying ethos of FedEx, people–service–profit. Get the first bit right and the other two objectives will quickly fall into place.

Appraisal

Appraisals these days are practised by many companies and are recognized as valuable means by which to assess morale and other issues. In FedEx, teams are asked to comment anonymously on the performance of their manager as part of a wider assessment of the company. You can't have satisfied customers unless you have satisfied employees. But how do you know whether they are content? To answer this question, FedEx 'takes the temperature' of the company with an annual questionnaire. *All* employees, from courier to chief executive, are invited to fill in the Survey Feedback Action (SFA) questionnaire. The first ten of approximately thirty questions are about 'my manager': for example, 'My manager keeps me informed about things I need to know', and 'My manager helps me find ways to do my job better'. In summary, these thirty or so questions are designed to elicit a team percentage approval/disapproval rating.

From this information the head office human resources analysis department tabulates the results, which are broken down by work group and then distributed back to both managers and employees in each group. At mandatory, formal feedback sessions, managers and their teams, often with a facilitator, meet to discuss the survey findings. This process helps to identify intra-group and inter-group concerns, from which formal written action plans for solving problems can be developed and then reviewed again on an ongoing basis.

Obviously, from this feedback every manager gets an immediate appreciation of how they are performing as leaders – as seen by their team. Even if the result is very favourable, managers are encouraged to improve. If the outcome is poor, then they are given every support to identify the issues and resolve them satisfactorily.

Every manager has an incentive to improve as their personal results from the SFA questionnaire are translated into a numeral measure known as the leadership index. First, this index establishes whether the company, as a whole, is successfully meeting its 'people' goal within the people–service–profit philosophy. Secondly, all managers' personal MBO plans incorporate leadership index goals. Meeting or exceeding people goals as well as service and profit goals, can qualify a manager for twice-yearly bonuses.

Of course, regularly monitoring the feelings and concerns of teams across the company also provides valuable management statistics that can identify broader issues or problems. For example, past surveys have identified health and safety issues, a lack of communications from 'the top' and so on, which it has then been possible to improve.

CUSTOMER SATISFACTION

504 As indicated earlier, FedEx has a clearly stated and consistent service quality

goal: 100 per cent customer satisfaction after every transaction with FedEx. That objective is enunciated frequently and pursued doggedly in innumerable ways, large and small, throughout the entire organization. But while this must surely be the objective of every company operating in increasingly competitive markets, in FedEx it isn't a fuzzy or intangible goal. Put simply, our job is to deliver something in perfect condition from A to B in the time we promise. Anything less than that is a service quality failure.

Service quality indicator (SQI)

FedEx has developed the service quality indicator (SQI) as a very effective mathematical measure of absolute service failures, designed as a catalyst to promote continuous quality improvement – a process, you won't be surprised to hear, involving teams.

Before looking at how teams are used in the process of continuous improvement it is important to understand how our SQI came about and how it works.

FedEx has always catalogued customers' complaints and in the early 1980s began to use this information in order to identify and eliminate the root causes of customer dissatisfaction. Dubbed the 'hierarchy of horrors', some common complaints were as follows:

- Wrong-day late delivery (a package delivered on a day later than that promised).
- Right-day late (package delivered on the promised day but after the promised deadline – even by one minute!).
- Pick-up not made (failure to make a pick-up on the day requested).
- Lost package.
- Customer misinformed by FedEx (mistakes or inaccurate information on rates, schedules and so on).
- No proof-of-delivery.
- Damaged package.

However, while offering a valuable insight into customer expectations and disappointments, this list also served to illustrate the fallacy in measuring customer satisfaction primarily in terms of on-time delivery. Although you may have delivered safely and on time, the customer may be disappointed or disgruntled with your service for any number of reasons (for example, a mistake in billing or an unhelpful voice at the end of a telephone). Also you need to differentiate the impact of different complaints on customer satisfaction. Simply saying, 'Oh, we get it right 95 per cent of the time' isn't good enough, and beware the company that uses such claims as an endorsement of their efficiency.

FedEx wanted to tap into the kind of information that would give management the capacity to be proactive in anticipating or eliminating customer complaints. The importance of understanding why a customer is disgruntled with your company cannot be underestimated in terms of achieving future growth and prosperity. For example, on a typical day FedEx handles 2 million *505* packages. If 99 per cent reach their destination on time, undamaged and with accurate paperwork, the remaining one per cent that fell short of those targets may represent 20 000 unhappy customers. Moreover, some customer service studies suggest that only 30 per cent of unhappy customers actually voice their complaints, which means that the remaining 14 000 customers could be looking for an alternative supplier and haven't bothered to tell us! You cannot afford to let that happen day after day if you want to stay in business.

Creating teams using teamwork is vital in solving those kind of problems, but to be effective there needs to be a structure within which to work and visible goals to work towards. With that thought in mind, a new approach to measuring service performance *and* customer satisfaction was developed. Service was defined from the customer's perspective as opposed to internal standards. A means of measuring actual service failures was evolved, as opposed to merely looking at overall percentage of service achievement. Each category of service failure was weighted to reflect its impact on customer satisfaction. With this information it would then be possible continually to track and measure (day-by-day as opposed to month-by-month) performance against the 100 per cent customer satisfaction and service performance goals. Once collated, the information could be fed back and employees could act accordingly.

From those objectives the *service quality indicator* was evolved. The various service failures and their weightings are listed in Figure 35.1.

Indicator	Weight
Complaints reopened	3
Damaged packages	10
Invoice adjustment requested	1
Lost packages	10
Missing proof of delivery	1
Overages	5
Right-day late deliveries	1
Traces	3
Wrong-day late deliveries	5

Figure 35.1 Service quality indicator

All are critical points in the service value chain. The higher the weighting, the higher the level of customer dissatisfaction.

It should be noted at this point, that a huge and continuous investment by FedEx in highly sophisticated tracking and tracing systems (which, incidentally, are also accessible to FedEx customers large and small) means that packages are monitored at every stage of the process, from pick-up to delivery. I mention this because access to such powerful technology makes identifying weaknesses and service failures a whole lot easier.

OWNING SERVICE QUALITY

Having created an *'open'* environment that is designed to empower people, along with the SQI providing detailed and accurate measurements of service failure and supported by sophisticated tracking systems, all the elements are in place to begin effectively to improve quality. Or are they? Unless there is a clearly defined quality structure within an organization and the concept of 'owning' quality understood by every employee from top to bottom, you will still find it very difficult to move forward.

FedEx has decentralized its quality structure (although various mechanisms remain for sharing information and quality success across organizational lines to spread the good news and ensure that nobody is trying to reinvent the wheel). Every division employs a quality administrator, who is responsible for fostering, coordinating and managing quality initiatives.

To achieve ownership of quality, the theory and necessary skills are developed in specific training programmes, for management and non-management employees alike. The FedEx Quality Academy (QA) develops and delivers training courses such as 'The Meaning of Quality', 'The Cost of Quality', 'Continuous Improvements', 'Problem Solving', 'Statistical Process Control', 'Leading Teams', 'Facilitation Skills' and so on. In essence, all FedEx employees learn about quality with the aim of equipping them with important process analysis techniques and problem analysis/solution tools, so that everybody in the company can speak a common 'quality' language.

As I said at the beginning of this chapter, FedEx isn't pioneering anything particularly new. Our *quality improvement process* (QIP) is constructed on techniques, terms and tools that have all been imported from existing management theory and literature, sometimes with the help of outside consultancies. Remember, the secret for success lies in the practical application of what has been learnt.

Quality action team

The *quality action team* (QAT) is our improved QIP technique taught in FedEx training programmes and then put into practice throughout the company. A QAT is, typically, an eight- to twelve-member, usually cross-functional, problem-solving team often comprising both management and non-management employees. These teams are formed to tackle persistent service-quality problems, pinpoint 'root causes', develop action plans to solve problems, and then implement and track the effectiveness of solutions.

At any given time there will be literally hundreds of QATs within the company dealing with a diverse range of problems. The issue could be entirely local and specific, such as finding a more advantageous way of transporting packages from an airport to a nearby sorting station. On the other hand, it could be a global issue such as making software enhancements to the company's main on-line tracking system.

Whatever the task, every QAT follows the same four-step problem *507* identification, assessment and solution process, known as FADE, which has the following structure:

1 **Focus** What is the problem opportunity? The **focus** phase represents the first big task in problem solving: selecting, verifying and defining the problem. A QAT selects a single 'critical' problem and defines it. The end product of the focus phase is a clear, written problem statement, which becomes the foundation for the remaining phases of the process.

2 **Analyse.** What do we need to know about the problem? The goal of the **analysis** phase is to understand the primary contributing factors, or root causes, that lie at the problem's source. Typically, this analysis includes gathering and evaluating related data stored in the myriad of information management systems within the company.

3 **Develop.** Development of an action plan/solution. At the **development** phase, a QAT builds on its analysis to brainstorm solutions that will eradicate the problem. Employees evaluate one solution against another and develop an implementation plan for the most promising one.

4 **Execute.** Implementing the agreed solution/action. At the **execution** phase, the team continuing commitment to its solution from within the organization, then executes the plan and monitors its effectiveness.

This process may seem straightforward and obvious. However, sit on any problem-solving group and you will be surprised at how many go from 'focus' to 'execute' in one step, and so fail to achieve the right solution first time because of a lack of analysis and a consequent lack of understanding of the problem's root causes.

For teams to succeed, responsibility and accountability are the keys to success. If the teams are managed to the last degree of detail they have no real need to think things through properly and be creative. Companies, to produce effective results, require the creative potential of teams, which all too often simply lies dormant. FedEx has found that genuinely giving responsibility and accountability to QAT teams is a great motivator. A word often abused in companies is 'empowerment'. If you really mean to empower people, give them all the tools, techniques and assistance they need, and then they'll succeed.

Recognition

Recognition is also important and FedEx has many reward and recognition schemes, which quite simply say to employees, 'Thank you and well done'.

Importantly, exceptional work by teams is recognised in a special way. Under the Quality Success Programme, teams are encouraged to submit their improvement projects to their relevant quality administrator. Following an evaluation process, about a dozen 'quality success stories', as they are called, are chosen from around the world. The relevant teams are then invited to present their success stories to the chief executive and the senior management

team at the FedEx corporate headquarters in Memphis, USA, the ultimate accolade. Once presented, they're free to enjoy a brief break from their usual activities and are able to experience FedEx's massive Super Hub in Memphis and also Gracelands!

Of course, quality success stories also present an opportunity beyond team building and employees motivation. By publicizing quality success stories on a quarterly basis within FedEx, good ideas can be replicated to progress continuous improvement throughout the company.

Dealing with problems

QATs look at the means to improve processes and systems as well as overcome obvious problems and failures. In the case of failures – whether it be failure in service, communications, training, safety or whatever – it's pointless trying to apply a superficial remedy to the problem, because that sort of solution is unlikely to last for long. So the emphasis is on eliminating the root cause of a problem.

This quest for root causes is vitally important. Often the concept is talked about as 'working on the main thing'. In other instances it is framed in the context of the 80:20 or Pareto principle, which separates problems into the significant few (that is, those that deserve the most attention and hold promise for the greatest positive impact) and the trivial many (that is, those which, even if solved, will not improve the problems in direct proportion to their numbers). This approach is certainly the one used to ensure that SQI 'failure points' decrease year over year against a corporate target.

If a category is not decreasing for some reason, *root cause teams* come into play. A root cause team can work locally, divisionally or by country. In Europe, the *service assurance board* oversees this kind of activity. It meets every six weeks to analyse SQI points in different areas and to identify any further areas of action. To date this has proved to be a powerful reinforcement for eliminating problems and improving service.

ISO 9001 ACCREDITATION

FedEx was the first air express transportation company to achieve global ISO 9001 accreditation, a process only made possible with concerted teamwork. Following the initial enthusiasm for ISO 9001 in industry and commerce, there has since been criticism from the pundits who claim that accreditation amounts to nothing more than documenting your own performance levels – good or bad. All I can say is that the critics can't have gone through what can often be the lengthy and expensive process of self-examination. No company would do it unless they were genuinely committed to providing service excellence.

Certainly as far as FedEx is concerned, achieving ISO 9001 has given an extra impetus to the importance of teams. During the accreditation process different teams examined local procedures, and identified and clarified previously unnoticed gaps that needed consolidation. In turn, the whole process clearly *509* verified, for both managers and employees, 'right things' which had to be done 'right' within the organization. Equally, we regard reviewing policies and procedures as an integral part of the continuing improvement process. Having a clear picture of *what you do* (that is, written documentation, flowcharts and so on), allows you to examine more clearly where improvements can be made.

Gaining ISO 9001 accreditation was time consuming. It did tie up resources. But the view throughout the organization is that it was a very worthwhile process to complete. However, as everyone who has been through the process knows, the difficult part is actually trying to maintain accreditation. With ongoing external surveillance audits being conducted every six months by Lloyds Register Quality Assurance to ensure that we are continuing to maintain the standards set by ISO 9001, teamwork will continue to be just as important as it was when working towards the initial accreditation.

CONCEPT OF INTERNAL CUSTOMERS

Another fundamental element to team development is the concept of internal customers. Again, this isn't particularly new, but it is perceived to have a high value and is rigorously applied within FedEx. It is supported by the inverted pyramid management hierarchy concept (see Figure 35.2), where the job of management is seen as supporting and serving the needs of front-line employees (that is couriers and customers service agents). These groups, after all, have more daily contact with external customers than most managers.

A shallow organizational hierarchy not only eliminates unnecessary bureaucracy, it also facilitates clear two-way communication of corporate goals.

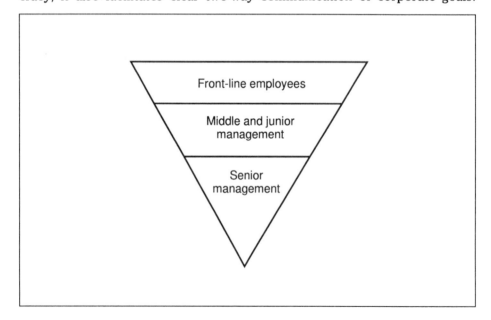

510 **Figure 35.2   The inverted management hierarchy**

Keeping a short distance between top management and front-line troops means corporate goals filter through the organization very rapidly and remain embedded within the working culture.

Teams are, of course, made up of individuals, and within any group there are bound to be cynics. Nevertheless, a lack of faith in team involvement and continuous improvement has to be addressed. Managers will only become enthusiastic 'converts' when they experience practical benefits. Perhaps the best anti-cynic measure is to communicate positive results. A continuous improvement programme should enable the manager to dissipate argument and clearly demonstrate practical results to the team. Simply, getting 'right things right' releases time and resources and gives you the opportunity both to motivate and to plan strategically.

CONCLUSION - PEOPLE FIRST

As I hope this chapter clearly demonstrates, effective teamwork is at the heart of everything FedEx does. The company is the first to recognize that the only certainty in the future is the permanence of change, and that in order to succeed, the people within the organization must constantly adapt to change. Ultimately, the only long-term competitive advantage is the people within the company – which is why we cultivate, at whatever cost, a people-first environment built on total team involvement at every level. That way we *can* achieve our main goal: *100 per cent customer satisfaction after every transaction with Federal Express!*

Part VI
MAKING THE MOST OF TECHNOLOGY

36 The call-centre concept

Dr Eve Carwardine

The use of the telephone in business is commonplace but frequently its usage is inconsistent and fragmented across differing departments, functions, teams and individuals employed by the organization. Therefore the perception of service through the telephone is equally patchy.

The use of the telephone by customers is, however, increasing. Some organizations have responded by setting up dedicated areas of their business to receive inbound telephone calls, and those employed in these areas are skilled in the business applications. These areas have evolved into the concept known as a *call centre*, which take one of several forms:

1 They may simply be a team known to be able to answer customer queries, with customers channelled to them via the switchboard, such as the accounts team.

2 As customer information centres, call centres have improved productivity for clerical processing within the organization by removing the interruption in the general business administration.

3 More sophisticated call centres have been designed to present the company image via the telephone and are staffed by specialists skilled in customer handling via the telephone channel. Today's well-known call centres have business objectives linked to customer service but there is still great scope for improvement.

4 Other organizations have developed business teams that utilize the telephone as an outbound channel to their customers. Whilst these are not necessarily described as call centres, they conduct business in a methodical manner, and together with inbound contact, should form part of the infrastructure for good customer service practice. The future of outbound calling will, however, be governed by European legislation.

The moment in which a customer comes into direct contact, whether face to face, over the telephone or via post, is the critical moment in that customer's perception of the service provided. Where the customer is channelled to a call centre, a number of aspects must be designed into the infrastructure to support the contact if the service is to be seen as good. A professional and consistent approach must be adopted, right from the opening conversation, through to a point of beneficial conclusion for both the customer and the organization, with seamless involvement by experts where required, explanations of activities when necessary, and all proper fulfilments and follow-ups.

Most ideas of customer service have their origins in the conception of pleasure – 'a pleasure to do business with', 'a delightful experience' and so on. Both parties gain from the encounter in a positive and beneficial way. Customers now recognize, or can be educated to recognize, that the more information they provide, and the better the relationship they develop with their service provider, the harder that organization will work for them. The customer must trust the organization not to take advantage of the information they have provided nor the relationship. The organization, in turn, must provide easy access to facilitate the relationship, and capture and utilize efficient processes to manage it, whilst still maintaining a cost balance. Call centres may have evolved to provide the economies of scale associated with these benefits, but it is a combination of the people, processes and technology in an operational infrastructure that must be applied in order to deliver cost-effective and innovative customer service that satisfies, delights and nurtures good relationships.

In summary, a call centre is that area in an organization where business is conducted by telephone in a methodical and organized manner, and its primary activity is consistently to execute telebusiness within a defined corporate style and procedures. A call centre is not a static business, and it must be reviewed and adapted at regular intervals to respond to the customer's needs. Benchmarking the call centre on all aspects is essential to ensure that the service is proactive to its customers. Each call centre is different because its customers are different, and what makes it different should be what makes it successful.

Whilst the call centre has developed as a concept, the term is often misused as a descriptor for telephony products associated with call delivery and handling, such as *automatic call distributors* (ACDs), *Centrex services, private branch exchange* (PBX) or *dialing direct inward* (DDI). Failures occur when calls are routed to areas of the business that cannot deliver service because they are not supported by an organizational structure, technical infrastructure and empowerment to respond to the customer. The infrastructure is not just the provision of access to core applications, nor simply the use of scripting tools. Best practice is achieved when processes are designed to support customer management and these processes should also include integration with customer databases, workflow and document management systems.

The technology of the call centre is realistically only the vehicle that delivers the service; it does not have to be completely owned by the organization. In fact, there are benefits in cost terms that can be achieved in outsourcing all or part of the call centre activities. However, much greater emphasis must be placed on the other principal component of the call centre, the people, and on the organizational infrastructure to support them, if call centres are truly to deliver exceptional customer service.

This chapter is therefore designed with the following objectives:

- to help you identify where you might be in the evolutionary path of call centre development;
- to demystify the technology of the call centre, both current and future; and
- to give pointers for improvements in call-centre procedures that will lead to better customer service practices in this evolving channel.

THE EVOLUTION OF THE CALL-CENTRE CONCEPT

Too much emphasis has been placed on the technology of the call centre. Nevertheless, in order to position your organization on the evolutionary path to better customer service practices it is important to describe here the technology involved.

Call-centre evolution is based on business applications which developed for inbound and outbound telephone activities. Like many technology-driven environments, the call centre concept has developed its own and sometimes confusing terminology. Staff who take and make the calls have differing job titles depending upon the industry and the task they perform, such as 'operator', 'clerk', 'customer service representative/CSR', 'telesales executive', 'credit controller', 'account manager' and so forth. Collectively, however, they are known as 'agents'.

Inbound business applications

Inbound business applications, where the call is originated by the customer, include the following:

- Help desks/advice lines
- Campaign response handling
- Customer care
- Account enquiries/transaction requests
- Dealer/broking
- Investor relationships
- Information provision/product enquiries

- Complaint handling
- Telephone banking
- Order processing
- Claims handling

- Credit authorization
- Repair services
- Emergency coordination

517

Initially, the provision of charge-free (0800 and 0500), local rate call (0345 and 0645) and newer 0990 services provided the impetus to use telephone response in marketing campaigns and so encouraged the development of tele-marketing units. Insurance and catalogue marketing companies, as well as specialist bureaux, sprang up using these services.

The development of specialist and proprietary computer software, known as scripting systems, followed. These systems provided a structure to telephone-based conversation as well as an ability to key in information and initiate fulfil-ments such as letter output, or activity scheduling. They made the telemarketing agents more efficient and equally they offered a consistent approach. Often, however, the systems were independent from the organiza-tion's PBX (private branch exchange or switchboard) and core computer sys-tems. They provided management information of agent performance and reporting capability for campaign success, whilst other organizations utilized PBX functionality (that is, call distribution and hunt groups) to direct calls to teams responsible for that aspect of the business.

Requirements grew for improvements in the quality of service to calling cus-tomers by reducing the delay in answering to a minimum and further increase agent performance. The *automatic call distribution* (ACD) and more sophisti-cated call-routing and call-handling systems were developed and employed to manage large volumes of incoming calls and also to distribute them among a dedicated group of extension users (see Figure 36.1). In addition, ACDs have the ability to cope with varying call volumes by managing the resources in peaks and troughs, giving measurements and performance feedback in the

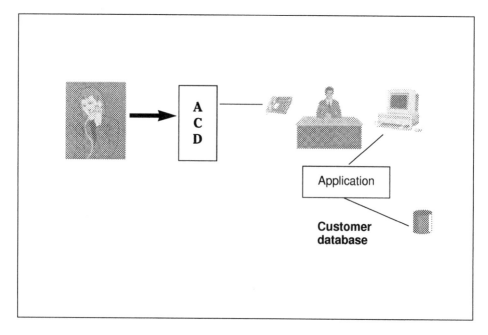

Figure 36.1   Call centre development/Stage 1: improving efficiency

form of call statistics that help managers to resource call centres in a cost-effective way.

When organizations employed the use of ACDs in conjunction with *dialling direct inward* (DDI), they were able to group agents together into functional groups. For example, a customer service unit could be divided into 'washing machine', 'dishwasher' and 'tumble drier' enquiry groups, thus allowing the customer the benefit of reaching a specialist first time and no longer requiring routing through an operator.

This stage in the evolution is where many successful UK operations are now established (for example, British Airways, First Direct and Directline). These organizations have demonstrated the power of the call centre in winning new, good quality business and in generating profits quickly. The two financial organizations – First Direct and Directline – have defined the word 'direct' as synonymous with doing business by telephone. Abbey National Direct, Bank of Scotland Direct, N&P (National & Provincial Building Society) Direct, and Virgin Direct (with Norwich Union) are examples of the followers.

The first steps towards technology-based improvements in customer service, related to the need not to repeat information, are achieved by the use of *computer-supported telephony* (CST) or *computer telephony integration* (CTI). Perhaps the important aspect of this stage is the ability for companies to have timely access to integrated management information on all aspects of customer handling, tracking the voice routing through the call centre and the data transmission history. Also new and faster access is available to customer profile information, enabling the transfer of data screen with calls within the call

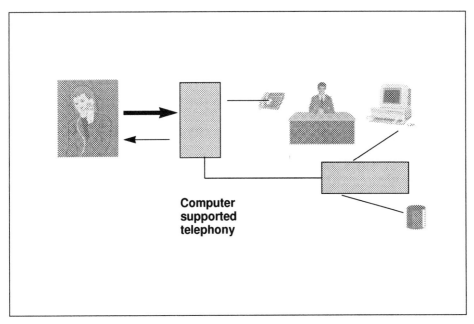

Computer supported telephony

Figure 36.2　Call centre development/Stage 2: integration

centre and then across a network, thus supporting the contact and improving the service offered to the customer.

This infrastructure allows the call centre to handle multiple campaigns for inbound and for *dialed number identification service* (DNIS) to automatically pull up – known as 'screen pop' – the appropriate screen with correct information about the customer or product. From the organization's perspective, this facility also allows the automation of outbound dialing for fraud prevention, telesales, customer reactivation and cross-selling.

Outbound business applications

Outbound business applications, where the call is originated by the service organization, include the following:

- Credit control/debt management
- Market research
- Building and maintaining marketing databases
- Fund raising
- Invitation to events

- Reactivating lapsed accounts

- Appointment setting
- Servicing small and low-margin accounts

- Telesales

- Testing marketing
- Account servicing and customer loyalty building
- Welcome call/anniversary call
- Lead generation/prospect tracking
- List building, cleaning and testing
- Fulfilment follow-up

In their simplest form, computer-generated lists are used to identify customer information prior to contact, and trained agents use standard telephone facilities to generate business. All cleaned lists are then returned for data entry. This system is inefficient in agent time because of the 'ring no answer' (RNAs) and 'engaged' call-backs which have to be manually rescheduled and, in addition, it is heavily dependent upon technicians to manage the data.

Various automated dialling techniques have been developed to improve the number of contacts made. For example, if a number is typed into a computer application it can then be sent to an autodialling device or telephony switch that would automatically generate the correct signals to emulate the telephone agent using the telephone handset. This is the simplest form of automatic dialling and is the basis of all other options. Generally, this capability is used in alliance with some form of computer software, which, at the lowest level, could be a personal electronic diary.

With preview dialling, the agent is presented with details of the customer to be rung prior to the system attempting to dial that customer and the call is initiated after a preset interval or by a keystroke. Customer information is bespoke to support the call and access is normally available, through the computer, to additional information (for example, a history of customer contact).

From this point, intelligent systems have been developed to boost sales and reduce waiting time between contacts. The main principal of intelligent dialling is that the agent is presented with a continuous series of voice connections. These technologies tend to be used with high call volumes usually linked to short call durations, or environments that have a high rate of replies which are 'busy' or 'no answer' – typically, the business process handled by consumer sales and marketing departments.

The terms used for the technology options are often interchangeable and are the domain of the power, anticipatory and predictive dialers. In general, power dialling is carried out by a special telephony device that is loaded with a file of numbers, either batch or on-line, which are then called at predefined intervals. They have answer detection capabilities and will route calls to an available agent. 'Busies' and 'no answers' are handled automatically and redialled as appropriate.

The next step up from this is available both on the type of device used for power dialling and on software which can control other telephony devices. Rather than simply dial at preset intervals based on the number of agents and number of calls answered, anticipatory devices 'anticipate' when an agent will be free. This system is based on a calculation of the average call duration and the number of calls to be dialled to provide an 'answer' connection, and by dialling ahead will attempt to provide agent connections as soon as each agent becomes available.

Predictive dialling technologies utilize an algorithm, based on factors such as average call-hold or queue time, number of agents available, call preparation time and the telephone contact rate, to drive the outbound dialling. This algorithm can be dynamically managed. Where connection was made and no agent was free, some systems fed to a voice response unit. This has been the subject of nuisance call debates and has had a poor impact on customer service, so this is now governed by Direct Marketing Association (DMA) code of practice in the United Kingdom. In the United States, recorded announcements (RANs) are often played until an agent is available.

Combined inbound and outbound technologies

Call-centre developments have encapsulated the use of inbound and outbound technologies as the next stage in their development (see Figure 36.3).

The market is littered with failure stories of the use of voice response systems linked to customer acceptance. These are related to the earlier low usage of *dial tone multi frequency* (DTMF) telephones and the older telephone exchanges, as well as the older and mechanical-sounding nature of these systems. There is also confusion with *automated voice response* systems which

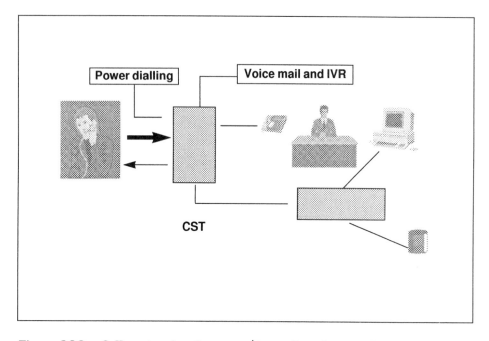

Figure 36.3   Call centre development/Stage 3: serious outbound calling

automatically answer calls and rely upon database vocabularies related to the purpose of the call.

Today modern call centres use *integrated voice response* (IVR) with greater success. With this system they are able to test and adjust the scripts, menus and use agent voice recording. IVR can be used as a front end to filter or to route callers to specific teams or messaging services, which is particularly useful to a customer who is waiting to be answered. Through effective IVR, the caller can be informed how long it will be before an agent is available or what his or her position within a queue is. The system also offers an alternative option for the caller to leave details of the nature of call, contact number and the convenience for call-back.

Other filters can be applied to cover the security angles, such as account number and personal identification number (PIN), so that the agent is in full possession of all necessary information at the start of the call, the customer's name. Live operators do provide greater warmth, and they can also deal with off-script queries and ask the caller to repeat unclear information, all of which ensures a higher percentage of useful calls. For example Nations Bank in the United States handles 77 per cent of its business by IVR alone.

At this stage, the call centre may introduce call recording for tracking financial instructions such as share dealing, and may use inbound RANs (for example, latest company information or music) on hold to improve customer service, ride out the peaks in call volumes and refine their internal efficiency.

522   Figure 36.4 shows the latest developments in call-centre technology where

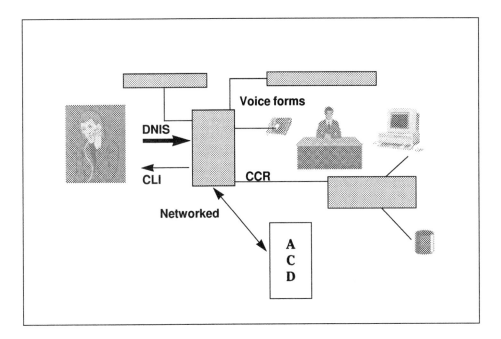

Figure 36.4   Call centre development/Stage 4: intelligent call blending

balancing is made between inbound and outbound traffic to suit the demands and opportunity. Many additional technologies can be integrated here as well (for example, fax, image, smart phones, personal computers (in the home), multimedia and so on).

BT has provided a service that transmits the number you have telephoned from, the *calling line identification* (CLI) to be displayed on caller identification equipment. Integration between the ACD and databases can then be used to prompt particular applications or customer information. The *call return service* (that is, where an organization or individual enters a code to hear the last caller's number or automatically dials that number) can be employed to check abandoned calls. It is still difficult to see how this can be used in some sectors, where customers phone from their place of work but it can be utilized in emergency services. For example, the AA use CLI integrated with a database to identify the location of the caller, and IVR to validate membership before contact with an agent and initiation of rescue services.

The dialled number identification service (DNIS) integrated with a database can be used to route calls to particular agents (for example, 0800 222000 for new prospect handling, 0345 100100 for customer service at First Direct). Customer controlled routing (CCR) is used to give the caller individual treatment. It is based on CLI and on the previous history of calls from that number and record of the previous agent handling those calls. New calls can be routed to the regular agent, account manager or at least that group.

ACDs can be networked to make the best use of the resources in peak times *523* or alternatively to provide call free routing to the service centre best placed to handle the call. They are sometimes known as 'virtual call centres'. In essence this is several groups of agents, usually in geographically separate locations, that are treated as a single call centre for management, scheduling and call-handling purposes. These virtual centres might take advantage of a private telephone network for sophisticated routing between locations, or they may use the public network along with features that are provided through the carrier. A good example of this is seen in BT's service centres: residential and business sales (150 and 152 respectively), and residential and business repairs (151 and 154). The caller dials one number and is routed to a location or specific *customer service representative* (CSR). This allows BT the choice of management of distribution dependent on volumes. They also stagger billing throughout the United Kingdom so that they can manage the resultant queries across the virtual call centre environment.

In terms of customer service, call centres must test their customer base to ensure satisfaction is measured and thereafter adjust the service in line with their findings. Benchmarking the service against the customer requirements is essential to proactive customer service improvements. For example, BT use independent *customer surveys* to measure the service they provide; the type of enquires are captured and analysed and what was done to resolve a problem. These data are then fed back into a service quality improvement programme so that business customers can be informed of developments in the improvement process. Residential customers only become aware when they next use the service.

Future call centre enhancements will be seen with the uptake of home or teleworking, where satellite office and telecottage industries are already developing (see Figure 36.5). Whilst this requires management and security controls, it provides an ability to use skilled staff who may not wish to travel into a dedicated centre.

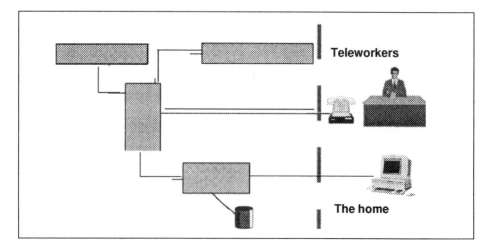

Figure 36.5   Call centre development/Stage 5: flexible working

Other chapters in this *Handbook* will cover in greater depth future developments in all related call-centre technologies.

BEST EXAMPLES OF US AND UK CALL CENTRES

Call centres in the United States are generally more advanced than their counterparts in the United Kingdom. They also provide a cost-efficient channel; in 1993, business worth $220bn was conducted through US call centres. In Europe, the Henley Centre predicts growth in employment in call centres from 0.7 million to eight million by the year 2000.

The *1994 World Almanac and Book of Facts* gave the numbers of people served by each telephone in individual countries. In this respect, the United States and the United Kingdom have the same profile (see Figure 36.6). So one might expect the take-up eventually to be similar in both countries. The UK population is seen to be one which uses the telephone more readily to contact each other than the US population. However, the US usage of the telephone is significantly higher than the UK usage in terms of minutes per day.

Unfortunately, due to the newness of the concept, no one organization in either country can be named as the best example. However, the organizations listed in Figure 36.7 have been awarded customer service accolades and they exhibit aspects of call centre development that put them in the top of their class.

CUSTOMER SERVICE BY TELEPHONE

What proportion of customer service is destined to be delivered by telephone in the next five to ten years? In the most recent survey conducted in the United Kingdom, by telecommunications marketing consultancy Schema, a spectacular rise in computer-supported telephony (telebusiness) systems over the next eight years was predicted, from the current European base of 600 systems to

Denmark	1.2	**United Kingdom**	**1.9**
Switzerland	1.2	Australia	2.0
Canada	1.3	Greece	2.2
Germany	1.5	Japan	2.3
Netherlands	1.6	Spain	2.5
Norway	1.6	Ireland	3.8
France	1.7	Hungary	5.5
Italy	1.8	Poland	7.5
United States	**1.9**	Guatemala	36.0
Belgium	1.9	Bangladesh	572.0

Figure 36.6   Numbers of people served by each telephone in individual countries

United States

Alverno Receivable	American Express
Ault Foods	Bank of America
Banc One Mortgage	Carlson Wagonlit Travel
Dow Jones	First Hawaiian Bank
First National Bank of Chicago	Gottschalks
(Cash Management Services Division)	(West Coast Retail Chain)
Kellogg	Novell
Massachusetts Registry of Motor	Los Angeles Department of Water &
Vehicles	Power
Pitney Bowes	San Francisco Chronicle
State of Illinois Department of Revenue	The Parri/Lee Agency
US Department of State	United States Postal Service

United Kingdom

Automobile Association	Abbey Direct
Alliance & Leicester/Girobank	Amex
Bass	Birmingham Midshires Building Society
Bristol & West Building Society – Asset	British Airways
British Telecom plc	Direct Line Insurance
First Direct	IPC Magazines
Mercury	National Breakdown
NatWest	RAC
Royal Bank of Scotland	Rover Group

Figure 36.7   Leading organizations in call service development

over 33 000 by the year 2000. The Henley survey showed that service applications currently account for some 40 per cent of all telebusiness applications, with sales and marketing at 27 per cent and information distribution at 9 per cent.

There is no doubt from my own consultancy experience in the United Kingdom that the benefits/costs/risks to customer services are now being strongly emphasized, and rigorous analysis of these parameters in the establishment of the telephone channel is being carried out. For instance, in the financial services and utilities business sectors in the United Kingdom, where service is seen as the differentiator, all the big institutions are setting up call centres or developing better front-line customer-handling capabilities with defined customer service objectives.

With Mondex (electronic cash), multimedia (ability to involve live transmission/video/contact with expert staff and sharing of other applications), services on demand via television at home, and the potential of the Internet, the telecommunications global infrastructure is gearing itself to handle dramatically more traffic of all types in the next five years. With margins greatly squeezed, the level of customer service delivered through these avenues will greatly affect which businesses survive and the way in which they conduct their business. In the short to medium term, the call centre can and will become the main vehicle for service, such as home shopping on the *digital superhighway*.

THE ADDITIONAL BENEFITS OF A CALL CENTRE

A call centre is more than just a place to receive calls! As can be seen from the call-centre developments outlined above, the working environment is uniquely designed to receive and update core business information on its customers (see Figure 36.8). Making it easier for the customer to access the organization, guiding them quickly and efficiently through the process of obtaining the service (whether at the time of contact or on subsequent follow-up), giving the customer the degree of control they require, measuring the behaviour and perception of the service process – these are all functions within this infrastructure.

The greater the role the customer has played in the service, the higher their emotional involvement. They become involved in the service, and as their

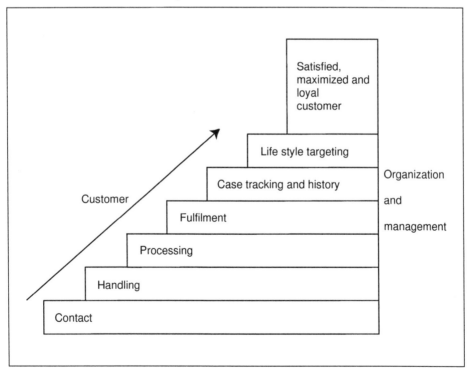

Figure 36.8   Gathering core business information on the customer   *527*

perception of 'good service' improves, so this is more likely to lead to loyalty and recommendation.

Accurate customer information can be collected – at the point of contact when the customer is keen to supply it – to update the core computer applications. If a customer database is integrated into the call-centre infrastructure, it can be refreshed with information, such as complete address, all contact telephone numbers and convenient times to call. With calling line identification (CLI) the number of the person that is calling can add information to that which did not exist historically on the accounts systems or customer databases, thus furnishing tangible benefits to customer contact management.

Cost benefits can be applied in terms of the corporate channel strategy. Here customer acceptance of outbound calling can be included in the customer profile so that when information is to be supplied to the customer, the most cost-effective method can be calculated. As a prime example, the banking code of practice will ensure that banks give 14 days' notice of charges to be levied on customers' accounts. A customer profile could show that this may be achieved through a cheaper telephone contact than via the postal service. Provided that this was audited the bank could show adherence to the code. Contact by the telephone could ensure that problems are addressed in a proactive manner and this results in a perceived improvement in service.

The term 'The Martini customer – any time, any place, anywhere' has been coined to describe a modern financial services customer. The channel the customer uses is dependent upon its convenience. Typically, contact can be made through branch, retail financial services outlet, intermediary and differing functions in the organization. Tracking this contact provides the opportunity to gain control, and to test requirements for further information and follow-up (for example, diarizing specialist resource, conformation of account change, new product introductions and so on). The call centre, as part of this unified environment, would have access to this information, or even be flagged to provide it and to qualify the customer for other products and services on an inbound call.

Call centres are therefore an alternative and more cost-effective channel than the retail outlets. They capture customer details that are not typically captured at retail point of sale, and they offer immediate results in comparison with the longer postal service.

Customer enquiries often lead to fulfilment activities such as output of letters, product information or financial services. Whilst fulfilment audit provides valuable information given to the customer, tracking this in workflow systems can generate benefits in customer control, customer service, customer reaction to and satisfaction with the service provided, and valuable marketing information, as well as controlling the efficient scheduling of work.

There are definite benefits to cost control here too. By doing more than just capturing the call, by feeding back information to organizational databases, costs are driven down. The payoff comes when a totally integrated approach is taken (see Figure 36.9).

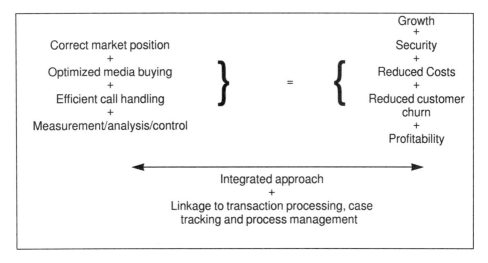

Figure 36.9 A totally integrated approach to customer management

DELIVERING SERVICE VIA THE TELEPHONE

Call centres can deliver service over the telephone by the following means:

- Providing a single point of contact and seamless access to other resources at a cheap rate to the customer.
- Resolving queries in one telephone call.
- Monitoring and managing customer expectation.
- Providing a consistent approach.
- Delivering timely, appropriate and relevant information.
- Providing reassurance and ownership of problem resolution.
- Providing an environment in which to learn about the customer and thus better place the organization to care for and react to its customer base.
- Treating the customer as a customer and not an account number.
- Providing the friendly and customer-facing contact point in an organization.

SUMMARY

It is far less painful to learn from someone else's mistakes than your own. Some important lessons have already been learned regarding setting up call centres, and these should be carefully considered, as follows:

- Corporate customer service objectives should be set in the strategic business plan.
- Benefit/cost/risk analysis is very necessary.

- Seek consultancy advice on implementation, but have an executive sponsor.
- This is not a traditional information technology (IT) area; IT just forms part of the bigger picture.
- Call centres deliver effective business process automation.
- Organizational structure is different from traditional business structure.
- The centres are often staffed by part-time staff who work non-traditional hours in rotas linked to call volumes.
- Call centres must interface to marketing and other business operations, with service level agreements established between them.
- All customer contact must be managed, and supporting information must be available in the call centre as well as other parts of the business.
- Businesses must accept that they cannot capture all calls and be cost-effective, but between 90 and 95 per cent of calls can be captured with dedicated operators.
- Customers must be offered an alternative to waiting in the queue.
- This environment provides a valuable cross-fertilization across different products.
- This is not a static environment.
- Benchmark against your customer base and 'best in class'.
- Don't accept assumptions – test, test and retest.
- Don't accept external 'norm'. Your customers are *your* customers.
- Management control and involvement is vital.
- Monitoring and reporting of exceptions aid control.
- Build a total support infrastructure. This can be achieved in phases, with each phase bringing benefits.
- There is a need for the *total quality* and *continuous improvement* mentality.
- Develop a customer services culture.
- Some activities – or even the whole call centre – can be outsourced.
- There are many ways to achieve integration, and all must be assessed for your organization and customer base in terms of benefits/costs/risks. Each step may provide improvements in effectiveness but 'the whole is greater than the sum of the parts'.

Remember, above all, that it is people who make the call centre work, not technology.

37 Harnessing new technology
Martin Meikle-Small

In many markets customers are now fully aware of how many organizations are vying for their business. Ever-increasing advertising opportunities, direct marketing campaigns and cross-selling strategies are raising customers' expectations of service when they do contact a business.

In parallel with this, there is an increasing motivation to 'shop around' for the product or service that the customer really wants. The modern customer is less likely to go for a year-on-year renewal of a service or repeat product purchase. Instead they will put a varied amount of effort into finding the 'best purchase'. Combined with the prevalence of the telephone as a tool with which to do business, it is not surprising that an efficient and effective telephony channel is such a powerful strategy for a modern organization.

The rise and rise of the telephone and the personal computer lead to a gradual acceptance (at least within certain segments) of other technologies as tools for provisions of an efficient service. For example, well-implemented voice response systems now encounter low resistance. On the computing side, the provision of service via on-line systems is set to expand dramatically. Multimedia kiosks are appearing in high-street locations as an adjunct to traditional forms of service, and are being used. The growth of the Internet community is climbing at a staggering rate, and as the multinational computer software and hardware suppliers join in, accessibility of service over the modem links will soar as well.

AUTOMATION

The drivers for automation

Whilst the brave new world that the media present is all very exciting and glamorous, however, the reality of the situation from the provider's perspective is the increasing competitiveness of the wider marketplace in which they find themselves. To help them in this climate, companies have a number of very clear business drivers for the automation of their operations which can be summarized into four main strategies: reduce unit cost; increase revenues; improve service quality; and segment the customer base (see Figure 37.1).

It is easy to claim that all four strategies are crucial to success, but segmentation of the customer base (for example by demographic factors, by product, or life-cycle analysis) allows for the identification of the most important driver for each segment. It is critical that the key driver is identified if you are to build a business case for automation and quantify the resultant benefits.

Reduce unit cost

Increasing competitiveness in the marketplace means that there is huge pressure on product and service margins. The high cost of sale and the ongoing cost of service have therefore to be reduced in order to make that customer segment or particular product profitable. This situation might require an increase in the overall productivity of call-centre agents. Using the analogy of the call centre as a machine, the need is to gain the same performance out of the machine for less input. Changing the method of sales and service using automation is one way of achieving this.

Increases revenues

In an environment where companies need to maximize the revenues available from every customer in order to maximize profitability, automation can pro-

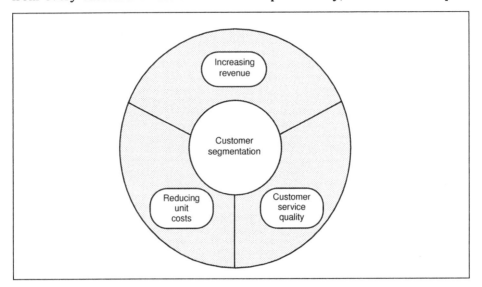

Figure 37.1 Four main strategies driving the automation of a company's operation

vide a valuable role. Analysis of call types will furnish data on how many of the incoming calls were real sales leads from important customers who value the service you offer and so remain loyal to you. Automation, by handling easily answered questions or by filtering out calls from people whose business you do not or cannot take, can enable you to deal properly with the most important calls. Alternatively you may wish to handle peaks in call volumes (for example caused by direct response television advertisements) by keeping people in a queue or by capturing their details and calling them back. In this way, any opportunity for additional revenue will be taken. Still following the machine analogy, this driver should enable you to obtain more output from the machine for the same input.

Improve service quality

In an environment where there are an increasing number of competitors, companies are looking for effective ways to differentiate their offering. Improving the level of service they can offer, or the efficiency of the sales process, are ways of achieving this. In this respect, automation can help in a number of ways. For example, it may be able to improve the speed or efficiency of the basic process or processes; or it may allow companies to offer a new service such as 24-hour information, or an anonymous service. Alternatively, companies might pass the savings made through automation on to the customer in reduced service charges.

Segment the customer base

Another widespread way of improving the level of service perceived by callers is to ensure that it is tailored to their needs, a process which requires segmentation of the customer base in some way. Much has been written on the subject of segmenting customers, but suffice to say that it can be achieved in a variety of ways (for example by spend level, stage in the product life cycle, demographic factors and so on). Once this segmentation has been carried out, automation helps by providing a different service to these different segments, possibly by routing a certain segment to specifically trained operators, or by providing customer details to the agent's screen at the same time as delivering the call, thus enabling the agent to provide a higher level of service.

Where to apply automation

In the tight budgetary environment common to most organizations, it is important that the finite resources available in the call centre are deployed in the most effective way to meet the drivers outlined above. The matrix in Figure 37.2 can help determine where to apply resources and where to automate. It requires you to assess each process in the call centre against the following two criteria:

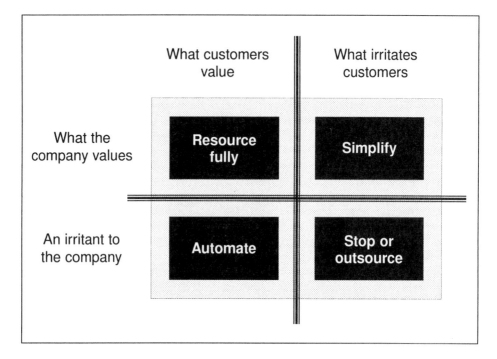

Figure 37.2   Matrix to determine the most effective deployment of resources

1   Do customers value this process, or are they irritated by it?
2   Does the company value the process or find it irritating to carry out?

The company's human resources should go into supporting processes in the top left-hand quadrant, such as answering in-depth questions on a high value product which might well lead to a valuable sale. Answering very basic queries on a simpler product might well fall into the bottom left-hand quadrant and so would be a target for automation, such as recorded information triggered from a voice-processing system menu.

Processes on the right-hand side of the matrix should require minimum effort on the part of the customer. Therefore simplify those that the company finds of value and if none values them, ask whether you should be doing them at all.

THE POTENTIAL INTERFACES TO A CUSTOMER

Most organizations have a number of channels for moving products and services to their chosen markets and for subsequently supporting them. In the past, sales channels have often been via a branch structure, or a third-party route such as a dealer network. The direct service channel, if it existed, tended to be via paper. However, companies are increasingly looking for a cost-effective and efficient channel for direct communication with end users. Hence the dramatic increase in the use of telephone-based sales and service.

Whilst covering the automation of the paper-based channel, this section con-centrates on the technologies applicable to the voice channel, and then goes on to consider the possibilities of moving to multimedia-based communica-tion. Here we will consider the possibilities for interactive video communica-tion as well as on-line service over the Internet and other PC-based computer networks.

Paper channel

Paper is still used primarily for legal purposes to offer, agree and pay for prod-ucts and services. The methods of improving efficiency are aimed at:

1 removal;
2 simplification; and
3 improved speed of handling.

The principle is to analyse the customer interface process including paper, voice and face to face. In many cases, introducing one extra contact with paper or voice will remove ongoing actions which increase cost. For example, explain-ing clearly the first bill a user will receive can reduce not only initial queries but also further telephone support calls. Simplification of text and messages or user instructions using simple English is a common theme in financial services, for it reduces end-user confusion and minimizes the need for help calls.

Another significant area of change is 'automation'. This includes scanning incoming paperwork using *document image processing* (DIP) hardware and software. The file can then be sent round the organization, using workflow soft-ware to follow the defined support process. Workflow is used to manage the hidden office processes using proven factory techniques. Management infor-mation is available to identify backlogs and problem areas. Electronic signa-tures can be used to sign off individual stages of the process, allowing greater empowerment whilst maintaining clear management procedures.

Preliminary applications have included departments handling insurance claims, which receive large volumes of claims documentation. Where a clear handling process has been established and implemented, efficiency improve-ments of up to 300 per cent have been achieved. Improvements have included improved speed of claims handling, accurate documentation, and implementa-tion of clear financial sign-off rules.

As hardware and software costs drop, these technologies are set to make a significant impact on call-centre efficiency. Agents will be used to handle inbound/outbound mail and telephone calls, thus minimizing back office func-tions and overheads.

Voice channel

To understand the possibilities for automation of the voice channel we will *535* consider a typical call as consisting of three main elements (see Figure 37.3), as follows:

1   The initial (and sometimes subsequent) handling of the call in order that it can be answered by the most appropriate agent.
2   The data that the agent needs to get from the caller in order to deal with the reason for the call.
3   The output from the transaction (for example, information provided back to the caller or the processing of an instruction from the caller).

The technologies that will be discussed in this section are each capable of automating or simplifying one or more of these elements.

Automatic call distributors (ACDs)

ACDs are the core technology component of most call centres, providing the basic call-handling capability required for an effective operation.

Basic private branch exchange (PBX) functionality found in a normal office telephony situation, is designed to allow one caller to reach a specific person, either from outside into the office or vice versa. Whilst an ACD consists of the same basic switching capability, the software is written to allow a queue of callers to be connected to any one of a pool of agents. The similarity of the basic components of ACD and PBX means that many PBXs also offer ACD function as an additional feature, although it is important to check that such software does not conflict with other configurations required in the main PBX functionality.

The main driver behind ACD functionality is the equality of distribution of calls. In essence it ensures that if there is ever an agent free who can handle a waiting call, then the call is routed to that agent. All agents therefore have an equal chance to handle calls and so the workload is shared evenly between these agents. In more complex environments this is not necessarily totally true (some exceptions are discussed later), but it is generally the case. For the caller this also provides equality, in that the calls are placed in a queue and answered in order. Moreover, queueing time is also generally reduced as calls are answered as efficiently as possible.

The other main function of an ACD is the essential management information

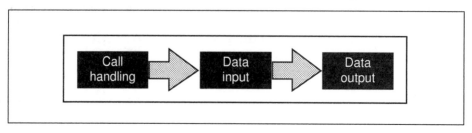

Figure 37.3   Three main elements of a typical call

that it provides on the calls being handled and on the agents themselves. Most ACDs offer both real-time information for an immediate view of the situation and historical data for analysis of performance over time. Real-time information is normally available to supervisors' and managers' computer screens for a detailed view, and sometimes on a large wallboard, which enables all agents to see basic, generally statistical, information, such as the number of calls being handled, currently queueing and, most importantly, not being answered before the caller hangs up. The information assists in the management of the call centre by providing a picture of the overall service level being provided to callers. Combined with a scheduling system this allows the managers and supervisors to plan the staffing levels required to maintain or improve performance. The system also gives information on individuals' performance for measurement and development purposes.

One other area of increasing importance in today's call centres is the control over call routing which an ACD provides. It is generally possible to have different queues of callers routed to different groups of agents, either on part of the same ACD or on one networked to that ACD which facility offers the following features:

1. The ability to vary the service provided, based on factors such as:

- time of day;
- number of agents with particular skills available;
- number of calls waiting to be answered;
- inputs from voice processing systems (see later section); and
- number dialled by customer (to provide special service lines).

There are many other factors and their extent depends on the functionality of any particular ACD. This is known as conditional routing. Often a system will have template routing tables that a supervisor can activate very quickly as necessary to deal with changing or special circumstances.

2. The ability to identify agents as having specific skills suited to handling certain calls, and then routing those calls to them whenever possible. The sophistication of the ACD determines the extent of this functionality. For anything other than a small call centre, when there are several skill requirements (for example, service, billing and faults call types in either English, French or German), the permutations can quickly become very complex.

The main impact of ACDs is in the improved quality of call handling with more calls being answered, or at least answered faster. For the agents, the handling of calls is improved with dedicated turrets that make all telephone-related operations simpler to do. For the supervisors and managers it is the information available which is critical. Most systems allow agents to enter a 'wrap up' code into the system to log the nature of the call, which affords very useful analysis of the actual service that the call centre is providing to callers. The ACD also allows callers to queue, often with messages to increase *537* patience, rather than simply being turned away whilst all agents are busy. It is always desirable to be able to divert overflow calls to other agents so as to ensure that all calls are answered by someone. ACDs generally provide the hooks to allow integration to further automation such as voice processing and computer telephony integration, which will be discussed below.

Not surprisingly, all these functions carry a premium and so a fully featured system is a significant investment. It should also be noted that the nature of ACD call handling is not suited to all environments. For example, a specific agent cannot usually be called directly (they may not even have an explicit extension number), which may not be acceptable when a highly personal service is required.

The market for ACDs can most easily be segmented by system size. Whilst there are large variations in the capacity and functions of the systems, it is broadly possible to identify the following categories:

1   Dedicated ACDs with upwards of fifty agents offering the most sophisticated functionality.
2   Standard systems with anything from 10 to around 80 agents, which are generally based on large PBXs with added software functionality.
3   Small systems suitable for help-desk environments of up to 15 agents. These are based on the smaller PBXs available, with the required software upgrade.

Selection of the most suitable system is dependent on first analysing the business requirements of your operation (discussed at the end of this chapter). However, issues for selection which must be considered are:

● Basic design parameters such as capacity, information provision and routing control, available interfaces, turret design and functionality.
● Company specific issues such as effectiveness of pre-sales and after-sales activity, software and R&D policies.
● Initial capital costs and the ongoing operational costs.

The future trends for ACDs are towards an integrated call-centre environment, where the ACD is fully integrated with computer systems to further enhance call handling. Such integration will become easier and cheaper as certain de facto standards emerge and are implemented by all suppliers. In addition, inbound and outbound calls can be integrated, with agents being automatically assigned to handle whichever calls are required to meet demand. Management information systems will become more sophisticated, simpler to read through the use of graphical user interfaces, and more widely available to anyone who might wish to access the information. Networking of ACDs over private or public networks will be more common, allowing the development of virtual call centres. For example, it will be possible to have several call centres distributed across Europe that can be managed as one operation, with skill and language routing across all sites. In addition, the ability to provide ACD functions to remote locations such as homeworkers will become simpler. This offers the possibilities of using remote staff as overflow in peak times or as a way of reducing office overheads, and also of attracting staff otherwise unavailable for work. In the longer term the intelligent network will provide increasing functionality within the public network to provide facilities such as network-based call-centre functionality or voice processing. The next generation of switching technology known as asynchronous transfer mode (ATM) may well provide the flexibility of capacity needed to handle the peaks and troughs of a call centre. Within the ACD, 'software agents' will be able to handle more of the basic transactions human agents currently handle, freeing them to handle more sophisticated enquiries.

Voice processing

For this discussion we shall define voice processing as the caller communicating over the telephone with a machine. Communication at present can be via the keys on their handset generating tones or pulses, or simple voice recognition. Interactive voice response (IVR) is defined as the situation where the voice processing unit is interfaced to company databases to allow exchange of data.

There are five basic areas of application for the call-centre environment (see Figure 37.4), as follows:

1   *Queue management* concerns maintaining a caller's patience whilst they are waiting to have their call answered. This might be achieved by

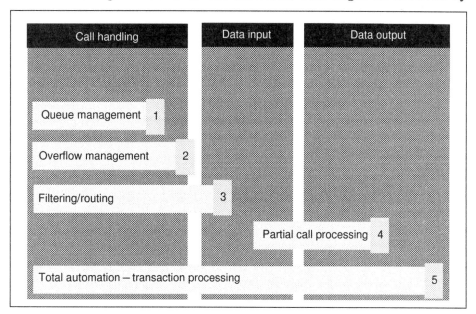

Figure 37.4   The five basic areas of application for the call-centre environment

playing music or a hold signal, or more effectively by playing various messages telling the customer, for example, about the services offered or about the current length of time to answer.

2 *Overflow management* is the handling of customers in a situation where their call is very unlikely to be answered. Such damage limitation may be a simple message or a request for them to leave details on a voicemail system to allow an agent to call back later.

3 *Filtering and routing applications* allow the caller to select the function they are trying to reach, or identify the nature of the call in some way, usually via a menu system. These allow calls to be directed to or away from particular agents as required.

4 *Partial call processing* aims to automate part of either the data input or data output elements of the call. This might involve prompting the caller to enter his or her account number via tones or voice recognition to save the agent having to ask and then enter this in to the system. Alternatively, it might be to speak back the output of a particular transaction such as the reading out of the telephone number in a directory enquiries call.

5 *Full transaction processing* is the replacement of a human agent with a totally automated solution. Examples of this are the automated telephone banking systems widely available now, or the automatic dialling available on many telephone credit cards, rather than dialling via a live operator.

The impact of voice processing should be measured in terms of the business drivers discussed in the introduction above. To recap, these are reducing unit costs, increasing revenues, improving customer service quality or further segmenting the customer base. Voice processing should in addition be planned to align with the 'value or irritant' model (discussed above under the automation matrix) so that it has a beneficial affect on processes which may cause problems for the company. Generally, any applications should achieve one of the following objectives:

● Reduce abandonment rate in peak traffic periods.
● Reduce agent time spent on unnecessary calls, either by filtering or total automation.
● Reduce talk time for calls, improving the percentage of time spent on the valuable elements only.
● Allow you to provide a faster or more efficient service, or offer services you were previously unable to offer (such as 24-hour operation).

These significant impacts should, however, be balanced against a number of caveats, and the factors leading to approval by the customer in order that the application is actually used should be carefully considered. In particular, you must consider the age and culture of the different segments that may use the service, as well as the penetration of tone-generating telephones in that segment. Estimates of tone penetration vary considerably from business-to-business situations to purely residential callers. There is a significant trend of increasing penetration across all call types in the United Kingdom. Figure 37.5 shows the UK picture in 1993/1994.

The other area of concern for more sophisticated applications is the integration to legacy databases with which the application must exchange data. This exchange is often a painful and costly element to implement.

The market for voice-processing platforms is most easily segmented by historical functionality. Platforms for call-handling applications were mostly developed by ACD and PBX manufacturers. Data input systems originated in voice mail applications and data output platforms were the domain of the audiotex equipment suppliers. There were also a number of dedicated IVR system suppliers providing high-end (that is, high-cost, high-functionality, hardware based) solutions. These definitions have become very blurred recently as suppliers have moved towards providing full IVR solutions.

The future will see increased blurring of the distinctions between the systems and a significant increase in the number of PC-based systems employing standard and widely available voice-processing cards. This progress will give increased flexibility and so less dependence on the suppliers in the development and maintenance of applications, as well as continuing the downward pressure on prices. The movement towards standards will make integration to the necessary legacy databases simpler. The emerging improvements to voice recognition will make it a viable option for telephony-based voice-processing applications, allowing word and phrase recognition as well as concatenation of digits, making any application far simpler to use. All these factors are likely to increase the penetration of IVR in the call centre significantly.

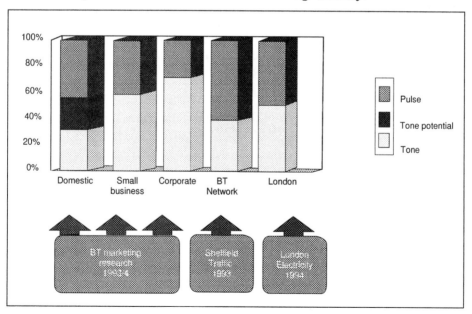

Figure 37.5   Tone penetration across call types in the United Kingdom, 1993/1994

Computer telephony integration

Computer telephony integration (CTI) is a diverse and complex area that is prob- ably most easily defined as the linking of the telephone and computer systems to enhance the functionality of both. Previously this has been something con- fined only to the largest call centres where significant capital outlay is justifi- able, or to the IVR applications discussed above. Also, most applications have been delivered via bespoke solutions integrating to a large mainframe com- puter. There are now, however, numerous published *application programming interfaces* (APLs) which can provide links to client server environments and to work stations directly, as well as to mainframes.

As detailed in Figure 37.6, the process is as follows:

1 *Intelligent routing* allows the computer to determine the most appropriate routing for a call based on data provided from the telephone system (for example, by passing the telephone number of the caller to the customer database and then determining that the call is likely to be a renewal query).

2 Subsequently, *intelligent answering* uses the data from the telephone sys- tem to provide the most appropriate information to the agent's screen at the time of answering the call, so that they can go straight to the most valuable part of the call. This might simply be to bring up a copy of a caller's last bill when they ring in to the bill enquiries department.

3 *Coordinated transfer* ensures that as the switch is transferring a call between extensions, the computer transfers data about the caller to the recipient's work station so that they can continue the call without having to recap on basic customer details. This is particularly useful when calls are transferred from the front office to a technical specialist. As the call is transferred, the specialist's screen will show specific details relating to that caller, thus avoiding any need to recap.

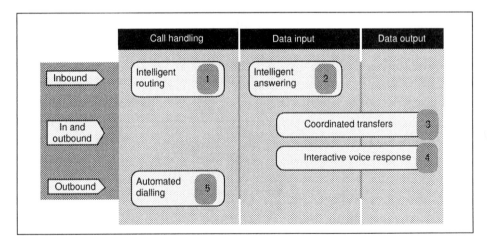

Figure 37.6   Computer telephony integration

4   *IVR* applications which exchange data with legacy databases have been discussed above, but are nonetheless CTI applications.

5   *Automated dialling* is another popular application of CTI, where the computer system holds work lists of calls that need to be made and then passes the dialling instruction to the switch as calls are completed by agents. Such systems are the subject of their own section later in the chapter.

Finally, one can consider the unified management statistics provided by CTI as another key element. Many organizations use the resultant data to provide more useful information on call-centre performance. For example, it allows detailed analysis of the amount of time agents are spending with a particular customer and how much of that time is spent on different types of calls. The detailed analysis of call traffic and talk times combined with in-depth call-type analysis provide the most exact view of what is happening in the call centre. Combined with information on the cost per minute of service, this provides an added dimension of cost management.

As with voice processing, the impacts of CTI applications should relate back to the originally defined drivers for automation.Typically, applications achieve at least one of the following objectives:

●   Maximizing agent productivity by concentrating them on the higher-value elements of calls.
●   Minimizing call handling by reaching the right person first time with the call.
●   Minimizing talk-time by putting customer data on the work-station screen at the start of the call.
●   Improving the understanding of the call centre in operation through the quality of information provided.

Unfortunately due to the complexity of such integration, solutions are expensive, and at present, significant call volumes are required to produce a return on the investment. Skills in both the voice and data sides are required and are difficult to find. There is also no clear view of which technologies are the best ones to implement to provide a future-proofed solution. There are numerous 'standards' and little proof that a standard really helps in providing a better solution.

The market for CTI is best divided up by API and application type. There are a number of proprietary APIs specific to the computer system with which they integrate. These are generally used to provide bespoke solutions for high-end call centres. These have been the most common solutions to date but there are now a number of system integrators providing hardware-independent solutions using their own or someone else's API. These solutions are either bespoke or may be 'templateware', where a basic solution is adapted to meet the specific needs of any particular operation. Yet to achieve a significant impact on the market at the time of writing are the solutions based on de facto *543* 'standards' devised by Microsoft and Novell. These are likely to be either the 'templateware' mentioned above or 'off the shelf' products that a company could buy and run with very little effort to provide simpler CTI applications.

The future of CTI is not really clear at the moment, with many different suppliers seeking to exert an influence on the market. The only sure outcome is the continuing drop in price of CTI solutions as their penetration into call centres increases. This situation will help to provide the gains in productivity that companies will need to remain competitive. As to the future of the different APIs, there are not really any solid predictions worth committing to paper in an area subject to constant and rapid change.

Automated outbound dialling

Early outbound dialling campaigns for telemarketing promotions or debt collection involved agents manually dialling successive call attempts from a list provided to them either on paper or sometimes on their work station screen. Using an automated dialler simply eliminates the need for the agents to dial the calls. Instead, CTI allows the computer holding the work list of calls to instruct the switch to dial them as required. There are a number of different methods of dialling available and the key terms are defined below, in order of efficiency gain:

- *Preview dialling* is where the application displays the customer details on the agent's screen and then places the call at the agent's request.
- *Power* (sometimes called *progressive*) *dialling* is where the system places a call as soon as one agent is free to handle another call. When it detects an answer, the call and the relevant screen of data are passed to the free agent.
- *Predictive dialling* is where the system monitors the performance of all agents in order to predict when it should place the next call so that agents do not have to wait between calls.

Because the system can detect whether there is an answer and even whether it is a real voice or an answering machine (dialling another call and placing numbers in a call-back list if necessary), agents are left to concentrate on the matter of the call itself. In addition, the system provides vital management information on the progress of any particular campaign, the percentage of 'live' answers, and individual agents' performance. As with ACDs, this information can be instantaneous or historical, as required. Another key area of functionality is the ability to integrate inbound and outbound calling. This may be simply the use of a single turret to allow agents to work on the ACD and dialler. In more sophisticated solutions, however, there is a CTI link between the two systems. By this means there is one overall management information system, and agents can be automatically diverted to and from inbound calls to ensure the best grade of service possible in the call centre.

The chief impact of such a system is the vast improvement in productivity achievable. This comes from the elimination of any dialling time as well as eliminating a large amount of time spent preparing for each call. In a large-scale project there may also be gains from the application of scripting to the calls, and from the overall focus for a team, that is provided by the dialler and associated telebusiness software.

However, the integration issues involved are complex. On the voice side, there are a myriad of different interfaces to the different switches, both for the simple voice channels and for the more complex CTI link to provide inbound and outbound blending. On the data side, it is necessary to interface to the existing corporate databases to extract work lists, as well as integrating at the work station level, providing the agents with multiple sessions to access customer databases as well as the dialler screens. As well as the technical issues, thought should be given to the organizational impact of blending. Many organizations find that they are not structured in a way that will allow them to cope with blending, nor are the staff trained to handle both inbound and outbound calls.

The phenomenon of nuisance calls, or 'hang-ups' must be considered. Whenever a system is dialling before an agent is actually free, it is possible that the call will connect before there is anyone available to take it. In this situation the machine will simply drop the call, but the called party may well already have heard the telephone ring, or may even have answered. Modern diallers have numerous mechanisms that aim to eliminate hang-ups, but the only guidelines at present (issued by the Direct Marketing Association) recommend that less than 5 per cent of calls made should hang up.

The market has traditionally been the exclusive domain of a few manufacturers. However, the algorithm for predictive dialling has now been developed by numerous other companies. Combined with the increase in computing power, solutions integral to an ACD, based on a CTI link, or on a PC platform, are starting to emerge. The defence of the established players has been increasingly sophisticated blending and management information capabilities as well as dropping prices. This trend is likely to continue for some time, so that automated dialling will start to appear in situations outside the call centre wherever there is a heavy dialling requirement. With the increasing use of the technology and the ability of the called party to identify the number of the person dialling (see below), then 'hang-up' rates will become more of an issue, encouraging more extensive use of functionality to eliminate hang-up calls altogether.

Buying a dialler has always been an expensive activity, both in terms of the equipment costs and then all the necessary integration. Therefore, it has until now been limited only to the high-end market, where the huge volumes of calls being placed provide enough return within a reasonable timescale. Prices are dropping, however, making smaller and smaller installations justifiable.

Calling line identity

In essence, *calling line identity* (CLI) services allow the called party to identify the telephone number of the calling party. This functionality has been opened to customers of certain network operators in the United Kingdom following the implementation of a technology to allow the transmission of the data down a normal telephone connection. The facility allows people to identify callers before answering the call as well as identifying people who called and rang off. The capture of CLI is also possible on *integrated services digital network* ISDN lines.

The main impact for the call centre is the ability to capture the number of callers before answering the call. This can be used for example to identify the customer for call routing or intelligent answering purposes, or for generating call-back lists at times of high inbound traffic loads. This capability will drive the implementation of CTI in the call centre because significant productivity gains from intelligent answering will be possible. However, there are some drawbacks to its implementation, most notably for outbound-calling operations, since hang-ups (see automated dialling section) can now be traced by the called party, generating return calls asking why you called but hung up. There are also some limitations to the service, due to the fact that customers can withhold CLI if they wish and, more importantly, they may well call from a telephone other than the number stored in the customer database.

Acceptance of CLI services in the United Kingdom has been swift. Within four months of launching in the United Kingdom, BT were able to provide service to approximately nine out of every ten lines. Business-to-business applications have demonstrated 95 per cent availability in that time frame and consumer-oriented call centres have recorded less than 2 per cent of callers withholding CLI despite early bad press about the data protection concerns for such a service.

In the near future the service should be rolled out by all network operators, along with agreements to pass CLI between networks, and the coverage should be improved to include nearly all lines. In addition, modifications to the service should allow identification of the extension number of the caller as well as the main PBX number, improving the usability of the captured number significantly. In the longer term, there may well be standardization on a single method of delivery rather than the two different systems currently operating.

Visual/Multimedia/Internet channel

As the telephone has now provided a 'direct channel' to reduce the cost of sale and service against face-to-face communication, businesses are looking for new areas to innovate.

Automation of the telephone channel has been discussed where the telephone is the user device to access company data via an agent or application. The next step is to integrate other front-end access mechanisms. The opportunities here seem almost limitless; examples to date have included:

1   An automated teller machine or cashpoint machine which functions as 'normal' until the user requires a service where added value can be

delivered by offering face-to-face communication (that is, loan confirmation). The screen becomes a video-conferencing link to an agent in a call centre. This application reinstated the bank's ability to offer a low-cost face-to-face relationship when required. It can be achieved consistently and managed within the call-centre environment.

2   An information screen providing data on holidays or hotels, with video clips and all local information, can be used to 'sell' the booking. If the user chooses payment by credit card, then it can be satisfied, and if the user required a face-to-face discussion, then it can be satisfied again using video conferencing.

Both examples are where customers use third-party computer-available publicity to access information on or provided by suppliers. The next sweeping trend will be the increasing availability of personal devices. This includes smart phones, personal computers, game machines and the next generation TVs under development.

Currently, computers using dial-up technology can access information resources throughout the world through bulletin boards, information networks and Internet. In recent years these have been solely used for data and e-mail with limited consumer market use. Consumers are changing rapidly, with the home PC sales outstripping office sales, the next Microsoft operating system release incorporating Internet access, and suppliers offering products and services on the Internet. Things are changing and changing quickly. There were 40 million Internet users in the world *before* Microsoft released Windows '95. The potential growth is staggering, but more importantly, its impact will determine how businesses respond to customers.

This is not the superhighway but the first step towards it, providing the complete picture:

- Face to face (that is, video-conferencing).
- Voice (that is, telephone).
- Text (interactive or office) (that is, Internet or mail).

Customers will use a combination of channels to contact suppliers, depending on their needs, expectations, time available and location. It is the suppliers' challenge to meet this as cost effectively as possible.

The call centre can develop to deliver customer service across multiple delivery channels. The main changes will be:

- Increased use of technology.
- Linking interactive voice or mail into one automated contact distributor system.
- Management information across all customer contact points.
- Improved automation of non-value-adding functions.
- Skill charges to include both verbal and written English.
- Keyboard and computer skills.

547

- Full-24 hour service will be increasingly required as global markets emerge.
- Language issues will develop as multilingual, verbal and written skills are required in the global market.
- The call centre may be distributed across continents but central management of service and costs will become increasingly important.

THE TECHNOLOGY PROJECT - HOW TO DO IT

Once the decision has been made to deliver a customer function using a call centre, then the detailed analysis and design is required.

In order to do this, use the generic business case shown in Figure 37.7, which can be adapted to suit your circumstances. First, identify what and how the call centre will operate and undertake a sizing analysis to meet expected customer demand. Second, within this analysis, peak call handling needs to be forecast,

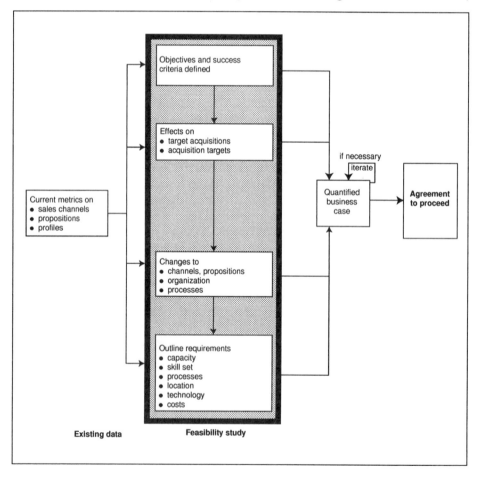

Figure 37.7 Generic business case for detailed project analysis and design

along with skill-set and multilingual requirements. Both factors affect the instantaneous peak requirements of agents. Once the sizing is known then the technology, process, skill-set and location can be defined. These elements must be linked in a coordinated design which meets the customer proposition. The design and costing should be developed with scalability in mind, along with flexibility to change with customer requirements and the introduction of new services.

Figure 37.8 shows the generic plan including the technical project and the human resources (HR) project. The HR project has been discussed in other chapters but is integral to the call-centre build project in timing, process, and technology requirements.

The technology project will include six generic areas as follows:

1 Telephony (ACD).
2 Network services.
3 Outbound dialling.
4 Data capture and tracking.
5 Information access.
6 Front-end systems.

It is the integration of these elements that causes most of the design work to ensure that the system meets the current and future process and automation requirements. For example, if a customer calls to purchase a service, then they expect it to be a seamless operation. Unfortunately, most organizations have historical legacy systems for different functions (for example sales information, order placement, credit check, customer registration, maintenance contract and so on). A new system may need to be designed that integrates these functions with the incoming call which triggers the process off. The front-end system requirement therefore spans ACD interconnection multiple host system access and third-party system access.

Planning the budget to meet these design requirements is fundamental and integral to the build project. Coordinating the requirements sign-off, design, ordering, installation and test within the people and property fit-out projects requires a detailed understanding of the total project integration. Project management to meet the timescales with a thorough understanding of the whole project is essential.

The main errors to avoid are as follows:

1 Running separate non-integrated areas of the project.
2 Designing the technology too late for the building fit-out.
3 Not designing the technology solution for the HR induction training project.
4 Applying technology in unsuitable manners to customers.
5 Not telling customers what to expect when automation is applied.

The most important factors for using an integrated plan are as follows: *549*

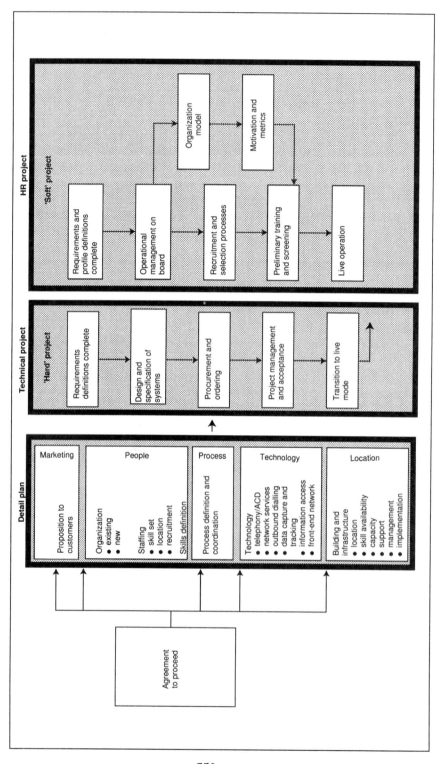

Figure 37.8   Generic plan, including the technical project and human resources project

1 Coordinating all actions back to the customer proposition.
2 Providing a holistic view of the customer requirements and process.
3 Building a management system which monitors all customer contact points.
4 The removal of any surprises and hitting the 'go live' date on time.

SUMMARY

Technology has revolutionalized how business operates, it has changed markets by 'selling direct', breaking country borders, offering convenient times to do business, and reducing the cost of sale and service. In this chapter, the main areas of technology have been addressed, together with where, how and why to apply them. It is their application in an integrated fashion which makes the difference. To deliver a competitive edge in this ever-changing environment is a challenge to all of us and technology is one of the tools to help.

In this model the organizational structure must also be considered, since in practice new processes, for best practice, may not be simple organizationally. If a new process cuts across existing internal boundaries then change has to be achieved in order to deliver the best practice. This one factor alone is often the reason new entrants to a market can achieve best practice before existing players.

38 Toll-free and local charge rate services

Jamie Clyde

In the United States if you advertise your products without a toll-free number, you do not take customer service seriously. In fact over 80 per cent of supermarket products carry free customer care line numbers on their labels. While the use of such numbers is significantly lower in the United Kingdom, an increasing number of UK companies are adopting free and reduced rate services as part of their customer service proposition. In attempting to provide a high level of service, does offering a free or cheap call actually improve the quality of the service in the eyes of the customer, or could the expense be more effectively invested elsewhere?

Offering a free call can make an organization more accessible and promote an image of efficiency and customer focus among its target audience. An airline, for example, may have to advertise either a toll-free or a local rate number in order to compete because of the expectations set by others in the marketplace. However, customers in other markets may not perceive the reduction in the price of the phone call to be a benefit. Instead, they would prefer shorter queues and more efficient call handling. One computer manufacturer recently abandoned their toll-free number after customer research indicated that the waiting time on a call before being answered mattered to customers considerably more than the cost of that call. The savings made through reverting to standard numbering enabled the company to invest in more staff and technology. As a result, the queue lengths were reduced and they succeeded in aligning their proposition to the needs of their customers.

Providing a low-cost call to the customer is not the only driver towards the use of these services. In fact, toll-free services have fundamentally two sets of benefits: those which concern the customer and those which assist the operation of the company through the efficient routing of calls. The latter is achieved because the telecommunications network operators are able to provide extra functionality that can determine the way calls are routed between an organization's call centres. Toll-free and local rate services are therefore part of a basket of products which are known as *intelligent network services* on account of their ability to be tailored to a particular company's needs. They differ from normal STD telephone numbers because they have special dialling codes such as 0800 and they are not fixed to any particular telephone line. The company simply nominates an STD number to which the calls are delivered. For example, the telephone number for sales enquiries might be 0171 489 0037. If the company decided to offer a toll-free service to prospects, they would simply order a toll-free number and request that it be delivered to their existing sales lines on the 0171 number.

THE SERVICES AVAILABLE

Intelligent network services are without doubt a strategically significant area within the telecommunications operators' portfolios. As the telecommunications industry becomes more deregulated and the pressure of competition rises between the players, these services will be increasingly offered to call-centre managers. This should result in greater choice, additional functionality and the ability to tailor services to the needs of individual organizations.

BT was the first UK carrier to offer intelligent network services (see Figure 38.1). The 0800 Freefone brand is now very well established. A company with the Freefone number pays for an initial connection charge plus a quarterly rental. Customers calling from within the United Kingdom pay nothing and the company is charged a flat rate for the call duration by BT, regardless of its origin. Subsequently, BT has launched a number of other related services that offer companies a range of tariff options, as follows:

- The Lo-call 0345 service enables customers to phone the company from anywhere in the United Kingdom and pay for the call at local rate. The company pays a flat rate for the call duration to BT which is effectively a reduced Freefone tariff.
- A National Call service was launched in 1994. This service assists companies which do not want to offer reduced rate calls to their customers but would like to benefit from the routing capabilities of intelligent network services. A National Call number has the prefix 0990 and the customer is charged at the same rate as a normal long-distance call. The company can select which centre the call is delivered to, based on the same range of criteria as for Freefone and Lo-call numbers.
- Three Premium rate services are offered on the 0891, 0894 and 0897 codes. They offer, respectively, a standard premium tariff per minute, a fixed charge independent of call length, and a high-value rate per minute.

Mercury offers free, local, national and premium rate services (see Figure 38.1). The Freecall brand is the most established of the three on 0500 and is used by a number of high-profile organizations. The 0645 and 0541 codes are Mercury's local and national rate offerings and are similar to BT's Lo-call and *553*

National Call services. The premium and higher premium rate services are on 0839 and 0991 respectively. While the public awareness of these codes is generally less, Mercury competes against BT by offering attractive tariff plans and connection charges, especially for existing Mercury customers who are directly connected to their network (2100 service).

Tariff	BT	Mercury
Toll free	0800	0500
Local rate	0345	0645
National rate	0990	0541
Premium rate	0891	0839
Premium rate (single charge)	0894	N/A
Higher premium rate	0897	0991

Figure 38.1   BT and Mercury network services tariffs

Many of the new operators such as Energis will shortly be launching their own services to compete against the two established players. The mobile operators are also interested in providing these services: for example, Vodata, a service provider for Vodaphone, has launched a toll-free service on the 0321 range. While this is primarily being aimed at mobile users and audiotex providers on the Vodaphone network, the service is available to landline customers. In addition, Vodata's 03745 and 0399 services are their equivalent to the BT's National Call and Lo-call.

WHAT NUMBER SHOULD YOU GIVE TO YOUR CUSTOMERS?

Before any decision is made on whether a company should adopt an intelligent network service, such as Freefone, it should consider its whole numbering strategy. This should address four factors: how many numbers, their memorability, their tariff and their associated image.

In order to provide an accessible service to its customers, a company must publish a set of numbers which makes it easy for them to contact a member of staff who can address their particular queries. If too few numbers are used, this results in a high volume of transfers between departments. On the other hand, too many numbers make the service less accessible and may still result in many transfers because customers dial the wrong number.

The multiskilling of agents within call centres has enabled companies to reduce the number of telephone numbers used as staff are trained to handle different types of calls. As a result, many leading-edge companies now advertise fewer numbers – in many cases, just to a single number, which has the added advantage of offering a very clear message to customers. When marketed properly, this single number can effectively become part of the brand.

Having fixed the number of separate telephone channels or numbers into an organization, the company must then select a tariff. If the US experience is followed in Europe, the increase in toll-free numbers will continue to the point that any company committed to customer service will use them. Toll-free numbers now appear on many direct response advertisements for customer acquisition, on products such as shampoo bottles for customer retention, and they are used increasingly by organizations internally (for example, remote voice mail access).

Reduced rate numbers have in the past suffered from a lack of identity. If they are not marketed properly they can easily be viewed as a poor man's freephone. Therefore, if such a service is to succeed, it needs to be promoted by firmly planting the notion of 'locality' in the customer's mind. While free calls conjure an image of a large national and centralized service, local rate numbers (which may or may not be run by the same large national and centralized organization) must convey the image of an accessible 'local' service that combines convenience with nationwide support.

First Direct is an example of a heavy user of both free and local rate numbers which are divided between prospects and customers. Prospects are given an 0800 freephone number in order to make the company as accessible as possible. However, on joining the bank the new customer is given an 0345 reduced rate number to use whenever they call in order to lower the overall costs.

On the other hand, free and local rate services can be allocated to different customer segments. Trusthouse Forte, for example, provide free calls to business customers and local rate to their residential customers. British Airways Executive Club offers different services to various segments of customers: blue and silver members are each given a local rate number for bookings while gold card members are given their own dedicated freephone number.

Free numbers have also shown that a company can become too accessible. A UK telecommunications operator discovered that its toll-free phone number increased the response from a marketing campaign. However, because the marketing message was not sufficiently targeted, the higher call volume actually caused a drop in the customer conversion rate as agents became less productive because they were handling a large number of untargeted calls.

While the effects of these services will undoubtedly depend on factors specific to your business, the cost will be significant. A number of different studies have found that the cost of telecommunications in the average call centre will rise from 25 per cent to 45 per cent of total spend after introducing toll-free numbers.

A toll-free or a local rate number gives the organization two different images which contrast with a company advertising a normal STD number. A 'free number' implies that the company is committed to customer service by being prepared to pay for the call. As the initial users of freephone were large organizations, the image of the free number still implies a nationwide and established company. Local rate calls on the other hand are intended to give the customer the impression of a nationwide company with a local presence.

One of the factors which determine the effectiveness of using toll-free or local rate services to boost corporate image is the public's perception of the services and their awareness of them. There is no point in publishing a toll-free *555* number if the customer does not realize that the call is free. Thus, BT's 0800 service commands a healthy 86 per cent (BRMB, 1995) awareness among the general public. In contrast, Mercury's 0500 is currently recognized by only 20 per cent, though this figure is now rising rapidly. BT has been trying to raise the profile of its 0345 service and, as a result, one in four of the population are aware of the code's significance, but Mercury's local rate service has a very low level of recognition within the population. While these figures may suggest that, with the exception of 0800, there is a poor general awareness of these services, research has indicated that their impact can be boosted significantly if the advertisement states the benefit (for example, 'Call us *FREE* on 0500 xxx xxx').

Market research has shown that toll-free numbers project a positive image for an organization. Various research projects (Direct Marketing Association, 1993, *Henley Centre Telebusiness Survey*) have found that the majority of consumers perceive that a company advertising Freefone number cares about their customers and wants their business.

Local rate numbers do not create such a strong image because they have a lower level of awareness within the population and the customer benefit is not as great. Also, they can be confused with the increasing number of premium rate and mobile codes, and so the customer must be told clearly that the call is charged at local rate whenever that number is advertised.

Premium rate numbers in most countries have been tarnished by the sex-line image, which they gained when the services were first launched. Now that such services have been either heavily regulated or effectively shutdown in the mature European markets, the newer premium rate codes are beginning to be used for serious business applications. Strong regulations governing how these numbers can be operated still exist, however. For example, special permission must be obtained through OFTEL if a company wishes to connect a premium rate number to a live agent as opposed to a recorded message. Nevertheless, despite the restrictions, there are considerable opportunities for organizations to recoup the costs of service provision through revenues gained from the calls. Several computer companies are investigating the use of premium rate numbers for telephone-based support. With the introduction of new high-premium tariffs, there is further potential for the use of premium rate, both for telephone information services such as legal advice and for the sale of low-value products where payment is taken through the cost of the call rather than by credit card.

Having decided on the tariff, the memorability of the number is the final factor which the company must consider if it is going to maximize the accessibility of its service. It is now possible to exercise some degree of choice over the ordinary telephone number you are allocated by BT. While the first seven digits containing the STD and local exchange codes are fixed, you can normally choose the last four digits of your number, assuming that combination is currently unassigned. However, even if you are lucky enough to obtain a distinctive set of final digits, it is still unlikely that the whole number will be very
memorable.

Therefore, a strong reason for opting for an intelligent network service is the access it affords to a more powerful number. Both BT and Mercury allow you to choose which number you have, although you may have to pay extra for the privilege. BT charges considerably more if you pick a particular 0800 or 0345 number, although many of the good 0800 ranges have already been taken (for example, 0800 800 800). Mercury normally do not charge for 0500/0645 numbers if you choose them, with the exception of a few 'golden numbers' such as 0500 x 00 x 00.

Even if you cannot get a so-called golden number, network providers recommend that you pick a number which is memorable for your business but is less attractive to other organizations. For example, TSB manipulates the letters in its name to produce the number 758; its main number is therefore 0500 758 758. Mercury 121 uses 0500 500 121, and Trusthouse Forte uses 0800 404 040, which can be written as 0800 40 40 40.

THE OPERATIONAL BENEFIT OF ONE NATIONWIDE NUMBER

The most important aspect of an intelligent network service such as toll-free or reduced rate numbers is that the number is independent of the location of both the customer and the company.

From the customer's viewpoint, the call is either free or charged at a given rate (for example, a local call). Therefore they know how much it will cost to call but do not know where they are calling, and thus the business can be located anywhere. Moreover, the calls can be routed to a single call centre or they can be divided between two or more offices, and it is the company that determines the criteria of the split. These criteria can be a combination of the following :

- *Volume*. This can be simply a straight division of calls by volume. For example, 55 per cent of calls are routed to site A and the remaining 45 per cent go to site B. Otherwise site B could be designated an overflow site from site A.
- *Time*. Routing can be time and date dependent. For example, calls are split between two sites during the day but all are routed to one main site at night and at weekends.
- *Location*. Calls can be routed depending on the customer's location. For example, Scottish customers could be routed to a Glasgow-based call centre while calls from England and Wales could be routed to an English office in Newcastle.
- *Emergency*. Routing plans can be activated in the event of a disaster, such as a fire at one call centre.

This flexibility helps the company in a number of ways, but the fundamental benefits are found in the staffing of the call centres. By making the operation geographically independent from the customer, the company can relocate to minimize staff turnover and costs.

557

Here are some examples of companies which achieved operational benefits through the introduction of intelligent network services:

- Prior to using local rate services, British Airways had a call centre on the outskirts of London to service the majority of London-based callers. By changing to 0345, the customer still paid for a local call but BA could relocate to the Midlands where staff retention was considerably higher and costs were lower.
- General Accident introduced a freephone number as part of a drive for better customer service. With the advanced routing as described above, GA was able to offer a new 24-hour service.
- Autoglass, one of the first users of 0800, have been able to match the peaks and troughs of calls much more effectively through the load-balancing features of the intelligent network, resulting in cost efficiencies and convenience to the customer.
- The RAC introduced free and reduced rate numbers when it moved from a branch network to a centralized service. The result was that more specialist staff could be deployed, creating a faster and higher level of service.

Other costs can also be reduced as a result of a having a nationwide number. If the company advertises in local press or TV regions, only one version of the advertisement is needed. By encouraging customers to phone because the call is free or local, the need for a mail coupon can be removed, hence saving press and magazine space.

With the introduction of intelligent network services which offer national rate tariffs (for example, BT's National Call), it is possible to gain the operational benefits described above without the extra cost of subsidizing the cost of the customer's call. This can, however, be achieved using traditional methods of routing through a private network.

Similarly, local rate calls can be provided for a customer through a number of regional numbers which are connected to one or more central call centres via a private communications network of leased circuits. A number of regional electricity companies (RECs) have opted for this route as they moved from many small regional branch offices to centralized call centres. As each branch office closed, calls were rerouted to the call centre using the private network. If the organization already has a private network, this may be a viable option. However, as the trend moves away from asset-intensive corporate networks towards virtual private networks (VPNs), this option may become increasingly costly, especially if a new or enhanced network is required to carry the traffic.

TOLL-FREE OUTSIDE THE UNITED KINGDOM

As companies look to develop pan-European and global markets, there is an increasing need to offer their customers accessible telephone-based services in a number of different countries.

Unfortunately telecom network providers in the majority of countries are still heavily controlled and regulated by their local government and have traditionally been slow to respond to the needs of their customers, particularly when international services are requested. In addition, telephone numbering has evolved separately as different countries adopted their own codes for special services such as toll-free. For instance, the complexity of European numbering is most easily appreciated by watching a direct response advertisement on satellite television. Instead of one freephone number the viewer is greeted with a list of up to sixteen different numbers, each with its own code.

Country	Toll free	Reduced rate	Premium rate
France	05	36 63	36 64, 36 65, 36 67, 36 70
Germany	0130	0180	0190
Italy	167	147	144
Netherlands	06 0, 06 4	06 8	06 3, 06 9
Spain	900	901, 902	903, 906
Sweden	020	077	071
United Kingdom	0800, 0500, 0321	0345, 0645, 0399	0891, 0660, 0839, 0894, 0897, 0898 etc
United States	800, 888	500	900

Figure 38.2   Telephone codes for special services in individual countries

The lack of uniform European numbering plans has a strong impact on a company's ability to market themselves across borders. Separate campaigns must be run with their own numbers in each country to avoid the satellite syndrome described above. This has an additional complication if customers need to contact you from more than one country. Examples of this include airline travellers and holders of telephone charge cards. Research into the use of the cards has shown that the complexity in accessing the service from different countries in Europe has resulted in a considerably lower take-up than in the United States.

North America, on the other hand, enjoys a common numbering strategy across the United States, Canada and the Caribbean. Its 800 toll-free service is universal across countries and carriers. Such is the success of the service, new numbers are rapidly running out and so a new range, 888, has been introduced to handle future demand. North America also benefits from having retained its lettering on the telephone keypad as telephone numbers can be encoded into words: Amtrak for example will always be remembered as 1–800–USARAIL.

While devoid of a common numbering strategy and lacking the foresight to introduce alphanumerics at an earlier stage, Europe is slowly becoming more integrated. The liberalization of the voice telephony market in 1998 will remove many of the barriers which telecommunications operators face when providing services beyond their national boundaries. The numbering plan is currently under review, with four options being considered. These range from *559* maintaining the *status quo* to a completely new pan-European plan similar to the North American area code system, which would remove the need for separate country codes. Any call within Europe would be deemed national and would not need the international dialling code or tariff. Such a move would clearly involve massive disruption to businesses across all countries in Europe and therefore it is highly unlikely that such a plan would be politically acceptable. The outcome of the various studies is more likely to be a compromise which minimizes the amount of change to existing numbers yet provides the capability of new pan-European numbering for specific organizations who require it.

Because of their income potential, toll-free services that offer one international number are being developed by a number of operators across Europe. BT and the Dutch PPT are separately investigating their own services, seeking to enable callers outside the United Kingdom and Holland to access their existing toll-free services. Callers simply dial the international access code, 00 in most countries, followed by the 0800 number. As with other international calls, the leading zero is dropped and so a single number can be advertised in a number of countries as +44 800 xxx xxx.

The ultimate goal for many international organizations is to have one toll-free number which can be dialled from anywhere in the world. Whether you need a hotel in Boston or Bangkok, for example, you need to remember only one number: 00 800 HILTONS. The International Telecommunications Union (ITU), the UN-based body that allocates international numbering, have for some time been considering the implementation of a global toll-free service. It is intended that this will consist of a new country code (800) which will be dedicated to toll-free services. Operators from around the world will be able to provide services on this number to global organizations who wish to have a single number for service.

There are many technical and operational issues which have to be resolved before the service is launched. These include fundamental issues such as the quantity of digits in the freephone number and whether letters can be used – the North American lettering on keypads is not present in some European countries and a different alphabetical layout is used in the Far East! Given the number of countries and systems which must be aligned, it is unlikely that the service will be available before the end of 1998.

39 Meeting the fulfilment challenge
Peter Hardingham

There is a view, to which I subscribe, that the enormous amount of technology available to us today has had very little impact on the quality of our communications. That is, we can all say things much faster than ever before, we are all capable of being contacted at any time of the day or night, but the quality of those communications has spiralled downwards. What we say seems to have declined in value, but is said far more frequently and quicker than ever before!

Within marketing generally, and customer services in particular, these developments have had serious effects on 'relationship marketing', and fulfilment material is one of the most obvious areas to have suffered. This chapter will therefore look at a practical approach towards alleviating these detrimental effects on fulfilment in the following terms: planning fulfilment; integrated communications; a typical 'integrated' fulfilment programme; what your customers think; and finally, a few hints for the future.

PLANNING FULFILMENT (IT BEGINS IN THE HOME ...)

Recently I had to invest in computer equipment that would assist my quest to become experienced in all matters of the Internet and the World Wide Web. There were two implications for the fulfilment of this desire:

1 Financing the purchase price.
2 Choosing the equipment.

Finance

You would imagine that finance would be an easy item to arrange, particularly in an industry that has had enormous experience in the direct sales and marketing of their products. Indeed, there is an amazing amount of very effective *561* lead generation campaigns from a huge variety of personal finance providers, of which I picked out four in order to compare their offerings. Two sent me an application form which was virtually impossible to understand (I should add that my agency does these all the time and so I ought to be reasonably conversant with the process) and an explanatory 'brochure' which might just as well have been a technical manual on the Financial Services Act! The third company did provide good material but the fulfilment brochures bore no resemblance to the lead generation campaign and it was difficult to find the product features (explained originally in the advertising) in the mailpack that followed.

The final provider – and the one with whom I finally negotiated – not only tied in the material supplied with their original proposition, but also made it very easy to fill out the application form, and had very helpful staff at the end of a 'helpline' to clarify any difficulties in the process.

Equipment

Contrast this with the second part of my task – dealing with the computer marketplace. All the leading hardware brands (for example Toshiba, Apple, Compaq and others) seem to be very efficient in tying in all the stages of the fulfilment process. Apple had an especially good campaign with a three-dimensional fulfilment 'box' that could not be ignored. But in all cases – because hardware manufacturers depend on resellers – there was a dearth of useful information on the actual process of purchase. The manufacturers preferred to leave it to the retailers to follow up – or not, as the case may be – and regrettably, they did not follow up! In the end I had to take the initiative and contact a retailer, otherwise nothing else would have happened.

Since then, the customer care programmes I have experienced with the finance company and the retailer have been 'interesting'. For example, I have received many additional mailings from the finance company offering me the same product that I had already taken up. It is worth remembering that sending lead generation material with no regard to the customer database is not the way to keep a customer happy!

What, then, is the moral of this story? Namely, that in order to plan fulfilment it is necessary to think in terms of 'planning to fail'. Sounds odd? Not really, once you start to examine what this means. Planning to fail involves looking at every significant eventuality in a 'start to finish' process for a marketing and customer care programme.

The process often starts out as a questionnaire for members of the marketing team. For example:

1 Who are we aiming our communications at? How does the target audience break down and how might these segments react to: awareness advertising (including PR); lead generation campaigns; and all stages of fulfilment material, including call-centre handling, and follow-up coordination with lead generation (that is, dedupes)?

2 What are the likely responses from your own organization to any

reaction of the target audience in item 1? This includes all areas of the company (for example, operations, sales, marketing, accounting, legal, policy committees and personnel). A typical question may be, what happens if demand exceeds supply?

3   What links exist between lead generation, conversion (to purchase) and customer care/loyalty processes? In some companies there are separate departments for each and when they do not talk to each other it becomes embarrassingly obvious to the customer.

We should now try to access the likely impact of any one element on all others. At the same time as considering what your overall marketing objectives may be for a campaign, you should also be considering the 'back end' process of fulfilment, how it fits into the entire campaign, and the consistency of tone and manner of the communication. In other words, analysing what you should be doing to maintain a successful marketing relationship involves planning for integrated communications.

INTEGRATED COMMUNICATIONS

My agency often receives briefs from clients on a 'tactical' basis. For instance, this might involve a lead generation advertising campaign where the main objectives and all other tactical elements have already been decided. When we go through our own internal briefing sessions, one of the most important elements we consider is one over which we have no control in these particular campaigns: that is, just what is a potential customer of our client going to receive in the way of lead conversion/fulfilment material?

I have to say that on occasion our copywriters are often frustrated by the poor quality of this element, which will often dictate the success or otherwise of the overall campaign (as in my own experiences outlined above). Similarly, when we are briefed on customer loyalty and customer growth strategies, we are again often constrained by the client's significant investment in corporate brochures and internal telemarking procedures which have little relevance for the successful coordination of the campaign, but which are often used as the main element of fulfilment.

How should one look at this area? A practical case history might serve as a good example here. One of my previous clients was one of the myriad of mobile telephone service providers that exploded on to the UK market in the early 1990s. These service providers do not actually sell mobile telephones in many cases but simply act as the company responsible for the contract with the consumer for usage of the 'airwaves'. The parties involved were as follows:

1   Mobile telephone manufacturers (for example, Motorola, Sony and so on).
2   Retailers selling the telephones (large retailers such as Dixons with hundreds of branches, and independent outlets with sometimes only one or two branches).

3 Companies possessing the licences to authorize sale of air time (for example, Cellnet, Vodaphone and so on).
4 Service providers who buy air-time packages from the licensed companies and resell it in the form of airtime contracts to the end user (for example, my client).

Therefore my client had relationships with three other bodies before they could get near the final customer. They needed the airtime of course, and also the relationship with the telephone suppliers in order to negotiate supplies of hardware compatible with their telephone identification systems. Also, without an agreement with the distribution channels (for example, the retailers) there could be no sales process!

Consider, then, this matrix of communication possibilities. Each organization had its own priorities for its customer relationships and its own idea for marketing campaigns and customer care strategies.

For my client to even contemplate success in its customer acquisition campaign, therefore, required considerable emphasis on the fulfilment process, as follows:

1 Capture of the customer's name and address from lead generation campaigns (including telephone responses).
2 Customized fulfilment material for retailers to use in their own marketing.
3 Coordination of the 'enquiry database' with actual customers and those who are almost customers (that is, those who have expressed a desire to buy a mobile telephone but have not yet gone to a retailer to make the purchase).
4 The initial customer care process (for example letters, welcome packs, 'member get member' promotions) must tie in with the entire purchase process and in some way show a seamless communications 'face' to the customer.
5 In-store point of sale for all retailers – this was critically important. It was all very well for a potential customer to be attracted to the idea of a mobile telephone, but in 99 per cent of cases the final decision as to which model (and therefore which service provider) would be made in the retailing outlet.

In these terms my client was forced to consider fulfilment at the same time as deciding on national advertising campaigns and dealing with operational matters, capital expenditure and many other areas. Thus it can be seen what is required to tie in all the thinking on fulfilment with other marketing issues. And even in cases where a decision is not so imperative, it is still wise to follow the same route in setting up fulfilment programmes.

A TYPICAL 'INTEGRATED' FULFILMENT PROGRAMME

564 Let us imagine a typical marketing scenario where a company has existing

customers but wishes to both acquire new customers and grow existing business. As we have already discussed, the initial decisions on overall objectives, corporate positioning and operations policies should have been considered side by side with fulfilment policies.

In the following areas of acquisition, requirements for the potential conversion of prospects into customers can now be assessed, as follows:

1 *Awareness advertising*. This area may or may not have a 'response' element, but in any event, materials such as product/service brochures must be available to meet enquiries, and follow-up fulfilment material must be ready to guide enquirers into purchasers.
2 *Lead generation campaigns*. Whether in broadcast media or print, these campaigns will necessarily require material consistent with that campaign in order to achieve data capture, follow-up, and lead conversion.
3 *Customer loyalty/growth campaigns*. Fulfilment material is absolutely crucial here, and, in fact, that material is often used as both the initial contact point and the conversion, combining it into a one-stage communication.

In all cases there may be a necessity for initial 'filtering' activity to weed out unlikely prospects from those whom are very likely to respond.

In a lead generation campaign, for example, the fulfilment matrix may typically look like that set out in Figure 39.1.

The levels of activity in the campaign here can be decided by the following methods:

1 *Score card modelling*. Pre-screening of mailing/customer lists can allow much of the decision making to be done prior to any marketing activity,

Days 'post enquiry'	'No hoper' enquirer	'Unlikely' enquirer	'Possible purchase'	'Highly likely purchase'
1	Low-cost pack	Low-cost pack	Standard pack	Standard+ pack
14		Follow-up letter	Follow-up telemarketing	Follow-up telemarketing
21–28		Follow-up letter 2	Follow-up letter	Follow-up telemarketing
29–45			Follow-up letter	Follow-up card pack

Figure 39.1   Fulfilment matrix for a lead generation campaign   *565*

by assigning a value to a segment of the database given from the 'score' attributed to several variables:

(a)   geodemographics;
(b)   psychographics;
(c)   financial indicators; and
(d)   lifestyle indicators.

2   *Neural networking.* A more recent technique, neural networking aims to predict propensity to respond and purchase through the computer's 'artificial intelligence' analysis of existing transactional or responsive data. In the United States, these techniques are used intensively in predicting attrition rates in a customer database in the early days of the customer relationship. The techniques require many data or sets of data to be truly predictive, but once in place they offer the possibility of cost effective marketing through more accurate targeting and suppression of potentially risky segments of a database.

3   *Good old testing!* In launch situations particularly, nothing can take the place of testing strategies, which may show some failures but thus affords a better guide for roll-out activities (again, 'planning to fail' providing the crucial data for future success).

Testing or some form of prescreening allows decisions to be made (and tested again) as to what the 'low cost' fulfilment pack should consist of. It might be the full pack but using two colours rather than four, or just a letter, or even a postcard. The standard or 'control' pack will of course need test packs set against it to verify its effectiveness over time and the standard+ (the '+' element can vary from nothing at all, through surveys and questionnaires, to masses of material relating to product specifications particularly in business-to-business environments).

Often, telephone 'scripting' will have to be the most carefully set up of all the fulfilment processes. Quite apart from the objectives of the exercise – varying from gentle enquiries and reminders through to a script verging on verbal assault! – is the question concerning the effect of different levels of scripting. Decision trees versus word-by-word scripts, computer screens versus handwritten notes – all of these depend on judgements about the skills of the staff involved and the level of quality control required.

However, having made decisions about what you intend to send to your prospects and customers, how do you know that they will want to receive it?

WHAT YOUR CUSTOMERS THINK

So far we have looked at fulfilment activity from the perspective of marketing planning. However, one of the issues which troubled my agency in the direct marketing context was that concerning what potential customers think about all the direct marketing campaigns they receive. Surprisingly, there were very few data available on this question in the United Kingdom or Europe.

Therefore, in late 1994 we set out to establish the best empirical evidence to date regarding respondents' reactions to lead generation and fulfilment activity. Our studies were designed to cover the following factors:

1   Receipt of direct mail: (a) from unsolicited cold mailings; and (b) in terms of quantity (that is, which industries were perceived to have sent most mailings).
2   Acceptability of direct mail. Which industries consumers find it acceptable to receive mailings from. (This data was also broken down by job type to assist business-to-business marketing decisions.)
3   Replies to direct response advertising. What communications were more likely to produce an initial enquiry.
4   Purchase (conversion). What channels were most likely to convert from enquiry to purchase.
5   Views on direct mail and telemarking. A general assessment of these two communication channels.

The studies were set up to monitor the following variables: sex, age, class, marital status, children in the household and job type. The geography was studied using TV regions.

The project work was conducted in conjunction with Gallup Research in November 1994, and in February and May 1995, and covered 3000 consumers across the United Kingdom. The top-line conclusions make fascinating reading for fulfilment strategists, and, in particular, those concerning what the public perceive as being most effective in generating enquiry and purchase of products or services from direct marketing material.

As Figure 39.2 shows, there is a significant difference in the level of enquiry

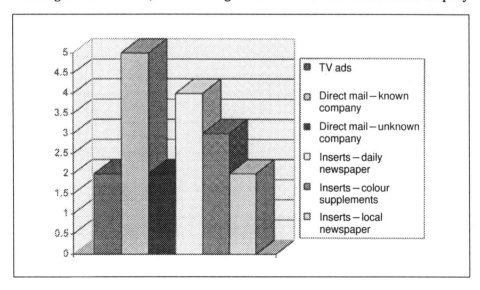

Figure 39.2   Enquiry (not purchase) from direct marketing channels   *567*

generated by direct mail from a company known to the respondent (5 per cent) versus mail from an unknown company (2 per cent). Direct response TV is effective (and will continue to grow as exposure increases in Europe). Press inserts work extremely well in large-scale print runs, delivering a variety of response quality and thus requiring decision on levels of fulfilment.

The figures for actual conversion to purchase are set out in Figure 39.3. These figures were even more dramatic, being five to one in favour of companies known to respondents. It is worth noting that this same trend applied throughout all the samples and segments (whether you look at age, class, job type or any other variable), which further underlines the importance of fulfilment material carrying the same 'tone and manner' as other communications. The adverse consequences of being mistaken for an unknown company can be clearly seen in these results.

Figure 39.4, which shows overall reaction to outbound telemarketing, is worth looking at in this context. As can be seen here, there is a very significant difference between the figure for acceptability of telemarketing from companies known to the respondent (under 10 per cent) and the figure for total opposition to all cold outbound telemarketing (87 per cent). Again this argues strongly for ensuring that prospects – and, in some cases, existing customers – are sufficiently aware of your likely intentions to call, before you embark on large-scale telemarketing.

These survey figures should not come as a complete surprise to marketing practitioners. Nevertheless, since they represent the UK public's perceptions of direct marketing and how they react to it, they are the first real indicator that some of the principles we preach are founded in fact!

Thus it seems clear that the integrated approach to prospect and customer communications which we have outlined above makes sense in practice. This

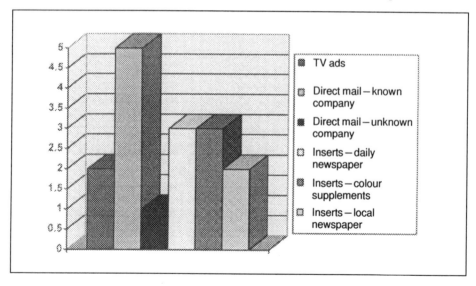

Figure 39.3   Purchase from direct marketing channels

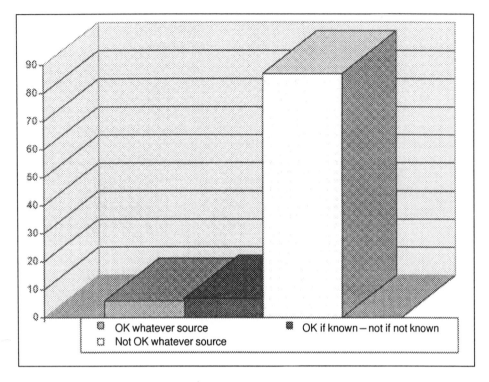

Figure 39.4   Overall reaction to cold outbound telemarketing

point is also confirmed by other research that we have done in financial services marketing, where one of the top factors in the choice of a product provider was the simplicity and quality of the fulfilment material. (In fact, it came a close second behind the advice of a reliable financial adviser and way ahead of both mainstream advertising and direct-marketing lead generation mailings!)

HINTS FOR THE FUTURE – THE INTERNET BELL TOLLS!

Marketing, in all its facets, is an ever-evolving management process. However, there is always a certain amount of 'reinventing the wheel' – for example, when personnel change within marketing departments, or when budgetary restrictions preclude testing strategies, or when there is a simple requirement for a company to change operating strategies – which then affects customer relationship marketing.

Many companies do not adopt the correct strategy at some stage, but most find this not to be critical in the overall scheme of things – particularly as it can be hard to identify what part of a company's operations is responsible for customer attrition, lack of business growth and the reduction in new customer acquisition. Market forces, the economy, legal changes, for example, can all cloud the issue, so as to make it almost impossible to isolate the effect of the customer relationship strategy employed.

569

Along with developments in computer hardware technology, however, has come the creation of a whole new method of customer communication which, sooner rather than later, will dramatically affect the success of marketing policies. This new arena is commonly known as the Internet, or the World Wide Web. The World Wide Web is the newest information service to arrive on the Internet. The Web is based on a technology called Hypertext and most of the development has taken place at CERN – the European Particle Physics Laboratory. The World Wide Web is basically a universe of information which is accessible through a computer network and works on the principle that information placed on the 'web' is available to any authorized user, in any country, from any computer and via a simple program. As we all know, the creation of a worldwide system of computer communications in the early 1990s was initially driven by the use of military data links by the educational institutions, initially in the United States and then around the world. After that, it was not long before the communications possibilities for the rest of humanity became clear. Now it is possible for any one of us with the correct equipment to send and receive messages and files from anywhere in the world – at local telephone call charge rates!

One of the most common uses for this new technology has been e-mail between company sites and employees. More recently, 'viewer' programmes (known as 'browsers') on the Internet have made it absurdly easy for anyone to exploit the facilities offered on a highly interactive and graphically organized interface. Just as the domination of Microsoft Windows has continued apace, so too will these browsers bring about enormous increases in Internet traffic.

But what will we talk about? At the beginning of this chapter I put forward the idea that in a retrogressive development parallel to the increasing communications possibilities, the substance of what we communicate has suffered rather than benefited. For the future, the area of transactional relationships has to be a clear exception to this decline in standards.

In transactional relationships we already have a great deal of experience of the new electronic world (for example bank transfers, ordering theatre tickets, playing computer games, satellite television and so on). The idea of expanding this range to include most of our everyday transactions (for example shopping, organizing travel, reading books on-line and so much more) will not be difficult for consumers to assimilate in the medium to long term.

Whilst this development may take a number of years to become fully apparent, we must take heed now of what it will mean for customer relationships and fulfilment strategies. These relationships will become 'real time' in their nature. When consumers decide for example, that they would like to apply for investment in a new financial instrument, or for details on the latest fashion craze, they will expect instant satisfaction. Increasingly, they will be offered this satisfaction over a Web site provided by finance companies, retailers, and almost any other company you can imagine. Indeed, already we can order flowers, wines, computer equipment and much more over the combination of telephone line and computer equipment that allows communication on the World Wide Web.

In these circumstances, if your fulfilment material is not adequate, or worse, if your product does not satisfy, the almost immediate response you will receive will be in the form of complaints. And should you choose to ignore these complaints, it will be possible for the aggrieved party to deluge you with e-mail – and persuade others to do the same.

At the same time, there will also be great possibilities for customer relationship research. We already know in direct marketing that questionnaires are a very effective means of soliciting response – it is easy and noncommittal to reply on paper. It will be at least as easy, then, to reply on electronic 'paper'. Such research, however, will in turn raise the need for a commitment to reply to the concerns and issues raised. It will not be possible to survive if you ask for response and then cannot cope with demand.

Customer database e-mail is likely to become the most significant method of obtaining feedback on marketing strategy that we have seen this century. How do we prepare for this? The most important principle will be to treat this medium as just another communications channel, which will require in place those elements we have already discussed:

1 A prospect and customer marketing database.
2 An operating policy on customer fulfilment.
3 A customer service strategy.
4 A coordinated and integrated awareness, lead generation, fulfilment and customer care strategy.

Admittedly these elements will need to be revised and updated as the speed of the relationship increases from lead generation through to transactional operations, but the principle remains the same.

Thus it seems quite possible that computers – having put a significant number of people around the world out of a job – will now require companies to reinvest in customer relationship departments in order to cope with demands for that element which fulfilment is all about, namely, good quality service.

FURTHER READING

Bird, D. (1989), *Commonsense Direct Marketing*, London: Kogan Page.

40 Forecasting volumes in a call centre

Peter Murley

The running of an ordinary, everyday call centre – if in fact there is such a thing – is an extremely challenging task. Managing a large centre or a number of linked locations is both demanding *and* difficult. Directing and controlling a large 24-hour, seven-day operation is unbelievably hard work in a constantly changing environment!

Technology eases the problem and will continue to do so (for example, automation call distributor data is an absolute prerequisite to any good activity models), but for every new item of technology-related help that springs up, the marketing department adds a different dimension, a new requirement or changes the speed of acquisition, so that the call centre manager finds it hard to keep up. The general rule is that whatever solution the technical people provide, the marketeers can render it obsolescent within days by specifying something else that nobody has previously considered.

THE NEED FOR FORECASTING: A CAUTIONARY TALE

Nevertheless, despite the fact that a campaign to double the new customer acquisition rate was communicated to you two days *after* it started – or perhaps two days *before* if you're really lucky – let us assume that you are expected to respond with no service standard degradation and no change in resources. And if, as the call centre manager, you don't respond, you are blamed for any problems that arise, and, as a result, you are upset. But you take it all on the chin and you live to fight another day.

Then someone decides to change the billing dates and the whole incoming call volume goes haywire. If that weren't bad enough, fifteen of your staff go on a training course on the following day, and even though the course was arranged months ago, you have forgotten about it, and, well . . . the rest doesn't really matter.

Next, budget time approaches, you're taking twice as many calls as last year, and marketing are looking to double the customer base next year. So you quadruple the resource budget and the managing director has a seizure on receiving your next year's request. He savages your budget and also that of the marketing department. The marketing department asks a few very key questions about the reasons why customers call, the number of times people ring to buy something and the percentage penetration – and you don't know the answers. The managing director is admitted to hospital for triple by-pass surgery!

His temporary replacement now decides to freeze all recruitment, take 10 per cent off all budgets, *and* sack half of the direct sales force, replacing them with telesales staff but only allocating 40 per cent of the previous direct cost to the new telesales function. The outlook seems grim.

This new managing director, however, knows more than you do. He comes from a business which has an amazing ability to forecast call types and volume on a weekly or monthly basis – a business that knows how much it costs to acquire and service a customer, can output peak hour staff schedules at the blink of an eyelid, can transform call centre activities into budgets, can produce and implement training schedules, and can use information to actually stop people calling if it doesn't result in added value for the customer or the business. And all this data is dynamic and can be utilized as a tool to help call centres and marketing functions work together and not against each other.

At this stage, some research on your part indicates the existence of some excellent software packages which appear to offer help with some of your problems. However, it turns out that you actually need three quite separate and non-linked packages: one for estimating call volume, one for busy-hour staff scheduling, and one for budgeting. They all tell a good story, but not one of the packages available provides you with a holistic solution and enables you to link in activity-based and call-based costing or Pareto processes (that is, 20 per cent of the call centre processes produce 80 per cent of the work activity/call volumes).

By contrast, the larger call centres can afford to buy big software and hardware products and train themselves in their use. But even they often discover the very ordinary and limited nature of off-the-shelf programs, whereas most companies want a very high-tech, advanced version at the least, and most probably a version that is custom-made. Thus *most* of a call centre volume model can now be developed through a spreadsheet and/or via a proprietary database. It then becomes *your* model with *your* data and under *your* control and almost certainly within *your* budget.

The situation described above is no fantasy or fabrication. It is a fact and it is happening every day in call centres of all sizes and shapes. And as for understanding the true cost of each new customer acquisition or servicing call, a recent survey clearly shows that most call centre managers and their senior management have very little appreciation of customer acquisition or of the costs of establishing and maintaining a relationship with a customer or a prospect by telephone. Some of the data from this survey does make one wonder how some *573* managers and their businesses actually survive, even though a number of the solutions to their problems should be relatively easy to implement.

DEFINITION AND DEVELOPMENT OF A FORECASTING MODEL

A good forecasting spreadsheet or model is a tool which enables you to input data in a flexible fashion, make changes to the data, and outputs the desired results, quickly.

Inputs

All models require inputs and for the call centre some of these might include the following:

1. Staff hours of work and effective utilization.
2. Business acquisition volumes by the month.
3. Business acquisition by different market sectors/products (where prospect/customer habits may vary).
4. Customer turnover or attrition percentage.
5. Types of calls and other administrative activities (business process linked).
6. Duration of calls and other role activities.
7. Percentage of calls via IVR (Interactive Voice Response)(for example).
8. Peak hour and day call/administrative/ activities as a per cent of a total weekly volume.
9. Staff salary levels, that is, hourly pay rate (used for example, to determine the basic 'cost per call').
10. Fixed and variable costs – capital and revenue.

Most of the inputs listed, in the case of an existing business, will, or should, be based on historical data (although many businesses may have difficulty in providing such data). For new, greenfield call centres, however, estimates will have to be made, some of which may be assessed through proper market research and/or participation in a benchmarking process.

Outputs

Given the above inputs, the following should be included in the outputs:

1. Gross, net and average customers by month, by business sector.
2. Call volume and role activity volumes (that is, work other than a telephone call, including, for example, post-call activities to fulfil a promise, responding to correspondence, regular file maintenance and so on).
3. Total work times, for both calls and non-call activities.
4. Total work times, for both calls and other activities, *by functional area and by 'process'*.

5   Number of staff required by day, by hour, and by week.
6   A budget.

It can also be used as the foundation for activity-based costing, whereby, for example, when marketing want to add or delete certain things to the calling pattern, or add, amend or delete a market sector or acquisition seasonalization, you can see the impact in resources and the impact in costs. This in turn helps to decide whether any ideas or plans for change are commercially viable.

Development

Developing this model is very simple and is subject only to three main principles, as follows:

1   The first of these is the necessity to understand the data that is being inputted – its relevance, its importance and its relationship within the model.
2   The second principle is an ability to decide what it is you are trying to get out of the model. You must be able to determine what your objectives are and how you want to present them. (This also involves understanding the questions that others might ask of you regarding the data in both inputs and outputs.)
3   The third principle is a basic understanding of how a spreadsheet, or a database works. You have to know some of the basic commands and functions and be able to use them in such a way that changes will give a new result, quickly.

ANALYSIS OF A FORECASTING MODEL

The following is a simple example of a forecasting model using an Excel[*] spreadsheet.

Staff utilization

The first area of the model considers the actual average available/productive/'on-the-job' time (that is, average over the year, and not placing any difference between a week where no absences arise versus a week where all absences arise). This results in a final, average percentage utilization figure – productive utilization – derived from the assumptions in Figure 40.1. Average percentage utilization is derived from deducting, from a basic full-time working week (in the example used 36 hours per week) all absences (holidays, sickness), training days, breaks 'wrap' (time spent completing a call prior to being able to take the next or another call) and 'idle' time (time waiting for a call to be put through). The result of these deductions, which are not necessarily all

*   Excel is a registered trademark of Microsoft Corporation.

Working week:	36 hours per week.
Annual holidays:	20 days per annum.
Bank holidays:	8 days per annum.
Breaks:	10 minutes per 2 hours work.
Training days:	12 days per annum (post initial training course).
Sickness/absence:	5 days per annum.
Wrap:	5% of the total net time remaining post the above items. (Wrap is time spent wrapping up actions from the call prior to going back into available to take another call.)
Idle:	5% of the total net time remaining post the above items. (Idle is time spent in available and waiting for the next call assuming there to be no other activities being performed.)

Figure 40.1 Data for calculation of average percentage utilization figure

inclusive, provides the *actual* number of working hours available for each individual to take ('answer') or make calls, on average (that is, some days the figure may well be higher or lower). In the example shown, 36 hours is 100 per cent and the 'deductions' equate to 28.02 per cent, thus the utilization percentage is 71.98 per cent. This percentage utilization is then used to calculate a number of productive seconds (on average) per month (see Figure 40.2), which in turn is one of the final drivers which establishes resources required.

Acquisition volumes

Gross new acquisitions

The model then lists 'gross new customers acquired per month' on a non-cumulative basis. These data are given by each of two market sectors (a

Hours per week		36			
= Minutes	60	2 160			
= Seconds	60	129 600			
= Seconds per annum	52	6 739 200	Per week 129 600	Per day 18 464	
			= Seconds	= Cumulative seconds	%
Annual holidays (days)		20	369 271	6 369 929	
Bank holidays (days)		8	147 708	6 222 220	
Breaks (minutes per two hours)	10	120	518 518	5 703 702	8.33
Training (days)		12	221 563	5 482 139	
Sickness/absence (days)		5	92 318	5 389 821	
Wrap (%)			269 491	5 120 330	5.00
Idle (%)			269 491	4 850 839	5.00
Final % utilization				71.98 %	
Seconds available (on average) per month				404 237	
Seconds available (on average) per annum				4 850 839	

Figure 40.2 Calculation of average productive seconds per month

market sector in this context, could be, for example, residential or business, or retail or wholesale). Each and every change to the business plan has an impact on resource requirements and must, therefore, be carefully considered before enacted.

In each of the sector plans, data exist for acquisition on a monthly basis and shows in sector (a) in this example increased activity during the run up to Christmas (see Figure 40.3). For sector (b), acquisition is, relatively speaking, evenly spread. In sector (a), this peak and trough acquisition activity has a marked effect on resource requirements and when the final resources are mapped and budgets derived, it may be necessary to conclude some manual adjustments so as to smooth net new hires/training programmes/and so on.

| | | Gross New Acquisitions | | |
		Sector (a)	Sector (b)	TOTAL
January	Year 1	2 333	300	2 633
February	Year 1	2 333	300	2 633
March	Year 1	2 333	300	2 633
April	Year 1	2 333	300	2 633
May	Year 1	2 333	300	2 633
June	Year 1	2 334	300	2 634
July	Year 1	2 000	300	2 300
August	Year 1	2 000	300	2 300
September	Year 1	2 000	300	2 300
October	Year 1	19 000	300	19 300
November	Year 1	19 000	300	19 300
December	Year 1	19 000	300	19 300

Figure 40.3   Gross new customers acquired per month by sector and date

Churn

The second business volume heading 'churn by month' then considers churn on a month-by-month basis and calculates that based on the formulae derived from the gross monthly acquisition inputs from above together with a churn formula for each of the two sectors (see Figure 40.4). If the gross new acquisitions in any given month are 2 333 and the churn rate is 0.42% (two decimal rounding based on 5.00% pa) per month then the number of customers who churn is 10 (rounded). Thus the net acquisition for the month is 2 333 minus 10 = 2 323.

| **Churn:** | Sector (a) | 5.00 % per annum | Sector (b) | 7.50 % per annum |
| | | 0.42 % per month | | 0.63 % per month |

Figure 40.4   Churn figures per month for end sector

Net monthly acquisitions

The third business volume heading is the result of deducting the month-by-month churn figures from the gross month-by-month acquisition figures, thus producing the net month-by-month acquisition figures, again by the two sectors (see Figure 40.5).

| | | Gross New Acquisitions | | |
		Sector (a)	Sector (b)	TOTAL
January	Year 1	10	2	12
February	Year 1	19	4	23
March	Year 1	29	6	35
April	Year 1	39	8	46
May	Year 1	49	9	58
June	Year 1	58	11	70
July	Year 1	67	13	80
August	Year 1	75	15	90
September	Year 1	83	17	100
October	Year 1	162	19	181
November	Year 1	242	21	262
December	Year 1	321	23	343

Figure 40.5   Percentage churn figures applied to figure 40.3

Average net customers per month

The fourth business volume heading 'average net per month' is based on previous inputs and shows the average net new customers per month. These figures are derived from simply adding the number from the previous month to the number from the current month and dividing by two to give an average for the month (see Figure 40.6).

The main drivers

The above four headings/sections are then recalculated to form the basis of the next four headings which are simply the cumulative versions of the first four.

The drivers which arise from all these headings are then just two (applied to each of the two market sectors). These are:

1. *Gross acquisition.*   See figure 40.11 together with the resource utilization figures above (which, in this example, is the same figure across the two sectors), gross acquisition figures drive the number of inbound acquisition staff (that is, calls and back office associated work) required and the number of outbound staff required (that is, all non-servicing aspects with the exception, for

		Net Acquisitions		
		Sector (a)	Sector (b)	TOTAL
January	Year 1	2 323	298	2 621
February	Year 1	2 314	296	2 610
March	Year 1	2 304	294	2 598
April	Year 1	2 294	293	2 587
May	Year 1	2 284	291	2 575
June	Year 1	2 276	289	2 564
July	Year 1	1 933	287	2 220
August	Year 1	1 925	285	2 210
September	Year 1	1 917	283	2 200
October	Year 1	18 838	281	19 119
November	Year 1	18 758	279	19 038
December	Year 1	18 679	278	18 957

Figure 40.6   Net customers acquired per month by sector and date

		Average net customers		
		Sector (a)	Sector (b)	TOTAL
January	Year 1	2 323	298	2 621
February	Year 1	2 318	297	2 616
March	Year 1	2 309	295	2 604
April	Year 1	2 299	293	2 592
May	Year 1	2 289	292	2 581
June	Year 1	2 280	290	2 570
July	Year 1	2 105	288	2 392
August	Year 1	1 929	286	2 215
September	Year 1	1 921	284	2 205
October	Year 1	10 377	282	10 659
November	Year 1	18 798	280	19 078
December	Year 1	18 719	278	18 997

Figure 40.7   Average net customers per month by sector and date

example, of welcome calls – calls prompted by a customer services function to welcome a new customer to the 'family' – which are a cost of customer service activity but which will be performed by outbound staff).

2. *Average net cumulative number of 'customers' per month*. Again this, together with the resource utilization figures above (which is the same figure across the two sectors) drives the number of inbound staff (that is, calls and back office associated work) required to deal with ongoing servicing of customers (for example, calls/mail in to query bills, report faults, detail changes (payment/address, and so on), add/delete products/services/features and so on). At this stage it is valuable to point out that 60 – 80 per cent of calls/mail in *579*

		Cumulative churn per month		
		Sector (a)	Sector (b)	TOTAL
January	Year 1	10	2	12
February	Year 1	29	6	35
March	Year 1	58	11	70
April	Year 1	97	19	116
May	Year 1	146	28	174
June	Year 1	204	39	244
July	Year 1	271	53	323
August	Year 1	346	68	413
September	Year 1	429	84	514
October	Year 1	592	103	695
November	Year 1	833	124	957
December	Year 1	1 154	146	1 300

Figure 40.8   Percentage churn figures applied to Figure 40.3 - cumulative version

		Net cumulative acquisitions		
		Sector (a)	Sector (b)	TOTAL
January	Year 1	2 323	298	2 621
February	Year 1	4 637	594	5 231
March	Year 1	6 941	889	7 829
April	Year 1	9 235	1 181	10 416
May	Year 1	11 519	1 472	12 991
June	Year 1	13 795	1 761	15 555
July	Year 1	15 728	2 048	17 776
August	Year 1	17 653	2 333	19 986
September	Year 1	19 570	2 616	22 185
October	Year 1	38 407	2 897	41 304
November	Year 1	57 166	3 176	60 342
December	Year 1	75 845	3 454	79 299

Figure 40.9   Net customers acquired per month by sector and date - cumulative version

to a customer service/call centre from new and established customers – as opposed to prospects (that is, those who are not yet active, buying customers) – will come as a result of a 'billing' or fault query/enquiry/report.

The ability for a model to allocate resource to categories of acquisition is a significant advantage, and this model has been built such that *some* of the building blocks for establishing cost of acquisition and cost of service are already in place.

		Average net cumulative customers		
		Sector (a)	Sector (b)	TOTAL
January	Year 1	2 323	298	2 621
February	Year 1	3 480	446	3 926
March	Year 1	5 789	742	6 530
April	Year 1	8 088	1 035	9 123
May	Year 1	10 377	1 327	11 704
June	Year 1	12 657	1 616	14 273
July	Year 1	14 762	1 904	16 666
August	Year 1	16 691	2 190	18 881
September	Year 1	18 612	2 474	21 086
October	Year 1	28 989	2 756	31 745
November	Year 1	47 787	3 037	50 823
December	Year 1	66 505	3 315	69 820

Figure 40.10   Average net customers acquired per month by sector and date – cumulative version

		Gross new cumulative acquisitions per month		
		Sector (a)	Sector (b)	TOTAL
January	Year 1	2 333	300	2 633
February	Year 1	4 666	600	5 266
March	Year 1	6 999	900	7 899
April	Year 1	9 332	1 200	10 532
May	Year 1	11 665	1 500	13 165
June	Year 1	13 999	1 800	15 799
July	Year 1	15 999	2 100	18 099
August	Year 1	17 999	2 400	20 399
September	Year 1	19 999	2 700	22 699
October	Year 1	38 999	3 000	41 999
November	Year 1	57 999	3 300	61 299
December	Year 1	76 999	3 600	80 599

Figure 40.11   Gross cumulative new customers acquired by sector

Calls and activities

The next area of the model is a set of narrative statements showing the broad types of calls and activities. These broad types of calls and activities are meant to cover the majority of matters in which the call centre will be involved. They also largely represent the main business processes and procedures.

		Average net cumulative customers[1]		
		Sector (a)	Sector (b)	TOTAL
January	Year 1	2 323	299	2 622
February	Year 1	3 485	448	3 933
March	Year 1	5 808	747	6 555
April	Year 1	8 131	1 046	9 177
May	Year 1	10 455	1 344	11 799
June	Year 1	12 779	1 643	14 422
July	Year 1	14 937	1 942	16 878
August	Year 1	16 928	2 241	19 169
September	Year 1	18 920	2 539	21 459
October	Year 1	29 376	2 838	32 214
November	Year 1	48 297	3 137	51 434
December	Year 1	67 218	3 436	70 653

[1] Figures prepared for customer servicing purposes

Figure 40.12   Average net cumulative customers by sector

Acquisition and servicing subdivisions

Each of the two market sectors is now subdivided into two, so that there are now four groups of data. This subdivision covers (previously referenced) activity/call types broadly considered to be in either the acquisition category (that is, largely prospects) or the servicing category (that is, customers). Thus there are now four categories, namely:

1   Sector (a): *acquisition.*
2   Sector (a): *servicing.*
3   Sector (b): *acquisition.*
4   Sector (b): *servicing.*

Each of these four categories are built around a common framework, which is constructed in the following manner.

Broad task areas

There are six subsections in each of the four groups covering six broad task areas or functions, as follows:

1   *Front office.* Tasks (calls) performed by staff trained to be on the front-line or the back-line and who are logged on to taking inbound calls.
2   *Back office.* Tasks (mainly activities and not calls) performed by staff trained to be on the front-line or the back-line and who are logged off from taking calls (mainly) but are dealing with mail (same as calls but

with no person at the other end of the transaction/activity).

3 *Fulfilment.* Tasks (not calls) performed by staff who are physically located within a fulfilment centre.

4 *Customer care.* Tasks (calls and activities) undertaken by staff trained to be on the front-line or the back-line, and of a more specialist, detailed or time-consuming nature.

5 *Outbound.* Tasks (calls and activities, but largely calls) undertaken by staff with additional skills/training to sell up, close a sale, make a sale (from cold or warm), plus additional functions such as welcome calls and first debt chase and so on.

6 *Credit and collections/billings.* Tasks (calls and activities) undertaken by staff in this specialist area.

Call/activity types

Within each of the six sub-areas there has been allocated sufficient space in which to enter up to 20 different call/activity types. Whilst there may be many hundreds of call/activity types, the representation of more than the likely top 20 often proves futile and will give diminishing returns. There is nothing to stop any sector performing detailed analysis/inputs before getting to the required figures in this section, but that is outside the scope of the model which by its very nature is reasonably macro rather than incredibly micro. Each of these 20 call/activity types is repeated automatically (by entering a formula) in each of the four sections. Examples of the 20 call/activity types used in each of the six sub-areas used in this model are as listed in the appendix to this chapter.

Data and calculations

Within each of the six stated sub-areas in each sector there is a group of data and calculations/formulae as follows:

1 *Percentage penetration.* To show the percentage of customers who are likely to use this particular service or call/mail to make an enquiry or complain, and so on. Within the acquisition parts of this area of the model this formula is used to indicate, for example, the proportion of enquiries versus conversions to customer (see below).

2 *Percentage agent intervention.* To show the percentage of the call or the activity where the agent (the customer services staff member) will be involved on a person-to-person basis with the customer.

3 *Call/activity duration (seconds).* To show the typical duration of the call or the activity in seconds. In overall terms, experience shows that the average call duration (calls and not activities) is in the order of 200/210 seconds across all types of acquisition and servicing calls. As with busy hour and busy day, this calculation is more or less true regardless of the product, the market sector or the geographical location of the call centre. *583*

4   *Number of calls per customer per annum.* The number of occasions in a twelve-month period when the customer will telephone customer services against that specific call/activity type.
5   *Number of seconds per acquisition/servicing.* This is a simple calculation: item 1 x item 2 x item 3 x item 4 = an annual number of seconds.

Example

In Figure 40.13 call/activity type number 1 in front office shows 567 per cent penetration and call/activity type number 2 shows 100 per cent. For the purposes of the model – and there are different ways in which this can be shown – for every 6.67 enquiries one (15 per cent) becomes a customer and 5.67 (85 per cent) do not (that is, they stay as prospects). It further says that for the enquiry, the customer service agent (CSA) will deal with all enquiries on a 100 per cent, one-to-one basis (that is, no automation/integrated voice response), that the average enquiry call duration will be 90 seconds (that is, salutation, take name, address/postcode, media source, actual request for information/

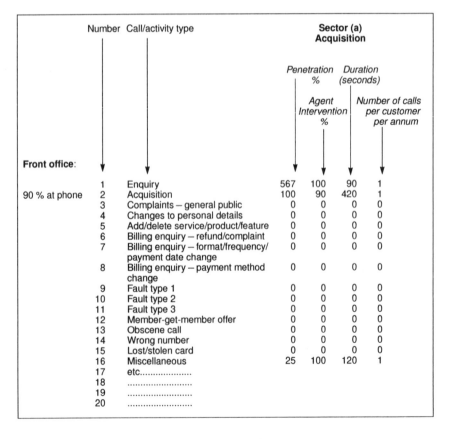

Number	Call/activity type	Sector (a) Acquisition			
		Penetration % / Agent Intervention %	Duration (seconds)		Number of calls per customer per annum

Front office:

	Number	Call/activity type	Penetration %	Agent Intervention %	Duration (seconds)	Number of calls per customer per annum
90 % at phone	1	Enquiry	567	100	90	1
	2	Acquisition	100	90	420	1
	3	Complaints – general public	0	0	0	0
	4	Changes to personal details	0	0	0	0
	5	Add/delete service/product/feature	0	0	0	0
	6	Billing enquiry – refund/complaint	0	0	0	0
	7	Billing enquiry – format/frequency/ payment date change	0	0	0	0
	8	Billing enquiry – payment method change	0	0	0	0
	9	Fault type 1	0	0	0	0
	10	Fault type 2	0	0	0	0
	11	Fault type 3	0	0	0	0
	12	Member-get-member offer	0	0	0	0
	13	Obscene call	0	0	0	0
	14	Wrong number	0	0	0	0
	15	Lost/stolen card	0	0	0	0
	16	Miscellaneous	25	100	120	1
	17	etc....................				
	18	....				
	19	....				
	20	....				

584   **Figure 40.13   Example of front-office call/activity type data: acquisition** fulfilment, attempt to connect/sell proposition, close), and that this will happen once for each prospect. Note that where the call/activity line is incomplete – that is, when it shows a series of zeros – the same call/activity type is repeated in the servicing section where it will be completed and the acquisition line items will be zeroed (see Figure 40.14).

In call/activity type number 2 at figure 40.12, those who go beyond the query to an actual customer, spend a total of 420 seconds becoming that customer. This is call time total and includes the 90 seconds above (or a proportion of it) plus additional time to check credit, take personal/financial details, advise of procedure from that point onwards and so on. Again this is done once, as each customer is only acquired once. It further says that 90 per

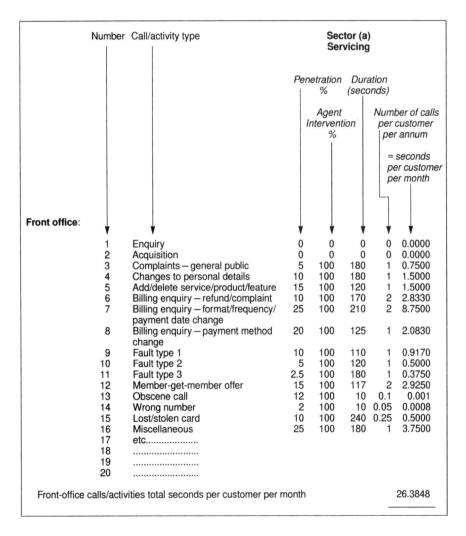

Figure 40.14   Example of front-office call/activity type data: servicing   *585*

cent (agent intervention column) of those acquired will be acquired via the telephone and not via the mail. To balance this 10 per cent shortfall of acquisition an identical call/activity type appears in the back office area for those customers who might be asked to or prefer to be acquired via the mail.

There is also a relationship between these two call/activity types and some of the activities in the outbound section (Figure 40.14). Any successful conversions of prospect chases in the 'outbound' category on figure 40.15 are shown under the 'acquisition' item in figure 40.13, although these would normally be displayed as two separate calculations (one at figure 40.13 and the other at 40.15 being those acquired at the front office by the inbound team and by the outbound team respectively). That is to say, the 567 per cent who just enquire

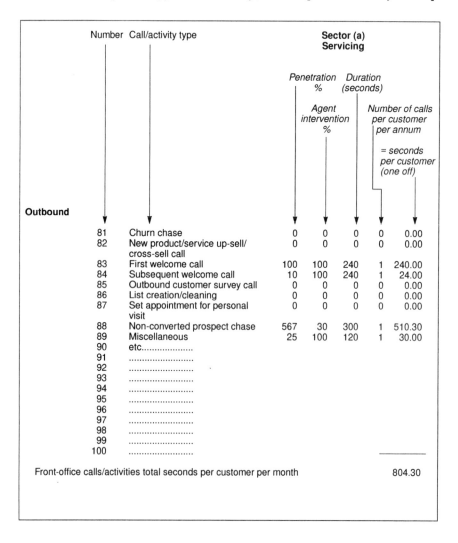

Figure 40.15   Example of outbound call/activity type data: servicing

go to an outbound chase list. In call/activity type/number 86 for sector (a), it can be seen that 567 per cent is shown in the penetration figure. In the next column a figure of 30 per cent is stated. This says that of the list of prospects to telephone in order to try and convert, 30 per cent are telephoned (which implies that 70 per cent of the chase list is either dumped and/or chased by mail).

If the gross acquisition business plan for the month is 1 000, then a 15 per cent conversion rate requires 6 667 calls, 5 667 of which are enquiries only and which result in, say, an information pack being dispatched from the fulfilment system. The balance of 1 000 are those who 'join' as customers. The model assumption is that they are all acquired by inbound staff at the first call (in a call centre, this is the best time to sell and close the proposition). However, 30 per cent of the 5 667 people (that is, 1 700) are going to be given to the outbound team to chase, and if they convert, say, 20 per cent of those, then we now have a total of 1 340 (1 000 plus 20 per cent of 1 700) customers which is a 14.5 per cent conversion ratio. Furthermore, if 50 per cent of the 70 per cent who were initial enquirers and who did not appear on the telephone chase list, are contacted/chased by mail (1 984) and 5 per cent of those convert (99), then we now have 1 433 customers from the initial 6 667 enquirers, which is a 21.5 per cent conversion rate. For simplicity, the examples in this model assumes that 15 per cent is the final total conversion percentage figure and that the detail behind that is subject to separate volumetrics.

Summary resource requirements (detailed level)

The model can now output a summation of resource requirements by market sector and by month. This information is given for each of the six sub-areas (front office, back office, fulfilment, customer care, outbound, and credit and collections), and by acquisition, by servicing, by acquisition and servicing as a total, or by whatever combination is required.

The model shown only outputs resources on a monthly basis for one year but can be easily adapted to go beyond this – perhaps over a three- or five-year cycle to match the strategic plan.

Within this section there are no assumptions, simply formulaic outputs derived from calculating all the above referenced inputs and outputs.

Resources summary at a high level

The above detail is summarized such that any changes made to the model are quickly visible in this section. Readers can look across this summation and see rounded numbers of full time equivalent (FTE) staff required per month by sector, or by acquisition or servicing, or by functional area and, within each functional area, by sector also. These are exclusive of management and support staff, who are not listed in the model but are entered on a different basis: that is, the number of CSAs per team leader, number of team leaders per manager and so on.

Busy hour/busy day

Broadly speaking the resources are then split into outbound and inbound (as they have different terminal utilization patterns/requirements) and a busy hour/busy day model applied to the weekly total number of hours which need to be filled.

An example of busy day/busy hour patterns for inbound calls is shown in Figure 40.12. (Generally speaking, these figures are regardless of market sector unless the product has a great deal of seasonality: for instance, car recovery services, or retail/high street purchases where a heavy Saturday calling activity is likely in the acquisition areas, but not servicing of existing customers). This figure also indicates that Sunday calling and activity traffic is on the upward curve.

Seven day a week operations (% of calls per week taken on a specific day)		Five day a week operations (% of calls per week taken on a specific day)	
Monday	19%	Monday	23%
Tuesday	18%	Tuesday	21%
Wednesday	17%	Wednesday	19%
Thursday	17%	Thursday	19%
Friday	16%	Friday	18%
Saturday	9%	Saturday	
Sunday	4%	Sunday	

Figure 40.16   Example of a busy day pattern

Beyond the busy day calling profile, the busiest hours are likely to be between 9.30 am and 11.00 am (any day) with another surge between 4 pm and 6 pm (and in some 24-hour operations, a late evening call surge). This information/knowledge is vital in, for example, planning for a direct response TV campaign (DRTV), where minimal staff may be employed during the hours when DRTV is most likely to occur.

Given the knowledge of the number of resources required to match the calling/activity patterns and the business plan acquisition and servicing numbers derived from the model (as described above), together with the peak/busy day and busy hour calling patterns, one can then spread resources to match peaks and troughs in the work patterns. Alternatively, one can match resources to the average pattern or minimum pattern for the day and outsource the balance of calls/overflows to a suitable (tightly controlled) third party. This can be done as follows:

1   Take the number of resources indicated by the model and multiply by the number of contracted hours employed per week. Both figures are taken from the model and calculated automatically if the model has been built correctly.

2   Against the busy hour/day framework which you have decided to use, the model then calculates: the busy day percentage × the busy hour percentage × the result from item 1 above.

3   Thus if resources required as indicated in the model output were 50 and hours per week per resource (pre-actual utilization due to the fact that utilization deductions have already been made within the model) were 36, then hours to be spread across the week are 1 800. If the busy day is Monday and the percentage of calls on that day represent 19 per cent of the total for the week, then Monday requires 342 hours spread across the 24-hour cycle. If the busiest hour on Monday is 10 am to 11 am and that is 12 per cent of the calls for that day, then 41 hours are required, as are 41 people and 41 terminals (that is, 82 per cent of the original FTE number of 50, which demonstrates why it is critical to employ a relatively high number of part-time staff in a call centre), in order to match the anticipated call volume.

Other outputs of the model

The model can also show a summary of the number of calls and activities (and time assigned) which go to make up an acquisition. This information could be further used to provide outputs regarding cost of acquisition and service. For example, let us say that for sector (a) a model shows that it takes a total equivalent of ten inbound calls and four outbound calls plus three activities (non-calls but work connected activities) to attract a signed-up customer. It also indicates that (as a result of the inputs regarding calling frequency and call/activity durations) the total time spent on these calls and activities is 3 000 seconds or 50 minutes (with productive utilization taken into account already). Furthermore, if the fully loaded cost of a member of staff on the front-line is say £15 000 per annum and support staff adds a further £5 000 (all excluding capital investment, initial training investments, selection costs and so on), then it is possible for the model to quickly establish an acquisition cost. This acquisition cost, because its components have been derived from a detailed model which breaks down the cost of each main process across specified functions (for example, front office, back office, outbound and so on), can be analysed piece by piece and business plan/process/call and activity duration changes and so forth, will rapidly indicate not only resource impacts but costs also. This also applies, of course, to the annual cost of servicing a customer beyond the acquisition stages.

Budget

The outputs of the model can be used in a dynamic way so as to be able, for example, to forecast budgetary requirements – both operational and capital expense items – on a month-by-month, quarter-by-quarter, year-by-year, sector-by-sector basis, using certain assumptions and formulae. Certain parts of the model can be manually adjusted to even out peaks and troughs   *589* experienced as a result of a variable acquisition plan, particularly in a sector which perhaps has a very heavy acquisition seasonality bias.

For training and budget purposes the budget aspects of the model should be regressed by two to three months (or whatever is the duration of the basic training programme) to allow for recruitment ahead of the required date. This means that recruitment/*the starting of new staff* must take place before the actual budgeted/modelled need by the equivalent of the duration of the training programme. If this does not happen then there will not be sufficient staff to respond to work volumes. An example would be that the model says that to answer 'x' calls/perform 'y' work activities on the first of April I would need one hundred staff. However, I have a two-month training programme before they reach full competency, therefore they need to start work two months *before* the first of April. This will enable the full training and accreditation programme to be implemented, thus ensuring that new staff are available and able to fully support the customer growth at precisely the right time. In many organizations the budget shows the new staff at the time it is required to be active/productive, and in a business where customers are being acquired continually, this will result in a degradation of service.

CONCLUSION

Whilst it is not possible in this chapter to indicate the detailed nature of a spreadsheet 'model', one thing is certain: it requires only a few skills, first, to design a dynamic document that will form an important and integral part of the business planning process, and secondly, to enter the correct calculations and formulae. The key to success is using and manipulating data intelligently, and to do that you must be able: to establish the parameters against which you are working; to understand the nature and relevance (or otherwise) of existing historical data; and to make informed estimates where data is unknown or unavailable. If you approach matters carefully the strength of the outcome is without doubt likely to have a crucial and positive impact on your ability to respond quickly and authoritatively to any questions from colleagues elsewhere in the organization. Knowledge is a road to salvation and the journey is worthwhile!!

APPENDIX: CALL/ACTIVITY TYPES

Each market sector is subdivided into two categories, *acquisition* and *servicing*, and each of these categories is divided again into six subsections: *front office*, *back office*, *fulfilment*, *customer care*, *outbound*, and *credit and collection/billing*. Each subsection is allocated sufficient space in which to enter up to 20 different call/activity types, as follows.

Front office

1   Enquiry
2   Acquisition
3   Complaints – general public
4   Changes to personal details
5   Add/delete service/product/feature
6   Billing enquiry – refund/complaint
7   Billing enquiry – format/frequency/payment date change
8   Billing enquiry – payment method change
9   Fault type 1
10 Fault type 2
11 Fault type 3
12 Member-get-member offer
13 Obscene call
14 Wrong number
15 Lost/stolen card
16 Miscellaneous
17 etc...................
18 ....
19 ....
20 ....

Back office

21 Acquisition by mail
22 Mailed enquiry by service/mailed response
23 Rekey returned applications
24 Recheck credit
25 Filing/passing on, etc. of forms/mandates
26 Account closing by mail
27 Changes to personal details by mail
28 Add/delete service/product/feature simple
29 Billing enquiry – refund by mail
30 Billing enquiry – format/frequency/payment date change
31 Miscellaneous
32 Survey analysis
33 Survey despatch
34 etc...................
35 ....
36 ....
37 ....
38 ....
39 ....
40 ....

Fulfilment

41 Open/distribute inbound mail
42 Log mail in
43 Collect and post outbound mail
44 Log mail collection
45 Fulfilment equipment loading
46 Letter/information pack collation and check
47 Reporting and quality checks on despatch
48 Miscellaneous
49 etc...................
50 ....
51 ....
52 ....
53 ....
54 ....
55 ....
56 ....
57 ....
58 ....
59 ....
60 ....

Customer care

61 Outbound fault warning
62 Complex fault handling – chase and call-back
63 Transferred call for resolution
64 Chase overdue fault/about to be escalated
65 Complex billing call – chase and call-back
66 Transferred billing call – chase and call-back
67 Complex product/service change request – chase and call-back
68 Complex add service/product – chase and call-back
69 Complex complaints – mail
70 Complex complaints – call-back and mail confirmation
71 Complex account closures
72 Lost/stolen cards – complex checking
73 Difficult acquisitions
74 Difficult and complex enquiries
75 Miscellaneous
76 etc...................
77 ....
78 ....
79 ....
80 ....

Outbound

81 Churn chasing
82 New product/service upsell/cross-sell call
83 First welcome call
84 Subsequent welcome call
85 Outbound customer survey call
86 List creation/cleaning
87 Set appointment for personal visit
88 Non-converted prospect chase
89 Miscellaneous
90 etc..................
91 ....
92 ....
93 ....
94 ....
95 ....
96 ....
97 ....
98 ....
99 ....
100 ....

Credit and collections

101 Overdue chase 1
102 Overdue chase 2
103 Overdue chase 3
104 Collate and check bills prior to despatch
105 etc..................
106 ....
107 ....
108 ....
109 ....
110 ....
111 ....
112 ....
113 ....
114 ....
115 ....
116 ....
117 ....
118 ....
119 ....
120 ....

Index

Note: Page references in *italics* relate to figures.

Dealing with Customer Complaints

Tom Williams

Increased consumer protection, government initiatives, changing
expectations on the part of the consumer - a number of factors
have combined to lead to a marked growth in complaints. At the
same time organizations are beginning to recognize the value of an
effective complaints handling system. Yet until now there has
been no systematic book-length treatment of this significant area
published in the UK.

Tom Williams starts by explaining the strategic importance of
complaints handling. He goes on to examine how people actually
complain and what their objectives might be. He shows how to
determine policy and how to set up and run an effective
complaints handling unit, considering both the point of view of the
complainer and the implications for staff on the receiving end.
With the help of case studies and examples drawn from the private
and public sector he identifies the principles and practices involved.
The book ends with a summary of key points and details of where
to find further advice and information. This is above all a practical
guide.

It is all too easy to regard complaints as a pain to be avoided or a
nuisance to be got rid of as fast as possible. In fact, as Tom
Williams demonstrates, they can be a valuable source of
information, of customer satisfaction and, ultimately, of
improvements in both reputation and profitability.

Gower

Handbook of Customer Satisfaction Measurement

Nigel Hill

With the current emphasis on service as a competitive tool, delivering customer satisfaction has become a key strategic issue. But there's only one group of people who can tell you what the level of customer satisfaction is in your business, and that's the customers themselves. Using worked examples and real-life case studies, Nigel Hill's comprehensive guide takes you step by step through the entire process, from formulating objectives at the outset to implementing any necessary action at the end.

Among the topics covered are questionnaire design, sampling, interviewing skills, data analysis and reporting, while a set of valuable appendixes points the way to sources of further information and support. The book will equip the reader both to carry out a survey themselves and to brief and monitor an external agency for optimum results.

Whether you are directly responsible for measuring customer satisfaction or simply need to understand the issues and methods involved, the *Handbook* represents an unrivalled source of knowledge and advice.

Gower